EASTERN EUROPE

EASTERN EUROPE

*An Introduction to the People,
Lands, and Culture*

VOLUME 3

EDITED BY RICHARD FRUCHT

A B C ● C L I O

Santa Barbara, California • Denver, Colorado • Oxford, England

Library of Congress Cataloging-in-Publication Data
Eastern Europe : an introduction to the people, lands, and culture / edited
by Richard Frucht.
    p.   cm.
  Includes bibliographical references and index.
    ISBN 1-57607-800-0 (hardback : alk. paper) — ISBN 1-57607-801-9
(e-book)
    1. Europe, Eastern.   2. Europe, Central. 3.   Balkan Peninsula.
I. Frucht, Richard C., 1951–

DJK9.E25   2004
940'.09717—dc22

                                                          2004022300

This book is also available on the World Wide Web as an eBook. Visit abc-
clio.com for details.

ABC-CLIO, Inc.
130 Cremona Drive, P.O. Box 1911
Santa Barbara, California 93116-1911
This book is printed on acid-free paper.

Manufactured in the United States of America

CONTENTS

EASTERN EUROPE

PREFACE

In *The Lexus and the Olive Tree* (Farrar, Straus, and Giroux, 1999) and *Longitudes and Attitudes* (Farrar, Straus, and Giroux, 2002), the award-winning reporter for the *New York Times* Thomas L. Friedman observed that the world has made a remarkable transition during the past quarter century from division to integration. What was once a world of separation, symbolized by the Cold War and "the Wall," evolved, especially with the collapse of the Soviet Union, into a world of globalization and global interconnectedness, symbolized by "the Net." That new reality has led to remarkable changes. Moreover, it is not merely a passing trend; it is a reality that affects every facet of human existence.

Regrettably, however, not everyone has become part of what amounts to a revolution; in some cases, an antimodernism has caused a lag in the developments of the critical trends of democratization and economic change. That gap, epitomized by the difference between the world of the Lexus and that of the olive tree, forms the core of Friedman's analysis of the Middle East, for example. As perceptive as he is of this clash in that region, in many ways Friedman's observations regarding the necessity of seeing the world in a more global and integrated manner are prophetic for many in the West as well. Although Friedman's emphasis is on an antimodernism that creates a gap between the world of the olive tree and the world of the Lexus, preventing interconnectedness from being fully realized, there are other barriers, more subtle perhaps, but no less real, that create gaps in the knowledge of so many areas of the world with which we are so closely linked.

Certainly in the United States, knowledge of other parts of the world is at times regrettably and, some might argue, even dangerously lacking. The events of September 2001 and the actions of a handful of al-Qaeda fanatics are but one example of an inattention to the realities of the post–Cold War world. Despite the fact that the organization of Osama Bin-Laden had long been a sworn enemy of the United States (and others) and his followers had already launched attacks on targets around the globe (including an earlier attempt on New York's World Trade Center), many, if not most, Americans knew very little (if anything) about al-Qaeda, its motives, or its objectives. What is troubling about that limited knowledge is the simple fact that if an organization with such hostile designs on those it opposed could be so overlooked or ignored, what does that say about knowledge of other momentous movements that are not so overtly hostile? In a world that is increasingly global and integrated, such a parochialism is a luxury that one cannot afford.

Although educators have at times been unduly criticized for problems and deficiencies that may be beyond their control, it is legitimate to argue that there are occasions when teaching fails to keep pace with new realities. Language training, for example, hasn't changed much in the United States for decades, even though one can argue that languages critical to the future of commerce and society, such as Japanese, Chinese, or Arabic, are less often taught than other "traditional" languages. Thus the force of tradition outweighs new realities and needs. Such myopia is born out of a curricular process that almost views change as an enemy. Similarly, "Western Civilization" courses, on both the high school and college level, for the most part remain rooted in English and French history, a tunnel-vision approach that not only avoids the developments of globalization or even a global outlook, but also ignores key changes in other parts of Europe as well. Provincialism in a rapidly changing world should only be a style of design or furniture; it cannot afford to be an outlook. In a world of rapid change, curriculum cannot afford to be stagnant.

Such a curriculum, however, especially on the high school level, is often the inevitable by-product of the materials available. When I was asked to direct the Public Education Project for the American Association for the Advancement of Slavic Studies in the early 1990s, I had the opportunity to review countless textbooks, and the regional imbalance (overwhelmingly Eurocentric in presentation, with a continued focus on England and France) present in these books was such that it could lead to a global short-sightedness on the part of students. Despite the fall of the Berlin Wall and the collapse of the Soviet Union, the books usually contained more on obscure French kings that on Kosovo. Educators recognized that, and from their input it was clear that they needed, more than anything else, resources to provide background material so that they could bring to their students some knowledge of changes that only a few years earlier had seemed unimaginable.

This need for general resource works led to the publication of *The Encyclopedia of Eastern Europe: From the Congress of Vienna to the Fall of Communism* (Garland, 2000). Its goal was to provide information on the rich histories of Albania, Bulgaria, Czechoslovakia, Hungary, Poland, Romania, and Yugoslavia. The reception the book received was gratifying, and it has led to this work, which is designed to act in tandem with the information in the *Encyclopedia of Eastern Europe* to offer the general reader a broad-based overview of the entire region running from the Baltic to the Mediterranean. In addition, this book expands the coverage to other areas in the region not addressed in the encyclopedia.

The three volumes of this work cover three groups of countries, each marked by geographical proximity and a general commonality in historical development. The first volume covers the northern tier of states, including Poland and the Baltic states of Lithuania, Estonia, and Latvia. The second volume looks at lands that were once part of the Habsburg Empire: Slovakia, the Czech Republic, Hungary, Slovenia, and Croatia. The third volume examines the Balkan states of Serbia and Montenegro, Bulgaria, Albania, Romania, Macedonia, Bosnia-Hercegovina, and Greece, lands all once dominated by the Ottoman Empire. Each chapter looks at a single country in terms of its geography and people, history, political development, economy, and culture, as well as the challenges it now faces; each also contains short vignettes that bring out the uniqueness of each country specifically and of the area in general. This structure will allow the reader not only to look at the rich developments in each individual nation, but also to compare those developments to others in the region.

As technology makes the world smaller, and as globalization brings humankind closer together, it is critical that regions once overlooked be not only seen but viewed in a different light. The nations of East Central and Southeastern Europe, that is, "Eastern" Europe, are increasingly a vital part of a new Europe and a new world. What during the Cold War seemed incomprehensible to many, namely, the collapse of totalitarianism and the rise of democracy in these countries, is now a reality all should cherish and help nurture; first, though, it has to be understood. It is the hope that this series may bring that understanding to the general reader.

Putting together this work would have been impossible without the scholarship, dedication, professionalism, and patience of the authors. The words are theirs, but the gratitude is all mine. In addition, I would like to thank a number of students and staff at Northwest Missouri State University who helped with the mountain of work (often computer-related) that a project of this size entails. Chief among them is Patricia Headley, the department secretary, who was not only my computer guru but also someone whose consistent good cheer always kept me going. I would also like to thank Laura Pearl, a talented graduate student in English who filled the role of the "general reader" by pointing out what might make sense to a historian but would not make sense to someone without some background in the region. Other students, including Precious Sanders, Jeff Easton, Mitchell Kline, and Krista Kupfer, provided the legwork that is essential to all such projects. And finally, I would like to thank the staff at ABC-CLIO, especially Alicia Merritt, for keeping faith in the project even when delivery of the manuscript did not match initial projections; Anna Kaltenbach, the production editor, for navigating the manuscript through the various stages; the copy editors, Silvine Farnell and Chrisona Schmidt, for their thoughtful and often painstaking work; Bill Nelson, the cartographer; and the photo editor, Giulia Rossi, for creating such a diverse yet balanced presentation.

And finally there are Sue, my wife, and Kristin, my daughter. Words can never express how important they are, but they know.

Richard Frucht
September 2004

INTRODUCTION

The use of the term "Eastern Europe" to describe the geographical region covered here is standard, but it is nevertheless something of a misnomer. The problem is that it not only makes a geographical distinction between this area and "Western Europe"; it also implies a distinction in development, one that ignores the similarities between Western and Eastern Europe and instead separates the continent into two distinct entities. It even suggests that Eastern Europe is a monolithic entity, failing to distinguish the states of the Balkans from those of the Baltic region. In short, it is an artificial construct that provides a simplistic division in a continent that is far more diverse, yet at the same time more closely linked together, than such a division implies.

Western Europe evokes images of Big Ben and Parliament in London, the Eiffel Tower and the Louvre in Paris, the Coliseum and the Vatican in Rome, the bulls of Pamplona in Spain. Eastern Europe on the other hand brings to mind little more than the "Iron Curtain," war in Kosovo, ethnic cleansing in Bosnia, orphanages in Romania, and the gray, bleak images of the Cold War and the Soviet Bloc. Just as colors convey certain connotations to people, so too do the concepts of "Western" and "Eastern" Europe convey very different impressions and mental images. The former is viewed as enlightened, cultured, and progressive; the latter is seen as dark, uncivilized, and static. Western Europe is democratic; Eastern Europe is backward and totalitarian, plagued by the kind of lack of fundamental humanity that leads inevitably to the horrors of Srebrenica.

Some of these stereotypes are not without some degree of justification. Foreign domination—whether German, Habsburg, Ottoman, or Russian (later Soviet)—has left parts of the region in an arrested state of development. All the peoples of the region were for much of the last half-millennium the focus and subjects of others rather than masters of their own destinies. Accordingly, trends found in more favored areas were either delayed or stunted. Albanian nationalism, for example, did not take root until a century after the French Revolution. The economic trends of the West as well as the post-1945 democracy movements (notably capitalism and democracy) are still in their infancy.

But labels are often superficial, and they can blind individuals to reality. Certainly, Tirana would never be confused with Paris. Estonia is not England. At the same time, the Polish-Lithuanian state was at its height the largest empire in Europe. Prague stuns visitors with its beauty no less than Paris; in fact, many remark that Prague is their favorite city in Europe. Budapest strikes people in the same way that Vienna does. The Danube may not be blue, but it does run through four European capitals, not just Vienna (Bratislava, Budapest, and Belgrade being the other three). The painted monasteries in Romania are no less intriguing in their design and use of color than some of the grandiose cathedrals in "the West." The Bulgarian Women's Chorus produces a sound no less stunning than that of the Vienna Boys' Choir. In short, to judge by labels and stereotypes in the end produces little more than myopia.

To dismiss Eastern Europe as backward (or worse, barbaric) is to forget that many of the Jews of Europe were saved during the Inquisition by emigrating to Poland or the lands of the Ottoman Empire. To cite the Magna Carta as the foundation of democracy in England, even though in reality it meant little more than protection for the rights of the nobility, is to ignore the fact that first written constitution in Europe was not found in the "West" but rather in the "East" (Poland). And although backwardness and even barbarity certainly can be found in the recent past in the region, no country in Europe is immune from a past that most would rather forget (the Crusades, the Inquisition, religious wars, the gas chambers of World War II, to name but a few). Myths are comfortable, but they can also be destructive. They can ennoble a people to be sure, but they can also blind them to reality and lead to a lack of understanding.

Eastern Europe is not exotic, and an understanding of it is not an exercise in esoterica. Rather the region has been and will continue to be an integral part of Europe. In one sense Europe became a distinct entity when Christianity, the cultural unifier, spread through the last outposts of the continent. In another sense, it has again become a unified continent with the demise of the last great empire that held sway over so many.

When former president Ronald Reagan passed away in June 2004, the media repeatedly recalled perhaps his most memorable line: "Mr. Gorbachev, tear down this wall," a remark made in 1984 as the American president stood in front of the Berlin Wall. In this case the American leader was referring to the concrete and barbed wire barrier behind him erected in the 1960s by the former Soviet Union to seal off its empire from the West. Yet, in many respects, the modern history of Eastern Europe was one of a series of walls, some physical (as in the case of the Iron Curtain), others geographical (all of the nations in the region were under the domination of regional great powers), and, one could argue, even psychological (the at times destructive influence of nationalism that created disruption and violence and has been a plague in the lands of the former Yugoslavia on numerous occasions in the past century). These walls have often determined not only the fate of the nations of the region but the lives of the inhabitants as well.

The past is the DNA that tells us who we are and who we can be. It is the owners' manual for every country and every people. Without that past there would be no nation and no nationalism. It is that past that provides the markers and lessons for nations and peoples. It gives direction to the present. It provides a bedrock upon which we build our societies. Whether it leads to myths that embody virtues or myths that cover up what we don't wish to acknowledge, it is the shadow that we can never lose. Thus, when each of the nations of East Central and Southeastern Europe was reborn in the nineteenth or twentieth centuries (in some cases twice reborn), the past was the compass directing them to the future.

Nations are a modern concept, but peoples are not. Poland, for example, once a great and influential European state in the Middle Ages, was partitioned in the late eighteenth century, only to rise again, like a phoenix, in 1918. And even when it again fell prey to the domination of outside influences following World War II, it was the people, embodied in Solidarity, the workers' union, who toppled the communist regime. Despite the fact that at one time or another all of the peoples and nations addressed in these volumes were under the rule or direction of a neighboring great power, the force of nationalism never abated.

Nothing is more powerful than an idea. It can inspire, unify, give direction and purpose; it can almost take on a life of its own, even though it may lie dormant for centuries. In his *Ideen zur Philosophie der Geschichte der Menschheit* (Ideas on the Philosophy of the History of Mankind), the eighteenth-century German philosopher Johann Herder captured the essence of nationalism in his analysis of the *Volk* (the people). Herder emphasized that a spirit of the nation (which Georg Hegel, the nineteenth-century German philosopher most noted for his development of the concept of the dialectic of history, later termed the *Volkgeist,* or "spirit of the people") existed that transcended politics. From the point of view of Herder and the other German idealist philosophers, peoples developed distinct characteristics based upon time and place (reflecting the *Zeitgeist,* the "spirit of the time"). Societies were therefore organic, and thus each had to be viewed in terms of its own culture and development. Accordingly, each culture not only was distinct but should recognize the distinctiveness of others, as characteristics of one culture would not necessarily be found in another. To ignore that uniqueness, which gives to each Volk a sense of nobility, would be to ignore reality.

For the peoples of Eastern Europe, language, culture, and a shared past (even if that past was mythologized, or in some cases even fabricated), exactly that spirit of the Volk that Herder, Hegel, and others saw as the essence of society, proved to be more powerful and more lasting than any occupying army or dynastic overlordship. And when modern nationalism spread throughout Europe and for that matter the world in the nineteenth and twentieth centuries, culture became the genesis of national revivals.

For centuries, Eastern Europe served as a crossroads, both in terms of trade and in the migrations (and in some cases invasions) of peoples. The former brought prosperity to some parts of the region, notably the northern and central parts of the belt between the Baltic and Mediterranean seas, while the latter left many areas a mosaic of peoples, who in the age of nationalism came to struggle as much with each other for national dominance as they did with their neighbors who dominated them politically. As the great medieval states in the region, from the Serbian Empire of Stefan Dušan to the First and Second Bulgarian Empires, to the Hungarian and Polish-Lithuanian states, fell to stronger neighbors or to internal difficulties, no peoples were left untouched by outsiders. Greece may have been able to remain outside the Soviet orbit in the 1940s, but for centuries it was a key possession of the Ottoman Empire. Poland may have been the largest state of its time, but it fell prey to its avaricious neighbors, the Russians, Prussians, and Austrians. Yet, despite centuries of occupation, in each case the Volk remained.

One of the dominant elements in modernization has been the establishment of modern nations. While the rise of the modern nation-state was late arriving in Eastern Europe, and some in Eastern Europe had failed to experience in the same manner some of the movements, such as the Renaissance or the rise of capitalism, that shaped Western Europe, it was no less affected by the rise of modern nationalism than its Western neighbors. Despite the divergent and, in some cases, the retarded development of the region in regard to many of the trends in the West, the nations of Eastern Europe in the early twenty-first century are again independent members of a suddenly larger Europe.

The story of Eastern Europe, while often written or at least directed by outsiders, is more than a mere tale of struggle. It is also a story of enormous human complexity, one of great achievement as well as great sorrow, one in which the spirit of the Volk has triumphed (even though, admittedly, it has at times, as in the former Yugoslavia, failed to respect the uniqueness of other peoples and cultures). It is a rich story, which will continue to unfold as Eastern Europe becomes more and more an integral part of Europe as a whole (a fact evident in the expansion of the European Union and NATO into areas of the former Soviet Empire). And in order to understand the story of that whole, one must begin with the parts.

CONTRIBUTORS

VOLUME 1

Terry D. Clark is a professor of political science and the director of the graduate program in international relations at Creighton University. He received his Ph.D. from the University of Illinois at Urbana-Champaign in 1992. A specialist in comparative politics and international relations, he was instrumental in developing Creighton University's exchange program with universities in Eastern Europe. He has published three books and numerous articles devoted to the study of postcommunist Europe. His research interests include the development of democratic institutions and the evolution of public opinion supporting such institutions in Lithuania and Russia.

Mel Huang is a freelance analyst on the Baltic states and is also a research associate with the Conflict Studies Research Centre (CSRC) at the Royal Military Academy, Sandhurst. He previously worked as the primary Baltics analyst for the analytical department of Radio Free Europe/Radio Liberty and served as the Baltics editor of the award-winning online journal Central Europe Review.

Aldis Purs received his Ph.D. in history from the University of Toronto in 1998. He has taught at Vidzeme University College, Wayne State University, and Eastern Michigan University. He is a coauthor of *Latvia: The Challenges of Change* (Routledge, 2001) and *The Baltic States: Estonia, Latvia, and Lithuania* (Routledge 2002) and a contributor to the University of Manchester research project "Population Displacement, State Building, and Social Identity in the Lands of the Former Russian Empire, 1917–1930."

Piotr Wróbel holds the Konstanty Reynert Chair of Polish Studies at the University of Toronto. He received his Ph.D. from the University of Warsaw in 1984. He has been a visiting scholar at the Institute of European History in Mainz, at Humboldt University in Berlin, at the Institute of Polish-Jewish Studies at Oxford, and at the United States Holocaust Memorial Museum in Washington, D.C. He has authored or coauthored some fifty articles and nine books, including *The Historical Dictionary of Poland, 1945–1996* (Greenwood, 1998). He currently serves on the advisory board of *Polin: A Journal of Polish-Jewish Studies,* on the board of directors of the Polish-Jewish Heritage Foundation of Canada, and on the governing council of the American Association for Polish-Jewish Studies.

VOLUME 2

June Granatir Alexander is a member of the faculty of the Russian and East European Studies Program at the University of Cincinnati. In addition to numerous scholarly articles, reviews, and encyclopedia entries, she is the author of two books: *The Immigrant Church and Community: Pittsburgh's Slovak Catholics and Lutherans, 1880–1915* (Pittsburgh, 1987) and *Ethnic Pride, American Patriotism: Slovaks and Other New Immigrants in the Interwar Era* (Temple University Press, 2004).

Mark Biondich is an analyst with the Crimes against Humanities and War Crimes Section of the Department of Justice of Canada. He received his Ph.D. in history from the University of Toronto in 1997 and is the author of *Stjepan Radić, the Croat Peasant Party and the Politics of Mass Mobilization, 1904–1928* (Toronto, 2000), as well as a number of articles and reviews concerning Croatian, Yugoslav, and Balkan history.

András A. Boros-Kazai was raised in a proletarian district in Budapest before coming to the United States, where he studied at Kent State University and the University of Pittsburgh. He earned his Ph.D. in history from Indiana University in 1982. He is currently a freelance translator, a researcher-consultant, and an adjunct member of the faculty at Beloit College.

Brigit Farley received her Ph.D. from Indiana University. She is an associate professor of history at Washington State University. A specialist on twentieth-century Russian and European cultural history, and the author of a number of articles, reviews, and encyclopedia entries, she is currently working on the life and death of a Moscow church.

Daniel Miller received his Ph.D. from the University of Pittsburgh, and is a professor of history at the University of West Florida in Pensacola. His research involves Czech and Slovak history, especially between the two world wars, and focuses largely on agrarian political history. He is the author of several chapters and articles along with *Forging Political Compromise: Antonín Švehla and the Czechoslovak Republican Party, 1918–1933* (Pittsburgh, 1999), which has been translated into Czech. He is also one of the coauthors of a volume in Czech on the history of the Slovak and Czech agrarian movement. In the preparation of his chapter, he would like to acknowledge the contributions and suggestions of Gregory X. Ference of Salisbury University, Lenka Kocková and Pavel Kocek (on several aspects of Czech culture and history), Alex Švamberk (on Czech popular music), and Ivan Lalák (on modern architecture).

VOLUME 3

Robert Austin is a lecturer and project coordinator with the Centre for Russian and East European Studies at the University of Toronto. He is also a project manager with Intermedia Survey Institute in Washington, D.C. His current research focuses on interwar Albania and media trends in contemporary Albania. He was aided in the preparation of his chapter by Brigitte Le Normand, who received her M.A. from the University of Toronto and is currently pursuing her Ph.D. in history at UCLA.

Richard Frucht is a professor of history and chair of the Department of History, Humanities, Philosophy, and Political Science at Northwest Missouri State University. He received his Ph.D. from Indiana University in 1980. The author of a number of books and articles on Eastern Europe, most recently he was the editor of *The Encyclopedia of Eastern Europe: From the Congress of Vienna to the Fall of Communism* (Garland, 2000).

Alexandros K. Kyrou is an associate professor of History and the director of the Program in East European Studies at Salem State College. He received his Ph.D. from Indiana University and was a Hanaah Seeger Davis Visiting Research Fellow in Hellenic Studies at Princeton University, a senior research fellow of the Kokkalis Program on Southeastern and East Central Europe at the John F. Kennedy School of Government at Harvard University, and a research scholar at the Institute on Religion and World Affairs at Boston University. He is also the associate editor of the *Journal of Modern Hellenism*.

Katherine McCarthy teaches history at Bradley University and is a research associate in the Russian and East European Center at the University of Illinois, Urbana-Champaign. She completed her Ph.D. in East European history at the University of Pittsburgh in 1996 and has written on peasant issues in the former Yugoslavia.

Nicholas Miller is an associate professor at Boise State University. He has written extensively on the Serbian community in Croatia, Serbian nationalism, and Serbia since 1945, including *Between Nation and State: Serbian Politics in Croatia, 1903–1914* (Pittsburgh, 1997). He is currently completing a manuscript on an intellectual circle in Serbia during the communist era.

James P. Niessen is World History Librarian at Rutgers University in New Brunswick, New Jersey, and Vice President for Research and Publications of H-Net: Humanities and Social Sciences OnLine. He earned a Ph.D. in East European history from Indiana University and taught history at several universities before pursuing a library career since 1994. His published works include more than fifteen studies on modern Romanian and Hungarian history, libraries, and archives.

Aleksandar Panev teaches history and philosophy at Appleby College in Oakville, Canada. He received his B.A. and M.A. degrees from the University of Belgrade and his Ph.D. from the University of Toronto. He is also an associate of the Centre for Russian and East European Studies at the Munk Centre for International Studies at the University of Toronto and has served as a faculty research associate at Arizona State University and the University of Skopje.

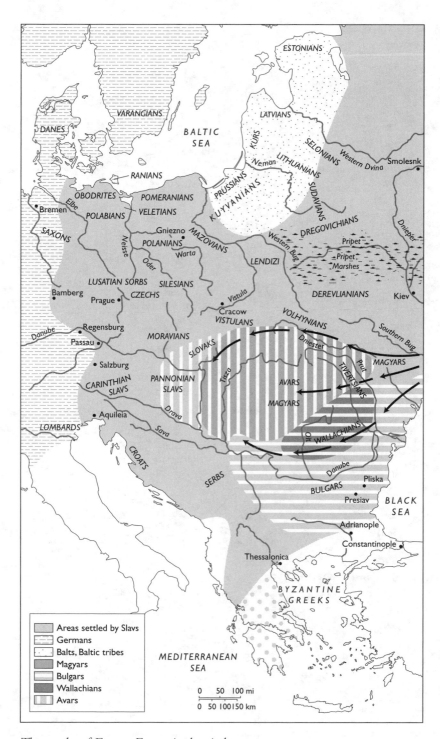

The peoples of Eastern Europe in the ninth century.

Territorial divisions in Eastern Europe in the thirteenth century (at the time of the Mongols).

Eastern Europe in the late sixteenth century.

Eastern Europe after the Congress of Vienna (1815).

Eastern Europe in 1914.

Eastern Europe between the World Wars.

Eastern Europe after World War II.

Eastern Europe in 2004.

1878–1912

Territorial changes in Southeastern Europe, 1815–1912.

SERBIA AND MONTENEGRO

NICHOLAS MILLER

LAND AND PEOPLE

The borders and political affiliations of Serbia and, to a much lesser extent, Montenegro have changed so often in history that one historian, Stevan Pavlowitch, recently titled his examination of the topic *Serbia: The History of an Idea*. From the eleventh to the fifteenth century, there was a Serbian kingdom. From 1453 to 1804, the lands inhabited by Serbs were controlled by the Ottoman Empire. During the nineteenth century, a Serbian state gradually emerged and grew at the expense of the Ottoman Empire. In 1918 Serbia merged with other lands from the Habsburg monarchy to form the Kingdom of Serbs, Croats, and Slovenes (known after 1929 as the Kingdom of Yugoslavia). This state allegedly reflected the commitment of its inhabitants to a supranational Yugoslav (South Slavic) identity. In 1941 Serbia became a puppet state of Nazi Germany. It reemerged as a republic within the new communist Yugoslavia in 1945. Montenegro meanwhile had enjoyed virtual independence

in the Ottoman Empire until 1918, when it too was included in the Kingdom of Serbs, Croats, and Slovenes. It also became a republic in communist Yugoslavia after 1945. In 1991 Yugoslavia collapsed, and Serbia and Montenegro were reconstituted in the Federal Republic of Yugoslavia (FRY), which lasted until 2003, when Serbia and Montenegro created a new constitution, and the official name of the country became the State Community of Serbia and Montenegro. With so many changes having occurred, Pavlowitch's title seemed to have been wise.

The standard definition of a Serb would be "an Orthodox Christian speaker of Serbo-Croatian." That strict definition has not always held true on an individual basis—there are plenty of Catholics and Muslims in former Yugoslavia who have considered themselves to be Serbs (such as Ivo Andrić and Meša Selimović, two important figures in Serbian culture)—but as a general rule, it works, with the religious component of the definition being more rigid than the inherently less manageable linguistic portion. To be Serbian has meant to be Orthodox Christian since the thirteenth century, with the founding of the church by Saint Sava. During the early modern period, the church became one of the foundations of Serbian identity, thanks in part to Ottoman administrative policies during the long era of Turkish occupation. Today, Serbs are not particularly religious, but they are nonetheless culturally Orthodox Christians. The church today has 3 metropolitan sees, 28 dioceses, 2,553 parishes, 2,019 ordained priests, and 179 monasteries. Of course, not all citizens of Serbia and Montenegro are Orthodox Christians; there is a Muslim Slavic population in the Sandžak of Novi Pazar, and there are various Protestant groups, especially in the

Saint Marco Church in downtown Belgrade. (Thomas Jouanneau/Corbis Sygma)

Vojvodina, where there are also Catholics (Croatian, Hungarian). The Albanian population of southern Serbia (outside of Kosovo) is also uniformly Muslim. Official figures state the following overall: Orthodox 65 percent, Muslim 19 percent, Roman Catholic 4 percent, Protestant 1 percent, and "other" 11 percent.

The language issue is more complicated, mostly because the modern language(s) spoken by Serbs, Croats, Montenegrins, and Bosnians are concoctions based on a variety of regional dialects that have attained the status of national languages, in spite of the fact that they are geographically based. The languages that were spoken by medieval and early modern elites are no longer the languages spoken by the various peoples. There are some certainties: all Serbs speak the *štokavian* dialect. The other dialects—*kajkavian* and *čakavian*—are spoken by Croats in northern Croatia and in Dalmatia respectively. Most Croats today, however, speak štokavian. Thus, it is not a "Serbian" language, no matter what intellectual language reformers and creators such as Vuk Karadžić might have said in the nineteenth century. Štokavian has three variants, known as *ekavian, ijekavian,* and *ikavian*. Ekavian and ijekavian have been rather imprecisely considered the "Serbian" and "Croatian" variants of the language. This notion received a big boost in 1954, when Croatian and Serbian linguists and literary figures

signed off on the Novi Sad Agreement, which proclaimed that the "Serbo-Croatian or Croato-Serbian Language" had those two variants, one to be considered Serbian, the other Croatian. The issue remained contentious through the communist period. Today, in Serbia, ekavian reigns supreme. Serbs, though, speak both the ekavian and ijekavian variants.

The national anthem of Serbia and Montenegro is "Hej Slaveni," composed by Samuel Tomasik (lyrics) and Michal Kleofas Oginski (music) in the nineteenth century and written as a general Slavic anthem. The country's national holiday is 28 June, St. Vitus's Day. In November 2001 a working group in the Serbian justice ministry proposed that Serbia's coat of arms inaugurated in 1882 be reestablished, that the national anthem should once again be "Božje pravde," as it was before 1918, and that the pre-1918 red, blue, and white tricolor flag once again become the national flag. Those proposals are now in limbo, as some concerns were raised about the crown in the coat of arms, which would imply that Serbia is a kingdom rather than a republic.

The population of the Federal Republic of Yugoslavia in 2000 was estimated at 10.6 million; the population growth rate in 2003 was 0.3 percent. The age structure of the Serbian and Montenegrin populations is as follows: 0–14 years: Serbia, 19.95 percent, and Montenegro, 22.05 percent;

The Serbian Language

Serbian is a Slavic language. It belongs to the South Slavic language group, along with Slovenian, Bulgarian, Macedonian, Croatian, and Bosnian. It accompanied the first Slavic migrants to the Balkan peninsula. Today's Serbian language has had a rather complicated history in which politics has played as important a role as linguistics.

The Serbian language is a rather complicated beast. It is clearly related in some way to the Croatian language, but that relationship has been defined and redefined in a variety of ways since it was (or they were) standardized in the mid-nineteenth century. Vuk Karadžić first standardized a Serbian tongue and orthography (using a Hercegovinian dialect, *štokavian,* as the basis) after years of ethnographic and linguistic work in the countryside with those who spoke a variety of dialects of what was potentially a unified language. It was his legendary view that all who spoke the Serbian language were in fact Serbs; thus, he adopted the approach that language defined nationality. Of course this approach was fundamentally flawed. The fact that Karadžić chose to define his own product as the language of Serbs and the fact that many Croats spoke the language he identified as Serbian were the primary flaws. Nonetheless, thanks to the influence of the German romantic philosopher Johann Gottfried Herder and the German ethnographers, by the late nineteenth century language and nationality were seen as united by an almost sacred bond; thus language became a subject of great contention between nationalists of various stripes.

In the aftermath of World War II, the unveiling of "brotherhood and unity" as the mantra of Titoist Yugoslavism dictated that attention be paid to the language that the Serbian and Croatian "brothers" allegedly shared. (Slovenes and Macedonians spoke languages that were not considered kin to Serbian and Croatian.) The Novi Sad Agreement of 1954, negotiated by representatives of the Croatian and Serbian linguistic and literary communities, established an acceptable approach: the language would be referred to as Serbo-Croatian or Croato-Serbian. Serbian and Croatian would be considered variants differentiated by the Croatian use of the *jat* and slightly different grammatical structures, and each variant would be used where appropriate. The language itself was the štokavian dialect of a broader language that included *kajkavian* and *čakavian* (both historically spoken by Croats).

The Novi Sad Agreement fell apart after 1967, when Croatian institutions and individuals protested the fact that in spite of the stipulations of the agreement, the Serbian variant was being used on Croatian soil. Thereafter, there was no official "guidance" on the subject. On the ground, as Yugoslavia collapsed, the situation remained as it had been since World War II: Croats primarily used the *ijekavian* form of štokavian, Serbs primarily used the *ekavian.* Nonetheless, there was plenty of crossover. Since the collapse of Yugoslavia, all of the peoples of the former Yugoslavia have been demonstrating just how powerful state intervention can be in recreating languages (the Croats are most active in this regard, as they have unsystematically been purging their press and educational systems of forms considered to be Serbian).

Today, Serbs speak štokavian in both the ijekavian and ekavian variants.

15–64 years: Serbia, 65.22 percent, and Montenegro, 66.16 percent; 65 years and over: Serbia, 14.83 percent, and Montenegro, 11.79 percent. The growth rates of the populations of the two republics are, for Serbia, 0.739 percent; for Montenegro, 12.22 percent. Their birthrates are, for Serbia, 12.20 births per one thousand inhabitants; Montenegro, 14.9 births per one thousand. Their death rates are, for Serbia, 11.08 deaths per one thousand; for Montenegro, 7.9 deaths per thousand (all 2000 estimates). The Serbian infant mortality rate is 20.13 deaths per thousand live births; the Montenegrin rate is 10.97 deaths per thousand live births. The life expectancy at birth for the total population of Serbia is 72.39 years; for Montenegro it is 75.46 years. For Serbian males, it is 69.31 years; for Serbian females, it is 75.72 years. For Montenegrin males, it is 71.45 years; for Montenegrin females it is 79.82 years (2000 est.)

Serbia encompasses 88,361 square kilometers. Serbia's border totals 2,397 kilometers. It shares borders in the east with Bulgaria, the north and east with Romania, the north with Hungary, the west with Croatia and Bosnia-Hercegovina, the southwest with Albania, and the south with Macedonia. It has a population of 10 million, of whom approximately 20 percent live in Vojvodina and 20 percent in Kosovo, two provinces of the Republic of Serbia. Its largest cities include Belgrade (population 1,602,226), Novi Sad (179,626), Niš (175,391), Kragujevac (147,305), Priština (108,083), Subotica (100,386), Čačak (71,550), Smederevo (63,884), and Leskovac (62,053). In addition, as of July 2001, there were 377,731 registered refugees in Serbia; 63 percent of those were from Croatia, and 36 percent from Bosnia-Hercegovina. Belgrade is the republican and federal capital, Priština is the capital of Kosovo, and Novi Sad is the

Arrival of the post in Cetinje, capital of Montenegro, ca. 1890. (Library of Congress)

capital of Vojvodina; Subotica is also in Vojvodina. The Republic of Serbia (including Vojvodina and Kosovo) is divided into twenty-nine counties.

Serbia's flatlands include the Pannonian Plain, Mačva, the Sava River valley, the Morava River valley, and parts of eastern Serbia. Serbia's mountainous districts are in the central and southern portions of the republic, including Kosovo. The republic is transected or bounded by several rivers: the Danube (588 kilometers), which runs through Vojvodina and divides Vojvodina from Serbia proper; the Zapadna Morava (308 kilometers) and the Južna Morava (295 kilometers) in central Serbia; the Ibar (272 kilometers) in Kosovo; the Drina (220 kilometers), bordering Bosnia; the Sava (206 kilometers), dividing western Serbia from Vojvodina; the Timok (202 kilometers) in eastern Serbia; the Velika Morava (185 kilometers) in central Serbia; the Tisa (168 kilometers) in Vojvodina; the Nišava (151 kilometers); the Tamis (118 kilometers); and the Begej (75 kilometers). Serbia has nine mountain peaks of over 2,400 meters in height: Deravica (2,656 meters), Crni vrh (2,585 meters), Gusam (2,539 meters), Bogdas (2,533 meters), Žuti kamen (2,522 meters), Ljuboten (2,498 meters), Veternik (2,461 meters), Crni krs (2,426 meters), and Hajla (2,403 meters). Serbia's land surface includes 46,746 square kilometers of arable land and 10,065 square kilometers of pasture. Fifty-five percent of Serbia is arable land, and 27 percent is forested. Those figures are further divided as follows: production of cereals, 24,534 square kilometers; meadows, 6,667 square kilometers; reed marshes and pond forage, 4,946 square kilometers; industrial herbs, 3,486 square kilometers; vegetables, 3,005 square kilometers; orchards, 2,569 square kilometers; vineyards, 858 square kilometers; uncultivated land, 647 square kilometers; forests, 869 square kilometers; and nursery gardens, 27 square kilometers. Serbia's railway network totals 3,619 kilometers, while its road network is 42,692 kilometers long (with 24,860 kilometers paved).

The Serbian industrial sector includes mining, the processing industry, the electric power industry, and the production and distribution of petroleum products and water. A breakdown of Serbian industry shows the following distribution: the processing industry (75.18 percent), production and distribution of electric power, petroleum products and water (19.69), ore and stone mining (5.31). Processing includes 23 areas: food and beverages (19.97 percent), tobacco (1.61), textiles (4.11), garment industry (3.00), tanning (1.23), wood industry (0.84), pulp and paper (2.68), printing and reproduction (0.97), production of coke and oil derivatives (1.14), chemicals (9.50), plastics and rubber

(3.63), nonmetal minerals (5.49), basic metals (5.74), metal manufacturing (3.20), machinery (3.11), office supplies (2.41), electronics (2.41), radio, television, and communications equipment (0.31), optical instruments (0.22), motor industry (3.10), transportation (0.76), furniture (0.02), recycling (0.011). There are 696,540 workers employed in industrial and mining companies, comprising 52 percent of the total active labor force in the Republic of Serbia. Small enterprises employ 82,273 workers. There are 146,972 in medium-size enterprises and 457,286 in large enterprises.

Vojvodina's area is 21,506 square kilometers. Its population was 2,013,889, according to the 1991 census, which is approximately 20 percent of Serbia's total population. The largest cities in Vojvodina are Novi Sad (estimated at 179,626 in 2001), Subotica (est. 100,386 in 2001), Zrenjanin (est. 81,316 in 2001), and Pančevo (a suburb of Belgrade, est. 72,793 in 2001). Serbs, with 1,143,723 (57 percent), make up a majority of the population of the province. Non-Serbs include Hungarians (339,491), Croats (74,808), Slovaks (63,545), Montenegrins (44,838), Romanians (38,809), Roma (24,366), Ruthenians (17,652), Macedonians (17,472), and others, including Ukrainians, Albanians, and Slovenians; furthermore, 174,225 people in Vojvodina declared themselves Yugoslavs (in other words, they chose to claim a supranationality rather than a specific one).

Kosovo's area is 10,849 square kilometers. The census of 1991 showed Kosovo with 1,956,196 inhabitants, which is, like Vojvodina, approximately 20 percent of the population of Serbia. Priština, Kosovo's capital, has an estimated 33,305 residents; other cities in Kosovo include Prizren (est. 24,617 in 2001), Kosovska Mitrovica (est. 18,595 in 2001), and Peć (est. 15,926 in 2001). Albanians are the dominant ethnic group, with approximately 90 percent of the population of the province, and (in 1991) 17 percent of the total population of Serbia. In 1991 Serbs (194,190), Muslim Slavs (66,189), Roma (45,745), Montenegrins (20,356), Turks (10,446), Croats (8,062) followed in numbers.

Montenegro's capital is Podgorica, while its cultural and historical center is Cetinje. Its area is 13,812 square kilometers, and its population as of the 1991 census was 650,575. It has 294 kilometers of coastline, and its borders (with Albania, Croatia, and Bosnia) total 614 kilometers. Montenegro is divided into twenty-one counties and has five urban areas: Podgorica (with 117,875 people); Nikšić (56,141), Pljevlja (20,187), Cetinje (15,946), and Kotor (5,620). The highest point in the republic is Mount Durmitor at 2,522 meters, and its biggest lake is Skadar, at 391 square kilometers. Montenegro has several national parks: Durmitor, Lovćen, Biogradska gora, and Lake Skadar. Montenegro has 5,227 kilometers of roads. Major roads total 1,720 kilometers; the rest are local and predominantly unsurfaced. There are 250 kilometers of railroad in the republic, and it has two airports, at Podgorica and Tivat. In Montenegro, five state holidays are celebrated (1 January, 27 April [celebrating the constitution of the Federal Republic of Yugoslavia], 1 May, 13 July [celebrating the uprising in World War II], and 29 November [Republic Day]) and three religious holidays (Christmas, Easter, and Bairam). The mean January temperature is 5 degrees Celsius; July's is 25 degrees Celsius. Montenegro's official currency is the euro.

Forests cover 54 percent of Montenegro's land surface, or 7,200 square miles. In the communist era Montenegro began to industrialize. The steel, aluminum, and energy industries dominated this development, and the building of a transportation infrastructure contributed mightily to industrial growth. Today Montenegro still produces steel, bauxite, glinice, aluminum, sea salt, and coal on a large scale. Montenegro has the capacity to produce 3 billion kilowatt-hours of energy yearly via its hydroelectric plants at Perućica and Piva and its thermoelectric plant at Pljevlja. To this industrial base, Montenegro adds the ability to produce metalworks, machinery, wood products, textiles, chemicals, clothing, and food products. Agriculture in the republic is limited to the production of meat, milk products, and some fruit. Montenegro also produces some highly sought after wines, including the famous Vranac.

Serbia and Montenegro have approximately 333 regularly occurring bird species (214 in Montenegro alone, with 379 recorded in total) and three dozen internationally recognized birding areas. One Serbian birding organization listed the following ten species as good reasons to visit the country: pygmy cormorant, ferruginous duck, great bustard, long-legged buzzard, Saker falcon, Syrian woodpecker, red-rumped swallow, wallcreeper, nutcracker, and black-headed bunting. In Montenegro, Lake Skadar, Ulcinj, and Mount Durmitor are key birding destinations. In Serbia, the Danube River is an important wintering area for wildfowl, including more than twenty species of ducks recorded in the last fourteen years. Other important mountain sites include Uvac and Milesevka Griffon Vulture Sanctuary, Ovčar-Kablar Gorge, Mt. Tara, Mt. Kopaonik, Djerdap (Iron Gates) National Park, Rešava, Sičevo, Jerma Gorge, and the Pčinja River valley; lowland areas of interest include Koviljski, Obedska, Carska Bara, Dubovac Wetland, Bečej Fishpond, Apatin-Monostor Wetlands, and Slano Kopovo. Serbia and Montenegro also are home to over 100 species of fresh-water fish, with 14 subspecies that are endemic to the region, over 150 species of amphibians and reptiles, and 96 mammals. Serbia and Montenegro have 4,300 plant species, over 400 of which are endemic to the region.

HISTORY
MEDIEVAL SERBIA

Serbs first came to the Balkan Peninsula in the seventh century C.E., a century after the Slavic migrations into the region began. The Serbs created numerous small states spotted through modern Hercegovinian, Montenegrin, and southern Serbian territory, with names like Trebinje, Konavli, Zahumlje, and Duklja (later Zeta). By the tenth century, Duklja had consolidated control over the territory that eventually constituted modern Montenegro. Raška, which was the core of the medieval Serbian kingdom that emerged in the twelfth century, split from Duklja in the eleventh century and quickly became the strongest Serbian state in the region.

In 1168 the lands of Raška, which had been divided, were united under the leadership of one man, Stefan Nemanja. The origins of Stefan Nemanja, who emerged as the strongest of four brothers, are unknown. By the time of his abdication in 1196, Zeta (as Duklja had come to be known) had been incorporated into Raška. Upon his abdication, Stefan became an Orthodox monk and moved to Mount Athos, in northern Greece, to join his son Rastko, who had joined the church a few years earlier and taken the name Sava. Together, they convinced the Orthodox patriarchate to approve a Serbian monastery on Athos. This monastery, Hilandar, became the cultural center of Serbia in the medieval period. By 1219, Sava was able to win the grant of an autocephalous Serbian Orthodox Church, which firmly established Serbia as an Orthodox kingdom and gave it a stable cultural identity.

Stefan and Sava thus established the two foundations of modern Serbia: the state itself, which later disappeared from the map of Europe but not from the memory of Serbs, and the faith that ensured the continuity of a Serbian people through the centuries that followed. At its greatest extent, under Stefan Dušan (r. 1331–1355), the Serbian kingdom extended from the Danube and Sava Rivers in the north to the Dalmatian coast in the west, through Epirus, Thessaly, and western Thrace. This kingdom became a powerful element in the fluid relations of the Balkan Peninsula, which included Bosnian, Byzantine, and Hungarian states. When Stefan Dušan died in 1355, however, the Serbian state fell into internal feuding such as had existed before Stefan Nemanja's consolidation of power. Stefan Dušan's son, Stefan Uroš V, lost to the invading Ottoman Empire in the Battle of Maritsa in 1371 and died in the same year, leaving no heirs. Between 1371 and 1389, the remaining Serbian aristocracy declared loyalty to Lazar Hrebeljanović, a Serbian notable, but they could not defeat the Ottomans at the historic Battle of Kosovo on 28 June 1389. Between 1389 and 1459, Serbia continued to exist as a vassal state of the Ottoman sultan. In the latter year, Ottoman armies finally brought Serbian statehood to an end at the Battle of Smederevo. Until the early nineteenth century, Serbia was extinguished as a state.

The Battle of Kosovo has become a key event in Serbian historical memory, thanks to two sources: the Serbian Orthodox Church and Serbian folk tradition. Modern Serbs' memory of the battle is that it was a critical defeat for Serbia, a defeat that spelled the end of medieval Serbian glory and the beginning of a centuries-long period of darkness for the Serbian people. Most historians today, however, agree that Serbia's medieval glory had already passed, that the Battle of Kosovo was neither a battle between Serbs and the Ottomans as such nor a military victory for either side. Memory, therefore, has transformed the event from a battle fought by multinational armies, which ended inconclusively, into an apocalyptic confrontation between good Serbs and evil Turks, which the good Serbs lost. That such a transformation could occur says much about what the Ottoman conquest did and did not bring to the lands of medieval Serbia.

SERBIA UNDER THE OTTOMAN EMPIRE

The Ottoman conquest socially leveled Serbia. The Serbian aristocracy did in fact disappear; Serbian aristocrats converted to Islam, lost their lands and privileges, or were killed. The result was a society consisting of peasants, which is what Serbia remained until the mid-nineteenth century. Thus one-half of the Nemanja dynasty's great achievement of statehood and political and military power disappeared from Europe. The other half, however, did not: Saint Sava's Serbian Orthodox Church remained and, with general though varying success, continued to define the Serbian population culturally. Together with a folk culture that maintained and passed on a historical understanding that was part myth, part reality, the church, ministering to its peasant flock via its peasant clergy, nourished the continued existence of a Serbia not as a state, but as an identity. Thus it was that the portion of the Nemanja inheritance that was lost (power) was defined in historical memory by the portion of that inheritance that remained (the faith). The fact that a continuous memory of "Serbianness" and Serbian medieval power remained throughout the four centuries of "darkness" testifies to just how permeable that darkness really was.

As inhabitants of the Ottoman Empire, Serbs both suffered and benefited. The classic accusation against the Ottomans is that they oppressed and discriminated against those who were not Muslim. There are various ways to evaluate the discrimination that non-Muslims suffered in the empire. One is to note that many Serbs, Bulgars, Albanians, Greeks, Romanians, and other originally non-Muslim people of the Ottoman Empire chose to convert, in which cases they instantly became members of the favored faith and thus part of the ruling class. On the other hand, those who chose not to convert became, by definition, peasants (thanks to the fact that Christians could not own land in the Ottoman Empire). Another is to note that while Orthodox Christian Serbs were subject to taxes and levies that Muslims did not pay, those burdens were balanced by the fact that Christians did not have to fight in Ottoman armies. Finally, the Orthodox Christians of the Ottoman Empire were administered via the millet system, according to which they were governed by their own church hierarchy.

The millet system reflected the Ottoman belief that one's identity is fundamentally religious. Thus, while one had the option to convert to Islam and enjoy the fruits of that conversion, one also had the right to maintain one's faith. Thus, the Ottomans administered their subjects as religious beings, and the Orthodox Church was given responsibility for the Orthodox Christians of the empire. The millet system was established in 1453 as a result of a decree by Sultan Mehmed II. For the Orthodox of the empire, the millet system meant that they were governed by the Orthodox patriarchate and its hierarchy. This hierarchy was not necessarily of the same ethnic group as those it governed: Bulgars, for instance, did not have their own church after 1394, and Serbs only had theirs from 1557 (with the reestablishment of the patriarchate at Peć) to 1766 (when its autonomy was removed as punishment for consorting with the Ottoman enemies Russia and the Habsburg monarchy.

Otherwise, the Orthodox of the Balkans were placed under the authority of the Greek patriarch in Istanbul (Constantinople). But on the local level, where contact between the believer and the church was most common, the parish priest was of the ethnicity of the flock. From the patriarch down to the parish priest, the church was made responsible for marriage, divorce, and the collection of dues to the church as well as the state. The Orthodox Church was one important face of the state for Orthodox subjects of the sultan. The millet system thus ameliorated some of the effects of the Ottoman conquest. Serbian statehood was gone, but a Serbian, Orthodox Christian identity was maintained through what many Serbs see as a dark age, thanks to a system that allowed a degree of self-administration.

Over the course of the Ottoman conquest and in subsequent centuries, many Orthodox Christians migrated northward and westward under the pressure of the Ottoman advance from the south and east. Thus, a large and important Serbian presence was established in the Habsburg monarchy from the fourteenth century onward. Population movements began in earnest after the Battle of Smederevo in 1459, and by 1483, up to two hundred thousand Orthodox Christians had moved into central Slavonia and Srijem (eastern Croatia). In the early sixteenth century Orthodox populations had also been established in western Croatia. Finally, in the 1520s and 1530s, waves of Orthodox immigrants made their way to the region known as Žumberak, which straddles the modern Croatian-Slovenian border. Thereafter, the Orthodox populations were supplemented following further Ottoman conquests, and existing Orthodox populations in Croatia and Hungary shifted with the flow of battles. The final major population shift occurred in the 1690s, following an Austro-Ottoman war, when at least 30,000 Orthodox Serbs, led by Patriarch Arsenije III Crnojević, made their way from Kosovo north to southern Hungary. This "Great Migration of the Serbs" has become legendary, due to its size and to the fact that it signified the end of a Serbian presence in Kosovo. Furthermore, the center of authority in the Serbian Orthodox Church moved with the migrants; the patriarchate at Peć, which was finally extinguished by the Ottomans in 1766, was replaced for all intents and purposes by the metropolitan see of Sremski Karlovci, in Croatia.

Through the late nineteenth century, two institutions, the military frontier and the metropolitan see, defined Serbian life in the Habsburg monarchy. The military frontier existed until 1881, when it was dismantled because it was no longer militarily necessary. During the centuries of its existence, however, it provided a framework for Serbian existence in the monarchy. The Orthodox Christians who had made their way from Ottoman territories to the Habsburg monarchy were given certain privileges; these tended to include a plot of land, freedom from taxation by the local aristocracy, and freedom of worship, paid for by military service in times of crisis. The most famous agreement of this kind was the Statuta Valachorum, issued in 1630 by Emperor Ferdinand II. Others were issued in the 1690s upon the arrival of the final large group of immigrants; this group of privileges included the right of the Serbian Orthodox Church to work among Serbs. Still other sets of local privileges were negotiated over the centuries. Settlement patterns, with Banija, Kordun, Lika in the west and parts of Slavonia in the east heavily populated by Serbs, were a result of these agreements.

These privileges gave the Serbian community the real sense that they were something apart from the monarchy itself, a corporate body that had negotiated its position vis-à-vis the authorities and could thus negotiate changes. The metropolitan see (the equivalent, in the Serbian Orthodox Church, of an archbishopric), a late arrival in the Habsburg lands, contributed to the sense of uniqueness that their privileges had encouraged among Serbs. The privileges themselves were negotiated by religious authorities, and when the church moved north, it inherited the authority to speak for its Orthodox flock in the Habsburg lands. By the nineteenth century, when political life began to expand under the impress of the ideology of nationalism and the striving for political democracy, Serbs in the monarchy tended to look to the strengthening of their church's position as a strengthening of their own. In other words, they remained wedded to the notion of corporate privilege, even in a time when others began to seek constitutional guarantees for democratic forms of government. The Serbian Orthodox Church offered a different sort of guarantee: its National-Church Congress acted as a pseudo-representative body for the Orthodox of the Habsburg lands and claimed to speak for the Serbs of the monarchy.

THE BIRTH OF MODERN SERBIA

The origins of a modern Serbian state can be traced to the late eighteenth century in the *pašalik* (an area governed by a *paša,* or pasha) of Belgrade. This region, south of the Danube and Sava Rivers and east of the Drina River, became the geographic core of modern Serbia. The first stirrings of rebellion among the Serbs of the region followed the Austro-Ottoman War of 1788–1791, during which Serbs had fought (as they had many times before) for the Habsburg monarchy. After the war, the Austrians, who had lost the war, left the Serbs of the region to their own devices. In spite of the Serbs' disloyalty to the sultan, both the Serbs (who had enjoyed some self-government under the Austrians earlier in the century) and the Ottomans desired peace and stability in the region. However, in the ever weaker Ottoman Empire, the borderlands had come under the sway of local janissaries (at this time only unruly remnants of the highly disciplined soldiers of earlier centuries), and the pašalik of Belgrade was no exception. The sultan and his Serbian subjects had a mutual interest in destroying the destabilizing influence of the janissaries, and the roots of the Serbian independence movement are thus paradoxically to be found in an alliance of local Serbian headmen with the Ottoman central government.

In January and February 1804, fearing a coordinated Serbian uprising, the janissary leaders in Belgrade began to systematically murder Serbian headmen throughout the pašalik. The Serbian uprising that immediately followed was the work of headmen who had escaped their death

Serbs attend the unveiling of a monument to Karadjordje, who was the leader of the first Serbian uprising against the Turks in the year 1804, in Orasac, 100 kilometers south of Belgrade, 15 February 2004. The ceremony was held on the occasion of Sretenje, the Serbian Statehood Day, marking its two hundredth anniversary. (Andrej Isakovi/AFP/Getty Images)

sentences and headed to the hills to resist the janissaries. Serbia at this point had about 400,000 people, 10 percent of whom were Muslim. Under the leadership of Djordje Petrović, known as Karadjordje ("Black George," a headman from western Serbia), the Serbs were able to overcome the warlords' forces by August of 1804 (when they captured and executed the four leading janissaries) and establish themselves as the political power in the region. What had begun as a rebellion with social and economic roots was quickly transformed into a potential national revolutionary movement, as the Serbs began to consolidate their influence in the region and to be tempted to expand their power.

Outsiders were essential to this transformation, as Russia in particular encouraged the Serbian movement as one that could benefit the Russian Empire as it fought in the Napoleonic Wars. Russia assisted the Serbian rebels sporadically through the summer of 1813, when Russia signed the Treaty of Bucharest with the Ottoman Empire, ending their hostilities as Russia made war on Napoleon's France. The Ottomans were then able to crush the Serbs, most of whose leaders fled into the Habsburg monarchy or beyond. In April 1815 those who had not fled, led by Miloš Obrenović (a headman from southwestern Serbia), rebelled anew, with the intent of negotiating a quick agreement allowing self-

rule with the Ottoman authorities. Miloš accomplished this task and was able thereafter to incrementally add to his power (and that of a small Serbian principality). Miloš had Karadjordje murdered in 1817, when the latter returned to Serbia in order to attempt to link Serbs to a wider anti-Ottoman uprising.

After 1815, the core of an independent Serbia existed in the form of a tenuously autonomous principality, although that status was not formally bestowed until 1830. Miloš governed this small state as a Turkish paša might have: it was his domain, to be milked for as much personal gain as he could get. In this regard, the difference between Turks and Serbs was minimal, and in fact one could argue that over the centuries, Serbs had adapted to the ways of the Turks quite nicely. Nevertheless, this Serbia also represented the possibility of a revived, modern Serbian state, and even if Miloš tended to be venal, others invested the principality with more national content.

Miloš's actions as absolute ruler of this Serbia were generally self-interested, but they often had beneficial results. For instance, in his desire to clip the wings of rival headmen, he made it easier for peasants to own and prosper on the land. Miloš also welcomed the help of better-educated Serbs, which had the result of encouraging national goals. Both Vuk Karadžić and Dositej Obradović, for instance, worked during and after the revolution to see their vision of a Serbian culture and nation develop, Dositej as Karadjordje's advisor on education, Vuk in various posts in Miloš's bureaucracy. Miloš also welcomed in Habsburg Serbs, better educated and more experienced in modern administration. These outsiders were resented by the Serbs of Šumadija, but they were needed nonetheless.

Miloš ruled absolutely till 1838, when the Ottomans approved a sort of constitution for the pašalik of Belgrade, by which Miloš would govern along with a council of elders. The Turks wished to rein in Miloš; he could not bear the restraint, so he left Serbia in 1839.

With Miloš's departure, the office of prince was given by the council to his son Milan, who died within a month. Then it passed to Miloš's second son, Mihailo, who lasted until 1842, when he was replaced by Aleksandar Karadjordjević, son of the original Karadjordje. Karadjordjević ruled until 1858, when he was replaced by Mihailo Obrenović, in a return engagement that lasted until 1868. Mihailo was assassinated in 1868, to be replaced by his cousin Milan Obrenović, who governed as prince and then king until 1889, when his own son Aleksandar Obrenović took over until his own assassination in 1903. Between 1830 and 1878, Serbia was an autonomous principality of the Ottoman Empire. Several sets of tensions defined its existence in this period: one was the continuing struggle between the notables on the council of elders and the princes, both desirous of gaining more power. Miloš, for instance, was opposed by a council of elders; their competition simply carried on earlier competitions between Karadjordje and his elders. Until the 1860s, the tug of war between prince and notables continued; after that point, politics began to expand to represent, or at least strive to represent, the interests of the ordinary Serb. Another tension came with the importation of political ideas from outside the Balkans, which resulted in pressures for a real constitution and the democratization of political life in Serbia (reflected in the growth of political parties). The third major source of tension was the growth of Serbian nationalism, as well as Yugoslav nationalism, which placed new burdens on the young Serbian government and society.

SERBIA EXPANDS

In an era of nationalism such as that in which the Serbian state emerged, it was inevitable that Serbia would become the focus of expansionist dreams, dreams of Serbs but also of others. Yugoslavism was and remains an intellectual construct. As an active political ideology, it is a product of the nineteenth century, when the concept of the nation first entered the vocabulary of politics. "Yugoslav" means "South Slavic," which is in turn a linguistic category; thus, the Yugoslav idea would bring unity to the speakers of South Slavic languages. Yugoslavism was therefore an alternative identity formulated by intellectuals in order to bypass some of the vexing problems of other national movements that were thriving in the South Slavic regions of the Balkans, primarily Croatian and Serbian nationalism, but potentially also Slovenian, Bulgarian, Montenegrin, and Macedonian

movements. In its first modern iteration, Yugoslavism took the form of "Illyrianism," in the Illyrian movement of the Croat Ljudevit Gaj. The Illyrian movement was an early, idealistic attempt to promote the unity of speakers of all of the dialects of Serbo-Croatian. It was also the most welcoming of national movements, as Gaj and his followers argued that the nation (which they called "Illyrian," from the term the Romans used for the region, because that name would help circumvent the competitiveness of Croats and Serbs) should adopt as its language the štokavian dialect of the language, which was not actually spoken by most educated, urban Croats (such as the followers of Gaj themselves), but was spoken by Serbs and a majority of Croats in general. The Illyrian movement was born in 1835 and survived until 1848, but did not succeed on its own terms. It did produce a newspaper, called *Danica* (The Dawn), which was written in the štokavian that it imagined as the new Illyrian tongue. But, in spite of Gaj's attempts to bring harmony to division, division won the day. Serbs, in particular, resented the suggestion that the extant national names (Serb and Croat) be jettisoned; they already had an identity, and it had been nurtured in fire over the Ottoman centuries.

While the Illyrian movement struggled for popularity and recognition, the development of a Serbian state south of the Danube and Sava Rivers continued. The principality had become the center of Serbian national aspirations. Until 1832, when he was expelled from the principality, Vuk Karadžić worked with Miloš Obrenović to nurture the new Serbian state as the core of a future expanded state. Karadžić was an intellectual child of the German philosopher Johann Gottfried Herder, who taught that a common language made a people a nation, and the founders of German philology, the brothers Grimm, and thus placed language at the center of his analysis. For him, as a Serb, then, all speakers of the language he spoke were by definition Serbs. In an article entitled "Serbs All and Everywhere" (1842), he developed this idea, presenting a new definition of Serbianness, which had in the past depended on religion rather than language. But it is easy enough to see what Karadžić's ideas did to the assertions of the Illyrians: metaphorically, Vuk told them that their graciousness was not appreciated; the speakers of štokavian were not Illyrians, they were Serbs. All of this is not meant to imply that national identities rose and fell with the intellectual and political capabilities of their authors; Vuk did not kill the Illyrian movement. Instead, we can say that Vuk's ideas better reflected the opinion of educated and influential Serbs than Gaj's did the opinions of educated and influential Serbs and Croats.

Croats too eventually gravitated to an exclusively Croatian national ideology, associated with Ante Starčević and his Croatian Party of Right. But the Yugoslav idea did not die; instead, it was adopted and nurtured in the 1860s by new forces, led by Bishop Josip Juraj Strossmayer. Strossmayer worked to build ties between Croatia's Croats and Serbs and the principality of Serbia to the south. He envisioned the creation of a large Yugoslav state, perhaps including Bulgaria, probably with its capital in Zagreb. Strossmayer worked with Ilija Garašanin in the late 1860s to create some sort of coalition between Serbia and Croatia.

This was an impractical goal, given the fact that Croatia was not a state at the time.

One Serbian "statement of purpose" regarding expansion and the nature of the Serbian nation has emerged from the period. It is entitled the *Načertanije* (Outline), and it was written by Garašanin, the Serbian minister of the interior, in 1844. One must be careful in assessing the importance of this document, since nobody outside of the Serbian government knew of its existence until 1906, and it is unclear how persuasive it was for any Serbian political figure other than Garašanin himself. It is probably best to consider the *Načertanije* to have been a general statement of aims that most Serbs could agree on regarding the future of the Serbian state. The *Načertanije* envisioned first the liberation of Serbs under Ottoman control in Bosnia; thereafter, Garašanin imagined the liberation of Kosovo and Macedonia. He was leery of antagonizing the Habsburg monarchy, so he described the unification of the Serbs of Croatia and Hungary with Serbia as a distant goal. The *Načertanije* has been the source of much debate over the century since it appeared: was it "Serbian" or "Yugoslav" in its orientation? On balance, however, it appears to have been a statement of Serbian aims: it never mentions unification with non-Serbs and assumes that Kosovo, Bosnia, and Macedonia are all Serbian lands (and, of course, that assertion was and remains absurd).

Garašanin composed the *Načertanije* at a time when Serbs had little interest in combining with other South Slavs. By 1860, however, when Mihailo Obrenović ascended the Serbian throne, the situation had changed. Prince Mihailo was Miloš's son and had grand plans for his Serbian state. His goal was to expel the Ottoman Empire from the Balkan Peninsula and create a large kingdom of South Slavs, including Serbs, Croats, Montenegrins, Macedonians, and Bulgars, and his method would be to bring about a grand alliance of Balkan Christians to fight the Ottomans. Although Garašanin had been Mihailo's political enemy, Mihailo kept him as an advisor after coming to the throne. Thanks to the growth of Yugoslavism in Croatia, Garašanin by 1860 had come to see the potential of cooperation with the Croats, not just as allies (as with the other Balkan Christians) but as Yugoslavs, or members of the same nation.

Thus the 1860s saw a flurry of diplomatic activity initiated by Serbia. In 1860 Mihailo sent Vuk Karadžić to Cetinje to talk about alliance with the Montenegrin prince, Nikola; in the early 1860s he provided assistance to Bulgarian nationalist revolutionaries; in 1861, Garašanin went to Novi Sad to discuss collaboration with the Serbs and Hungarians of the Habsburg monarchy, and later that same year he went to Istanbul to discuss alliance with the Greek ambassador there. The problem generally with Mihailo's plans was that neither Serbia nor its prospective allies were strong enough to defeat the Ottomans. Nonetheless, in 1866 it seemed that the moment might be at hand. The Habsburg monarchy was defeated by Prussia in the Six Weeks War, and the Cretan Uprising forced the Ottomans to abandon their garrisons in Serbia. Garašanin concluded a formal alliance with Montenegro, and he entered negotiations with Strossmayer in Croatia on cooperation with the Croats. It all came to naught, however, when Prince Mihailo was assassinated on 9 June 1868 by opponents of his authoritarian domestic system. With his death, the alliances all dissolved, which was evidence of their tenuousness in the first place. The entire episode reinforced the fact that at this early stage in its modern history, Serbia could do little to liberate its brethren, however defined, without help from one or more of the great powers (Great Britain, France, Germany, Russia, Italy, and the Habsburg monarchy).

Until the Balkan Wars (1912–1913), Serbia required outside assistance, whether intended or not, to expand territorially. Between 1875 and 1878, the so-called Eastern Crisis offered just such assistance. With a modest contribution of its own, Serbia was able to add a bit of territory and achieve independence from the Ottoman Empire. The Eastern Crisis of 1875 began, as did so many other crises, with a peasant uprising, which began in July when Orthodox leaders in Hercegovina rebelled against Ottoman tax collectors. Prince Milan hoped to avoid war, but his people had become deeply involved in a romantic nationalism that would not tolerate inaction when fellow Serbs were rebelling against the Ottomans. The crisis spread to other districts of Bosnia, and the Ottomans stationed an army on Bosnia's border with Serbia. In December the great powers got involved when Austria's foreign minister, Gyula Andrassy, issued a demand that the Ottoman Empire reform its administration in Bosnia. The Russian government wished Serbia to remain out of the crisis, but as in Serbia, the Russian populace had come under the sway of Pan-Slavists (as those were called who looked to unite Slavs under some political or cultural association), who wished to push Russia into war with the Ottoman Empire.

While this complicated situation played out, the Bulgarians rose in rebellion in April of 1876, bringing a brutal Ottoman response. Public opinion in much of Europe became violently anti-Ottoman. In the spring of 1876 Russian general Mikhail G. Cherniaev, a decorated veteran of campaigns in Central Asia, showed up in Belgrade. Cherniaev, in the service of Pan-Slavists in Russia, let the Serbs believe that he represented official Russia; the Serbs fell for his ruse. He was made a citizen of Serbia and sent off to lead Serbia's troops against the Ottomans in a war that began in July 1876.

Serbia's four armies fought horribly, and there was no general Balkan uprising. The end came in November 1876, when Serbia, supported by an ultimatum from Russia, sued for peace. At the same time, the Russian government began to put pressure on the Ottomans, with the threat of war looming. But Serbia had lost its chance at Russian patronage; its war effort had been woeful, and after Russia saved Serbia from annihilation in November, the Serbs made territorial demands on Russia (that Bosnia and the Niš district should go to Serbia in the event of victory against the Turks that were bold enough to insult Russian leaders).

The Russo-Turkish War of 1877–1878 began in June with a Russian attack south across the Danube into Ottoman territory in Bulgaria. It ended in January 1878, with an armistice signed in Edirne. Throughout this war, Russia treated the Serbs as second-rate fighters; Russia now placed Serbian interests below Bulgarian needs. The Treaty of San Stefano, which ended this conflict in March 1878, was a bracing setback to the Serbs, who gained 388 square kilometers of almost meaningless territory around Niš and recognition of independence. This treaty also created an enormous Bulgaria that swallowed nearly half of the Balkan Peninsula. It offended everyone, however, but Russia and Bulgaria, so Russia was forced to submit to a European congress at Berlin, which convened in June and July 1878. Here, Serbia gained another 129 square kilometers of territory, but Bulgaria was partitioned into three separate units. Serbia, Montenegro, and Romania were declared independent states. Perhaps the most important results of the Eastern Crisis of 1875–1878 were that Serbia was now in the Austro-Hungarian sphere of influence, and that Bosnia and Hercegovina were occupied and administered by Austria-Hungary (as the Habsburg monarchy was now known). Serbia now had to proceed without the patronage of Russia, and without the possibility of uniting with its northern and western neighbors, who were part of the now-allied Habsburg monarchy.

Between 1878 and 1903, Serbia found itself in the unlikely position of being an Austro-Hungarian client. Russia, Serbia's Orthodox Christian patron for three-quarters of a century, had chosen to view Bulgaria as its ticket to the straits for one good reason: geographically, Bulgaria was right on the road to Istanbul, whereas Serbia was oriented to the western Balkans. It is true that, for Russia, Bulgaria was an unknown quantity, and the fact that it had been divided into three separate entities at Berlin in 1878 made it more likely to be an unstable client. Nonetheless, Serbia remained uncomfortably in Austria's sphere of influence. The relationship, understood after 1878, was formalized in 1881 with a trade treaty and a secret treaty of the same year. The trade treaty made Serbia a virtual colony of Austria-Hungary and stunted its industrial growth for years. The secret treaty placed Serbia in a completely subordinate position to its northern neighbor. Serbia could not negotiate or conclude a treaty with another state without Austria's permission; in return, Prince Milan could proclaim Serbia a kingdom, and himself king, whenever he wished. He did so in March 1882.

Serbia's political spectrum began to diversify after the Russo-Turkish war and its aftermath. A new Progressive Party, representing younger Serbs, often educated abroad, emerged before the war, and with the support of Prince Milan Obrenović, became the governing party in 1880. More importantly, though, the Radical Party was formed in the mid-1870s. Its original leaders, including Pera Todorović and Nikola Pašić, had been educated abroad and were close to Svetozar Marković's Serbian socialist movement. Eventually moving more to the center of the political spectrum, the Radicals were known for their advocacy of peasant interests and the notion of local self-government, a term that became their slogan and the name of the party newspaper: *Samouprava*. The party's 1881 program called for universal male suffrage, local self-government, free public education, support for Serbian unification, and freedom of the press and association. The party became a virulent critic of the reign of Milan Obrenović and his son Aleksandar, largely because of the corruption of their regimes and their complete failure to further Serbian national interests as the Radicals understood them (the unification of Serbs, in other words).

SERBIA'S GOLDEN AGE

In June 1903 a group of officers in the Serbian army conspired to murder the king and queen of Serbia, Aleksandar Obrenović and his wife Draga. The murders of the king and queen were motivated by two factors: the conspirators' belief that Aleksandar was an incompetent and a patsy of the Austrian government, and thus unable to fulfill Serbian national goals as they understood them; and the belief that the scandalous behavior of Aleksandar and Draga (Belgrade society believed her to be a "woman of ill repute") had rendered them embarrassments to Serbia on the European stage. The murders were carried out with great brutality, the king and queen being shot to death and then hacked into pieces, behavior that actually served temporarily to worsen the reputation of Serbia abroad. But eventually, after Petar (Peter) Karadjordjević, grandson of the original Karadjordje and member of the Obrenovićes' rival dynasty, ascended the Serbian throne with the death of Aleksandar, Serbia's fortunes began to take a turn for the better.

Historians have often termed the period from 1903 to 1914 a sort of golden age for Serbia, as the state more successfully defended Serbian national interests, projected Serbian power on the Balkan Peninsula, and perhaps enjoyed a period of true democracy. On the other hand, it all happened in the shadow of World War I, which was an enormous tragedy for the country. Petar Karadjordjević proved to be an uninvolved ruler; power was in the hands of the Radical Party, which benefited from the change in dynasties and became the most powerful political party in Serbia through the interwar period. Led by Nikola Pašić, the party had been founded in 1881 as an expression of peasant interests. By the end of his career, Pašić had been alternately revered and detested: revered for the expansion of Serbia that occurred on his watch and for his stewardship of Serbia through extremely violent times, detested for his stubbornness and his party's corruption, and his own insensitivity toward non-Serbs in interwar Yugoslavia. In the earlier era, however, Serbia was plagued by the conspirators who had murdered Aleksandar Obrenović and who continued to act as an extra-constitutional force in Serbian politics. In 1911 they formed an organization called Union or Death (colloquially, the Black Hand), which played a critical role in the origins of World War I.

The obstacles facing the Radicals and King Petar after June 1903 were sizable. Serbia's image had been tarnished by the brutality of the murders of royalty, and several of the European courts (most importantly, Great Britain) required a period of waiting before they would recognize the new king. Furthermore, the Karadjordjevićs and the Radicals alike were known to be Russophile, while Serbia under the Obrenovićs had had a special relationship with

Nikola Pašić

Nikola Pašić was born in 1845 in Zaječar, Serbia, and died in Belgrade in 1926. He was one of the original members of the Radical Party in Serbia, which he, Pera Todorović, and Adam Bogosavljević founded in 1880, and which was the dominant party in Serbia and Yugoslavia from 1903 through the Great Depression. Pašić was educated in Belgrade and in Zurich, Switzerland (from 1868 to 1872), where he received his degree in engineering. In Switzerland, he was influenced mightily by the ideas of Mikhail Bakunin, the Russian anarchist. His original circle included Svetozar Marković, who later became the first influential Serbian socialist. When Pašić returned to Serbia in 1873, he took a government job. By 1875, though, he had determined to go into politics. In 1878 he succeeded in being elected to the Skupština (the Serbian legislature). He, Todorović, and others soon (1880) officially formed the Radical Party, which at that point was perhaps not as radical as its leaders' résumés would suggest. In its first program in 1881, the party demanded universal male suffrage, self-government for local communes, the usual press and speech freedoms, a more effective banking system that would make money available locally, a modernized judicial system, and an assertive foreign policy with the unification of Serbs as its goal.

Pašić's glory years were between 1903 and 1918, when he served as prime minister of Serbia and the Radical Party governed essentially unchallenged. By that time, the party's socialist roots were virtually invisible; the party no longer filled its role as representative of the peasant landholder, having shifted its focus to carrying out its aggressive foreign policy. Coming to power on the heels of the assassination of King Aleksandar Obrenović and firmly tied to the Karadjordjević house and King Petar (Peter), the Radicals pursued a policy of the unification of Serbian communities throughout the Balkans and worked closely with Russia. The key events of this era included the so-called Pig War, a customs war with Austria-Hungary that lasted from 1905 to 1911 and served to sever Serbia's close ties with that empire; the two Balkan Wars of 1912 and 1913, which expanded Serbian territory to the south; and finally, Serbia's participation in World War I. All bore the signs of Pašić's uncompromising belief that Serbs should be unified and independent, no matter the cost.

During World War I, in Entente diplomacy and in relations with the Yugoslav Committee in London, the Pašić government steadfastly refused to concede that any other entity than Serbia should be responsible for the unification of the South Slavs. When the new country was formed and its government created between late 1918 and 1921, Pašić and Serbia were able to enforce their will on an extremely disparate variety of opposition forces. For better or for worse, the Kingdom of Serbs, Croats, and Slovenes could rightly be considered Pašić's gift to the South Slav peoples.

The last years of Pašić's life were spent managing his unstable creation. The Radical Party earned a reputation less for its consistent pursuit of Serbian interests (though it certainly continued that pursuit) than for its corruption and unwillingness to adapt to circumstances, which had changed radically since the prewar period. When Pašić died in 1926, the constitutional monarchy that he had helped found was only to last another two years.

---

the Habsburg monarchy. Petar Karadjordjević was crowned king in September 1904. Austria and Russia were the first to recognize the new situation, given their rivalry for influence in the kingdom. By 1906, relations with Great Britain had been reestablished. However, recognition did not mean stability: in fact, the Austro-Russian rivalry was only heightened after 1903, since Serbia's subservience to Austria had been called into question by the overthrow of the Obrenović line. Serbian attempts to act independently in economic and foreign affairs prompted punitive actions by the Austrian government, which wished to retain its predominance in Belgrade. The so-called Pig War was one result. Provoked by the Serbian government, which negotiated trade and political agreements with Bulgaria in 1904 and 1905 without Austrian consent, the Pig War was a customs war, by which Austria

hoped to prove that Serbia could not go it alone internationally (it lasted from 1906 to 1911). But the new Radical government in Serbia wished to demonstrate that it could in fact act without Austrian support. Serbia survived the customs war, but its relationship with Austria was now destroyed (as the Serbian government had intended). Serbia's attachment to Russia and competition with Austria were now assured.

The period between 1908 and 1914 saw Serbia aggressively pursuing perceived national interests. Since the mid-nineteenth century, Serbian governments had considered two likely avenues of expansion: one to the west and north, into Bosnia and perhaps Croatia and Hungary, the other to the south, into Ottoman territories of Macedonia ("South Serbia") and Kosovo ("Old Serbia"). All of those regions were seen by Serbs as Serbian by virtue of their populations

Portrait of Nikola Pašić, prime minister of Serbia (1891–1892, 1904–1905, 1906–1908, 1909–1911, 1912–1914, 1914–1918) and of Yugoslavia (1921–1926). (Hulton Archive/Getty Images)

many issued an ultimatum in support of its Austrian ally. Serbia followed suit. But Serbian anger did not subside, and the attention of the Serbian government only turned away from Bosnia for the time being. Beginning in late 1909, the Pašić government began to court the Bulgarian government, with the goal of creating a military alliance that would push the Ottoman Empire out of Europe. Over the course of the next two and a half years, with the help of local Russian representatives (who were more aggressive than their superiors back home), an alliance was formed of Serbia, Bulgaria, Greece, and Montenegro. This "Balkan Alliance" was intended to provoke war with the Ottomans, defeat the Ottoman Empire, and then divide the territorial spoils. By late summer 1912, the alliance was prepared to go to war. When it did so in October, it took its Russian patron and the rest of Europe by surprise.

The Balkan Wars were accompanied by an outpouring of support for Serbia in Croatia and Bosnia, a reflection of the growth of the popularity of the idea that Serbia should serve as the South Slavic Piedmont (in reference to the role that the Piedmont played in the unification of Italy). Strossmayer's Yugoslavism was a Croatian movement, but the idea of Yugoslavism made advances among the Serbs of the Habsburg monarchy as well. The Serbian National Church Congress spoke for Serbs as members of a church rather than as individuals, and therefore came under fire in the late nineteenth century by Serbs who viewed such an identity as stale and retrograde. In the early twentieth century, powerful opponents of this corporatist inclination had emerged. Two political parties dominated Serbian life in Croatia and Hungary: the Serbian Radical Party and the Serbian Independent Party, the first of which remained loyal to the privileges that had been granted to the Serbs who had migrated into the Habsburg monarchy to escape Ottoman rule, starting in the fifteenth century, whereas the second sought security via a constitutional order within the monarchy. Both were devoted to the security of Serbs as such, although the Independents believed that such security could only be found in agreement rather than competition with Serbs' Croatian neighbors.

The Serbian Independent Party was the more dynamic of the two, thanks to its more modern political ideology and its more aggressive leadership, which included Svetozar Pribičević, who was to lead Croatia's Serbs through the 1930s. Pribičević was responsible for two innovations in Serbian politics within the Habsburg monarchy: he advanced the cause of constitutionalism over the politics of corporate privilege, and he was an adherent of the notion that South Slavs were all members of the same nation (Yugoslavism). His (and his party's) embrace of Yugoslavism breathed life into the concept, whose popularity had waned in Croatia in the last two decades of the nineteenth century. Pribičević and the Serbian Independent Party in Croatia were largely responsible for building the Croato-Serbian Coalition, the most popular political organization in Croatia after 1905.

Until 1903, the notion that Serbia could provide the basis for an independent and unified South Slav state seemed laughable, but in the aftermath of the assassination

or histories (Bosnian, Croatian, and Hungarian territories were considered Serbian because of their demographics, Macedonia and Kosovo because of their historical ties to Serbian states of the past). The new, confident Radical government, along with an overconfident and overly influential military (parts of which had brought King Petar and the Radicals to power) saw themselves as eventual unifiers of the Serbs. Accordingly, when the Habsburg government announced the unilateral annexation of Bosnia-Hercegovina (as it had come to be known) in October 1908, the Serbian government responded hostilely. Bosnia was populated by a mix of South Slavs: in 1879, 43 percent Orthodox Serbs, 39 percent Muslim Slavs, and 18 percent Catholic Croats. Most Serbs viewed Bosnia as an incontestable Serbian inheritance from the Ottoman Empire. When the Habsburg monarchy annexed the region, a negative Serbian response was inevitable.

Between October 1908 and March 1909, Serbia, joined by its Russian patron (which had its own reasons for hostility to the annexation), threatened war against Austria. After six months of posturing, Russia backed down when Gerof Aleksandar and Draga in that year, Serbia's reputation grew among South Slavs outside Serbia itself. The fact that Russia had replaced Austria-Hungary as Serbia's great power patron contributed; Russia could afford to be much more aggressive in Balkan diplomacy than the more conservative Habsburgs, who were wary of taking on new commitments to the south. The fact that Serbia had so valiantly (if futilely) opposed the annexation of Bosnia also brought some luster to the little state. But beyond those reasons, the fact was that Serbian intellectual, cultural, and political life had begun to embrace the glorious goals of the Yugoslav movement. By the time of the Balkan Wars, younger Croats and Serbs were even more militant proponents of the unity of Serbs and Croats. They viewed Serbia as the standard bearer of Yugoslavism, and the Balkan Wars as their wars.

The First Balkan War was a surprising success. Bulgarian armies were able to take Kirk Killisi by October 24 and threaten Istanbul thereafter. The Serbian military defeated the Ottomans at Kumanovo on October 24, and the Montenegrin and Greek armies besieged Skadar and Ionnina, respectively. A problem arose, however, when it came time to determine the fate of the conquered territories. Originally, the Serbs and Bulgars had agreed on a set of territorial dispositions that called for Bulgaria to receive a large portion of Macedonia and Serbia to receive Kosovo, with a contested zone in between whose fate would be decided by Russia. That agreement was wrecked by the fact that the Serbs did not gain access to the Adriatic, which had been envisioned by the original treaty of alliance; at the London Conference, which convened to negotiate an end to the war, the Habsburg monarchy had refused to allow Serbs access to the sea. The Serbs demanded compensation in Macedonia, which the Bulgars rejected. The key region, in Macedonia, had not been assigned to either state in the original treaty, instead being left to Russian mediation.

The result of the disagreement was the Second Balkan War, which began on 29 June 1913, as ally fought ally, meaning in this case all of the allies plus Romania, in for spoils, fighting Bulgaria. Of course Bulgaria lost this unequal struggle, and the result of the Treaty of Bucharest which ended the war was a radically enlarged Serbia and Greece. The territory that Serbia incorporated following the Second Balkan War included Kosovo and modern Macedonia. The demographic structure of these regions was complicated: the Sandžak, Kosovo, and Macedonia were all multiethnic regions. Serbia expanded from 48,300 square kilometers to 87,300; its population rose from 2.9 million to 4.4 million people. For the Serbian government, the annexed territories were a headache, as military and civilian authorities contested the right to administer them. This struggle, which reflected the power of the military in Serbian life and the uncertainty of constitutional authority, was not finished when World War I began, less than a year after the end of the Second Balkan War; historians often consider the two Balkan wars and World War I to be one long conflict, which makes perfect sense from the Serbian perspective.

SERBIA IN WORLD WAR I

The immediate cause of World War I could be found in Serbia, or at least among Serbs: on 28 June 1914, a young Serb named Gavrilo Princip assassinated the heir to the Austro-Hungarian throne, the Archduke Franz Ferdinand, and his wife, Sophie. Princip was one of several young conspirators who were armed in Belgrade by the organization Union or Death in order to carry out the assassination. The conspirators themselves were members of Young Bosnia, a nationalist organization that sought the creation of a Yugoslav state. In the aftermath of the assassination, the Austrian government placed an ultimatum before the Serbian government on 23 July 1914: the ultimatum made ten demands, all but one of which were deemed acceptable by the Serbian government. The rejected demand was that the Serbs allow Austrian investigators to come to Belgrade and examine government documents, which the Serbs deemed too grave a breach of Serbian sovereignty to allow. As a result, the Habsburg monarchy declared war on Serbia on 28 July 1914. This war, between Austria and Serbia, could easily have been foreseen as a result of the assassination. However, the war became a European affair quite quickly, as the Russian government jumped to the defense of Serbia, which brought Germany into the fray as well. France and then Britain followed, and a Balkan conspiracy became an extremely destructive war, in both human terms and for the damage it did to European stability in the long term.

Serbia was at war with Austria-Hungary from 28 July 1914. Most historians would probably agree that, according to the values and the logic of international affairs prevailing in 1914, Austria's war against Serbia was just. The Serbian government did not participate in the planning for the assassination, but members of the officer corps (involved in the organization Union or Death) of the Serbian army did. There is evidence that the Serbian government wished to avoid war in 1914 at all costs. At the very least, though, the crisis revealed that Serbia's constitutional order was unstable, and the persistent violence emanating from Serbia (or the work of Habsburg Serbs) had reached proportions that Austria could not and would not stand any longer.

Serbia disappeared as a state by November 1915, but not before some stunning victories. On 12 August 1914, Austro-Hungarian invaders pushed through Belgrade into northern and western Serbia, but were repulsed at the Battle of Kolubara on 15 December, which drove the Austrians out. In October 1915 the tide changed. Austrian armies were now under the command of the German general August von Mackensen, who attacked Serbia anew on 6 October. On 9 October, Bulgaria also attacked, and the result was a rout. On 28 November, the notorious "flight in winter" of Serbian troops and civilians over the Albanian mountains began; 240,000 Serbs died, while about 200,000 survivors made it to the coast and refuge on the island of Corfu, where the Serbian government set up shop for the duration of the war. From that point, Serbia's focus during the war was to be sure that its Russian, French, and British allies did not forget its sacrifices. This was essentially a diplomatic war, which only occasionally demanded a military effort.

Diplomatically, Serbia was caught between great power allies with agendas of their own, Habsburg South Slavs who were (at best) uncertain about unity with Serbia and a contingent of "Yugoslav" exiles from Croatia, Slovenia, Dalmatia, and Bosnia who united to form a "Yugoslav Committee," whose purpose was to agitate among the British and French for the creation of an independent Yugoslav state. This was a predicament for the Serbian government, which, in the person of Nikola Pašić, attempted to act pragmatically and in the interests of Serbia rather than idealistically and in the interests of a visionary Yugoslavia. Pašić the pragmatist thus reacted to events as the war progressed. Until 1917 (when the United States entered and Russia withdrew from the war), Pašić understood that his Entente allies and protectors (Britain, France, and Russia) had no interest in destroying the Habsburg monarchy; instead, they wished to convince it to sign a separate peace and to sustain it as a force for stability in Central Europe.

In such conditions, the Serbian government could gain little by agitating for the creation of a Yugoslav state; instead, it could and should work, at most, toward the aggrandizement of Serbia. The Serbian government did so in the best tradition of nineteenth-century horse-trading. For instance, the Serbs gained the agreement of the British and French to the eventual annexation of Bosnia and parts of Dalmatia when the Entente was tempting Bulgaria with a promise of Serbian territory, but that deal died with Bulgaria's adherence to the Triple Alliance in 1915. The clearest example of this sort of diplomacy came with the Treaty of London in April of 1915, by which the Entente bought the entry of Italy into the war. The price: much of the Dalmatian coast, the homeland of some of the most idealistic and aggressive "Yugoslavs" among Croats. With no apparent support for the creation of a Yugoslav state, Serbia could comfortably seek limited, Serbian goals: the reestablishment of the Serbia of July 1914 and perhaps some pieces of territory at the expense of the Habsburgs at war's end.

There was always pressure to expand those goals, however, and from mid-1917 forward, more expansive goals made a bit more sense. Nicholas II, the tsar of Russia, always Serbia's best friend, abdicated in March 1917; the United States, with the idealistic Woodrow Wilson as president, entered the war; and, perhaps most importantly, separate peace negotiations with Austria-Hungary were finally broken off, which meant that the Entente could now consider the dismemberment of the monarchy. As early as November 1914, several influential Croats had gathered in Italy to begin agitating for the creation of a Yugoslav state; with the Treaty of London in April 1915, these émigrés began to work as the Yugoslav Committee.

The Yugoslav Committee was headed by Frano Supilo, a dynamic Croat from Rijeka (Fiume) whose Yugoslavism was unquestioned. Other members included Ante Trumbić, a Croat and convinced Yugoslav, Ivan Meštrović, the great sculptor, and other Croats, Slovenes, and Serbs. The committee feared most that the war would end with Italy incorporating South Slavic territory, especially Dalmatia. It operated from a position of great weakness from the outset,

since it had no legal standing and the Entente really did not need to satisfy it. It was also not clear whether the committee represented the general opinion of the Habsburg South Slav populations. Nevertheless, with the change in composition of the Entente, and with the end of separate peace negotiations with the Habsburg monarchy, the British and French governments began to consider the Yugoslav Committee a useful tool. Pašić refused to consider the Yugoslav committee an official, legal representative of the Habsburg South Slavs, and in this he exemplified Serbian opinion in general. For Pašić, Serbian interests took precedence over the interests of a committee that represented people in an enemy state, people he knew were to be found fighting loyally for the Habsburgs against Serbia. But, given the attitudes of its allies, Serbia needed to come to some sort of agreement with the committee.

The Corfu Declaration of June 1917 was signed by Ante Trumbić for the committee and Nikola Pašić for the Serbian government. The assumption of the Corfu Declaration was that the Serbs, Croats, and Slovenes were all one people, an assertion that the Serbian government had endorsed as early as December 1914 in the Niš Declaration. The declaration proclaimed the goal of the creation of a Kingdom of Serbs, Croats, and Slovenes under the Karadjordjević dynasty in a constitutional monarchy. The constitution would be promulgated by a constituent assembly to be elected at a later date. The symbols (flags, coats of arms) of each of the three named peoples of the new state would be respected by all; Orthodoxy, Catholicism, and Islam would be equal; the scripts would be equal as well. The various peoples of the state would have "the opportunity to develop their individual energies in autonomous units" (Petrovich 645). So the Corfu Declaration endorsed the creation of a unified state for Serbs, Croats, and Slovenes. It also laid out fairly clearly how that state should be constructed once the war was over. What it could not do was predict the course the war would take; nor could it make the Serbian government (in the person of Pašić) respect the Yugoslav Committee as its legal equal.

Had the war ended without contention, with Habsburg, German, and Bulgarian armies withdrawing from the lands that the Serbs, Croats, and Slovenes considered to be theirs, with a peaceful transition to power by (especially) Croats and Slovenes who wished to form a state with Serbia, the prescriptions of the Corfu Declaration might have been valid. What happened, however, was that the war ended chaotically; not all Croats and Slovenes wished to join Serbia in a Yugoslavia, and the enemies did not withdraw in an orderly fashion. A reconstituted Serbian army fought north through Macedonia via the Salonika front. There were those who did not wish for union with Serbia, and while the enemy was in no position to continue the war, Italy, an Entente ally, attempted to take territory in Dalmatia and Istria that most Croats felt to be Croatian. It was above all the fear of Italy that drove Croatia and Slovenia into the arms of Serbia, the one actor that had the military to defend South Slavic territory from Italy. In November 1918 there were numerous negotiations between various bodies and individuals representing a variety of interests. The most prominent players were the Serbian government of Nikola Pašić; the crown, in the person of Crown Prince Aleksandar; the National Council, which had proclaimed itself sovereign in Croatia and Slovenia; and the Yugoslav Committee, whose position was now in question, given the fact that the war was over.

The most concrete negotiations that took place produced the Geneva Declaration on 9 November; the Serbian government was displeased with this declaration because it placed Serbia in an equal or subordinate position to Habsburg South Slavs. On 1 December 1918, after the National Council in Zagreb, other regional bodies, and the Prince-Regent, Aleksandar, had agreed on terms for unification, the Kingdom of Serbs, Croats, and Slovenes was proclaimed in Belgrade. The act of declaring unity papered over problems that continued to plague the new state throughout its existence. The key difficulty was to determine the relationship of Serbs to Croats, Slovenes, Muslims, and others, as well as the relationship of the various newly unified regions to Belgrade.

INTERWAR SERBIA

The prewar Kingdom of Serbia became the postwar Kingdom of Serbs, Croats, and Slovenes. The monarch (now King Aleksandar, the son of King Petar), the government, the military, the currency, the bureaucracy, all were simply expanded to envelop the territories that were now incorporated with Serbia into the new state. The constitution of the new state, known as the Vidovdan Constitution for the day on which it was approved by the Yugoslav parliament (28 June 1921, St. Vitus's Day, a Serbian holy day), was a centralizing constitution that passed by a bare majority of the representatives in the parliament, many of whom (primarily Stjepan Radić's Croatian Peasant Party representatives) abstained in opposition to the document. Such a document gave some assurance to Serbian interests that they would not be ignored but left many of the other nations of Yugoslavia feeling deeply aggrieved at the outset of the new state's existence. The Vidovdan Constitution was not designed to promote harmony between the disparate nations of the Kingdom of Serbs, Croats, and Slovenes.

From 1921 to 1928, the kingdom was governed as a parliamentary monarchy. Politics in the kingdom was dominated by the Radical Party and Nikola Pašić, but that party, always a plurality but incapable of gaining a majority of seats in the Yugoslav parliament, found it impossible to create stable coalition governments. Pašić tried to collaborate with Svetozar Pribičević, the leader of Croatia's Serbs, and then even with Stjepan Radić, the mercurial head of the Croatian Republican Peasant Party, but in both cases the personalities and the overwhelming administrative and constitutional issues made it impossible to govern coherently. When Stjepan Radić was gunned down in the Yugoslav parliament on 20 June 1928 by Puniša Račić, an otherwise unremarkable Montenegrin deputy, the parliamentary experiment came to an end. Seven months later, King Aleksandar proclaimed a renamed Kingdom of Yugoslavia and abolished the Vidovdan Constitution. Yugoslavia became a royal dictatorship for five years.

King Aleksandar initiated several flashy changes in Yugoslav administration. Aside from changing the name of the state, he also abolished all existing administrative districts and established nine *banovine,* or counties, each named after geographic features, mainly rivers. Of these new banovine, the Drava banovina resembled Slovenia, but the others were largely ahistorical. Serbs inhabited four banovine, and in each they were a majority. To this clear attempt to eliminate historical national consciousness from political discourse in Yugoslavia, Aleksandar added a new constitution in 1931 that had provisions designed to further degrade regional loyalties. Candidates running for the parliament needed to get signatures from voters in each of Yugoslavia's three hundred new electoral districts in order to be on the ballot. In an upper house, or senate, members would be split between royal appointees and those appointed by councils in each banovina. These were creative and perhaps admirable attempts to overcome national rivalries such as that which had resulted in Stjepan Radić's murder, but it was too little, and much too late. By 1934, forces devoted to the destruction of Yugoslavia had grown strong, including the Macedonian revolutionaries in the Internal Macedonian Revolutionary Organization (VMRO) and Croatian nationalists in the Ustaša. The Ustaša, formed in 1929 in Italy under the leadership of Ante Pavelić, became notorious during World War II as the leaders of the Independent State of Croatia. Now, though, in the 1930s the organization was marginal and quite weak, capable only of the occasional outrage. After three years of rather futile attempts to make the new constitution work, Aleksandar was assassinated in Marseilles by a Macedonian gunman in 1934.

In the summer of 1935 a regency headed by Aleksandar's cousin Prince Paul designated Milan Stojadinović to head the government. Stojadinović remained in that position until early 1939, the longest tenure of any interwar Yugoslav prime minister. He was able to maintain power by reaching out to Croats and by putting into effect successful economic policies that relied on trade with Germany. When he fell, it was thanks to an unexpected controversy over a concordat that he negotiated with the Vatican, regulating the Catholic Church's position in Yugoslavia. Opposition from Serbs, led by the Orthodox Church, destroyed Stojadinović's power base and led to his downfall.

By the time of Stojadinović's fall from power, the question of Croatia's place in Yugoslavia had become preeminent. Prince Paul arranged the formation of a government amenable to compromise with the Croats, and the result was the Cvetković-Maček *Sporazum* (Agreement) of 20 August 1939. This agreement gave Croatia autonomy within Yugoslavia, within historical Croatian borders, with some Bosnian territory added. The new Croatian banovina comprised 30 percent of Yugoslavia's territory and included a Serbian minority of nearly 20 percent. This agreement satisfied only Croats, and not all of them. Serbs wondered where their banovina was; Slovenes had the same concern. More extreme Croats demanded that more or all of Bosnia be included in the banovina. The Sporazum was an unstable first step in a solution to the national question in Yugoslavia. Further steps in that solution did not come before World War II broke out a little over a week later.

Yugoslavia remained out of the conflict until the spring of 1941. Prime Minister Cvetković relied on the hope that Germany did not really need Yugoslavia to prosecute its war; nonetheless, by March 1941, the Germans had determined that Yugoslavia must sign on to the Tripartite Pact, which the government did on 25 March. As a result, on 27 March, Serbian military officers led by General Dušan Simović, profoundly angered by an alliance with a traditional Serbian enemy, executed a coup d'état and declared underage Prince Peter the new king of Yugoslavia. As a result, German forces invaded Yugoslavia on 6 April.

SERBIA IN WORLD WAR II

Yugoslavia disintegrated in April 1941, and the parts went in disparate directions. In Serbia, a quisling regime was established; Bosnia and Croatia constituted the Independent State of Croatia, a fascist state whose leadership attempted to kill all of its Jews and Gypsies and kill, convert to Catholicism, or expel all of its Serbs; Macedonia became part of Bulgaria; and Slovenia was split between Italy and Germany. Serbian society was more fragmented than most. Territorially, parts of Serbia, as defined by most Serbs, went to Italian-occupied Albania (Kosovo), Italy (part of Montenegro), Hungary (western Vojvodina), Bulgaria (Macedonia), and the Independent State of Croatia (Serb-populated regions of Croatia and Bosnia). Politically, the destruction of Yugoslavia in April 1941 left several groups of Serbs: Serbians loyal to the government in exile (Prince Peter), who were loosely gathered under the leadership of former Royal Army colonel Dragoljub (Draža) Mihailović, known as Četniks; members of the fascist paramilitary group Zbor, led by Dimitrije Ljotić, whose allegiance was to the puppet Serbian state headed by Milan Nedić; others loyal to Nedić; those who fought with Tito's communist Partisans; and those who chose not to choose sides.

The Serbian experience of World War II was more tragic than that of any other Yugoslav people, but unfortunately there is not enough space available to go deeply into it here. The war in Yugoslavia is best described as a civil war, with three main forces contesting the outcome: the Četniks; the Partisans; and the Ustaša, the insurgent Croatian nationalist force that stood behind the Independent State of Croatia, which in turn consisted of prewar Croatia and Bosnia–Hercegovina. Of course, the German and Italian forces that invaded and occupied various portions of Yugoslavia remained in the country, the Italians until late 1943 and the Germans until the end of the war. But while the invaders provided the excuse for the hostilities, they were rarely the focus.

It would be a mistake to view the Četniks as a unified fighting force, for there were various focal points for the movement, with different leaders and different goals and methods. Nonetheless, there was one acknowledged leader, Draža Mihailović, whose Ravna Gora movement was the best known among Četniks. Mihailović was a standard-issue Serbian nationalist, one who believed that Serbs should have a state of their own and that the interwar Yugoslav state had been a mistake, and who was rabidly anticommunist. Mihailović and his Četniks were, until late 1943, the resistance movement recognized as "official" by the British and Americans, and Mihailović himself was minister of defense in the Yugoslav government in exile. Over the course of the war, his movement came under increasing suspicion of being less interested in resistance than in awaiting the end of the war in good position to take power. Certainly one important reason for this reluctance to fight was the overwhelming retaliations of the Germans. Nevertheless, with the Italian surrender of late 1943, the British and Americans switched their own support to the Partisans, who at least appeared to be more willing to engage the Germans.

The Partisans began their war in late summer 1941, following the German invasion of the Soviet Union, which freed up all European communists to begin open resistance. For the first year or so of the war, the Partisans approached the war as a social revolution, treating "liberated" territories to the full gamut of Stalinist measures. Soon they realized, however, that they could attract more support by shifting the focus of their efforts from social revolution to opposition to nationalism. The Četniks and the Ustaša had alienated or frightened enough Yugoslavs—and especially Serbs—that it became fruitful policy for the members of the Communist Party to position themselves as seekers of "brotherhood and unity" rather than as virulent communists. As such, the Partisans became ever more powerful and popular as the war progressed, at the expense of the national resistance and collaboration movements.

The Ustaša—the third major force that affected Serbs—did so in a negative way, which is to say that they never competed for the hearts and souls of Serbs. Instead, Serbs were the focus of the collective rage of this extremist, fringe Croatian nationalist group, which only had the opportunity to act because its leader, Ante Pavelić, was put in place by the Germans as Croatia's wartime collaborationist leader. The Ustaša was a crudely violent organization, which attempted to rid wartime Croatia of Serbs. They tried all available methods: forced emigration, conversion to Catholicism, and murder, to do so. They murdered Serbs on an individual and a collective basis, by slaughtering the inhabitants of Serbian towns and villages and by creating death camps like that at Jasenovac. They only appealed to Croats, and probably can be credited with making the Partisans a more viable option for Serbs than they otherwise would have been. Ultimately, the Ustaša have been credited with killing anywhere from 10,000 to 1.7 million Serbs (obviously, both these numbers are the absurd extremes). The most reasonable, and generally accepted, estimate is that a total of something less than 500,000 Serbs were killed during the war. The Ustaša are believed to have been responsible for several tens of thousands of those. This was not the Nazi killing machine, but it was nonetheless wholesale and mindless slaughter in the name of a racist variant of Croatian nationalism. It clouded Serbo-Croatian relations thereafter, for obvious reasons.

SERBIA IN TITO'S YUGOSLAVIA

The political configuration of Serbia in the new Yugoslavia was determined by a series of wartime and postwar decisions by the Communist Party of Yugoslavia (Komunistićka partija Jugoslavije, KPJ). Serbia, a republic within the federation, had two autonomous units: Vojvodina, a province, and Kosovo and Metohija, a region, of lesser status than Vojvodina. The Party also decided to add to Vojvodina some territory that had belonged to Croatia and to create republics of Montenegro, Bosnia-Hercegovina, and Macedonia, all of which could conceivably have been added to Serbia or partitioned between Serbia and some other federal unit. Serbia was thus one of six Yugoslav republics in a fictitious federal system. The republics were intended as sops to the national feelings of their namesake nations. Only Bosnia did not fit that model, as at that point there was no nation calling itself Bosnian. Bosnia's fate, however, was contested by Serbs and Croats; its establishment as a republic reflected the instrumental nature of Yugoslavia's federal organization, as it was a compromise designed (ironically) to maintain stability in an extremely fractured society. As for the decision to make Kosovo and Metohija, which most Serbs considered a Serbian territory, an autonomous region of the Republic of Serbia, it clearly came at the expense of the Serbian republic, as did the designation of Vojvodina as an autonomous province (slightly higher in status than an autonomous "region"). In both cases, the intent was twofold: to satisfy a national minority (Albanians in Kosovo, Hungarians in Vojvodina) and to weaken Serbia. The Communist Party and then the Tito regime blamed Serbs for the failure of interwar Yugoslavia; keeping Serbia institutionally weak would work against a recurrence of the interwar situation.

Serbs in communist Yugoslavia were dispersed among all of the republics, with especially high concentrations in Croatia and Bosnia-Hercegovina; Montenegro, nationally Montenegrin in the Titoist taxonomy, was nonetheless considered by many Serbs and Montenegrins alike to be a Serbian territory; and many Serbs found it difficult to acquiesce in the existence of a Macedonian republic and nationality (a Titoist construction, since Macedonia had never been a political unit but rather a geographical expression). Furthermore, Vojvodina and Kosovo-Metohija ("Kosmet" for short until 1963, when it was raised from autonomous region status to become the autonomous province of Kosovo) were now separate-from-but-part-of Serbia, which further atomized the Serbian community.

Unitl 1948, Tito and his colleagues governed Yugoslavia repressively, following the Stalinist model. In June 1948, however, Cominform (the Communist Information Bureau, the coordinating body of world communism, controlled of course by the Soviet Union) expelled Yugoslavia from its ranks. Stalin had grown weary of Tito's independence in foreign and domestic affairs, in spite of Tito's absolute adherence to the Stalinist precedent. Stalin's expectation was that the Yugoslav Communist Party would overthrow Tito and his leadership and install a more compliant one. The reverse occurred. In Yugoslavia, Tito and his regime became more popular, and loyalists to the Cominform were purged from the Party. The Tito regime survived under overwhelming pressure (both economic and military). By 1950, it had also begun its highly influential rethinking of Stalinism, which eventually resulted in the formulation of "self-management," a novel approach to the building of socialism by which workers were to control the workplace. Politically, the split with Stalin resulted in Yugoslavia moving closer to the West. In the realm of culture, the rethinking that followed the split with the Cominform resulted in the abandonment of socialist realism and a long period of relative cultural freedom.

The most important problem for the Tito regime remained the national question. New cultural norms were expected by most Serbian intellectual and cultural figures to contribute to the safety of their communities outside of Serbia proper. Titoism had to deal with certain antagonisms: non-Serbs wished to protect their cultures from assimilation, while Serbs wished to protect their diffused population. The combatants in this struggle utilized language drawn from past experience: Slovenes and Croats feared Serbian "centralism," "hegemonism," and the like, while Serbs would eventually discover words like "genocide" to characterize their fears of other nationalities. But Serbian fears were not kindled until the 1960s. During the first two decades of communism, it was the Serbs who engaged in the most substantive discussion of how to generate a new Yugoslav culture, because they needed one.

By 1961, economic performance in Yugoslavia had begun to slow noticeably. For the first time, the LCY (League of Communists of Yugoslavia, as the Yugoslav Communist Party was now called) reexamined the organization of the state, albeit from a purely economic perspective, and Serbia was in the end deeply affected. The debate on economic reform acted as a spur to camouflaged political debate. The conservative position found support among some, but not all, Serbian economists; many Serbian economists nonetheless gravitated to the conservative position out of a sense of national loyalty. Their logic held that centralization protected the Serbs of Yugoslavia, and central planning was integral to the centralized state. The fruits of this ongoing discussion included the 1963 constitution, which initiated a gradual devolution of economic decision-making power from the center to enterprises and local governments. The Eighth Congress of the League of Communists of Yugoslavia, held in December 1964 in Belgrade, placed the Party seal of approval on economic reforms supported by the liberals. The congress cleared the way for reforms of the economy that brought decentralizing political reforms with them. This decentralization came to make many Serbs doubt their own commitment to Yugoslavia and to Titoism.

An incoherent but growing Serbian opposition to Titoism began to be heard after 1966. There were a series of events that influenced and indicated the direction and character of that opposition: the demotion of Aleksandar Ranković in 1966, a language controversy in 1967, the student movement of June 1968, and the rebellion in Kosovo in November 1968. Those events were unrelated, but together they eventually provided the foundations of a relatively coherent Serbian critique of communism in Yugoslavia. That critique focused on Serbia's (and the Serbian people's) unequal position in the state. It argued that Serbs and Serbia, unfairly blamed for the failure of the interwar Yugoslav state and wrongly castigated for their na-

Aleksandar Ranković, Josip Broz "Tito," and Milovan Djilas during the Second World War. (Bettmann/Corbis)

tionalist proclivities, had purposely been territorially and culturally divided by the Tito regime. That territorial and cultural division had resulted in the rewarding of the other peoples, republics, and provinces of Yugoslavia, primarily Croatia, Bosnia, Macedonia, Vojvodina, and Kosovo. The reforms of the early 1960s, according to this view, had by their decentralizing tendencies exacerbated the fragmentation of the Serbian community of Yugoslavia.

In July 1966 Aleksandar Ranković, the ethnic Serb who was vice president of Yugoslavia and, until 1964, the head of state security in Yugoslavia (UDBa; uprava državne bezbednosti), was purged from his positions and eventually kicked out of the League of Communists. The first step in this process came on 1 July 1966, when the Fourth Plenum of the Central Committee of the League of Communists of Yugoslavia met on the island of Brioni (a meeting known as the Brioni Plenum). Here Ranković and his recent replacement as head of UDBa, Svetislav Stefanović, were condemned for a limited number of infractions. They boiled down to one critical accusation: that state security answered to only one man on the Central Committee of the League of Communists, Aleksandar Ranković, instead of the committee as a whole. Thus, in the words of Krste Crvenkovski, the Macedonian who chaired the commission, "Comrade Aleksandar Ranković became synonymous with the Central Committee" (Kesar and Simić 59).

The Central Committee of the League of Communists of Serbia (CC LCS) set up its own commission to examine the evidence regarding UDBa a few days after Brioni; it presented its report on 5 September 1966 to the Central Committee; the Sixth Plenum of the CC LCS met on 14 and 15 September to hear the results. The League of Communists of Serbia moved beyond the limits set at Brioni, which had only asserted that under Ranković and Stefanović UDBa had abused its power. At the Sixth Plenum, a report of the Regional Committee of the League of Communists of Kosovo and Metohija was entered into the record. This report concluded that the security services in Kosovo actively persecuted those of Albanian nationality: "The ideological foundation of such policy under the competence of Serbia is nationalism and chauvinism" (Kesar and Simić, 92). Other than those accusations related to Kosovo, the Serbian conclusions mirrored the Yugoslav version. For a growing number of Serbs, however, the removal of Ranković came to be interpreted (especially after 1974) as an example of the latent anti-Serbianism of those in power in Yugoslavia; any Serbs who acquiesced in Ranković's removal were, from this point of view, traitors to Serbia.

If Ranković's dismissal betrayed the fact that the foundations of Titoism were changing on the party and state level, on the cultural plane Titoism's midlife crisis could be felt as well. In particular, a brouhaha regarding the nature of the Serbian and Croatian languages went public in the spring of 1967. The "Declaration on the Name and Position of the Croatian Literary Language" (Deklaracija o nazivu i položaju hrvatskoga književnog jezika, henceforth "the Declaration") was issued by nineteen Croatian institutions and signed by 130 people (80 of them Party members, including Miroslav Krleža, Croatia's leading writer) on 15 March 1967, and sent to the federal parliament as a petition on the same day. The Declaration made two demands of the federal government. First, in place of the usual formulation that held that in Yugoslavia there were three official literary languages ("Serbo-Croatian or Croato-Serbian," to give it its full name, Slovenian, and Macedonian), the constitution should be amended to read that there were four: Serbian, Croatian, Slovenian, and Macedonian. Second, the Declaration demanded "the consistent use of the Croatian literary language in the schools, the press, the public and political forums, on radio and the television networks whenever the broadcasts are directed to a Croatian audience." Furthermore, "officials, teachers, and public workers, irrespective of their origin, should use in their official dealings the language of the milieu in which they live." This amounted to a unilateral revocation of the Novi Sad Agreement (1954), which had given the language a name, "Serbo-Croatian or [odnosno] Croato-Serbian," which was designated one language "with two pronunciations, ijekavian and ekavian" (Spalatin 6–9).

The response of the League of Communists was straightforward: it proclaimed the Declaration an attempt to destroy the brotherhood and unity of the Serbs and Croats. The Declaration, however, also moved many of Serbia's leading literary lights to action. The "Proposal for Consideration" (Predlog za razmišljanje, henceforth "the Proposal"), drawn up during a meeting of the Serbian Writers' Association, remains somewhat mysterious, largely because it was unofficial and less widely disseminated. Of some 300 writers present at the meeting of the Serbian Writers' Association on 19 March when the Proposal was presented, 42 apparently signed (the authors were known as "a group of writers"). Of these, 21 were members of the League of Communists. The group characterized the Declaration as a "significant and epoch-making document." It also concurred that the institutions that issued the Declaration were "competent ones in matters pertaining to the Croatian literary language"; these Serbs therefore declared the Novi Sad Agreement void (Spalatin 6–9).

The Proposal responded to the assertion that the Croatian language should become official on the territory of the Socialist Republic of Croatia—in other words, the linkage of a national attribute to a piece of land. The tit-for-tat Serbian response hinted that the equation of nations with territory could establish a messy precedent. "Our Constitution guarantees to all our nationalities and minorities the right to an independent development of language and culture." Thus they demanded that the constitutions of the Socialist Republic of Serbia and the Socialist Republic of Croatia add regulations guaranteeing to all Croatians and Serbs:

the right to a scholastic education in their own languages and scripts according to their national programs, the right to use their national languages and scripts in their dealings with all authorities, the right to found their cultural societies, local museums, publishing houses and newspapers, in short, the right to cultivate unobstructedly and freely all aspects of their national culture. (Spalatin 6–9)

The group thus argued that if Croats wished to equate language with territory, Serbs would do the same, which would result in their linguistic secession from the Croatian republic. Never mind that the Serbs of Croatia largely used the same officially designated "literary language" *(ijekavian)* as the Croats; all Croats and all Serbs, after all, spoke what amounted to the same language (štokavian). The point that the "group of writers" wished to make was that once national rights were linked with territory in this Yugoslavia, the logic of secession (whether geopolitical or cultural) would leave the state a tattered patchwork of national sectors, or as they came to be called in actual practice twenty-five years later, cantons. Under growing evidence that the noble Yugoslav dream was being allowed to wither on the vine, many Serbs began a great withdrawal, from a form of Yugoslavism to a frantic attempt to rescue that which was Serbian from the wreckage.

To this day, a small but influential segment of the Serbian intellectual community remains convinced that the student demonstrations of 1968 were the last great chance for Yugoslav communism to fulfill its promise. The student movement began innocuously on the night of 2 June 1968, at around ten o'clock, when a number of students living in dormitories in New Belgrade tried to crash a concert put on for the benefit of a local workers' brigade. Members of the brigade fought with the party crashers, and the police were called in. The police separated the two groups, but the disturbance had already brought more students into the streets, where they milled peacefully if edgily. Shouting "Jobs for All," "Workers-Students," and "Tito-Party," students made their way to an underpass near the building housing the Federal Executive Council, where they came upon a cordon of riot police, who allegedly stoned and shot at them.

The nature of the student movement changed during the day on 3 June. Two factors propelled the movement forward: the behavior of the police, which was more brutal than the occasion had demanded, and the writing of the press, which gave the impression that the students were nothing more than a self-interested rabble. From a fairly unfocused series of protests and clashes with the police in the vicinity of the underpass, the students were able to pull together a more coherent and organized movement centered on the university buildings downtown. Students, under leaders drawn from the League of Students of Belgrade University, occupied the Law, Philosophy, and Philology Faculties, the Academy of Fine Arts, and other buildings and created "Action Committees," which coordinated the protests. Here, in the occupied university buildings, a disorganized series of demonstrations was transformed into a sophisticated protest against changes in the nature of Yugoslav socialism under the pressure of the economic reforms that had begun in 1963.

One of the first "resolutions" of the student movement appeared on 3 June in the student village in New Belgrade, signed by the "Action Committee of the Demonstrators." Its demands included a call for the government to work against corruption and the enrichment of the "red bourgeoisie," the demand that the student body of universities reflect the social structure of the country, and demands for the freedom to meet and demonstrate, the democratization of political and social organizations (including the League of Communists), and better material support for universities in Yugoslavia. The slogans that the students used included "We Fight for a Better Man, Not a Better Dinar," "The Revolution Is Not Yet Finished," "Against Enrichment at the Expense of the Worker," "We've Had Enough of the Red Bourgeoisie," "Self-Management From Bottom to Top," "Tell a Bureaucrat That He Is Incapable, and He Will Show You Just What He Is Capable Of" (Arsić and Marković, 86). On balance, if we can accept slogans chanted and displayed as reflecting ideology, the students were at least as upset by corruption in the Party as they were by their own lack of jobs.

On Belgrade television on 9 June, Tito gave a speech that brought the student movement to an end, to the initial joy but eventual chagrin of many of its participants. Tito was masterful and apologetic. The Presidency and the Executive Committee of the Central Committee of the League of Communists had been meeting since March, he said, to deal with the problems facing the state. Just as they were about to make public their responses, the student demonstrations broke out. "That was our mistake" (Arsić and Marković 117–122). They had met that very day to consider the student movement, and according to Tito, they agreed that there were problems to be addressed in Yugoslavia, especially relating to the "enrichment" of undeserving people. In the most famous portion of his speech, Tito paid homage to that portion of the student demonstrators who had acted out of the most loyal and consistent motives: "Thus I must say here today that I am happy that we have such a working class. And I can also say that I am happy that we have such a youth, which has proved itself mature. . . . Our youth is good, but we need to pay more attention to it" (Arsić and Marković 117–122). Tito's speech was greeted by the students as an affirmation of their position. A week later, the Central Committee of the LCY met to approve its "Guidelines," which amounted to a further acknowledgment of the failure of the League to adequately address issues of concern to the students.

The student movement did not occur in a vacuum: there were good reasons for the students' discontent. They were influenced by critical thinkers within Yugoslavia, and they had examples to follow. Problems with the universities were well publicized before the movement began, and they went beyond the question of employment into the realm of ideology. For instance, enrollment at Belgrade University grew between 1960 and 1965, but the percentage of students with stipends fell from 25.5 to 14.2. Furthermore, the percentage of working class and peasant children in the university fell from 15.1 to 12.4 between 1962 and 1967. The satirical magazine *Jež* constantly harped on the problems of unemployment, the development of a "red bourgeoisie," and the university. Indeed, it would have been a real dereliction of duty had the central committee and the presidency *not* been discussing these problems before the student movement began. Furthermore, critical thought about the nature of self-management and Yugoslavia's path to a socialist future had erupted in the mid-1960s in response to reform plans formulated on the party level. The so-called Praxis group had made it their business to attack corruptions in the real world of the Yugoslav administration and the economy, including the emergence of a new class of privileged communists and the persistence of Stalinist forms of authoritarianism in Yugoslavia.

March 1968 saw student demonstrations in Poland; the spring and summer of 1968 witnessed the Prague Spring and the short-lived period of openness in Czechoslovakia; and, finally, May 1968 saw the grandest student rebellion of that summer, in France, where millions of workers and students went on strike, entire factories and even one city were turned into workers' communes, small children struck their classes at school, the Left Bank burned, and revolution seemed a real possibility. The student rebellion of 1968 in Belgrade achieved nothing; perhaps, however, it was yet another example of the distance that was growing between the regime and the people of Serbia.

Finally, the tumultuous sixties were capped by events relating to Kosovo. In May 1968 Dobrica Ćosić, the most famous living novelist in Serbia, as well as an important nationalist leader, gave a speech to the Central Committee of the Serbian League of Communists that blasted the League for its treatment of Kosovo and Vojvodina. To be precise, he warned that the new order in Yugoslavia—the move to more substantive federalization, christened in Ćosić's view by the fall of Ranković—offered too prominent a place to the Albanians of Kosovo and the non-Serbs of Vojvodina. For Ćosić, these were fundamentally Serbian territories, in which national minorities lived by the grace of Serbs. The Tito regime, however, was allowing, even encouraging, these two autonomous provinces of Serbia to become more autonomous than ever. Serbs were being removed from important positions in the two provinces, and local minorities were taking control. For Ćosić, this portended not merely the end of Serbia as a republic, but the eventual ruin of Yugoslavia as a state. The Serbian League

Dobrica Ćosić. (Emil Vas/Archive Photos/Reuters)

of Communists distanced itself quickly from the sentiments found in Ćosić's speech, because it was obvious that they were hostile to the direction that the Tito regime had taken. Ćosić was labeled a nationalist for his efforts. However, we need to understand that although Ćosić clearly was and remains a Serbian nationalist, the sentiments he expressed in his speech were relatively moderate and, most importantly, shared by many Serbs. When, in November 1968, an Albanian rebellion took place in Kosovo, Ćosić's warnings seemed timely indeed to many Serbs. The problem of the Serbs' attitude toward Kosovo would have to be addressed constructively if stability were to be maintained in Yugoslavia.

The events of the 1960s—from the beginnings of reform, through the fall of Ranković, the language crisis, the student rebellion, and the rebellion in Kosovo—resulted in the beginnings of a consensus that Serbia was consciously, purposely, being mistreated in Tito's Yugoslavia. Each of those events awakened a different opposition constituency, two of which eventually emerged clearly. One was nationalist, and built on the perceived threat of Croatian and Albanian nationalism and the sense that Tito encouraged those movements; the other was socialist, and was founded on the belief that Titoism had parted from its own stated goals and from a pure Marxism. The former strand of opposition coalesced around Ćosić and other outsiders to the Party. The latter was embodied in the Praxis group, named for the journal that it founded, in which it expressed its critique of Titoism.

In light of the events of the late 1960s, the Serbian League of Communists entered a tempestuous phase. In the aftermath of the student demonstrations, Tito is reported to have exclaimed that "all of them should go," referring to the leaders of the Serbian Party. With the ascent of Marko Nikezić and Latinka Perović to the top of the Serbian Party hierarchy, the era of the so-called liberals in Serbian politics commenced. Until 1968, Nikezić had devoted most of his public life to diplomacy, having served as ambassador to Egypt, Czechoslovakia, and the United States, and as the minister of foreign affairs in Yugoslavia. Perović had risen through the Party ranks as a member of the presidency of the Yugoslav Youth organization and of the Ideological Commission of the LCY. Together, they attempted to fundamentally alter the way politics was done in Serbia and Yugoslavia. The liberals have become the objects of a Serbian cult of "what might have been." They are credited with having tried to modernize the Serbian Party, with having been the best and the brightest of their generation, and with having been the tragic victims of Tito's jealous desire to remain the single arbiter in Yugoslav political life. Nikezić later identified five principles that guided them: a market economy, a modern Serbia, freeing Serbia from the "ballast of Serbian Yugoslavism," creating capable and expert cadres, and cooperation rather than confrontation with other republics.

Unfortunately for Nikezić and his colleagues, their arrival came at an inopportune time—not only were the student demonstrations fresh in the minds of Serbs and of Tito, but the Croatian mass movement was gaining momentum, and an Albanian national rebellion broke out in Kosovo on the third day after Nikezić and Perović were installed. Aside from those tangible crises, it also appears in hindsight that Tito was in the process of concluding that the Party needed to reassert control of political life in Yugoslavia, undoubtedly under the impress of those same events. And finally, while the liberals attempted to navigate those events and put their stamp on a new, economically sound communism in Serbia, a non-Party Serbian opposition to Titoism began to be heard, with Dobrica Ćosić as its alleged leader (although this opposition was not a coherent or consistent one). All in all, it is difficult to say whether Serbia lost a historic opportunity when the liberals fell, because Nikezić and Perović had little chance to pursue coherent policies aggressively.

They resigned their positions in November 1972, eleven months after the Croatian leadership of Savka Dabčević-Kučar, Mika Tripalo, and Pero Pirker, who fell from power in December 1971 when the Croatian Spring movement, which they had embraced, got out of hand. The comparison with the Croatian situation disturbed Serbs: Croatian Party leaders embraced a nationalist, in the end even separatist, movement; Serbian Party leaders wished to modernize Serbia and Yugoslavia, were not nationalists *or* centralists, yet lost their positions as well. The liberals could not overcome the complexity of their position; unlike Dabčević-Kučar and Tripalo, who are still revered by Croats for their efforts, the liberals were loved neither by Tito nor Serbs in general. Mijalko Todorović, a former Partisan who was an integral part of the liberal group in Serbia after the fall of Ranković in 1966, believed that the liberals "did not have enough support in Serbia itself, i.e., that they did not express the majority mood" (Inić 166). Instead, they were caught between two forces: Tito and a Serbian intelligentsia that was growing more and more restive.

When, in 1974, a new constitution was unveiled for Yugoslavia, the political and administrative changes initiated in the early 1960s reached their logical conclusion. The constitution institutionalized all of the changes that had prompted the antagonism of many Serbs from the mid-1960s through the early 1970s: republics gained initiative, while the central government in Belgrade became virtually powerless, and the autonomous provinces of Serbia achieved something akin to the status of republics, which, given the enhancement of republican status, was a double blow to those who feared the administrative parcelization of Serbia. Beyond those geopolitical structural changes, the widely held Serbian position on the constitution of 1974 is that it made centralized decision making virtually impossible, because in the federal parliament republican and provincial delegations voted as one, and any given delegation could veto legislation. Those republican and provincial delegations were elected by their own leagues of communists. Of particular concern to Serbs was the fact that the autonomous provinces were equal actors in this drama; beyond that, of course, the political will of the Serbs of Bosnia and Croatia was subsumed by the leaders of those republics. Because those leaderships had been purged in 1971/1972 by Tito, the republican delegations that were empowered by the

1974 constitution consisted of nonentities. Because the new constitution put a premium on the republic, or province, as the source of authority in the federation, and because both the Serbian and Croatian Leagues of Communists had been thoroughly purged of experienced, somewhat independent, competent people before the constitution was proclaimed, the space available to intellectuals to influence affairs in Yugoslavia had become as small as it had ever been.

SERBIA AFTER TITO

In April 1980 Tito died. Initially, it appeared that little had changed. Yugoslavs mourned the loss of their leader, who had sustained a cult of personality throughout his period in power, but the government did its best to act as though he still lived. "After Tito—Tito!" became the operative political slogan in Yugoslavia. The rotating presidency, established in 1970, now consisted of nine people, each of whom would act as president for a one-year term, beginning in the month of May. These people were not authoritative figures in Yugoslavia; they owed their positions to the system, which in turn owed its existence to Tito. Thus "After Tito—Tito" symbolized the death of initiative and creativity in a Yugoslavia that faced many obstacles upon the leader's passing. Serbia and Slovenia became the two primary centers of change in post-Titoist Yugoslavia, as each in its own way sought an escape from the zombie-like insistence that Tito had not really died; he lived on, in the system that he created.

In Serbia, the push for reform in Yugoslavia came from intellectuals, not from within the Party. Openness became one of the issues that galvanized a Serbian opposition to Titoism after the president's death. The post-Tito period in Yugoslavia could be dated from October of 1980 and the failed attempt to create a new "independent socialist" journal, to be entitled *Javnost* (The Public), after a journal founded by Svetozar Marković a century before. Dobrica Ćosić and Ljubomir Tadić, in the name of a committee of nine, appealed to 410 intellectuals across Yugoslavia to support such a journal. They claimed to have received 120 positive responses, with only 4 outright nays. In suitably vague language, the letter addressed the problem of responsibility and succession in Yugoslavia, so compromised by Tito's egoistic establishment of a weak rotating presidency and Party leadership. The government refused *Javnost*'s application to publish in November 1980.

The cause of openness gained strength in March 1981, when protests about bad food at the University of Priština grew over the course of several weeks into demonstrations of Albanians demanding that Kosovo be granted republic status by the Yugoslav government. Some demonstrators demanded union with Albania. By April the demonstrations had encompassed many cities and towns in Kosovo. On 2 April, the federal government declared a state of emergency, and the Yugoslav People's Army took to the streets of major cities, crushing the uprising. The army killed Albanians, although there is no number that all sources can accept (the government claimed, incredibly, that only nine demonstrators and one policeman were killed). The government lifted the state of emergency in July, but the political reckoning had only just begun. Immediately, over 1,000 Party members were expelled, and the Kosovo Party president, Mahmut Bakalli, lost his position. About 350 Albanians were immediately fired from their jobs (about half as educators). One credible estimate holds that over 4,000 Albanians were arrested and jailed in the aftermath of the demonstrations. In response, in November 1981 the LCY issued its "Political Platform for Action of the LCS in the Development of Socialistic Self-Mananagement, Brotherhood and Unity, and Togetherness in Kosovo." Then, in December 1981, the Central Committee of the Serbian League of Communists met to summarize the lessons of the demonstrations and propose measures to control the situation in the future. These meetings revealed, to the shock of many Serbs, that the demonstrations were no surprise to the Kosovo Party leadership and probably should not have been a surprise to those outside of Kosovo.

The cause of openness was served by revelations about Kosovo, but it was also served by the multitude of examples of the government crushing artistic freedom. *Javnost* had failed to get off the ground, but another underground initiative had an impact. The Committee for the Protection of Artistic Freedom (CPAF) was formed on 19 May 1982 at a meeting of the Belgrade section of the Serbian Writers' Association, at the urging of Dragoslav Mihailović, a survivor of Goli Otok and author of *When the Pumpkins Blossomed, Petra's Wreath,* and other novels. The most pressing reason for its formation was that a Serbian poet named Gojko Djogo had been arrested and was being tried for a crime against the state as the result of a book of poems that attacked the Titoist personality cult (the book was entitled *Woolen Times*). The committee's members included Desanka Maksimović, Borislav Mihajlović Mihiz, Stevan Raićković, Predrag Palavestra, Milovan Danojlić, Raša Livada, and Biljana Jovanović. The CPAF drafted an outline of its goals at its meeting of 20 September 1982. That draft included the following points: the CPAF would (a) nurture the protection of artistic freedom; (b) help expand support for artistic freedom in society; and (c) take it upon itself to inform the public when artistic freedom was violated. The committee also agreed that its votes would be taken by simple majority (although Mihiz later stated that every communiqué issued by the committee was supported unanimously).

By early 1983, the CPAF had issued several protests, addressing all of the known offenses against artistic and literary production to that point, including the cancellation of Jovan Radulović's play *Golubnjaći* (Pigeon Hole) and attacks on several notable books: Dobrica Ćosić's *Stvarno i moguće* (The Real and the Possible), Antonije Isaković's *Tren II* (Flash II), and Vuk Drašković's *Nož* (The Knife). On 28 March 1983, Gojko Djogo left for prison to serve a reduced one-year sentence. That night, the Serbian Writers' Association (UKS) held its first "protest Monday," as they would come to be called. Forty writers came to the UKS that night, including Ćosić and Mihiz (neither of whom was then a member). Other meetings followed, on 11 April, 18 April, and 25 April. Francuska 7 (the address of the Serbian Writers' Association) became from that point a symbol of democratic renewal in Serbia. The nature of that renewal changed over time, but in 1983 there can be little doubt that the Serbian Writers' Association was the single institution in Serbia that had decided, collectively, to attempt to come to grips with the country's subservient past.

They challenged Tito's legacy in some ways, but not others. Djogo's poetry clearly criticized Tito ("the rat from Dedinje"), but Djogo and his supporters argued that he had been misinterpreted, claiming that poetry cannot be understood literally—it has multiple meanings *(višeznaćnost)*. Why did they not just acknowledge the truth and send Djogo off to prison as a martyr to a petty regime? Apparently, they believed that the *višeznaćnost* argument had more potential for universal application. From the freedom of speech "flows all political freedoms," as Mihiz put it in 1991 (Krivokapić). The regime's opponents believed more good could be accomplished by arguing that the government should simply stay away from artistic speech than by creating a one-time martyr. Unfortunately, however, the free speech movement defended the right to speech, but it did not successfully establish the necessity of criticizing that speech. The result was that Serbian intellectuals discovered the euphoria of speaking truth to power but paid no attention to the ideas contained in the free speech they defended. Serbian questioning of Tito's legacy and the nature of Yugoslav statehood went deeper than that of other Yugoslavs. Ironically, while the Serbian republican government persecuted Gojko Djogo, it also harbored the most revisionist members of any republic's communist hierarchy. Most importantly, the Serbian League of Communists, whose leaders included Dragoslav (Draža) Marković, Petar Stambolić, and Ivan Stambolić, wished, as did most aware Serbs, to revise the constitutional status of Kosovo and Vojvodina. But the glazed eyes and the droning rhetoric of the Serbian leadership's mediocrities ultimately failed to inspire confidence, and as survivors of the 1972 purge and proponents of the 1974 constitution, their credibility was shot in any case.

By 1984, the Yugoslav government's dedication to its own pathetic slogan, "After Tito—Tito," had prompted it to extremes of petty harassment and persecution. While the Party shrank in fear of action that might disrupt the stagnant equilibrium following Tito's death, intellectuals embraced the opportunity to shake up that equilibrium. The jailing of Djogo, the cancellation of two plays (*Golubnjača* and *Karamazovi* [The Karamazovs]), various less publicized abuses—all betrayed a frightened government that attempted to maintain the Yugoslavia that existed when Tito died. In 1983 and 1984, though, the sheer number of arrests, trials, imprisonments, and proscriptions drove the free-speech movement to a new, more open stage in its development, out of the UKS and into society at large, as it were. But, importantly, that movement remained chained to the UKS strategy of defending speech per se, without critiquing the content of that speech.

Then, in April 1984, Dr. Vojislav Šešelj, a lawyer from Sarajevo, was arrested in Sarajevo, and twenty-eight people, including Milovan Djilas, were arrested in Belgrade. Šešelj's crime was to have written a contribution to a poll in the Party organ *Komunist* on the subject "What Is to Be Done?" That contribution was confiscated, and Šešelj was arrested before the piece could be published. The twenty-eight people arrested in Belgrade were accused of engaging in enemy propaganda over a period of seven years as part of the "flying university," an underground institution that saw different apartments hosting lectures on various topics, it goes without saying subversive ones, on a regular basis. Djilas was far and away the most notable catch in this sweep. After the initial arrests, all were set free. But then, on 30 April 1984, several days after his release, Radomir Radović, one of the original twenty-eight, was found dead in his apartment. Understandable suspicions that Radović had been killed by the police fed public outrage. On 23 May, six of the original twenty-eight were rearrested and charged with counterrevolutionary activity. The Belgrade Six, as they came to be known, together with Šešelj, became powerful symbols of the intransigence and insecurity of the regime.

Under these tense conditions, a new, and ultimately far more influential committee, the Committee for the Defense of the Freedom of Thought and Expression, was formed in November 1984. It was the brainchild of Ćosić, Taras Kermauner, and Rudi Supek, who envisioned a broadly Yugoslav forum that would take on causes similar to those embraced by the Committee for the Protection of Artistic Freedom. The presence of Ćosić, in the eyes of the government the standard-bearer of Serbian nationalism, and Supek, one of the leading leftist critics of Yugoslav socialism, made this committee a much more high-profile undertaking. Ćosić was responsible for bringing critical Serbian intellectuals into the fold, while Kermauner and Supek worked in the Slovenian and Croatian communities. Kermauner and Supek failed to convince their colleagues to join the Serbs: the Slovenes, Kermauner found, wished to create such a committee composed just of Slovenes, while the Croatian response was resounding silence.

The eventual members, all Serbs, included a cross-section of Belgrade's intelligentsia, with members of the Praxis group (Mihailo Marković, Ljubomir Tadić), historians (Radovan Samardzić, Dimitrije Bogdanović), young but established critics (Kosta Ćavoški, Ivan Janković), painters (Mića Popović, Mladen Srbinović), writers known to be hostile to the regime (Matija Bećković, Dragoslav Mihailović), veterans of the CPAF (Nikola Milošević, Predrag Palavestra, Mihiz), of course Ćosić, and five others: Neca Jovanov, Tanasije Mladenović (a writer of Ćosić's generation), Gojko Nikoliš, Andrija Gams (an economist and strong critic of the constitution of 1974), and Dragoslav Srejović.

In their initial declaration, the committee noted that "trials of human thought, . . . [which are] ever more common in our country, [are] becoming an ideologically and legally legitimate method of political reckoning for the government with those who disagree with it" ("Saopštenje Odbora," no. 361). Noting particularly the case of the Belgrade Six and Vojislav Šešelj, as well as the application of the notion of moral-political suitability in the workplace, they proclaimed that "freedom of thought and expression are not

Milovan Djilas

Milovan Djilas was born in 1911 in Montenegro and died in 1997 in Belgrade, Serbia. He joined the Communist Party of Yugoslavia in 1932, while a student at Belgrade University. He served time in prison for his activities between 1933 and 1936 and was elected a member of the politburo of the party in 1940. During World War II, Djilas was acknowledged to be one of the top four communists in the Party as it led the Partisan resistance movement. His own area of expertise was ideology and propaganda. After the war, he was one of the leaders of the new regime's agitation and propaganda division. He later (1961) published his reminiscences of his meetings with Stalin, entitled *Conversations with Stalin,* a book that is still regularly (and justifiably) used in history courses. Djilas and Edvard Kardelj were the original architects of self-management, which became the signal innovation of a regime that needed desperately to find a new source of legitimacy once it was rejected by Stalin.

Djilas is best known, though, for his own falling-out with the Tito regime, which came in January 1954, when he was purged from the leadership of the League of Communists of Yugoslavia. The cause of his fall was his growing advocacy of political pluralism in Yugoslavia, coupled with his ever more open critiques of the behavior of members of the communist leadership in the country. He probably could have passed his enforced retirement peacefully had he not chosen to publish a series of books that served collectively as a profound critique of the Yugoslav regime and its leader, Tito, and that opened the party and the state to more scrutiny than it was willing to bear. *The New Class,* which was published in 1955, was Djilas's first major post-purge work. In it, he detailed the rise of a new power class in communist systems, which had been supposed to put an end to class structures. This book earned him a nine-year prison sentence (he served time until 1961). Then *Conversations with Stalin* landed him another four-year spell in prison. His four-volume memoir, published between 1972 and 1986, is a brilliant evocation of his times. The first volume, *Land without Justice,* is of high literary quality, but it is the remaining three volumes—*Memoir of a Revolutionary, Wartime,* and *Rise and Fall*—that seem most significant, serving as wonderful excursions into the complex and deeply intriguing recent past of Yugoslavia.

Djilas was unable to publish or speak publicly in Yugoslavia until the late 1980s. His own complicated history of intellectual engagement—first as a militant communist, then as a supporter of pluralism, never as a nationalist—rendered him an outsider until his death in 1997.

the possession, gift, or privilege of any class, social group, party, or power of state; that freedom and that right belong to all human beings, and their fulfillment or endangerment are the business and conscience of all of the citizens of the social community. On that assumption, the Committee for the Freedom of Thought and Expression is organized" (Djukić 265). The committee continued to operate through 1989, but its effect was minimal, even in the view of the notoriously self-congratulatory Ćosić: "No matter how much the petitions reflected honorable democratic resistance to the autocratic and bureaucratic regime, their political meaning was small" (Djukić 265).

Again, as with the Committee for the Protection of Artistic Freedom, having denied themselves the freedom to debate the ideological and practical content of those causes they chose to adopt, members of this new committee in essence blessed any persecuted idea, regardless of its meaning. Laudably, this included the ideas of non-Serbs, some of which were contentious from a Serbian nationalist viewpoint. The committee defended the speech of, and protested the arrest of, anyone who was tried on the basis of Article 133 of the Yugoslav constitution, which enunciated a broad definition of enemy propaganda. Thus the two committees not only tackled Serbian causes, but also condemned the persecution of Bosnian Muslims like Alija Izetbegović, Albanian nationalists like Adem Demaci, and assorted others, especially in Croatia and Slovenia.

By 1984, a full-blown opposition movement existed in Yugoslavia. Founded upon the principle of free expression, which the movement's leaders presented as a means of discovering the "truth," a counterbalance to the regime's manipulative lies, this movement retained its principled purity through 1985. At that point, it underwent a transition with fateful consequences for Yugoslavia. In 1985 and 1986 several things happened that turned the principled movement for free expression into a cathartic Serbian nationalist movement over the fate of Kosovo. On 1 May 1985, a Serbian farmer named Djordje Martinović was found injured, bleeding from his rectum, a mineral water bottle by his side, on his fields near Gnjilane, Kosovo. The farmer survived, but to this day there is no agreement on what happened to him. Serbs (and Martinović) argue that he was attacked by young Albanians who forced the bottle into his anus. Albanians respond that Martinović injured himself while masturbating. The truth will probably never be known, but it did not matter. The Martinović episode fed Serbian fears that Kosovo had been lost to them, handed over to a Titoist-Albanian bureaucracy that would never allow the truth, so long as it hurt Albanian interests, to be heard. In this case, the movement for truth found a new catalyst.

The linkage of free speech and openness with Kosovo received another stimulus in October 1985, when over two thousand Serbs from Kosovo presented a petition to various governmental bodies. The designers of the petition produced an aggressive, challenging document, which they sent to the presidencies, assemblies, governments, and central committees of the Serbian and Yugoslav parties and state governments, as well as to the Serbian Academy of Arts and Sciences, the Serbian Writers' Association, four individuals, and a few other institutions in Yugoslavia. One suspects that the forcefulness of the petition might have come as a shock to the Serbian and Yugoslav public consciousness, had it not been for the Martinović episode, which was barely five months old. This petition gave more formal structure to the fears engendered by the Martinović incident:

Exposed to violence unheard of in history . . . we the undersigned Serbs from Kosovo and Metohija undertake our final effort to protect our families' right to life using legal means. . . . The situation is in reality stunning: a part of Yugoslavia is occupied, the region of our historical and national essence, and genocide by fascists against us Serbs of Kosovo and Metohija has achieved the status of a civil right. (Zahtevi 2015 stanovnika Kosova" 3)

Two claims in this initial section of the petition became the ritualized basis for Serbian grievances regarding Kosovo: that Kosovo was the core of Serbs' historical "essence," and that the law of this Yugoslavia was—inexcusably and unjustly—on the side of the Albanians, who were committing genocide against the Serbian population. The petition finished off with fourteen demands, including the following: that Serbia be given the same status as the other republics of Yugoslavia (that is, that it be unified and the autonomous provinces eliminated); that the names of those responsible for the genocide of Serbs be publicly announced; that no more Albanians be allowed to immigrate from Albania; that all agreements to sell Serbian property to Albanians be nullified; that Serbian families be enabled to return to Kosovo; that Ballists (Albanian nationalists from World War II) be rooted out; that the ethnic key be eliminated in determining employment in the province; and that the parliament of the Federal People's Republic of Yugoslavia be convened, with the petition's signatories present, to answer this petition by 30 October 1985.

When the federal and republican governments refused to consider the demands of the petitioners in the parliament and labeled them counterrevolutionaries, the transformation of Kosovo into the central grievance of the movement for free expression was complete. In January 1986 over two hundred influential Serbs forwarded a second petition to the federal parliament, demanding nothing specific of that body but announcing their hope that the Yugoslav public would rise in opposition to the government's collaboration in genocide, by Albanians, of Serbs in Kosovo. As the work of Serbia's intellectual elite, this document included a much more florid choice of words than the October petition:

The methods [of persecution of Serbs] have remained the same: on old stakes there are again heads. The new Deacon Avakum is named Djordje Martinović, and the Mother of the Jugovićes is Danica Milinčić. Old women and nuns are raped, the feeble are beaten, cattle are blinded, stalls are built of grave stones, the church and its historic holy places are profaned and shamed, economic sabotage is tolerated, people are forced to sell their property for nothing. (Magaš 49–52)

Aside from wildly exaggerated claims expressed in lavish prose, the petitioners pointed out the duplicity of the government. "In 1981," the petition continued, "it was publicly acknowledged that the true situation in Kosovo had been hidden and falsified; the hope was stoked that it would not happen again. For five years already we have witnessed uninterrupted anarchy and the collapse of hope that social and national relations in Kosovo and Metohija could be changed" (Magaš 49–52). For these petitioners, the competition for Kosovo became a competition between public truths and governmental deception. The refusal of the government to receive the earlier Kosovo Serb petitioners became an attack on their right to speak. By cloaking the truth, the authorities became complicit in genocide, and thus did the movement for free expression come to focus primarily on Kosovo.

This second petition was signed by representatives of virtually all possible factions within the Serbian critical intelligentsia. Signatories included Dobrica Ćosić, Borislav Mihajlović Mihiz, Mića Popović, Vera Bozičković-Popović, Vojislav Djurić, Mihailo Djurić, Bata Mihajlović, and Žika Stojković; Ljubomir Tadić, Mihailo Marković, and Zagorka Golubović-Pešić of the *Praxis* group; over thirty members of the Serbian academy; a number of retired military officers; several priests; and dozens of others. Particularly surprising were the contingent from *Praxis,* who were called to answer for their signatures on what appeared to be an outlandish petition based on a romantic understanding of historical processes, rather than the dispassionate socioeconomic analysis that might have been expected of them. To one commentator's attack on them for signing on to Serbian nationalism, three signatories responded that (a) there was nothing inconsistent in their support for an oppressed minority, be it Serbian or of some other nationality, and (b) that "all three of us are members of the *Committee for the defense of freedom of public expression* in Belgrade and raise our voices against all forms of repression in our country" (Magaš 57).

Their justification for their signatures was telling: Kosovo turned into just another occasion for the defense of freedom of expression, and the fight for the freedom of expression validated any interpretation of the roots of the crisis in Kosovo. Speech repressed became, by definition, good speech. The merging of two strands of opposition: the legalistic, reasoned, cerebral support for free expression, and the mystical, cathartic, visceral support for the Serbian minority in Kosovo, was now complete; they may have been intuitively incompatible, but in the progression of Serbian thought in the 1980s they were fully complementary.

The infamous Memorandum of the Serbian Academy of Sciences and Arts completed the transformation of the free speech movement into a movement of rage. On 23 May 1985, just after the Martinović episode and several months before the petitions of the Kosovo Serbs and the Belgrade intellectual elite were sent to the Federal Parliament, the Serbian Academy of Sciences and Arts met in general session and decided to produce a document outlining the problems Yugoslavia faced. The academy apparently debated long and hard over whether it should assemble such a document in the first place, since its bylaws required it to remain out of politics. But the general assembly of the academy ultimately agreed that Yugoslavia's crisis demanded contributions from all of those resources at Yugoslavia's disposal. "No one has the right to shut his eyes to what is happening and to what might happen. And this particularly holds true for the most venerable institution of scientific and cultural achievement of this nation" (Mihailović and Krestić 94). It was intended that the document eventually be sent to the various governing bodies of the state. On 13 June 1985, the presidency of the academy appointed a committee to prepare the outline. Members of the committee wrote those sections that fell within their expertise. When a draft of a section was completed, Antonjije Isaković (the vice president of the academy and the informal chair of the committee) would convene meetings, which several additional academicians, including Dobrica Ćosić and Ljubomir Tadić, attended. By January 1986, the first full draft of the Memorandum was prepared. In late September, after several months of editing, as the document neared completion, the Belgrade newspaper *Večernje novosti* (Evening News) revealed that the academy was preparing it.

This synopsis of the origins of the Memorandum is included because it clarifies some areas of real and alleged confusion regarding the document. First, it was not prepared secretly as many critics claimed. The academy had acknowledged that it was working on such a project. Second, it was not written by Ćosić, although he has long been credited with authorship by non-Serbian commentators and he unquestionably had promoted such a project. This is not to say that his ideas did not find their way into the document. Third, it was not completed. This point, repeated ad nauseum by the academy, its members, and supporters, is accurate but ultimately beside the point, for none of the document's authors or admirers have ever disavowed its contents. In any case, the Memorandum, unfinished (and until 1989 unpublished), entered the realm of public and political discourse in September 1986. It also entered the realm of the mythology accompanying the collapse of Yugoslavia.

The Memorandum is formally divided into two parts: one on the "Crisis in the Yugoslav Economy and Society," the other on the "Status of Serbia and the Serbian Nation" (Mihailović and Krestić 94–140). That first portion can be further broken down for the sake of clarity into three subsections: one on the economy, one that considers Yugoslavia's constitutional order, and a third that treats cultural questions. Putting a strong emphasis on the economic crisis, which took up much of the Memorandum, the committee wrote that "a particular cause for anxiety is that official political circles are unwilling to acknowledge the true reasons for the economic crisis, making it impossible to take the steps necessary for economic recovery" (95). Aside from that, the Memorandum noted the Party's unwillingness to "acknowledge" the truth—as it had also failed to do in the 1981 Kosovo crisis. The Memorandum's complaints can be reduced to what the committee saw as the one fundamental problem: the confederalization of Yugoslavia, as enshrined in the 1974 constitution, whose antecedents it traced to the early 1960s. That constitution unfairly penalized Serbs. Underlying the great mistake of 1974 was an attitude that was born in the international communist movement: "The roots lie in the ideology propagated by the Comintern and in the CPY's national policy before the Second World War" (Mihailović and Krestić 137).

The second half of the Memorandum is the part that is most often quoted, for it includes the most inflammatory language and tenuous claims. Entitled "The Status of Serbia and the Serbian Nation," it foreshadowed many of the themes that dominated Serbian political and intellectual discourse in the following years, during which, among other things, "genocide" became an extremely elastic concept in Serbia. This section first identifies the three situations that the committee felt needed to be discussed: the "long-term lagging" of the Serbian economy, "unregulated legal relations with Yugoslavia and the provinces," and "the genocide in Kosovo"(Mihailović and Krestić 118).

Although much of the Memorandum retains a scholarly, or at least analytical, tone, the portions concerning Serbia's relations with its autonomous provinces, and the life of Serbs in those provinces, are quite extravagant. The Memorandum initiates its discussion of these topics by pronouncing them existential, rather than constitutional, issues.

> The relationships between Serbia and its provinces cannot be seen solely or even predominantly in terms of an interpretation of the two constitutions from a legal standpoint. The question concerns the Serbian nation and its state. A nation which after a long and bloody struggle regained its own state, which fought for and achieved a civil democracy, and which in the last two wars lost 2.5 million of its members, has lived to see the day when a Party committee of apparatchiks decrees that after four decades in the new Yugoslavia it alone is not allowed to have its own state. A worse historical defeat in peacetime cannot be imagined. (Mihailović and Krestić 126)

Serbia's relationship to its provinces was thus removed from the realm of administrative efficiency and legal consistency and raised to the level of a question of historical justice, as the Memorandum itself moved from the cerebral to the visceral. With regard to Kosovo, the Memorandum stated that "in the spring of 1981, open and total war was declared on the Serbian people." That war, which brought "the physical, political, legal, and cultural genocide of the Serbian population of Kosovo and Metohija," had now continued for five years. Fantastically, the authors of the Memorandum claimed that Kosovo was "worse than any defeat experienced in the liberation wars waged by Serbia from the First Serbian Uprising in 1804 to the uprising in 1941" (Mihailović and Krestić 126).

The Memorandum, which was never openly released (only leaked to the public), met with a predictably weak response from the Serbian Party leadership. Ivan Stambolić, the president of the Serbian Party, asserted that "we [Communist Party leaders] do not accept the Memorandum's call for Serbia to turn its back on its own future and the future of Yugoslavia, for it to arbitrarily accuse the proven leaders of the revolution and of socialist development, for Serbian communists to be seen as the illegitimate leaders of the working class and people of Serbia" ("Stambolić Criticizes Memorandum Authors"). The decline of the Party's legitimacy in the eyes of the Serbian public could only accelerate in the face of such a weak response.

Where the Party missed the point, others did not. Ćosić approved of the Memorandum and defended the integrity of the academy. The other half of the non-Party opposition consisted of members of the Praxis group. Their position outside of the Party had been long established. Yet their opposition to the Party had always been essentially Marxist. The fact that they now joined a nationalist consensus is thus intriguing and somewhat shocking. Four members of the group, Ljubomir Tadić, Zagorka Golubović, Mihailo Marković, and Milan Kangrga, had signed the January 1986 petition that first labeled Albanian behavior in Kosovo as genocidal. Their gravitation from Marxism to nationalism was abrupt. Their anti-Titoism was of long pedigree, and their democratic inclinations were well publicized. Their transition can be explained in two ways: their democracy, like that of other Serbs (and Croats, and the rest), was not rooted in a belief in individual liberties but founded on a collective conception of society and rights; and they found it easy to move from one homogenizing, collective ideology (class-based Marxism) to another (cultural-based nationalism).

THE ARRIVAL OF SLOBODAN MILOŠEVIĆ

Both general approaches reached their fullest development in Slobodan Milošević's so-called anti-bureaucratic revolution, which began in 1988, played on Serbs' hatred of the Titoist Party, and demanded a complete turnover in the Party elite. Milošević had been a rather unremarkable Party apparatchik until 1987, when he orchestrated the purge of his mentor in the Serbian League of Communists, Ivan Stambolić. To do so, Milošević harnessed the growing power of the alleged persecution of Serbs in Kosovo as an issue dear to the Serbian people. After 1987, when he became president of the Serbian League of Communists, Milošević became ever more popular as his control of the press grew and he was able to both feed and be fed by the hysteria over Kosovo. Milošević took advantage of the general Serbian

belief that the Party did not have the capability to end the "terror" in Kosovo. Instead of droning on using Titoist phraseology about the ability of "self-management" to produce solutions, he took the old Ćosić idea of anti-bureaucracy and made it his own. This anti-bureaucratic revolution, by cleansing the Party, allowed Milošević to install his own men, who supported his new nationalist proclivities, whether cynically or not. Milošević thus achieved a historic fusion of the attitudes of the Party and of the non-Party oppositionists.

From late 1987 forward, the now "revolutionary" Party incorporated more and more of the ideas of the Serbian Academy nationalists and their non-Party allies. The fusion could best be seen in the celebrations of the 600th anniversary of the Battle of Kosovo in June 1989. With the backdrop of the "field of blackbirds," on which the Battle of Kosovo was fought and which is considered by Serbs one of their sacred places, Milošević pronounced his determination to redress the balance of history. The Battle of Kosovo was lost due to "lack of unity and betrayal." "Therefore," he continued, "words devoted to unity, solidarity, and cooperation among people have no greater significance anywhere on the soil of our motherland than they have here in the field of Kosovo, which is a symbol of disunity and treason" ("Milošević Delivers Speech"). By linking the fate of a disunited Serbia in 1389 with that of the allegedly disunited Serbia of 1989, Milošević linked the subtle revisionism of the Serbian Party with the overt nationalism of the Memorandum authors.

It was an unlikely combination, and an explanation of how it came about requires more discussion of the background. The opposition movement had inflamed Serbian public opinion over Kosovo. Its goals were to push the Serbian (and potentially the Yugoslav) League of Communists to address the unequal position of Serbia in Yugoslavia. Practically, their success would have meant reincorporating Kosovo and Vojvodina into Serbia proper, a position they had not occupied in the communist era. Neither the Serbian League of Communists nor the Party organizations of the other republics of Yugoslavia were receptive to the Serbs' position. It is easy now to forget that the Serbian Party actually had been quite critical of the division of Serbia, especially in light of the 1981 Albanian rebellion. Under the leadership of Ivan Stambolić, however, it insisted on going slow, seeking incremental change in alliance with other Yugoslavs. By 1987, though, the intellectual movement had reached a point where it could not be ignored. Typically, the Party and the Party press portrayed the movement as nationalistic and destructive of the brotherhood and unity of the Yugoslav peoples. Both accusations were true, but they had become so much a part of the Titoist mantra that they were largely ignored by Serbs. Ultimately, it was probably inevitable that some person or group within the Party would try to harness the power of the opposition to their own ends.

In 1987 Slobodan Milošević did just that. In April of that year, Milošević had visited the town of Kosovo Polje to address the locals and to hear the grievances of a delegation of Serbs. Outside the building, Serbs were demonstrating and

Slobodan Milošević. (Petar Kujundzic/Reuters/Corbis)

struggling with the police, who were Albanians. When Milošević poked his head out the window and said to the Serbs, "No one dares beat you," he instantly became the hero of the Serbian movement in Kosovo. The entire episode had been scripted beforehand: Milošević understood that the Serbian movement in Kosovo was a powerful one, which he could use to gain and hold power in Serbia. Over the course of 1987, Milošević had built a strong relationship with the directors of *NIN* (*Nedeljne Informativne Novine* [Weekly Informative News], the leading Serbian newsweekly) and Radio-Television Belgrade. Using his media allies, he had been able to stoke the fears of ordinary Serbs over the fate of Serbs in Kosovo. By November of 1987, he had been able to bring about the fall of Ivan Stambolić, his best friend and political mentor, as president of Serbia. Thereafter, Milošević, feeding on the power of the Kosovo issue, was able to create and fund a massive organization (allegedy populist, but actually quite professional) of demonstrators who moved from city to city in the Serbian portions of Yugoslavia, demanding that the Parties of Montenegro, Vojvodina, and Kosovo reform, get rid of the dead wood, and embrace the anti-bureaucratic revolution of Slobodan Milošević. Frightened Party leaderships in Vojvodina and Montenegro resigned en

masse in the fall of 1988. By the spring of 1989, Milošević had been able to proclaim a new constitution for Serbia, which reincorporated Vojvodina and Kosovo into the republic proper.

Milošević was now extremely popular among Serbs. He was able to portray himself as a true "people's revolutionary," one who understood that the Party had grown away from the people and needed to return to them. However, for the same reason that he became popular among Serbs, he was a frightening figure to most other Yugoslavs. Slovenes and Croats feared that Milošević would try to use the power of Serbian nationalism to take power in Yugoslavia; Albanians recognized that he had manipulated Serbian opinion to inflame racist hatred of Albanians among Serbs. The result of Milošević's takeover of power in Serbia was the growth of national movements in other republics. In Slovenia and Croatia, in particular, latent nationalism reemerged in the late 1980s.

Thus the celebration of the 600th anniversary of the Battle of Kosovo was simply Milošević's coming-out party, if you will, which he and Serbia in general celebrated at Gazi Mestan, the scene of the battle. With all of the republican leaders from around Yugoslavia in attendance, he presided over a celebration that capped the Serbian revival of the 1980s, during which he announced the readiness of Serbs once again to defend themselves militarily, if necessary.

Milošević's popularity peaked that summer of 1989. Thereafter, as Serbian society became more fully politicized, as competitors and new political parties emerged, he necessarily lost some of his luster. Virtually all of the new parties embraced a Serbian nationalist platform that differed very little from that which made him so popular in the first place. As a result, differentiation among the parties tended to be ideological and historical—in other words, nationalist parties arrayed themselves from right to left. Milošević and his now renamed Socialist Party of Serbia suffered among many Serbs for being communist. Others who had once approved of his defense of Serbian interests soon became disillusioned by his willingness to use coercive measures to defend his power (a topic discussed more fully in "Serbian Politics and Political Evolution"). Milošević's ambiguous position came into full relief in March 1991, when a rally against his control of the media turned into a days-long movement against the regime's authoritarian methods. The army was called into Belgrade to quell the movement, and two people were killed (one student demonstrator, one policeman). The rally did not achieve much in the way of its goals, but it did become a touchstone for opponents of the Milošević regime thereafter. Since it came, however, a mere three months before the outbreak of war, opponents of the regime were unable to capitalize on its momentum.

SERBIA AT WAR

The war of Yugoslav succession broke out when Croatia and Slovenia declared their secession from the state on 25 June 1991. Serbia, as such, was not at war at that point. But it was clear to all observers and participants—even when it was not openly acknowledged at the outset—that the Yugoslav

People's Army fought thereafter as a Serbian force, and it went without saying that many of the Serbian paramilitaries who were responsible for much of the Croatian fighting were being directed from Serbia. The war with Slovenia lasted a mere seventeen days; thereafter, a truce having been negotiated, the open war in Croatia began. For all intents and purposes, however, the war in Croatia had begun in the summer of 1990, when Serbian leaders in Knin and other towns openly resisted the imposition of certain new measures—largely symbolic—by the newly elected regime of Franjo Tudjman. In August 1990, under the leadership of Milan Babić, the "Autonomous Province of the Serbian Krajina" had been proclaimed, with Knin as its center in western Croatia. For another ten months, hostilities were local but often vicious. When the declared war began in July 1991, the most shocking fighting took place in eastern Croatia, around the cities of Vukovar and Osijek, which Serbs hoped to incorporate into a unified Serbian state. There, the "Serbia Autonomous Region of Slavonia, Baranja, and Western Srem" was formed and proclaimed in July 1991. By early 1992, Serbian forces controlled about 30 percent of the territory of the prewar Republic of Croatia, and they continued to do so until the summer of 1995.

In April 1992 the focus of the war shifted to Bosnia, which declared its own independence on 6 April. Sarajevo was immediately beseiged by Yugoslav People's Army forces, acting in essence as the military of the Serbian Democratic Party, the Bosnian Serb political party headed by Radovan Karadžić. Like the war in Croatia, the war in Bosnia was really several different struggles, whose nature was more local than general. Serbian forces attempted to clear eastern Bosnia (Goražde, Višegrad) and north central Bosnia (Banja Luka) of non-Serbs in order to complete an envisioned independent Serbia. As in Croatia, Serbian forces in Bosnia were quickly able to conquer and control a large part of the former republic—in Bosnia's case, well over 50 percent. And also as in Croatia, this conflict was not to end until the summer of 1995. The war in Croatia, quiet after January 1992, flared up again in the spring of 1995. Croatian forces had been upgraded—better armed (thanks to Germany), and trained by Western (especially American) advisors—and now went on the offensive to regain territory controlled by Serbs. In early May Croatian forces overran western Slavonia, centered on the town of Okučani. Then, in July and August 1995, Croatian forces overran the Krajina (western Croatia), liberating Knin and prompting a massive exodus of Serbian refugees, estimated to be as many as 200,000.

The story of the 1990s is a chronicle of wars; once Croatia and Bosnia were finished, Kosovo loomed. There, the Albanian population had hunkered down after 1990; by the mid-1990s, however, younger Albanians were no longer willing to tolerate the absence of political autonomy and any semblance of a cultural life in the region, and many of them opted for armed resistance to the Serbs. The result was that an armed insurgency began in 1996 and reached substantial proportions by late 1998. Serbian military and police forces used maximum force to put down the movement, which was led by the Kosovo Liberation Army. A NATO (North Atlantic Treaty Organization) bombing

Bosnian Serb leader Radovan Karadžić. (Reuters/Corbis)

campaign in March and April 1999 effectively drove the Serbs from Kosovo. At the end of the decade of wars, Serbia had thus lost all four areas: Slovenia, Croatia, Bosnia, and Kosovo.

POLITICAL DEVELOPMENTS IN THE POSTCOMMUNIST ERA

There are a couple of factors that are critical to any understanding of how Serbia's "democratization" in the 1990s proceeded. One is that by 1990, people across virtually the entire Serbian political, cultural, and intellectual spectrum agreed that Titoism—in other words, communism in Yugoslavia—had victimized Serbia; thus, all believed that Serbia needed to assert itself by protecting Serbs' interests and projecting Serbian power. In other words, virtually all political Serbs were nationalists. However, this unity was crosscut by a source of great disunity: the legacy of the Serbian past (especially World War II) lay heavily on Serbian political parties. Regardless of their shared nationalism, these parties fell across the spectrum from left to right and were often quite hostile to each other in ideological terms. Thus, for instance, the two parties that were initially most popular in Serbia were the Socialist Party of Serbia (SPS, the party of Slobodan Milošević) and the Serbian Renewal Movement

(SRM, the party of Vuk Drašković). Both thrived on the growth of Serbian nationalism (the SPS was, arguably, not nationalist itself), but the SPS was communist and the SRM was royalist. One was the heir to the Partisans, the World War II group led by Tito; the other was the heir to the Četniks, the Serbian World War II fighters led by Colonel Dragoljub (Draža) Mihailović. The two leaders were rivals, and their constituencies loathed each other. Shared nationalism was not a guarantee of political harmony in Serbia.

The period under discussion here is often referred to as one of democratization, especially elsewhere in Eastern Europe, which began that process after the fall of the communist regimes in 1989. In Yugoslavia, though, the process followed a different logic. The year 1989 did have meaning for Yugoslavia, but not the same kind of meaning as for the rest of Eastern Europe. In Yugoslavia, 1989 was the year that Serbian nationalism reached its crescendo with the celebration of the 600th anniversary of the Battle of Kosovo. For Serbs, the celebration symbolized the unity of the Serbian people in the face of enemies far and wide. For other Yugoslavs, the celebration symbolized the fear that a unified Serbian people could provoke. The rise in Serbian nationalism actually resulted in pressure to democratize in two other Yugoslav republics, Slovenia and Croatia, each of which held democratic elections in the spring of 1990. The pressure to hold free elections in Serbia came from two parties formed in early 1990: the monarchists of the Serbian Renewal Movement (SRM) and the liberal democrats of the Democratic Party (DP), both of whom were intensely anticommunist. In June a large demonstration of the opposition parties was held in Belgrade, and soon thereafter, opposition parties were legalized. Aside from the SRM and the DP, several dozen parties registered, including the reformed and renamed League of Communists of Serbia, which called itself the Socialist Party of Serbia (SPS).

These parties were to be the three major parties in Serbia during the transition phase. The SPS retained the resources and the pedigree of the League of Communists, but it also welcomed in many of the opposition figures of the past decade whose loyalties were to the Left (including, for instance, the Praxis philosopher Mihailo Marković and the novelist Antonije Isaković). The SRM was extremely nationalistic and bitterly anticommunist. Its leader was Vuk Drašković, who earned a reputation as a demagogic speaker, one who evoked links to the Četnik past in Serbia. The Democratic Party was the party of the urban intellectual elite, and thus found it difficult to appeal across the social spectrum in Serbia. Its parliamentary principles and somewhat muted nationalism made it the favorite party of Western observers of the Serbian political scene. This party underwemt a major split within a year, but its early leadership included Zoran Djindjić and Vojislav Koštunica, the premier and president of Yugoslavia following the October 2000 fall of the Milošević regime. The constituencies of all three parties described themselves as "nationalist"; a majority of the members of the SPS actually described themselves as "authoritarian," whereas the SRM was split between "authoritarian" and "antiauthoritarian" and the DS was heavily "antiauthoritarian." Other parties ranged the political spectrum, but none would compete with the three described above, until the emergence of the Serbian Radical Party of Vojislav Šešelj in 1992.

The most important issue preceding elections in Serbia was the decision whether to promulgate a new constitution before or after the vote. On 26 June 1990, the Serbian skupština (parliament) voted that the question should be decided by a referendum to be held a week later. The regime preferred to produce a constitution before the elections, and the opposition was unable to counter the regime's influence in the one-week window it was given. The regime announced that 97 percent of voters had favored promulgating a new constitution before holding elections (Miller, "A Failed Transition" 158–159). Accordingly, the SPS had the advantage of creating a political system in its own image. The result was a presidential system with a weak parliament. The constitution was designed to assure the power of Slobodan Milošević. In the same preelection period, the Serbian skupština passed electoral laws that established single-member constituencies. In such a system, representatives are chosen by constituency rather than being allotted according to the countrywide vote. Furthermore, any organization with 100 members and a program could be registered as a party. These laws made it more difficult for the serious opposition parties to get elected.

The elections of 1990 empowered the government that was to run Serbia for a decade. In these December elections, 71 percent of the citizens of Serbia (including Vojvodina and Kosovo) voted. The SPS won 78 percent of seats in the skupština. No other party received more than 8 percent of the seats (the percentage gained by the SRM). Parties representing minorities did win a few seats: the Hungarian, Muslim, and Croatian organizations each did so, whereas the Albanians of Kosovo boycotted the election and thus gained nothing but an unimportant moral triumph. With Slobodan Milošević's victory in the presidential election (in which he received 63 percent of the vote to Drašković's 16 percent), the parliamentary elections rewarded a party and a politician who were popular, but not all that popular in Serbia. Why? One answer is that Serbs had grown comfortable with authoritarian rule, and that the SPS had taken over the nationalist issues that Serbs found so compelling in the late 1980s. So, even if Drašković was more stridently nationalist, voters did not feel compelled to opt for him; he was an unknown quantity, after all. Another explanation is also convincing, however: the Milošević regime had resources that the opposition parties simply could not match, and thus could campaign more effectively. In any case, Slobodan Milošević retained power in an era in which communist parties throughout Eastern Europe—and Yugoslavia—were falling like flies. It seems ironic that he probably had nationalism to thank for his victory.

The Milošević regime thus had the aura of power and authority in Serbia. Nonetheless, it faced great hostility, especially in Belgrade, where the core support of the Democratic Party resided, and in other urban areas of Serbia. Street demonstrations in Belgrade in March 1991 illustrated the depth of the hostility to the regime in that city, especially from supporters of the SRM and the DP. Neverthe-

Zoran Djindjić (1952–2003)

Zoran Djindjić was born in Bosanski Šamac in 1952. He was murdered in Belgrade in February 2003. He graduated with a degree in philosophy from the University of Belgrade in 1974 and was jailed soon thereafter for attempting to form an independent student union. After his release, he moved to Germany, where he earned a doctorate in philosophy from the University of Frankfurt. In 1990 he was one of the founders of the Democratic Party, one of the three leading contenders for power in the first free postwar elections held in Serbia in that year. By 1994, he had taken over leadership of that party. Throughout the wars in Croatia and Bosnia, Djindjić maintained a somewhat ambiguous position in Serbian politics; he himself was not a radical nationalist, but it was difficult to appeal to a Serbian population that was deeply nationalist itself without playing to that extreme nationalism. When the war in Bosnia was over, Djindjić remained one of Slobodan Milošević's most aggressive opponents. In late 1996 Djindjić, along with Vuk Drašković, the leader of the Serbian Renewal Movement, and the leaders of the Civic Alliance of Serbia, led demonstrations against the regime following clear election fraud in the elections of that fall. By early 1997, the demonstrations had wrested concessions from the Milošević regime and Djindjić was installed as the mayor of Belgrade. In the aftermath of this victory, he and Drašković sabotaged their own positions by fighting a bitter personal battle. As a result, the gains of early 1997 were lost soon thereafter.

During the NATO bombing campaign of 1999, Djindjić fled Belgrade for safe haven in Montenegro, whence he continued to criticize the Milošević regime. Branded a traitor for his choice of flight, he proved his political savvy by nonetheless emerging once again as one of Milošević's opponents. In 2000, recognizing that his own political baggage made him an unlikely victor in the presidential election of that year, he threw his party's support to Vojislav Koštunica, who won the election. After bitter street battles on 5 October 2000, the Milošević regime collapsed. Koštunica became president of Serbia, and in January 2001 Djindjić, as the leader of the party with the most representation in the Serbian parliament, became prime minister of Serbia.

As prime minister, Djindjić advocated doing all that was necessary to build a strong relationship with Western Europe and the United States. This necessitated his support for the handing over of those who had been indicted to the Hague, including Milošević himself. Unfortunately for Djindjić, political power in Serbia still required the support of factions within the security services, organized crime, and the extremely corrupt business community. When Djindjić made it clear he was seeking the arrest of many of those who had thrown him their support in 2000, he was assassinated in February 2003. The man responsible, Milorad Ulemek, known as "Legija," had been Djindjić's own man in the security services in October 2000—the man, in other words, who arguably assured the success of the demonstrations of 5 October.

less, the regime had little trouble ending the demonstrations with only cosmetic losses. When the wars in Croatia and Slovenia began in June 1991, Milošević was able to capitalize on the fact that virtually all Serbs, regardless of ideological persuasion, favored the aggressive defense of Serbs and projection of Serbian power in areas with large Serbian minorities (Croatia and Bosnia). The SRM and the DS could not compete with a Milošević who was aggressively prosecuting the war against (through 1991) a Croatian government that actively courted the legacy of the Ustaša, the Croatian ultranationalist organization.

Interestingly, as the war progressed, Drašković, one of the most vitriolic of Serbian nationalists before the war, began to express pacifist sentiments, which opened the door to another extreme nationalist, Vojislav Šešelj. Šešelj had been the founder of the Serbian Četnik movement. From the early 1980s, he had been a hero of the free speech movement in Serbia, as he had been persecuted by the government for the expression of the view that Yugoslavia's federation should be reorganized, with Serbia gaining territory at the expense of Bosnia and others. The Četnik movement was illegal in Serbia, but behind the scenes Šešelj and Milošević had contacts. Šešelj came in fifth in the presidential elections of 1990, and was actually elected to the skupština in a 1991 by-election in a Belgrade suburb. A latecomer to the political scene, Šešelj became one of Serbia's most important political actors in the mid-1990s, in spite of his ostentatious and even atavistic nationalism. His party, renamed the Serbian Radical Party (SRP) in memory of the Radical Party of Nikola Pašić in the early twentieth century, occupied an interesting niche in Serbian politics: its membership profile was almost identical to that of the SPS, with the exception of the fact that the SRP attracted anticommunists.

From the summer of 1991 on, Serbian political developments had a surreal air. Outsiders could note that there was a great degree of agreement in Serbia on the need to prosecute the war aggressively, while Serbs themselves undermined that apparent unanimity, as they continually fought among themselves. The key to this paradox is that while virtually all Serbian parties were nationalist, they were ideologically quite distinct from and hostile to each other. Inside Serbia, then, the years of the war saw constant attempts to combine and overthrow the Milošević regime. In May 1992, for instance, some opposition parties (SRM, an offshoot of the DP called the Democratic Party of Serbia, the Serbian Liberal Party, New Democracy, and the People's Peasant Party) formed a coalition called the Democratic Movement of Serbia (DEPOS). It pursued the overthrow of Milošević, sponsoring demonstrations during the summer of 1992. In July 1992, though, DEPOS found itself allied with a new federal prime minister, the Serbian-American Milan Panić, whose appointment Milošević had arranged in order to appease American opinion. In spite of American material and moral support for Panić, Milošević and the SPS won elections held in December 1992 with 40 percent of the seats in the skupština and 56 percent of the presidential vote. With the Radical Party of Šešelj, the SPS controlled 70 percent of the seats of the skupština. The results were demoralizing for the opposition. Elections in 1993 did not result in any real changes, except that the SRP lost support to the DP and to DEPOS. The most important change to occur during the war in Bosnia was that the Milošević regime lost its Radical allies when it allowed monitors to observe the Serbian-Bosnian border, an affront to the Radicals' nationalist sensibilities.

The Bosnian and Croatian wars ended in the summer of 1995. In the Croatian case, a motivated Croatian army, trained by the United States, overran the various Serbian communities that had achieved a level of independence in 1991. It appears that Milošević ordered the Serbian forces defending those Krajina communities to abandon the region to Croatia. The end of the Bosnian conflict came in August, after NATO bombing and an offensive by combined Croatian and Bosnian armies. Such a dismal end to a long war might have endangered the Milošević regime, which could only suffer from its failure to defend important Serbian territories. Unfortunately, it did not. With the Bosnian and Croatian wars concluded, Milošević's fate became the key issue in Serbian politics. And here there was an unpleasant fact that had to be faced by both Serbs and outsiders: many Serbs simply felt comfortable voting for Milošević. Pensioners, workers in state-owned enterprises, civil servants, people who saw themselves still on the Left, all voted for Milošević, albeit for different reasons. Furthermore, although Serbia had a democratic electoral system, the regime still possessed undeniable advantages, primarily in its control of the press, its control of the police, its ability to assure supplies of important goods like paper, and its general sophistication.

Except for one brief moment of hope in late 1996, when a coalition of the Democratic Party, the Serbian Renewal Movement, and the Civic Alliance (called *Zajedno,* or "together") won municipal elections in many of Serbia's cities, Milošević was unbeatable. In the case of Zajedno, in-

ternal squabbling ruined the coalition's victories within a year. Arguably responsible for the amazingly destructive wars of the 1990s, Milošević could not be beaten even after losing those wars.

Of course, today Milošević is out of power. The explanation cannot, however, be found in the Serbian electorate; instead, his removal from power was a result of developments in Kosovo. Beginning in 1989, with the promulgation of the new Serbian constitution, which reincorporated Kosovo into Serbia, the Kosovo Albanian community chose to respond to increased Serbian oppression in the province by withdrawing from public and political life. Albanians in Kosovo chose to create a parallel society, using the model of Solidarity and its associated organizations in Poland in the late 1970s and 1980s. Since the University of Priština had already been purged of its Albanian professors and turned into a Serbian university, and since the ethnically Albanian professionals in Kosovo's cities had been removed from their positions, the Albanian population chose to boycott Serbian elections and work as though they were free.

In December 1989 the Democratic League of Kosovo (DLK) was founded. In July 1990 approximately 90 percent of the Albanian members of the provincial parliament voted that Kosovo be proclaimed a republic in Yugoslavia. In September 1991 those deputies announced a referendum on Kosovo's independence. In October that referendum, illegal but not obstructed by the Serbs, saw an alleged 99.87 percent of those who voted choose independence. In underground elections for a parliament of this independent Kosovo, held in May 1992, the DLK won a solid victory. The DLK's leader, Ibrahim Rugova, was elected president. The Serbian authorities allowed all of this to happen, but did not allow the parliament to meet. There was a tacit understanding on both sides that the Albanians would lie low, and that Serbia, engaged elsewhere, would not react violently to the limited Albanian moves.

This truce lasted as long as the wars in Croatia and Bosnia. After the Dayton Accords ended the Bosnian conflict, however, younger, more combative Albanians began to question the tactics of the DLK. The Kosovo Liberation Army (KLA) was the result of this questioning. The first guerrilla actions of this new organization came in the spring of 1996; over the next two years, it acted sporadically, attacking police stations and provoking retaliation by the Serbs. In 1998 the KLA's activity took on greater proportions, although it was still an exceedingly small organization (perhaps 150 men in 1997). In March 1998 the first of several large-scale massacres of Albanians took place when the Serbian police encircled and destroyed the home of Adem Jashari, one of the leaders of the KLA. Fifty-eight people were killed in the compound, including twenty-eight women and children. The Serbian government had decided to attempt to wipe out the KLA at any cost. Because the cost turned out to be amazingly high, the Milošević government eventually brought on foreign intervention. The most important of these massacres came at Račak in January 1999. The administration of American president Bill Clinton decided at that point to issue an ultimatum to Milošević: pull out of Kosovo and allow a NATO occupa-

Serb soldiers display a Serbian flag as they depart Priština early on 14 June 1999 as NATO troops sought to establish control over the province of Kosovo. (Reuters/Corbis)

tion to begin, or be attacked by the NATO alliance. Milošević refused the ultimatum, and in late March 1999 NATO did in fact attack Serbia.

The DLK's authority had weakened in the mid-1990s, when many Albanians became frustrated with Rugova's pacifism. The KLA had emerged as a result of that frustration, with the ultimate result that the policies of the Milošević regime resulted in a month of heavy bombing by NATO forces in the spring of 1999. The key here, in this section of the study, is to understand how the Kosovo situation affected Milošević's ability to govern. It had in fact two opposite effects: first, in fighting NATO ultimatums and arms, he was defending a Serbia under attack by an enemy of overwhelming strength, and this was a positive role in Serbs' eyes; second, though, his policies could easily be blamed for having brought on that very bombing. In the end, the NATO bombing achieved its goal, which was to drive Serbian forces from Kosovo; however, all, inside and outside of Serbia, understood that the removal of Milošević from power and the destruction of Serbian military power were tacit goals of the bombing, and here NATO failed. When the bombing ceased, Milošević could claim to have successfully defended Serbia from aggression. This claim resonated with Serbs. However, once the enormity of the bombing's destruction was known, and once the political

reality set in that Milošević had now fought and lost four wars—in Slovenia, Croatia, Bosnia, and Kosovo—the president's position became more tenuous.

In August 2000 a new coalition called the Democratic Opposition of Serbia (DOS) emerged, which united all of the parties in opposition to Milošević, save one, the Serbian Renewal Movement of Vuk Drašković. Drašković may have been motivated by his strong dislike for Djindjić, he may have feared assassination (which had been tried at least twice), or he may have wanted to avoid offending Milošević and losing his power base in Belgrade. Regardless, the absence of his party was a blow to the coalition. Still, the key element turned out to be the choice of presidential candidate: Vojislav Koštunica, the head of the Democratic Party of Serbia, was unsullied by the politics of personal rivalry that had poisoned the relations of Djindjić and Drašković, which had doomed Zajedno in 1997. Koštunica's pedigree had the right components: he was both a sincere nationalist and a sincere democrat, who believed that Serbs would be best served by a parliamentary democracy and the rule of law, but who could not be accused of ever having sold out his nation. Perhaps most importantly, Koštunica condemned U.S. involvement in the Balkans. He could compete for the vote of sincere democrats, and his nationalism could pull voters away from people like Šešelj.

In the presidential elections of September 2000, Koštunica received approximately 52 percent of the vote to Milošević's 35 percent (government figures, of course, showed a closer race). When the government refused to acknowledge Koštunica's victory, instead insisting that a second round of voting occur, Serbia rebelled. Between 2 and 5 October, Serbs took to the streets, and miners in Kolubara went on strike; Milošević finally agreed to respect the results of the election. On 7 October, Koštunica was sworn in as president.

Koštunica remained president until the fall of 2002, and until his assassination in March 2003 Djindjić, as the leader of the most popular party in the parliament, was prime minister. The two men were not friends and only barely remained political allies. The divisions between them were clearest in foreign affairs: Djindjić believed that Serbia should cooperate with the International Criminal Tribunal for Yugoslavia (ICTY) at the Hague, whereas Koštunica wished to see Serbia punish its own people for their crimes. The need for international economic support has made it very difficult for Koštunica to realize his vision. Since this problem is still very much alive at the time of this writing, it is discussed more thoroughly in "Contemporary Problems and Challenges."

No account of the political evolution of Serbia in the postcommunist period would be complete without a discussion of the troubled relationship between Serbia and Montenegro. According to the 1992 Constitution of the Federal Republic of Yugoslavia, the state was composed of two republics, Serbia and Montenegro. The constitution was promulgated after virtually no public debate, as an expedient to fill the vacuum left by the international recognition of Croatia and Slovenia and the secession of Bosnia-Hercegovina and Macedonia. For several years, there was little contention between Serbia and Montenegro, and certainly none of the sort that could be expected to lead to a Montenegrin independence movement. Nonetheless, historically the Serbo-Montenegrin relationship had not been without conflict. The best example of this came in the aftermath of World War I, when Montenegrin "greens" (supporters of independence) and "whites" (supporters of union with Serbia and Yugoslavia) had fought pitched battles. When an independence movement did arise in Montenegro, it was partly a continuation of older competitions and partly the result of the politics of personality, as Montenegro's president harnessed the strength of Montenegrin separatism to enhance his own popularity.

The crisis that has developed in recent years has its origins in the mid-1990s, after the Dayton Agreement ended the war in Bosnia. At that time, a faction of the Montenegrin leadership, led by Milo Djukanović, began to urge that Montenegro become more open to the international community, in order both to take advantage of economic development opportunities and to shed the pariah state status that Serbia had attained. Djukanović more and more openly criticized the Milošević regime in Serbia, which opened him up to criticism from the government-controlled media in Serbia and Montenegro alike. However, somewhat surprisingly, Djukanović survived the onslaught and saw his own popularity grow. In Montenegrin presidential elections in October 1997, Djukanović defeated Momir Bulatović, Milošević's ally in Montenegro, by a slim margin. In May

1998 parliamentary elections in Montenegro, Djukanović's party, the Democratic Party of Socialists, outpolled Bulatović's, the Socialist People's Party, gaining forty-two seats to the latter's twenty-nine. From that point on, Djukanović's challenge to federal authority gained strength.

The war in Kosovo exacerbated the situation. Djukanović kept Montenegro out of the conflict, assuring that NATO would not target Montenegrin territory and that Montenegro might receive favorable treatment from the West after the conflict ended in June 1999. In August the Djukanović government presented the Serbian government with a document entitled "The Basis for Defining the New Relationship between Montenegro and Serbia," in which Djukanović proposed an "asymmetric confederation," in which the republics would share only a currency and defense and foreign policy. Rebuffed by Serbia, Montenegro has begun to create a separate state, having divorced its economy from the federal economy by late 2000. With the fall of Milošević in October 2000, a pragmatic Serbian response came in the form of "the Platform," written by Vojislav Koštunica and Zoran Djindjić, president and prime minister respectively of the Republic of Serbia. The Platform suggests that Serbia and Montenegro form a commonwealth, following the German model. Djukanović responded that first Serbia and Montenegro should constitute themselves as sovereign states, and that when they joined, they should do so on the basis of confederation, retaining separate seats in the United Nations, and (as had been suggested before) sharing only defense policy, monetary policy, and foreign affairs.

In April 2001 parliamentary elections were held in Montenegro. Djukanović's "Victory for Montenegro" alliance won thirty-three seats, a plurality, but the victory was much narrower than expected, with pro-union parties receiving the same number (six seats were won by a Djukanović ally, the Liberal Alliance of Montenegro). The elections nevertheless demonstrated the strength of independence sentiment in Montenegro, which had been negligible only a few years before. It took the influence of European Union High Representative Javier Solana to push the Montenegrins to the bargaining table, where Djukanović, Djindjić, Koštunica, and others hammered out the Belgrade Agreement in March 2002. According to this agreement, a federal state called the Union of Serbia and Montenegro was to be formed. After three years the union was to become permanent. If Montenegro chose to leave the union at that time, Serbia would be the FRY's legal successor. Other than that, the agreement was extremely vague, presumably in order to allow the two republics to further work out their relationship. Since the problem of the nature of the new state, which did in fact officially come into existence on 4 February 2003, under the name State Community of Serbia and Montenegro, is an ongoing one, it is discussed more fully in "Contemporary Challenges."

CULTURAL DEVELOPMENT

Their culture sustained the Serbs as a nation through several centuries of governance by the Ottoman Empire. Without

Milo Djukanović, Montenegrin president and leader of the ruling Democratic Party of Socialists (DPS) and the pro-independence "Victory for Montenegro" coalition, casts his ballot at early parliamentary elections in Podgorica, 22 April 2001. On the left is his wife, Lidija Djukanović. (Reuters/Corbis)

the consolidation of a cultural identity over that time, Serbs as a people would likely have disappeared, assimilated by Ottoman Muslim culture. Furthermore, their cultural identity as Serbs developed in stark and purposeful contrast to that of the dominant empire. Thus, to be Serbian came to mean to be Orthodox Christian (not Muslim), and it came to involve opposition to the Turk as a foreign element in Europe, upon whom the Serb people had a special duty to avenge themselves. This identity developed under the special circumstances that existed in the Ottoman Empire, in which Orthodox Christians were governed on a day-to-day basis by their own church. Finally, a powerful oral folk tradition developed that eventually expressed in mythical terms what it meant to be Serbian.

In the nineteenth century, as the modern Serbian state emerged from the chaos of the collapsing Ottoman Empire,

Serbs gained confidence from the achievement of renewed statehood; that achievement made them less inclined to imagine themselves anything but Serbian. Therefore, although Serbs were part of a cultural-linguistic complex that obviously included Croats, Slovenes, and Bulgarians, they nurtured a self-image of uniqueness that ultimately made it difficult for them to imagine themselves part of any larger cultural community. Ironically, others from that larger community were instead drawn to Serbian culture.

So, although one may be tempted to adopt an easy definition of Serbianness, as "Orthodox Christian, speaking Serbo-Croatian," shaped by the conditioning of centuries of oral folk culture embodied in the Kosovo cycle of songs, in fact Serbian culture has attracted people with different origins. For instance, novelist Ivo Andrić was born to Catholic parents in Bosnia, but felt himself to be a Serb.

Meša Selimović, another outstanding novelist, was a child of Muslims who chose to think of himself as a Serb. Emir Kusturica, the brilliant film director, also hails from a Muslim background but now considers himself to be a Serb. Danilo Kiš, the author of *A Tomb for Boris Davidovich* and several other stunning novels, was the son of a Hungarian Jewish father and an Orthodox mother. Today's Serbs enjoy a rich and varied cultural heritage.

Serbian culture begins with the Serbs' oral folk tradition. By the end of the seventeenth century, in patriarchal peasant villages throughout the central Balkans, *deseterci* (songs with ten-syllable lines) were being sung. These songs—poems sung to a melody, words and melody handed down orally from generation to generation—fell into two general categories: love songs and heroic historical songs. When they were collected and catalogued in the nineteenth century by Vuk Karadžić, they were being sung (or recited without melody) by male and female singers who had learned them at the feet of their predecessors. Vuk's collection, entitled *Narodna srbska pjesnarica* (Serbian People's Songbook, Leipzig, 1823–1833) includes songs from the lyrical tradition and the heroic tradition. The heroic songs in this collection include those of the Kosovo cycle (which describe and mythologize the Battle of Kosovo, the devastating loss to the Turks in 1389), which

are some of the most important and impressive of the entire opus, as well as other deservedly renowned songs such as "Banović Strahinje," "The Wedding of King Vukašin," and the various songs describing the feats of Kraljević Marko (an Ottoman vassal, one of the remarkable heroes of Serbian culture). In the end, according to Michael Petrovich, the songs "preserved and transmitted from generation to generation [the Serbs'] own idealized memory of their past, a chronicle of their present, and their hopes in future freedom, all in a spirit of folk democracy." The songs also taught Serbs to oppose oppressors violently if necessary, and that the Turk was that oppressor. The legacy was both uplifting and incendiary: Serbs were raised on mythical heroes and the promise of revenge in the future. These are the foundations of modern Serbian culture and identity.

The oral culture described above competed with a high culture that was dominated by the religious hierarchy of the Serbian Orthodox Church and used a language, Old Church Slavonic, that bore little resemblance to the language of ordinary people. For an understanding of modern Serbian culture, two men, the aforementioned Vuk Karadžić and Petar Petrović Njegoš, are of critical importance, as they were the authors of the transition from an early modern culture that was divided between folk and

Yugoslavian novelist and poet Danilo Kiš (1935–1989) sits near a typewriter and a bookshelf in his writing room. (Sophie Bassouls/Corbis Sygma)

high religious elements to a modern culture that became pervasively Serbian. Karadžić (1787–1864) was born in a small village in western Serbia. He took part in the Serbian revolution and become one of Prince Miloš Obrenović's civil servants in the first autonomous Serbian state. But Vuk's eminence stemmed from two other sources: his standardization of a modern Serbian language and his collection of folk songs. As discussed above, both tasks marked him as a child of Johann Gottfried Herder, a romantic, a member of the first generation of ethnographers, working in the spirit of national revival and consolidation, along with the brothers Grimm and others like them throughout Central and Southeastern Europe. Vuk's central premise was that the only true language was the language spoken by the people. His aphorism "write as you speak" (piši kako govoriš) became one of the most recognizable Serbian sayings. The results of Vuk's lifetime of work were a grammar (finished in 1814), a dictionary of the Serbian language (printed in 1818), a monumental collection of folk songs and proverbs (published over several decades), and a New Testament translation into Serbian.

Vuk's work brought him into conflict with more traditional authorities in Serbian life, primarily the Serbian Orthodox Church, which resisted his belief that the true language of the Serbs was that spoken by the Serbian peasant, favoring instead a Serbian more closely tied to Old Church Slavonic and thus Russian. Vuk also found himself in conflict with other national "awakeners" of his time, especially Croats, thanks to his belief that those who spoke the štokavijan dialect of the language that Serbs and Croats shared were, by definition, Serbs. This was an early example of the ideology of nationalism riding roughshod over facts on the ground; the fact in this case was that people who considered themselves Croats as well as those who considered themselves Serbs spoke this dialect of the language. Thus Vuk's gifts to nineteenth-century Serbs were a simplified orthography and a modern literary language; his gift to Serbian, and Yugoslav, posterity was his argument that all speakers of štokavijan were Serbs, an idea that competed with several other conceptions of the relationship between Serbian and Croatian and bore unpleasant fruit down the road.

The second critical figure in modern Serbian culture is Petar Petrović Njegoš, prince-bishop of Montenegro and author of The Mountain Wreath. Njegoš became the spiritual and political leader of Montenegro in 1830 at the age of seventeen. He had been educated in a monastery in Cetinje and then in a boarding school in Dalmatia, which was about the best a Montenegrin could hope for at that time. As the political leader of Montenegro, Njegoš was a modernizer who attempted to bring unity to the divisive Montenegrin tribes and progress to the extremely backward Montenegrin countryside. He worked to gain recognition of Montenegrin sovereignty, traveled through Central Europe and to Russia, and met and corresponded with Vuk Karadžić. Between 1833 and 1845, he wrote four books of poetry, which were modeled on Serbian folk poetry and betrayed his dedication to the goal of the liberation of Serbs from the Ottomans.

In 1845 Njegoš published The Ray of the Microcosm, and in 1847 The Mountain Wreath, his two greatest works. Called one of the greatest achievements in Serbian literature by Vasa Mihailovich (in his introduction to the 1997 edition of the work, page 15), The Mountain Wreath is a long, complex, and beautiful poem based loosely on a historical event. But it is not a historical analysis or interpretation at heart; instead, it is a meditation on freedom. Njegoš's final work was entitled Stephen the Small, the Pretender and was published in 1851. Mihailovich argues that Njegoš's importance to Serbian culture was in "his appearance at the time when Serbian literature was making its first unsure steps after centuries of dormancy. . . . Njegoš's use of the vernacular, which he patterned after folk poetry, assured the success of this all-important linguistic reform" (xxi).

After the two founding figures, the first prominent representative of modern Serbian literature was the critic Jovan Skerlić (1877–1914), who wrote in pre–World War I Belgrade and helped introduce Serbia and Serbian writers to literary modernism. He was an urbane, socially conscious presence in the small Belgrade literary scene, and his critical standards affected and informed all writing of the period. His books included The Younger Generation and Its Literature (1906), Serbian Literature in the Nineteenth Century (1909), and The History of Modern Serbian Literature (1914). He edited the Srpski književni glasnik (Serbian Literary Herald), which became the leading literary journal in Serbia and introduced Serbs to the work and criticism of other Europeans, especially the French, who thereafter became the role models and critical guides for generations of Serbian writers and artists. Skerlić was also a political Yugoslav, who helped open the eyes of his generation's educated and cultured Serbs to the vision of a Yugoslav future. He died young, in 1914, but his influence was felt for another thirty years and beyond in Serbian cultural life.

The main interwar Serbian writer whose reputation has lasted is Miloš Crnjanski, the author of Migration and a large body of fiction and poetry. Many Serbs would argue that Crnjanski is Serbia's most distinguished writer; the fact that other Serbs would not agree probably has something to do with politics, as Crnjanski was a monarchist who was for a time sympathetic to the fascist regimes in Italy and Germany. As a result, many of his interwar contemporaries who found a home in the communist Yugoslavia rejected him; he was unable to return to Yugoslavia until the 1970s. Nonetheless, Migration (1929) is regarded as one of the best novels written in the Serbian language. Its plot is rather unadorned; it concerns the movements of two Serbian brothers and soldiers as they fight for the Habsburg monarchy against France in the mid-eighteenth century. Its language, however, is beautiful, and its theme, migration, is one that is near and dear to Serbs' hearts.

After World War II, Serbia, like the rest of Yugoslavia, initially suffered under the strictures of the official Stalinist cultural orthodoxy of socialist realism. In Yugoslavia, the socialist realist period did not last long; the doctrine was discredited along with Stalinism not long after the 1948 Tito-Stalin split. Since socialist realism reflected nothing natural in Serbian culture, it left nothing of note behind.

Beneath the veneer of Stalinist orthodoxy, Serbian culture was thriving. From the late 1940s through the mid-1960s, Serbian letters were dominated by writers of the Partisan generation, men and women who did not question the Titoist order. Instead, the dominant theme in their writing was World War II, focusing on the Partisan experience in the struggle against the multiple enemies the Partisans faced during the war: Četniks, Ustaša, and Germans. In the late 1960s, for reasons developed in the history section of this article, many Serbs began to examine their place in Yugoslavia more critically. This development could be seen chiefly among playwrights, but also in a few novelists. The regime attacked critical writers effectively until the death of Tito. Thereafter, a flood of novels, plays, and stories critical of aspects of the communist era, including the Tito-Stalin split and its aftermath, poured out.

In a survey such as this, the most important figures to consider are those writers whose work is accessible to an English-speaking audience. Among these are several who are of unquestioned importance in Serbian literary history in general: Ivo Andrić, Meša Selimović, Dobrica Ćosić, and Danilo Kiš. Of the first postwar generation, Ivo Andrić (1892–1975) is unquestionably the most famous Serbian novelist. (The reader will also find him covered in "Bosnia-Hercegovina" as a Bosnian novelist.) Winner of the 1961 Nobel Prize for literature, he is best known for his historical novel *The Bridge on the Drina,* which was published in 1945. In that same year, two other novels, *The Woman from Sarajevo* and *The Bosnian Story* were also published; Andrić had written all three in Belgrade during World War II. Along with *The Devil's Yard,* published in 1954, these are Andrić's most famous works, although he also wrote short stories, essays, historical meditations, and poetry.

Andrić was born into a Catholic family in Travnik, Bosnia, in 1892; he lived for a brief time as an infant in Sarajevo and attended elementary school in Višegrad (the site of the actual bridge on the Drina). He was active in various nationalist and literary clubs and attended university in Zagreb, Vienna, and Cracow. After World War I (during which he spent some time in internment), he moved to Belgrade, where he entered the foreign service. In February 1939 he was named Yugoslav envoy to Germany, a position he occupied through the March 1941 adherence of Yugoslavia to the Tripartite Pact and the bombing of Belgrade two weeks later. He spent the war in an uncomfortable "retirement" in Belgrade, during which he wrote his best-known work. Although *The Bridge on the Drina* is occasionally cited as a novel that explains the allegedly violent history of Bosnia, it actually speaks of the binding power of place and the ability of shared lives and traditions to ameliorate conflict. The central character in this novel is actually the bridge itself. Beginning with its construction, Andrić takes the reader through four centuries of the history of Višegrad, focusing on the bridge's power to link rather than divide. With the bridge as a place where peaceful solutions are negotiated, Andrić's novel testifies to the ability of people to overcome what seem to be insurmountable cultural and political differences. It is a brilliant novel.

Another Bosnian, Meša Selimović (1910–1982), also belongs to the Serbian literary tradition, like Andrić by choice rather than by birth or religious faith. Selimović was born in Sarajevo. He would probably be considered rather run of the mill were it not for his final two novels, *Death and the Dervish* and *The Fortress. Death and the Dervish* is an examination of authoritarianism set in the distant Ottoman past in Bosnia. Its lead character, Sheikh Nuruddin, is caught in a web of deceit and uncertainty while trying to help his brother, who has disappeared into the shadows of Ottoman rule. The book is based on a personal experience for Selimović, whose brother, a Partisan, was arrested and executed by the communist regime for corruption just after World War II. *The Fortress* deals with similar themes, but in a more lighthearted manner and through a central character (Ahmet Shabo) who is more human and humorous than Naruddin.

Serbia's most celebrated living novelist is Dobrica Ćosić (b. 1921), who played such an important role in Serbian history as a nationalist. Ćosić was a Partisan during World War II and a member of the postwar Serbian Party leadership until 1968, when he resigned from the central committee of the Serbian League of Communists in protest of its policies toward Kosovo and Vojvodina. Ćosić's novels include *Far Away Is the Sun* (1951), *Roots* (1954), *Divisions* (1961), *Time of Death* (1972–1975), *Time of Evil* (1985–1990), and *Time of Power* (1996). He was self-taught as a writer, and one can sense Ćosić feeling his way through the various influences that affected him during his career. *Far Away Is the Sun* is a war novel, written in the aftermath of the Tito-Stalin split and reflecting Ćosić's (and Yugoslav society's) critical spirit toward Stalinism and the mythology of the Partisan war effort. It was not socialist realism, which was unique; but it was a formulaic and turgid first effort. *Roots* is set in a Serbian village and concerns the conflict between generations and between the village and the city in turn-of-the-century Serbia. It is clearly influenced by the writing of William Faulkner, right down to the creation of a fictional village, Prerovo, which was the center of most of the rest of Ćosić's literary output, just as Yoknapatawpha County was for Faulkner. *Divisions* is a long (three-volume) examination of the roots and dynamics of the Četnik movement in wartime Serbia; considered a critical analysis at the time it appeared, today it seems to demonize those Serbs who became Četniks more than it explains them.

Politics changed the nature of Ćosić's literature. In the early 1960s he became disillusioned with the status of Serbs in Tito's Yugoslavia. By 1968, he had withdrawn from active political life and become a spokesman for Serbian concerns in Yugoslavia. Over the next twenty-five years, he became the central figure in a Serbian opposition movement that wished to destroy the Titoist order of Yugoslavia and establish a unified Serbian community within the state. His novels reflected those commitments: *Time of Death* is a monotonous three-volume meditation on Serbia and the Serbs as the country is being overrun by Habsburg and Bulgarian armies in 1915; *Time of Evil* (also three volumes) and *Time of Power* consider the effects of Bolshevism on

Serbia. Ultimately, Ćosić's appeal—unlike that of Andrić, Selimović, or Danilo Kiš—does not extend beyond Serbs. His themes are so introspectively Serbian that they have no universal appeal. Ćosić remains popular (as a writer) in Serbia, but a provincial everywhere else. Contemporaries of Ćosić include Antonije Isaković, whose work has not been translated.

If there is a polar opposite to Ćosić to be found in Serbian letters, it is Danilo Kiš, whose themes are universal and who was only provincial when forced to be. Kiš (1935–1989) wrote some of the most impressive novels in modern Serbian letters, including *Garden, Ashes* (1965), *Early Sorrows* (1968), *Hourglass* (1972), and *A Tomb for Boris Davi-*

dovich (1976). Never formally an exile from Yugoslavia, Kiš nonetheless spent the majority of his time after the late 1960s in France, where he did most of his writing. *A Tomb for Boris Davidovich,* the second-to-last of Kiš's novels, was really the first to gain an audience in the West, and it did so by virtue of the uproar it caused in Yugoslavia itself. The novel is a series of vignettes that address the nature and effects of Stalinism; several of the chapters incorporate the writing of others, a literary collage method that should have raised no eyebrows. Nevertheless, Kiš was attacked as a plagiarist by Serbian literary critics. The issue was complicated by the fact that a literary critic from Zagreb, Croatia, rose to Kiš's defense, which further inflamed members

Danilo Kiš (1935–1989)

Danilo Kiš was born in 1935 in Subotica, Yugoslavia, and died in Paris in 1989. His father was Hungarian and Jewish, and his mother was Montenegrin. Kiš's parents had him baptized in the Orthodox church in 1939 in order to protect him from anti-Semitism. Kiš's family fled Novi Sad for Hungary proper in 1942, following anti-Semitic violence in Novi Sad. His father perished in Auschwitz in 1944; the rest of the family returned to Montenegro in 1947. Kiš's mother, Milica, died in 1951. Danilo Kiš's first poem was published in 1953. In 1954 he enrolled in Belgrade University, where he became one of the first graduates in its new History of World Literature program in 1958. His first two novels, *The Attic* and *Psalm 44,* were published in 1962. In 1965 the first installment in a three-volume autobiographical cycle, entitled *Garden, Ashes,* was published. *Early Sorrows* and *Hourglass* followed in 1969 and 1972, respectively. In 1973 *Hourglass* won the award for fiction given by *Nedeljne Informativne Novine,* the leading Serbian newsweekly.

Garden, Ashes, Early Sorrows, and *Hourglass* are all loosely autobiographical novels (although *Early Sorrows* is rather a collection of stories) of childhood and adolescence. The first two are unencumbered narratives that deal directly with the world through the eyes of a child; *Hourglass,* on the other hand, is a quite complex story of a man (Kiš's father) caught up in the Holocaust.

In 1976 *A Tomb for Boris Davidovich* was published. It brought Kiš his greatest fame and enormous controversy. The novel, a collection of stories that examine the nature of totalitarianism, was criticized by an influential segment of the Belgrade literary community for having allegedly plagiarized other authors. In fact, Kiš used methods familiar to readers of the Argentine author Jorge Luis Borges and others when he incorporated fragments of other authors' prose in his own work. What was considered avant-garde elsewhere was ferociously attacked in Belgrade. The polemics that ensued eventually lapsed into the sort of frenzy that only Yugoslavia and its complicated ethnic situation could produce, as Croatian writers came to Kiš's defense and Serbian critics accused "outsiders" of meddling in a Serbian literary controversy. It is impossible not to conclude that Kiš was a victim of his own lack of interest in daily politics; many accused his attackers of anti-Semitism. Kiš responded to his critics with the book *The Anatomy Lesson,* in which he explained his own literary roots and influences in his typically combative way: labeling the controversy a witch-hunt, he noted that much of the so-called debate took place in literary salons and clubs, where only the officially acceptable writers were allowed to speak.

Ultimately, the controversy drove Kiš permanently out of the country of his birth. He spent the majority of his remaining years in France, where he had periodically taught and lived since the early 1960s. He published only one more book, *The Encyclopedia of the Dead,* in 1984.

Kiš is now remembered outside of Yugoslavia mostly for *A Tomb for Boris Davidovich;* in Yugoslavia, he was mourned universally after his death, as if he had not in fact been driven from the country by the provincialism that always repelled him. As Susan Sontag has written, we have an idea how he would have responded to the collapse of Yugoslavia, which came two years after his death: "An ardent foe of nationalist vanities, he would have loathed Serb ethnic fascism even more than he loathed the neo-Bolshevik official culture of the Second Yugoslavia it has replaced" (viii).

of the Serbian literary community, who believed that the Kiš affair should be the business of the Serbian milieu. So accusations of plagiarism became intertwined with a kind of nationalism that could only have reared its head in Tito's Yugoslavia, where republics were considered the possessions of nations, and the institutions of those republics were reflections of national prerogatives. Kiš defended himself admirably, and his detractors emerged as ridiculous figures. Still, the affair led many to wonder if Kiš, half Hungarian Jew, was being persecuted for his ethnic background.

The writers described above satisfy two demands: they are translated into English, and they are acknowledged literary stars in Serbia. But they certainly do not exhaust the list of outstanding Serbian writers. Aside from the experience of World War II, which produced some of the best literature of the postwar period, the most dynamic phase in modern Serbian literature undoubtedly came with the death of Tito and the outpouring of novels, short stories, and plays questioning his legacy and the events of his period in power. In particular, survivors of imprisonment on the island of Goli Otok, who were victims of the purge of "cominformists" after the Tito-Stalin split, stand out. Dragoslav Mihajlović, the author of *When the Pumpkins Blossomed, Petra's Wreath,* and other novels (several of which are devoted to Goli Otok directly), may be the best and best known of this group of writers. Antonije Isaković, otherwise a respected novelist and short story writer, wrote the path-breaking novel *Tren II* (Flash II), though not himself a survivor of the island. Dušan Jovanović's play *Karamazovi* (The Karamazovs) questioned the nature of the split and the attack on cominformists that followed. Jovan Radulović's play *Golubnjača* (Pigeon Hole) brought up the suppressed memory of wartime slaughters in Dalmatia. Milan Martov's *Isterivanje Boga* (The Expulsion of God) dealt with the brutal nature of collectivization in Yugoslavia.

As for Serbian art, it has tended to follow trends set in Europe, with a lag of a few years. After World War II, Serbia's artistic community found itself more bound by the socialist realist faith than writers were. There were no true socialist realist painters in Serbia in 1944, although there were traditions in Serbian painting that lent themselves to the new form. The social painters of the 1930s had possessed a social conscience and chosen themes that they judged close to the people. Many of them were close to the Communist Party and became Partisan painters during the war. But those were the exceptions. Impressionism, which came late to Serbia (between approximately 1907 and 1920, in the work of Nadežda Petrović, Mališa Glišić, Kosta Miličević, and others) became the bête noire of the new communist elite in Yugoslavia. Impressionism's heirs (expressionism, abstract painting, surrealism) had also made inroads in Serbia. The new regime rejected them all. In the words of Oto Bihalji Merin, one of Yugoslavia's leading cultural figures in the early period of communism, the art of the interwar period left "a clear picture of the sickness and weakness of capitalism. It did not create a harmonious style, nor even a unified character. It is chaotic, restless, and far from its true calling: to create not an artistic work, but [one] for humanity, and that in the great, convincing, and

universally understandable language of formation" (Trifunović 251).

The socialist realist critics demanded painting that reflected the unity of form, content, and the era in which it was produced. This demand for coherence and engagement led the critics to promote the painters of the Renaissance, the baroque, and the romantic eras. In Serbian painting, they reached for models beyond the impressionists to a slightly earlier period, when painters like Uroš Predić and Paja Jovanović produced their imposing testaments to romantic national revival. These paintings were complements to the romantic literary work of Njegoš. The goal of the proponents of socialist realism was not to turn painters into automatons who would replicate the work of old masters. Painters were, however, urged to replicate the synthesis of era and art that the ideologues of socialist realism believed those earlier periods reflected. Jovan Popović wrote in 1947 that "Socialist idealism must permeate the content and form of the work of art, it must be inseparable from the most intimate feelings and thoughts of the artist. . . . Thus work on ideological education is crucial" (Trifunović, 253). They sought to create a new yet authentic art for the proletariat of the new socialist society being created.

Its lofty goals aside, the new regime had to accept what it could find in Serbian art after 1944. The most likely candidates to initiate the development of Serbian socialist realism were the social artists of the 1930s, who painted the lives of the impoverished and the backward and who thus became weapons in the hands of the eft. These painters included Djordje Andrejević Kun (*Witness to Horror*) and Petar Lubarda, whom critics differentiate by noting that Kun became a true adherent of socialist realism, whereas for Lubarda it was just a passing wartime fancy. Their shortcomings magnified the need for a truly new painter, one raised, trained, and produced fully within the socialist realist school. That demand was answered with the arrival of Boža Ilić. Ilić, a Montenegrin who studied art during the war and was by 1947 a student of a leading Serbian painter, Milo Milunović, first exhibited his work in June 1947 in Belgrade, reaching his peak in late 1948 with the painting *Sounding the Terrain in New Belgrade.* His rapid rise, facilitated by the overwhelming approbation of regime critics and exhibition juries, was matched by his precipitous fall after 1950, when socialist realism was eclipsed by a *new* new order brought by the break with Stalinism.

The end of the socialist realist period came in 1950, with the death knell being sounded by Mića Popović, a young painter whose exhibition in that year featured 160 paintings that owed a clear debt to interwar painters. His catalog notes were written in consultation with representatives of the official organization, the Association of Fine Artists of Serbia (ULUS), and in them he attacked socialist realist precepts openly. From 1950 on, Serbian painting again followed the lead of French painting, going through various phases. First the dominant style was abstraction (represented by the December Group, with Miodrag Protić and Stojan Ćelić), and then, through the mid-1960s, came a particular emphasis on what was called *art informel* (art without form, unformed art), abstract expressionism inspired by the French model, which was deeply suspicious of power and order in art and society (represented by Lazar Vozarević and Mića Popović, among others). Then followed the "new figuration," a return to figural painting, which again found perhaps its most influential representative in Popović, whose *Scenes Painting* embodies a healthy critique of the Tito regime's social and economic policies (*Scenes* was inspired by the student rebellion of 1968 in Belgrade). While Popović returned to figuration in a traditional yet politicized form, others, such as Dragoš Kalajić, embraced Pop Art. Still others pursued the informal artists' use of materials in their painting. After 1970, Serbian art grew ever more experimental; by the 1980s, Serbian artists had begun to incorporate elements of the postmodern into their work.

Turning to film of the postwar period, Serbia produced the most sophisticated filmmaking in Yugoslavia during that time. The film industry went through predictable phases: the first years of Partisan films, designed to glorify the war effort and the building of the new socialist society (to 1950); a period in which the film industry broadened its horizons, treating historical, comedic, and classical themes drawn from literature (to 1960); the "new film" (also known as "black wave") period, which lasted to the early seventies and saw the emergence of a highly critical spirit with nihilistic tendencies, which came under harsh attack by the communist regime. Perhaps the most well-known films from this period were the works of Dušan Makavajev *(WR: Mysteries of the Organism, Sweet Movie, Man Is Not a Bird,* and *Love Affair)* and Zivojin Pavlović *(When I Am Dead and White, Ambush);* and finally, from the late 1970s, films from a new period of critical but less confrontational filmmaking, dominated by a new generation of filmmakers who continued to work throught the 1990s (these include Goran Paskaljević, Emir Kusturica, Srdjan Dragojević, and others). Many of the films of these incisive filmmakers are available in subtitled versions for an English-speaking audience, including Makavajev's *WR: The Mysteries of the Organism* and *Montenegro,* Paskaljević's recent *Cabaret Balkan,* Dragojević's *Pretty Village, Pretty Flame* and *Wounds,* and virtually all of Kusturica's opus.

The films of the black wave were a distinguished but very diverse lot. Makavejev made films that subtly undermined the orthodoxies of the one-party, scientifically socialist state. Pavlović's films were violent depictions of the underside of Yugoslav society. Mića Popović, better known as a painter, made two films that were part of the black wave. One was *Man from the Oak Forest,* which examined the irrational roots of communal violence, and the other was *Hoodlums,* which dealt with soldiers at the end of World War II. Živojin Pavlović's *When I Am Dead and White* and *Ambush* both aggressively question critical aspects of the Titoist myth. What united the black wave films was their irreverence toward the sacred myths of the Tito regime; they tended to use violence to make their points about the new communist order, which had promised such a peaceful future to the Yugoslav people.

Emir Kusturica, like Andrić and Selimović, is a Bosnian whose ethnic background is not Serbian (his family is Muslim) but who considers himself to be a Serb. His films are uniformly challenging, but also rewarding; they are not overtly political, which is refreshing given the heavily politicized output of Serbian writers who are Kusturica's contemporaries. Kusturica's films include *Do You Remember Dolly Bell, When Father Was Away on Business, Time of the Gypsies, Underground,* and *Black Cat, White Cat.* The first two are both set in Kusturica's native Sarajevo, and both concern events within families. *Dolly Bell* is a coming-of-age story set in a working-class family. *When Father Was Away on Business* examines the interrelationship of politics and private lives, using the effects of the Tito-Stalin split on one Sarajevo family as a prism. It is an extraordinarily rich film. *Underground* was savaged by some critics as a political apologia for Serbian aggression in the wars of the 1990s, but that is a ridiculous dismissal of this brilliant film, which, by narrating the story of a group of World War II resistance fighters who never find out the war has ended, presents a metaphor for the effects of communism on an entire society.

The wars of the 1990s led to the production of other outstanding Serbian films, including *Cabaret Balkan* and *Pretty Village, Pretty Flame.* Goran Paskaljević's *Cabaret Balkan* (1999) is a fascinating study of a society falling apart, with a series of vignettes that testify to the chaos and violence that have ripped Serbia and the rest of Yugoslavia apart (although this film is set almost entirely in Belgrade). The vignettes illustrate relationships destroyed by the mendacity of friends and lovers, petty and not so petty vengeance, and general moral breakdown, with the wars as an unmentioned backdrop. Paskaljević also made *Someone Else's America* (1996), depicting immigrants from Montenegro and their attempts to adapt to their new country. *Pretty Village, Pretty Flame* (1996), the work of Srdjan Dragojević, presents the story of two Bosnians, one Serb and the other Muslim, who grow up as friends but are divided by the war. The film has proved equally appealing to those who are interested in the destruction that the war brought to Yugoslav society and those who love a good war film (it made critics' lists on both counts). His other best-known film, *Wounds,* on the other hand, is a thoroughly chaotic but riveting account of the underbelly of Serbian society during the 1990s; it examines two teens who become leaders of Belgrade's criminal underground and the lawless amorality of their milieu.

ECONOMIC DEVELOPMENT

Until the 1880s, Serbia was typical of Balkan peasant societies, with livestock raising and agriculture as the foundation and trading centers spotted along a couple of important trade routes. Montenegro was an extremely poor mountain region. Economic development in both countries was nevertheless quite similar, involving transition from an agricultural to an industrial economy; the process began in the late nineteenth century, with accelerated change occurring only after World War II.

In the medieval era, Serbia's consolidation as an independent kingdom was helped along by the increase in royal revenues brought by exploitation of mineral wealth, thanks to an influx of German mining talent from Transylvania. Dubrovnik also provided much needed artisans and traders, as well as a center for their economic activity. The Ne-manjićes, founders of the first Serbian state, also benefited from the establishment of the Byzantine system of land grants in return for military service. In other words, Serbian monarchs followed a familiar path in consolidating their power. Serbia might well have continued down that path, had it not been for the Ottoman advance, which by the middle of the fifteenth century had fully incorporated the medieval Serbian state into the Ottoman Empire.

As a part of the Ottoman Empire, the Serbian economy changed greatly. Muslims benefited from a land grant system that rewarded those who did military service (*sipahis*) with land grants known as *timars* for their military service. Christians tended to move northward ahead of the Ottoman advance or into the mountains, leaving the more fertile lowlands to the Muslims who now moved in. In this way, Kosovo became the preserve of Muslim Albanians after the fifteenth century. The mining industry withered under Ottoman administration. Trade routes were dominated by Greeks and Jews, and towns that had begun to thrive as trade centers earlier now became military outposts, populated mostly by Muslims in Ottoman service.

At the time of the first uprising, in 1804, Serbia was a province distant from Istanbul that thus had a significant degree of self-administration. Wealthier Serbs in this under-populated region maintained ties with the Habsburg monarchy, trading mostly pigs. Under Prince Miloš Obrenović, there was rapid growth within a limited framework. Miloš demanded and received full control of the autonomous Serbia's economy, and he put that control to good use: he encouraged land-ownership with a three-year tax break and gave away lands abandoned by Muslim landowners for nothing. In general, he promoted an influx of Serbs into the Serbian lowlands. He also encouraged immigration and land clearing and arranged for all payments for lands taken from Muslims to be part of the general tribute payment. Miloš controlled trade in autonomous Serbia through the issuance of trade permits, which the state sold. These steadily increased in number (from 56 in 1820 to 1,341 in 1829). Until the 1890s, this trade was mostly in pigs and other animal products. Serbia actually had to import grain on occasion. Capital was difficult to come by in Serbia; much came from the Serbs of the Habsburg monarchy, who had expertise, money, and markets. Another impediment to Serbian economic development was that the region was overwhelmed by oak forests, with only a couple of roads that could handle horses and carriages on a good day. The principality had about 450,000 inhabitants in 1815. Of the inhabitants, 90 percent were Serbs, and 80 percent of those were recent arrivals. In 1834 the first official census showed a population of 678,192.

In the second half of the nineteenth century land under grain cultivation doubled, a growth that was matched by the decline in animal husbandry. There were "more pigs than people" in 1866, according to the historian Michael Petrovich (526). By 1900, there were 2.5 million people in Serbia and a mere 1 million pigs. This was progress, of a sort, but Serbia's real problem was the lack of investment capital and any concomitant industrial growth. Foreign banks were not interested in promoting an industrial Serbia—they were more interested in maintaining Serbia as a captive source of raw materials for their own industrial economies. Before the chartering of the national bank in 1883, the state did lend money, but it required that collateral equal two-thirds of the loan amount, which was safe but tended to reward the wealthy and perpetuate the poverty of the peasantry. And Serbia was a land of peasants: 55 percent of the land was in the hands of smallholders (units of five hectares or less).

Serbia's only heavy industrial concern was an ironworks in Kragujevac, founded in 1847 in Belgrade. Otherwise, new industries were of the light variety, including mills and breweries, but nothing that promised to grow radically or to employ a large number of people. Independence brought new opportunities. In 1878 the government agreed to the minting of 6 million new silver dinars, the first Serbian currency. The first Serbian railroad, from Belgrade to Vranje, was approved by the Serbian parliament in 1880. It was to be one section of Serbia's portion of the Orient Express. Between 1884 and 1904, 1,664 kilometers of rails were laid, resulting in a relatively complete network around Serbia. The chartering of the National Bank in 1883 finally provoked some industrial growth in Serbia. In 1898 there were 28 industrial businesses in Serbia, and by 1903 the number had risen to 105. By 1910, following the chartering of several other banks, including the Export Bank, Belgrade Cooperative, Belgrade Merchant Bank, and the Commercial Bank, there were more than 400 enterprises.

World War I affected Serbia as much as it affected any state. Serbia's population loss in the war, as a percentage of its total population, was larger than that of any other European state, or 2.5 times that of France. Even if Serbia had emerged from the war within the same borders, its economy would have been staggered by the war. But Serbia emerged as a part of the new Kingdom of Serbs, Croats, and Slovenes, with all of the attendant economic complications of bringing together a new state virtually overnight. The story of this new kingdom was similar to that of Poland; in Yugoslavia's case, Slovenia, Croatia-Slavonia, Bosnia, Serbia, Montenegro, and the Vojvodina were each a part of a different legal entity before the war (and Macedonia and Kosovo had only recently become part of Serbia). Their transportation systems were oriented differently, and their trading partners were not the same. Thus, Croatia found it easier to trade with Austria and Hungary than to supply other regions of Yugoslavia; Vojvodinian exports moved north as well. Serbian railroad tracks had been sabotaged during the war, and its power sources had been destroyed as well. The result was a difficult transition period, but one in which Serbia's dominant position in the new state's power structure guaranteed it some favorable treatment. For instance, the prewar Serbian currency was to be the basis for the new currency, and Serbs could exchange their currency at a 1:1 rate, while the Habsburg crown was exchanged at a 5:1 rate.

One pressing concern for most of Yugoslavia, but not Serbia, was land reform. Serbian holdings were already small. While a land reform law was passed by the parliament in 1919, it was inefficiently applied and indemnification was promised but not forthcoming. Furthermore, when the government established a colonization program for under-populated or expropriated lands in Bosnia, Kosovo, Macedonia, and Vojvodina, it was limited to Serbian war veterans. Still, in the end, Serbs only received about 8 percent of the redistributed land, which totalled 10 percent of the kingdom's arable land. According to those who have looked at the situation, such as historian John Lampe, the "balance sheet" on the reform looked "surprisingly good by the end of the 1920s." In the 1920s the Serbian economy lagged behind that of Croatia, in part because Zagreb survived the war with its superior trade connections intact, in part because it had a series of wealthier investment banks on hand. Overall, according to Lampe, Yugoslav economic growth was "in the upper ranks for interwar Eastern Europe," which was a result of the growth of manufacturing in the north-west and mining in the south and east, that is, in Bosnia, Kosovo, and Macedonia (148). Serbia gained some industry at Croatia's expense, thanks to its lower wages.

World War II interrupted what, for Yugoslavia as a whole, had been a fairly successful encounter with the Great Depression. After the war, until 1948, Yugoslavia was not only a communist country, but a communist country intent on replicating Stalinist norms at home. Thus, a combination of central planning and idealistic enthusiasm were counted on to help the devastated country rebuild. The war had thoroughly ruined the country's transportation network, and 40 percent of prewar industry had been damaged or destroyed. Yugoslavia, never a fully integrated country, now had several regions in which starvation threatened. United Nations assistance contributed mightily to the fact that the country pulled through that initial postwar period. UN programs not only provided food, but also machinery and help with rebuilding the transportation system. The assistance of the United Nations was needed but not necessarily loved by the Tito regime, which preferred to think that its own efforts were responsible.

Ideology drove economic policy through the late 1940s. Upon the liberation of Belgrade in October 1944, the new regime began to implement a series of nationalization decrees. These were never all-encompassing: Yugoslavia had privately owned businesses throughout the communist era. In agriculture, Yugoslav peasants were subjected to the now notorious *otkup,* according to which peasants were required to make a certain level of deliveries to the state (all the while keeping their land). Peasants who failed were subject to arrest as enemies of the state. The otkup was an utter failure. The first and only Yugoslav five-year plan (1947–1951) was overly complex, set unachievable industrial goals, and slighted agriculture to the point of near rebellion in the countryside. Collectivization was then tried, mostly in order to answer Soviet accusations after June 1948 that the Yugoslavs were not good Stalinists. This too was a failure, one that was acknowledged only later.

The struggle to redeem themselves as true Stalinists ended within a couple years of the break with the Cominform. According to Milovan Djilas, the Yugoslav communist and dissident, Edvard Kardelj, Boris Kidrič, and Djilas himself debated the merits of transferring control of enterprises from the state central planning apparatus to the enterprises themselves sometime in early 1950 (*Rise and Fall* 268–269). Convincing themselves that such a move would be more in line with Marx's Marxism than Stalinism was, the idea gestated and eventually—by that summer of 1950—emerged as "workers' self-management." Formally inaugurated with the passage of the "Law on the Management of State Economic Associations by Work Collectives," self-management was largely fictive in its first few years. But it served the Tito regime's need for ideological self-justification and differentiation from Stalinism. After 1952, self-management meant that workers' councils for each enterprise made certain limited decisions on investments, pricing, production levels, and wages; these councils were controlled by local committees with representation from the League of Communists, which assured a high degree of central control. At this point, self-management did not have any republican attributes.

Through the early 1960s, the Yugoslav economy grew at a pace typical for European communist states: industrial output increased markedly, but productivity rates did not. Unemployment grew to 7 percent by 1962, one signal of the need for reform. By the early 1960s, the less-developed republics in Yugoslavia had grown even weaker in comparison with the developed republics, and Serbia, formally a developed republic, had lost ground to Croatia and Slovenia. Demands for reform, which came from all corners, did not agree on the proper course for a reform to take.

For the first time, the LCY (the League of Communists of Yugoslavia) reexamined the organization of the state, albeit from a purely economic perspective. At this point one begins to hear of "liberal" and "conservative" approaches to economic reform. Liberals favored increased room in the economy for entrepreneurialism, which implied expanded civil liberties; conservatives wished to retain a centrally governed economy and saw no need to reduce the Party's monopoly on power. Tito's own impulse was to favor the conservatives, which he did publicly in a May 1962 speech at Split. But in December 1962 and January 1963 two conferences of economists produced reports that called into doubt the conservative position. The result of expanded dialogue about economic change was a series of proposals, ranging from the creation of a virtually free market to the return to central planning. The debate on economic reform acted as a spur to camouflaged political debate. The conservative position found support among some, but not all, Serbian economists; it has been suggested that in spite of the economic logic of the liberal (market reform) position, many Serbian economists gravitated to the conservative position out of a sense of national loyalty.

The fruits of this ongoing discussion included the 1963 constitution, which, while not empowering the republics as such, did initiate the gradual devolution of economic decision-making power from the center to enterprises and local governments. The Eighth Congress of the League of Communists of Yugoslavia, held in December 1964 in Belgrade, placed the Party seal of approval on economic reforms supported by the liberals. In his opening speech to the congress, Tito himself attacked nationalism of the "centralist" variety, obviously referring to Serbian nationalism, which he accused of looking forward to the elimination of nationalities and the creation of an "artificial" Yugoslav nation. The rhetorical thrust of Tito's speech was meant to clear the way for reforms of the economy that would bring decentralizing political reforms with them.

From the onset of the reform period of the 1960s forward, economic development became one of the most potent political issues in Yugoslavia. This was so primarily because the various republics of Yugoslavia saw their economic interests as in competition. Broadly speaking, two blocs emerged: the more developed and less-developed republics. Montenegro was a less-developed republic, whereas Serbia was labeled a more developed republic (although Kosovo clearly belonged in the former category). Specific issues, however, transcended the more or less developed categorization. In fact, a more telling division was between those who argued for devolution of economic decision-making authority to the republics (Croats and Slovenes), and those who favored centralization (Serbs).

In 1965 the first major reform of Yugoslavia's economy after the advent of self-management was announced. It reduced the number of banks in the country from nearly 400 to about 40, which were governed by regional authorities; a fund for the development of the underdeveloped republics and provinces was established; prices, still controlled, were raised to make them more comparable to those of the world market; and peasants were given access to bank credit to modernize their operations. The goals of these reforms were increased efficiency, competitiveness, and agricultural production. Only the third goal was approached. By 1970, the percentage of rural population throughout Yugoslavia had dropped from 64 percent (1950) to 38 percent (1970). Other indicators of socioeconomic advance were similarly positive, showing improved access to doctors, a lowered infant mortality rate, and increased autombile ownership. By the mid-1960s, Serbia's industrial employment had grown by a factor of five over its prewar numbers, to 1.25 million. Illiteracy still remained a real problem: 41 percent of Kosovo's population was illiterate in 1961. Many of the advances described, however, may have been attributable to the inauguration of a thirty-year period of labor exportation in the form of "guest workers."

The guest worker became an institution in Yugoslavia by the late 1960s; there would be so many of them that Yugoslavs would refer to them as a "seventh republic." The phenomenon began in the early 1960s, accompanying the economic reforms and political liberalization of that era. Whereas, before that point, working outside of Yugoslavia had been considered officially "in contradiction to social-political norms," afterwards it came "to be identified . . . as one of the key defining features, along with market socialism and self-management, of what was distinct and positive in the Yugoslav socialist variant" (Zimmerman 76). From the point of view of those more critical of the phenomenon, open borders were being allowed, not to increase freedom, but simply to alleviate some of the economic pressure brought by market reforms, which resulted in immediate unemployment inside Yugoslavia. Of course, it was normal for the Yugoslav communists to frame an economic (or cultural, or political) necessity as an ideological innovation and justification for their own power.

Regardless of the justification, the number of Yugoslav workers abroad soared between 1960 and 1979: 18,000 in the former, 680,000 in the latter year, with a peak of 860,000 in 1973. (These figures do not include family members who accompanied the workers, which one author estimates brings the total to 1,080,000 Yugoslavs abroad in 1979.) In the early years (1960–1969), the guest workers tended to be from Croatia: 56 percent of total workers abroad in 1960, down to 37.8 percent in 1969. The Serbian numbers rose significantly in the same period: from 10.6 percent in 1960 to 27.1 percent in 1969. Considering nationality rather than republic of origin, the numbers show that in 1971 guest workers of Croatian nationality were heavily over-represented (39 percent of workers, 22.2 percent of the population of Yugoslavia) and Serbs were quite under-represented (28.5 percent of workers, 39.9 percent of the population of Yugoslavia). Members of different Yugoslav nations tended toward different destinations: the Croats and Bosnians to Germany, the Serbs to Germany but also in higher proportions to France and Austria, the Macedonians to Australia.

Yugoslavia's post-Tito political crisis was fueled by an economic decline that began in 1979, when the effects of the second oil crisis began to be felt. Unemployment and inflation grew at extraordinary rates after that year (unemployment stood at over 16 percent in 1985), and real earnings fell by 25 percent between 1979 and 1985. The economic collapse did not lead to credible action: instead, the positions of the republican leaderships hardened on the question of whether Yugoslavia had become too decentralized or not, with the Serbian answer being a resounding "yes."

CONTEMPORARY CHALLENGES

The contemporary challenges facing Serbia and Montenegro are less prosaic than those of most countries. Having engaged in an intense political and social radicalization between 1989 and 1991, followed by four years of war, several years of an Albanian insurgency in Kosovo that ended with the NATO bombardment of 1999, and the overthrow of Slobodan Milošević in 2000, the country today needs to achieve political normalcy. "Normalcy" would mean the establishment of a government that rests on constitutional principles and responds to the will of the Serbian electorate; a government that can rebuild economic and cultural ties with the rest of Europe; and a society that has come to terms with its role in the destruction of the second Yugoslavia after 1991. These goals are not easy ones to achieve. Many obstacles stand in the way, most of them associated with the troubled history of Serbia in the 1990s.

The political rivalries that plagued the opposition from the time of the advent of a postcommunist multiparty system in Serbia in 1990 have certainly left an unhappy legacy. Usually, these rivalries resulted in polarization and occasionally violence between supporters of one or the other

Hundreds of thousands of mourners line the streets and walk in a funeral procession for assassinated Serbian Prime Minister Zoran Djindjić, 15 March 2003, in Belgrade, Serbia. Djindjić was fatally shot by two sniper bullets on 12 March 2003 in downtown Belgrade as he stepped out of his armored car. Djindjić's body was laid to rest in Belgrade Cemetery's Alley of the Great Men. (Getty Images)

party; the intense rivalry between Milošević and Vuk Drašković in the early 1990s led to Drašković being beaten and jailed on occasion. Rivalries between members of individual parties weakened those parties. One thinks of the splits in the Democratic Party, which led to the ouster of Dragoljub Mićunović by Zoran Djindjić in 1991 and the defection of Vojislav Koštunica, who formed the Democratic Party of Serbia. At their worst, though, these rivalries could destroy promising opposition movements. Most critically, the opposition's gains in the 1996 elections were squandered over the course of 1997 by the antagonism between Vuk Drašković and Zoran Djindjić. Following the transition of October 2000, Djindjić was again at the center of the storm, this time as premier of Serbia, in competition with the new president of Yugoslavia, Vojislav Koštunica. Unlike the Drašković-Djindjić rivalry, which was almost entirely personal and which never had the chance to develop into a principled conflict, Djindjić and Koštunica not only did not like each other, they disagreed on some fundamental issues—*and* they both held power.

In October's aftermath, several sources of disagreement between Djindjić and Koštunica arose. Some were purely personal: Koštunica, according to many of his DOS part-

ners, received too much credit for the transition; he was, after all, the head of a relatively minor party who had never been particularly popular until DOS made him its presidential candidate. President only by virtue of chance and the hard, decade-long spadework of others in the coalition, he should have allowed others to guide the transition to real democracy. Koštunica resisted, though. He demonstrated early on a conservative approach to change. He resisted the urge to revolutionary reckonings with members and institutions of the old regime. He insisted that in dealing with accused criminals, legal means be used. Koštunica feared that any other approach would lead to the establishment of a new criminal regime, one in which the business allies of his coalition partners would come to dominate in place of Milošević's cronies. He is also a virulent anticommunist, who believed that revolutionary justice smacked too much of Tito's violent consolidation of power after late 1944.

In practical matters, the Djindjić–Koštunica rivalry made consensus and cooperation on several vital matters virtually impossible. The most glaring example concerned the potential arrest and extradition of alleged war criminals, including most prominently Slobodan Milošević himself. After Milošević's fall from power in October 2000, his potential extradition became one of the hottest of hot topics in Serbia. Koštunica argued that the prosecution of alleged war criminals was a Serbian domestic task and that those indicted should not be turned over to The Hague. Here he probably reflected the beliefs of most Serbs, who saw the trial of Serbs as a domestic concern, not least because of their perception that Serbs had been unfairly singled out by the prosecutors of the Hague Tribunal. Djindjić, however, probably recognizing the importance of cooperation to Serbia's future, argued that the indicted should be transferred to The Hague. In June 2001 the Serbian government unilaterally issued a law mandating cooperation with The Hague, under the pressure of deadlines imposed by the international community. The difficulties in extraditing Milošević did not help with the normalization of Serbia's relationship with the rest of Europe, and the problem did not end when he was finally extradited to The Hague in June of 2001. He has been indicted for war crimes in Croatia, Bosnia-Hercegovina, and Kosovo, and his trial began in February 2002. With one break (the result of health problems), his trial has lasted since then. Milošević has acted as his own defense lawyer, which has made the trial somewhat more chaotic— and much longer—than expected originally, since Milošević has been a vigorous cross-examiner and has relied on information he gets from Belgrade sources about some of the witnesses against him.

Although Milošević is the best known among the indicted, he is not the only one by a long shot. Ratko Mladić, the commander of the Bosnian Serb army, is believed to be living in Serbia, and three Serbian military figures indicted for actions taken during and after the siege of Vukovar in 1991 are also on the list, as are several who served in government, security, and military positions before and during the bombing of Kosovo in 1999, including Milan Milutinović, Yugoslav army chief General Dragoljub Ojdanić, and Milošević's former aide for Kosovo, Nikola Šainović. Several of those, including Milutinović (former president of Serbia, who surrendered in January 2003) and also Vojislav Šešelj (indicted for crimes in Croatia and Bosnia) have gone to the Hague voluntarily. The danger and difficulty for any Serbian government in arresting an indictee of, say, Mladić's stature is that authorities would court violence. It is obvious that such problems make it difficult for Serbia to rebuild ties with the rest of Europe. Certainly, until they are resolved, Serbia will have no hope of joining the European Union.

The interrelationship of crime, business, and politics in Serbia has been of more profound real significance for ordinary Serbs and their economic and political fate. The Milošević regime was never a legitimate expression of the political desires of most Serbs; it was, from the outset, a criminal enterprise that manipulated the perceived interests of Serbs in order to remain in power and enrich its members. Thus, from its inception, it spawned a series of laughably obvious but nonetheless effective pilferings of the pocketbooks of ordinary Serbs. From Jezdimir Vasiljević and his Jugoskandik Bank, which collapsed in early 1993, to Dafina Milanović's Dafiment Bank, which failed at the same time, pyramid schemes left Serbs without long-saved hard currency. Other bank schemes included that of the brothers Karić, who founded a bank using Serbian state funds and kept it afloat by lining the pockets of the SPS. Having switched loyalties to Djindjić after October 2000, the bank still exists, the core of a brothers Karić empire that may continue to act as a conduit for the transfer of funds to offshore accounts. One of Milošević's early cronies, Mihalj Kertes, who served the Dafiment Bank as security chief, later became the director of the customs administration, from which position he stole up to 4 billion dollars for Milošević.

Milosević's wife, Mirjana Marković, founded the political party Yugoslav United Left (JUL) in 1994. That party brought together financial interests and became, after its founding, the primary link between the regime and organized crime, although there was also competition between JUL and the SPS in this regard. Infamous paramilitaries like Željko Raznatović, known as "Arkan," were less military figures or patriots than they were organized criminals who enriched themselves and their followers with a combination of war booty and special grants in return for military favors.

The variety and complexity of the relationship of crime and politics in Serbia has been staggering. The result for the present and future of Serbia is that it has become an extremely violent society where the rule of law is meaningless. Assassinations have been a constant curse since the early 1990s, but their pace has picked up since the end of the Bosnian war in November 1995. The list of victims is astounding: Željko Raznatović, Miroslav Bizić (JUL), Žika Petrović (director of JAT airline), Pavle Bulatović (Yugoslav defense minister), Boško Perošević (SPS), Radovan Stojičić (deputy interior minister of Serbia), Zoran Todorović (JUL), Vlada Kovačević (JUL), Vladimir Bokan (businessman ally of Milošević), Zoran Sokolović (former Yugoslav interior minister), and former Belgrade police chief Boško Buha have been among the well-known who have been murdered since 1997. Hundreds of smaller fish have also been murdered in that period.

When Zoran Djindjić was assassinated on 12 March 2003, he became the latest in a long line, a victim of his own ambivalent relationship to organized crime in Serbia. Police immediately ascertained that Djindjić had been murdered by members of the so-called Zemun Clan, the organized crime family headed by Miroslav Luković, known as "Legija." One possible immediate cause for the assassination was that Djindjić had in previous days applied for warrants to arrest many Serbian organized crime figures, among whom may have been Luković. There is also, however, an important deeper history between the two men. Luković worked for state security under Milošević and has been accused of crimes committed in Srebrenica, Bosnia, in 1995 and in Kosovo in 1998 and 1999.

In October 2000 Luković, recognizing that the Milošević regime was about to fall, offered his services to Djindjić in return for unknown concessions. Djindjić, then, apparently owed his position to Luković and others like him. By early 2003, however, Djindjić had come under intense pressure to rein in organized crime and was known to have begun playing the Zemun Clan off against its rival organization, the Surčin Clan. Djindjić may have simply played too closely with fire. But did Djindjić have a choice? One of the great dilemmas faced by anyone hoping to lead Serbia out of the morass created by Milošević's relationship with the military and organized crime is the existence of people like Luković, who are able to place conditions on political change thanks to their ruthlessness and to resources that cross borders between the legitimate and the illegitimate.

In the aftermath of Djindjić's assassination, there are more mundane matters than war crimes and organized crime for Serbs to be concerned with. For instance, in late 2002 Serbs tried twice to elect a new president, and both times they failed to reach the 50 percent threshold of voter turnout necessary to validate the elections. What had been a reasonably principled campaign in September 2002 between two men with serious platforms (Koštunica, who attempted to move from the presidency of Yugoslavia to the presidency of Serbia, and Miroljub Labus, an economist) turned into farce as a result of voter apathy. The turnout issue is complex and points to the continued strange legacy of the Milošević era: the voter rolls in Serbia contain up to 600,000 names of those who are somehow ineligible to vote (they are either dead or have emigrated). Thus experts argue that to achieve the 50 percent threshold, something like 65 percent of actual voters would have had to turn out. Labus refused to run in the second election in December, which suffered the same lack of turnout. The result was that until 2004 Serbia did not have a president. At that point, Boris Tadić of the Democratic Party was elected, which served as a sign that Serbs are more interested now in political and economic reform than they are in supporting overt nationalists who thumb their noses at the international community. Koštunica's position as president of the Federal Republic of Yugoslavia disappeared with the country of that name in February 2003, and then Djindjić's murder put another position of power into doubt. Since his murder, a succession of ineffective premiers has occupied the office without much effect.

The reorganization of what was the Federal Republic of Yugoslavia (FRY) now overshadows the more substantial problem of the deep involvement of organized crime in politics and political rivalries, detailed above. On 4 February 2003, the FRY disappeared, renamed the State Community of Serbia and Montenegro. Designed to head off a Montenegrin independence referendum (which was postponed for three years under the current agreement), the new arrangement gives Serbia and Montenegro some autonomy within a confederal framework. Serbia and Montenegro were supposed to adopt new constitutions by June of 2003. Serbia and Montenegro will share defense and foreign policy. They will enjoy autonomy in economic, trade, and customs spheres. The military and current government assets are to be divided between the two. A federal parliament will be appointed by the governments of Montenegro and Serbia, which means that Milo Djukanović and the Serbian premier effectively control the federal government. Critics of the plan, who are in the vast majority, believe that it will stultify economic reforms and result inevitably in independence for the two units. Djukanović does not hide the fact that independence for Montenegro is his goal.

The issue of Montenegro's potential independence from (former) Yugoslavia is only part of the Serbian geopolitical uncertainty. The status of Kosovo is still formally undetermined, although for the time being it is an international protectorate still formally under Serbian sovereignty. Where will it be in a few years? How will Serbs respond in the short, medium, and long term to the loss of Kosovo? Also, experts and pundits predict on occasion that even the Serbian portions of Bosnia-Hercegovina, known as the Republika Srpska, will (or should) someday become part of a larger Serbian state. These are speculations that will not go away.

The question that may overshadow all others is whether Serbs can individually and collectively come to terms with their recent past. This issue is broader than it might seem at first glance. It is not only that in some intangible way Serbs should feel guilty about this past; it is also that Serbs need to be able to ascertain what they should keep from that past and what is better discarded. For instance, since all of the current political parties and political leaders appeared before or during the nine years of war in the region, should some sort of litmus test be applied? Who is too tainted by activities in the 1990s, and what should constitute the test of that taint. Beyond those relatively basic questions, there is the question of how to rebuild a sense of Serbian citizenship in a society fragmented brutally by ideology and attitudes toward the war.

SELECTIVE BIBLIOGRAPHY

Arsić, Mirko, and Dragan R. Marković. '68: Studentski bun i društvo ('68: The Student Rebellion and Society), 2d ed. Belgrade: Istrazivačko-izdavački centar SSO Srbije, 1985.

Banac, Ivo. The National Question in Yugoslavia: Origins, History, Politics. Ithaca: Cornell University Press, 1984.

———. With Stalin against Tito: Cominformist Splits in Yugoslav Communism. Ithaca: Cornell University Press, 1988.

Bokovoy, Melissa K. Peasants and Communists: Politics and Ideology in the Yugoslav Countryside, 1941–1953. Pittsburgh: University of Pittsburgh Press, 1998.

Bokovoy, Melissa K., Jill A. Irvine, and Carol S. Lilly, eds. State-Society Relations in Yugoslavia, 1945–1992. New York: St. Martin's Press, 1997.

Cohen, Lenard. Broken Bonds: The Disintegration of Yugoslavia. Boulder: Westview, 1995.

———. Regime Transition in a Disintegrating Yugoslavia: The Law of Rule vs. the Rule of Law. Pittsburgh: University of Pittsburgh Center for Russian and East European Studies, 1992.

———. Serpent in the Bosom: The Rise and Fall of Slobodan Milošević. Boulder: Westview, 2002.

Colin, Matthew. Guerilla Radio: Rock 'n' Roll Radio and Serbia's Underground Resistance. New York: Thunder's Mouth Press/Nation Books, 2001.

Denitch, Bogdan. Ethnic Nationalism: The Tragic Death of Yugoslavia. Minneapolis: University of Minnesota Press, 1993.

Djilas, Aleksa. The Contested Country: Yugoslav Unity and Communist Revolution, 1919–1953. Cambridge: Harvard University Press, 1991.

Djilas, Milovan. *Land without Justice: An Autobiography of His Youth.* New York: Harcourt, Brace, 1958.

———. *Memoir of a Revolutionary.* New York: Harcourt Brace Jovanovich, 1973.

———. *Wartime.* New York: Harcourt Brace Jovanovich, 1977.

———. *Rise and Fall.* New York: Harcourt Brace Jovanovich, 1985.

Djogo, Gojko. *Vunena vremena* (Wooly Times). Belgrade: Srpska knjizevna zadruga, 1992.

Djukić, Slavoljub. *Čovek u svom vremenu: Razgovori sa Dobricem Ćosićem* (A Man in His Times: Conversations with Dobrica Ćosić). Belgrade: Filip Višnjić, 1989.

Dragović-Soso, Jasna. *"Saviours of the Nation": Serbia's Intellectual Opposition and the Revival of Nationalism.* Montreal: McGill-Queen's University Press, 2002.

Fine, John V. A., Jr. *The Early Medieval Balkans: A Critical Survey from the Sixth to the Late Twelfth Century.* Ann Arbor: University of Michigan Press, 1983.

———. *The Late Medieval Balkans: A Critical Survey from the Late Twelfth Century to the Ottoman Conquest.* Ann Arbor: University of Michigan Press, 1987.

Gordy, Eric. *The Culture of Power in Serbia: Nationalism and the Destruction of Alternatives.* University Park: Pennsylvania State University Press, 1999.

Gorup, Radmila J., and Nadežda Obradović, eds. *The Prince of Fire: An Anthology of Contemporary Serbian Short Stories.* Pittsburgh: University of Pittsburgh Press, 1998.

Goulding, Daniel. *Liberated Cinema: The Yugoslav Experience, 1945–2001.* Bloomington: Indiana University Press, 2003.

Holton, Milne, and Vasa D. Mihailovich, eds. *Songs of the Serbian People: From the Collections of Vuk Karadžić.* Pittsburgh: University of Pittsburgh Press, 1997.

Inić, Slobodan. "Serbia's Historic Defeat." *New Politics* (Summer 1993): 166.

Ignja, Petar. "Studentsko pitanje—materijalno" (The Student Question—A Material One). *Nedeljne Informativne Novine* (Weekly Informative News), 4 February 1968, p. 4.

Jelavich, Charles. *South Slav Nationalisms: Textbooks and Yugoslav Union before 1914.* Columbus: Ohio State University Press, 1990.

Judah, Tim. *Kosovo: War and Revenge.* New Haven: Yale University Press, 2000.

———. *The Serbs: History, Myth and the Destruction of Yugoslavia.* New Haven: Yale University Press, 1997.

Kesar, Jovan, and Pero Simić. *LEKA: Aleksandar Ranković.* Belgrade: Biblioteka 'Misterije politike,' 1990.

Krivokapić, Boro. "Srbi su dvoglav narod" (The Serbs Are a Two-Headed People). *Nedeljne Informativne Novine* (Weekly Informative News), 12 April 1991.

Lampe, John R. *Yugoslavia as History: Twice There Was a Country.* Cambridge: Cambridge University Press, 1996.

Lampe, John R., and Marvin R. Jackson. *Balkan Economic History, 1550–1950.* Bloomington: Indiana University Press, 1982.

Lilly, Carol S. *Power and Persuasion: Ideology and Rhetoric in Communist Yugoslavia, 1944–53.* Boulder: Westview, 2000.

Magaš, Branka. *The Destruction of Yugoslavia: Tracking the Breakup 1980–1992.* London: Verso, 1993.

Malcolm, Noel. *Kosovo: A Short History.* New York: New York University Press, 1998.

Mertus, Julie A. *Kosovo: How Myths and Truths Started a War.* Berkeley and Los Angeles: University of California Press, 1999.

Mihailović, Kosta, and Vasilije Krestić. *The Memorandum of the Serbian Academy of Sciences and Arts: Answers to Criticisms.* Belgrade: Kultura, 1995.

Mihailovich, Vasa D. Introduction to *The Mountain Wreath,* by Petar II Petrović Njegoš. Belgrade: Srpska evropa, 1997.

Miller, Nicholas J. "A Failed Transition: The Case of Serbia." In *Politics, Power, and the Struggle for Democracy in South-East Europe.* Edited by Karen Dawisha and Bruce Parrott. Cambridge: Cambridge University Press, 1997.

———. *Between Nation and State: Serbian Politics in Croatia, 1903–1914.* Pittsburgh: University of Pittsburgh Press, 1997.

"Milošević Delivers Speech." Federal Broadcast Information Service (FBIS), Daily Report, 3 July 1989.

O'Malley, Martin, and Owen Wood. "Who Is Vojislav Kostunica?" *CBC News Online,* http://www.cbc.ca/news/indepth/facts/kostunica_vojislav.html (accessed 12 August 2004).

Pavlowitch, Stevan. *The Improbable Survivor: Yugoslavia and its Problems, 1918–1988.* Columbus: Ohio State University Press, 1988.

———. *Serbia: The History of an Idea.* New York: New York University Press, 2002.

Perica, Vjekoslav. *Balkan Idols: Religion and Nationalism in Yugoslav States.* Oxford: Oxford University Press, 2002.

Petrovich, Michael. *A History of Modern Serbia, 1804–1918.* New York: Harcourt Brace Jovanovich 1976.

Pinson, Mark. *The Muslims of Bosnia-Hercegovina: Their Historic Development from the Middle Ages to the Dissolution of Yugoslavia.* Cambridge: Harvard University Press, 1994.

Ramet, Sabrina. *Balkan Babel: The Disintegration of Yugoslavia From the Death of Tito to the War for Kosovo.* Boulder: Westview, 2002.

———. *Nationalism and Federalism in Yugoslavia, 1962–1991.* 2d ed. Bloomington: Indiana University Press, 1992.

Ramet, Sabrina, and Ljubiša Adamović, eds. *Beyond Yugoslavia: Politics, Economics, and Culture in a Shattered Community.* Boulder: Westview, 1995.

Rusinow, Dennison. *The Yugoslav Experiment, 1948–1974.* Berkeley and Los Angeles: University of California Press, 1978.

"Saopštenje Odbora za odbranu slobode misli i izražavanja" (Notice of the Committee for the Defense of Freedom of Thought and Expression). *Naša reč* (Our Word) (London), January 1985, no. 361.

Sell, Louis. *Slobodan Milošević and the Destruction of Yugoslavia.* Durham: Duke University Press, 2002.

Shoup, Paul. *Communism and the Yugoslav National Question.* New York: Columbia University Press, 1968.

Sontag, Susan. Introduction to *Homo Poeticus: Essays and Interviews,* by Danilo Kiš. New York: Farrar, Straus and Giroux, 1995.

Spalatin, Christopher, "Serbo-Croatian or Serbian and Croatian? Considerations on the Croation Declaration and Serbian Proposal of March 1967." *Journal of Croatian Studies* 7–8 (1966–1967): 6–9.

"Stambolić Criticizes Memorandum Authors." Federal Broadcast Information Service (FBIS), Daily Report, 31 October 1987.

Stokes, Gale. *Legitimacy through Liberalism: Vladimir Jovanović and the Transformation of Serbian Politics.* Seattle: University of Washington Press, 1975.

———. *Politics as Development: The Emergence of Political Parties in Nineteenth-Century Serbia.* Durham, NC: Duke University Press, 1990.

Thompson, Mark. *Forging War: The Media in Serbia, Croatia, and Bosnia-Hercegovina.* London: Article 19, 1994.

Tomasevich, Jozo. *Peasants, Politics, and Economic Change in Yugoslavia.* Stanford: Stanford University Press, 1955.

———. *War and Revolution in Yugoslavia, 1941–1945: The Chetniks.* Stanford: Stanford University Press, 1975.

———. *War and Revolution in Yugoslavia, 1941–1945: Occupation and Collaboration.* Stanford: Stanford University Press, 2001.

Trifunović, Lazar, *Srpsko slikarstvo, 1900–1950* (Serbian Painting, 1900–1950). Belgrade: Nolit, 1973.

Vucinich, Wayne. *Serbia between East and West.* Stanford: Stanford University Press, 1954.

Wachtel, Andrew. *Making a Nation, Breaking a Nation: Literature and Cultural Politics in Yugoslavia.* Stanford: Stanford University Press, 1998.

Wilson, Duncan. *The Life and Times of Vuk Stefanović Karadžić, 1787–1864.* Oxford: Oxford University Press, 1970.

Woodward, Susan. *Balkan Tragedy.* Washington DC: Brookings Institution Press, 1995.

———. *Socialist Unemployment: The Political Economy of Yugoslavia, 1945–1990.* Princeton: Princeton University Press, 1995.

"Zahtevi 2015 stanovnika Kosova" (Demands of 2015 Residents of Kosovo). *Knijiževne novine* (Literary News) (Belgrade), 15 December 1985.

Zimmerman, William. *Open Borders, Nonalignment, and the Political Evolution of Yugoslavia.* Princeton: Princeton University Press, 1987.

CHRONOLOGY

Seventh century	Serbs first arrive on the Balkan Peninsula.
Tenth century	Duklja consolidates control over territory that will eventually constitute modern Montenegro.
Eleventh century	Raška, the core of the medieval Serbian kingdom, splits from Duklja.
1168	The lands of Raška, which had been divided, are united under the leadership of one man, Stefan Nemanja.
1219	Sava (later Saint Sava) gains the grant of an autocephalous Serbian Orthodox Church.
1331–1355	Stefan Dušan governs the most powerful medieval Serbian state.
28 June 1389	The Battle of Kosovo, traditionally considered a defeat by the Turks and the end of Serbian independence.
1389–1459	Serbia continues to exist as a vassal state of the Ottoman sultan.
1459	Battle of Smederevo ends Serbian statehood.
1557	Serbian Patriarchate established in Peč.
1630	Statuta Valachorum issued by Emperor Ferdinand II.
1690s	At least 30,000 Orthodox Serbs, led by Patriarch Arsenije III Crnojević, make their way from Kosovo north to the Habsburg monarchy (the Great Migration).
1766	Serbian Patriarchate dismantled by Ottoman authorities.
1787	Vuk Karadžić (1787–1864) is born in a small village in western Serbia.
January and February 1804	Janissary leaders in Belgrade systematically murder Serbian headmen throughout the *pašalik* of Belgrade.
August 1804	Serbian insurgents under Karadjordje establish themselves as the political power in the region.
1813	Russia signs the Treaty of Bucharest with the Ottoman Empire, effectively ending the Serbian insurrection.
1814	Vuk's grammar of the Serbian language completed.
April 1815	Miloš Obrenović leads the second Serbian insurrection.
1817	Miloš has Karadjordje murdered.
1818	Vuk's dictionary of the Serbian language published.
1822–1833	Vuk's collection entitled *Narodna srbska pjesnarica* (Serbian People's Songbook) published.
1830	Serbia's autonomy proclaimed.
1830	Njegoš becomes the spiritual and political leader of Montenegro at the age of seventeen.
1838	The Ottomans approve a constitution for the pašalik of Belgrade, by which Miloš is to govern along with a council of elders.
1839	Miloš leaves Serbia.
1839	Miloš replaced by his second son, Mihailo.
1842	Publication of Vuk Karadžić's "Serbs All and Everywhere."
1842	Aleksandar (Alexander) Karadjordjević, son of the original Karadjordje, begins his period in power in Serbia.

1844	The *Načertanije* (Outline) is written by Ilija Garašanin, the Serbian minister of the interior.
1845	Njegoš's *The Ray of the Microcosm* published.
1847	Njegoš's *The Mountain Wreath* published.
1858	Aleksandar Karadjordjević is replaced by Mihailo Obrenović, in a return engagement as prince of Serbia.
1868	Prince Mihailo assassinated. Milan Obrenović becomes prince of Serbia.
1869	A second constitution proclaimed in Serbia.
1876	Russian general Mikhail G. Cherniaev arrives in Serbia to lead its troops against the Ottomans.
July 1876	War begins.
November 1876	Serbia sues for peace in its war with the Ottoman Empire.
March 1878	The Treaty of San Stefano ends the conflict.
June 1878	The Congress of Berlin meets. It revises the Treaty of San Stefano.
1881	The Radical party founded.
1889	Milan Obrenović abdicates; his son Aleksandar Obrenović becomes king of Serbia.
June 1903	A group of officers in the Serbian army murder the king and queen of Serbia.
September 1904	Petar (Peter) Karadjordjević is crowned king.
March 1905	The Croato-Serbian Coalition founded in Croatia.
1906–1911	The customs war with Austria.
October 1908	The Habsburg monarchy annexes Bosnia and Hercegovina.
1911	Union or Death (The Black Hand) founded.
1912	The First Balkan War begins in October.
29 June 1913	The Second Balkan War begins.
28 June 1914	Gavrilo Princip assassinates the Archduke Franz Ferdinand and his wife Sophie.
23 July 1914	The Habsburg government presents Serbia with an ultimatum.
28 July 1914	Austria-Hungary declares war on Serbia.
December 1914	Niš Declaration.
15 December 1914	The Battle of Kolubara.
April 1915	Treaty of London.
9 October 1915	Bulgaria attacks Serbia.
28 November 1915	The notorious flight in winter of Serbian troops and civilians over the Albanian mountains begins.
June 1917	The Corfu Declaration.
9 November 1918	The Geneva Declaration.
1 December 1918	The Kingdom of Serbs, Croats, and Slovenes is proclaimed in Belgrade.
28 June 1921	Vidovdan Constitution promulgated.
20 June 1928	Stjepan Radić gunned down in the Yugoslav parliament by Puniša Račić.
January 1929	King Aleksandar (Alexander) proclaims a renamed Kingdom of Yugoslavia and abolishes the Vidovdan Constitution.
1931	Aleksandar announces a new constitution.
1934	Aleksandar is assassinated in Marseilles by a Macedonian gunman.
20 August 1939	"Sporazum," also known as the Cvetković–Maček Agreement, signed.
25 March 1941	Yugoslavia signs the Tripartite Pact.
27 March 1941	Serbian military officers, led by General Dušan Simović, execute a coup d'état and declare underage Prince Peter the new king of Yugoslavia.
6 April 1941	German forces invade Yugoslavia.
20 October 1944	Liberation of Belgrade.
1945	Three novels by Ivo Andrić (*The Bridge on the Drina, The Woman from Sarajevo,* and *The Bosnian Story*) are published.
28 June 1948	The Cominform (Communist Information Bureau) expels Yugoslavia.
1954	The Novi Sad Agreement signed.
1 July 1966	The Fourth Plenum of the Central Committee of the League of Communists of Yugoslavia meets on the island of Brioni (the Brioni Plenum) to condemn Aleksandar Ranković.
19 March 1967	The Proposal for Consideration signed.
28–29 May 1968	Dobrica Ćosić gives a speech to the Central Committee of the Serbian League of Communists in which he blasts the League for its treatment of Kosovo and Vojvodina.
2 June 1968	The student movement at Belgrade University begins.
November 1968	Albanian rebellion takes place in Kosovo.
1974	A new constitution is unveiled for Yugoslavia.
April 1980	Tito dies.
March 1981	Rebellion in Kosovo begins.
19 May 1982	The Committee for the Protection of Artistic Freedom is formed.
April 1984	Dr. Vojislav Šešelj is arrested in Sarajevo, and twenty-eight people, including Milovan Djilas, are arrested in Belgrade for antistate activity.
November 1984	The Committee for the Defense of the Freedom of Thought and Expression is formed.
1 May 1985	A Serbian farmer named Djordje Martinović is found injured, bleeding from his rectum, a mineral water bottle by his side, on his fields near Gnjilane, Kosovo.
13 June 1985	The presidency of the Serbian Academy of Arts and Sciences appoints a committee to prepare a document that will address Serbian concerns about Yugoslavia.

October 1985	Over two thousand Serbs from Kosovo present a petition to various governmental bodies.
September 1986	After several months of editing, as the document nears completion, the Belgrade newspaper *Večernje novosti* reveals the existence of what comes to be called the Memorandum.
April 1987	Slobodan Milošević visits the town of Kosovo Polje and gives his famous declaration that the Serbs of Kosovo should not be "beaten."
November 1987	Milošević is able to bring about the fall of Ivan Stambolić as president of Serbia.
1988	Frightened party leaderships in Vojvodina and Montenegro resign en masse in the fall.
1989	Milošević is able to proclaim a new constitution for Serbia, which reincorporates Vojvodina and Kosovo into the republic proper.
28 June 1989	The 600th anniversary of the Battle of Kosovo celebrated.
December 1989	The Democratic League of Kosovo is founded.
1990	Two opposition parties are formed, the Serbian Renewal Movement and the Democratic Party.
July 1990	Approximately 90 percent of the Albanian members of the provincial parliament vote that Kosovo be proclaimed a republic in Yugoslavia.
August 1990	Under the leadership of Milan Babić, the Autonomous Province of the Serbian Krajina is proclaimed in Croatia.
December 1990	First free postwar elections in Serbia give victory to Milošević's Socialist Party of Serbia (SPS).
9 March 1991	A rally against Milošević's control of the media turns into a days-long movement against the regime's authoritarian methods.
25 June 1991	Croatia and Slovenia declare their secession from Yugoslavia.
July 1991	The Serbia Autonomous Region of Slavonia, Baranja, and Western Srem is formed and proclaimed in Croatia.
September 1991	Referendum on Kosovo's independence announced.
October 1991	The referendum results in affirmative vote.
6 April 1992	The focus of the war shifts to Bosnia, which declares its own independence on this day.
December 1992 1993	Milošević and the SPS win elections. Elections do not result in any real changes, except that the Serbian Radical Party (SRP) loses support to the Democratic Party (DP) and to the Democratic Movement of Serbia (DEPOS).
1995	The war in Croatia, quiet after January 1992, flares up again in the spring.
December 1996	A coalition of the Democratic Party, the Serbian Renewal Movement, and the Civic Alliance (called *Zajedno*, "Together") wins municipal elections in many of Serbia's cities. Demonstrations compel the government to respect the outcome of the elections.
October 1997	In Montenegrin presidential elections, Djukanovic defeats Momir Bulatović, Milošević's ally in Montenegro.
1998	The Kosovo Liberation Army becomes active.
March 1998	The first of several large-scale massacres of Albanians by Serbian security forces.
January 1999	The Račak massacre.
March–April 1999	NATO bombing campaign in Kosovo.
August 2000	A new coalition called the Democratic Opposition of Serbia (DOS) is formed.
September 2000	Vojislav Koštunica receives approximately 52 percent of the vote to Milošević's 35 percent in the presidential election.
2–5 October 2000	Serbs take to the streets, and miners in Kolubara go on strike; Milošević finally agrees to respect the results of the election.
7 October 2000	Koštunica is sworn in as president of Serbia.
April 2001	Parliamentary elections are held in Montenegro.
March 2002	Djukanović, Djindjić, Koštunica, and others hammer out the Belgrade Agreement.
4 February 2003	The Federal Republic of Yugoslavia disappears, renamed the State Community of Serbia and Montenegro.
March 2003	Zoran Djindjić is assassinated.

MACEDONIA

ALEKSANDAR PANEV

LAND AND PEOPLE

The name "Macedonia" refers to what is probably the most contested geographical entity in Southeastern Europe. The Republic of Macedonia's territorial integrity, language, name, symbols, nationality, and history are challenged either openly or covertly by its neighbors, as well as by various internal and external lobby groups and organizations.

Recent internal interethnic clashes, greatly exacerbated by the situation in Kosovo, call into question the very survival of the Macedonian state. Many in Bulgaria assert that the Macedonian language is a dialect of Bulgarian and that Macedonian nationality is only a recent communist invention. A similar and often much better-developed campaign of the Greek state challenges the validity of giving the name Macedonia to the newly established independent Macedonian republic. The inexperienced and self-centered Macedonian leaders (often accused of corruption and nepotism), together with an inefficient and untrained state bureaucracy, have produced a mixed and ambiguous impact on the internal development and external position of the country. Despite the odds, however, the new state has succeeded in surviving for more than a decade.

At present, the term "Macedonia" can refer not only to the territory of the independent Republic of Macedonia, which is in greater part positioned around the River Vardar, but also to two other adjacent regions. One of those regions is the central northern part of Greece, bounded to the south by the Aegean coast, Mount Olympus, and the Pindus Mountains; to the west by the Haliakmon (Bistritsa) River; and to the east by the lower Nestos (Mesta) River. The other is a region in southeastern Bulgaria around the Pirin Mountains. Based on the main geographic characteristics of each region, students of the region often employ the terms *Vardar, Aegean,* and *Pirin* Macedonia to distinguish these three different parts. In the early twenty-first century, however, the international community uses the name Macedonia predominantly to refer to the independent Republic of Macedonia, strongly as that usage has been challenged by Greece. Only a full account of the troubled history of the region can explain adequately the current debates over the name and status of Macedonia, but some preliminary account of the origins of the name and the various ways it has been used may be helpful.

Macedonia traces its name to an ethnic group that lived mainly on the territory situated around the Haliakmon (Bistritsa) River and its tributary Moglenitsa in present northwestern Greece. In the period between the seventh and second centuries B.C.E., the ancient Macedonians established a kingdom that at times had as its boundaries the Danube, the Black Sea, the Peloponnesus, and the Adriatic. In the centuries that followed, Macedonia was a Roman

and then a Byzantine province whose boundaries frequently and radically changed, but generally encompassed the greater part of Southeastern Europe.

At the turn of the ninth century, the Byzantine Empire lost effective control over the greater part of Southeastern Europe. It then established a province for which it used the name Macedonia on the territory of present-day southern Bulgaria and northeastern Greece, and that province harbored refugees from Macedonia proper. The Ottoman Empire, which had conquered the Balkans in the thirteenth and fourteenth centuries, did not identify either officially or unofficially any area in its holdings by the name Macedonia. For centuries, only Western geographers, certain historians and travelers, and Eastern Orthodox Church officials used this name to denote a geographical space in the Balkans. However, the interpretation of the boundaries and exact location of the geographic area called Macedonia varied greatly from author to author. That clash of interpretations has been the source of much of the friction over the region.

At the turn of the nineteenth century, the modern geographical definition of the term "Macedonia" began to emerge. This occurred as a result of Western influences, closely interwoven with the attempts of several indigenous and mutually exclusive national movements to use the aura of ancient Macedonia (and its most famous hero, Alexander the Great) in order to foster the emergence of national consciousness among the local population. By the 1890s, local inhabitants, ruling elites of the neighboring states, and the representatives of the great powers clearly understood that the present-day territories of the Republic of Macedonia, as well as the aforementioned regions in Greece and Bulgaria (Aegean and Pirin Macedonia), denoted a region called Macedonia. At the time when this name gained widespread use, these three areas represented a whole and unbroken unit of the Ottoman Empire.

Then Serbia, Greece, and Bulgaria conquered and partitioned this part of the Ottoman Empire during the Balkan Wars (1912–1913). It was at this time that the terms Vardar, Aegean, and Pirin Macedonia were introduced to designate respectively the Serbian, Greek, and Bulgarian territorial gains. The Republic of Macedonia was established mainly on the territory of Vardar Macedonia, first in 1944 as an integral part of the Yugoslav federation, and finally as an independent state in 1991.

The Republic of Macedonia, which comprises approximately 26,000 square kilometers, or 39 percent of the territory of Macedonia as it came to be defined in the nineteenth century, is a landlocked state in the heart of Southeastern Europe. It is slightly smaller than Belgium or the state of Vermont in the United States. Pastures (encompassing 6,700 square kilometers) and meadows (530 square kilometers) form approximately one-quarter of the Republic of Macedonia. Arable land (6,650 square kilometers), which includes vineyards and orchards, makes up another quarter of the territory. Forests are present on roughly 37 percent of the land, and the remainder of the territory of the Republic of Macedonia is comprised of barren terrain (8 percent), lakes (2 percent), and cities (3 percent). The av-

General view of a Muslim part of the city of Skopje, the capital of Macedonia. (AFP/Getty Images)

erage altitude of the country is 850 meters, a result of the fact that approximately 80 percent of Macedonian territory is mountainous and hilly.

Through the valleys of the Rivers Vardar and Strumitsa as well as the Pelagonia plain, Macedonia is open to the Mediterranean in the south. To the north, the low and easily passable Kumanovo-Preševo hills form the watershed between the Vardar and the Danube tributary Morava, while the Kačanik pass connects the upland basin of Kosovo with the Vardar Valley. In this way, the Republic of Macedonia provides longitudinally the shortest land connection between Central Europe and the Near East. The Skopje plain provides the key access to all the routes that interconnect Kosovo, Bosnia, Serbia, Greece, Albania, and Bulgaria. The famous ancient Roman road Via Ignatia, a main communication line between the western and eastern Balkans, passed through the Pelagonia plain in the southern part of today's Macedonian state.

The principal geographic features of the Republic of Macedonia consist of large and massive mountains with fertile basins and terraces. The Republic of Macedonia represents a transition between the Dinaro-Pindus range and the Rhodope massif. The Dinaro-Pindus massif, which is situated around the western and northern basins of the country, is wide and generally high. Its main mountains (Šar Planina, Stogovo, Baba, Nidže, Galičitsa, Korab, and Kožuv) are cut by the upper Vardar, Treska, and Crna Reka Rivers. Its highest peak is Golem Korab, which reaches 2,764 meters. Osogovo, Maleševo, Ogražden, Belasitsa, and Plačkovitsa represent the main mountains of the Rhodope massif in eastern Macedonia. They consist mainly of crystalline and granite rocks. In general, most of the republic is mountainous and hilly.

The principal basins of the Republic of Macedonia were filled with water in the Pliocene era (approximately 10 million years ago, about the same time that the North American landmass was uplifted). With the sinking of the Aegean Sea region in the geological periods that followed, these basins started to drain toward the Thermaic Gulf in present-day Greece. The result was the formation of the ravines and passes in the region that stand today. These movements created not only lakes and valleys that are mutually connected by deep, ravine-like passages and saddles, but also a number of riverbed terraces. While the Polog, Pelagonia, Ohrid, and Skopje basins developed in western and northern Macedonia, the Ovče Pole, Kočani, and Tikveš are the main valleys in eastern Macedonia.

These basins, which contain the sediment of early lakes and present-day rivers, have a variety of extremely fertile soils. Some basins are covered with black soil, while others have clays and sands of earlier lakes or volcanic deposits. The arable lands that were formed by the nearby rivers are suitable for cultivation of grain, garden plants, poppy seeds, and even rice. The edges of the basins, which were formed through accumulation of early lakes' sediments, are suitable for cultivating grapes and tobacco, and when irrigated, for various types of fruits. The existence of salty soils in certain parts of the Skopje and Ovče Pole valleys provides an opportunity for the development of pastures, as well as for cultivation of livestock plants. The higher mountain regions and terraces, which contain mainly rocky and shallow grounds of dark brown hue, are used for potatoes, rye, and barley.

Lakes Ohrid, Prespa, and Dojran represent the main standing waters of the republic. Lake Ohrid, which occupies an area of 348 square kilometers, is located in the far southwestern part of the state. Over 229.9 square kilometers is found in the Republic of Macedonia, while the rest is part of Albania. It is 30.35 kilometers long and 14.5 kilometers wide. The surface of the lake is at an elevation of 695 meters above sea level. The lake is 287 meters deep, while the transparency of the water is 21.5 meters. The lake has an average temperature of 23 degrees Celsius. Lake Ohrid, with its scenic features and clear waters, is a well-known resort, visited by thousands of local and international tourists every year.

Over half of Lake Prespa (approximately 174 square kilometers out of a total surface area of 274 square kilometers) is contained inside the boundaries of the Republic of Macedonia; it is situated west of the Vardar River, on the border with Greece and Albania. The surface of the lake is at 853 meters above sea level. It is 28.6 kilometers long, 16.9 kilometers wide, and 54 meters deep. Its average tempera-

ture in August is 24 degrees Celsius, while its transparency is 7.20 meters. Lake Dojran, situated 148 meters above sea level in the southeastern part of the republic, covers an area of 43.1 square kilometers. It is divided between the Republic of Macedonia (27.3 square kilometers) and the Republic of Greece (15.8 square kilometers). It is 9 kilometers long, 7 kilometers wide, and 10 meters deep. Because of its small size and shallowness, its water warms up to 28 degrees Celsius. Several small glacial lakes exist in the high ranges of the Šar, Pelister, Jablanitsa, Jakupitsa, Korab, and Stogovo Mountains. Mavrovo, Globočica, Debar, Tikveš, Matka, Kalimantsi, Streževo (on the river Šemnica), Glažnje, Lipkovo, and Mantovo are lakes that are artificially constructed for energy and irrigation purposes.

The Vardar River and its tributaries irrigate more than 80 percent of the territory of the Republic of Macedonia. From its spring on the edge of Šar Planina, where it flows at 1.5 cubic meters per second, the Vardar's flow increases to an average of 174 cubic meters at Gevgelija (which is situated on the border between the Republic of Macedonia and Greece). Its main tributaries from the western part of Macedonia are the Treska, Markova Reka, Topolka, Babuna, Tsrna, and Bošava, while from the eastern part come the Lepenets, Pčinja, and Bregalnitsa. Tsrn Drim and its tributary, the Radika, in southwestern Macedonia, belong to the Adriatic river-system. This river, together with Lakes Ohrid and Prespa, irrigate 13 percent of the territory of the country. Waters from the spring well of the Binečka Morava belong to the Black Sea basin.

The territory contains various minerals. Traces of gold are found in the Kratovo and Zletovo region in the eastern parts of the Republic. Silver, copper, zinc, and iron are also found in these areas. Tin is mined northeast of Ohrid at Velomej. There are chrome mines north and west of Skopje and in Pelagonia south of Prilep. Asbestos appears near Skopje and Gevgelija, while bauxite is found in eastern parts of Macedonia. Lignite is present in the vicinity of Skopje and in Pelagonia near Bitola. There are iron ores in the basins of Skopje, Kičevo, and Demir Hisar. Mica appears in Pelagonia near Prilep, while manganese ore, arsenic, and antimony are present in the Stogovo Mountains and the Mariovo-Moglena region. Serpentine, carnelian, travertine, and fine marble occur in several places throughout Macedonia. There are sulphurous mineral springs in Katlanovo and Štip in northeastern and eastern Macedonia.

The Republic of Macedonia, which is situated between 40° 51′ and 42° 30′ north latitude, is in a transitional zone between the continental and Mediterranean climates. The basin of the Vardar, which reaches the Aegean Sea, acts as a funnel, endowing the region with Mediterranean influences. The low hills between the Morava and Vardar Valleys expose Macedonia to continental climate features. As a result, this region has hot, torrid, and dry summers, as well as snowy and cold winters. The average annual temperature is 11.5 degrees Celsius. July is the warmest month with an average of 22, while January is the coldest with an average of minus 3 degrees Celsius. The precipitation in the Republic of Macedonia, which equals approximately 680 millimeters per square meter per year, is extremely low.

Moreover, it is significantly irregular: the mountainous part of western Macedonia gets over 1,000 millimeters, while the Vardar Valley receives under 500 millimeters precipitation. The most frequent winds in Macedonia, known under the names of Vardarets and Jugo, are characteristic of the Vardar Valley.

The location of the country at one of Europe's geographical crossroads and the topographic features dictate the type of flora and fauna present in Macedonia. There are over 3,500 species of plants, as well as 55 known species of fish and 78 species of mammals. Approximately 330 species of birds are also known to appear in the area. Reptile and invertebrate species are insufficiently studied. It also has a number of endemic plant species, some of which are very rare, such as *Atrolagus cerjavski, Tulipa marianae, Ferulago macedonia,* and *Sambucus deborensis.* The lynx, the rarest of the cat family in Europe, can be found in the western parts of the country.

The predominant deciduous tree types, which spread over the greater part of the wooded area, are drought-resistant oaks and beeches, while the most frequent evergreen trees are the white and the black pine. Low forests, mainly represented by the hornbeam, ash, and hazel trees, are present in the dry regions. The annual growth of wood mass is small: only 202 cubic meters per square kilometer, compared to 700–1,000 per square kilometer in the rest of Europe.

The territory of the Republic of Macedonia is subject to frequent and violent earthquakes, which result from the tectonic movements in a zone that extends from the Mediterranean and Caspian seas to the Himalayas. Within this zone, the movement of the continental landmasses produces quakes, which occur at relatively shallow depths. The impact of these tectonic disturbances is often devastating for certain parts of Macedonia, especially the Skopje valley. In 1963 more than a thousand citizens were killed in an earthquake that destroyed the city.

In 2002 the Macedonian GNP (gross national product) per capita was approximately $1,859, or approximately twenty times lower than the GNP per capita in the United States, a fact that clearly reveals that the country's economy is underdeveloped and characterized by a low industrial output. This situation is a result of a long historical development, communist management in the Yugoslav federation, and problems of transition from a planned to a free economy in the period from 1990 to 2000, as well as political instability, corruption, and the recent ethnic conflict. The unemployment rate in 2004 has soared to over 36 percent, while the average monthly salary for those who remained employed has been less than $160. Only 12 percent of the population make their living directly from agriculture (which produces over 20 percent of the GDP). The industrial sector provides employment for approximately 36 percent of the workforce.

Agriculture, which never was compelled to build large collective farms on the model of the Soviet Union, is characterized by small and barely productive landholdings, while industry is based on outdated technologies that do not comply with the European Union's standards and requirements. The backward nature of both sectors combines to hinder the country's overall economic development.

The major agricultural products of the country are wheat, barley, corn, rice, and tobacco, as well as sheep and some cattle. The mining of minerals, iron ore, lead, zinc, and nickel provides additional sources of revenue and employment for the inhabitants. The industrial sector mainly produces steel, chemicals, and textiles.

Environmental conditions are comparable to those found in many other Eastern European and former Soviet countries. According to the communist ideology that guided Macedonian society in the period from the end of World War II until the collapse of Yugoslavia, development was measured through increased production of industrial goods and energy. This approach led to overexploitation of natural resources, lack of interest in environmental issues, and significant environmental degradation.

The most important environmental challenge facing Macedonia is that of air pollution, which is caused by various industries such as metallurgical and thermal power plants, as well as unregulated emissions from numerous old and unchecked vehicles used on the roads. As a result of environmental problems, half of the urban population of Macedonia is often exposed to unhealthy concentrations of gasses such as sulfur dioxide, carbon oxides, and hydrocarbons, as well as heavy metals such as lead, zinc, and cadmium. Various studies clearly demonstrate that, especially in Veles and Skopje, a large number of children suffer from respiratory diseases associated with poor air quality.

Water pollution and inadequate solid waste management are endemic for Third World countries. Macedonia is not an exception. Only one official wastewater treatment plant operates properly, while none of the approximately twenty-five known landfills possess environmental safety features. In addition, numerous unregulated casual disposal waste sites exist in the rural areas. Major cities and various industrial sites in most cases do not possess any waste treatment equipment; they dispose of their waste in the rivers and in the existing landfill sites. This approach to dealing with wastewater and solid waste leads to heavy pollution of the environment and a negative effect on biodiversity in the country. Numerous governmental and nongovernmental institutions monitor and allegedly work on the improvement of the environmental situation in Macedonia. In 1996 the Macedonian parliament adopted a special Act on Environment and Nature Protection and Promotion, which requires creation of an ecological plan both on the national and municipal level, as well as its full implementation. The act itself and the policies specified in it are in compliance with the European Union standards and requirements in order for Macedonia to gain access to Western markets. The existing institutions, however, including a specially created Ministry of Environment, have failed to implement this legislation. The actual indolence of the state organizations is a result of the extremely precarious financial situation in the country, political infighting, the recent armed conflict that began in Kosovo and spread to Macedonia, and the inability of post-communist governments to establish professional, effective, efficient, and responsible administration.

Macedonians make up the majority of the population of the country; the minority ethnic groups are composed of Albanians, Turks, Roma (Romany, Gypsies), Serbs, Vlachs, and Bulgarians. The country and its major cities are divided along ethnic lines. Most of the Albanian and Turkish population live in compact settlements in the northwestern part of Macedonia and along the border with Albania, as well as in the towns of Skopje and Kumanovo. The Roma, who are dispersed throughout the country, very often live in isolated and secluded areas.

The 1994 Macedonian census, conducted under international supervision, was marred by political problems and confrontations. In contrast to the censuses in developed countries, where the interest and the impetus is predominantly on economic, gender, and social issues, in Macedonia the conflict revolved around the number of members of the various ethnic groups in the country. In order to procure more rights, privileges, and financing for their followers (usually at the expense of others), the political leaders of the various nationalities deliberately inflated the numbers within their particular ethnic group. When the figures claimed by the political leaders of the ethnic groups were added together, the country found that it had at least twice as many inhabitants as actually existed.

The international community accepted the complaints of the Macedonian Albanians that the previous census was deliberately inaccurate and unjust. The European Union (EU) and the Council of Europe decided to monitor the 1994 population census closely and even finance it. Despite this heavy international involvement, the Albanians remained at odds with the government, and even abstained in certain counties from taking part in the census. The Kosovo crisis in 1999, which led to a rise in terrorist activities on the part of Albanian militant groups inside Macedonia, and continued interethnic conflict in Macedonia during the greater part of 2001, delayed the implementation of a new census until 2002 and the reporting of results until December 2003.

According to the 2002 census, Macedonia had 2,022,546 inhabitants. Of those, 64.18 percent were Macedonians, 25.17 percent were Albanians, 3.85 percent were Turks, 2.66 percent were Roma, 1.78 percent were Serbs, 0.84 percent were Muslims, 0.48 percent were Vlachs, and 1.04 percent belonged to "other" nationalities.

The figures for the Macedonians remained consistent throughout the second half of the twentieth century. In 1953 they represented 66 percent of the population. In contrast, the Albanians constituted only 12.4 percent of the inhabitants of the country. The people who declared themselves to be Turks represented approximately 16 percent of the population in 1953; many of them either left for Turkey or declared themselves Albanians in the years that followed. The other two main reasons for the rise in the Albanian population were natural increase and migrations. On the one hand, Albanians have a significantly higher birthrate than Macedonians. On the other hand, the breakdown of the former Yugoslavia left Macedonian borders open to uncontrolled immigration of Albanians from Albania proper, who in the wake of the 1997 state meltdown were looking for a more stable and prosperous environment. The uncontrolled influx of Kosovar Albanians into Macedonia resulted from the actions of the Yugoslav government of Slobodan Milošević, a nationalistic and overtly anti–Albanian regime in the late 1980s and throughout the 1990s.

The Macedonian population is relatively young: 25 percent of the inhabitants are less than fourteen years of age, while approximately 65 percent are over fourteen and younger than sixty-five, according to the 2002 census. The increasingly higher number of births among the Albanians, which makes its population the youngest in Europe, produces fear among the Macedonians that they will eventually become a minority within their own country. This situation only fuels the existing conflict between Macedonians and Albanians. The annual 1 percent population increase among ethnic Macedonians is quite low in comparison to North American and European standards, due to the high (though still not precisely measured) rate of permanent emigration of predominantly Macedonians to North America, Australia, and Europe. The infant mortality of approximately 16 percent is substantially lower than that found in many countries of the former Soviet Union; the relatively small number of fifty divorces per thousand marriages reveals that the patriarchal outlook and approach to family and social life present in Macedonia for centuries remains. The relatively low life expectancy—68 years for men and 72.5 years for women—reflects the relatively underdeveloped and overburdened health care system, as well as suggesting that the environmental and industrial problems in the country take a heavy toll on the lives of the people in the region.

HISTORY

The Republic of Macedonia has a lengthy historical and cultural heritage. Several archaeological sites confirm that the area has been inhabited from late Neolithic times. During the Bronze Age (1900–1200 B.C.E.), the Indo-European people settled in the area and gradually assimilated the existing population of the region. This period also witnessed a closer connection with the Mycenaean and Aegean societies in the Greek lands (which had developed earlier). The latter initiated a lucrative trade with the people living in Macedonia.

The principal inhabitants of the territory of the present-day Republic of Macedonia were the Paeonians, with their capital in Astibo (present-day Štip in eastern Macedonia), who are mentioned in Homer's *Iliad* as allies of the Trojans. Other tribes are mentioned in early sources, such as Dardanians in the northwest, some Illyrian tribes in the southwest, and some Thracians in the eastern parts of the present state. The fact that these groups, some of them organized in kingdoms, did not develop a literacy of their own, leaves the question of their ethnic affiliation, interrelationship, and origin subject to diverse interpretations. Some present-day nationalist movements in the Republic of Macedonia, as well as its neighbors, have attempted and indeed still make an effort to interpret the origins of these groups in accordance with their political and nationalistic agendas.

The Macedonian Language

Macedonian is the official language of the Republic of Macedonia. In addition, parts of the population in western Bulgaria and in Aegean Macedonia, the inhabitants of a number of villages in Albania and Serbia, and numerous immigrants in Canada, Australia, the United States, and Europe speak the Macedonian language.

Greece has prohibited the use of the Macedonian language both in private and public use, denying its existence and the existence of a Macedonian nationality. Parts of Bulgarian officialdom, some Bulgarian scholars, and part of the Bulgarian public still approach the Macedonian vernacular as a dialect of their own language. On the other hand, Greece published a primer for the Macedonian language in 1924, and Bulgaria allowed Macedonian to be taught in the schools of Pirin Macedonia in the period from 1946 to 1948. It has to be asserted therefore that Macedonian is a separate language, one that is spoken by approximately 2.5 million people.

Macedonian belongs to the group of South Slavic languages, which also includes Slovene, Serbian, Croatian, and Bulgarian. The spoken language of the Slavic tribes who settled in geographic Macedonia during the sixth and the seventh centuries provided the basis for the formation of the modern Macedonian literary language. Although Macedonia is a relatively small country, in the period before World War II the extremely difficult communication lines and outdated roads infested with gangs of robbers facilitated the isolation of the various localities, which were left alone to speak their local vernaculars. As a result, several dialect areas emerged, of which the most notable are the western and the eastern, as well as the northern, which cuts across the major east-west division. As a result of consistent governmental actions aimed at suppressing the Macedonian language, the distinctive dialects of the Macedonians in Greece and Bulgaria have not been much studied.

In the nineteenth and early twentieth centuries Macedonians attempted to codify their language and win its recognition, though, as a result of the specific political and social circumstances, they did not succeed. Partenija Zografski (1818–1876), Gjorgija Pulevski (1838–1894), and Krste Petkov Misirkov (1874–1926) were the most prominent representatives of this movement. Only with the formation of Macedonia as a federal unit of Yugoslavia in 1944 did Macedonians gain the right to use their language freely. Macedonian scholars developed the modern Macedonian literary language based on the dialects used in the central and southwestern parts of the Republic. Its official orthography is a modified Cyrillic alphabet that meets the phonetic needs of the language.

Macedonian shares with the other Slavonic languages a rich morphological system in which nouns are divided into three genders. As in the Bulgarian language, the case system has been entirely lost. In addition, Macedonian has been influenced by Turkish, Greek, and Albanian and contains sounds that are unique to literary Macedonian.

The name Macedonia comes from the Macedonians, who mainly inhabited Aegean Macedonia (now in northern Greece) and during the fourth century B.C.E. expanded their power over the tribes living on the territory of Vardar Macedonia, the present-day Republic of Macedonia. The court used Greek as its medium for keeping records and written communication. Their political, cultural, and social organization, however, was different enough from Greek ways that the Greeks labeled them barbarians, aliens, and intruders. The Macedonian kingdom, which reached its apogee during the reign of Alexander the Great (336–323 B.C.E.), gradually weakened, and finally became a province of the Roman Empire in 148 B.C.E. When the Roman Empire broke into its eastern and western parts in the fourth century C.E., Macedonia remained under the control of the eastern half of the empire (later known as the Byzantine Empire). The Byzantine emperors succeeded in controlling this province only until the seventh century, when numerous Slavic tribes started to move from the territory beyond the Carpathian Mountains in Eastern Europe into Central and Southeastern Europe.

In order to clarify what the Slavic tribes found when they arrived, it is necessary to look again at the period just covered. As mentioned above, the ethnic makeup of the ancient Macedonians is unclear. What is clear is that during the time of the domination of the Macedonian kings (the fourth to second centuries B.C.E.), the territory of the present-day Republic of Macedonia and its population, along with the population of Macedonia as a whole, came under the influence of Hellenistic culture. During the long period of Roman rule (from the second century B.C.E. until the fourth century C.E.) this region, bisected as it is by the important north-south Morava-Vardar passage from the Danubian lands to Thessaloniki, as well as by east-west routes between Asia Minor and Italy, experienced population migrations and the settlement of various ethnic groups in the area, including Romans and Greeks. Moreover, when the Macedonian Empire collapsed in 148 B.C.E., the Roman conquerors enslaved and displaced more than 40,000 local inhabitants. Macedonia truly became cosmopolitan and intermixed, as evidenced by the extremely diverse tombstones (*stellas*) of its inhabitants.

Cathedral of Stobi: Baptistery from the late fourth century C.E. Stobi, Republic of Macedonia. (Vanni Archive/Corbis)

The South Slavic tribes that settled in Macedonia during the seventh century initiated numerous ethnic, demographic, social, and economic changes. The Slavs became the dominant ethnic group, but they also came under the cultural, economic, and social influence of the native population. Some of the native population were assimilated by the Slavs; others immigrated to cities and areas that remained under Byzantine rule. Many towns ceased to exist, money was replaced with barter, the slaveholding system disappeared, and the agricultural system underwent significant changes. At the same time, the influence of the Byzantine Empire remained, as evidenced by the fact that the Great Church of Constantinople began to make inroads among the Macedonian Slavs, which eventually resulted in their conversion to Christianity of the Byzantine rite, the establishment of a Slavic alphabet, and the emergence of a rudimentary literacy among the population.

In the seventh and eighth centuries, the Slavs who lived in Macedonia were organized in loose tribal alliances, which gradually became dependent on a newly emerging Bulgarian state. During this period, a classical feudal order of the Byzantine type emerged in Macedonia. Its main characteristic, as in Western Europe, was the presence of strong feudal lords who controlled large territories and often claimed their independence from the central power. From the mid-eighth to the mid-ninth century, the Byzan-

tine Empire succeeded in checking the power of the Bulgarians and reasserting its control over Macedonia. In the times that followed, Bulgaria fought a number of successful wars against the Byzantine Empire and expanded into the greater part of the Balkan Peninsula. By the beginning of the last quarter of the tenth century, however, the Byzantine Empire had crushed the Bulgarians and temporarily become the undisputed ruler of Southeastern Europe. Several years later, the uprising of the young prince Samuel and his brothers in southwestern Macedonia fundamentally changed the situation in the Balkans.

The differences in the various historical accounts of Samuel, who ruled a short-lived kingdom centered in Prespa and Ohrid from 976 to 1014, reflect recent nationalistic controversies and scholarly discourses that have emerged in the scholarly literature of modern Macedonia and Bulgaria. The dispute focuses on Samuel's ethnic affiliation and the alleged nationality of his subjects. On one hand, scholars from the Republic of Macedonia tend to emphasize the cultural, social, and even linguistic distinctiveness of Samuel's kingdom. On the other, Bulgarian scholars emphasize the fact that Samuel used the Bulgarian name for himself and his kingdom and the beginnings of his career in southwestern Macedonia are rarely mentioned. Both approaches clearly aim to support present-day nationalistic claims and agendas. The Macedonians need

The so-called fortress of Emperor Samuel (ruled 976–1014) stands on a hill above the city of Ohrid, Republic of Macedonia. (Arthur Thévenart/Corbis)

this approach in order to demonstrate that they have long been a separate nationality with their own language and history; the Bulgarian interpretation, on the other hand, supports the claim that Macedonians are essentially Bulgarians by ethnic origin, as well as by cultural and linguistic characteristics. Both approaches are anachronistic. It is indeed difficult to speak about the national consciousness of a short-lived medieval ruler and his subjects and to discuss his impact on national development at a time when the majority of the population was illiterate and boundaries were fluid. Moreover, the only primary source that discusses the ethnic affiliation of Samuel asserts that he was an Armenian by origin. Bulgarian and Macedonian ethnic groups only began to acquire national consciousness in the nineteenth and early twentieth centuries. Only during the past century and a half have Southeastern European Slavs gradually begun to assert their nationality and unify around several urban centers. Thus, the national affiliation of Samuel can neither be determined nor could it be relevant to today's situation in the region.

In many aspects, Samuel was a typical medieval ruler who was primarily interested in maintaining and expanding his power. As such, he executed his only surviving brother and entered on a long period of expansion and conquest. It is most likely that Samuel perceived and proclaimed his state

as the heir to the recently defeated Bulgarian empire (enabling him to establish a degree of international recognition and respect). He successfully expanded his rule over the entire territory of Macedonia (except for the town and immediate vicinity of Thessaloniki). Moreover, Samuel gradually took over the formerly Bulgarian territory between the Danube River and the Balkan Mountains (Stara Planina), Thessaly, Epirus, present-day Kosovo, and southern Serbia, as well as parts of Albania. After the death of the previously captured Bulgarian emperor in a Byzantine prison, Samuel proclaimed himself emperor and probably received some confirmation of a princely title from the Church of Rome. His kingdom, however, was short-lived. In 1014 the Byzantine emperor Basil II defeated Samuel's forces at Belasitsa and inflicted a terrible punishment on the 14,000 captured soldiers. He blinded almost all and released them from his custody. The story is that Samuel died of a stroke caused by grief after the arrival of his blinded and defeated army at Prilep. By 1018, Basil II defeated Samuel's successors, triumphantly entered into the capital, Ohrid, and reasserted Byzantine control over Macedonia.

Overall, Samuel and his kingdom established an important legacy. Although it is clear that Samuel used the Bulgarian name for political purposes, he never sought to expand into Bulgaria proper, or transferred his state capital to the former Bulgarian capital, Preslav. His political interests instead focused on Macedonia, Albania, and northern Greece. In this regard, the Macedonian territories and Slav population around Ohrid and Prespa represented the core of Samuel's kingdom. Therefore, the social, cultural, and ethnic composition of this newly established state, as well as the political and territorial aspirations of its leader, significantly differed from similar political units established earlier in the region. In addition, Samuel's legacy was important in one more respect: the establishment of an independent (autocephalous) Christian ecclesiastical unit with its center in Ohrid.

Christianity played an important role in the development of South Slavic culture and society. The Byzantine rulers and their main partner, the Patriarchate of Constantinople, succeeded in converting the Macedonian Slavs to the Orthodox branch of Christianity. In contrast to the Church of Rome, which used only Latin throughout Western Europe, the patriarchate did not preach its doctrines and beliefs exclusively in Greek. The Byzantine clerics realized that the use of the local vernaculars would bring much better results among the illiterate Slavic tribes. To this end, in the middle of the ninth century, on the basis of the southern Macedonian Slav vernaculars, the Byzantine cleric Cyril and his brother Methodius invented the first Slavic alphabet, called Glagolitic. In honor of its founder, the simplified version of Glagolitic used later received and has retained the name Cyrillic.

While Cyril and Methodius worked in Moravia, several of their disciples went to Macedonia to evade the persecution of the Roman Church, which did not approve of the ecclesiastical use of non–Latin vernaculars. The most famous of them were Clement and Naum, who worked in Ohrid in the second half of the ninth and the beginning of the tenth centuries. They not only translated into Old Church Slavonic (the language of the Orthodox Church in the region, based upon the local Slav dialect around Thessaloniki and sometimes referred to as Old Bulgarian) numerous religious texts and composed homilies for ecclesiastical use, but they also established a school in which they taught basic literacy and theology in the local Slav vernacular. As a result, the population accepted Christianity relatively quickly and easily, and the religious roots of Christianity established in this way have run deep, withstanding the challenges of time and religious pressures. In contrast, the Albanian tribes, which lived in the area west of the Ohrid region, accepted Islam more easily, in the aftermath of the Ottoman conquest in the fourteenth and fifteenth centuries. It should be noted here that at this point there was no differentiation in the written vernacular among the South Slavic tribes, whether they lived on the territory of Macedonia, Bulgaria proper, Kosovo, or Moravia. Clement and Naum worked under the auspices of the Bulgarian autonomous and later autocephalous church, which was essentially a Slavic ecclesiastical institution.

The Ohrid archbishopric survived its founder Samuel for more than seven centuries, consistently enjoying a large measure of autonomy and independence. In 1767, however, the Ottoman government abolished it under pressure from

Macedonian Orthodox Christian believers light candles in front of the Saint Mother of God church, one of the many old churches and monasteries dotting the shores of Lake Matka near the Macedonian capital, Skopje. Thousands of Macedonians celebrate the Orthodox holiday Saint Mother of God. (AFP/Getty Images)

the Great Church of Constantinople, which wanted to increase its revenues and establish better control over the Christian Orthodox population in the Balkans.

In contrast to the situation in Western Europe during the Middle Ages, Byzantine and later Slavic ecclesiastical institutions were heavily dependent on the secular rulers and their decisions. Therefore, the establishment of an independent state was necessarily followed by the founding of independent, self-governing (autocephalous) churches, most often called patriarchates, metropolitan sees, archbishoprics, or exarchates. With the rise of nationalism in the nineteenth and early twentieth centuries, these churches, or the memory of them in areas in which they had previously been abolished, served to rally popular support for national movements.

Despite numerous external and internal challenges, in the period after Samuel's death, the Byzantine Empire succeeded in retaining control over Macedonia until the end of the twelfth century, increasing the taxes and exploiting the population to meet the demands of frequent wars. During the thirteenth century, the power of the Byzantine Empire started to dwindle; as a result, various independent feudal

The Macedonian Orthodox Church

In 2003 the Serbian Orthodox Church renewed its opposition to the Macedonian Orthodox Church, thereby negating Macedonian national identity through anti-Macedonian propaganda. The issue was whether Macedonians, who are predominantly Orthodox, have the right to have their own independent ecclesiastical organization. The archbishopric of Ohrid had had periods of independence, starting in the eleventh century, but otherwise the church in Macedonia was considered to be under the authority of other jurisdictions, especially the Serbian Patriarchate. The government of Yugoslavia insisted on the creation of the Orthodox Church of Macedonia after World War II, but only in 1967 did the governing body of that church formally (and unilaterally) separate from the Serbian Orthodox Church and become autocephalous (independent). In this way the Macedonian Orthodox population came to be led by their own indigenous prelates, who in turn were not subject to any kind of external power. The Orthodox Church in Macedonia acquired the right to choose its own bishops, as well as the head of the church, without any obligatory expression of dependence to another external body. Moreover, the Macedonian Orthodox Church gained the right to resolve all its internal disputes on its own authority.

Macedonian ecclesiastical independence is still not widely accepted; the Serbian Patriarchate has declared that the proceedings by which the Macedonian Orthodox Church asserted its full independence were against canon law, and the patriarch of Constantinople has agreed. The Serbian Patriarchate has always been opposed to any kind of independence for the church in Macedonia, but in 1959, under pressure as some say from the communist government of Yugoslavia, which wished to strengthen Macedonia and weaken Serbia, the Serbian church's governing body recognized a separate Macedonian Orthodox Church, autonomous, but not autocephalous. The Serbian patriarch was still the head of both churches. Serbian bishops consecrated Macedonian bishops, and the Macedonian Orthodox Church began to function. When the new church petitioned the Serbian Patriarchate for autocephalous status in 1966, the request was rejected, and when the new church went ahead and unilaterally proclaimed its own autocephaly, the governing body of the Serbian church declared it schismatic and broke all ties.

Those who criticize the actions of the Macedonian Orthodox Church accuse it of not following Orthodox canon law and of being influenced by political motives. Those who take the other side argue that in fact the church is really following Orthodox tradition. Every independent Orthodox nation has had its own autocephalous ecclesiastical entity. In this way, the Orthodox people have had the opportunity to shake off external cultural and political attempts aimed at assimilation. The process of granting autocephaly has always involved the interference of the secular authorities (in the beginning, the Byzantine emperor) and has followed the establishment of new borders. The medieval Serbian church (and later the Serbian Patriarchate) in the thirteenth and then again in the fourteenth century unilaterally declared its own autocephaly. During the nineteenth century, state and national leaders used the Orthodox Church in the Balkans for their political and national goals. Thus it can be argued that the Serbian refusal to grant autocephaly to the Macedonian church is more against the accepted practices and rules of Orthodox Christianity than anything the Macedonian Orthodox Church has done.

The clash between the Macedonian and the Serbian church was exacerbated in 2003. The Serbian church offered to recognize the Macedonian church if it would accept autonomous status, but Macedonians refused to accept a widened autonomy in the framework of the Serbian church; rather, they perceived the Serbian approach as a denial of Macedonian nationality and a return to the nightmare of the nineteenth-century struggle for the partition of Macedonia and the attempts to impart a Serbian national identity to the Christian population of Macedonia. As a countermeasure to the Macedonian refusal, the Serbian church appointed a parallel, pro-Serbian set of prelates, who were young and devoted to the Serbian cause in Macedonia; the Serbian ecclesiastical organization empowered these prelates and their supporters to Macedonia to convert the population to its agenda. For Macedonians, the actions of the Serbian church have tarnished the reputation of Orthodox Christianity in the area, and as a result an increasing number of people have converted to other forms of Christian worship. The friction, which seemed to contradict the very essence of Orthodox virtues, such as patience, understanding, and compassion, is another sign that relations in the region can be frayed, even by that which should bring people together.

lords, the Crusaders, the second medieval Bulgarian empire, and the newly emerging Serbian Nemanjić dynasty fought for control over Macedonia. The frequent wars over the territory exhausted the population and its wealth. The situation somewhat stabilized during the first three-quarters of the fourteenth century, when Serbia and its feudal lords ruled the area. Then, with the defeat of the Serbians at Maritsa in 1371 and Kosovo in 1389, Macedonia came under direct Ottoman rule.

The Ottoman Empire governed Macedonia for over five centuries, a period in which the social, ethnic, and cultural situation in the region fundamentally changed. The major impact of Ottoman rule on Macedonia was that the area became much more ethnically and religiously diverse, in a way that was greatly influenced by the establishment of a special type of government called the *millet* system.

In order to establish better control over its new territory, the Ottoman government encouraged Turkish settlers to come to Macedonia. As a result of the constant influx of settlers, governmental officials, and army soldiers, Muslims of diverse ethnic origin came to outnumber Orthodox Slavs in the towns, though not in the countryside. There was also a steady immigration of Jews and Roma (Gypsies) into the area. In addition, the authorities encouraged (although not forcibly) the process of conversion of the indigenous Macedonian Slav population to Islam. Many nobles, as well as peasants, accepted the new religion in order to retain or improve their social and economic standing; for example, taxes were lower on Muslims than they were for Christians. For all practical purposes, the Slav population that converted to Islam identified itself with the ruling classes and did not acquire a national consciousness until the late nineteenth and early twentieth centuries. (The attempts by the present-day Macedonian governments to discourage the identification of the Slavic-speaking Muslims with the Turks, or in some cases, the Albanians, has had an adverse effect on the country and has even led to the emigration of some of the affected population.) By the end of the nineteenth century, Macedonia had approximately 1,715,000 people, including 746,000 Muslims, 929,000 Christians, and 40,000 Jews. Moreover, in addition to modern Macedonian, part of the Christian population had developed Greek, Bulgarian, or even Serbian national consciousness.

To return to the Ottoman Empire and the position of the Slav population under its authority, it is important to emphasize that the framework within which Orthodox Christians functioned under Ottoman rule was called the millet system. This term refers to a specific political, sociocultural, and communal institution based on religion. The millet system was based on the Islamic belief that Roman Catholics, Orthodox Christians, members of the Armenian Apostolic Church, and Jews are People of the Book. As a result, the Ottomans granted them protection in return for the acceptance of a subordinate status and payment of a poll tax. In legal terms, the Ottoman state made a perpetual contract with these various non-Muslim groups, which was automatically revoked when the contract was breached. The religious institutions, with their hierarchies, functioned as the representatives of their faithful before the state. Ottoman sultans granted its Orthodox subjects extensive cultural self-rule in perpetuity without being subject to renewal or limitation. After the abolition of the Orthodox Archbishopric of Ohrid in 1767, the Patriarchate of Constantinople established direct and undisputed jurisdiction over the entire Orthodox population in Macedonia.

The millet system had a profound impact on Macedonian communities. The isolated localities were the main units of this type of organization; they acted at the same time as a religious congregation, social community, and administrative entity. Moreover, the extremely difficult communication lines, outdated roads that were infested with gangs of robbers, and often ineffective bureaucracy further contributed to the isolation of the villages, which were left to exist on their own, according to their own customs.

Life for Orthodox Christians was most difficult during the eighteenth century, when the Ottoman Empire experienced a weak central government and a rise in lawlessness. Rural brigands and robbers posed a constant threat for the population and in some cases jeopardized major centers like Bitola and Ohrid. The local rulers governed and taxed the population at will. Under these circumstances, inhabitants had to rely on their internal community's unity to safeguard their lives and property. Although the central government in Istanbul (Constantinople) began to reassert its power in the provinces in the second quarter of the nineteenth century, many of the old attitudes and habits remained. Even in the early twenty-first century, small gangs of robbers still operate in the countryside, especially in the western part of the independent Republic of Macedonia. Consequently, one could argue that the particular organization of the millets could be credited with the preservation of the cultural, religious, ethnic, and linguistic identity of the various Christian groups, even up to the present.

At the beginning of the nineteenth century, it was clearly the Orthodox Church that governed the social and religious life of its followers in Macedonia. Its clergy was sharply segregated into several categories. Real power was in the hands of the prelates, who were most often Greek by origin and who constituted an integral part of the Ottoman bureaucratic and revenue system. The hierarchs, also primarily of Greek ethnic background, enjoyed the right to appoint, dismiss, tax, and punish the clergy in their eparchies. The metropolitans and bishops, who also enjoyed the right freely to tax the population, focused their activities on collecting the revenues they needed for repaying the levies to the Ottoman state, for repaying debts encountered in the process of ascension in the ranks of the ecclesiastical hierarchy (bribery was endemic in the church in the eighteenth and nineteenth centuries), and for a comfortable living. Ottoman officials and certain local lay notables, guided by financial interests, assisted them in this process. The parish priests and monks, on whom the state did not bestow any administrative or representative rights, originated mainly from the localities in which they served. By their lifestyle, dress, and education, this stratum of the clergy was virtually indistinguishable from the lay inhabitants, and it shared their fortunes. The prominent local lay members, and not the lower clergy, managed the greater part of the church possessions in their communities. The local churches and monasteries served as savings and credit unions and generated profits. The prelates received a part of the profits from the ecclesiastical establishments, and the remaining part was channeled toward various communal and social endeavors.

During the first centuries of Ottoman rule, the peasants made their living by working on their small plots of land, or on the holdings of the cavalrymen (sipahi) and their descendants who held fiefs. The Ottoman government undertook land reforms beginning in 1831, in which the landowners lost control over the process of tax collection, the main source of their income. In the wake of the new state ordinances and actions, the fief holders had to derive their main revenues from the core holdings, called čiftliks, which were primarily cultivated by landless peasants. The čiftliks, for their part, being small and having been long neglected, furnished little profit. The Ottoman government imposed further restrictions on sipahis' exercise of power over their tenants by prescribing a 10 percent maximum for the tithe on the peasants who worked on sipahis' land. As a result of these changes, in addition to the decrease in grain prices after the Crimean War (1853–1856) and a series of bad harvests, the Muslim owners started to leave their landholdings, selling them to the peasants and local Christian notables.

The socioeconomic changes that took place in the course of the second and third quarters of the nineteenth century disrupted the traditional way of life and distribution of power. The early stages of national awakening among the Macedonian Slavs were related to the general process of cultural and economic modernization in the Ottoman Empire, as well as to the specific Macedonian communities themselves. The enactment of new land laws, a tariff system, and export and import conventions, along with the gradual tightening of state control over isolated and self-contained communities, resulted in the gradual disappearance of the influential craftsman class and in the decline of the influence of the Muslim landowners and the local Christian notables.

At the same time, a modernized entrepreneurial class emerged, winning substantial wealth through the export-import trade, tax farming, and extending money on credit; it was organized into factions held together by commercial and family ties. Certain financial cliques, comprised of merchants of Slav origin whose profits depended on trade with the Slav peasant population, came under the economic sway of the far more developed Bulgarian commercial and national groups from Istanbul and Bulgaria proper. The local commercial competitors of these entrepreneurs were the Hellenic cliques, composed mainly of ethnic Greeks, as well as Hellenized Vlachs and Albanians. The Hellenic factions controlled far greater wealth, relied closely on the Greek commercial circles in Europe, Athens, and Constantinople, and formed stable financial relations with the prelates, with whom they shared a common language and culture. As social and economic modernization progressed, the financial factions composed of merchants of Slav origin who used the Slav vernacular in their homes and commerce, and who depended economically on the Bulgarian entrepreneurs,

started to perceive the Byzantine Greek used in the ecclesiastical services and the Greek language and culture of their commercial competitors as parts of an alien and hostile element in their midst.

The local Slav businessmen attempted to create an alternative public realm, which would correspond to Western European bourgeois developments. They needed this public sphere in order to voice their individual political, economic, and social perceptions and concerns, to form a clear public opinion on various issues, and to represent these opinions to officials for their own benefit and for the benefit of the state. In contrast to the Western European experience, however, the public sphere in Macedonia was first created in the ecclesiastical domain, through the transformation of the existing legally recognized ecclesiastical bodies and the formation of affiliated organizations. The church-building process mobilized the Slav Orthodox public, fostered communal self-organization, established a feeling of self-respect and local identity, and facilitated the formation of viable, responsible, and democratically organized parish committees in almost every urban and village community. These informal bodies, controlled by the entrepreneurs, worked toward the formation of a literate public, which in turn was one of the main prerequisites for the formation of public institutions. By the beginning of the 1870s, almost every Slavic-speaking community had a modern secular primary and in many cases secondary school for boys and girls. At the same time, reading and social clubs, as well as charitable organizations, appeared in the main urban centers. Yet the revenues from ecclesiastical property and the donations of the local wealthy merchants were insufficient to sustain the newly formed Slav educational and cultural institutions. Moreover, the local Slav businessmen did not have the resources to establish the printing presses that would provide the pupils with textbooks and the general public with newspapers, journals, and monographs.

Therefore, in order to complete the process of establishing a viable Slav public life, and to open new avenues for fostering social modernization, local entrepreneurs attempted to take full control of the property and rights of the church and to manage the election of the prelates. In the period before 1878, almost every Macedonian community attempted to take over the local church establishment. In this way, all the resources available through the church could have been used toward the development of schools, cultural institutions, and various social organizations and endeavors. Moreover, the hierarchs would have become sincere advocates of local social and economic interests before Ottoman officials. The Great Church of Constantinople, however, unable to adjust to the changes in the communities, attempted to preserve its medieval social rights by suppressing by force any modernizing tendencies.

The members of the Ottoman bureaucracy, who originated from a different culture and ideology, possessed neither the power nor the will to support the prelates effectively against the population. Therefore, in order to retain their fiscal and social powers, the prelates sought the assistance of the members of the Hellenic factions. These factions, in turn, came under the influence of the Greek national movement, which sought to incorporate the Slavs into its national entity and the territory of Macedonia into its national state. Both sides therefore found a common cause in suppressing the emerging elements of a Slavic public life and discourse. As a result of the lack of a medieval, pre-Ottoman historical heritage bearing any specific Macedonian name, the Orthodox Slavs of Macedonia instead used the Bulgarian and Serbian national labels to safeguard their local vernacular as well as their way of life, while at the same time distancing themselves from the Greek language and culture propagated by the prelates and the members of the Hellenic factions.

As a result of strong opposition from the prelates and the Hellenic faction, the economic weakness of the emerging entrepreneurial class, the small numbers of intellectuals, and an insufficiently organized and mobilized public, the Slav residents of Macedonia were unable to take over the ecclesiastical domain and to complete the process of public sphere formation. In addition, Macedonia did not have an economically, socially, and intellectually powerful Slav center that could organize, unify, and channel the actions of the Macedonian localities. Moreover, Macedonia occupied a central position in European Turkey, being left without direct contact with Western, Central, and Eastern Europe. Consequently, all the relevant foreign influences came to the area through Serbian, Bulgarian, and Greek channels. In order to produce the desired change, the Macedonian Slavs had to turn toward these external factors for assistance, and beyond that, toward the Catholic Church.

During the 1850s and 1860s, Serbian institutions, as well as Bulgarian organizations from Constantinople and Bulgaria proper, responded to the pleas of Macedonian residents and began to dispatch the required printed materials, financial support, and teachers to the region. In contrast to the objective of the Macedonian Slavs, who wanted to foster the process of public sphere formation, Serbian organizations and the Bulgarian National Circle aimed at bringing a Serbian or Bulgarian national consciousness to the Macedonian Slavs. Because Macedonian entrepreneurs depended economically and commercially on the far wealthier and more nationally conscious Bulgarian businessmen from Bulgaria proper and Constantinople, Bulgarian organizations and activities gained greater influence among the residents of Macedonia. Meanwhile, France, and later Austria, with the intention of exercising influence in the internal affairs of the Ottoman Empire, supported attempts by certain Macedonian communities to enter into church union with Rome, as a counterforce to Greek influence through the office of the patriarch. In the early 1870s the Macedonian communities hoped that through the Bulgarian Exarchate, which was a product of the Bulgarian national and social movement, they would accomplish their goal.

It became clear by the mid-1870s, however, that these external entities—the Bulgarian national movement, the Bulgarian Exarchate, the Serbian Principality, and the Catholic Church—were failing to assist the Macedonian Slavs in the process of taking over the ecclesiastical establishment and creating a viable public sphere. As a result, the Macedonian residents attempted to create that sphere in their communities by using entirely their own resources. As had Orthodox Slavs from Bulgaria proper, Macedonian notables and intellectuals attempted to form a distinct Macedonian church, independent from both the patriarchate of Constantinople and the Bulgarian Exarchate. In the mid-1870s, for the first time, a separate Macedonian movement organized by Macedonian communities, with its center in Veles, attempted to beat the odds and produce the desired change and formation of a distinct Macedonian church.

This movement built on the ideas and actions of a small group of indigenous intellectuals, who noticed the linguistic and cultural differences between the areas of their origin and activity and those of the populace of Serbia and Bulgaria. They promoted the vernacular and culture of the Macedonian Slav communities, and even came up with a theory of the separate historical development and identity of the Macedonian Slavs. For example, in 1868 Kuzman Šapkarev asserted that among the inhabitants of western Macedonia "nobody, from the youngest to the oldest," knew the Bulgarian vernacular that originated in eastern Bulgaria (Šapkapev 3). What is more, according to Šapkarev, many inhabitants, because of local patriotism and self-respect, refused to learn and use the Bulgarian vernacular. Approximately a decade later, Giorgija Pulevski stressed that "a nationality are the people *(luge)* with the same ethnic origin, who speak the same language. . . . In this regard, Macedonians are a nationality *(narod)* and their place is Macedonia." Pulevski further declared that "our fatherland is called Macedonia, and we are named Macedonians" (Pulevski 81–97). For him, the language of this area was Macedonian, which belonged to the family of the Slav languages and had equal standing with Russian, Croatian, Bosnian, Serbian, Polish, and Bulgarian.

Thus, in the process of attempting to complete the formation of a viable public sphere, a number of Macedonian Slavs became more and more aware of their linguistic and historical distinctiveness. They voiced the idea that they were a separate national entity, which should bear the name Macedonian. Although the advocates of a separate Macedonian church and Macedonian nationality were few, and although they failed to accomplish their program, they did show that the idea of Macedonian distinctiveness could appeal to the population; and thus they planted the seeds for future national developments.

Moreover, in the period of the late 1870s, the Macedonian population and its leaders started to combine political, cultural, and military struggle in order to improve its situation. Several insurrectionist movements paralleled the Russian military advance into European Turkey in 1877 and 1878 (during the Russo-Turkish War of 1877–1878). The Razlog (1876) and Kresna (1878–1879) rebellions, which took place in eastern Macedonia, followed the pattern of a series of revolutionary movements in the Balkans against Turkish rule. The 1875 insurrection in Bosnia-Hercegovina precipitated the Serbian-Turkish war of 1876, and the April 1876 uprising in Bulgaria paved the way for Russian intervention in the Balkans. The intervention of the great powers in Balkan affairs resulted in the rise to arms and demands for independence of a significant portion of the Macedonian Slav population; however, Macedonia in its entirety remained under Ottoman control, while Bulgaria proper gained limited independence in 1878. During these rebellions, many of the leaders came to a clear understanding of the complexity and unity of the Macedonian ethno-geographic territory, the concept of an autonomous Macedonia, and elements of a separate national consciousness. Moreover, they recognized Macedonia as an area with an ethnically mixed population, in which different beliefs and cultures should be equally appreciated and respected. Accordingly, the manifestos and proclamations of the leaders of these insurrections addressed all ethnic communities and emphasized common goals of modernization, justice, and equality.

The national awakening of the Macedonian Slav populace, which had started in the first quarter of the nineteenth century, took a divergent path following the economic turmoil in the Ottoman Empire in the 1870s, the Russo-Turkish war of 1877–1878, and the formation of the autonomous Bulgarian Principality in 1878. During the 1870s, fiscal crisis, government bankruptcy, and the Russo-Turkish war produced famine and hindered international trade in the Ottoman Empire. The 1892–1896 economic depression and fall of industrial output in Europe diminished the West's need for raw materials and agricultural products. Moreover, after 1870, the increased involvement of Western capital in the Ottoman Empire brought into being various credit unions and banks, including the state-funded Agricultural Bank, which started to extend loans. This situation undermined the financial standing of the Macedonian local entrepreneurs, who based their wealth on the export of agricultural goods and money lending. As a result, the social stratum that had facilitated change in the local communities began to disappear. At the same time, the main political goal, indeed the obsession, of the new Bulgarian principality established in 1878 became the incorporation of Macedonia and Thrace into its national and state framework. This policy marked the beginning of the "Macedonian struggle," since Greece, Serbia, and even Romania also had expansionist ambitions in this area.

At the same time, the Slav Macedonian intelligentsia began to leave Macedonia on a huge scale. This was the result of direct pressure from the Ottoman authorities, who perceived the members of the Macedonian intelligentsia as potential dissenters and instigators of popular revolt. This process was further facilitated by the lack of any prospects for advancement, change, and better conditions of life in this part of the Ottoman Empire. As recent research has indicated, out of the 959 people in Macedonia who could be identified as intellectuals, only 111 remained after 1878 (and of these, only 7 had some level of higher education). The others left their homeland for good. In the years that followed, their places were taken by people sent and paid for by the Bulgarian principality, the independent kingdoms of Greece and Serbia, or in some cases even Romania. The main task of these newcomers was to encourage the linguistic and cultural assimilation of the Macedonian Slavs. These occurrences in the early to mid-1870s marked the end of the early stages of the national awakening process of the Macedonian Orthodox Slavs.

However, it did not mark the end of the process. The members of the Macedonian intelligentsia who lived and worked outside Macedonia came under the influence of diverse national ideas and movements. Some of its members not only developed Macedonian national consciousness, but also started to propagate their ideas among other Macedonian immigrants and the representatives of the great powers. They formed a number of cultural societies, which contained in their name the term Macedonia. These organizations, mainly centered in Bulgaria, Serbia, and Russia (but also in other European capitals), argued for the liberation of Macedonia and canvassed economic, political, and social support for this cause. This process included the formation of the Macedonian Scholarly and Literary Society in St. Petersburg in 1902 as the kernel of Macedonian national endeavors; it formulated a succinct strategy for national liberation. Moreover, in the period from 1903 to 1905, the first book and the first journal in the modern Macedonian language and orthography emerged, as well as the first textbooks for the projected Macedonian schools.

Meanwhile, within Macedonia, the formation of a secret national liberation organization, known as the Internal Macedonian Revolutionary Organization (IMRO), or by the generic name of the Macedonian Revolutionary Organization (MRO), introduced a more radical approach in the national struggle. Formed in 1893, this organization, at its congress in 1896, clearly defined its goal of full political autonomy or independence of Macedonia, to be acquired through a revolution of the people in Macedonia. The Christian Slav population formed IMRO's principal membership base. Like all secret organizations, IMRO established a clear hierarchical structure and started to collect the necessary military and economic means for the achievement of its task. At the same time, Greek, Serbian, and Bulgarian organizations that started to operate in Macedonia with the ultimate goal of annexing this Ottoman territory for their prospective states greatly hindered and influenced IMRO's activities.

In effect, the Greeks feared the possible connections of an autonomous Macedonia with Bulgaria and worked against IMRO and the rebellion. As a result, the August 1903 Ilinden-Preobraženski Uprising was not only badly prepared and premature, but was also left without any external help. Although the insurgents were poorly equipped, untrained, and outnumbered, they scored a number of initial successes in the Bitola, Adrianople, and Salonika regions. Despite those successes, the Bulgarian state and church were unable to support the uprising, the Greeks fought against it, and the great powers were not willing to interfere in the internal affairs of the Turkish state. As a result, the Ottoman regular army, despite its own weaknesses, swiftly and easily crushed the rebellion and enacted a set of humiliating reprisals that victimized especially women, children, and the property of the Christian Slavs. More than 5,000 people were killed, and 70,000 were left homeless.

Macedonian insurgents, ca. 1912. From the late 1800s through the Balkan Wars (1912–1913), such groups as the Internal Macedonian Revolutionary Organization fought against the Ottoman rule. (Library of Congress)

After the rebellion, the great powers, especially Russia and Austria-Hungary, came under pressure to push the Ottoman state to initiate a number of reforms in Macedonia. The Mürzsteg reforms, which called for foreign control over the Ottoman police, internal administrative delineation along ethnic lines, and financial support to the victims of the rebellion in Macedonia, were never fully enacted. Instead, Macedonia became the playground of Bulgarian, Greek, and Serbian efforts, each nation hoping to achieve decisive influence among the Christian Slav population and prepare the grounds for future annexation.

The problem remained that there were too many parties interested in the partitioning of Macedonia; the territorial appetites of the interested parties were too large to allow all of them to be accommodated. At first there was an agreement among Bulgaria, Serbia, and Greece to attack Turkey and partition its remaining European territories, among which the greatest part was Macedonia. In the first Balkan War (1912), this coalition was very successful: Turkey was pushed almost entirely out of Europe. However, the division of the spoils was not as easy a task. In the summer of 1913, the inability of the partners to resolve their differences led to the breakdown of their comradeship and to another war, this time with Bulgaria against Greece, Serbia, Romania, and even Turkey. This second Balkan War ended swiftly with the defeat of Bulgaria (sanctioned at the Treaty of Bucharest in August 1913). The treaty clearly outlined the partitioning of Macedonia; the greatest part, Aegean Macedonia (which constituted 50 percent of the whole), was allotted to Greece. Bulgaria, as the defeated party, gained only 10 percent of the land, the so-called Pirin Macedonia. Serbia gained, in addition to Kosovo, the Sandjak, and numerous

territories in present-day southern Serbia, the remaining part of Macedonia, Vardar Macedonia.

In this period, as the Macedonian scholar Blaže Ristovski has asserted, an authentic Macedonian movement, plagued by a so-called dualism, started to take clear shape. The encroachment of foreign nationalistic propagandas resulted in a split among the Macedonians. Some of them began to express their individuality by labeling their language a "dialect" of the Bulgarian vernacular, and their national denomination became "Macedonian Bulgarians." In the same way, Greek and Serbian cultural, political, and social actions in Macedonia produced the birth of similar labels among other indigenous intellectuals. Yet some leaders of the Macedonian movement always envisaged and continued to argue for the establishment of a separate, independent Macedonian entity, which would exist in a federal or confederation framework. The most prominent Macedonian leaders continued to harbor the idea of the distinctiveness of the Macedonian people, for which they were branded "separatists."

In March and June 1913 two Memorandums for the Independence of Macedonia were submitted to the Russian government; these asserted that "Macedonia should remain a single, indivisible, and independent Balkan state within its geographical, ethnic, historical, economic and cultural borders." During World War I, similar efforts on the part of Macedonian societies and organizations continued to mount. In 1917, in Russia, the Macedonian Revolutionary Committee produced a democratic program that advocated the formation of a Balkan federation that would include not only Serbia, Bulgaria, and Greece, but also Macedonia as a separate and equal political and territorial entity. Macedonians approached not only the Russians for help, but also the representatives of the Paris Peace Conference in 1919 with the same pleas. Unfortunately, attempts by the Macedonian immigrants to influence the European and Balkan powers in their decision-making process did not produce the desired results.

Instead, the Paris Peace Conferences sealed the partition of Macedonia among Serbia, Greece, and Bulgaria. In this regard, the pro-Bulgarian branch of IMRO, which supported the inclusion of Macedonia in "Greater Bulgaria," continued to play an increasingly important role in the Vardar and Pirin part of the territory. Its leaders initially declared that the aim of the organization remained the same as before: winning freedom, in the form of autonomy or independence, for Macedonia within its ethnic and economic borders. Using Pirin Macedonia as a base, IMRO became a powerful armed force that initiated a number of incursions into Vardar Macedonia and even Aegean Macedonia. The results were disastrous—the population in Macedonia found itself not only subject to the terror of IMRO but also oppressed by the Serbian and Greek authorities, who cracked down on the region.

At the same time, the Serbian and Bulgarian governments began a forced colonization of their newly acquired territories. In Vardar Macedonia, thousands of Serbian agricultural colonists received lucrative plots of arable land, while the population of Macedonia was left without adequate sustenance. The Serbian government allotted farms to its colonists by appropriating the land of the Turkish population (which gradually started to leave the country due to a rising fear of oppression). The Serbian language was introduced into the schools, and the Macedonian name, vernacular, and culture were banned and suppressed. In the interwar Yugoslav Kingdom, Slav Macedonians were destined to become "South Serbians." The Serbian state employed all possible means to implement its goal.

In the period from 1919 to 1941, Greece adopted several approaches aimed at eradicating the presence of the Slav population from its newly acquired territories. In 1922 Greece compelled the defeated Bulgarian state (Bulgaria had been an ally of the Central Powers in World War I) to sign a Convention for the Exchange of Population. In other words, as there was not a significant number of Greeks in Bulgaria, ethnic cleansing was implemented in Greek Macedonia. Greece simply expelled the Slav population from its new territorial acquisitions in the Balkans. The Western allies, looking to forget the horrors of the war and move on, turned a blind eye to Greek actions. As a result, more than 100,000 Slav Macedonians were forcefully relocated to Bulgaria; their property was confiscated, and they left their ancestral homes as refugees. Greece initially toyed with the idea of providing certain rights to the Slav minority. To this end, a primer in the Macedonian language was printed for the needs of the Macedonian children in Aegean Macedonia. But the Greek government rejected the idea and withdrew the primer before it reached the schools. In addition, Athens resettled more than half a million ethnic Greeks who had fled from Turkey in Macedonian lands. The remaining Slav Macedonians were declared Slavophone Greeks who had to learn again their paternal Greek language and culture, forgotten in the times of Slavic "occupation" of the area (a policy that remained in force in Greece for decades).

The only international organization that accepted the Macedonians as an independent, separate, and distinct national entity was the Communist International (Comintern). In 1934 its Executive Committee approved a motion that recognized Macedonians as a separate nationality with their own language and distinct culture. This document furthermore charged that the partitioning powers were determined to suppress and eradicate any expression of Macedonian national individuality in order to carry out their expansionistic plans. It asserted the continuity of Macedonian national development and provided the Macedonian national movement with a new international dimension, which in turn led to the codification of the Macedonian vernacular and the establishment of an indigenous literature.

The full circle of the Macedonian national development and affirmation was completed at the First Session of the Anti-Fascist Assembly of the National Liberation of Macedonia (ASNOM) on 2 August 1944. But first, following German expansion into the Balkans in April 1941, Vardar Macedonia was divided between Bulgaria and Italy, with the former occupying four-fifths and the latter one-fifth of the territory. In fact, however, the armed struggle of the Macedonian people against the fascist regimes took place on the entire Macedonian territory, namely in Pirin, Vardar, and Aegean Macedonia. During 1941, a number of Partisan detachments were established as a part of the Macedonian National Liberation Army. By 1943, certain free territories had been created, mainly on the territories occupied by Italy. In October 1943 the first Allied (British) Military Mission visited the liberated territories in western Macedonia, which represented the first international recognition of the Macedonian national liberation movement. By the end of the war, the Macedonian National Liberation Army numbered over 56,000 soldiers. More than 25,000 Macedonian recruits were killed during the war. A complete system of government was created on the liberated and semi-liberated territory, which together with the Liberation Army represented the foundations of the modern Macedonian state.

On the basis of the inviolable, permanent, and inalienable right of the people to self-determination, the establishment of the modern Macedonian state was proclaimed at the First Session of ASNOM, held on 2 August 1944. The Macedonian state was established only on the territory of Vardar Macedonia; Aegean and Pirin Macedonia remained integral parts of Greece and Bulgaria respectively. The assembly passed a number of resolutions in which ASNOM was proclaimed the supreme legislative and executive national representative body; the Macedonian language was proclaimed the official language of the Macedonian state; and the citizens of Macedonia, regardless of their ethnic affiliation, were guaranteed all civil rights, as well as the right to their mother tongue and faith.

ASNOM actually marked the beginning of the legal and constitutional existence of Macedonia as a constituent and integral part of the Yugoslav federation. At the outset, the Macedonian state bore the name Democratic Federate Macedonia. After the proclamation of Yugoslavia as a Federal People's Republic at the session of the Constitutional Assembly of Yugoslavia on 29 November 1945, the Macedonian state adopted the name People's Republic of Macedonia. This name was also established in its first constitution, adopted by the Constitutional Assembly of the People's Republic of Macedonia on 31 December 1946. In accordance with the constitution of 7 April 1963, the name was changed to the Socialist Republic of Macedonia. On 7 June 1991, the Macedonian National Assembly passed a constitutional amendment deleting the designation "Socialist" from the state's name and thus created the present name of the country: the Republic of Macedonia. During this period, the Macedonian people further strengthened their national identity, and the Republic of Macedonia obtained broad international affirmation and recognition. The modern world accepted the reality of the existence of the Macedonian people and its state within the framework of the Yugoslav federal community. However, this situation existed only in Vardar Macedonia.

The situation was markedly different in Aegean Macedonia, which remained under Greek control. By the end of 1944, at the moment of the liberation from the German occupation, Greece stood in need of a new constitutional, social, and national order. The factions that vied for political influence over the state promoted their particular agendas with an exclusiveness and mistrust that destroyed any chance for genuine compromise and reconciliation. The Partisan movement, which had gained significant respect among the population for its guerrilla actions against the German occupiers during the war, was to a great extent controlled by the Communist Party (KKE). It was, however, effectively disarmed, pursuant to the Varkiza agreement of February 1945. This enabled the right-wing forces to gain the upper hand, bring the king back to the throne, and start a political persecution of the pro-Soviet elements. The dissatisfaction on the part of the leftist Partisan leaders, a part of the population, and the repressed Slav Macedonian minority, resulted in an insurrection that led Greece into a bloody and lengthy civil war. By the end of the summer of 1949, the hostilities had ended with the defeat of the communists. During the conflict, and especially during its last stages, tens of thousands of people fled from Greece, ending up as refugees in Yugoslavia, Albania, and the countries of the former Soviet bloc. A unique phenomenon occurred during the exile of the population: over 25,000 children were separated from their families and transported across the borders into the neighboring countries, many of them later scattered throughout other Eastern European countries and the Soviet Union. In the aftermath of the Greek Civil War, many others emigrated to Western Europe, North America, and Australia.

Mass evacuation, as a deliberate part of military strategy during the conflict, was used first by the monarchist side. Its purpose was to cut off the insurrectionists, led by their military organization, ELAS (People's Liberation Army), from its sources of food and to make recruiting more difficult for them. This policy was feasible because the monarchists controlled enough relatively safe areas in which the refugees could be temporarily housed. They also started forcibly to gather children under the guise of saving them. These children were then sent to various regions in Greece (particularly the Greek islands). By April 1947, approximately 14,500 children had been separated from their parents. The details of the actions of the monarchist government and the fate of the children taken into its custody are mostly unknown; the Greeks withheld all information, and the United Nations never investigated the matter.

By late 1947, the civil war in Greece had entered its most intense phase. Incessant Greek monarchist army attacks focused heavily in the frontier region where the Slav Macedonian minority lived. Scores of children died of malnutrition, disease, and injuries. However, ELAS did not control an area within the frontiers of Greece where any large number of refugees could be accommodated. The extreme difficulty in providing adequate supplies for the soldiers as well as for the general population was a powerful argument for evacuating the most vulnerable and least useful individuals. In this regard, some action was called for to save the children in the war zone from its hardships.

Toward the end of 1947, ELAS made an appeal to the governments of the people's republics in Eastern Europe and the Soviet Union to offer refuge, at least on a tempo-

rary basis, to the children from the increasingly exposed areas of Aegean Macedonia. A commission was established for this purpose, composed of cultural and educational officers from the resistance organizations. Not surprisingly, a Slav Macedonian, Lazo Angelovski, was its director. The members of this body visited the villages under the control of the ELAS and acquainted the population with its mission. Parents were asked to volunteer for the program of evacuation of minors. It was agreed that children under the age of three years should stay with their mothers, while the rest should be moved from the war zone to the countries of East Central Europe and the Soviet Union. Parents who agreed to be separated from their offspring confirmed their participation by signing formal agreements.

According to statistics published by the United Nations, which relied on documents prepared by the United Nations' Special Committee on the Balkans (UNSCOB), between 25,000 and 28,000 children left Northern Greece in 1948–1949 and were resettled in various Eastern European countries. And children were not the only ones who sought safety in the countries controlled by communist regimes. The total number of refugees from Greece that fled into the Soviet bloc surpassed 100,000. As a result, both the parents and their children ended up as displaced persons, though often in different camps and countries. The UNSCOB report confirms that the villages with a Slav Macedonian population were in general far more willing to let their children be evacuated. Their decision was guided by the experiences of the past, when various Greek governments attempted to assimilate them, employing brutal police force to accomplish this task. At the same time, the willingness of ELAS to recognize the national rights of the Slav Macedonian population, establish schools in their Slav Macedonian vernacular, and provide a certain level of local self-government caused the members of this ethnic group to join the ranks of the Liberation Army. In addition, ELAS effectively controlled only parts of northern Greece, where the Slav Macedonians represented a clear majority. Therefore, the majority of children sent to the countries of the Soviet bloc had a Slav Macedonian origin and spoke their native Slav vernacular.

The Greek Civil War and its effect upon the Macedonian Slav population in many ways represent a microcosm of the political and ideological clashes that after World War II marked not only Greek and Balkan history, but the history of the Cold War world as well. Children affected in different ways by the war found themselves in the center of the ideological struggle. They became the victims of the complex conflict in Greece and remained the most vulnerable long after the cessation of military operations in 1949.

Yugoslavia, which strongly supported the attempts by the communist-led ELAS to overthrow the monarchy, was instrumental in the process of evacuating the children to the countries of the Soviet bloc. Only Yugoslavia and Albania had an effective territorial contact with the areas in Greece controlled by the Liberation Army. As a way of fulfilling humanitarian and internationalist obligations, Yugoslavia accepted children who were transported to its territory from the rebel areas. It accepted around 11,000 children, 2,000 of which were placed in homes specially established for this occasion. Of the ten special homes, most were in Serbia (primarily in Vojvodina), Croatia, and Slovenia. The Yugoslav Red Cross managed these institutions, which in the early postwar years (which were accompanied by frequent famines and political instability) barely met the most basic living standards. The remaining 9,000 children were placed in families in Macedonia. At the same time, over 14,000 children were transported through Yugoslav territory to the various East Central European countries. In addition to the 11,000 individuals who remained in Yugoslavia, Albania harbored 2,000, Bulgaria 2,660, Hungary 3,000, Poland 3,000, Romania 3,801, and Czechoslovakia 2,235.

It is extremely difficult to trace the destinies of the refugees in all these countries. Part of the problem in the past was the closed archives, both in the former members of the Soviet bloc and in Greece, as well as the animosities between the various players. The United Nations, in October 1948, called for the reunification of the displaced victims with their parents. As frequently happens with the decisions of this organization, the practical results of the UN declaration were few and insufficient, because the problem was not purely humanitarian or nonpolitical. In addition, the lists of the refugee children were assembled in haste and were often mixed and misplaced during the transport, while their ages caused difficulties in the process of finding reliable information about the parents. Greece, which most vehemently insisted on the repatriation, often supplied misleading data. Consequently, the repatriation process, which was strongly supported by Yugoslavia in the early 1950s as a result of its break with the Soviet bloc in 1948, had meager effects: less than six hundred children were reunited with their families in Greece by the end of 1952, though the process did continue in the following years.

The overwhelming majority of these minors remained in exile. In the light of existing political tensions, even today it is almost impossible to track their lives and wanderings. The destiny of the ones who remained in Yugoslavia was at first influenced by the Tito-Stalin split. The children who stayed in the foster homes controlled by Belgrade were exposed to an ideology in which the principle of "socialist pedagogy" was applied. They were drawn into the conflict about their nationality and language. Their teachers, influenced by the decisions of the Greek Communist Party, accepted the Stalinist arguments during the breakdown in relations between Yugoslavia and the Soviet Union in 1948. As a result, Yugoslavia expelled them, replacing them with ideologically and politically loyal instructors. The existing division between the refugees of Slav and Greek ethnic background, the removal of their former instructors, the abysmal living conditions, youthful frustration, and disappointment with their position now produced a wave of revolts in the foster homes. The children demanded to be transferred to other Eastern European countries loyal to the Soviet Union, expressing support for the communist cause in its Stalinist form. The Yugoslav State Security Police (UDB) suppressed these insurrections.

With the improvement in relations between the countries of the Soviet bloc and Yugoslavia in the mid-1950s, several hundred of these refugees, who had by now come of age, started to move, curiously enough, toward the colonies of Greek expatriates in Tashkent and Alma Ata in the Soviet Union, as well as to Romania, Czechoslovakia, Bulgaria, and Hungary. It seems, however, that many of them continued to live in their new countries, graduated from various schools, found jobs, married, and fitted in more or less successfully to their new surroundings.

Some of them, it is known, continued their emigrant odyssey. By the 1970s, hundreds of individuals from the countries of the Soviet bloc had moved into the Republic of Macedonia, a federal unit of the Yugoslav federation; the more relaxed political climate in Yugoslavia proved to be an attractive magnet for the refugees. Disillusioned by the Soviet experience, a number of young adults who had earlier moved to Tashkent now came to Macedonia. Many of them used this opportunity as a first step to move to the West. For example, more than 550 child refugees of Slav Macedonian descent moved to Australia. Still, the question remains why the majority of the displaced persons went to the Republic of Macedonia and did not return to Greece, even after the latter declared and enacted full amnesty in the early 1980s. The problem was that the Greek state denied repatriation of the ethnic Slav Macedonians to their homes and the right to reclaim their citizenship and property. (In 1982 and again in 1985, the Greek parliament passed several laws that allowed only political émigrés who were "Greek by origin," that is, ethnic Greeks, to return and regain their possessions.) This official attitude of Athens mobilized the émigrés to demand the recognition of their ethnic and minority rights by the Greek government.

The plight of the Macedonian refugees in many respects is a metaphor for the struggle for Macedonian independence. If World War II began the process of the end of colonialism and the development of national self-determination, for Macedonians this development required the end of another conflict, the Cold War. Only then could an independent Macedonian political entity become a reality. Until then, "Macedonia" remained divided between Yugoslavia, Greece, and Bulgaria, with no completely independent state bearing the name. Only in Yugoslavia did a Macedonian political unit exist (as one of the republics in the Yugoslav federation), but, fittingly, it was one of the least important and most overlooked regions in the Yugoslav state. It was not until the 1990s that a national anthem, composed in 1943 by Vlado Maleski, a poet from Struga, and later adopted as the anthem of the Yugoslav Macedonian republic, truly proclaimed Macedonia's independence.

Denes nad Makedonija se ragja	Today over Macedonia
Novo sonce na slobodata,	A new sun of freedom rises,
Makedoncite se borat	Macedonians fight
Za svoite pravdini,	For their rights,
Makedoncite se borat	Macedonians fight
Za svoite pravdini!	For their rights!
Odnovo sega znameto se vee	Now once again flies

Na Kruševskata Republika	The flag of the Kruševo Republic,
Goce Delčev, Pitu Guli,	Goce Delèev, Pitu Guli,
Dame Gruev, Sandanski.	Dame Gruev, Sandanski.
Goce Delčev, Pitu Guli,	Goce Delèev, Pitu Guli,
Dame Gruev, Sandanski!	Dame Gruev, Sandanski!
Gorite Makedonski šumno peat	The Macedonian woodlands sing brightly
Novi pesni, novi vesnici,	New songs, new awakenings.
Makedonija slobodna	Free Macedonia
Slobodna živee!	Lives free.
	Free Macedonia lives free.

POLITICAL DEVELOPMENTS

The gradual collapse of SKJ (Communist Union of Yugoslavia) and the slow and painful disintegration of Yugoslavia, along with the rapid democratization process in Slovenia and Croatia, influenced the democratic processes in the Republic of Macedonia. The SKM (Communist Union of Macedonia) simply had no choice but to step down voluntarily and to agree not to be the sole politically organized force in Macedonia. In less than six months, from March to September 1990, more than thirty political parties and movements were established in Macedonia. Their membership, with rare exceptions, consisted of Macedonians only. However, it was quite obvious that most of the thirty political parties in the upcoming first free elections in 1990 would just be part of the decor. It furthermore became apparent that ethnic Macedonian votes would be divided among three political parties: SKM (Communist Union of Macedonia); SRS (Union of Reform Forces), a pro-Yugoslav party led by the last and most popular Yugoslav prime minister, Ante Marković; and VMRO-DPMNE (Internal Macedonian Revolutionary Organization–Democratic Party of Macedonian National Unity). The only question was how many votes each of these parties was going to win.

It seemed clear that these Macedonian parties would win the first parliamentary elections in Macedonia, but they were scarcely united among themselves. The majority membership of VMRO advocated an independent Macedonia throughout the whole period of the campaign. The basis of their election program was the constant emphasis on their cause of making the Republic of Macedonia the state of the Macedonian people. SKM took the opposite side on the issue, advocating the preservation of the Yugoslav federation, but with serious amendments to the Federal Constitution in favor of the republics (with special attention given to democratization of foreign policy). The members of the sole Yugoslav party in Macedonia, SRS, also advocated the preservation of the Yugoslav federation, with special attention given to strengthening the market economy in Yugoslavia and canceling barriers between the republics.

The Albanian portion of the population established two political parties (the Democratic Prosperity Party and the National Democratic Party). The National Democratic Party never managed to develop into a serious political force; it created a coalition with PDP (the Democratic Prosperity Party). This coalition sent a clear and serious message that the Albanian sector, through political homogenization, would make an attempt to achieve a significant presence in the first Macedonian parliament in order to achieve its program objectives.

The behavior of the leadership of PDP should be seen within the context of the overall relations in the Albanian political movement within the territory of federal Yugoslavia. Kosovo, whose population was preponderantly Albanian, and which had for a time experienced a degree of autonomy within the Yugoslav federation, was until 1998 controlled by a Serbian state that implemented repressive methods against Albanians. The clash between Serb and Croat interests in Bosnia-Hercegovina, together with the oppression of Bosnian Muslims, seemed to suggest that the Serbs would not allow any rights to its minorities. These two developments, along with the long-standing Serb desire to control the Vardar Valley, made Macedonian Albanians feel that if Macedonia remained in a Serb-controlled Yugoslavia they would be discriminated against. They also feared that the Macedonian majority would oppress them. Therefore, Albanian politicians in Macedonia chose to advocate a separate political identity in Macedonia; this new Albanian state would be called "Illyrida." This advocacy was interpreted by part of the Macedonian population as a sign of disloyalty toward the Republic of Macedonia.

The verbal political propaganda and the terminology used in the pre-election period, as well as the events that took place in the other Yugoslav republics, especially in Bosnia-Hercegovina, had a direct impact not only on Macedonian-Albanian relations in the Republic of Macedonia, but also on the relations within the Macedonian political parties. The closer the time came for voting, the more obvious it became that the Albanians would only vote for the coalition of PDP and NDP. While the Albanians experienced a growing unity, the division and degree of mutual animosity within the Macedonian ethnic block, between SKM and SRS (which advocated a federalist option) and VMRO (which advocated full separation), gradually increased.

Given that a majority vote was required to win in these elections, the results of the first round of voting were not surprising. In the predominantly Albanian areas, the unified Albanian party was able to win a majority and gain seats. In many of the predominantly ethnic Macedonian areas, no candidate won a majority. The result was that in the first round, the Albanian party, the PDP-NDP, actually won a majority of the seats that were decided in that round.

Where no one won a majority (that is, in the ethnic Macedonian areas), generally either SKM or SRS candidates came in first, with VMRO either second or third. It thus seemed obvious that even VMRO's powerful rhetoric had not resulted in serious inroads in city and rural areas. At the same time, it is clear that it was not only party affiliation that influenced voters in the first round; the personalities and roles of the candidates were also very significant. SRS and SKM selected candidates who were prominent doctors and directors of the biggest enterprises in the districts in which they stood for election. Due to the structure of its membership, which mainly consisted of people left on the margins of society and repressed throughout the whole communist period, VMRO did not have candidates who could stand on an equal footing with the candidates from the other two leading ethnic Macedonian parties. That contrast also suggests the serious economic interests that lay behind the political struggle. The idea of an independent Macedonia implied restructuring the communist class structure, which the ruling elites wanted to avoid doing. Still, in ethnically mixed environments such as Macedonia, economic and social interests often have less impact on citizens and their voting practices than other factors. The results from the second round were an indication of this.

What had the most impact on the voting in the second round was the victory of the Albanian coalition in the first round. The arrival of an Albanian on a white horse celebrating the victory of the PDP in the streets of Tetovo in predominantly Albanian western Macedonia brought Macedonia to the brink of civil war. Ethnic Macedonians were horrified by the power that seemed about to be won by what they saw as a separatist party and were almost ready to join in a war to defeat this threat to the unity of their state. Moreover, the results from the elections in Bosnia-Hercegovina, where the national parties had won and the SRS party and the Communist Party of Bosnia-Hercegovina had been defeated, influenced the outcome of the elections in Macedonia by greatly strengthening the cause of independence. After the second round, VMRO acquired a plurality of the seats in the parliament, a total of thirty-eight. In addition, SKM acquired thirty-one, PDP-NDP twenty-three, and SRS twenty-five.

Despite this marked increase in votes for VMRO, the results of the election indicated very clearly that the majority of ethnic Macedonians still saw membership in the Yugoslav federation as the most secure way of balancing interethnic relations and maintaining acquired benefits. Regardless of how hard VMRO-DPMNE tried to create the illusion that it was the sole protector of the interests of the Macedonian ethnic group, still many did not hold it to be very reliable. VMRO-DPMNE's occasional use of warrior rhetoric could not compensate for its disadvantages, such as the lack of human resources for handling (even with violence) the impending Albanian danger (as they typically referred to it).

Even with strong factors in their favor, the allocation of seats in the first free multiparty parliament indicated clearly that the pro-Yugoslav forces were not in a position to impose their political will, although together they had a plurality of seats in the unicameral parliament (56 out of 120). They not only had to form a coalition between themselves, but they then had to form another coalition, either with the Albanian political block or with VMRO-DPMNE, in order to form a government. At the same time, VMRO-DPMNE found itself in a situation where the only suitable partner for creating a coalition was the former Communist Party (SKM), whose members were less inclined to keep Macedonia in the Yugoslav federation than SRS. For VMRO-

DPMNE, any coalition relationship with the Albanian political block or with SRS would have meant abandoning their own political platform completely. As a result, the difficulty of forming workable coalitions was such that a situation was created in which it seemed that all relevant political forces had to forge a minimum mutual understanding in the interest of the stability of the Republic of Macedonia and the security of its citizens.

After the presidential elections, all political parties supported the idea of forming an "expert" government. The idea was a failure, as this government was supported by everybody and nobody; it did not survive the passing of the new constitution a few months later. Moreover, the main issue was not settled: whether Macedonia would declare its independence or remain in the Yugoslav federation.

The proclamation of independence on the part of the Republics of Slovenia and Croatia in 1991, in addition to the resulting military conflicts in the northern and western parts of the former Yugoslav state, pushed the Republic of Macedonia toward declaring independence. The federalists (SKM and SRS) in the Macedonian parliament, the largest political bloc, had no more arguments at their disposal to confront the pressures from the separatist VMRO-DPMNE. The delay in coming to a decision to hold a referendum on independence was simply a tactic for winning time to define the contents of the referendum question in order to preserve political positions. By peaceful and democratic means, Macedonia asserted its independence from the Yugoslav federation during the period between January and November 1991. This process may be seen as having occurred in three stages: the promulgation of the Sovereignty Declaration in January 1991 by the newly constituted and democratically elected parliament; the holding of a referendum on independence in September 1991; and the establishment of a new constitution in November 1991.

The January declaration generally stipulated that in case the problematic issues among the six republics in the Yugoslav federation remained unresolved and were further aggravated, or the sovereignty of Macedonia was jeopardized, the republic would declare independence. During the September referendum, attended by 75.74 percent of the electorate, 95.26 percent supported this decision. The results from the September 1991 referendum clearly indicated that most of the citizens of the Republic of Macedonia saw their future in an independent state. The fifty-year political (and at times repressive) conflict between the federalists and the separatists was finally concluded with victory for the latter. Attention was then directed toward the constitutional regulation of the Republic of Macedonia. Due to the ethnic structure of the population, this issue was even more significant for the internal stability of the country.

The Albanian political parties, both in the parliament and on the referendum, refused to support the independence of the Republic of Macedonia. Their rationale was very simple: they would not support an independent Republic of Macedonia without guarantees that in the new state they would not be second-class citizens. Their stance led to new, even harsher political struggles. It was very obvious that VMRO-DPMNE would make the Macedonian language and culture dominant and exclusive in the new state, while minority rights would be suppressed. On the other hand, the Social Democratic Party of Macedonia (SDSM, as the formerly communist SKM was now known) and SRS, in accordance with their own objectives, advocated a nonnationalistic constitution. This position did not attract much support from ethnic Macedonians. It also was not enough for the Albanian political bloc in the coalition, which was demanding that the Republic of Macedonia be defined as the State of the Macedonian and Albanian Peoples and calling for the use of both languages at all levels in the Republic of Macedonia.

As the Macedonian parties were unable to meet the Albanian requirements for support, there was no chance of concluding an agreement between SDSM, SRS, and PDP-NDP and obtaining the necessary two-thirds majority for passing the new constitution (as the existing laws required). As a result, the Macedonian political parties, one way or another, had to find a way to cooperate with each other in order to adopt a constitution that would reflect a compromise; and they did. The Albanian political parties simply were given the choice of either accepting or refusing the compromise that resulted. In essence, the compromise brought a modern civic constitution that asserted the dominant role of the Macedonian language and culture in society. Unlike VMRO-DPMNE (which accepted the compromise with a sinking heart), PDP-NDP did not participate in the voting.

Regardless of how much justification there was for such a decision, this move did not improve the interethnic relations in the Republic of Macedonia. Moreover, it was an act that was remembered and brought forward in any subsequent dispute between the Macedonians and Albanians. It also provided the Albanians with political fodder and justification for their armed insurrection in 2001. In effect, the refusal on the part of the PDP to support the referendum and the constitution initiated the process of political erosion that erupted in a violent conflict ten years later.

The adoption of the first democratic constitution that defined the Republic of Macedonia as a state of its citizens marked the third step in the nonviolent political transformation of the country. The road to establishing the first political government was open, especially since in the phase of adopting the constitution it became apparent that both SDSM and SRS had gradually developed a closer relationship with each other, as well as with the leading Albanian party. Another important factor in making it possible to establish a government was the nature of the man who held the position of president. Seasoned former federal Yugoslav politician Kiro Gligorov was able to acquire the personal support of the parliamentary groups of the former federalists, as well as the favor of most of the members of the Albanian parliamentary group, and so to arbitrate the establishment of the first political government. His shaping of a political parliamentary majority composed of SDSM, the former SRS (now renamed the Liberal Party), and the small socialist party, as well as the Albanian political parties, assured a politically stable government and gave additional power to the personal position of the president vis-à-vis the

Portrait of Macedonian president Kiro Gligorov, in Skopje. (AFP/Getty Images)

parliament. Thus the role of President Gligorov was crucial in the political development in the country; he continued to play a crucial role during the second multiparty elections in 1994.

In the 1994 elections, the coalition built by Gligorov was in the end completely victorious, and the opposition parties, especially VMRO-DPMNE, contributed to the coalition's victory by boycotting the second round of elections. International observers did not support the opposition's claim that the ruling parties had tampered with the results of the first round. Accordingly, the results from the elections were validated, and the second parliament of the Republic of Macedonia was formed without an opposition. The consequences of this situation have continued to be difficult to overcome. The absence of the opposition from the parliament enabled concentration of power in the hands of a small party elite composed of the former federalists. Constitutional violations, bribery and corruption, and numerous financial scandals, along with the already established system of patronage and blatant nepotism, made it more difficult for the Republic of Macedonia to move on with the critical process of becoming integrated into Europe. Even more

Kiro Gligorov

Just as Krste Petkov Misirkov's life illustrates the wanderings of Macedonian intellectuals and the challenges that they met at the turn of the twentieth century, the life of Kiro Gligorov, the first president of the independent Republic of Macedonia, embodies the national and ideological pressures that the Macedonian people had to endure through the course of the twentieth century.

Gligorov was born in 1917 in Štip in Vardar Macedonia, a territory controlled by the Bulgarian military at the height of World War I. In 1918 his town became a part of the newly formed Kingdom of Serbs, Croats, and Slovenes (later renamed Yugoslavia). Gligorov finished high school in Skopje and university in Belgrade. After graduation, he returned to Skopje to work as an attorney for a bank. With the outbreak of World War II, he found himself again in territory annexed by Bulgaria.

His star began to rise with the fall of the Bulgarian fascist regime and the communist takeover of Yugoslavia. He participated in the antifascist struggle during World War II, as well as in the most important meeting in modern Macedonian history: the antifascist Assembly of the National Liberation Movement of Macedonia (ASNOM). In 1944–1945 he became a member of its Presidium in charge of finances. Gligorov further elevated his status by becoming a member of the antifascist Assembly of the National Liberation Movement of Yugoslavia (AVNOJ), the governing body of the communist-controlled federal state. In the years that followed, he was assistant general secretary of the federal Yugoslav government (1945–1947), assistant minister of finance (1952–1953), and federal secretary of finance (1962–1967). At the beginning of the 1970s, he was elected as a member of the Yugoslav presidency (1974–1978), and as president of the Yugoslav federal parliament. In 1978 his signature sealed the last Yugoslav constitution, which led to decentralization of the federal state, to the transfer of power to the hands of local communist bosses and leaders, and finally to the dissolution of the former Socialist Federal Republic of Yugoslavia (SFRY). He then gracefully retired for the next twelve years.

As elected president of the Macedonian state in the period from 1991 to 1999, Kiro Gligorov masterfully orchestrated the peaceful separation of the republic from the crumbling Yugoslav federation. He is to be credited with the fact that Macedonia became the only part of the former federation to acquire full independence without bloodshed, without conflict with the Serbian-controlled army. Moreover, his cunning diplomatic skills brought international recognition of the new republic and its admission to the United Nations, despite the Greek campaign aimed at undermining and isolating the new Macedonian state. He also steered Macedonia away from the internal conflict that plagued much of the former Yugoslav state. In October 1995 an assassination attempt was made on his life with the aim of destabilizing Macedonia. The bomb killed his chauffeur, but the seventy-eight-year-old president survived the attack (although he lost an eye as a result of the blast). He resumed his functions, then withdrew from political life in 1999. He recently published his memoirs. In many polls, he is still the most popular politician in the country.

The importance of Kiro Gligorov in maintaining stability in Macedonia seems underscored by the troubles that have befallen the country since he retired in 1999—although perhaps he cannot escape all responsibility, since he did not use his power to address the underlying problems when he was in office.

importantly, these problems prevented any significant foreign investment of the kind that was instrumental in the development of many Eastern European countries. Moreover, the coalition government utterly failed to resolve the ethnic tension between the Macedonians and Albanians.

As a consequence, the conflicts between the government and the Albanians multiplied and intensified. The main Albanian parties were participating in the government as equal coalition partners, but a separate Albanian party emerged that advocated the resolution of the main unresolved grievances. The pro-government media portrayed this party as a radical anti-Macedonian warmongering party, a counterpart of VMRO-DPMNE, which was going to push the country into a civil war. The third free multi-party elections were

fast approaching, and the government's propaganda machinery intended to send a message to the electorate that the only way to prevent the events of Bosnia from spreading to the Republic of Macedonia was to keep in power the former communists and federalists.

Several months before the third parliamentary elections, a new political party formed, led by the last Macedonian representative of the former Yugoslav presidency, Vasil Tupurkovski. Members of the old communist apparatus who had not participated actively in the political life of the country since 1990 became Tupurkovski's closest political collaborators. Because Tupurkovski was associated with the former Yugoslav federation, this new political creation was acceptable to an electorate that had traditionally supported the former federalists. VMRO-DPMNE joined Tupurkovski, and in this way softened its image as a radical party, making it also more acceptable to the electorate. For the first time, the Macedonian public had strong coalitions that presented two political options: former communists and new nationalists. An even greater pre-election surprise was the public announcement by VMRO-DPMNE that it would not try to impose ethnic Macedonian nationalism. In their official party programs, as well as in the campaigns of the party leaders, the new coalition members expressed agreement with a liberal approach to individual and collective human rights. As the electorate was tired of the nepotism and corruption of the government parties, it accepted the Tupurkovski–VMRO-DPMNE coalition with a renewed hope for change. As a result, in the third parliamentary elections, the ruling parties were ousted from power; most importantly, the new Albanian party joined Tupurkovski and VMRO-DPMNE in forming the new cabinet. This peaceful transition, especially given the presence of the new Albanian party in the victorious coalition, was a very clear sign that the citizens of the Republic of Macedonia had managed to win three big victories in less than ten years of peaceful transformation. They had resolved the conflict between those who wanted to remain part of a larger Yugoslavia and those who wanted independence, and they had embraced peaceful, legal means of interethnic conflict resolution.

Despite the people's high hopes, however, the new coalition failed to keep its promises; the new leaders started to rule the country like a medieval fiefdom. The new coalition partners' pursuit of fast financial enrichment, together with the de facto division of Macedonia into an Albanian and a Macedonian part, ruled by the governmental Albanian and Macedonian parties respectively, disillusioned an electorate that had overwhelmingly expected positive changes and an end to corruption. Despite this division of the country, interethnic tensions did not improve. Rather they became so serious that an actual civil war resulted in Macedonia. These tensions remain the most serious problem faced by the Republic; accordingly, the war and its causes and results will be discussed in the final section, "Contemporary Challenges." The result of the failures of the Tupurkovski–VMRO-DPMNE coalition, which consistently blamed the former communists for all its problems, was their total defeat in the fourth parliamentary elections in 2002. Tupurkovski's party vanished from the political scene, and VMRO-DPMNE received less than two dozen seats in the 120-member parliament. Their Albanian coalition partner shared their fate. After the election, SDSM came back with a vengeance, imprisoning and persecuting the leading figures of the defeated opposition parties.

At the same time that the difficult internal process of shaping a democratic political future for the state unfolded, the matter of Macedonian independence became an international issue that threatened stability in the region. In the midst of the crisis in Southeastern Europe, under exceptionally difficult circumstances, Macedonia was the only republic from the former Yugoslav federation to have gained independence without bloodshed. Yet the country immediately found itself in the unenviable position of having failed to gain full international recognition, even though its independence was widely acknowledged and its borders were not disputed. After a protracted period of diplomatic struggle, described in what follows, Macedonia was accepted as a member of the world community. However, a number of foreign relations issues remained unresolved, which still render the international standing of this newly independent state fragile and problematic.

To understand this international aspect of Macedonia's problems, it is essential to go back to the first stages of international involvement. The inability of the members of the Yugoslav federation to find a peaceful solution to their problems was recognized by the European Community (EC) Council, which on 16 December 1991 in Brussels declared that the European Community and its members agree "to recognize the independence of all Yugoslav Republics" (Türk 73). The Council further appointed a special commission, under the presidency of Robert Badinter, which had to examine the claims of the Yugoslav republics to independence and present an assessment before 15 January 1992. On the basis of the ruling of this commission, the EC committed itself to recognizing the "successful applicants" from the former Yugoslav federation. For its part, the Macedonian assembly, with its Declaration of 19 December 1991, asked for full international recognition. On 6 January 1992, the assembly also promulgated two constitutional amendments that explicitly renounced any future territorial aspirations. These amendments were aimed at reassuring Greece that Macedonia had no intention of creating problems among Greece's Slav population. Moreover, after the signing of the February Agreement between the Macedonian government and the former Yugoslav army, Yugoslav troops had left the republic by 15 March 1992. On the basis of the political, social, ethnic, and juridical situation in the republic, the Badinter Commission declared on 11 January 1991 that Macedonia met the requirements for full international recognition.

In its meeting on 15 January 1992, however, the EC, despite its solemn declarations and commitment to the rule of law, did not follow the recommendation of the commission; it failed to recognize Macedonia as an independent state. Greece, a member of the European Union (EU), represented the main impediment to the recognition of the republic, claiming that this state had usurped the name Macedonia, which rightly belonged to Greek heritage and could not therefore be used by other countries. This southern neighbor of Macedonia demanded as a condition for its recognition of the new state that the republic refrain from using the name Macedonia, either internally or externally.

The part Greece has played in the controversy over what the Republic of Macedonia should be called has its origins in both foreign and domestic considerations. In Greece, where economic decline has rendered people generally more receptive to intensified chauvinistic rhetoric, nationalists, curiously enough led by the foreign minister, Andonis Samaras, decried the adoption of the name "Republic of Macedonia" by the new state to the north. A groundswell of popular anger grew in Greece, and the prime minister,

Constantine Mitsotakis, faced a political crisis in 1991 as a result. He evidently chose to adopt the nationalist line in order to preserve the government. Gradually he became more moderate, a change in orientation that was probably given impetus by adverse world reaction to the Greek position, and perhaps the realization that a confrontation on this issue could have devastating consequences not only for Macedonia, but for Greece and the Balkans as a whole.

For the Macedonians in the republic, the question of the country's name was directly tied to national identity. In the heat of their nationalist and anti-Greek fervor, the Macedonians adopted signs and symbols that the Greeks associated with their national heritage. Among them was the emblem that in 1992 formed the centerpiece of the Macedonian republic's flag: a motif from a casket found at the site of Philip of Macedon's grave in Vergina. Moreover, a number of articles in the Macedonian press asserted that the modern Macedonians were in fact descendants of the ancient Macedonians, and thus Alexander the Great.

Greeks feared that the next step in such an argument would be the claim that what was Alexander's—namely, northern Greece—should belong to today's Macedonians. The government of Macedonia, however, stood firm in its repudiation of any irredentist design on Greece. Greeks also feared Macedonia's potential for stirring up irredentist yearnings among the Slavic-speaking minority in northern Greece, whom the Greek government officially called Slavophone Greeks, and whose ethnic, national, and human rights had been violated in the aftermath of the Greek Civil War. The Greeks' fears were puzzling, both to Macedonians and to a number of foreign political scientists. How, they asked, could a landlocked country with an ethnically and linguistically mixed population of approximately 2 million people, which at the same time was economically impoverished and without an army and military equipment, jeopardize the ethnically homogeneous Greek state of 10 million people, a member of the EU and NATO?

Nevertheless, Athens successfully lobbied against recognition of Macedonia by the European Community and the United States. No EU member challenged Greece on the Macedonian issue, thus preserving an aura of solidarity in the Western alliance. Under strong Greek pressure, the EU position was officially laid out in the Lisbon Declaration on 27 July 1992, when the EU foreign ministers declined to recognize Macedonia until Greek demands were met. Denial of recognition left Macedonia, the poorest of the former Yugoslav republics, ineligible for critically needed financial assistance from world organizations, including the International Monetary Fund, the European Bank for Reconstruction and Development, and the World Bank. Moreover, the economic embargo imposed by Greece's unilateral closure of its border with Macedonia, as well as the UN sanctions on rump Yugoslavia (Serbia and Montenegro), left Macedonia, a landlocked state, on the brink of total economic, social, and political collapse. Furthermore, the Lisbon Declaration brought despair and disorientation to the Macedonian politicians and people. In those circumstances, the center of power in the republic, and especially foreign relations, gradually shifted toward the

president, Kiro Gligorov. It was he who guided the country along the sometimes tortuous path to international recognition. Gligorov actually became the central figure who managed to keep the ship of state afloat, without serious internal upheavals.

Fearing the total breakdown of the country in the aftermath of the Lisbon Declaration, Gligorov became extremely adept at his pursuit of recognition and needed international aid. His recurring theme was that Macedonia had gained its independence peacefully and legally, had stayed out of the wars of Yugoslav succession, had secured interethnic peace, had carried out democratic and economic reforms, and had fulfilled the conditions for recognition laid down by the EU and the Conference on Security and Cooperation in Europe. He repeatedly pointed out that Macedonia renounced territorial claims on other states, proclaiming that the Republic did not wish to interfere in the internal affairs of its neighbors. Gligorov also stated that he was willing to enter into a bilateral agreement with Greece, guaranteeing the inviolability of borders and establishing friendship and cooperation. At the same time, he shifted the country's external efforts toward the admission of Macedonia into the United Nations, an organization that did not function in the same unsympathetic manner as the EU and where the Western European supporters of Macedonian recognition had more space for diplomatic maneuvers.

The conciliatory assertions of the president and, even more importantly, the mounting instability in Southeastern Europe placed the Western European countries in a difficult position. They realized that an unstable Macedonia could open the door to old irredentist territorial aspirations on the part of Albania, Bulgaria, Greece, and Serbia. The Western European countries needed to decide whether withholding recognition of Macedonia would create another Bosnia, or worse, and whether granting recognition would begin a process of Balkan healing by enabling the nascent country to receive financial aid and thus have an opportunity to establish some degree of economic stability. Having been scarred by the Bosnian example, European and U.S. politicians were understandably worried. As a result of the peaceful and pragmatic diplomacy of the Macedonian president and the concern about peace in the region, France, the United Kingdom, and Spain decided to break the deadlock between Greece and Macedonia by finding a temporary solution with a compromise name.

On 8 April 1993 Macedonia was finally admitted to the United Nations under the temporary name "the Former Yugoslav Republic of Macedonia" (FYROM). After its recognition by the United Nations and subsequent incorporation into a number of international financial institutions, Macedonia began to show signs of cautious optimism. Moreover, with the outbreak of civil war in Bosnia and Croatia, Macedonian diplomacy succeeded in convincing the UN that an international protective force, which would prevent the spillover of the Yugoslav war, needed to be positioned in Macedonia. In the winter of 1993, 700 international peacekeepers and 300 U.S. soldiers, under the auspices of the UN, were assigned to the Macedonian border with Serbia and Albania. This deployment of troops further strengthened the international acceptance of the republic.

Still, the main barrier to Macedonian recognition remained: Macedonia's dispute over its name with Greece. The Greek position significantly influenced the EU as well as the UN and NATO countries in their dealings with the Republic of Macedonia throughout most of 1993. In November of that year, however, the patience of the Western European democracies ran out. Germany and the UK broke ranks and lobbied EU members to grant Macedonia full recognition before Greece was to take over the rotating EU presidency on 1 January 1994. Greece was enraged, and diplomatic relations among EU members became strained. On 1 December 1993, Greece again voted against Macedonia's membership in the Conference on Security and Cooperation in Europe. Two weeks later, on 16 December, Germany, the UK, Denmark, and the Netherlands announced that they had initiated a process to grant Macedonia full recognition. France and other EU countries followed their lead. Macedonia and Greece were now under pressure to find a workable solution to the issue.

During the following twenty months, Macedonian diplomacy was focused on finding some kind of solution with Greece, which was still blocking the attempts of the republic to obtain wider incorporation in international political and financial organizations. At the same time, the Macedonian president actively lobbied the world community for the recognition of his country. As a result of complex international factors, especially after the admittance of Macedonia into the UN, a number of countries, including Russia and China, extended formal recognition to the Republic and established diplomatic relations with it under its constitutional name. Furthermore, some Western states tried to help Macedonia and Greece find a solution to their dispute. Especially important was the increased involvement of the United States in this process, which led to the appointment of the U.S. diplomat Cyrus Vance as the principal negotiator. The United States henceforth became increasingly involved in the internal and external affairs of the republic.

As a result, Greece found itself under mounting international pressure to soften its approach toward the new Balkan state. On 13 September 1995, a temporary solution of the dispute between Greece and Macedonia was finally reached. According to the complex agreement, entitled "Interim Accord" and signed in New York by the Greek foreign minister, Carolos Papoulias, representing the unnamed "First Side," and the Macedonian foreign minister, Stevo Crvenkovski, representing the "Second Side," the First Side recognized the sovereignty of the Second Side. The First Side guaranteed not to impede the other's incorporation into international institutions and to allow transit of goods through its border. For its part, the Second Side had to refrain from any use of symbols offensive to the First Side and to change its flag. The two sides agreed to proceed with their negotiations over the name of the Second Side under the auspices of the UN and open representative offices in their respective capitals. As could be expected, at this writing the negotiations are still under way in the UN, under a

veil of secrecy. Occasionally both sides leak information and speculate on the name issue for internal political purposes. Most importantly, both sides now possess a formula for addressing each other and concluding various bilateral agreements. In the aftermath of the agreement, Macedonia was admitted into various European institutions, including the Organization for Security and Cooperation in Europe (OSCE) and the Council of Europe. Moreover, by the end of 1998, Macedonia had diplomatic relations with approximately a hundred countries, more than half of them being established under its constitutional name, the Republic of Macedonia.

In the period following its declaration of independence, Macedonia attempted to join the European Union and NATO. Already in December 1993, the Macedonian parliament decided to ask for full incorporation into NATO. In October 1995 it was admitted into the Partnership for Peace program, hosting on its territory a number of military exercises of NATO and allied countries. In regard to Macedonia's attempts to become a member of the EU, the situation seems even more bleak. The European Union has put Macedonia in the "third circle" of applicants, together with Albania, Bosnia, and Serbia.

Macedonia has already succeeded in concluding a cooperation agreement with the EU, which was implemented on 1 January 1999. The agreement has successfully been put into practice since then, as shown by the positive trend in Macedonian foreign trade. In fact, the EU has offered Macedonia a new kind of contractual relationship as an intermediary stage before granting this Balkan country an associative membership. Macedonia, which has showed significant progress in the political, economic, and juridical arenas, would have to implement the necessary reforms fully in order to be able to cope with the competitive pressure it will encounter when it enters the European Union. Moreover, the EU requires further administrative reform in the republic. In order to help Macedonia with these reforms, the European Commission has entered into a continuous political dialogue with the republic at every level.

After the declaration of its independence, Macedonia's relations with its neighboring countries, Bulgaria, Yugoslavia, and Albania, varied between extremely problematic and flourishing. The Macedonian president defined the foreign policy of his country as one of "maintaining equidistance," which meant nonpreferential treatment for any of its neighbors. Yet the republic's foreign relations depended on the actual circumstances in the region. Although Bulgaria was one of the first countries to recognize Macedonia in 1992, it continued to withhold recognition of a Macedonian nationality and language; this position resulted in a diplomatic deadlock between Skopje and Sofia, as well as an inability to conclude economic bilateral agreements that lasted until 1999. The problem between the two countries was as bizarre as the one between Greece and Macedonia: Bulgaria, which in 1992 and 1993 signed eight bilateral agreements with Macedonia, later on refused to sign any, since their official versions were written in the "Macedonian and Bulgarian languages." The Bulgarian government argued that the "Macedonian language" was a nonexistent communist fabrication, being simply a dialect of Bulgarian. The underlying Bulgarian thesis was that the Bulgarians and Macedonians belong to the same people, though they live in two different countries. The deadlock was resolved in early 1999, when again a curious formula was found to please both states. The agreements were signed in the "official languages" of both parties.

Relations between Macedonia and "rump" Yugoslavia (Serbia and Montenegro) remained strained as a result of a border dispute and the problem of the disposition of the assets of the former federation. The border between the two countries when they were members of the Yugoslav federation was never fully delineated. After the Macedonian declaration of independence, the Serbian side began to assert that a number of fertile fields and strategic posts should enter into its possession. A committee composed of representatives of the two countries was convened.

Only after losing Kosovo did Serbia actually agree to resolve the border dispute. Still, the Serbian-Montenegrin state claimed to be the sole successor to the former Yugoslavia, declaring that Slovenia, Croatia, and Macedonia had seceded unilaterally. Only after the downfall of the Milošević regime did the Serbian-Montenegrin state start to participate more constructively in the negotiations; this new attitude has led to a solution to the question. Macedonia and rump Yugoslavia had already established agreements in the sphere of commerce, as a result of the compatibility of the two economies (which had operated jointly for fifty years in the former Yugoslav Federation). Moreover, they concluded a free trade agreement, which has worked successfully for a number of years.

As for Albania, the main dispute between the two countries had to do with the ethnic Albanian minority in Macedonia. As this minority started to campaign for greater rights and more autonomy within the republic, the Albanian government began to press the Macedonian government to accede to their demands. At the same time, however, the Albanian president, Sali Berisha, cautioned Macedonian Albanians to be prudent in their quest for greater rights and to seek these rights by legal, peaceful means. Some of the progress made in bilateral relations suffered setbacks due to the shooting of Albanian smugglers and border guards. With the breakdown of the Albanian civil government as a result of the collapse of the pyramid schemes in 1997, which devastated the Albanian economy, Albania became increasingly unable to control its territory and border, thus losing its prestige and its ability to develop better economic and diplomatic relations with its eastern neighbor.

An important supporter of Macedonian independence was Turkey. During the struggle for recognition, Macedonia depended on the economic and political aid provided by Ankara, which established diplomatic relations with the republic almost immediately after its declaration of independence. Moreover, on 7 September 1999 the two countries concluded a free trade agreement. Turkey was, and still is, interested in Macedonia because of the latter's Turkish minority, as well as its location, which allows Turkey to have an ally on Greece's northern border.

Three important factors influenced the international standing of the republic in the period from 1998 to January 2000: the victory of the opposition parties in the parliamentary elections, the Kosovo crisis, and the Albanian insurrection, which ended with the signing of the so-called Framework Agreement. The new Tupurkovski–VMRO-DPMNE government, composed of right-wing and centrist parties, recognized Taiwan immediately after its ascension to power in 1998. This move produced a harsh diplomatic reaction in Beijing. As a result, China immediately suspended its diplomatic relations with Macedonia and vetoed the extension of the presence of the UN peacekeepers in this Balkan country. UN forces then left Macedonia, and with the increasing tension between the Western powers and Serbia over Kosovo, NATO troops began to pour into the republic, reaching a total of almost 30,000 soldiers at the peak of the Kosovo crisis. (By comparison, Macedonia has a standing army of approximately 15,000 soldiers.)

The recognition of Taiwan by the new Macedonian government was perceived by certain foreign relations specialists as a U.S.-orchestrated move for gaining full control over the military and security situation in the region. The official U.S. State Department position, however, is that the United States supports a one-China policy and did not favor this act in Macedonian foreign relations. Whether that is true or not, the recognition of Taiwan certainly damaged the diplomatic standing of the republic, which had not been able to honor its previously concluded international agreements with a world power that was among the first to recognize and support Macedonian independence.

The Kosovo crisis highlighted the importance of Macedonia in the world. Macedonia hosted almost 300,000 refugees from Kosovo. In proportion to the population of the republic, this influx of refugees is equivalent to 40 million refugees in the United States. Furthermore, most of the financial costs of hosting the refugees were covered by the Macedonian government. The international community, which pledged full diplomatic and political support for the republic, promised certain help, but that help was slow to come. As a result of the crisis, Macedonian indebtedness to international financial institutions skyrocketed, increasing the international vulnerability of the country. On the other hand, during the NATO war against Serbia many Western politicians and high-ranking diplomats visited Macedonia, including U.S. president Bill Clinton. Macedonian diplomats were reassured of the inviolability of their country's integrity by almost every Western capital. As explained by the U.S. president, the Kosovo war was partially conducted for the protection of Macedonia, which might have suffered from the spillover of hostilities from Kosovo. All of a sudden, Macedonia appeared in the news, and stories around the globe referred to the country simply as Macedonia, and not the Former Yugoslav Republic of Macedonia (FYROM). Thus, although the Kosovo crisis led to the insurrection of the Albanian minority in Macedonia in the summer of 2000 and lingering problems since (all covered in the final section), at least the war in the former Yugoslavia resulted in Macedonia being acknowledged by most people around the world as a distinct entity.

Kosovo Albanian refugees in Macedonia. The refugees reach Macedonia by following the rail tracks. (Yannis Kontos/Corbis Sygma)

CULTURAL DEVELOPMENT

The most important element in the cultural development of modern Macedonia was the establishment of a distinct Macedonian language and the appearance of a distinctive Macedonian literature. One crucial factor that influenced the development of a Macedonian literature was the fact that this area did not have any direct contact with the independent states of Western, Eastern, and Central Europe. This part of the Ottoman Empire was surrounded by the Serbs to the north, Bulgarians to the east, Greeks to the south, and Albanians to the west. By comparison, the Bulgarian national movement, centered in the central and eastern parts of the Ottoman European provinces close to Constantinople, benefited from the printing presses and activities of Slav inhabitants in neighboring Wallachia, Moldavia, and Russia. The Habsburg Empire, with its bureaucratic apparatus, its effective officialdom, its large numbers of organized Serbian settlers, and its burgeoning national movements, had a significant impact on the Serb population in the Ottoman Empire. This situation, together with access to the financial resources provided by a flourishing bourgeoisie, fostered the development of the Serbian and Bulgarian national movements much earlier than in Macedonia. These movements, due to the claims of the Serbs and Bulgarians (as well as the Greeks) upon Macedonian territory, in turn had a major impact on the Macedonian lands, influencing the development of the indigenous members of the Macedonian intelligentsia by providing textbooks, newspapers, and journals. In many cases, the Serbian and Bulgarian

national organizations even financed the education of Slavs from Macedonia in their centers.

Nineteenth-century Macedonian literati can be divided into several generations, which were interdependent and closely interconnected with each other. The first generation of public activists who initiated the national awakening of the Orthodox Slavs in Macedonia was made up of members of the clerical estate. They published their religious texts in a church language heavily influenced by the local Slav vernacular, realizing that only numerous printed copies of a book could produce wider popular interest in the written word and a well-informed public able to voice its opinion. In the period from 1814 to 1819, Joakim Krčovski, a member of the local clergy, who most probably came from western Macedonia and who lived and worked in eastern Macedonia in the towns of Kratovo and Kriva Palanka, published five religious books in his native vernacular in Budapest. In 1816 Kiril Pejčinovik, who served as a monk in the monastery Prečista near Kičevo, as priest-monk at St. Mark's monastery near Skopje, and as an abbot of the monastery of Lešok in the same area, published his book *Ogledalo* (Mirror) in Budapest. In 1840 his work *Utešenije Grešnim* (Consolation for Sinners) was published by Teodosij Sinaitski's press in Thessaloniki, thus bringing his total printed output to approximately two hundred pages. In 1838 Anatolij Zografski, a prominent member of the Zograf monastic brotherhood, who spent much of his career in the Russian capital, published a small, simplified primer at the same printing press.

St. Panteleimon church near Skopje. (Courtesy Turistkomerc)

The last literary endeavor of Pejčinovik establishes the link of the first generation of activists in the Slav cultural and linguistic sphere with the next generation, which appeared in the 1840s. The main representatives of this second generation were Jordan Hadži Konstantinov Džinot and Dimitar and Konstantin Miladinov. Jordan Hadži Konstantinov Džinot was born in Veles—one of the most economically and socially developed Slav communities in Macedonia at the time—into the family of a craftsman. Džinot spent all his life teaching in the local Slav schools in Veles, Skopje, and Prilep. Dimitar Miladinov and his brother Konstantin were well-known public activists who made a significant impact on cultural and social life in the Macedonian communities. Born to a family of a petty pottery craftsman of Slav origin in Struga, Dimitar Miladinov completed his studies at a three-year Greek school in Jannina. After working as a teacher in Greek educational institutions in the area, he served as a secretary to the patriarchal prelate in Mostar for less than a year. From 1857 to 1861, Dimitar Miladinov asserted himself as a capable organizer of education in the local Slav vernacular, an advocate of the Slav ethnic identity and ideas, and a compiler of folk materials. His charismatic personality and teaching skills made a favorable impression on the inhabitants of Kukuš, where he held the position of instructor from 1857 to 1859. From April to September 1860 he raised donations for the construction of the Bulgarian church in Constantinople. Konstantin Miladinov provided assistance to his brother, taught a short period of time in the schools of western Macedonia, and went to study in Moscow.

The remaining intellectuals from this generation were laymen who focused their activities on improving the educational and cultural conditions of the local communities. Grigor Prličev, a native of Ohrid and a pupil of Dimitar Miladinov, gained his fame as the winner of a poetry contest in Athens, where he started his studies in medicine. His poem, written in Greek, was widely acclaimed in Athens in 1860. Although Prličev had an opportunity to make a career in Greek circles, he dismissed this option and returned to his homeland to work on educating the general public. Kuzman Šapkarev, from Ohrid, was schooled entirely in the Greek urban schools of western Macedonia. In 1850 he began teaching in the Greek schools. Between 1861 and 1865, under the auspices of the Greek prelate Venedict, he was a teacher in Prilep. The Slav inhabitants there distanced themselves from Šapkarev suspecting he was an agent of Hellenization, the promotion of Greek culture and language. Šapkarev's activity in the field of education in the Slav vernacular began when he started teaching in the Kukuš schools in 1865; he remained there until 1872, moving afterwards to continue his teaching career in Prilep, Bitola, and Ohrid. Gjorgi Dinkov-Dinkata, from Thessaloniki, attended the Greek schools in his native town, and in Athens, as well as the patriarchal seminary in Halki. Moreover, he completed several courses at a gymnasium in Moscow. He taught in the Slav schools in Salonica, Prilep, Bitola, and the Kostur village of Zagoričani.

These intellectuals noticed that the books printed in distant Belgrade, in the Bulgarian communities of the Danube *vilayet* (the Ottoman administrative unit), and in the Bulgarian presses in Constantinople were not easily compatible with their local vernacular, customs, and perceptions, producing difficulties for the local population in the educational process. Moreover, the Serbian principality used a language significantly different in its grammatical structure from the western Macedonian vernacular, while the Bulgarian intelligentsia was moving toward codifying its language by basing it firmly on the dialects from the central and eastern parts of the Danube vilayet, which was geographically and linguistically the most distant area from western Macedonia. Consequently, the third generation of Slav intellectuals saw the language used in the Serbian and Bulgarian textbooks as alien, difficult to use in the primary schools, and not readily acceptable to the local communities. Writing for the Bulgarian newspaper *Pravo* (Law) in 1870, Venijamin Mačukovski clearly defined the problems that the intellectuals from western Macedonia faced: "Learning Bulgarian grammar in Macedonian schools represents one of the most difficult subjects for the pupils . . . [it] takes them a long time [and] without any result. This situation arises from the existing differences between the grammatical forms in the already published Bulgarian grammars and the Macedonian vernacular" (Koneski, 84–85).

The principal contribution of the first Macedonian intellectuals to the formation of a distinct Slav educational and cultural realm was the publishing of simple religious texts using the local vernacular and aimed at providing basic instruction in Christianity. However, the situation changed when the new generation of activists appeared. The members of the second and third generations of intelligentsia advocated Western democratic models of accountability by officials and the introduction of the elements of a viable bourgeois public sphere.

The most active members of the intelligentsia that advocated local interests originated from the area west of the Tetovo-Veles-Salonika line. The Slavic-speaking inhabitants in this part of Macedonia were linguistically and culturally most distant from the Serbian principality, as well as from the central and eastern parts of the Danube vilayet, which represented the most active region of the Bulgarian national movement. At the same time, because of the isolation imposed by geographical, social, and economic factors, these people developed a strong feeling of local identity. The Macedonian intellectuals from these areas noticed clear linguistic differences between the language used in the regions of their origin and activity and the Serbian and Bulgarian literary languages. On the other hand, these indigenous intellectuals from western Macedonia were a relatively small, insufficiently educated, and noncohesive group. As a result,

they were unable to produce a consistent national ideology and transform their Slavic-speaking ethnic group into a separate nationality. Nevertheless, they clearly voiced a demand for the establishment of a literary language, which would correspond to the linguistic situation in Macedonia. Also, as was the case with numerous movements in Central and Southeastern Europe, they did develop an intellectual construct that asserted the separate historical development and identity of Macedonian Slavs.

During the last quarter of the nineteenth century, Gjorgija Pulevski in Sofia formed the Slavonic-Macedonian Literary Group, to revive popular Macedonian literature. He also published numerous textbooks that asserted the independence and distinctiveness of the Macedonian ethnic group and its language. Three years later and again in Sofia, Kosta Šahov, a publicist and a publisher from Ohrid, launched the Young Macedonian Literary Group. In 1892 this group began the publication of the journal *Loza* (Vine). The ideas propagated by this journal (published from 1890 to 1894) played a paramount role in the formation of a modern Macedonian language and literature.

It was Krste Petkov Misirkov who most succinctly summarized and brought the ideas of his literary predecessors to fruition, in his work *On Macedonian Matters* (1903). This work became the most important scholarly and literary work in modern Macedonian cultural and national history. First and foremost, it was written in the contemporary Macedonian language. Moreover, *On Macedonian Matters* made the key assertions that formed the basis of the Macedonian national emergence: Macedonians constitute a separate Slav nation that has its own history, language, and culture; in order to win their national liberty, the Macedonian population should first reject any Bulgarian, Serbian, and Greek connections and denominations, start to use the Macedonian name for itself, and work for its acceptance by the Ottoman state; the Ohrid archbishopric should be reestablished as an independent Macedonian national church, which would serve to counteract foreign propaganda that sought to deny Macedonian identity; the central Macedonian Veles-Bitola-Prilep dialect should be accepted as the literary language of the whole of Macedonia, and this language should be taught at schools; and a full Macedonian national movement should be brought into being by intensified national and cultural agitation.

In the period before the end of World War II, Misirkov's ideas were embraced by several Macedonian authors, who presented their works in the popular vernacular. The most important among them were Vojdan Černodrinski and Nikola Kirov Majski, as well as the playwrights Risto Krle, Vasil Iljoski, and Anton Panov. The appearance of the poetry collection *White Dawns* by Kosta Racin in 1939 further led to the formation of modern Macedonian literature. The poems of Venko Markovski and Mite Bogoevski contributed to the development of verse expression in the Macedonian language.

This first generation of twentieth-century Macedonian writers was soon joined by the novelists Stale Popov and Jordan Leov, as well as poets Lazo Karovski and Vasil Kunoski. In the 1950s the new generation of Macedonian

Krste Petkov Misirkov

Krste Petkov Misirkov (1874–1926) is the first modern Macedonian intellectual and political activist who clearly and succinctly argued in a scholarly manner that Macedonians are a separate nation, with their own history, language, and culture. Most importantly, he not only declared that a distinct Macedonian vernacular does exist, but also established the scholarly principles for its evolution into a literary language. As a result, he wrote the book *On Macedonian Matters,* the first book written in modern Macedonian.

Misirkov's life, ideas, and approaches depict the challenges that Macedonian intellectuals encountered at the turn of the twentieth century. Born in a village near Pella, the capital of the ancient Macedonian kingdom, he finished primary school in Greek. In 1889 he received a scholarship to study in the Serbian capital, Belgrade; it was provided by a Serbian cultural and political organization in charge of spreading Serbian propaganda in Macedonia (which was still under Ottoman rule). However, Bulgarian propaganda and promises of a better life convinced Misirkov to declare himself a Bulgarian, leave Belgrade, and start to study in Sofia. However, once in Sofia, he realized that the true intentions of the Bulgarians were the same as the Serbians': educating young people from Macedonia as Bulgarians so that, once indoctrinated, they would return to their homes and teach children to be Bulgarian in the local schools. Deeply disappointed with this attitude, the young Misirkov again declared himself to be Serbian and returned to his former Belgrade school. Consequently, by the age of twenty-one, when he finished his schooling in Belgrade, he had experienced three official national identities, one of them more than once: Greek, Serbian, and Bulgarian. He went to Russia, where after a dramatic struggle to keep body and soul together, he finished his studies at the Faculty of History and Philology. It is important to note that he consistently declared on his university forms that he was a Macedonian.

His most significant legacy in the Russian capital was the establishment of the Macedonian Literary and Scholarly Society. His intention to help his unhappy homeland led him to a teaching post in Bitola, the most important administrative center in Macedonia; he started his work in the year of the Ilinden Uprising, the unsuccessful 1903 revolt initiated by the Internal Macedonian Revolutionary Organization (IMRO) aimed at gaining Macedonian autonomy. As a witness to the assassination of the Russian consul, who was intensely disliked by the Ottoman government (which very likely approved of the murder), he had to leave Macedonia. Later that same year, he published his seminal work, and he continued his struggle for the affirmation of the Macedonian language and culture until his death in 1926.

writers (Srbo Ivanovski, Gane Todorvoski, Mateja Matevski, Cane Andreevski, Cvetko Martinovski, Simon Drakul, Blagoj Ivanov, Dimitar Solev, Ante Popovski, Branko Pendovski, Georgi Stalev, Tome Arsovski, Aleksandar Spasov, Milan Gurčinov, Aleksandar Aleksiev, and Georgi Stardelov, among others) explored new literary dimensions and established new trends. The third generation of Macedonian writers (Živko Čingo, Petar Boškovski, Jovan Kotevski, Petre M. Andreevski, Petar Širilov, Metodija Fotev, Ljuben Taškovski, Taško Georgievski, Vlada Urošević, and Radovan and Jovan Pavlovski) was in closer contact with world literary trends. In the 1960s and 1970s the fourth generation, with its representatives Bogomil Gjuzel, Atanas Vangelov, Eftim Kletnikov, Sande Stojčeski, Katica Kiulafkova, and Goran Stefanovski, developed individual and uniquely Macedonian styles.

Numerous writers in Macedonia express themselves in Albanian and Turkish as well. Among the most distinguished Albanian-language authors are Murteza Peza, Ljutvi Rusi, Murat Isaku, Abdulazis Islami, Sefedin Suleymani, and Adem Gaytani. Turkish language works include those of Shukri Ramo, Nedzhati Zekiriya, Mustafa Karahasan, Fahri Kaya, Ilhami Emin, Esad Bayram, Nusret Dishu Ulku, Suad Engulu, and Alaetin Tahir.

Contemporary Macedonian poets and authors have the opportunity to meet their international counterparts in two well-known international meetings held annually in Struga and Veles. Local and national events are also held in Macedonia during the course of the year, such as the Days Below Kozyak, the Vevčani Meetings, the Little Messenger Meetings in Kičevo, the Feast in Podgorci, the Galičnik Meetings, the Bigorski Meetings, and the Shaking Hands in Dojran.

Cultural development in Macedonia is not confined to literature. At the end of the last century, the first choirs and groups devoted to modern, Western-style European music emerged in Macedonia. They were gradually complemented by small bands using folk instruments. These groups introduced oriental elements to Macedonian music. In 1934 the first music school was established in Skopje; its most prominent contributors were Trajko Prokopiev and Todor Skalovski, who continued their work in independent Macedonia. After the end of World War II, a creative upsurge of Macedonian artists resulted in the creation of Macedonian opera and ballet.

Macedonia is well known for its medieval ecclesiastical architectural and visual arts heritage, which was first seen during the days of the Byzantine Empire and which displayed a distinctly Byzantine influence. One of the architectural masterpieces of Macedonia, which dates from the early period of Slavic culture, is the Church of St. Sophia in Ohrid, renovated by Archbishop Leo between 1037 and 1056. Its size and the arrangement of the frescoes in the sanctuary seem to suggest that it was constructed as a cathedral.

Other important ecclesiastical buildings erected in the period before the Ottoman conquest of the area at the end of the fourteenth century that are preserved in their entirety include the Churches of St. Clement and St. Naum near Ohrid, St. Panteleimon near Skopje, and the churches in Matejče and Staro Nagoričane near Kumanovo. The frescoes in the preserved churches were the equal of the greatest and most beautiful works of the Byzantine Empire. It should be noted here that the territory of the Republic of Macedonia represents one of the richest regions in terms of medieval wall paintings, both in the Balkans and in Europe as a whole.

The coming of the Ottomans led to a substantial change in architectural patterns. The church was replaced by the mosque as the focus of religious architecture, while inns and baths started to occupy a central place in the urban settlements. The most famous Islamic places of worship that are still preserved are to be found in Skopje: the Mosque of Isaac Bey built in 1438; the Mosque of Murad Hainukyar, built in 1436; the Mosque of Kodja-Mustapha Pasha, built in 1491; and the Mosque of Yahya Pasha, built in 1504 (which includes a fifty-meter-high minaret). In Bitola can be found the Isac Mosque, finished in 1509; the Yeni Mosque, built in 1559; and the Mosque of Jahdar-Kadi, built in 1562 by Kodja Sinan, the most prominent Ottoman architect of the time. Secular architecture dating from the early Ottoman period includes the Kuršumli and Suli Inns in Skopje. In addition, several exceptional baths, which today serve as museums and art galleries, survived centuries of wars and natural disasters. Another typical trait of Turkish architecture present in Macedonia includes burial chambers (turbeh) of notable Ottomans, as well as dervish dwellings (tekeh). Particularly fine architectural examples of burial chambers are the Mustapha Pasha and the open Kral K'zi turbeh in Skopje. In addition, the Sultan Emir Tekeh in Skopje and the Arabati-baba Tekeh in Tetovo represent exceptional historical and cultural monuments.

ECONOMIC DEVELOPMENT

During the last century of Turkish rule, Macedonia was economically an agricultural country. The economy of the

The Church of St. Sophia (Ohrid)

The church of St. Sofia is one of the largest medieval churches in the region. It was probably built in the tenth or eleventh centuries and served as the cathedral church (Great Church) of the medieval autocephalous Archbishopric of Ohrid. The original church had only one main dome; in the fourteenth century, however, a luxurious external part was added. With the arrival of the Ottoman Turks, the church of St. Sofia was converted into a mosque. The new masters modified the interior of the church; the frescoes were whitewashed; the ornamented plates from the iconostasis were used for constructing the internal staircase; and a minaret was built above the northwest dome.

During the period between 1950 and 1957, extensive restoration took place. Many fresco paintings, which date from the eleventh to the fourteenth centuries, again saw the light of day. They are indeed among the highest achievements in medieval painting in the region. The oldest are eleventh-century frescoes, situated primarily in the altar section and at the ground level. They depict the early saints of the church, as well as the most prominent patriarchs, archbishops, and clergy. Among the most important portraits are those that represent St. Basil, known as Basil the Great, fourth-century church father and reformer of monasticism; St. John Chrysostom, fourth-century Syrian bishop and renowned preacher; and St. Gregory of Nazianzus, the great fourth-century theologian.

Portraits of six Roman popes and representatives of the Alexandria, Jerusalem, and Antioch patriarchates are painted on the side section of the altarspace. Among all these eminent figures, the portraits of the two most important saints of Slavic origin were painted: St. Cyril (after whom the Cyrillic alphabet was named) and his disciple St. Clement of Ohrid. Both were prominent cult figures in eleventh-century Ohrid. A number of important frescoes dating from the twelfth century have also been preserved. The most significant among them are the portrait of the Holy Mother and the scenes depicting the sufferings of the Apostles. The last painted in the church of St. Sofia was the fourteenth-century Gregorius gallery, which contains a heterogeneous composition of more than a hundred scenes and portraits. The portrait of St. Naum, another disciple of St. Cyril, already known in the Middle Ages as the healer of the mentally challenged, is among the numerous portraits of healers and martyrs painted in the western section.

Turkish province of Macedonia was characterized by primitive and backward production. The landmark events in Ottoman economic, social, political, and juridical history that propelled the appearance of new entrepreneurial strata and local intelligentsia include the destruction of the janissary corps (the former elite military units of the empire, which had by the seventeenth century become more of a political force than a military one) in 1826 and the reform edicts of 1839 and 1856 (the so-called Tanzimat, "reform," period in Ottoman history). As a result of the sultan's destruction of the janissaries, who were leaders of the urban craftsmen and the most powerful advocates of commercial protectionism, the local guilds, including the ones in Macedonia, lost their most important defenders. After the elimination of the janissaries, these professional organizations began to disintegrate, while their prominent members gradually lost wealth and social status. The reforms of 1839 and 1856 were significant because they publicly endorsed the new Westernizing process in the Ottoman Empire; in this case, Westernization meant implementation of administrative policies and means of social, economic, and fiscal control characteristic of France, Britain, Prussia, and Austria. The new governmental edicts committed the Ottoman state to a policy of modernization and equal justice for all subjects, whatever their religious affiliation.

The transformation of Ottoman economic life after the abolition of the janissaries was further advanced by the conclusion of the Anglo-Turkish convention of 1838. While the sultan signed it under duress to gain support for the struggle with the Egyptian rebel Muhammad Ali, Britain endorsed this agreement to utilize the Ottoman economy for importing cheap raw material and agricultural products and as an export market for its vastly expanding industries. This treaty abolished the remaining Ottoman monopolies that were protecting the local guilds and removed obstacles for European merchants. The convention allowed foreign businessmen to trade anywhere in the Ottoman Empire, liable only to a number of specifically prescribed duties. Consequently, with the 1838 accord, the Ottoman economy became far more open, perhaps more than any state in the world, but it was at the expense of its domestic industries and producers. As a result of this laissez-faire policy, the Macedonian lands were reduced to the role of a minor exporter of agricultural goods, while the initial attempts at promoting greater industrialization in the region were destroyed by a flood of cheap Western products.

The main exports of Macedonia continued to be wheat, rough unprocessed skins and hides, wool, and tobacco. The export of cotton flourished only during the period of the American Civil War, when the Northern blockade of the South choked off exports of high-quality American cotton to the mills of Europe. In the early 1800s 40 percent of the annual cotton crop was woven locally in the homes of the inhabitants, and not only sold to internal markets, but also exported beyond the area. However, after 1830, British cottons overflowed Macedonian markets and replaced local products. Even this domestic industry, then, gradually vanished from Macedonian towns and villages as a result of increasing imports. As a result, industrial enterprises that

employed larger numbers of workers did not emerge in Macedonia during nineteenth-century Ottoman rule.

Furthermore, Macedonian fields continued to be tilled in an outdated and unproductive fashion. Their owners did not bother to expand their holdings by farming abandoned or unused land. This situation in many respects resulted from the attitude of landlords toward production as well as their ethnic composition. Turkish and Albanian soldiers and local officials owned most of the land during the period before 1850. Their approach had little in common with Western ideas about investment and improvement of farming methods. Their main concern was how to raise enough money to secure a comfortable living in the towns where they resided. In the end, the system functioned in such a way that the large landowners sold their share of the crop at fairs or directly to the grain merchants, while the free services of their tenants reduced their expenses.

As a result of this neglect by landowners and the negligent attitude of the government toward agriculture, cereals remained the principal crops during the period until 1944, although Macedonia had proven potential for the production of silk, cotton, rice, tobacco, and other industrial cultures. Thus the crops harvested served mainly to meet the basic subsistence needs of the population. Consequently, domestic consumption remained a greater concern than possible lucrative exports. In the early 1860s wheat, maize, barley, rye, and millet fields covered almost 90 percent of the cultivable land in the district of Thessaloniki. Contrary to the assertion of a number of scholars, industrial agricultural cultivation remained extremely marginal. For example, cotton was grown on only 3 percent of the land.

The ineffective transportation system further contributed to the retarded nature of industrial and agricultural development. Routes were often available only to animal-back transport, in caravans usually composed of twenty to fifty pack animals with twenty to eighty men. The price for transporting agricultural goods on packhorses represented at least half of the market value. The attempts by the Ottoman central government to improve the road structure and security usually ended in embezzlement of funds, increased labor pressure on peasants, and greater local taxation. For example, in the late 1850s the only visible results of months and months of toil and financial constraint of the population in the process of building a road from Salonika to Bitola were two small ramshackle wooden bridges.

The period between the two world wars, with its economic crises, centralized and exploitative Serbian (Yugoslav) government, as well as inherent hostilities in the region, did not contribute to any significant economic development in Macedonia. Only with the formation of a federal state in Vardar Macedonia at the end of 1944 did some economic changes take place. Macedonia entered the new federal Yugoslavia not only as a region devastated by war, but as an extremely underdeveloped region that based its economy on primitive agricultural practices. After 1944, investments in the economy helped the region of Macedonia gradually develop an industrial standing. In accordance with the policy on equal regional development, Macedonia received significant economic support from the Yugoslav federation. In about thirty years this undeveloped area in the Balkans acquired a standard of living higher than that of any neighboring countries with the exception of Greece.

In the 1990s, with the collapse of the former Yugoslav state, Macedonian independence did not bring a spurt of economic growth, or even increased development. On the contrary, this period witnessed the closure of the otherwise protected market of the former Yugoslav republics. Macedonian products now had to fight their own way amidst fierce international competition. Moreover, the transformation of the economic system brought many industrial enterprises to a standstill. In the transition era, state managers needed to diminish the value of state property in order to afford to buy it. As a result, many Macedonian enterprises were intentionally run down, brought to bankruptcy, and then sold for a token of their real value. Some previously flourishing industries (the best example is the textile industry) were never able to gain a new momentum in the changed economic, social, and political environment, suffering as they did from the internal mismanagement, loss of markets, and lack of investment.

It is worth noting that there has been a noticeable decrease of foreign investment in the Republic of Macedonia in recent years. According to the State Statistical Office of Macedonia, in 1990 foreign investments amounted to 15,140,000 U.S. dollars, but three years later, in 1993, they were almost halved to $811,700. After an initial rise in investment and production characteristic of the mid to late 1990s, the situation significantly worsened during and after the 1999 NATO intervention in Kosovo. The subsequent insurrection of the Albanian population in the northwestern parts of the republic only further exacerbated the situation. One of the main legacies of the decade of the 1990s, marred by wars, instability, and insecurity in the Balkans generally and the republic specifically, was the rise in corruption and the fall of economic output. Three hundred thousand unemployed, a downtrodden industry, and Macedonian-Albanian hostilities do not bode well for future economic development. Foreign investment, on which Macedonian economic recovery depends, will only increase if it is possible to transform an economic climate that now appears corrupt, insecure, and burdened by political instability.

CONTEMPORARY CHALLENGES

The 2000 Albanian insurrection in Macedonia heavily affected the social, economic, and political situation, not only in the country itself but also in the region. With the outbreak of that war, this part of the western Balkans seems to have returned to the era of the uncertainties of the early 1990s. Moreover, the entire security situation in Macedonia has started to resemble that of the early nineteenth century, when groups of outlaws jeopardized the security of large urban centers like Bitola and Ohrid. The grievances found on both sides of the conflict—Macedonian and Albanian—have been debated, not only internally but also internationally.

To deal first with the causes that led to civil war, within the Republic of Macedonia, Albanians were paying a price

for their support nearly a half-century earlier of the idea of Greater Albania (during World War II). Their support for this Italian creation, as well as their nostalgia for the idea of a larger Albanian state during the postwar period, contributed to Albanian exclusion from social life in the Republic of Macedonia during the communist period. Their attitudes and their exclusion had repercussions on the social level as well. The Albanian population remained mainly rural, living in traditional village and tribal communities. As a result of this general isolation of the Albanian minority, women received few rights, and generations of younger Albanians were left undereducated.

An imbalance in the birthrate in Macedonia also played a role. That imbalance developed between the most often urban ethnic Macedonians and the rural Albanian population. According to census figures, the latter rose from 12.5 percent of the total number of inhabitants in the country in 1953 to 25.17 percent in 2002. The reasons for this increase were many; the effect was a dramatic shift in existing demographic patterns. The most important impact of the demographic shift has been the building of compact blocks of mono-ethnic Albanian population groupings. The imbalance between the rural, undereducated, and rapidly growing Albanian population and the Macedonian population, which moved to the city and started to staff the oversized and ever growing bureaucracy, had an impact, not only on the overall development of the Republic of Macedonia, but on interethnic relations within the fledgling nation.

The main external factor at work was the autonomy of Kosovo. The establishment of a university there in 1970 based on Albanian language instruction and the creation of an Albanian Academy of Sciences in 1976 made Priština (the capital of Kosovo) and not Skopje (the capital of Macedonia) the cultural, educational, and intellectual center for Macedonian Albanians. Every action of the Albanian Kosovo elite aimed at further improvement of the situation of the Albanians within Kosovo in turn directly impacted interethnic relations in Macedonia.

Important as the role of these recent developments was, conflict between Macedonians and Albanians is not simply a recent development, as has already been mentioned. Interethnic tensions, dating in part from the Middle Ages, frayed internal Macedonian-Albanian relations during the time of the Yugoslav federation. Moreover, the educational system has never acquainted ethnic Macedonians with Albanian history and culture, thus contributing to a situation in which the majority population sees all developments only from its own point of view. Seen from this perspective, it is no surprise that the irredentist and separatist movements and actions in Kosovo and western Macedonia during the 1980s and 1990s increased mutual distrust. The most surprising development, however, was the severity with which the central government in Belgrade and Skopje responded. A series of repressive actions took place against the Albanian minority, including depriving them of the opportunity to be educated in their mother tongue in the secondary schools. The number of Albanians in civil administration, the police, and the army, as well as in the university, was quite low. For example, according to the

1994 census, the number of Albanian students in the 1993–1994 school year represented only 2.8 percent, almost a 2 percent decrease from 1983–1984. Thus, agriculture, cattle-breeding, and small private businesses became the essential means of income for ethnic Albanians deprived of opportunities elsewhere.

While the Macedonian ethnic group, in most cases, depended economically on the state, the Albanians thus started to learn the tools of a market economy. This situation, on the one hand, and the cash inflow from the Albanian emigration in Western Europe, on the other hand, increased the economic power of the Albanian minority in Macedonia. This increased economic power, coupled with the apparent discrepancy in the birthrate (which created among the Macedonians a belief that they would eventually become a minority, due to the high birthrate among Albanians in comparison to their own), strengthened the perception that the Albanians were a national threat to the Macedonians. Since the Republic of Slovenia and the Republic of Croatia in that period were on the side of the Albanians from Kosovo, the Macedonian statesmen in the 1980s and even the early 1990s turned for support to the Republic of Serbia and the Serbs.

The outbreak of the civil war in Macedonia was a natural result of the removal of Serbian control over Kosovo as well as the inability of the Georgievski-Tupurkovski-Xhaferi government to control the territory of the republic effectively and to fully address the grievances of the Albanians in Macedonia. In March 2001 the so-called National Liberation Army (NLA) proclaimed itself a protector of the Albanian population in Macedonia. Its leader was Ali Ahmeti, who created and commanded the Kosovo Liberation Army in its fight against the Serbian state. The NLA was successful in expanding the conflict and gaining control over Macedonian territory. In the period between March and June 2001 the confrontations between Macedonian government forces and the NLA spread from Tetovo (which had a 90 percent Albanian population) to the outskirts of Kumanovo and Skopje. By June 2001, Ahmeti's insurrectionists captured Aračinovo, a village less than ten kilometers from the capital and in the vicinity of the international airport. The rebels were now effectively within rocket-firing range of the parliament building.

The precarious national unity government—a coalition of the four major political parties which was formed at the beginning of the crisis—effectively collapsed when the leaders of the two Albanian parties who were included in it signed a joint declaration of support with NLA leader Ahmeti in Priština on 22 May 2001. It was clear that the Macedonian army and police were unable to suppress the revolt. As a result, the EU and NATO decided to play a more decisive role and impose pressure on the fighting parties. On 5 July 2001, NATO mediated a cease-fire between Albanian rebels and Macedonian government forces, which became permanent with the signing of the Framework Agreement. Ali Ahmeti was elevated from the status of terrorist and rebel to the prestigious post of a political leader. In 2002 he was elected to the Macedonian parliament. It is difficult to establish the list of casualties on the both sides,

Special forces bombard Albanian rebels in the area northwest of Tetovo, 23 March 2001. (Yannis Kontos/Corbis Sygma)

but it is clear that several hundred people were killed during the hostilities. There is still an extensive list of missing and displaced persons.

The outbreak of civil war in Macedonia was a natural result of the fact that the grievances of Albanians had not been seriously addressed. As discussed above, the governing party at the time of the civil war was a coalition between Vasil Tupurkovski, VMRO-DPMNE, and a recently formed Albanian party. Even though that party had come into being to work for resolution of Albanian grievances, in practice its politicians were content to settle for local power. VMRO-DPMNE, meanwhile, which held the most power in the coalition, continued to play on strong nationalistic and even chauvinistic Macedonian feelings; the result was the division of the republic into medieval fiefdoms in which local politicians ruled over the population. In such a context, laws on the books that reflected advanced, modern European ideas of equal rights for all in a multi-ethnic state remained dead letters, reflecting wishful thinking, an almost utopian ideal. The problem was not legal discrimination against the Albanian minority, but rather the practical exclusion of the Albanians from public life. In essence, the Macedonian government and its institutions were corrupt, ineffective, and inappropriate.

During the conflict in Macedonia, the international community at first denounced the insurrection and encouraged a quick suppression of the revolt; with the passage of time, however, it realized that the Macedonian government could not produce a military solution to the problem. Despite attempts by the Macedonian government to suggest that the international community was mistreating Macedonia, it is evident that it was in the interest of the EU to maintain a stable and undivided Macedonian state. It also seems clear that, despite accusations by the Macedonian government, NATO did not support militarily or politically any incursions of armed Albanian gangs into Macedonia. What does seem to be true is that, given their concern with maintaining the fragile peace in Kosovo, the United States and the EU lacked the political and military will to prevent the logistical and military support given by Kosovo paramilitary groups to the Albanian insurrectionists in Macedonia. It is also true that, when the Macedonian government revealed itself to be corrupt and ineffective, the Western powers tried to find a peaceful solution to the crisis, and so shifted into a new role. It is clearly Macedonian politicians, who put their own economic pursuits before the interests of the state, who must bear the responsibility for the loss of life in the country and, perhaps more damaging in the long run, national humiliation. It was only the activities of the Western negotiators that prevented a much more devastating conflict from erupting.

The ruling VMRO-DPMNE actually wanted to persuade the Macedonian population that the government was forced to avoid using full military power against the terrorists and to open a dialogue with them. If the government had used the military as they intended, the results would have been catastrophic. Widespread carnage would have led to a widespread civil war, along the lines of that which had occurred in the early 1990s in Bosnia. Nevertheless, the result of the internal anti-Western propaganda was that the Macedonian population attacked the U.S. embassy. The Macedonians wanted to interpret their inability to control the situation as due to pressure imposed by the international community. It was the Framework Agreement, imposed by threats and cajoling on the fighting parties by the EU and the United States, that actually saved Macedonia from a Bosnian scenario. This agreement, concluded in Ohrid in August 2001, cut short a rapidly evolving civil war.

The real causes of the conflict, however, have not yet been eliminated. The viability of the agreement depends on the development of democratic institutions and a market economy. The Framework Agreement again and again improves the situation on paper, but the social, popular, and to a certain extent political support and will is still missing. The main objective of the Framework Agreement is to preserve the unitary character of the Republic of Macedonia, to promote the peaceful and harmonious development of civic society, to respect the ethnic identity and the interests of all citizens, and to ensure that the constitution fully meets the needs of all citizens. The Framework Agreement calls for a number of important constitutional amendments and structural reforms, primarily in the use of Albanian and other minority languages in government bodies, municipalities,

and the courts. It calls for the decentralization of the government and development of local self-government, as well as improvement in the representation of the minorities in the composition and distribution of police forces. In addition, this document stipulates the institution of the office of ombudsman, access to primary and secondary education for all minorities in the students' native languages, and reform of the public administration to assure equitable representation of minorities.

The actual situation makes the carrying out of the agreement virtually impossible. Macedonia, especially in certain areas in which there is a clear ethnic majority, is now more than ever divided into fiefdoms run by what amounts to local warlords. Albanian and Macedonian taxi drivers, policemen, state officials, and ordinary citizens do not dare to enter certain parts of the republic. Murders are up by a third over three years, and a series of bombings, kidnappings, and shootings have added to the sense of lawlessness. Poor communication on security matters often stokes the flames of ethnic tensions within the government and between communities; this, rather than any organized "pan-Albanian violence," is the greatest current threat to stability. The corruption that eats away at the country is in many ways a cross-community, shared enterprise. At a minimum, it is highly damaging to the economy and increases the chances for social instability. At the same time, it invites outright collusion between ethnic leaders to heighten tensions and plays a substantial role in making the country ripe for conflict. In light of recent developments, Macedonia could be viewed as one of the failures for multicultural society in the Balkans. In contrast to the enthusiasm and high hopes of the early 1990s, the dawn of the new millennium brings disillusionment, poverty, increased ethnic tensions, and an uncertain future. According to a recent UN survey, two-thirds of Macedonians and Albanians expect more conflict amid growing concerns over a stagnant economy. It is true that the Albanian minority has gained more rights and continues to become more powerful, but it has also lost the trust of Macedonians completely, and Albanians inevitably feel that in daily life. Society has already split more than ever into two opposing camps. Living together has become less realistic in Macedonia; if there is a possibility for a united, multicultural Macedonia, then it lies in the distant future. Aid workers continue to describe ethnic polarization in the former crisis areas, as minorities continue to face multiple pressures. Bitter disputes over schools defy mediation. Unemployment remains high and has created the potential for ambitious labor leaders to spark unrest. The prospect of yet more instability keeps foreign investment low and the economy almost paralyzed, a factor that only increases the internal tensions, perpetuating a vicious cycle.

What appears most likely is that the situation will remain unstable. Europe will have to take care of its unofficial protectorate; as the question remains as to what is to be done with Afghanistan, or U.S.-controlled Iraq, or Kosovo, or Bosnia, the question that imposes itself in the Macedonian case is whether any other option than an independent and unified Macedonia exists. The only other option that seems even remotely possible is that Macedonia will split into virtually independent cantons, one Albanian, one Macedonian, and that the federal state will follow the Canadian and Swiss political model.

SELECTIVE BIBLIOGRAPHY

Adanir, Fikret. "The Macedonians in the Ottoman Empire, 1878–1912." In *The Formation of National Elites.* Edited by Andreas Kapeller, Fikret Adanir, and Alan O'Day. New York: New York University Press, 1992, 161–191.

Bakalopoulos, Konstantinos. *Historia tou boreiou hellenismou: Makedonia* (History of Northern Greece: Macedonia). 3d ed. Thessaloniki: Oikos Adelfon Kiriakide, 1992.

Bitoski, Krste, et al., ed. *Istorija na Makedonskiot Narod* (History of the Macedonian People). Vols. 3–5. Skopje: Institut za Nacionalna Istorija, 2003.

Ekmečić, Milorad. *Stvaranje Jugoslavije, 1790–1918.* 2 vols. (The Making of Yugoslavia). Belgrade: Prosveta, 1989.

Friedman, Victor A. "Macedonian Language and Nationalism during the Nineteenth and Early Twentieth Centuries." *Balkanistica* 2 (1975): 83–98.

———. "Macedonian." In *The Slavonic Languages,* edited by B. Comrie and G. Corbett. London: Routledge, 1993, 249–305.

Gounaris, Basil. "Social Cleavages and National 'Awakening' in Ottoman Macedonia." *East European Quarterly* 29 (1996): 409–425.

———. *Steam over Macedonia, 1870–1912: Socio-Economic Change and the Railway Factor.* Boulder, CO: East European Monographs, 1993.

Karpat, Kemal. *Ottoman Population, 1830–1914: Demographic and Social Characteristics.* Madison: University of Wisconsin Press, 1985.

Kofos, Evangelos. *Nationalism and Communism in Macedonia.* Thessaloniki: Institute for Balkan Studies, 1964.

Koneski, Blaže. *Kon Makedonskata Prerodba* (Macedonian National Awakening). Skopje: INI, 1939.

Lunt, Horace. "On Macedonian Language and Nationalism." *Slavic Review* 45 (1986): 729–734.

Milosavlevski, Slavko, and Mirche Tomovski. *Albanians in the Republic of Macedonia, 1945–1995.* Skopje: NIP Studentski Zbor, 1997.

Nikolovska, Natalija, and Gordana Siljanovska-Davkova. *Makedonskata Tranzicija vo Defekt* (Problems of Macedonian Transition). Skopje: Magor, 2001.

Palmer, Stephen, and Robert R. King. *Yugoslav Communism and the Macedonian Question.* North Haven, CT: Archon Books, 1971.

Pavlovski, Jovan, and Mishel Pavlovski. *Macedonia Yesterday and Today.* Skopje: Mi-An, 1996.

Perry, Duncan. *The Politics of Terror: The Macedonian Liberation Movements, 1893–1903.* Durham, NC: Duke University Press, 1988.

Poulton, Hugh. *Who Are the Macedonians?* Bloomington: Indiana University Press, 1995.

Pulevski, Giorgija. *Odrani stranici* (Selections). Edited by Blaže Ristovski. Skopje: Mak kniga, 1978.

Ristovski, Blaže. *Istorija na Makedonskata Nacija* (History of the Macedonian Nation). Skopje: MANU, 1999.

———. *Krste Petkov Misirkov (1874–1926): Prilog kon pručivanjeto na Makedonskata nacionalna misla* (Contribution to the Study of Macedonian National Thought). Skopje: Kultura, 1966.

———. *Macedonia and the Macedonian People.* Vienna: Simag Holding, 1999.

Rossos, Andrew. "Macedonianism and Macedonian Nationalism on the Left." In *National Character and National Ideology in Interwar Eastern Europe.* Edited by Ivo Banac and Catherine Werdery. New Haven, CT: Yale Center for International and Area Studies, 1995.

———. "The Macedonian Question and the Instability in the Balkans." In *Yugoslavia and Its Historians.* Edited by Norman Naimark and Holly Carse. Stanford, CA: Stanford University Press, 2003.

Šapkapev, Kuzman. *Naračno blagovestvovanie ili sabor* (Selections of Gospel Readings). Constantinople: Makedonija, 1868.

State Statistical Office of the Republic of Macedonia. http://www.stat.gov.mk (accessed 13 August 2004).

Todorovski, Gane. *Makedonskata Literatura 19–20 vek* (Macedonian Literature, 19th–20th Centuries). Skopje: Detska Radost, 1993.

Türk, Danilo. "Declaration on Yugoslavia." *European Journal of International Law* 4, no. 1 (1993): 73.

CHRONOLOGY

808 B.C.E.	The geographic term "Macedonia" emerges, with the establishment of an independent kingdom of that name in present-day Northern Greece.
359–336 B.C.E.	Philip II enhances the prestige of his country by conquering Greece.
336–323 B.C.E.	Philip's son, Alexander III (the Great), defeats and conquers the Persian Empire. The name "Macedonia" becomes well known throughout the ancient world, and the exploits of Alexander the Great will provide an endless source for literary and political imagination up to the present day. After the death of its most famous king, the Macedonian kingdom dissipates into smaller political entities.
146 B.C.E.	Macedonia proper becomes a Roman province.
51–63 C.E.	The Apostle Paul and his followers come to Macedonia to preach Christianity.
500–600	Various Slavic tribes settle in Macedonia, Greece, Illyria, and Thrace.
855–886	The brothers Cyril and Methodius from Salonika create the first Slavonic alphabet (called Glagolitic) and promote Christianity among the Slavic peoples. Their disciples simplify it and rename it the Cyrillic alphabet in honor of Cyril. Cyril and Methodius's disciples, Clement and Naum, settle in Ohrid, spread

	Christianity in the Slavic language in this area, and establish a school in Ohrid.
976–1018	Samuel establishes his short-lived kingdom in Macedonia.
1371–1389	The Ottoman Empire overruns and conquers Macedonia.
1689	The uprising of Karpoš in northern Macedonia.
1767	Under pressure from the Greek Patriarch in Constantinople, the Turks abolish the Archdiocese of Ohrid, which had become a church that held its services in the local vernacular.
1822	The unsuccessful Neguš Uprising against Ottoman rule.
1828–1878	Greece, Serbia, and Bulgaria gain broad autonomy or independence from Turkish rule and display territorial aspirations for Macedonian territory, thus beginning the story of the so-called Macedonian Question.
1876	The failed Razlovtzi Uprising in eastern Macedonia against Ottoman rule.
1878–1879	The Macedonians rebel, again unsuccessfully, in eastern Macedonia.
1893	The Internal Macedonian Revolutionary Organization (IMRO) is founded in Salonika. Its objectives are national freedom and establishment of an independent Macedonian state. Goce Delčev becomes its leader.
1903	On 2 August 1903, IMRO launches the Ilinden Uprising against the Ottoman Empire. Although the revolutionaries briefly hold the small town of Kruševo and establish a republic with a government, the uprising is crushed by the Turks. Krste Petkov Misirkov publishes his work, *On Macedonian Matters.*
1912–1913	Balkan Wars. Greece, Serbia, and Bulgaria join forces to defeat the Ottoman army and conquer Macedonia in the First Balkan War. Bulgaria, angry over its share of the spoils, subsequently attacks its allies and in the Second Balkan War is defeated. Macedonia is denied independence, and in the Treaty of Bucharest (August 1913), it is partitioned.
1915–1918	Macedonia is occupied by the Germans and afterwards annexed to Bulgaria, which sides with the Central Powers.
1919	At the Paris Peace conference, the demands of the Macedonians for an independent and united Macedonia are ignored. The peacemakers instead sanction the partition of Macedonia.
1922	The exchange of population between Greece and Bulgaria. Thousands of

	Macedonians have to leave their ancestral homes in Aegean Macedonia.
1924	The Communist Party of the Kingdom of Serbs, Croats, and Slovenes issues the May Manifesto, which emphasizes the right of the Macedonian people to self-determination.
1934	The Resolution of the Communist International (Comintern), which provides the Macedonian language and nationality with international recognition.
1936	The Macedonian Literary Society is founded in Sofia by outstanding Macedonian writers.
1940	The Fifth Conference of the Communist Party of the Kingdom of Yugoslavia passes a resolution on the equality and right to self-determination of the Macedonian people.
1941	Bulgaria, as an ally of Hitler's Germany, annexes almost the entire territory of Macedonia (both Vardar and Aegean). On 11 October 1941, the Macedonians launch a war for liberation of Macedonia from the Bulgarian occupation.
2 August 1944	On the forty-first anniversary of the Ilinden Uprising, the Anti–Fascist Assembly of the National Liberation of Macedonia (ASNOM) proclaims a Macedonian state.
16 April 1945	The first government of the People's Republic of Macedonia is founded, with Lazar Koliševski as its president.
1946	The first constitution of the People's Republic of Macedonia is adopted. Bulgaria, under the leadership of Georgi Dimitrov, officially recognizes the existence of the Macedonian nation and of a Macedonian minority in Bulgaria.
1946–1949	In the Greek Civil War that follows World War II, an overwhelming majority of Macedonians from Aegean Macedonia support the Greek Communist Party (KKE), which promises them their rights after the war. After the communists are defeated, all national and minority rights of the Macedonians in Greece are denied.
1956	In the Bulgarian census of 1956, the majority of the population of Pirin Macedonia again declares itself as Macedonian. Bulgaria, however, under Todor Zhivkov, reverses its decision of recognizing the Macedonian nation and once again forbids free expression of Macedonian nationality and language in Bulgaria.

1958	The Archdiocese of Ohrid, abolished in 1767 by the Ottoman Turks under Greek pressure, is restored with an autonomous status.
1967	The Macedonian Academy of Arts and Sciences is founded. The autocephaly (independent status) of the Macedonian Orthodox Church is proclaimed.
1990	First multiparty elections in Macedonia. The nationalist party VMRO–DPMNE wins the greatest number of seats, but it is not able to form a majority government. The former communists (SDSM) forge a coalition government with the Albanian parties and SDS.
1991	Federal Yugoslavia disintegrates, as Slovenia, Croatia, and Bosnia declare independence. In a referendum on 8 September, the Macedonians proclaim independence. Kiro Gligorov is elected first president of independent Macedonia. A new constitution is adopted, declaring the Republic of Macedonia to be a sovereign, independent, civic, and democratic state, and recognizing complete equality of the Macedonians and the ethnic minorities in the country.
1993	Macedonia is admitted to the United Nations.
1994	Afraid that Macedonia might put forward a historical, cultural, and linguistic claim over Aegean Macedonia, Greece insists that there is no Macedonian nation and that the Macedonians have no right to use the name "Macedonia." Greece imposes a trade embargo on Macedonia because of the Macedonian refusal to rename the country, the nation, and the language. In

the second free elections in Macedonia, SDSM wins and forms a coalition government, again with the Albanian parties.

1995	Macedonia becomes a member of the Council of Europe. Human Rights Watch condemns Greece for the oppression of its large ethnic Macedonian minority, which Greece denies exists. Both Amnesty International and the European Parliament also urge Greece to recognize the existence of the Macedonian language and stop the oppression of ethnic Macedonians on the territory it appropriated in 1913.
1998	Opposition parties win the third free elections in Macedonia and oust the former communists (SDSM) and their Albanian allies from power.
1999	NATO intervention in Kosovo. More than 300,000 Albanian refugees come to Macedonia.
2001	Albanian insurrection in Macedonia. Short and violent war, which ends with the signing of the Framework Agreement.
2002	SDSM again comes to power and forms a coalition government with the former leader of the 2000 Albanian insurrection, Ali Ahmeti, who is granted amnesty. The country strives to implement the stipulations of the Framework Agreement, which grant Albanians equal rights and representation in the institutions of the system.
2004	The second president of the Republic, Boris Trajkovski, dies in a plane crash. Former SDSM leader Branko Crvenkovski is elected president.

BOSNIA-HERCEGOVINA

KATHERINE MCCARTHY

LAND AND PEOPLE

The Republic of Bosnia-Hercegovina declared its independence in 1991 and was recognized by the United Nations in 1992. Following a bloody war with Serbia and Montenegro (and sometimes Croatia), the American-brokered Dayton Peace Accords (negotiated in Dayton, Ohio) recognized the outlines of the new Bosnian state in 1995. The republic is a parliamentary democracy with universal suffrage at eighteen, but voting rights for employed citizens at sixteen. The Dayton Accords created a weak federal state and one of the most complicated constitutions in the world. Its three-member rotating presidency (representing each of the three main ethnic groups) is subordinate to a non-Bosnian UN High Representative, who may dismiss any member of the presidency. The republic consists of two entities: the Federation of Bosnia-Hercegovina (referred to as the Federation) and Republika Srpska (RS), both of which maintain their own armies and may negotiate binding treaties with other countries. The Federation (51 percent of the territory) is primarily Bosniak (Bosnian Muslim) and Croat. It includes the important cities of Tuzla, Maglaj, Bihać, Goražde, and Mostar. Republika Srpska (the remaining 49 percent of the country) is now principally Serb and includes the cities of Srebrenica, Banja Luka, Žepa, and Pale. Sarajevo, the capital of the republic, and Brčko have a special federal status. Strongly contested during the war, Brčko lies in the Posavina corridor, a 5-kilometer wide strip of land along the Sava River that connects the eastern and western portions of RS. It is also the Federation's only access to the Sava River, with its vital trade and communication links to the Danube and the rest of Europe. Its designation as a federal district means that Brčko remains outside of Federation and RS authority. As the capital of Bosnia-Hercegovina, Sarajevo also makes up its own district and is not subject to control by either entity.

Bosnia-Hercegovina covers 51,129 square kilometers, an area slightly smaller than West Virginia. According to the 1991 census, the prewar population was 4.4 million people. Current population estimates vary from 2.9 to 3.9 million, due to unreliable statistics stemming from the widespread fatalities and displacements during the 1992–1995 war. The Republic of Bosnia-Hercegovina is bordered to the north by Croatia and the Sava and Una Rivers, to the east by the Drina River and Serbia, to the west by the Dinaric mountain ranges and the Primorje region of Croatia, and by Montenegrin mountains to the southwest. Its coastline consists of one 20-kilometer stretch of land on the Adriatic Sea near the Croatian island of Pelješac, which provides no port facility. The republic has been using the Croatian port of Ploče near the mouth of the Neretva River for access to the sea.

Historically, the country is composed of two regions, Bosnia and Hercegovina, which are characterized by their mountain and river systems. Most of the country's cities grew up next to its 2,200 kilometers of river. In Bosnia, the major

Sarajevo, the capital of Bosnia-Hercegovina, 1983. (Dean Conger/Corbis)

rivers (and their cities) are the Una (Bihać, Bosanski Du-
bica), the Sana (Sanski Most, Prijedor), the Vrbas (Jajce,
Banja Luka), the Bosna (Zenica, Doboj, Sarajevo), and the
Drina (Goražde, Zvornik). These rivers flow north into
Bosnia's largest river, the Sava (Brčko, Bosanski Brod,
Bosanska Gradiška), itself a tributary of the Danube that
empties into the Black Sea. Bosnia derives its name from the
Bosna River, which flows from the Sarajevo-Zenica basin
into the Sava River. With no coastal facilities, the republic
maintains four inland waterway ports on the Sava River at
Bosanska Gradiška, Bosanski Brod, Bosanski Samac, and
Brčko. Hercegovina accounts for 10 percent of the population and 20 percent of the area in the state. This region was
called Hum until 1448, when Stefan Vukčić declared himself *herceg* (duke) of the region. Ever since, it has been identified as Hercegovina. The core of Hercegovina surrounds
the slender Neretva River valley, where Mostar, Hercegovina's principal city, is located. The Neretva River is the
country's only navigable river that flows into the Adriatic
Sea. However, the Neretva meets the Adriatic through a
narrow strip of Croatia.

The four traditional geographic regions of Bosnia-
Hercegovina (North Bosnia, Central Bosnia, the High
Karst, the Hercegovinian lowlands) do not correspond to
the Dayton Peace Accords' entity divisions. North Bosnia,
Central Bosnia, and most of the High Karst lie in historic

Bosnia, while the southern stretch of the High Karst and
Hercegovinian lowlands form the smaller area of historic
Hercegovina). North Bosnia, an area oriented to the Sava
River, made up of lowlands and hills, is the largest and most
densely populated of the four. With its major cities of Banja
Luka in the west and Tuzla in the east, North Bosnia incorporates 40 percent of the country and 55 percent of the
pre-1992 population. Central Bosnia, the core of the medieval Bosnian state, is a mountainous region. Centered in
the Sarajevo-Zenica basin, Central Bosnia covers 27 percent
of the state and includes 32 percent of its population. The
two remaining regions are sparsely populated, with little industrial development. The High Karst, covering 21 percent
of the country, consists of high mountain ridges *(bilo)* and
sunken valleys *(polje)* in western Bosnia and Hercegovina. It
contains no major cities and only 6 percent of the population. Finally, the lowlands of Hercegovina form a small sub-
Mediterranean region made up of polje and low plateaus.
With its major city in Mostar, this area supports 7 percent
of the population on 12 percent of the territory.

Rising dramatically from the Adriatic coast, the Dinaric
mountain ranges dominate Bosnia-Hercegovina's landscape.
These mountains cover virtually all of Hercegovina and
most of Bosnia, extending 563 kilometers in a northwest-
southeast direction and 100 to 160 kilometers across. Of the
country as a whole, 57 percent (almost 29,000 square kilo-

meters) is at elevations over 700 meters, while only 8 percent (4,000 square kilometers) is below 150 meters. The mountains average 1,200 to 1,800 meters with seventy peaks above 1,500 meters and ten over 2,000 meters high. Mt. Maglić, the highest peak, reaches 2,386 meters above sea level. Cut only by the Neretva River valley, the Dinaric Alps have long isolated Bosnia-Hercegovina from the Adriatic Sea. Geographers divide these mountains into three sub-zones: the Inner Dinaric Range, the High Karst, and the Adriatic coast (primarily in Croatia). The Inner Dinaric Alps slope toward the Sava River to form the southern part of the Pannonian Plain, called the Posavina. Here, narrow canyons are interspersed with open valleys and logging and mining predominate.

The most distinctive region in Bosnia-Hercegovina's topography is the High Karst. The term *karst* originates from a geological description of an area in Slovenia but is now applied wherever this type of terrain is found (such as areas in Florida, Kentucky, the American Midwest, the Causses plateaus in southwestern France, the Kwangsi area of China, and Mexico's Yucatan Peninsula). The High Karst reaches its greatest height in the south and west, extends the length of the Dinaric Alps and is 80 kilometers wide at its widest point. More rugged and barren than the Inner Dinaric Alps, the High Karst lacks above-ground lakes or streams. It is characterized by its cave networks, sinkholes, sunken fields, underground rivers, and short, widely spaced river valleys (such as the Zrmanja, Krka, Cetina, Neretva, and Morača).

The karst formation requires heavy rainfall and good underground water circulation to erode the dolomite and limestone rock near the surface. Widening cracks in the rock eventually evolve into a cave system or an underground stream network. Most of the principal cave areas in the world are in karst regions. If a cave becomes large enough (as well as close enough to the surface), the top collapses, producing a sinkhole. Sinkholes commonly run together and form larger depressions called polje, flat floored "fields" covered with a red arable topsoil made up of the insoluble limestone residue. Most polje have an elongated floor with steep enclosing walls that range from 50 to 100 meters. Large polje can be 259 square kilometers or more, forming arable islands in the harsh karst terrain. The country's largest polje, Livanjsko Polje, covers 652.6 square kilometers. In many karst areas, water is scarce in spite of heavy rainfall because so much water disappears into the sinkholes. In other areas underground rivers surface and then disappear, creating natural springs and thermal baths.

NATURAL ENVIRONMENT

Bosnia-Hercegovina's mountains and valleys are heavily forested. Forest covers 53 percent of Bosnia-Hercegovina (2.7 million hectares), making it the fourth most forested country in Europe. Although 78 percent of this forest is publicly owned, only 0.55 percent is protected. Nevertheless, much of the forest has remained intact and relatively unpolluted because of the lack of road access to it. A temperate continental forest of deciduous willow, poplar, ash, elm, and oak predominates in North Bosnia's Pannonian Plain area. This region also holds marshlands and saline areas where native steppe plants grow. Mountain forest containing oak and hornbeam is found in lower karst areas, while beech and fir prevail in the High Karst. Near the Adriatic Sea, the forest becomes dominated by holm oak (similar to the live oak in the American southwest) and aleppo pine.

Forests provide the habitat for most of the country's flora and fauna. Species from both the prehistoric tertiary (1 to 70 million years ago) and pre–Ice Age periods, as well as from the modern Balkan era, can be found in Bosnia-Hercegovina. Unfortunately, animal and plant life had not been extensively documented before 1992, and much of the existing information was lost during the 1992–1995 war. Still, biologists believe that Bosnia-Hercegovina's extensive karst region is rich in biodiversity and endemic species. The government estimates that the country has almost 4,500 vascular plant species, including 675 widely used in medicine. Although the area is most known for its bears, wolves, wild pigs, wildcats, chamois, otter, fox, badgers, and falcons, Bosnia-Hercegovina also provides habitat for hundreds of other animal species. Many of these plants and animals have become rare or threatened.

The International Union for the Conservation of Nature (IUCN) has a red list of globally threatened species, which names sixty-one animals and sixty-four plant species in Bosnia-Hercegovina (the number threatened at the state level is much higher). The vast majority of these are found only in the Balkans, in three countries or fewer. For example, the Serbian spruce, common throughout Europe millions of years ago, is now thought to consist of only one thousand trees on four mountains near the Drina River in Eastern Bosnia. The slender-billed curlew, common in the nineteenth century, has suffered a decline of 80 percent or more in the last ten years. Today it breeds only in Russia, and with as few as fifty left in the wild, the slender-billed curlew has an extremely high likelihood of extinction. The Danube salmon, found in the Danube River system, is one of the largest freshwater fish in the world, reaching up to 2 meters in length and weighing up to 100 kilograms. Its population has declined by 50 percent in the last decade. Today it lives in fewer than six locations and its habitat is limited to 777 square kilometers. Pollution, overfishing, and shrinking habitat are expected to halve the Danube salmon's population in the next ten years, placing it at a very high risk of extinction in the wild.

The Republic of Bosnia-Hercegovina protects 28,127 hectares of land. The five largest national parks account for 89 percent of the protected area. Located near the Montenegrin border, the largest, Sutjeska National Park, encompasses mountains (including Mt. Maglić), old-growth forest, lakes, extensive woodlands, and mountain pastures. Perućica Primeval Reserve, connected to Sutjeska National Park, is the largest old-growth forest sanctuary in Europe. Five smaller Primeval Reserves and part of the Kozara National Park also shelter these old growth forests. South of Mostar, at the state's one bird reserve, Hutovo Blato, the fast-moving Krupa River joins four lakes and their marshes, meadows, and riverside poplar and willow woods to shelter 240 kinds of birds, as well as many varieties of eel and freshwater fish. This is the best place to find endangered birds such as the pygmy cormorant, the ferruginous duck, and the corncrake (a type of rail).

Bosnia-Hercegovina's economy is based on its natural resources: arable land and pasture (food, food processing, tobacco, tobacco products, textiles), mines (coal, iron ore, bauxite, lead, zinc, manganese), forests (logging, timber, construction materials, wooden furniture, cellulose, paper, medicinal herbs), and rivers (hydroelectric power, fishing). In addition, the state produces steel, arms, chemicals, and domestic appliances. It refines oil, constructs aircraft, and assembles ground vehicles. After 1991, huge increases in oil prices, declines in trade, hyperinflation, food and medicine shortages, as well as insolvent banks created a large black market. Federal economic data are limited because official statistics are published by each entity, but there are no national statistics available. In addition, the country's large black market does not show up on official records. The 1992–1995 war caused the economy to shrink by 80 percent according to CIA statistics. Since independence there has been some economic recovery, but with the annual per capita gross domestic product at $1,700 per person, production remains well below 1990 levels. The Bosnian mark, the republic's new currency (tied to the euro) is the only accepted currency. Since the war destroyed much of the region's economic infrastructure, the state still needs massive reconstruction. Almost 3 million square hectares of land remains mined, and rivers (especially parts of the Sava River) are still blocked by destroyed bridges, silt, and debris. Most of the country's 1,020 kilometers of rail need repair from war damage. The war also destroyed utilities, water supplies, and treatment facilities, which has created water shortages, solid waste build-up (including 800 metric tons of expired medicine sent as humanitarian aid), and health hazards.

In 1998 agriculture in Bosnia-Hercegovina took up 2.63 million hectares. Even at the height of collectivization in 1951, Bosnia-Hercegovina's agriculture remained overwhelmingly private. However, after 1953, strict limits on the size of individual farms and inadequate investment kept agriculture throughout former Yugoslavia inefficient and undeveloped. Although 19 percent of the country's land is used for arable crops and another 20 percent for permanent pastureland, Bosnia-Hercegovina is a net food importer. The most and best arable land lies in North Bosnia, where the Inner Dinaric Range merges into the Pannonian Plain. In addition, the areas in Central Bosnia between the Vrbas and Drina Rivers contain fertile valleys that stretch toward the Sava. Some of the bigger polje in the High Karst (Livanjsko Polje, Imotsko Polje (shared with Croatia), Popovo Polje (Dubrovink hinterland) also sustain commercial agriculture. However, summer drought and heavy spring and fall rains make both the karst and plains regions susceptible to flooding.

Commercial agricultural produces crops, livestock, and industrial goods. The state's principal grain crops include corn, wheat, and barley. Vegetable and fruit crops, including soy, potatoes, apples, pears, and almonds, are also important. The sub-Mediterranean lowland region of Hercegovina produces wine grapes, early fruit and vegetables, tobacco, citrus, and flower crops. Plums, especially from northeast Bosnia, are used for making jam and the popular plum brandy (šljivović). Both Bosnia and Hercegovina are well known for livestock raising. Cattle predominate near the Sava River, and swine dominate in the northern borderlands adjacent to Serbia. Sheep raising is a significant part of the economy in the High Karst, which is renowned for its lamb and its wool textiles.

In addition to supplying food and wood for timber, furniture, cellulose, and paper products, Bosnia-Hercegovina's forests provide rich mining reserves. Beneath the forests lie coal, metals, and mineral deposits that have been mined for centuries. Copper, gold, silver, lead, and zinc were excavated before Roman times. In the medieval period, Bosnian and Serb smelters were in demand all over Europe. Today, coal (both lignite and bituminous), iron ore, and bauxite are the most economically important mined commodities. Most mines are found in Hercegovina and eastern Bosnia; however, important reserves of coal and iron ore are also located near Banja Luka and in the Kozara mountains in North Bosnia. Lignite and bauxite mines near Mostar predominate in Hercegovina, while Bosnian miners extract lignite, manganese, and iron ore. Although zinc, mercury, and manganese are still mined, they are less significant today than coal and heavy metals.

POPULATION

Bosnia-Hercegovina, like its Ottoman, Habsburg, and Yugoslav predecessors, is a multinational state. Today, most citizens identify themselves as one of three Slavic groups: Bosnian Croats (17 percent), Bosnian Serbs (31 percent), or Bosniaks (Bosnian Muslims; 44 percent). In addition to Slavs, smaller groups of Bosnians living in the region for centuries include Albanians (descended from Illyrians), Germans, Roma (Gypsies), Jews, Romanians, Turks, and Hungarians. With no independent state between 1463 and 1995, no distinctive language, no single dominant ethnicity, and no common religion, it is difficult to describe one Bosnian people. An independent Bosnian state did govern the region from 1180 to 1463. Subsequently, Bosnians belonged to the Ottoman Empire (1463–1878), the Habsburg monarchy (1878–1918), and Yugoslavia (1918–1992). Language neither unified Bosnians (as it did German speakers) nor did it adequately distinguish them from neighboring Serbs and Croats. The establishment of three medieval Christian churches in Bosnia-Hercegovina precluded a common religious identity from taking hold. Indeed, religion has divided the Slavs of Bosnia-Hercegovina since 1054. Religious identity became central during the Ottoman period. At this time, many Slavs turned to Islam; the Serbian Orthodox Church grew, as it officially represented all Christians in Ottoman Bosnia; and Jewish immigrants formed small, vibrant communities. While neither ethnicity nor religion can define Bosnian identity, they both played key roles. Geographically isolated by rugged terrain, Bosnians developed their unique culture and distinct national identity by blending the diverse and often divisive characteristics of Bosnia's many peoples.

Language in Bosnia-Hercegovina

There are three official languages recognized in Bosnia-Hercegovina today: Bosnian, Serbian, and Croatian. Before 1995, these languages were officially known as Serbo-Croatian. The definition of these languages today, as in the past, has both etymological and political roots. Bosnian, Serbian, and Croatian are variants of Serbo-Croatian, one of the major South Slavic languages. This language group includes Slovene, Serbo-Croatian, Macedonian, and Bulgarian. There are three basic dialects of Serbo-Croatian, based on the word of each for "what" (*kaj, ča,* or *što*). In Bosnia-Hercegovina (as well as in Croatia, Serbia, and Montenegro), people speak *štokavian*. Within this dialect, variations in vowel pronunciation make up three general subdivisions: *ikavian* (spoken in eastern central Bosnia), *ijekavian* (spoken in central and northwestern Bosnia as well as Dalmatia), and *ekavian* (spoken in east-central Bosnia and in Serbia). In addition, each region and linguistic subdivision has specific word choice preferences. These differences in speech patterns vary by region rather than by nation.

In the medieval period, Bosnians wrote their language using two alphabets: Glagolitic and a Bosnian Cyrillic script known as Bosančica. During the Ottoman period, educated Bosnian elites wrote official, religious, and literary works in Latin, Greek, Persian, Arabic, and Turkish. The Bosnian vernacular also continued to be spoken. In the seventeenth century, two accessible Bosnian vernacular literatures emerged. Bosnian Franciscan literature introduced West European literature to Bosnian Catholics using a modified phonetic Bosnian Cyrillic script. Alhamijado literature used the Arabic script to write the Bosnian language, appealing to middle-class Bosnian Muslims. These vernaculars were eclipsed in the nineteenth century by the standardization of Serbo-Croatian.

The nineteenth-century linguist who standardized Serbo-Croatian, Vuk Karadžic, believed that in spite of religious and regional differences, South Slavs possessed a common culture that set them apart from the surrounding Albanians, Hungarians, Romanians, Greeks, and Germans. Karadžić believed that language defined the nation, an idea that reflected nationalist movements that were sweeping Europe at the time. The appeal of language to unify peoples in multinational states and distinguish themselves from the monarchies that ruled them was particularly powerful. Serbo-Croatian was a common national characteristic of South Slavs from the Habsburg monarchy, the Ottoman Empire, Serbia, and Montenegro. He wanted to use language to unify as many South Slavs as possible into one distinct nation-state. Karadžic also sought to provide the vernacular with a phonetic alphabet that would increase literacy. In doing so, he chose a dialect from Hercegovina as the basis of a standardized spelling that all Serbs, Croats, and Bosnians could understand. (Ljudevit Gaj, a Croatian grammarian and leader of the Croatian national revival, also advocated using štokavian found in Hercegovina as a literary language.) Karadžic urged schoolchildren to write as they spoke and to speak as they wrote. He modified the Latin alphabet and the Cyrillic alphabet to create a phonetic Serbo-Croatian with two alphabets that corresponded to each other letter for letter. Serbs generally write Serbo-Croatian using the Cyrillic alphabet, while Croats favor the Latin alphabet. Typically, Bosnians read both the Latin and the Cyrillic alphabets. The country's biggest daily, *Oslobodjenje* (Liberation), for example, is written in both alphabets. Thus Serbo-Croatian emerged as the standard, vernacular literary language in the early to mid-1800s.

The politics of the day has also influenced whether Bosnian, Serbian, and Croatian are viewed as one language or three. Under both the Yugoslav monarchy (1918–1941) and the communist period (1945–1990) of Yugoslavia, Serbo-Croatian was seen as one language, and similarities among dialects were stressed. As nationalism increased before the breakup of Yugoslavia, Serbs, Croats, and Bosnians emphasized the differences in regional usage and highlighted their own distinct pre-1800 literary traditions, arguing that each national group had its own language. Since 1995, the various dialect subdivisions that correspond to distinct national groups have led to the relabeling of Serbo-Croatian as Bosnian, Serbian, and Croatian.

Language played an important role in defining groups within the Romani (Gypsy) and Jewish communities as well. The oldest Jewish community in Bosnia-Hercegovina consisted of Sephardic Jews who spoke Ladino, a sixteenth-century form of Spanish. (It was in the sixteenth century that Jews expelled from Spain first settled in Sarajevo.) Any Yiddish-speaking Ashkenazi Jews from Belgrade or Vienna who settled in Bosnia-Hercegovina assimilated, and the community remained Ladino-speaking. After Habsburg annexation of the territory in 1878, a much larger group of Yiddish speakers from the Habsburg Empire (principally from Hungary, Galicia, Poland, and the Czech

(continues)

(continued)

lands) swelled the population from 2,000 to 9,300 by 1900. As the Sephardim had lived in the region for hundreds of years, they looked down on the more rural Ashkenazi newcomers. The Jewish community remained divided along cultural and linguistic lines, each with its own synagogues, schools, and cultural organizations.

Some historians have also divided the Roma population along linguistic lines. The most assimilated were known as "white gypsies," who no longer spoke much Romani and lived in settled areas by 1900. In Bosnia, these white gypsies practiced Islam (whereas in Serbia and Macedonia they were Orthodox). Nomadic "black gypsies" spoke a Romanian-influenced language, indicating that they may have come from Transylvania. These Roma worked as tinkers, lived in tents, and also practiced Islam; they were the most affected by the Serb massacres of Muslims in World War II.

ETHNIC IDENTITY

Bosnians are mainly a mixture of Slavic peoples who absorbed those living in the region before them. Scholars believe the original inhabitants of Bosnia-Hercegovina were Illyrians and Scordisci (an Illyrian-Celtic people). Most Slavs in the area trace their ancestry to the sixth-century invasions that followed the fall of Rome in 476. In the waning decades of the Roman Empire, many peoples migrated into the area. Goths inflicted massive defeats on the Romans in the Balkans in the third and fourth centuries before reaching Rome. By the fifth century, Huns and Iranian Alans lived in Bosnia. Slavs and Avars, a Turkic-speaking tribe from the Caucasus, arrived in the region in the sixth century, when Slav settlers established themselves throughout the Balkan Peninsula. At first the Avars dominated, but the combined forces of the Byzantine, Croat, and Bulgarian armies drove them out of the Balkans in the seventh century.

At this time, two new Slavic tribes arrived in the Balkans: the Serbs and the Croats. By the second quarter of the seventh

Muslims pray in Sarajevo's Gazi Husrevbeg mosque, built in 1531. (Dean Conger/Corbis)

century, Serbs controlled the southwest portion of modern Serbia (medieval Raška), Montenegro, and Hercegovina (medieval Hum), while the Croats dominated modern Croatia and most of modern Bosnia (except for the eastern Drina valley). This Slavic ethnic base, primarily Serbs and Croats, absorbed the peoples who had come to the region earlier: Illyrians, Celts, Goths, Alans, Huns, Avars, and Romans from all over Europe.

RELIGIOUS IDENTITY

In identifying themselves, each of the three main peoples of Bosnia-Hercegovina points to a distinct historic religious culture. The Bosnian Croats tend to be Roman Catholic, the Bosnian Serbs are overwhelmingly Orthodox, and the Bosniaks identify with a specifically Bosnian Islamic culture. Members of these groups may or may not practice these religions. Christianity first came to Bosnia in the first century C.E., but it had no mass following before the ninth century. In the medieval period (800–1463), Bosnia-Hercegovina became the home of three Christian religions: Roman Catholicism, Serbian Orthodoxy, and the Church of Bosnia. However, these medieval churches and popular identification with them were weak. In the Ottoman period (1463–1878), Bosnians acquired strong religious identities. At this time, both the Islamic and the Orthodox churches grew. In contrast, the Catholic presence receded, and the Church of Bosnia, disbanded in 1459, did not survive into the early modern period. Finally, Jewish exiles formed permanent settlements in the region in the early 1500s.

THREE CHRISTIAN MEDIEVAL CHURCHES

The presence of two rival Christian churches (Roman Catholic, Serbian Orthodox) in Bosnia-Hercegovina is primarily a consequence of medieval states using religion to extend their political influence after the fall of the Roman Empire (476). Emperor Diocletian (284–305) divided Rome into two halves, with Bosnia-Hercegovina in the western half. Emperor Constantine (324–337) moved Rome's capital to Byzantium (modern Istanbul), shifting the empire's political center to the eastern half. Constantine designated Christianity as Rome's official state religion, renamed the capital Constantinople, and transformed it into the center of Roman power and Christianity. Nearly a century after Rome fell, despite many attempts to reunite the empire, Rome and Constantinople emerged as rival seats of power, each claiming political authority beyond its borders. When the Western Roman Empire was defeated, invaders did not sack the monasteries. After the destruction of the western half of the empire, six successor states emerged. The Catholic Church provided support to various states in exchange for protection from invaders. By 814, the Papal States emerged as a Catholic state with the pope as its ruler. The pope claimed jurisdiction over all Christians, but the Papal States was a weak shadow of the former Roman state. In contrast, the emperor Justinian (527–565) refashioned the eastern part of the Roman Empire into a strong and dynamic Byzantine Empire, which claimed Bosnia-Hercegov-

ina, among other provinces. The Byzantine Empire became the world's preeminent Christian state, based on Roman law, Greek culture, and the Greek language. Thus, the division of the Roman Empire ultimately led to the creation of rival states and two rival Christianities (with no doctrinal differences before 1054).

In the ninth century, both Rome and Constantinople sent missionaries to Christianize Bosnia-Hercegovina, where neither state had real political control. Roman missions had great success in Croatia and Dalmatia, while Byzantine priests converted those living in Bulgaria, Macedonia, and much of Serbia. Since these missions carried civil and legal authority, they spread not only Christianity but also papal and Byzantine political influence. Although both empires claimed to lead the Christian Church, there were no significant doctrinal differences in these missions before the Great Schism of 1054 established Roman Catholicism and Christian Orthodoxy. After the Great Schism, popular church affiliation fell along political lines. At this time, Bosnia (which had been conquered by Catholic Croatia in the eleventh century and later annexed by Catholic Hungary in 1101) became primarily Roman Catholic, under the supervision of Croatian archbishops. Hercegovina, under Serb dynastic rule, became overwhelmingly Orthodox. In 1219 the Orthodox Church in Hercegovina became subordinate to the archbishop of Serbia, the head of the newly autocephalous Serbian Orthodox Church. Thus, Bosnia-Hercegovina became divided between Catholic Bosnia and Orthodox Hercegovina.

Political rivalry in the mid-thirteenth century produced a third Christian church, the Church of Bosnia. After a failed bid to dominate an independent Bosnian state (1180–1463), Hungarian rulers persuaded the pope to declare the Bosnian Catholic Church heretical and proclaim a crusade (1235–1241) against it. The crusade failed, but the pope removed the Catholic Church in Bosnia from the jurisdiction of the archbishop of Dubrovnik (in Croatia) and placed it under Hungarian control. The Bosnian clergy refused to recognize the Hungarian bishop's authority and drove him out of Bosnia into neighboring Slavonia. As a result, the Church of Bosnia established itself as an independent schismatic Christian church with its Catholic theology intact. From 1342 to 1878, Bosnia's Catholic clergy was limited to Franciscan monks.

Church membership in all three Christian churches tended to be regional. By the 1300s, the Church of Bosnia dominated in central Bosnia, as far east as the Drina and south to Hercegovina. Orthodoxy dominated in southern and eastern Bosnia (especially along the Drina River valley) and in Hercegovina. Catholicism predominated in northern and western Bosnia, especially around Franciscan monasteries and neighboring market towns. Bosnia was unlike many other European medieval states, however, in that all of its churches remained weak and none developed into a state church. Bosnian rulers and nobles intermarried and formed political alliances across religious denominations, changing confessions easily. From 1347, all the medieval rulers of Bosnia were Catholic, except for Ostoje (r. 1398–1404, 1409–1418), who belonged to the Church of

Church of Bosnia

The Church of Bosnia was one of three Christian churches that existed in medieval Bosnia. It has long been mistakenly associated with the dualist Bogomil heresy, which had pockets of adherents throughout the Balkans. The Church of Bosnia's liturgy, however, contained no doctrinal differences from contemporary Roman Catholicism. Rather, the Church of Bosnia emerged as a direct consequence of Hungary's attempt to dominate medieval Bosnia-Hercegovina.

In contrast to Bosnia, Hungary was a Catholic state, and the king was the head of the Hungarian Catholic Church. Papal denunciations of clerical illiteracy and ignorance of basic sacraments among Bosnia's monks fueled an unsuccessful Hungarian crusade (1235–1241), which used unspecified heresy charges to justify military conquest and the imposition of Hungarian religious authority. Subsequent attempts to politically dominate Bosnia by placing its Catholic clergy under Hungarian diocesan authority also failed. Instead of accepting the pope's 1252 appointment of a Hungarian bishop to supervise them, Bosnia's clerics broke with Rome and established their own Church of Bosnia. They remained theologically Catholic and monastic, but no longer recognized Roman Catholic church hierarchy. Since the Vatican recognized only Orthodoxy as a schismatic church, it labeled the Church of Bosnia heretical, despite the absence of any doctrinal differences. In spite of continual papal calls for a crusade against the Church of Bosnia, the country's rulers protected it and banned Catholic clergy from entering Bosnia until 1342, when the Orthodox Ban (governor) Kotromanić designated the monastic Franciscan order as the state's sole Catholic institution. The Franciscans remained the sole Catholic institution in the region until the Habsburg occupation over five hundred years later.

Papal heresy charges against the Church of Bosnia became more specific after 1440, a period in which the papacy was pressuring Bosnian nobles to convert to Catholicism. At this time, the Vatican asserted for the first time, on the basis of confessions made under torture, that the Church of Bosnia followed the dualist Bogomil theology. In 1459 the papacy demanded that the Bosnian king Tomaš suppress the Church of Bosnia because of its dualist heresy. In exchange for promised military aid against the impending Ottoman invasion, King Tomaš directed all Church of Bosnia clerics to either convert to Catholicism or to seek asylum in Orthodox Hercegovina. According to the pope, only forty fled. The Church of Bosnia did not survive this suppression. Papal military aid never materialized.

The accusation that the Church of Bosnia belonged to the dualist Bogomil sect lacks evidence to connect the church to the small number of dualists in the region. Dualists believe in the struggle between two powerful spiritual forces: a good, other-worldly God and an evil, materialist Satan. In contrast, the Church of Bosnia professed one omnipotent God. Bogomils rejected the Trinity, sainthood, and the Old Testament, all of which the Church of Bosnia accepted. Dualists rejected religious art, but Church of Bosnia gospels are lavishly illustrated. In fact, Hrvoje's Missal, an illuminated Church of Bosnia missal, confirms the church's adherence to Roman Catholic theological doctrine. The preference for conversion to Catholicism over emigration to Hercegovina in 1459 also suggests close theological ties between the Roman Catholic Church and the Church of Bosnia.

(continues)

Bosnia. In exchange for the promise of papal aid in fighting the Ottoman army in 1459, King Stefan Tomaš gave Church of Bosnia leaders the option of conversion to Catholicism to avoid expulsion. Most converted, and the Church of Bosnia ceased to exist.

ISLAM, CHRISTIANITY, AND OTTOMAN RULE

When the Ottomans conquered Bosnia in 1463, there was virtually no Orthodox presence in the country, only a small Catholic contingent of Franciscans and a defunct Church of Bosnia. The last fortress in Hercegovina capitulated in 1482, with the region's Orthodox character intact. Over the fifteenth and sixteenth centuries, most Christian Slavs slowly became Muslim. The Ottomans did not settle Turkish peoples in Bosnia-Hercegovina as they did in some other parts of the Balkans. There was no state policy of Islamicization in Bosnia-Hercegovina as there was in Albania. Using Ottoman tax records, Noel Malcolm estimates that, in 1468, 194,625 Christians and 1,660 Muslims lived in the Bosnian *sandžak* (military-administrative district; 1483–1580). In 1469 fewer than 1 percent of households professed the Islamic faith. By 1520, roughly 98,085 Christians and 84,675 Muslims lived in the sandžak of Bosnia. This area had experienced population stagnation, and no significant Muslim immigration since 1485, when there were fewer than 22,000 Muslims. By the early seventeenth century, Bosnia-Hercegovina had become a predominantly Muslim region,

(continued)

Nonetheless, the identification of the medieval Church of Bosnia with the Bogomils became widespread beginning in the mid-nineteenth century because it served the interests of those with political claims on the region, who wanted to deny the existence of a distinct Bosnian identity and culture. To account for the large number of conversions from Christianity to Islam, the Bogomil theory claimed that Bosniaks were the descendants of members of the Church of Bosnia, who had converted en masse to Islam after the Ottoman conquest. This explanation did not support claims that Bosniaks were "really" Croats or Serbs, but it did help nationalists (who identified religion with nation in Bosnia) deny that Catholics and Orthodox church members converted to Islam and maintain the fiction of Croat and Serb national identity in medieval Bosnia. The identification of Bosniaks with allegedly Bogomil Church of Bosnia descendants obscured the appeal of the dynamic Islamic faith, the absence of any national identity, and the weakness of the Roman Catholic and Orthodox churches in the region. Nationalist claims required the existence of strong medieval Catholic and Orthodox communities to argue that Croats and Serbs were "ancient" nations that had been subjugated by the Habsburg and Ottoman states and deserved to live in their own nation-state. After 1878, the Habsburg administration also encouraged this theory because it divided Bosnians by emphasizing three separate, competing cultures.

The denial of a distinct Bosnian culture was so strong that artifacts not found in the Catholic Croat or Orthodox Serb traditions were designated as "Bogomil" rather than Bosnian. For example, Bosnia's massive medieval gravestones, known as stećci, continue to be referred to as "Bogomil tombstones." Unknown outside of Bosnia-Hercegovina, stećci were not part of the wider Catholic Croat, Orthodox Serb, or Bogomil cultures. In contrast to any of the Christian churches in medieval Bosnia, Bogomils rejected the cross (an important feature in stećci design) and shunned religious art. Stećci are not found in centers of Bogomil belief. Within Bosnia-Hercegovina, however, Bosnians of all faiths used stećci to mark their graves. The existence of the stećci suggests that Bosnia's medieval Bosnian culture existed independently from Serbia and Croatia. By relegating the stećci to the marginal Bogomils, Serb and Croat nationalists maintained their claims to Bosnia's medieval heritage, while Habsburg officials could diffuse claims that Bosniaks were "really" Serbs or Croats. In 1909 Austrian archeologists looking for Roman artifacts discovered the tomb of Kulin, Bosnia's Catholic Ban (1180–1204), in a church that had been buried under the fourteenth century Saint Nicholas Church in Visoko. The strong identification of the stećci with the Church of Bosnia led the archeologists to break the 700-year-old stećak into pieces and leave it unlabeled in the basement of Sarajevo's Provincial Museum.

The Church of Bosnia was a striking example of a medieval schismatic church. In contrast to other medieval states, Bosnia developed no official state church and no privileged religion. This feature gave it religious tolerance but also made the state vulnerable to political attack and military invasion. Although all but one of Bosnia's kings were Catholic, they protected the Church of Bosnia for over two hundred years in spite of papal attempts to suppress it. The political use of the vague heresy charges against the Bosnian Catholic Church before 1252 and later accusations of Bogomilism in the Church of Bosnia has maintained debate over the nature of this borderland church for over 500 years after its demise.

with roughly 150,000 Catholics, 75,000 Orthodox, and 450,000 Muslims.

Under Ottoman rule, religious affiliation became a fundamental part of Bosnian identity. The Ottoman Empire (1463–1878) was a feudal state that categorized its people by religious community (each community forming a *millet;* in Bosnia: Muslim, Christian, and Jewish) and by legal status (the categories being Ottoman, or subject peoples, called *reaya* [ra'ya]). Each millet was responsible for its members' obligations to the state. Thus, religious affiliation became an integral part of one's identity, regardless of the extent of one's devotion. The state's recognition of Jewish and Christian millets gave each of these groups limited self-government and the freedom to practice their faiths. Muslims participated in the dominant culture, enjoyed legal privileges denied non-Muslims, and adhered to a separate tax code. However, conversion to Islam did not free those considered subject peoples from inclusion in the reaya, to which both Muslims and non-Muslims belonged. According to the 1468 tax records, 1,170 (70 percent) of Bosnia's 1,660 Muslims were reaya. As in other European feudal states, a military-administrative class (called Ottomans) ran the state and enjoyed most of its real advantages. The Ottoman conquest of the region was not a religious crusade; it was intended to extract soldiers, treasure, and income from Bosnia to pursue further wars.

In Ottoman Bosnia-Hercegovina, not only did Islam expand but the Orthodox Church grew at the expense of Catholicism. Until the Ottoman period, the Orthodox Church had been important in Hercegovina but barely active in Bosnia. When the Ottoman state designated the Serbian Orthodox Church to represent the Christian millet, that church acquired a privileged status among Christians. Catholics were required to pay taxes to the Orthodox Church (in addition to their Catholic contributions). At this time, many Bosnian Catholics left the region. Their land was resettled by Orthodox Christians from Hercegovina and Serbia, adding to Orthodoxy's growing strength in Bosnia. New Orthodox churches took over Roman Catholic ones. Sometimes it was difficult to get Ottoman permission to repair a Catholic church. Ottoman judges often favored Orthodox members in legal disputes with Catholics. Therefore, some Catholic parishes converted to Orthodoxy in order to remain Christian. Despite these relative advantages over Catholicism, many members of the Orthodox Church converted to Islam.

The Ottoman conquest brought a well-organized, popular, and dynamic Islamic church, one that attracted many converts in Bosnia. Before 1463, the Catholic and Orthodox Churches in the region had little institutional organization, no established parishes, and few clergy. A church member might see a priest less than once a year. Islam filled the religious vacuum left by the weak medieval Christian churches. With only fragile ties to Christianity, Islam's privileged legal status (including possible freedom from slavery) and the dominant culture attracted many Bosnians.

Conversion to Islam did not bring great economic advantages. Muslims were exempt from some financial burdens but acquired others, from which non-Muslims were exempt. For example, only non-Muslims were required to pay an annual tax of one to four ducats (equivalent to the price of twenty to eighty kilograms of wheat). On the other hand, Muslims paid an alms tax as part of their religious obligations and were subject to military draft, from which Christians were exempt. As the Ottoman armies swept through the Balkans, they used cavalrymen (spahis), who were given land holdings (usually small *timar* estates of four to twenty hectares) as payment for their military service. Until the early sixteenth century, spahis could be (and many were) Christian. However, these timar estates carried heavy financial burdens. In return for the use of a timar estate, a spahi was committed to six to nine months of military service per year, during which time he had to provide his own horses, weapons, and salaried soldiers. Thus increased obligations offset the economic advantages of being Muslim.

The biggest practical advantage for becoming Muslim was acquiring a privileged legal status. The Ottoman state placed many restrictions on non-Muslims, including forbidding them to ride horses, wear turbans and other Muslim style clothing, or carry weapons. Contemporary observers reported Christians and Jews doing all of these things without reprisal, but this behavior remained officially banned. The most important regularly enforced legal handicap against free non-Muslims was their inability to use the courts to resolve disputes with Muslims. Non-Muslims could use courts for disputes among themselves, but they could not bring suit or testify in court against a Muslim. Conversion to Islam also allowed slaves to apply for and often win their freedom. When the Ottomans conquered the Balkans, they took prisoners of war as slaves from Bosnia, Dalmatia, Croatia, and Slavonia. After converting to Islam, freed Bosnian slaves often returned and went to work in the newly expanding towns. In 1528 8 percent of Sarajevo's population were freed slaves.

During the Ottoman period, Bosnia-Hercegovina gained an identity as a single historic region with a dominant Islamic culture. An administrative reform in 1580 designated Bosnia, with its capital in Sarajevo, as an Ottoman province *(eyalet),* the largest administrative unit in the empire. While most of the other regions in the Balkans were carved up, the Bosnian eyalet continued as a single entity (one that included all of modern Bosnia-Hercegovina) until Hungarian occupation in 1878. Thus, Bosnians enjoyed three centuries of continuous Bosnian and Hercegovinian regional identity. The region's major cities developed as a result of Ottoman advances and improvement and were predominantly Muslim. Bosnia-Hercegovina developed a strong Islamic culture, especially in urban areas. The older cities of Banja Luka, Travnik, and Livno became new seats of government. Sarajevo and Mostar both grew primarily as a result of the Ottoman presence in Bosnia. For instance, Sarajevo benefited enormously from Ottoman patronage. Even before the entire Bosnian state capitulated in 1463, the Ottomans had built Sarajevo's first mosque, a lodge for travelers, baths, a bridge, a large market in the center of town, and a governor's courtyard (from which the city derives its name), and they had installed a city-wide piped plumbing system. Between 1521 and 1541, the governor, Gazi-Husrev beg, built Sarajevo's first theological school, a library, a second mosque (the city's finest until it was destroyed in 1993), and a cloth market. By the end of the sixteenth century, Sarajevo boasted five theological schools, over ninety primary schools, over one hundred mosques, and six bridges. Over three hundred years, the regional continuity, the influence of the millet system, and Bosnian Islamic culture formed the basis for modern Bosnians' diverse but coherent identities.

JUDAISM IN BOSNIA-HERCEGOVINA

Jewish communities also became established in Bosnia-Hercegovina during the Ottoman period. Always a small minority in Bosnia, Jews exercised important cultural influence. The largest number of Jews came to Bosnia in the sixteenth century after Queen Isabella expelled them from Spain during her Inquisition. These Jews spoke Ladino, a sixteenth-century Spanish. Many of these Sephardic Jews settled first in the trading centers of Salonika (Greece) and Skopje (Macedonia) before moving to Sarajevo. From the 1530s to the 1730s, Sarajevan Jews' main trading contacts continued to be with the Jews in Skopje and Salonika.

Under the Ottomans, Jews and Christians enjoyed roughly the same legal status and experienced similar restrictions. Despite these limitations, Jews in the Ottoman

Empire had more rights and fared better than in late medieval and early modern Christian Europe. As the Ottoman state prospered, so did the Jewish community, especially in Sarajevo. As a sign of their rising status, the Ottomans allowed Sarajevan Jews to move out of the Muslim quarter and into their own Jewish quarter near the main market in 1577. They built their first synagogue in 1580–1581. Nevertheless, the Jewish community remained small, and Ottoman records make little mention of it in the seventeenth century. By the 1720s, about 330 Jews lived in Sarajevo, working as traders, physicians, pharmacists, tailors, shoemakers, butchers, wood and metal workers, glassmakers, and dyers. In the 1770s the Sarajevan Jews established their own yeshiva (rabbinical school), and by 1779, just over 1,000 Jews lived in the city. By 1876, Jews had attained legal equality and had elected representatives in government. This co-equal status continued under both Hungarian and Yugoslav administrations until World War II.

At the time of the Austro-Hungarian occupation of Bosnia in 1878, the Jewish population of Bosnia numbered about 2,000. Yiddish-speaking Ashkenazi Jews (culturally distinct from the Sephardim) began arriving in Bosnia from Hungary, the Czech lands, and the Habsburg monarchy's Polish territories in 1878. By 1900, over 9,300 Jews lived in Bosnia, and the Ashkenazim had their own synagogue. Most of the Sephardic Jews looked down on the Ashkenazi newcomers. In general, the two Jewish populations lived as separate communities. Under Habsburg administration, the three leading factories were Jewish owned, and some Jews started to send their children to secular secondary school. By 1941, there were Jewish communities in every major market town in Bosnia-Hercegovina totaling 14,000 people (74,000 in Yugoslavia). In addition to Sarajevo, the largest communities were in Travnik, Banja Luka, and Bijelina. Most Bosnian Jewish communities perished in the Holocaust. In 1958 only 1,258 Jews remained in Bosnia-Hercegovina, with most living in Sarajevo. By the 1960s, the Jewish population in Yugoslavia stabilized at about 6,500, with the largest communities to be found in Zagreb, Sarajevo, and Belgrade. With 1,000 Jews living in Sarajevo, the city's Jewish population remained virtually unchanged from 1968 to 1991.

HISTORY

By the seventh century, Slav settlers had established control in a number of areas in what is now known as Bosnia-Hercegovina. In the ninth century Slav rulers controlled three new medieval states: Raška (southeast of Bosnia), Croatia (west of Bosnia), and Duklja (roughly modern Montenegro). The region that became known as Bosnia was mostly inaccessible and little known to these rulers, even though they all claimed to rule it. Warfare among Serb, Croat, Hungarian, Montenegrin, Bulgarian, and Byzantine rulers over Bosnia dominated the two centuries preceding Bosnian independence. In the tenth century Bosnia became part of Serbia. However, when Serbia's ruler, Časlav, died in 960, most of Bosnia came under the rule of the Croatian king Kresimir II. In 997 Samuel of Bulgaria conquered part

of the region, before the Byzantine Empire vanquished the Bulgarian army in 1018. Later in the century, Duklja and Croatia divided Bosnia. Part of Bosnia seceded from Duklja in 1101, but Hungary (which annexed Croatia in 1102) took control of the area in 1137. Thirty years later the Byzantine Empire regained Bosnia from Hungary. None of these states ruled Bosnia long enough to gain popular loyalty or to establish any historic claim to the region before it became independent in 1180.

MEDIEVAL BOSNIA, 1180–1463

Medieval Bosnia emerged as an independent feudal state in the late twelfth century and survived until the Ottoman Turks annexed it 283 years later. It was characterized by weak kings, a strong yet contentious nobility, and diverse (and politically weak) religious communities. Until 1377, when the sovereign crowned himself king, Bosnian rulers held the title of *Ban* (governor). Bosnia's first ruler, Ban Kulin, established independence in 1180 and reigned until his death in 1204. He maintained cordial relations with neighboring states, especially with Hum (modern Hercegovina) and Dubrovnik. For most of the medieval period, Bosnia was separate from Hum, which was ruled by Serbs in the twelfth and thirteenth centuries.

Politically, Bosnia distinguished itself from other feudal states by its strong, feuding, and autonomous nobility. The Bosnian king had less power over his nobles than his European counterparts. As in other medieval states, the ruler granted nobles estates in return for military service and loyalty. Unlike elsewhere, however, the king did not grant lifetime peerages, but bestowed private and hereditary estates on his nobles. In addition, each grant had to be approved by a noble assembly, which also elected the ruler. Under weak kings, the noble assembly wielded influence. Under the strong fourteenth century rulers, however, its importance receded. In the fifteenth century some Bosnian nobles actually held more wealth and power than the king. At this time, domestic power struggles led to shifting internal alliances among nobles, who invited various Serb, Croat, Hungarian, Montenegrin, papal, and Ottoman armies to intervene on their behalf. These tactics created periods of great instability and weakened the Bosnian state.

Bosnia-Hercegovina also differed from other feudal states by the absence of a strong privileged state church. Bosnia's Bans were both Catholic and Orthodox. The archbishop in Dubrovnik supervised and consecrated the Catholic Bosnian bishops, and Hercegovina became part of the autocephalous Serbian Orthodox Church in 1219. The Dubrovnik archdiocese only loosely supervised the small, poor, and isolated Bosnian Catholic Church. By the thirteenth century vague accusations of heresy surfaced that concerned the low educational level of priests, lax observation of Catholic ritual (such as not enough crosses in a church), and the preservation of some practices associated with Orthodoxy. In an era when popes dominated Europe's rulers, the weakness of the Bosnian Catholic Church left the state vulnerable to politically motivated charges of heresy.

The greatest single threat to medieval Bosnia's political existence was the Hungarian crusade (1235–1241). In 1232 Pope Innocent IV claimed that the Catholic bishop in Bosnia was illiterate and ignorant of basic sacraments. He replaced the Bosnian cleric with a German Dominican priest, charged by the pope with rooting out such "heresies." In 1234 the papacy renewed its call for a crusade against Bosnia, even though there were no doctrinal differences between the Church of Bosnia and mainstream Catholicism. The Hungarian crown, which had unsuccessfully attempted to conquer Bosnia and had been unable to place the church under a Hungarian-controlled archdiocese, answered the pope's call. In 1235 Hungarian crusaders attacked the devout Catholic Ban Ninoslav. In 1238 Ninoslav's army was close to defeat when the Mongols attacked Hungary and the crusade collapsed. By 1241 Ban Ninoslav had regained power and expelled the Dominicans.

After the crusade, Hungary continued its attempt to control Bosnia through church politics, an attempt that unintentionally resulted in the creation of a new Christian church in Bosnia and the expulsion of Catholic clerics from the country. In 1252 the pope placed the Catholic Church in Bosnia under a Hungarian bishop. Fearing the political consequences of the change, the Bosnian clergy refused to recognize the new bishop. Instead, they drove the newly appointed bishop out of Bosnia into Hungarian-controlled Slavonia. Having rejected the pope's authority, Bosnia's Catholic clergy established its own independent Church of Bosnia in schism with Rome. Catholic clergy were prohibited from practicing in Bosnia. Thus, the Church of Bosnia came about as a consequence of Bosnian resistence to Hungarian expansion. Since the Catholic Church recognized only Orthodoxy as schismatic, it labeled the Church of Bosnia heretical, even though the new church remained theologically Catholic. At no time during or following the crusade were the Bosnian clerics accused of being part of the dualist Bogomil heresy. These accusations first emerged two hundred years later. By the 1300s, the Church of Bosnia dominated in central Bosnia. Until the Habsburg occupation of Bosnia-Hercegovina in 1878, Bosnia's Catholic clergy was limited to a small number of Franciscan monasteries that were permitted to operate, beginning in 1342. In sharp contrast to the medieval trend of establishing a strong state church, Christian Bosnia-Hercegovina was thus fragmented into three politically weak Christian faiths.

Medieval Bosnia was at its height in the fourteenth century under the leadership of Stjepan Kotromanić and his successor Stefan Tvrtko. Kotromanić greatly expanded Bosnia's territory through diplomacy and conquest. He first united southwest Bosnia with the northern territories and then annexed Hum. By 1330, he had doubled the size of his state. Bosnia benefited most from Kotromanić's alliances with the Hungarian kings Charles Robert and Louis I. Kotromanić won Hungarian support by subduing Croatian rebellions in 1322 and 1340 and helping to defend the coastal city of Zadar against Venetian attacks in 1346. The alliance was further cemented when Kotromanić's daughter Elizabeth married King Louis in 1353. In exchange for Kotromanić's aid, Hungary ceded to Bosnia parts of western Croatia, including 320 kilometers of Dalmatian coast between Dubrovnik and Split. He improved relations with Venice, signing treaties with Dubrovnik (1334) and Venice (1335). His dealings with the powerful Serbian king Stefan Dušan also remained cordial, except at the time of Dušan's incursion into Hum in 1350.

Kotromanić's diplomatic skills were most evident in his religious policies. He fended off papal attempts to launch a new military crusade to displace the schismatic Church of Bosnia. Kotromanić recognized the legitimacy of the Church of Bosnia, and at the same time he did not interfere in church activities after his expansion into Orthodox Hum or into Catholic Dalmatia. In return for Bosnia's military aid in the 1322 Croatian uprising, Charles Robert supported Kotromanić against the pope's attempt to launch a Croat crusade against Bosnia. In a conciliatory gesture, Kotromanić invited the Franciscans to set up a Vicariate of Bosnia (extending far beyond Bosnia's borders) in 1342. Thus, three regional Christian churches (Catholic, Orthodox, Church of Bosnia) coexisted in medieval Bosnia, but none developed into a state church.

In 1347 Kotromanić converted to Catholicism, and except for King Ostoja, all of his successors were Catholic. In contrast to elsewhere in medieval Europe, however, the Catholic Church in Bosnia remained a regional one. With its small following and weak economic base in market towns and mining areas, it remained subordinate to the state. Although some Franciscans were personally influential as advisors to the king and some nobles, they were small in number. By 1385, the Franciscans had built four friaries, adding only twelve more before the Ottoman conquest in 1463.

Although Kotromanić held enormous personal authority and had created an independent and prosperous Bosnia, he did not create a strong state. When he died in 1353, the state promptly dissolved amid foreign invasion, renewed papal calls for crusade, and domestic rivalry. Kotromanić's heir was his fifteen-year-old nephew, Stefan Tvrtko, a Catholic descended from the Orthodox Nemjanić family that had ruled Serbia. Upon Tvrtko's succession, King Louis I demanded most of western Hum as a dowry for his marriage to Kotromanić's daughter Elizabeth. Bosnian nobles loyal to Kotromanić had no loyalty to Tvrtko. Without strong allies, Tvrtko lost Hum and surrendered Kotromanić's Croatian acquisitions. At the same time, Pope Innocent VI renewed calls for a crusade against the Church of Bosnia. In 1363 Tvrtko was again at war with Hungary. However, when Tvrtko's brother Vuk deposed him in 1366, Tvrtko took refuge in Hungary.

Ultimately, Tvrtko regained power and became medieval Bosnia's most powerful ruler. He became Bosnia's first king and further expanded Bosnian territory. By the end of 1367, he had suppressed the noble revolt against him. In 1370 Tvrtko supported Lazar Hrbljanović's bid for power in the Serbian civil wars. In return for Tvrtko's support, Lazar gave him control of Hum, southern Dalmatia (between Dubrovnik and the Bay of Kotor), and the region later known as the Sandžak of Novi Pazar (including the Orthodox monastery at Mileševo, with the relics of the Orthodox Saint Sava). In 1377 the Catholic Tvrtko had himself crowned King of Bosnia and Serbia at Mileševo. Between 1382 and 1390, a power struggle for succession to the Hungarian crown enabled Tvrtko to regain lands Louis I had taken from him thirty years earlier, to expand his influence over most of Croatia-Slavonia, and to rule the Dalmatian coast between Zadar and Dubrovnik. By 1390, Tvrtko had added "King of Croatia and Dalmatia" to his titles.

When Tvrtko died in 1391 without any legitimate heirs, three noble families used the Bosnian noble assembly to assert political authority over an elected and much weaker king. Thereafter, Bosnian kings depended on internal coalitions with these powerful nobles and an alliance with a powerful non-Bosnian sponsor to maintain power. These politics led Bosnian nobles to pursue their own short-term interests by joining ever shifting alliances between rival claimants for the Hungarian crown. Even more ominous were Bosnian nobles' ever changing coalitions with Hungary and the Ottoman Empire.

OTTOMAN CONQUEST OF BOSNIA-HERCEGOVINA

The medieval Bosnian state fell piecemeal to Ottoman forces between 1440 and 1463. Although King Stefan Tomaš surrendered in Ključ in 1463, the last fort fell in Jajce only in 1527. Despite an increasing Ottoman military threat, Bosnian nobles continued to fight each other rather than form a united defense. After the Turks' conquest of Serbia in 1439, Bosnia shared a common boundary with the Ottoman Empire, and border raids became frequent. By 1440, Ottoman officials increasingly mediated Bosnian nobles' disputes, and Dubrovnik merchants sought Ottoman guarantees for commerce in Bosnia. Bosnia's last years of independence were marked not only by its failure to unite or enlist outside aid against the Ottoman threat, but also by its own internal weaknesses. Constant internal warfare had weakened Bosnia's nobles. The strongest noble, Stefan Vukčić, seceded from Bosnia to form Hercegovina in 1448. At the pope's request, King Tomaš suppressed the independent Church of Bosnia, which the state had protected for 235 years.

Despite the Ottoman threat, the Bosnian nobles fought each other for no real gain. For example, Tvrtko II, Tvrtko's illegitimate son, used an international crusade against the Ottomans as an opportunity to strike his rival Stefan Vukčić, who was busy attacking Venetian holdings in Dalmatia. Tvrtko's successor, Stefan Tomaš, was no more perceptive concerning the Ottoman threat. Papal requests to both Tomaš and Vukčić went unheeded. Although lesser nobles committed as many as 700 troops, Tomaš and Vukčić were too busy fighting each other to participate. In 1446, having defeated the crusade, the Ottomans helped Vukčić reestablish prewar borders.

As Bosnia's most successful noble, Stefan Vukčić used his power to secede from Tomaš's realm in 1448 as the Ottoman army approached Vukčić's and Tomaš's lands. Vukčić dropped his title as *vojvod* (count) of Bosnia and declared himself "*Herceg* (duke) of Hum and the Coast." These lands have been known as Hercegovina ever since. The divisions that plagued Bosnia were, however, recreated in Hercegovina. Vukčić (hereafter Herceg Stefan) found himself constantly at war to meet increasing tribute demands after the fall of Constantinople in 1453. Stefan also faced civil war from his son, Vladislas. In 1451 Stefan took his son's potential bride for his own mistress and threw Vladislas in jail. After escaping, Vladislas enlisted the support of Dubrovnik, Bosnia, and some nobles in Hum to oust his father. Herceg Stefan survived only because an Ottoman attack forced Tomaš to withdraw his troops to defend Bosnia. The war ended in 1453, when Church of Bosnia clerics mediated peace between Vladislas and Stefan. Vladislas reinitiated the civil war with Ottoman aid in 1462 and encouraged the Ottomans in their spring 1463 assault on Bosnia. The Ottoman Empire ultimately conquered Hercegovina in 1481.

Fighting among Serbia, Bosnia, and Hercegovina lessened each state's ability to defend itself, at a time when the Ottomans had already annexed parts of Bosnia and had conquered neighboring Serbia. Between 1436 and 1448, the area around Sarajevo alternated between Hungarian and Ottoman control. In 1451 the Turks took permanent control of the city. Constant fighting between Bosnian nobles and against Ottoman incursions weakened Bosnia's nobility. For example, the Pavlović nobles, once the most powerful family in eastern Bosnia, became Herceg Stefan's vassals after 1450. By 1444, Serbia had resurrected itself as a state but continued its squabbling with Bosnia. The wealthy silver mining city of Srebrenica changed hands several times before Serbia secured it in 1451. Despite increasingly frequent Ottoman raids, Tomaš used the death of Serbian noble George Branković in 1459 to take eleven towns in eastern Bosnia (including Srebrenica) from his successor, Lazar. Tomaš made peace with Lazar, whose daughter married Tomaš's son, but fighting weakened the region and allowed the Ottomans to recapture all of Serbia in 1459.

After Tomaš's sudden death in 1461, his son Stefan Tomašević tried unsuccessfully from 1461 to enlist military help from the pope, from Venice, and from Hungary. In 1462 Tomašević wrote to the pope, arguing that the Ottomans were about to invade and that they intended not only to conquer Bosnia and the Balkans, but to penetrate deep into Catholic Central Europe. Bosnia's defenses could not withstand such an attack alone. Inexplicably, Tomašević stopped paying tribute to the sultan. As a result, in 1463 the Ottoman army launched a surprise attack. Bosnian forts fell rapidly. In Ključ, the Ottomans captured Tomašević, who quickly surrendered all of Bosnia in writing on the condition that he not be killed. After accepting defeat, he was quickly beheaded. Meanwhile, Tomašević's commanders obeyed his written surrender orders. Most of Bosnia fell in weeks. Bosnia and Hercegovina became part of the Ottoman state for the next four hundred years. By the time of the conquest, the size of Bosnia had been whittled down through seventy years of near-constant warfare. Most Bosnians had become more anti-Hungarian than anti-Ottoman, and peasants noted that their Ottoman counterparts rendered fewer obligations to the state.

OTTOMAN RULE, 1463–1600

The Ottoman conquest of Bosnia was a small part of its rapid expansion into Europe. Sultan Mehmet II took Constantinople in 1453, renaming it Istanbul. In addition to Bosnia-Hercegovina, he also captured northern Serbia, part of Anatolia, and Wallachia. His armies raided Moldavia and Hungary and destroyed the Venetian army in Greece. His successor consolidated Mehmet's power, while pursuing expansion in Moldavia, Poland, Hungary, and Venice. Süleyman the Magnificent brought the Ottoman Empire to the height of its power. By 1533, he had conquered most of Hungary, and he nearly captured the Habsburg capital of Vienna before signing a peace treaty.

During the next 350 years, Venice, France, and Russia all challenged Ottoman control over Bosnia-Hercegovina; the Habsburg monarchy, however, posed the greatest threat. After 1533, the Habsburg and Ottoman states built up military frontier zones along their common border (much of it along today's Bosnian-Croatian border). This military frontier consisted of forts manned by peasant-soldiers under loose governmental control. Raiding between these frontier zones was common, especially during military campaigns in what became a mostly static conflict between the two empires.

The Ottoman Empire was divided administratively into provinces (eyalets). After 1463, Mehmet II set up the eyelet of Rumelia, covering most of the Balkan Peninsula, each containing several military districts (sandžaks). Appointed on a rotating basis, a *sandžak-beg* (a junior-level pasha) commanded the cavalry in his sandžak. As long as the sandžak-beg's territory remained peaceful, he enjoyed great autonomy. With its seat in Sarajevo, Bosnia was the first sandžak organized in Rumelia. By 1470, sandžaks in Zvornik and Hercegovina had been established; in 1554 these were placed under the jurisdiction of the Bosnian governor (vizier). In 1580 administrative redistricting created a Bosnian eyelet with seven sandžaks, covering Bosnia-Hercegovina and parts of Slavonia, Croatia, Dalmatia, Montenegro, and Serbia. The Bosnian eyalet, which lasted until 1878, gave Bosnians a long-term regional-administrative identity that no other South Slavs enjoyed.

Ottoman Bosnia-Hercegovina was run by a Muslim military-administrative landowning elite who were pledged to behave according to Islam's highest ethical principles and cultural standards. However, most Muslims belonged to the *reaya,* or subject peoples. In local, civil, and spiritual matters, Muslim, Christian, and Jewish religious leaders governed their respective millets. In Bosnia-Hercegovina most Muslims and Christians were either peasant freeholders or serfs. Ottoman rulers also developed flourishing cities and mining towns throughout the region, where Jewish and Roma (Gypsy) immigrants settled. As in other parts of Europe, cities enjoyed tax and guild privileges denied villagers.

Like medieval Bosnia and early modern Europe, the Ottoman Empire was a decentralized, feudal, military state. The Ottoman army consisted of salaried infantry, known as janissaries, and two types of cavalry: spahis and spahis of the Porte (the Ottoman government). Spahis of the Porte, like janissaries, were salaried, but spahis received estates *(timars*

in exchange for their ongoing military service. To maintain his timar, each spahi supplied his own arms, horses, and salaried soldiers. He also spent six to nine months of the year on military maneuvers. The spahis' estates were nonhereditary lifetime grants, awarded by the sultan. As long as the empire kept expanding, providing opportunities to acquire timars, this system worked well.

The Ottomans also established the office of *kapetan* in the Military Frontier, an area on the border with the Habsburg Empire. Initially, a kapetan administered a *kapetanije* (a military area within a sandžak) in the Military Frontier. He raised troops, kept roads safe from bandits, checked travelers at the borders, and performed various police and administrative duties. By the end of the sixteenth century, one had to be Muslim to join the military or the government. However, in frontier areas the Ottoman army supplemented its military with local Christian forces. Kapetans also employed Christians to guard road and mountain passes and to organize supplies.

The most important Christian involvement in the Ottoman state was through the child-tribute (*devshirme*) system, which affected about 200,000 Serbo-Croat speakers before it was ended in the 1660s. The government randomly took boys from Christian villages to Istanbul as tribute. In Istanbul these boys converted to Islam and received education and training as janissaries or as servants. This practice is usually portrayed as an example of oppression of the Christian population. Yet, in 1515 Bosnian Muslim families made special arrangements to have 1,000 Muslim boys taken for training in Istanbul. High-ranking servants worked for the sultan and various departments of state, some reaching the rank of grand vizier. The Porte sent Bosnians trained in Istanbul back to govern Bosnia as early as 1488. Some ambitious Christian families volunteered their boys for tribute, hoping that they would eventually become viziers or senior pashas and return home to enrich their families. The biggest Bosnian success story of the devširme system is the Orthodox Sokolović family, who produced nine grand viziers during the sixteenth and seventeenth centuries.

Most Bosnians, Muslim and Christian alike, lived as peasants on timar estates and paid some labor dues (an in-kind tithe of 10 to 25 percent of a peasant's produce) and a land tax to the sultan. Altogether, these obligations were less than those imposed in Western Europe. Unlike the spahis, the peasants held hereditary leases, which could be sold or passed on to their children. A peasant who converted to Islam enjoyed a more secure land tenure, with full ownership of the smallholding (*čiftlik*).

OTTOMAN DECLINE, 1600–1815

The Ottoman Empire spent much of the seventeenth and eighteenth centuries at war. Sustained military losses created a perpetual fiscal crisis, which eroded its political and economic structure. As it steadily lost territory to the Habsburg and Romanov empires, the Porte turned to ever increasing taxes to support its military and government bureaucracy. Since nobles and cities enjoyed tax exemptions, the tax burden fell disproportionately on peasants and serfs. To collect

Stari Most, or Old Bridge, crossed the Neretva River in Mostar, Hercegovina's capital. In 1566, Ottoman architect Hajrudin built this arched bridge, which became a symbol for ethnic unity as it connected Croat and Muslim quarters of the city. Croat forces destroyed it in 1993. (Otto Lang/Corbis)

more revenue, the sultan created hereditary private tax farms (lands that derived income from taxes rather than raising crops or livestock) that were free of military obligation. The ongoing fiscal crisis increased Istanbul's dependence on taxes and local military forces, allowing the local aristocracy to become more independent. Such autonomy enabled tax farmers to strip peasants and serfs of their traditional feudal rights and greatly increased rural poverty. The rise of this landed military elite and the impoverishment of the rural

economy transformed Ottoman society in Bosnia. Continued economic decline between 1760 and 1815 and peasant tax revolts clearly demonstrated the need for military, administrative, tax, and land tenure reforms. Bosnian lords, however, had become powerful enough to block or ignore any significant reform that threatened their privileges.

Ottoman decline began after the Ottoman army failed to take Vienna in 1683. In their 1684 counteroffensive, the Habsburg military gained control over Hungary and sent

130,000 Muslim refugees (mostly from Slavonia) into Bosnia before reaching Kosovo in 1689. Ottoman troops drove the Habsburg army back, with at least 30,000 Kosovo Serbs retreating with the Habsburgs. After 1689, a military stalemate ensued, broken only in 1697, when the forces of Prince Eugen of Savoy seized Sarajevo. His forces plundered and burned the city to the ground. When the Habsburg army retreated, many Bosnian Catholics went with it, breaking the Catholic domination of trade in Bosnia. The 1699 Treaty of Karlovci ended the war with the permanent cession of Hungary and Transylvania to the Habsburgs. The Ottoman state never recovered, even though their military policy became fixed on regaining their losses.

Habsburg advances after 1683 allowed Venice to take territory in Dalmatia. In 1685 Venetian gains sent 30,000 Muslim refugees from the Lika area into Bosnia. The remaining 1,700 Muslims were forced to convert to Catholicism. The Treaty of Karlovci also ended these wars (ongoing since the 1640s), granting large parts of Dalmatia and Greece to Venice. However, after repeated Venetian treaty violations, Ottoman troops were soon at war once more. With Austrian aid, Venetian troops defeated the Ottomans (1714–1716) and acquired more Dalmatian territory. More Muslim refugees flooded into Bosnia. In 1736 Ottoman forces finally repelled an Austrian attack at Banja Luka, enabling the Porte to recover some of its 1718 losses at the 1739 Treaty of Belgrade.

Ottoman military losses were so great that by the late eighteenth century, the Habsburg ruler, Joseph II, considered annexing Bosnia. In 1788, Austria overran Bosnia, and Joseph II and Russia's Catherine the Great agreed to split Ottoman possessions in the Balkan Peninsula. In 1789 European diplomatic pressure in the wake of the French Revolution convinced Austria to withdraw. However, the sultan agreed to let the Habsburg emperor act as "protector" of Christians in the Ottoman lands. Although the Serb revolt of 1804 weakened Ottoman control in Serbia, Napoleonic conquests in Central Europe blocked Austria's ability to exploit local unrest for its own political ambitions. After Napoleon's victories over Austria and Venice in 1805, French troops helped the Ottomans subdue resistance in Serbia and Hercegovina.

The effects of these long-term military losses and the growing importance of the infantry in waging war transformed both the Bosnian economy and Ottoman politics in the region by ushering in the ascendancy of tax-farming landlords, janissaries, and kapetans. Changes in seventeenth-century warfare rendered infantry forces more important than the cavalry. Thus, the Porte became more dependent militarily on its salaried janissary forces than on its timar-holding spahis. As the influence of the janissaries increased, many spahis became impoverished. Permanent Ottoman military losses in Hungary and Slavonia and Dalmatia drove spahi refugees into Bosnia. Since these spahis had lost their estates and could not earn new ones, they became an economic burden on Bosnia.

To alleviate its financial crisis, the Porte increased taxes. Beginning in the seventeenth century, the sultan consolidated timar lands and created a new type of estate (čiftlik)

for janissaries and the descendants of imperial officials. These non-peasant estates were hereditary and carried no military obligations. Instead, landlords were required to collect taxes from peasants living and working on the estate and deliver them to the Porte. As Istanbul became increasingly dependent on cash taxes, the new čiftliks, on which revenue could be more efficiently collected, eventually replaced the timars. Even though these large landowning tax-farmers had no military obligations, many maintained their own militias. At this time, the nobility (*begs* and *agas*) acquired and enlarged their own čiftlik estates in a number of ways. They converted their timars, bought land from peasants, took deserted lands, seized farms, and appropriated land on which they had a right to collect a tithe.

By the eighteenth century, Istanbul's reliance on cash taxes had failed to resolve its revenue shortfalls, but it had transformed the traditional rural economy and its feudal land tenure system. On čiftliks, landlords' obligations to provide and maintain housing, tools, and seed were reduced. On the other hand, peasant obligations increased, and they lost many of the legal rights and protections that timar estates provided. As spahi lands dwindled, two types of non-peasant čiftliks developed: *agaluk*s and *beglik*s. Lesser nobles known as agas held agaluk estates, whose feudal character was never disputed. On agaluks, landlords increased peasant labor dues and in-kind payments, while peasants' personal security and independence decreased. Peasants deeply resented the agaluks, citing their rights under the timar system. The peasants claimed to possess hereditary control and property rights over the land they farmed. In contrast, the upper nobles (begs) denied the feudal character of their beglik estates. They asserted the fiction that their beglik estates were private property and peasants living on them were freely contracted laborers, not entitled to even limited feudal rights. The tax-farming čiftlik system essentially placed peasants at the mercy of the landlord, encouraging abuse and corruption.

These hereditary estates became the economic and political base for local elites' autonomy from Istanbul. Janissaries not only obtained čiftliks, they also exerted political influence in city government, especially in Sarajevo and Mostar. As in the rest of Europe, late medieval and early modern Bosnian cities enjoyed some autonomy because of tax exemptions and guild trade monopolies. Sarajevo had enjoyed an autonomous status since the Ottoman conquest. After the office of grand vizier moved from Sarajevo to Travnik in 1698, Sarajevo became even more independent. In the seventeenth century janissaries in Sarajevo formed a guild to protect their social and military privileges. By the nineteenth century, most of Sarajevo's 20,000 janissaries did not serve in the army, but they still held formidable political and military power.

In addition to the janissaries, the office of kapetan had become politically powerful in Bosnia-Hercegovina. In contrast to the rest of the empire, the office of kapetan, which had various police and administrative duties in military frontier districts, expanded its powers, spread to non-frontier regions, and became hereditary. In 1700 there were twelve kapetans; by 1800, when they began to collect taxes, thirty-nine kapetans administered territory covering most of Bosnia-Hercegovina. Since the office had become hereditary and kapetans raised their own militias, they could enjoy more independence from the Porte than either the sandžak-begs or the viziers, who served fixed terms of office. Beginning in the eighteenth century, their efficient tax collection and effective military service enabled the kapetans to ignore the authority of the sultan's vizier and the sandžak-begs and disregard centralizing Ottoman reforms.

The power of the Bosnian landowning-military elite was curtailed only in 1849–1850. To meet its financial and military commitments, the Porte continued to convert timars to čiftliks and to increase taxes in the region, further increasing the nobles' power and impoverishing the peasantry. Ignoring Ottoman law, begs and agas illegally converted crownlands to private estates, failed to deliver taxes they owed to the central government, and disregarded Istanbul's limits on peasant obligations to their landlord. At a time when landlords were extracting more and more from peasants, less and less revenue found its way into the Ottoman treasury. Despite these encroachments on the sultan's power, Bosnian nobles played a key military function in the Ottoman state, by providing trained troops from their own militias who defended the Ottoman state throughout the empire. For example, the Ottoman troops fighting Napoleon in Egypt came from Albania and Bosnia.

Economic decline and military defeats resulted in widespread depopulation from death, disease, and displacement. In the 1730s 20,000 Bosnians died of plague. Higher taxes, together with the failure to implement land tenure reforms and to effectively limit peasant obligations to their landlords, created an increasingly impoverished and resentful peasantry. Villagers rebelled against new taxes and ever increasing obligations to their lords in 1727, 1728, 1729, and 1732. After the 1739 Treaty of Belgrade, the state imposed more taxes, and revolts continued. As Bosnian peasants became more and more rebellious, Bosnia became increasingly difficult to govern.

Bosnian peasants and urban elites found common cause in opposing new taxes, an opposition that sometimes led to armed conflict with the state. Villagers opposed new taxes because they already paid a disproportionate share. As Ottoman officials tried to shift some of the tax burden to non-peasants, nobles and urban elites blocked any infringement on their traditional tax-exempt privilege. Sarajevo became one of the centers of tax resistance. It had enjoyed a semi-autonomous status since the fifteenth century for its role in aiding the Ottoman conquest. Since Sarajevo officials often refused to pay taxes, officials in other cities looked to Sarajevo before they would comply with new levies. In 1748 new tax revolts exploded throughout the region. The largest rebellion was in Mostar, where janissaries joined the insurgency. The 1748 rebellions were crushed only after the sultan assigned a new vizier, Mehmet-pasha Kukavica, to reconquer Bosnia. In 1768 a rebellion of senior Muslim officials defending their tax privileges could be subdued only with large army forces. In 1814 Mostar elites led another revolt, which required 30,000 troops to put down.

The seventeenth and eighteenth centuries brought a steady decline of Ottoman military power and increasing peasant rebellions. It also consolidated elites' political resistance against any reforms that undermined their privileges or autonomy. As in early modern France, the Ottoman state sought to centralize power and subordinate the autonomy of lords by enacting military, tax, and land tenure reforms. Unlike France, however, strong Bosnian resistance stymied the sultan's attempts to subordinate nobles' power. This failure left the Ottoman state in perpetual financial crisis, militarily vulnerable, and politically weak. Increased poverty and rural taxes supplied the socioeconomic basis for resentment, not only against the Porte but also between Bosnian Serbs and Muslims in the nineteenth century.

THE AGE OF REFORM, 1815–1878

In the last sixty years of its rule, Ottoman reforms transformed Bosnia-Hercegovina. These reforms, known collectively as *Tanzimat,* not only introduced postal services, established an official newspaper, provided new schools, and professionalized government bureaucracy, but they fundamentally restructured Ottoman political, legal, and economic institutions. The main purpose of the reforms, however, was to centralize Ottoman military and political control. In Bosnia-Hercegovina, Tanzimat threatened the privilege and power of the province's landowning military class. By 1815, the local Bosnian nobility had become so strong that it could ignore the Porte's authority. When the Bosnian viziers began to impose the sultan's reforms, conservative Bosnian lords rebelled. Only after 1850, when these lords' power was finally curtailed, could the Bosnian viziers implement significant military, legal, and land tenure reform to bring the region in line with the rest of the empire.

As in other parts of the empire, the power of the Bosnian lords rested on their dominance of the military. By the nineteenth century, the lords had become so powerful that they could challenge the sultan's authority. To reassert his own power, the sultan had to subordinate the janissaries to a centralized Ottoman military authority. Not only did they use their position to extort money from both the government and the local population, they poorly defended the empire and sometimes refused to fight at all. After several attempts to control the janissaries failed, Sultan Mahmut II crushed them and abolished the office in 1826. Provincial armies came under a central authority in Istanbul, undercutting local commanders.

Curtailing janissary (and kapetan) power in Bosnia-Hercegovina required another twenty years. In 1827 Bosnian janissaries rebelled against the new vizier. The sultan sent a Belgrade army to Sarajevo to quash the rebellion. Mahmut's troops were successful, but the rebels still forced the vizier out of Sarajevo. After the janissaries were defeated, Bosnian kapetans took up the cause. In 1830–1833 Husein, a kapetan from Gradačac, led a revolt for Bosnian autonomy within the Ottoman Empire and the end of Tanzimat reforms. He also demanded that the sultan always appoint a native Bosnian beg or kapetan to the post of vizier. While Ottoman officials at first agreed to Husein's demands, in

1832 the Porte reneged on its promises and defeated Husein. As reward for his role, Ali-pasha Rizvanbegović became vizier of a newly separated Hercegovina in 1833. After Husein's defeat, Mahmut replaced the thirty-nine kapetans with four much weaker *musselims*. A musselim held the same administrative duties as a kapetan, but served a non-hereditary life-term and possessed no private militia. He represented the vizier, who had held power to appoint and dismiss the musselim. Therefore, he held no power in his own right. Eliminating the office of kapetan set off separatist kapetan-led revolts in 1836, 1837, 1840, and 1849–1850. Only after 1850 did meaningful reforms progress in Bosnia.

Following his military reforms, Mahmut also implemented administrative, legal, and economic changes. He formed new legislative bodies and an advisory cabinet representing the administrative departments to enact new laws systematically. As in the military, government officials became salaried (instead of collecting fees for services). Building on his father's reforms, Sultan Abdulmecit I's 1839 *Hatt-i Şerif of Gülhane* abolished the reaya (which had come to include only non-Muslims) and guaranteed all male subjects equality of life, honor, property, and security. Granting legal equality had far-reaching consequences. It required revising statutes and overhauling the judicial system to secure civil and property rights. Since military conscription, tax assessment, and property rights had all depended on religious and social-status criteria, the Şerif demanded restructuring of military, financial, and land tenure institutions. For example, the Şerif's pledge to eliminate tax inequalities required ending the tax-farm system and redefining feudal relationships to accommodate modern ideas of private property. The elimination of tax farming (like ending the non-Muslim poll tax and the prohibition against Christian military service) required creating a more extensive and reliable census-taking bureaucracy. The state became much more involved in activities that had been left to religious charities and millet administration: schools, job creation, building and infrastructure projects, commerce, and law.

Of all these reforms, the most intractable and the most contested concerned land tenure. Reworking a system that had evolved piecemeal over four hundred years required overcoming enormous logistical obstacles. For example, both landlords and tenant sharecroppers claimed title to the same land, but it was unclear whose rights to uphold. Legally, there was no provision for serfdom in Ottoman law. In the Ottoman system, all land formally belonged to the sultan, and peasants enjoyed secure hereditary use-rights. By the nineteenth century, however, spahis had been displaced by janissaries and other elites, whose čiftlik estates the Porte treated as hereditary private property. Thus, the distinction between private property and use-rights was blurry. The agaluk and beglik estates provided landlords with their tax-exempt status and formed the basis of their economic power. In addition, since tax farms were the principal source of state revenue, these landlords were valuable to the state. On the other hand, those farming the land (serfs, sharecroppers, and free peasants) claimed that the lords had illegally and extralegally usurped their land and their rights.

They strenuously objected to shouldering virtually the entire tax burden and demanded lower taxes and recognition of their property claims.

Reforming land tenure required clarifying and redefining peasant-landlord relationships, restructuring the tax system, and creating a bureaucracy to carry out these changes. To resolve conflicting property claims, the state had to determine whose ownership rights to recognize and what rights nonowners could claim. The state then had to create new property tax criteria to replace tax farming and its privileges. Since landlords were to become taxpayers, tax assessment, collection, and enforcement would have to revert to the authorities in Istanbul. Thus, the state needed to create an extensive bureaucracy with highly skilled administrators, who could rely on an accurate census of landowners, sharecroppers, and their assets as well as trained crop and livestock assessors and enforcement procedures. Under the best of circumstances, such sweeping reform would be difficult. In the nineteenth century it proved impossible. In Bosnia, such comprehensive land reform was not implemented until the 1930s.

Increasing Ottoman control over Bosnia slowly subdued noble resistance to land tenure. In 1847 Bosnia's vizier, Tahir-pasha, began to codify the region's feudal land-tenure system in terms favorable to the begs. Both begliks and agaluks had feudal origins, but Tahir-pasha recognized only agaluks as subject to feudal land tenure regulations. He defined begliks as the landlords' private property and the serfs on these estates as freely contracted laborers, despite their obligation to pay taxes, tithes, and labor dues to the beg. This definition exempted the begliks from reform and left sharecroppers on these estates without legal property claims. He abolished labor dues (usually two to three days per week) on agaluk estates, but raised grain obligations. In addition, peasants continued to pay a 10 percent land tax to the state. Landlords strenuously contested these mild reforms, but they remained in effect until 1918.

Bosnian elites' opposition to Ottoman military and economic reforms came to a head in 1849–1851. Although Tahir-pasha's reform was minimal compared to the abolition of serfdom in Serbia (1833) and Croatia (1848), landlords resented and ignored it. Tahir-pasha's military reforms led to the last kapetan revolt (which included agas contesting agaluk reform) in 1849. After Tahir-pasha died in 1850, the new vizier, Pasha Lataš, crushed the rebellion and exiled or jailed many begs, expropriating their lands. Lataš divided Bosnia-Hercegovina into nine districts and subordinated those districts to his own authority. Over opposition from both Christians and Muslims, he disarmed the entire population. After curtailing the power of the Bosnian elites, the Ottoman state slowly implemented its reforms and brought the region into line with the rest of the empire. In 1855 the poll tax for non-Muslims was rescinded and the ban on Christian military service lifted. Since most Christians opted out of military service, a new levy on nonmilitary subjects offset the elimination of the poll tax. Written law replaced legal tradition, and sandžak administrators became accountable to Istanbul. The power of Bosnia's military landowning class was finally broken.

The government attempted to introduce land tenure reforms that protected landlords' interests. This strategy produced anemic proposals that everyone opposed. In 1858, Sultan Abdulmecit issued legal property definitions (in effect in Bosnia until 1945) that included private property, state property, religious-charitable property, and common property. In 1859 the Safer Decree (in effect until 1918) confirmed Tahir-pasha's 1847 reform and limited the most egregious excesses on agaluks by limiting peasant obligations. It defined agas as landowners and serfs as tenants, who worked on a contract of limited duration. In most cases, obligations totaled about 40 percent of the sharecropper's harvest, plus the tax in lieu of military service. It required that landlords provide and maintain housing for their tenants. Serfs could leave the land if they chose, and landlords could obtain permission to evict them for poor work or nonpayment of their obligations. At the same time, the Safer Decree (like Tahir-pasha's before it) exempted beglik estates from the reform by defining them as private property and identifying beglik serfs as free labor, whose grievances were governed by civil law. This meant that beglik serfs' property claims lost legal legitimacy and that these sharecroppers had no legal protection from excessive landlord demands. In addition, peasants despised this reformed system. Assessors based dues on projected crop revenue before harvest. If a crop failed, the government did not adjust obligations downward. Therefore, levies could exceed 40 percent. Thus, the Safer Decree strengthened beg property claims, protected their wealth, and reinforced their political influence. Between 1859 and 1918, landlords continuously converted their agaluks to begliks.

The most significant development in nineteenth century Bosnia-Hercegovina was the emergence of religiously informed, class-oriented national identities. Bosnian Christians and Muslims were all ethnic Slavs; they shared the same history and the same Serbo-Croat language. Yet Bosnian Croats, Bosnian Serbs, and Bosnian Muslims accepted different religious traditions. This religious affiliation became the key to identifying national groups in Bosnia. Not only did Orthodox Bosnians come to identify themselves as Bosnian Serbs, so did many Orthodox Roma and Vlachs (semi-nomadic herdsmen today concentrated in the Pindus Mountains). Similarly, Roman Catholic Bosnians became Bosnian Croats, as did Roman Catholic Germans and Hungarians who had lived in the region for generations. These national identities allowed Bosnian Serbs and Bosnian Croats to retain their Bosnian identity and still be a part of a larger national group. It also fueled competing nationalist separatist movements.

In the last twenty-five years of Ottoman rule, a Christian religious revival fed emerging nationalist political movements that wished to separate from the Ottoman Empire. Nationalists sought to unite with Croatia, join Serbia, or form a single South Slav state. It is at this time that non-Muslims began to claim that Bosnian Muslims had been Croats or Serbs before the Ottoman conquest. In fact, before 1463 most Bosnians characterized themselves simply as Christians belonging to one of three regional churches, none of which had any secular clergy or parish organization. In the nineteenth century the effort to join Serbia was the strongest of these nationalist movements. Bosnian Serbs looked to Serbia for inspiration and support against the Ottoman Empire. By 1878, Serbia had grown from an autonomous region in north central Serbia to an enlarged independent parliamentary monarchy that was a regional political power, with territorial claims on Bosnia. Serbia's nineteenth-century expansion was accompanied by massacres, robberies, and coerced baptisms of Slavic and Turkish Muslims, most of whom were forced into Bosnia.

Istanbul's failure to enact meaningful land reform allowed these national movements to transform peasant grievances against landlords into Christian-Muslim conflicts. Landlords squeezed as much as possible from their rural laborers, both Christian and Muslim, in order to offset long-term economic decline, political losses, and new taxes. Nobles' sustained resistance to mild land reform measures created rising hostility between Muslims and Christians. Rebels increasingly turned to Christian powers and to Serb or Croat nationalists outside of Bosnia-Hercegovina for support. For example, in 1860 Montenegrin troops invaded Hercegovina to aid an Orthodox peasant tax revolt. The Montenegrins, blaming all Muslims for landlord brutality, slaughtered Muslim villagers. The massacre ended only when Ottoman forces put down the conflict. Russia, Serbia, and Montenegro justified their aid to peasant rebels as helping to protect Christians, and the Habsburg monarchy invoked its 1789 concession from the sultan to act as "protector" of Christians in the Ottoman lands.

Centuries of Ottoman rule had created a small Slavic elite that was mostly Muslim and a very large, very poor Slavic underclass that was mostly Christian. Though the vast majority of Bosnia's 870,000 Muslims were sharecroppers and peasants (about 1 percent were landlords), most landlords were Muslims. The majority of Christians were also peasants and sharecroppers, but only a few hundred were landlords. Muslim peasants and serfs hated the mostly Muslim landlords as much as their Christian counterparts. Christian-Muslim resentments became an important element of rural conflict; Christians increasingly associated all Muslims with the brutality of all landlords, Christian and Muslim.

The emergence of religiously affiliated, peasant-based national movements overshadowed important Bosnian achievements after 1815. Under Vizier Topal Osman-pasha, Bosnia made cultural advances, while continuing economic and political reforms. To support education and literacy he funded new Muslim schools and allowed Catholic and Orthodox churches to construct more school buildings. Even so, by 1875 only 10 percent of the population received any schooling at all. He started a new library at Sarajevo's Gazi Husrev-Beg mosque and set up a printing press, which published textbooks and the weekly *Bosna,* in Serbo-Croat and Turkish. In Sarajevo, the vizier completed the first public hospital in Bosnia-Hercegovina, with forty beds open to all confessions. In an attempt to make his administration more inclusive, Topal Osman-pasha sought counsel from Muslim, Christian, and Jewish representatives. Beginning in 1866, each of the seven sandžaks sent representatives (two Muslim and one Christian) to a consultative assembly that met annually for forty days to advise the vizier on regional economic issues such as agriculture, taxes, and roads. In addition Osman-pasha's executive committee (made up of three Muslims, two Christians, and one Jew) met with him twice a week. In contrast to these strides in education and administrative reform, his economic endeavors were much more modest. He built new roads and a limited rail system, but outside of Bosnia's traditional craft production, the government did little to support industry. Manufacturing suffered from internal duties and from international trade agreements that placed lower taxes on imported goods than on domestic products. Nonetheless, by 1878, Ottoman political and economic reforms had completely transformed the Bosnia of 1815.

END OF OTTOMAN RULE IN BOSNIA, 1875–1878

Foreign powers' interest in Bosnia did not wane over the nineteenth century. European powers used the religiously defined national movements to justify foreign intervention and occupation. In 1875 foreign involvement caused a local conflict to spiral into a series of wars engulfing the Balkans and ending Ottoman rule in Bosnia-Hercegovina. The 1875 uprising began as a village tax revolt in Hercegovina pitting Christian and Muslim peasants against tax collectors, Ottoman officials, and local landlords. However, Serbian and Bulgarian nationalism and great power intervention internationalized hostilities, setting Christian powers against the Ottoman Empire. Romanov and Habsburg backing of Bulgarian, Montenegrin, and Serbian nationalists gave the rebels license to ethnically cleanse hundreds of thousands of Muslim villagers in the Balkans. The nationalist-religious wars left thousands dead and homeless, ending in 1878 with the Congress of Berlin, which redrew national boundaries in the Balkans and expelled the Ottoman Empire from Bosnia-Hercegovina.

The 1875 uprising began as one of the frequent peasant revolts in late-nineteenth-century Bosnia-Hercegovina. Despite efforts to reform the Ottoman land tenure and tax system in Bosnia-Hercegovina, peasants continued to bear most of the tax burden. In the summer of 1875, following the customary practice, tax officials (two Muslims and one Christian) demanded payment based on pre-harvest estimates. The crops, however, had failed, and when peasants in Nevesinje (east of Mostar) refused to pay, officials used force. By July, both Christian and Muslim peasants throughout the entire region had retreated to the mountains, where they engaged in armed resistance. This uprising was followed by another in northern Bosnia. At this time, many peasants fled to Croatia or Montenegro to avoid the violence and the taxes. As in other tax revolts, the Bosnian vizier raised an army to suppress the rebels.

The tax revolt took on nationalist and religious dimensions when outside forces intervened. Responding to the nationalism of the age, some Orthodox leaders' declarations of loyalty to Serbia convinced many abroad that the tax revolt was a nationalist rising against Ottoman power. Serb nationalists seeking a larger Serbian state and pan-Slav nationalists from the Habsburg monarchy and Russia came to Bosnia to fight the Ottomans. Serbs and Montenegrins associated Muslim peasants with Ottoman rule, despite the fact that both Muslim and Orthodox peasants had revolted against Ottoman taxes. When Christians, mostly from Serbia, attacked Muslim villages and Muslims retaliated with counterattacks on Serb villages, religious resentment rather than taxes became the driving force of the revolt. European powers claiming to protect Christians escalated the conflict along religious lines into a regional Muslim-Christian war, with Christian forces (Serbia, Montenegro, Russia, and the Habsburg monarchy) arrayed against the Ottomans. Guns flowed from the Catholic Habsburg monarchy through Orthodox Montenegro to the Christian rebels in Bosnia-Hercegovina. The Three Emperors' League (the Russian, Habsburg, and German emperors) demanded that Ottomans abolish tax farming, lower peasant taxes, and make other reforms. The Ottomans agreed to these conditions and pardoned the rebels; nevertheless, the rebellion continued until the Bosnian army suppressed it. Reacting to accounts of Christians fleeing Bosnia, but ignoring reports of Muslim suffering, the European powers made new demands on the Ottoman state, and their attitude against it hardened.

When Bulgaria, Serbia, and Montenegro entered the conflict, it became internationalized. In May 1876 Bulgarian nationalists (with Russian diplomatic backing) rebelled against Ottoman rule. In the first days of revolution, 1,000 Muslim peasants were killed. Since Ottoman forces were still occupied in Bosnia, the Porte armed local Turks (some of them massacre survivors) and recent refugees who had settled in Bulgaria to defend the empire. They brutally suppressed the Bulgarian revolution, killing from 3,000 to 12,000 Christians. In July 1876 Russia supported Serbian Prince Milan's declaration of war on the Ottoman Empire. Serbia and Montenegro had agreed that Serbia would annex Bosnia and Montenegro would take Hercegovina. By August, however, Ottoman troops had defeated Serbian forces, which required Russian reinforcements to fend off an Ottoman reconquest. By the November 1876 armistice, hundreds of Bosnian villages had been burned, leaving about 5,000 peasants dead and over 200,000 refugees.

Despite the armistice, hostilities continued. In 1877 Russia declared war on the Ottoman Empire, after promising the Habsburg monarchy possession of Bosnia-Hercegovina in exchange for its neutrality. The campaign targeted Muslims; Russian troops surrounded villages and burned them to the ground. Russia defeated the Turks so decisively in 1878 that the tsar dictated the terms of the Treaty of San Stefano to the sultan. However, at the July 1878 Congress of Berlin, the great powers revised this treaty to lessen Russian influence in the Balkans. They redrew international boundaries, recognized Serbia, Montenegro, and Romania as independent states, and created an autonomous Bulgaria. As promised, the great powers gave most of Bosnia-Hercegovina to the Habsburg monarchy to occupy and administer. Serbia gained over 300 square kilometers to the south, including the provincial city of Niš, and part of Hercegovina became Montenegrin.

Under the terms worked out at the Congress of Berlin, Bosnia-Hercegovina remained part of the Ottoman Empire, but under Habsburg occupation. The Habsburg monarch agreed to accept Ottoman currency as legal tender, to use Bosnian revenues locally, to staff Bosnian administrative positions with native Bosnian or Turkish personnel, to guarantee religious freedom, and to allow the sultan's name in Friday prayers. The Habsburgs, however, had no intention of returning Bosnia to Ottoman rule and honored only the last two provisions.

HABSBURG RULE IN BOSNIA-HERCEGOVINA, 1878–1918

Russia and the Habsburg monarchy had vied for political and economic influence in Southeastern Europe since the eighteenth century. Ottoman weakness, growing Russian influence in the area, and the realization that Serbia was becoming a formidable regional power led the Habsburgs to occupy (1878) and later annex (1908) Bosnia-Hercegovina. Under Habsburg rule, certain areas of education and industrial infrastructure improved. However, the most significant characteristics of this period were the sharp decline of Bosnian Muslims in the region, the imposition of colonial rule, and the maintenance of feudal property relations. Instead of using the occupation period to implement reforms and extend rights that other peoples in the monarchy enjoyed (such as abolition of serfdom, creation of political parties, and an elected assembly) in order to build support for Habsburg rule, Vienna governed Bosnia as a colony and neglected its economic and political development. Despite achievements in certain areas of education and in building an industrial infrastructure, Austrian policies fueled anti-Habsburg, nationalist politics in the region.

The 1875 rebellion and Habsburg occupation brought about the greatest demographic shift in Bosnia-Hercegovina since the massive Christian conversions to Islam in the sixteenth century. In contrast to that earlier, more gradual shift, the steep drop in the number of Muslims living in Bosnia during the Habsburg era (1878–1918) was the result of war, displacement, and ethnic cleansing. For the first time since the sixteenth century, the number of Muslims fell below the Serb population, which maintained its demographic plurality until 1945. The mortality rate from the 1875–1878 wars had been extremely high among both Serbs and Muslims. By 1879, the Bosnian Serb population had declined by 7 percent; the number of Bosnian Muslims had decreased by 35 percent. In 1870 Bosnian Muslims had comprised 48 percent (690,000) of a total population of 1.44 million. By 1879, the Bosnian Muslim population had fallen to 39 percent in a total population of 1.16 million (449,000). Between 1878 and 1918 another 100,000 Muslims emigrated. Despite pressure from the great powers, 200,000 Bosnian war refugees never returned home. At the same time, Habsburg policies encouraged Austrians, Hungarians, and western Slavs to immigrate to Bosnia-Hercegovina. In 1880, 4,500 Austrian and 12,000 Hungarian citizens lived in Bosnia. By 1910, these numbers had skyrocketed to 47,000 Austrians and 61,000 Hungarians.

A pattern of ethno-religious "cleansing" had been established in Southeastern Europe in the nineteenth century as part of the process of nation building. The results were even more dramatic in Bulgaria and Serbia than in Bosnia. Only half (700,000) of the pre-1878 Muslim population remained in Bulgaria in 1890. 216,000 had died from disease, starvation, or murder, and the balance had emigrated. Ethnic expulsions had accompanied Serbia's expansion since the 1820s. By 1888, only 17 percent of Serbia's pre-1820 Muslim population remained.

Austria-Hungary kept Bosnian regional (sandžak) boundaries and placed its religious hierarchies under Habsburg supervision. The modest political gains of the late Tanzimat period were revoked. The advisory councils became defunct, and political dissent was criminalized. Politics degenerated to presenting petitions in person to the emperor, who could have the signatories arrested for antistate activity. While Bosnia was reduced to politics by petition, Serbia became a parliamentary democracy. Even Habsburg Croatia benefited from its own assembly and modern political parties, which did not become legal in Bosnia until 1906. The Habsburgs permitted a Bosnian assembly, though still with no direct legislative power, only in 1910. Serfdom (abolished in the rest of the monarchy in 1848) continued. The land tenure and tax system that had set off the 1875 uprising remained unchanged.

Habsburg colonialism had to be imposed by military force. In contrast to the Ottoman reliance on local Bosnian forces, Austria-Hungary depended on vastly increased numbers of foreign troops and civilian officials to maintain control. In 1878, believing that Bosnians would welcome them as liberators, Austrian officials sent a telegram to inform the Bosnians of their impending occupation. Instead of embracing the army that rescued them from Ottoman rule, Bosnian newspapers warned of an Austrian invasion. Austrian troops crossing the border met with armed resistance from both Muslims and Serbs. Bosnian Serbs had opposed Ottoman rule, but did not favor replacing it with Austrian occupation. Ottoman army garrisons, charged with upholding the Berlin Treaty, mutinied and joined the resistance, but proved to be no match for Austria's forces. After fifty-three battles and nearly 1,000 Austrian deaths and another 4,000 casualties, Habsburg forces took possession of Bosnia-Hercegovina. In the first months of occupation, Austria-Hungary committed 268,000 troops to secure Bosnia-Hercegovina, one-quarter of its active military.

A new universal male conscription law sparked the second major rebellion of the Habsburg period. In November 1881 the government announced the unprecedented policy of a mandatory military draft. Both Christian and Muslim men had been subject to Ottoman military obligation since the mid-nineteenth century. Most Bosnians, however, fulfilled this duty by paying a tax in lieu of military service. In Hercegovina, 1,000 Christian and Muslim peasants and villagers revolted in January 1882, attacking army and police posts. The Austrian army easily crushed the revolt in March and executed its leaders. There were no more large rebellions, although peasant resistance through "banditry" continued until 1895.

Beginning in 1882, Bosnia-Hercegovina's civil administration was under the common finance ministry in Vienna, thus avoiding the problem of assigning the region to either half of the Dual Monarchy. With the appointment of Benjamin Kállay as joint finance minister, the role of the civilian governor eclipsed that of the military governor. The civilian administration grew exponentially. Before 1878, the Ottomans had run Bosnia-Hercegovina with 120 officials; in 1908 the Habsburgs employed 9,533 officials to administer a slightly smaller area. The first step in imposing civilian rule on Bosnia was controlling the religious hierarchies that had played such a prominent role in the Ottoman government. Austria negotiated the right to appoint the Bosnian heads of the Orthodox, Catholic, and Muslim churches, established its authority to appoint and dismiss religious leaders, and then placed them on the state payroll. In 1880 the ecumenical patriarch in Istanbul gave the Habsburg emperor, Franz Joseph, the right to select Serbian Orthodox bishops in Bosnia, as well as the right to dismiss them for failure to fulfill either their state or religious duties. Moreover, Serbian Orthodox finances came under state control. In 1881 the pope agreed to allow the emperor to nominate (not appoint) Roman Catholic bishops in Bosnia and to require a loyalty oath from priests working in the region. In return, the Franciscans lost their status (enjoyed since 1342) as the only Roman Catholic order allowed in Bosnia. This loss of exclusivity enabled the Catholic Church to establish a secular clergy in Bosnia and increase Catholic influence. After 1881, there was a large influx of priests and nuns, who actively promoted Muslim conversions to Catholicism. The position of Islamic leaders was complicated because the Ottoman sultan was also the caliph, Islam's highest religious authority. Since Bosnia-Hercegovina technically remained part of the Ottoman state (the 1878 Treaty of Berlin having granted Vienna the authority to occupy and administer Bosnia-Hercegovina, while it remained legally a possession of Istanbul), the Habsburg government could not appoint the Bosnian mufti (the highest Muslim cleric in Bosnia) without violating international law. Instead, Vienna created the state salaried office of *reis ul-ulema* to lead a new, independent Bosnian Islamic religious hierarchy, which included a four-man advisory committee *(medžlis)* to interpret and preside over *shariat* law (the Islamic equivalent of Catholic canon law).

Austria-Hungary strengthened its control in Bosnia by nationalizing its *vakuf*s (Muslim religious-charitable organizations), which had acted like family trusts to fund charities since the sixteenth century. These organizations had built mosques, schools, dervish lodges, inns, and bridges. Elite families could safeguard their assets by placing them in vakufs, which could never revert to ordinary ownership. By 1878, many vakufs had been family-administered for generations and had become very large. They owned and managed nearly one-third of Bosnia's usable land and controlled most commercial real estate, including virtually all of downtown Sarajevo. By 1883, Austria had placed them under a state-appointed Vakuf Administration (dominated by Sarajevans), which managed the property under a Bosnia-wide plan for funding schools and mosques.

Kállay continued the earlier practice of limiting politics to intermittent petitions because he believed political activism was nationalistic and seditious. In order to isolate the Bosnian Muslims from Istanbul and dilute Croat and Serb nationalism, Kállay promoted a pan-Bosnian identity. He did not recognize that Serbs, Croats, and Muslims had developed clear and distinct national identities. His conception of "Bosnian" required loyalty to the Habsburg monarchy but rejected the possibility of Serb, Croat, or Muslim identities coexisting with a Bosnian one. Despite Bosnia's medieval heritage and regional continuity under the Ottomans, Kállay prohibited the teaching of Bosnian history and denied the existence of a distinctive Bosnian culture. Moreover, his policies divided Catholic, Orthodox, and Muslim religious hierarchies in Bosnia in order to control them better. With no political alternative, Bosnia's Muslims, Serbs, and Croats developed their respective political affiliations with Istanbul, Belgrade, and Zagreb. Kállay's nationality policies and his ban on any local political organization not only failed to create a Bosnian identity, they fueled anti-Habsburg resentments.

Beginning in the mid-1890s, renewed grievances against Habsburg rule produced a sustained political revival that led to the creation of a modern political system aimed at carving out spheres of cultural autonomy. Building on resentments following the conscription revolt, Bosnian Serb opposition constructed a mass base around the issue of Orthodox school and church autonomy. After 1880, Austria-Hungary's Catholic emperor had the right to appoint Orthodox bishops and control church finances. Catholic control over the Orthodox Church hierarchy caused especially bad feelings concerning schools. The state compelled Serb schoolteachers to take a loyalty oath that was not required of their Croat counterparts, allowing Croat immigrants to dominate schools. After a prolonged struggle, Bosnian Serbs received autonomy for Orthodox churches and schools in 1905. Bosnian Muslims also sought cultural and religious autonomy. Muslim elites' issues centered on property rights defined in the 1859 Safer Decree, which remained in effect throughout the Habsburg period. Bosniaks complained that land defined as private property was arbitrarily redefined as state property. This change limited serf obligations to the landlord and provided sharecroppers with a few legal rights. Beginning in 1881, elites formally contested increasing Habsburg control of vakuf property, objecting both in principle and to specific Vakuf Administration policies. Despite regional divisiveness among the Muslim elite, their interests converged on the need for an elected Vakuf Assembly (rather than an appointed Vakuf Administration), a reform that Austria finally granted in 1909.

Since Kállay's efforts to promote an isolated Bosnian identity had clearly failed, his successor Istvan Burián eventually recognized political parties (1906) and a Bosnian Parliament (1910). At the same time, however, Burián made concessions with each separate national-religious group, exploiting divisions to keep the region politically weak. In 1906 Burián recognized Bosnia's first political party, the Muslim National Organization (MNO). This party emerged from the ongoing effort of the Bosnian autonomy movement to create an elected Vakuf Assembly and to preserve Ottoman property law. Predominantly consisting of Muslim landlords, the MNO speciously claimed to represent all Bosnian Muslims. Like Bosnian Muslims in general, however, the MNO rejected existing national labels, preferring to use the traditional "Muslim" moniker for an increasingly secular identity. Bosnians founded the Serb National Organization (SNO) in 1907. The SNO grew out of efforts to promote the autonomy of Orthodox churches and schools dating from the late 1890s. It represented propertied Serb interests but had a mass base. It also supported Serbian claims that Bosnian Muslims were really Serbs.

In 1908 the Croat National Union (CNU) established itself as Croats' secular, liberal, middle-class political party. The CNU claimed that Bosnian Muslims were really Croats. They advocated joining Bosnia-Hercegovina to Croatia and forming a third political entity within the Habsburg monarchy to rule as co-equals with the Austrian and Hungarian political entities. In 1910 the Croatian archbishop in Sarajevo, Josef Stadler, formed a small clerical party, the Croatian Catholic Association (CCA). The CCA was an exclusively Catholic party that rejected CNU proposals to annex Bosnia-Hercegovina but advocated converting Muslims to Catholicism. It was the only political party in Bosnia-Hercegovina that called for the end of serfdom.

All groups benefited from the creation of a Bosnian Parliament of the kind that all other Habsburg regions enjoyed. Consistent with Austria-Hungary's general policy of divide and rule, election rules for the Bosnian Parliament disenfranchised all but a small sector of middle- and upper-class Bosnians. By imposing a religious "curia" electoral system that set aside an assigned number of seats according to religion, Vienna encouraged national-religious political divisions over Bosnian cohesion. The government reserved thirty-one seats for Orthodox, twenty-four for Muslims, sixteen for Catholics, one for Jews, and appointed another twenty representatives itself. In the first elections, the MNO took all the Bosnian Muslim seats and the SNO won all the Orthodox seats available to them, while the Catholic vote was split between two Croat parties. The first act of the new parliament was a call for a broader electoral franchise. Parliament could debate issues on the province's finances, taxes, rail, police, public works, and civil or criminal law. Since the crown could veto any legislation, the parliament held no direct legislative powers.

As in the political arena, the Habsburg monarchy's colonial policies led to some economic progress, but inadequately addressed the region's most pressing problems. Unlike its Ottoman predecessor, the Habsburg state wanted to industrialize the region. It expanded iron ore, coal, copper, and chrome mining and built iron and steel works in western Bosnia. In order to facilitate its new forestry and steel industries in Zenica, the regime built roads and railways. By 1883, there was a rail connection between Sarajevo and the Croatian border. In twenty-eight years of occupation, the Habsburgs built 121 bridges, 111 kilometers of broad-gauge railroad, and 1,000 kilometers of major roads. It laid down 911 kilometers of narrow-gauge rail and an-

other 1,000 kilometers of local roads. By 1913, Bosnia-Hercegovina had an industrial workforce of 65,000. Many of these workers were organized into trade unions strong enough to strike. Habsburg industrialization efforts were significant, but they benefited non-Bosnian interests most. Instead of developing a manufacturing sector, the monarchy concentrated on extractive industries, whose wood, metal ores, and steel could be shipped to other parts of the state and finished for vastly increased profits elsewhere. Railroads facilitated trade with Austria-Hungary, but shipping by narrow-gauge rail was expensive, increasing the cost of production for Bosnian products. Finally, the state developed a logging industry on what landlords claimed was their private property, redefined by the Habsburgs as state property, increasing friction.

Progress in agriculture was even more limited. Bosnians benefited from improvements in agricultural education. The state set up model farms and established an agricultural college with training in modern farming techniques for rural schoolteachers, but it maintained feudal landlord-tenant relations with their ambiguous private property rights. It did not extend its own 1848 abolition of serfdom to Bosnia either in 1878 when it occupied the territory or after the 1908 annexation. Instead, Austria-Hungary relied on the 1859 and 1876 Ottoman land reform laws to maintain enserfed labor on begliks and required agaluk serfs to buy their own freedom. At the same time, it encroached on landlords' property rights, creating deep resentments among elites. By failing to enact a land tenure reform to resolve inconsistencies in landlord-tenant relations and to provide a legal basis for protecting private property, the government ensured that the agricultural sector could not modernize.

The failure to implement meaningful agrarian reform abandoned the more than 75 percent of the population who worked as free peasants or serfs and intensified popular resentment to Habsburg rule. Sharecroppers and serfs typically worked on scattered micro-holdings that might *total* 1 hectare and had to scrape together capital to buy their freedom. By 1913, despite these onerous conditions, 41,500 households managed to free themselves from serfdom. Free peasants (mostly Muslims) also faced the perennial problems of scattered holdings, smallholding, rural overpopulation, and insufficient credit (with usurious interest rates). While Habsburg officials refused to enact land reform for Bosnians, they granted foreign farmers special tax concessions, as well as twelve-hectare farms rent free for three years and a low mortgage for the next ten years. In all, Vienna established fifty-four agrarian "colonies" totaling 10,000 people. The "colonization" program created deep resentments among Bosnians. Since local landowners resented Habsburg rule as much as their tenants, one of the first acts of the Bosnian Parliament was to end the program.

Despite the importance of economic and political reform, Austria's annexation of Bosnia-Hercegovina (1908) and the Balkan Wars (1912, 1913) overshadowed these issues in Burián's administration. The successful Young Turk revolt in 1908 panicked the Habsburg government because it called into question the legitimacy of Austria-Hungary's presence in the Balkans. According to the Berlin Treaty

(1878), Bulgaria, Bosnia-Hercegovina, and the Sandžak of Novi Pazar all remained part of the Ottoman Empire (as did what is today Macedonia, Albania, and much of northern Greece). Since Bosnia and Bulgaria formally remained in the Ottoman Empire after 1878, they were invited to send representatives to the new assembly. The Young Turks offered Bosnia a more democratic constitution than the Habsburgs had provided. Despite its obligations under the terms of the Berlin Treaty, Austria-Hungary had no intention of relinquishing control in Bosnia-Hercegovina. The Habsburgs blocked Bosnian representatives from attending the assembly and formally annexed the region on 5 October 1908. Bulgaria, formerly an autonomous state within the Ottoman Empire, declared its independence soon thereafter.

The 1908 annexation deeply alienated Bosnians. Bosnian Muslims became more isolated from their Ottoman patrons, and Bosnian Serbs saw it as ending Serbia's territorial claims in the region. Despite objections from Serbia, Russia, Turkey, Britain, and France, no military action ensued. In February 1909 Turkey accepted the Bosnian annexation in return for Austrian withdrawal from the Sandžak of Novi Pazar (where Austrian troops had been since 1878), the promise of freedom of religion in Bosnia, and a payment of 2.5 million Turkish pounds to Istanbul.

Annexation secured Austria-Hungary's status in Bosnia-Hercegovina, but strained its relationships with both Serbia and Russia. Vienna's relations with Serbia had become tense in 1903 when the Russophile Peter Karadjordjević became king of Serbia, following a palace coup that left pro-Austrian King Alexander Obrenović dead. Thereafter, Russia became Serbia's patron. The Habsburg annexation rendered Serbia's territorial claims in Bosnia moot. The SNO claimed that Bosnia (with its "Serb" majority, which included Bosnian Muslims who were "really" Serbs) should be part of Serbia, but the Serbian government's acceptance of the annexation led some military officers to form quasi-secret societies aimed at uniting all Serbs through revolution. The annexation also embarassed Russia, which also had claims in the region since Russia was dealing with domestic turmoil from the consequences of the 1905 revolution and its losses in the Russo-Japanese War (1904–1905). Tsar Nicholas II did not support Serbian demands in 1908.

The Balkan Wars of 1912 and 1913 did not affect Bosnian territory, but the governor of Bosnia still declared a state of emergency, dissolved the parliament, suspended the courts, assumed control over all Bosnian schools, and closed down many Serb associations. Many members of radical underground groups such as Young Bosnia fought with Serbia in the First Balkan War, including some Muslims. Most Bulgarian troops fought the Ottomans on their common border, where they forcefully converted Bulgarian-speaking Muslims to Orthodoxy. Serb and Greek forces occupied Macedonia and Albania. In these areas, Serbs, Greeks, and their allies slaughtered Muslim Albanians, and 10,000 Macedonian Muslims fled their villages. The Balkan Wars reduced the Ottoman state's European possessions to eastern Thrace and further isolated Bosnian

Muslims. It also established an independent Albania. Serbia doubled in size, gaining the former Ottoman territories of Vardar Macedonia and the eastern half of Novi Pazar. Bulgaria kept Pirin Macedonia, the Struma valley, and western Thrace. Greece and Montenegro also made gains. The Balkan Wars left Serbia as the region's strongest power. Serbia's relationship with Austria-Hungary remained antagonistic, and the Habsburg administration in Bosnia-Hercegovina became anti-Serb.

Growing anti-Habsburg sentiments found voice in support for Bosnian autonomy. Croat politicians had long worked for "trialism," the creation of a third Croatian administrative region to govern on a co-equal basis with Austria and Hungary. After annexation, trialists envisioned Bosnia-Hercegovina as part of the Croatian territory. Archduke Franz Ferdinand, heir to the Habsburg throne, favored this trialist resolution of the monarchy's Slavic question. After 1910, however, a Yugoslav solution gained momentum. Many anti-Habsburg politicians favored creating a multinational state made up of South Slavs from the Habsburg lands (Slovenes, Croats, Serbs, Bosnian Muslims), Montenegro, and Serbia. In contrast to trialism, which worked through existing government structures, Yugoslavism was revolutionary, requiring secession from the Habsburg monarchy. The Yugoslav solution was vague regarding whether this union would have a federal or centralized government, a question that plagued Yugoslavia throughout its existence. Yugoslavism became most popular among Bosnian Serbs, but it drew adherents among Slovene, Croat, and Serb politicians, intellectuals, and radical student groups. Young Bosnia was one such pro-Yugoslav underground student group. Bosnian Muslims were split between trialist and Yugoslav ideas.

Following the Balkan Wars, the tension in Bosnia's political climate grew stronger. On the Bosnian-Serb border, peasant disturbances and border skirmishes with Habsburg officials kept the area in turmoil. Weapons from Serbia crossed into Bosnia. Secret Serbian nationalist societies worked on plans to unify all Serbs regardless of place of birth or religion. Young Bosnia sought out two of these societies, National Defense (established in 1908) and Black Hand (established in 1911) for training and weapons to pursue their Yugoslav ideals. Influenced by socialist thinkers, members of Young Bosnia were not only anti-Habsburg, they called for the abolition of serfdom, were fiercely anticlerical, and they viewed Bosnian politicians in the assembly as collaborators with Habsburg rule. Between 1910 and 1914, high school and university students from Young Bosnia and other revolutionary organizations attempted a string of political assassinations.

Archduke Franz Ferdinand's support of trialism made him a target of those who favored Bosnian incorporation into Serbia. Despite warnings about security risks, he came to inspect Habsburg troops on summer maneuvers in Sarajevo. Despite repeated assassination attempts on high-level officials and Serbia's unofficial warning to the joint minister of finance (Serbia took no official action despite knowledge of the plot), his visit was planned for 28 June 1914, the 525th anniversary of the 1389 Ottoman defeat of the

Serbs, which preceded the Ottoman conquest in 1439. Habsburg officials were insensitive to the fact that this battle had been mythologized into a celebration of Serb nationalism and revenge against occupation. On a parade route to a hospital to visit wounded soldiers, Franz Ferdinand's limousine convoy passed at least six student rebels armed with bombs and pistols. One bomb thrown hit the car behind the archduke. As his car drove slowly past Gavrilo Princip, his driver took a wrong turn and then backed up, again slowly passing this teenage assassin, who shot twice before people standing next to him subdued him. All the political parties condemned the attack; anti-Serb rioting broke out on the streets of Sarajevo, and parliament was permanently dissolved.

All of the eight arrested coconspirators were members of the revolutionary Young Bosnia, which viewed the formal Bosnian political parties as collaborators with Habsburg rule. Seven were Bosnian Serbs and one a Bosnian Muslim. At his 1914 trial, Princip declared himself a Yugoslav nationalist, who desired freedom from Vienna above all else. Princip was convicted and died of tuberculosis in a Theresienstadt prison in 1918.

The Habsburg government immediately blamed the Serbian government for the assassination, citing Black Hand ties with both Young Bosnia and the Serbian military. On 23 July, Vienna issued a ten-point ultimatum to Belgrade, condemning its toleration of anti-Habsburg organizations and literature. The Serb government agreed to suppress anti-Austrian groups, stifle hostile publications, and arrest those named as terrorists. They also agreed to keep the monarchy informed of their investigation into the assassination, but refused to allow Habsburg officials to participate directly in their assassination investigation. On 28 July, despite French, British, and Russian diplomatic efforts to continue negotiations, Franz Josef declared war on Serbia. Within days, Europe was at war.

World War I did not physically touch Bosnia-Hercegovina except for local skirmishes on its eastern border, but the Habsburg government treated the region as captured enemy territory, embittering politicians and the general population. It suppressed local government, conscripted teenagers and the elderly, and conducted sham political trials. Harsh crop requisitions to feed troops and Habsburg cities fueled rebellions, property seizures, and demands for land reform. Bosnian politicians demanded amnesty for political prisoners, restoration of constitutional rule, and new elections for a parliament.

Bosnian Serbs were singled out for Habsburg repression. The military governor of Bosnia-Hercegovina from 1914, General Sarkotić, systematically arrested and deported Bosnian Serbs. About 5,000 Bosnians, including Bosnian Muslims, joined Serbia's forces, including three volunteer battalions from Hercegovina. This desertion prompted Sarkotić to resettle up to 50,000 Serbs from the Drina Valley of eastern Bosnia to western Bosnia. Another 5,000 Serbs were driven into Serbia and Montenegro, and 3,300–5,500 Bosnians (mostly Bosnian Serbs) were held in internment camps during the war, where many died. Political trials for members of radical underground groups such as Young Bosnia and National Defense, begun in 1909, intensified during the war. Hundreds of Bosnians were tried for treason, espionage, and aiding the enemy, and hundreds received death sentences, which Vienna later commuted. Others were killed or imprisoned without the benefit of any legal proceeding. Since the Bosnian Serbs were singled out for repression, they associated Bosnian Muslims and Bosnian Croats with the Habsburg regime and turned increasingly to Serb nationalism. By early 1918, an estimated 50,000 Serb guerrillas were fighting Austria-Hungary.

In August 1914 the Yugoslav idea had the support of only a few intellectuals and some romantic revolutionaries. Throughout most of the war, most Bosnian politicians favored some kind of autonomy within a Habsburg framework. Until the fall of 1918, most politicians in Slovenia, Croatia, and Bosnia-Hercegovina favored postwar autonomy within the Habsburg Empire. Bosnian Croats and Bosnian Muslims wanted to preserve their own culture and identity and were wary of Great Serb aspirations. The Slovene politician Monsignor Korošec led a South Slav voting bloc in the Austrian Parliament that sought to unite Slovenes, Serbs, and Croats in a trialist Habsburg administration. They did not exclude the possibility of a South Slav state but emphasized that the Habsburg territories must unite together before joining another state. Their more inclusive May 1917 declaration for South Slav autonomy won over many Bosnian Serbs and moderate Bosnian Croats. However, Bosnian Muslims were less enthusiastic. Given the Catholic conversion scandals and Croat politicians' assertions that Muslims were really Croats, many Bosnian Muslims preferred Bosnian autonomy to avoid Croat domination.

The Yugoslav cause was taken up by a group of émigré Serb, Croat, and Slovene intellectuals from the Habsburg lands who had previously worked on Serb-Croat coalition building. Led by Croat politicians Ante Trumbić and Franjo Šupilo, these intellectuals formed the London-based Yugoslav Committee. Initially, the Allies opposed the self-appointed Yugoslav Committee because creating such a state would require breaking up the Habsburg monarchy. In Bosnia, many Serb and Croat politicians favored a Yugoslav state, while most Bosnian Muslims still preferred autonomy. Two influential politicians, Džemaludin Čaušević, the reis ul-ulema, and Mehmed Spaho, the founder of the Yugoslav Muslim Organization in 1919, had had enough of rule by "Turks and Germans" and favored a South Slav state. Serbia, intent on remaining a centralized Serbian nation-state after the war, rebuffed the committee's overtures to participate in a Yugoslav state. Thus, the pro-Allied Yugoslav Committee had little influence. The Treaty of London, which granted Italy large parts of Dalmatia and Istria, confirmed its fears of Italian expansion.

Serbia's 1915 defeat and its heroic, fighting retreat through Albania to the island of Corfu had left the government in exile weak and with little tangible Allied support for its war aims. Serbia had hoped to acquire Bosnia-Hercegovina, an Adriatic port, and the Vojvodina, if possible. Once in exile, the Serbian government's authority declined. The prince regent, Alexander, could not control the military, which he feared was planning his assassination. Montenegro refused to follow the government's lead, and rebels for an independent Macedonia were regaining strength. After the fall of Nicholas II in 1917, Serbia lost its best advocate among the Allies. In this context, the Serbian prime minister, Nikola Pašić, invited the Yugoslav Committee to Corfu to negotiate the basis of a Yugoslav state. The 1917 Corfu Declaration became a nonbinding statement of intent to form a South Slav state if the Habsburg monarchy dissolved. It called for the creation of a constitutional monarchy led by the Serbian Karadjordjević dynasty. Whether the state would be ruled as a unitary or a federal government was left to the future constitution.

In addition to Serbia's increased receptivity, by mid-1918, international conditions had changed markedly. Late in the war, the Allies decided to dismember Austria-Hungary. By November, this decision had become clear, nullifying autonomy as an option for any of the Habsburg provinces. Faced with a choice between a Yugoslav state (including Serbia) and partition among Italy, Austria, Hungary, and Serbia, the regions of Croatia, Slovenia, and Bosnia chose Yugoslavia. In October 1918 Korošec and his followers formed various National Councils to run provincial affairs. The National Councils granted the Yugoslav Committee the authority to represent them in negotiations for a Yugoslav state. The National Council met in October 1918 and renounced Habsburg rule; Croatia declared its own state. On 3 November 1918, the first National Government of Bosnia-Hercegovina was formed.

Neither this declaration nor the 11 November armistice ended the armed conflict. As in much of the rest of Europe and Russia, uprisings against the old regime ensued. Germany was swept by a wave of industrial strikes and revolts. In rural Eastern Europe and Russia, peasants in rebellion seized and set fire to landlords' property. In some places, including Bosnia, rebels declared their own peasant republics. As the largest landowners in Bosnia, Muslims sustained the greatest losses. To restore order, the Bosnian government asked the Serb army to put down the violence. When Serb soldiers entered the region in November 1918, the anti-landlord violence turned anti-Muslim, as Muslim smallholders (half of Bosnia's free peasants) and villages became targets. Serb soldiers believed that the Muslims had been loyal to the Habsburg government and had participated in its anti-Serb repression. Most of this anti-Muslim hostility came from non-Bosnian Serbs who did not live in the region. Some 270 Muslim villages were pillaged. To counter Serb reprisals, Muslims formed political parties that crossed class boundaries; the most influential became the Yugoslav Muslim Organization (YMO) led by Mehmed Spaho. As in 1878, another wave of Bosnian Muslim emigration began in 1918.

In an attempt to catch up with events following the sudden collapse of the Central Powers, the Allies met in Paris in February 1919 to redraw European political borders by arbitrarily applying Woodrow Wilson's principle of national self-determination which sought to systematically apply nineteenth-century principles of nationalism. They created several weak new "nation-states" (Poland, Czechoslovakia, Latvia, Lithuania, Estonia, Austria, Hungary, Yugoslavia), enlarged Romania, and constricted Germany's borders. However, all the new states either contained substantial national minorities or had a sizable population of co-nationals living outside the new nation-state. In addition, Yugoslavia and Czechoslovakia were explicitly multinational states. Thus, resolving political disputes over the "national question" became the defining challenge of the interwar period.

BOSNIA-HERCEGOVINA IN ROYALIST YUGOSLAVIA, 1918–1941

The new Yugoslav state (originally called the Kingdom of Serbs, Croats, and Slovenes) united Serbia with the former Habsburg lands of Slovenia, Croatia, Bosnia-Hercegovina, and the Vojvodina. These former Habsburg lands agreed to a South Slav state based on the 1917 Corfu Declaration and its specific call for a negotiated constitution. In December 1918 delegates chosen from prewar political parties established an interim government to rule until elections for a constituent assembly could be held. The interim government lacked popular legitimacy, both because it excluded new parties and because the pre-1914 political parties represented only middle- and upper-class interests. Characterized by divisiveness, the interim government failed to pass three-quarters of the legislation before it (including a budget). After waiting two years, the government held elections loosely based on universal manhood suffrage.

From the beginning, Constituent Assembly deputies were divided about the type of constitution it should adopt. In 1921 the assembly narrowly adopted a controversial constitution by a vote that many members boycotted. Subsequent attempts to revise the constitution became the focal point of the polarizing nationalist politics that dominated interwar Yugoslavia. The largest Serbian parties favored a unitary state, but most non-Serbs preferred a federal model. As a rule, Serbs saw Yugoslavia (ruled by the Serbian Karadjordjević monarchy from the Serbian capital of Belgrade) as an extension of pre-1914 Serbia. Serbs, however, did not form even a simple majority in the kingdom. In contrast, most Croats saw Yugoslavia as a collection of nations that could only be ruled on a decentralized federal model, with each nation having substantial authority within its own historic region. Slovenes also favored the federal paradigm. The Communists, the Social Democrats, and the Agrarians, the most important nonnational parties, also preferred a federal structure. Leftist independents and factions from the Social Democrats and Nationalist Youth (a collection of Yugoslavist young activists, including Young Bosnia) groups in prewar Habsburg territories and in Serbia merged to form the Communist Party of Yugoslavia (CPY) in 1919. Its strongest appeal was among the nationally disaffected, the politically unorganized, and those in the urban centers of Zagreb and Belgrade.

In Bosnia-Hercegovina, Bosnian Serb and Bosnian Croat parties tended to reflect the positions of their co-nationals outside of Bosnia. The main Bosnian Serb party, the Radical Democrats, favored a centralized state and demanded far-reaching social reform, including the abolition of serfdom. In contrast, the Bosnian Croat parties argued for a federal Yugoslavia. The largest Bosnian Muslim party was Mehmed Spaho's Yugoslav Muslim Organization (YMO). The YMO represented Bosnia's urban professionals, but it sought common ground with all classes to defend against anti-Muslim policies and actions, such as systematically replacing Muslims with Serbs in regional and local Bosnian government. The YMO was a specifically Bosnian party and did not organize in Muslim areas outside of Bosnia. On federal questions, the YMO was allied with the autonomist Cemiyet party, which represented Muslims in Kosovo, Macedonia, and the Sandžak of Novi Pazar. The YMO was split between conservative, pro-Serb members led by Ibrahim Magljajić, who favored a centralist Yugoslavia, and more progressive federalists like Spaho. Whether Yugoslavia became a unitary state or a federal one, most Bosnians favored autonomy within the monarchy.

The 1920 election results split between unitary parties and federalists, with the YMO receiving twenty-four seats. In order to achieve a unitary constitution, the Serbian parties set aside their differences and extended minor concessions to the YMO, the Agrarians, the Slovene's People's Party (SLS), and the Croatian Union (HZ) in exchange for their support. Contrary to the Corfu Declaration, the Constituent Assembly agreed to ratify a constitution based on a simple majority plus one. Nevertheless, negotiations remained contentious, and the YMO's bloc of votes proved critical for the constitution's ratification. Despite his preference for federalism, Spaho agreed to support the constitution in exchange for Islamic religious equality, autonomy for Islamic religious and educational institutions, including *sharia* courts, landlord compensation, and the preservation of Bosnia's territorial integrity. On St. Vitus's Day (Vidovdan), 28 June 1921, the anniversary of the Battle of Kosovo, the so-called Vidovdan Constitution passed, by a slim majority (with nearly half of the delegates abstaining).

The 1921 constitution placed state power with the parliament, the courts, and the Serbian king, Alexander. The king held legislative and executive powers, but the judiciary was independent. Alexander confirmed and issued every law, appointed all state officials, and served as supreme commander of the military. Instead of using national or historic criteria to determine administrative units, the constitution divided the kingdom into thirty-three districts (*oblasti*). The king appointed loyalists to the head of each district. Ruled by a Serbian royal family, the Kingdom of Serbs, Croats, and Slovenes ignored the historic roles that Macedonians, Montenegrins, Albanians, Bosnian Muslims, Hungarians, Roma, and Jews had all played in the Yugoslav lands.

The government used the centralist Vidovdan Constitution (ratified against the will of most non-Serbs) to rule an authoritarian kingdom. The government drove the CPY, the largest opposition party, underground in 1922 and reneged on its promises to the YMO. Pašić's promise of territorial integrity for Bosnia-Hercegovina's six historic districts (Bihać, Tuzla, Banja Luka, Travnik, Sarajevo, and Mostar) evaporated in 1922. The districts remained as oblasti, but Bosnian Muslims held none of the king-appointed leadership positions in them. This betrayal caused

Spaho to resign his government posts, and the pro-Serb wing of YMO formed its own party. By 1923, Spaho and the YMO had joined the major Slovene and Croat parties in a federalist bloc opposed to the Vidovdan Constitution. Finally, in 1925, the government extended anticommunist legislation to include the Croatian Peasant Party (CPP) and arrested its leadership. In the attempts to revise the Vidovdan Constitution that followed, the main conflicts were between the Serbian and Croatian parties, with the YMO and Slovene People's Party (SLS) providing crucial swing votes.

The YMO primarily represented urban middle-class interests, but Spaho did negotiate government compensation for families losing land in the 1919 agrarian reform. In a population of nearly 2 million Bosnians, the agrarian reform affected about 4,000 landlords. Long overdue, the agrarian reform abolished serfdom and resolved the most important property disputes. Landlords were limited to 50 hectares (the size of a small American family farm) unless the property owner himself tilled the land. Most forests became state property. Setting a precedent for the 1945 land reform, the state also expropriated all land that had been enemy property (German, Ottoman, or Habsburg) without compensation and made war veterans eligible for land. Ultimately, the agrarian reform affected 25 percent of Yugoslav land (over 2.43 million hectares) and one-third of peasants. It not only terminated feudal labor practices in Bosnia and the former Ottoman lands, but it also ended the system of compulsory labor in Croatia. Only Serbia was exempt from the reform.

The Bosnian Muslim landlords of 1921 were not what they had been in the seventeenth and eighteenth centuries. Ottoman inheritance laws, war, and economic decline had reduced the size of most property. More than 60 percent of Bosnian landlords owned less than the 50-hectare limit. Only seventeen Bosnian families held more than 1,000 hectares, all in the Bosanska Gradiška region by the Sava River. In Bosnia-Hercegovina, the 1919 agrarian reform affected only peasants on agaluk estates, because they were legally recognized as operating under a feudal tenancy system. As in the past, peasants on beglik estates had been legally classified as free labor on private property and were excluded from the reform. Many landlords were reduced to poverty because they lost income from rents and tithes and the state's indemnity was insufficient to modernize their farms. The government paid compensation to agaluk owners in cash (125 million dinars) and in 4 percent bonds maturing in fifty years (130 million dinars) at below market value. Further, most landlords sold their bonds at or below face value because they had no other source of income. Beginning in 1925, these bonds were traded on the Yugoslav stock exchange at less than 30 percent of their original value. Thus, the mostly Muslim landlords' compensation for their land was not enough to keep them from post-expropriation poverty.

Full implementation of the agrarian reform and other land reform legislation remained incomplete by 1941. Throughout the interwar period, however, the government enlarged the category of those entitled to receive land. Between 1919 and 1928, 14,000 war veterans and their families received 34,000 hectares of forestlands. In 1921 the government extended the Agrarian Reform to include beg-lik peasant households, who had worked under tenancy arrangements similar to agaluk estates since February 1909, whose tenancy contract had no limited duration, and whose livelihood depended on working the land. Between 1928 and 1930, the state included more customary tenants on beglik estates and agreed to pay compensation of 500 million dinars in 6 percent government bonds amortized over forty-three years. As with the agas, the begs sold most bonds to creditors, and their value shrank to 76 percent of their face value when they started trading on the Yugoslav stock exchange. A 1936 decree legalized peasant encroachments and cultivation of government forestland, estimated at up to 600,000 hectares. In all, an estimated 168,000 families (some families counted twice) obtained 1,175,000 hectares of land (1,156,000 arable, 162,000 forest, 47,000 pasture) in Bosnia-Hercegovina from large holders, vakufs, and "enemies of the state," and by peasant encroachments.

The agrarian reform held tremendous significance for Bosnia-Hercegovina. Disputes over land tenure, taxes, and labor obligations had been the root of Bosnian Serb–Muslim animosity in the nineteenth century and the cause of many revolts, including the 1875 Rebellion that ended Ottoman rule in Bosnia. The agrarian reform replaced ambiguous Ottoman-era property laws that blurred the distinction between state and individual property with modern concepts of private property. However, receiving title to their land and eliminating rents and tithes did not resolve all the peasants' problems. Peasants continued to pay a disproportionate share of the tax burden. Inadequate roads and transportation infrastructure discouraged market-oriented farming. Peasants still held their property in scattered micro-plots rather than in one piece of land. Therefore, most peasants remained subsistence farmers. As the agrarian depression of the 1920s gave way to the worldwide depression of the 1930s, farmers received too little for their produce and spent too much for manufactured goods to maintain their farms. Despite the agrarian reform, micro-holding and rural poverty increased in interwar Yugoslavia.

After June 1928, when a Serb deputy shot the Croat leader Stjepan Radić in the Skupština (assembly), the political system grew even more authoritarian. Radić's subsequent death in August set off mass demonstrations. In January 1929 King Alexander installed himself as royal dictator. He abolished the Vidovdan Constitution, suspended civil liberties, disbanded political parties and trade unions, placed all newspapers under state control, and made any "anti-state" activity a capital offense. He renamed the state the Kingdom of Yugoslavia and consolidated the thirty-three oblasti into nine *banovine,* each administered by a king-appointed governor *(ban).* After redistricting, Serbs enjoyed a majority in six of the nine banovine. The new regime shredded Bosnian territorial integrity and ended Bosnian Muslim religious autonomy. For the first time in over four hundred years, the region was partitioned. The king divided Bosnia-Hercegovina's six historic districts among four banovine (Vrbas, Drina, Zeta, Primorija), each with a Bosnian minority. The king merged the Sarajevo-based Bosnian Muslim religious community with Skopje-centered Muslims from Macedonia and Kosovo and moved the office of the reis ul-ulema to Belgrade.

Alexander issued a new constitution in 1931. It confirmed his dictatorship and provided for legislative and judicial branches of government accountable solely to the king. Alexander fired "incompetent judges." The constitution established a Senate and a National Assembly elected by open ballot. The king allowed only political parties with significant representation in all nine banovine. Since none of the pre-1929 parties met this criterion, Alexander filled the legislature with loyalists. In 1932 Maček, Korošec, and Spaho all issued resolutions calling for the return to democracy. Alexander's authoritarianism did not dispel political tension or end violence. In 1934 the extreme nationalist Ustaša had Alexander assassinated in Marseilles. (The Ustaša had been formed by Ante Pavelić following Alexander's royal coup. The government immediately exiled Pavelić to Italy.) In 1934 Alexander's cousin Paul became regent for Prince Peter until his eighteenth birthday in 1941.

After 1931, the YMO specifically called for the resurrection of the country along national-historic lines with Bosnian autonomy. Spaho and the YMO participated in each of Stojadinović's governments. However, the government's 1939 *Sporazum* (Agreement) with Croatia further complicated the territorial integrity of Bosnia-Hercegovina. Brokered by Vladko Maček (CPP leader since 1928) and Prime Minister Dragiša Cvetković, the Sporazum established an autonomous Croatian banovina and provided for the division of Bosnia-Hercegovina based only on its Serb and Croat population. Therefore, if a county were 35 percent Muslim, 33 percent Croat, and 32 percent Serb, it became Croat despite the Muslim plurality. The Croatian banovina contained thirteen historically Bosnian counties, including Mostar, Stolac, Brčko, Gradačac, Derventa, Travnik, Fojnica, and Livno. By August 1939, Bosnia had been whittled down to two rump banovine with majority Serb populations. After Spaho's death in 1939, his successor Džafer Kulenović demanded a new Bosnian banovina to include the two rump banovine plus the Sandžak of Novi Pazar.

WORLD WAR II

While Slovene, Croat, Bosnian, and Serb politicians in Yugoslavia negotiated for greater autonomy in 1939, World War II began in Europe. After 1939, the German Reich used the close political and economic relationships it had developed with the Yugoslav government in the 1930s to pressure the Yugoslav government to join neighboring Italy, Romania, Hungary, and Bulgaria in the Axis alliance. By 1941, Germany had annexed Austria (1938), occupied the Czech lands (and set up a client state in Slovakia), and defeated both Poland (1939) and France (1940). In 1941 Prince Paul's reluctant signing of the Tripartite Agreement led to a military coup and the regent's abdication in favor of Prince Peter, still a minor. On 6 April, German forces attacked Yugoslavia, defeating it in eight days. Subsequently, Germany annexed Slovenia, set up quisling regimes in Serbia and in an enlarged Croatia (renamed the Independent State of Croatia, NDH), and gave Italy jurisdiction over

Montenegro and the western half of the NDH. On 10 April 1941, the German puppet state of Croatia officially proclaimed itself the Independent State of Croatia, with the exiled Ustaša leader, Ante Pavelić as its *Poglavnik* (leader). Before Pavelić took power, his extreme nationalist movement had only 12,000 followers. Bosnia-Hercegovina, divided among eleven provinces, became part of this highly authoritarian state. Initially, many Croats in Croatia and Bosnia welcomed the NDH as relief from Serbian rule. Within days of taking power, Pavelić guaranteed religious freedom and invited eleven YMO politicians to join the NDH's paper parliament.

Known as the National Liberation Struggle, World War II consisted of three wars in Yugoslavia: a war against foreign occupation, a social revolution, and a war of ethnic cleansing. Unlike World War I and the Balkan wars, World War II was fought in Bosnia, and its citizens were drawn into all three conflicts. Each of these wars originated and was driven by forces (Axis, NDH, Četniks, communists) from outside the region.

Two competing resistance movements associated with the Allies, the communist-led Partisans and the royalist Četniks, waged separate campaigns against German and Italian occupation forces and their puppets. Initially, the Allied Command recognized and materially supported Colonel Draža Mihailović's forces as the official Yugoslav resistance. Mihailović represented the London government and fought to restore the interwar monarchy. However, many Serbian resistance bands called themselves Četniks without any connection to Mihailović. While the Četniks fought to save the monarchy, the communist-led Partisan movement sought to abolish it. An illegal political party since 1921, the Communist Party of Yugoslavia (CPY) began to recover in 1937, when Josip Broz "Tito" became party secretary. However, it counted only 6,000 members in 1940.

By the winter of 1941–1942, the Četnik and Partisan resistances were also fighting each other. The Četniks expelled the weaker Partisan resistance from Serbia in late 1941, forcing it into an unreceptive Bosnia-Hercegovina and a long trek through Bosnia's Dinaric Alps to Bihać, where Tito regrouped. The Partisans championed themselves as fighting both against the Axis powers and for a Yugoslavia with national and social equality. In 1942 Tito established the Anti-Fascist Council for the Liberation of Yugoslavia (AVNOJ) to vie with the government in exile for Allied support in the postwar political settlement. The London government's passivity, as well as the Partisans' appeal to national equality, led a large number of Croats and Muslims to join the Partisans in 1943. By this time, the Četniks were openly collaborating with the Germans. In September the Allies recognized the Partisans as the main resistance force in Yugoslavia and transferred their backing to Tito. The 1943 Italian surrender meant large amounts of arms and equipment fell into Partisan hands. By this time, Partisan resistance had become a mass movement of over 100,000, and it was still growing.

The National Liberation Struggle also became a social revolution, as Mihailović's and Tito's resistance forces each aimed to establish its own vision of postwar Yugoslavia. Mi-

hailović's royalist forces, representing the prewar government in exile, were determined to restore the Serbian dynasty that had ruled the Yugoslav monarchy from 1918 to 1941. As noted above, the interwar regime had disillusioned many. As Serb nationalists, Mihailović's Četnik forces recruited few non-Serbs. In contrast, the Partisans, who promised national and social equality, a new round of land reform, and economic development, appealed particularly to peasants (both Serb and non-Serb), the small number of urban poor, and those adversely affected by Serb chauvinism. However, most Muslim, Catholic, and Orthodox clerics opposed the communists' atheism, and many allied with the government in exile or a quisling regime. The YMO had been excluded from the London government but opposed the CPY's atheism and its socialist goals. The CPY had little support in Bosnia-Hercegovina. It had polled poorly in 1920, and by 1939 there were only 170 Communist Party members, most Bosnian Serbs, in the region.

Finally, World War II also became a war of ethnic cleansing. Led by the ultranationalist Croat Ante Pavelić, the NDH's Ustaša leadership massacred and expelled Serbs, Jews, and communists of all ethnicities in order to create an ethnically pure Croat nation-state. Since Croats did not form a demographic majority, the NDH identified Bosnian Muslims as ethnic Croats, who had converted to Islam four centuries earlier, and set about eliminating the small Jewish and sizable Serb population. In retaliation, Serbs massacred both Croats and Muslims, whom they collectively associated with the NDH's anti-Serb atrocities.

German occupation and NDH rule in Bosnia (as in Milan Nedić's quisling regime in Serbia) were accompanied by anti-Semitic pogroms. On 16 April 1941, one day after they arrived in Sarajevo, German soldiers attacked the old synagogue. Within two days, all of Sarajevo's synagogues had been ransacked. Although one German officer called for the confiscation of the Sarajevo Haggadah from the National Museum, its Muslim director hid the manuscript in a mountain village throughout the war. On 18 April, the NDH issued its first anti-Jewish law. On 30 April, laws on citizenship and racial identity and on the protection of Aryan blood and the honor of the Croatian people were announced.

Croats and Muslims quickly became disillusioned with the NDH and its campaign of ethnic cleansing against Serbs, Roma, and Jews. The state also killed and deported Bosnian Muslims and communists as enemies of the regime. In June mass internments of Jews began throughout the NDH. By December 1941 most Jews in the NDH and in Serbia had been sent to internment camps. By the end of World War II, all Bosnian synagogues had been looted and many destroyed. In 1945 only 14,000 Jews remained in Bosnia; another 12,000 had been killed.

The NDH's Serb population of 1.6 million (out of a total NDH population of 6.3 million) required a much larger ethnic cleansing project. The state planned to convert to Catholicism, expel, and kill the Serb population in equal thirds. Widespread terror began in May, and mass arrests of Serbs followed in June. In Mostar, the Ustaša shot hundreds of Serbs and threw them in the Neretva River. NDH atrocities also occurred in Bihać, Brčko, and Doboj, and the state destroyed entire Serb villages around Sarajevo. Serb resistance, especially from Hercegovina, "liberated" some areas from NDH control by collaborating with the Italian occupation. Many Serbs responded to Ustaša massacres by joining the Četnik resistance and retaliating against Croats and Bosniaks.

In contrast to Bosnian Croats and Bosnian Serbs, the National Liberation Struggle left Bosnian Muslims politically isolated. The London government excluded the Bosnian Muslims' most prominent interwar political party, the Yugoslav Muslim Organization (YMO), from the government in exile. Some Bosniaks joined the NDH, but some also joined the Četnik resistance. In December 1942 an estimated 4,000 Muslims were fighting with the Četniks (roughly 8 percent of their troops). However, nationalist Serb calls for the annexation of Bosnia and the expulsion of all non-Serbs made Muslim participation with the Četnik guerrillas difficult. Then Serb massacres of thousands of Muslims in Hercegovina and eastern Bosnia beginning in late 1941 rendered Bosniak participation in the Četnik resistance impossible. The YMO's opposition to socialism and atheism also prevented easy alliance with the Partisans.

Since the NDH defined Bosnian Muslims as ethnically Croat despite their traditional Islamic faith and culture, Bosniaks were not targets of Ustaša atrocities. However, relations between Bosniak leaders and the NDH were tense despite this special status. Beginning in August 1941, Muslim clerics issued a series of resolutions condemning the NDH's violations of civil and religious rights. These resolutions reported numerous crimes, abuses, and forced conversion of Orthodox Serbs and others to Catholicism. They complained of theft and looting of Serb and Jewish property. One hundred prominent Sarajevans demanded security of life, dignity, property, and religion for all and denounced violence against Serbs and Jews. By the end of 1942, Bosnian Muslim leaders, complaining of NDH killings of Muslims, requested autonomy and the end of Ustaša activity in Bosnia.

Beginning in the winter of 1941–1942, Četnik guerrillas and local Serbs forces retaliated against Ustaša ethnic cleansing by killing thousands of Bosniaks. The worst violence was in Hercegovina and in eastern Bosnia. In August 1942 a single Četnik commander, Zaharia Ostojić, killed at least 2,000 Muslims in Foča-Čajniča. In February 1943 9,000 Muslims were massacred, including 8,000 elderly, women, and children, in the same region. Leading Četnik intellectuals tacitly approved these actions. For example, Dragiša Vasić called not only for Serbia's annexation of Bosnia, Dalmatia, Montenegro, and parts of Croatia, but also advocated the postwar expulsion of all non-Serbs from this Greater Serbia. As more Bosnian Muslims began to join forces with Tito in early 1942, nationalist Serbs slaughtered Muslims for their Partisan affiliation, and the massacres intensified.

Many Bosnian Muslims formed local defense units to protect themselves and tried to avoid contact with all combatants. One such group was the Young Muslims, which was founded in 1939 to promote the role of Bosnian Muslims after the creation of the Croatian banovina. During the war, the Young Muslims did charitable and social work to aid refugees and organized rural and urban Muslim youth into cultural and religious organizations.

As Ustaša attacks on Muslims increased in 1943, some Bosnian leaders sought German intervention. They wrote to Hitler requesting an end to Ustaša activity, autonomy for Bosnia, and an expansion of the Muslim Volunteer Legion (similar to volunteer SS divisions in France, Holland, Belgium, and Denmark). Germany dismissed Bosnian autonomy but did form the Bosnian Muslim SS division, "Handžar," in April 1943. (The term "handžar" refers to a scimitar, a type of curved dagger of Ottoman origin.) This division had all ethnic German officers, and at its height contained 21,000 troops. Most volunteers believed the division would be used to protect Muslim towns and villages. However, it was sent to France. In November 1943 Muhamed Pandža, one of the principal recruiters for the Handžar division, called for the overthrow of the NDH and the creation of an autonomous Bosnia with equal rights for all religions. In March 1944 the Handžar division was sent back to Bosnia for "peacekeeping" in Tuzla, Gradačac, Brčko, Bijelina, and Zvornik, where it dispensed indiscriminant reprisals against local Serbs. The division began to break up in the summer of 1944 when two thousand of its members joined the Partisans. By October 1944, the division had disintegrated. In 1944 the NDH tried to intimidate the Muslim population with summary executions.

Tito's victory can be attributed to the Partisans' populist appeal, Allied military aid, and Partisan military success. The Partisan promise of national "brotherhood and unity" appealed to those in all national groups who were opposed to the ethnically motivated Četnik and Ustaša violence. The Partisans' willingness to resist the NDH and occupation forces eventually won them substantial support, both from the Allied Command and from anticommunist leaders in the Croatian Peasant Party (CPP) and the YMO. Among Bosnian Serbs, the Partisans recruited most successfully in the Bihać and Jajce areas, where Tito formed his Popular Front government. Tito's military successes in turn weakened clerical Muslim resistance to the Partisans. When the NDH collapsed in 1944, thousands more disaffected Serbs, Croats, and Muslims joined the Partisans. The German withdrawal began in the summer of 1944. On 6 April 1945, Partisan forces liberated Sarajevo, and they formed a government on 28 April.

The war devastated Bosnia-Hercegovina. Forces from outside the region (NDH, Četniks, communists) led the fighting, but Bosnians participated on all sides. Thus, much of the fighting crossed ethnic, religious, and class barriers, as Bosnians were caught in the war's whirlwind. Some Bosnian Serbs fought with the Četnik resistance; others chose the Partisans. Some Bosnian Croats allied with the government in exile; others with the NDH or the Partisans. Bosnian Muslims served either with the NDH, the German army, the Četniks, or the Partisans. The NDH systematically attempted to create an ethnically pure Croat nation-state by eliminating its Serbs and Jews. In retaliation, nationalist Serb forces massacred both Bosnian Croats and Bosnian Muslims because of their ethnicity. However, the Ustaša also killed

Bosnian Muslims and sent them to death camps at Jaseno-vac, Buchenwald, and Auschwitz despite their special ethnic status. Serb, Croat, and Bosniak Partisans not only fought Croats associated with the NDH and Serbs associated with the Četniks, they opposed anyone they perceived as loyal to the interwar regime. When Partisans came into villages, they rounded up Muslims of higher social standing and intellectuals and shot them.

By the time hostilities ended in 1945, the CPY had a communist-dominated Popular Front government ready to put in place. The war's death toll in Yugoslavia was staggering (up to 1.7 million) and continues to be a subject of much debate. In Bosnia, 8.1 percent of Bosnian Muslims and 7.3 percent of Bosnian Serbs were killed. Only Jews and Roma suffered greater losses. The end of the war brought uncertainty, as widespread homelessness (3.5 million), a devastated economy, and starvation threatened in 1945 and 1946. When the Communist Party of Yugoslavia (CPY) took power in 1945, it ruled over a divided, war-devastated country seething with resentments.

BOSNIA-HERCEGOVINA IN COMMUNIST YUGOSLAVIA, 1945–1992

Tito and his Partisans came to power in 1945 offering democracy and social equality to replace monarchy, national equality to replace ethnic chauvinism, and economic development (above all, further land reform and industrialization) to replace backwardness. The Communist Party of Yugoslavia (CPY), like its predecessors, used democratic rhetoric, but never intended to allow political pluralism in Yugoslavia. Instead, it replaced the nationalist royal dictatorship with a communist dictatorship and equated political opposition to the Party with treason. The politicians who led Yugoslavia and Bosnia after 1945 used their war records to obtain government positions and then ruled through old-fashioned patronage networks. Nevertheless, Tito and the CPY proved to be remarkably flexible.

Tito's Stalinist state transformed itself after its 1948 ouster from the Soviet bloc. In 1952 the CPY changed its name to the League of Communists of Yugoslavia (LCY) and began to implement a series of reforms, placing it, as has so often been observed, between East and West. Its diplomatic relations with the West improved. Yugoslavia became a founding member of the Non-Aligned Movement, a bloc of developing states opposed to the Soviet and American alliances of the Cold War. As an alternative to the Stalinist model, the Party developed its economic ideology of socialist self-management that theoretically gave workers (rather than the state) control over their workplace and became one of the cornerstones of the communist state. This control was mostly fictional, but employees did enjoy a high level of job security. The 1953 land reform officially ended collectivization and reconfirmed the legitimacy of private property. In the 1960s restrictions on small business eased, consumer goods improved, and travel to foreign countries to work and shop became easier. In most of Yugoslavia, life improved dramatically. The economy industrialized and grew at a rapid pace. The state built roads and rail lines.

Cities urbanized. Universal access to basic social services improved health care, nutrition, and housing. Mass education virtually wiped out illiteracy.

When the CPY came to power in 1945, it pledged to eliminate the nationalist violence that had plagued the interwar regime and had exploded in World War II. Despite the CPY's political monopoly and Tito's dictatorial role, the CPY took on a federalist form to accommodate South Slavs' national aspirations. Six republics (Serbia, Croatia, Bosnia-Hercegovina, Slovenia, Macedonia, and Montenegro) and two autonomous provinces (Kosovo and Vojvodina) within Serbia replaced the interwar banovine. Except for multinational Bosnia-Hercegovina, which had no demographically dominant nation, each of the republics represented the historic territory of each region's single dominant nation. Thus, Tito's Yugoslavia recognized six distinct South Slav nations, each represented by a theoretically sovereign republic. Each republic had the formal right to secede from Yugoslavia. The autonomous provinces represented historic regions dominated by national minorities (defined as a national group living outside of the established nation-state). Since Kosovo (majority Albanian, historically Ottoman) and the Vojvodina (no majority, until 1918 Hungarian) were historically, demographically, and culturally distinct, the CPY designated them as autonomous provinces within the Serb republic.

In a government premised on the politics of nation-building, multinational Bosnia-Hercegovina was in an ambiguous position. Although no nation formed a majority, Bosnian Serbs were the most numerous national group. The CPY designated Bosnian Muslims as a special ethnic group, not a nation. However, the Party recognized that Bosnia-Hercegovina was a culturally distinct historic region and understood that the region's Serb, Croat, and Muslim populations were too mixed to be separated without mass expulsions. Therefore, instead of absorbing Bosnia into Serbia, the CPY restored the region's territorial integrity and designated it a republic. Since the CPY had defined the Bosniaks as an ethnic group and the Bosnian Serbs and Croats as fragments of their respective nations, the peoples of Bosnia-Hercegovina were at a political disadvantage vis-à-vis the other nationally defined republics. Representing only a small portion of their respective nations, Serbs and Croats in Bosnia were politically weaker than their counterparts in Serbia and Croatia. The CPY's insistence that Bosnian Muslims were nationally undecided gave them a second-class political status. The weakness of Bosnians (Serbs, Croats, and Muslims) rendered them less effective in pursuing their own regional interests than other republics.

Postwar Bosnian Muslim politics focused on obtaining recognition of Bosnian Muslims as a nation. In contrast to Serb, Croat, and communist claims, the 1948 and 1953 census showed their overwhelming aversion to identifying themselves either as Croats or Serbs. In the 1948 census Muslims identified themselves as Muslim Serbs (72,000), Muslim Croats (25,000), or Muslims undetermined (778,000). In the 1953 census there was no Muslim option, but 891,800 Bosnians declared themselves Yugoslavs, "nationally undeclared," rather than Serbs or Croats. The 1961 census allowed Bosnians to identify themselves as "Muslims in the ethnic sense." Over the objections of Macedonians and nationalist Serbs, the LCY finally recognized Bosnian Muslims as a nation in 1971. Macedonians, only recognized as a nation in 1945, objected to Muslim national identity because they believed Macedonian Muslims might declare themselves as Muslims. However, Macedonian Muslims were historically, culturally, and linguistically Macedonian and identified themselves as such. In fact, Muslims living in Serbia, Croatia, and Macedonia overwhelmingly identified with the dominant nation (83 percent in Serbia, 70 percent in Croatia, 95 percent in Macedonia). Since there was no pre-Ottoman Serb or Croat national identity for Bosnians to revert to, and modern religious affiliation had determined Bosnian Serb and Bosnian Croat national identification, Bosnian Muslims maintained their identity.

The initial denial of Bosnian Muslims' national identity allowed the CPY to attack Bosnian Muslims as a community. The crackdown on the Catholic and Orthodox Churches was aimed at clerical institutions, not at the Croat or Serb communities. Viewing the Roman Catholic Church as an NDH collaborator, the CPY destroyed some churches and closed some monasteries, convents, and seminaries after 1945. The Orthodox Church experienced similar repression, but because some Orthodox clergy had served with the Partisans, reprisals were less harsh in some areas. In contrast, the CPY viewed Islam as a particularly backward Asiatic faith that encompassed a wide spectrum of social practices. Since the CPY did not recognize Bosnian Muslims as a nation, its attacks on Islam embraced the entire community, interfering in styles of dress, diet, and family rituals. It legally prohibited women from wearing the veil, forced some Muslims serving in the military and in labor brigades to eat pork, and instructed Muslim communist officials not to circumcise their sons.

Acting on a much broader scale than either the Habsburg or Karadjordjević monarchies, the communist state shut down active Bosnian Muslim cultural organizations as well as centuries-old Bosnian Muslim economic and religious institutions. The politically and economically important vakuf administration, still functioning much as it did under the Habsburgs, was placed under state control. The 1958 law nationalizing rental property (most of which was vakuf property) forced the charitable foundations, established as early as the 1530s, to close. The expropriations allowed the state to turn Muslim graveyards into parks, office building sites, and housing. In 1946 the state suppressed sharia courts. It banned independent Islamic cultural associations in 1947. The Young Muslims, resentful of the CPY for its harsh actions and for denying Bosnian Muslim national identity, tried to organize a political party to succeed the YMO. Between 1946 and 1949, 200 of its members were tried, the organization was banned, and defendants were given long jail sentences (including Alija Izetbegović, the future president of Bosnia-Hercegovina); 4 were executed. By 1950, 200 of the 750 mosques damaged in the war remained unusable, either because they still needed repair or because they had been converted to museums, warehouses, or stables. In 1950 the state closed

Alija Izetbegović, president of the Republic of Bosnia and Hercegovina, in the Pentagon, 1997. (Department of Defense)

Muslim elementary schools and banned Bosnia's dervish religious orders. Teaching children in mosques became a criminal offense. Only one *medressa* remained open for training clergy. The state shut down the last Muslim printing house in Sarajevo. Yugoslav publishers printed no Islamic texts until 1964.

Bosnia-Hercegovina's lack of political clout was evident in the lack of economic investment there and by the relative decline in living standards. At a time when the Yugoslav economy was experiencing high rates of sustained economic growth, the Bosnian portion of Yugoslavia's per capita production fell 10 percent. Very little economic investment in the region took place after 1952. In 1961 the Party declared it an economically underdeveloped region. In 1947 Bosnia's per capita income had been 20 percent below the national average. After experiencing the lowest growth rate in all of Yugoslavia since 1952, per capita income sank to 38 percent below the national average in 1967. By the 1970s, Bosnia had the highest infant mortality rate, the highest illiteracy rate, the highest percentage of adults with less than four years' education, and the fewest people living in cities in Yugoslavia, except for Kosovo. It also had the highest rate of emigration, consisting mostly of Bosnian Serbs moving to Serbia.

Tito's Yugoslavia began to unravel in the 1970s, but the roots of its decline lay in the Party's failure to achieve real political reform in the 1960s. Tito ruled Yugoslavia as a unitary state and would not compromise the LCY's political monopoly. To defuse widespread interest in political reform, he legitimized national cultural associations and began a process of political decentralization. The Party tolerated Serb, Croat, and Bosnian Muslim cultural associations, which in turn facilitated liberal democratic political revivals in the late 1960s and early 1970s. In the late 1960s Serb students and workers demonstrated and went on strike. A reformist communist movement in Croatia ("Croatian Spring") advocating increased political liberalization exerted influence in 1971. Both the Serb and the Croat cultural revivals included those who were more religious (Orthodox or Roman Catholic) and those who were more secular. Tito crushed both movements.

In contrast to the Serb and Croat revivals, distinct secular and religious movements emerged among Bosniaks. Since the Habsburg occupation, a secular identity had been developing among many Bosnian Muslims. They viewed observances of customary religious practices as cultural traditions rather than spiritual obligations. Islamic prohibitions against alcohol and portraying living things in art had never been widely observed in Bosnia-Hercegovina. Secular Muslims focused on political issues, such as the underrepresentation of Muslims in the LCY and the League of Communists of Bosnia-Hercegovina (LCBH) and Bosnia-Hercegovina's lower political status. By the mid-1960s, Bosnian Muslims had become the largest national group in the republic, and Bosnian Muslims' participation in the Party had increased tremendously. Linking Bosnia's economic decline to its lack of national status, secular Bosnian Muslims worked for national recognition and to bring more investment into the region. By the 1970s, Bosnian Muslims dominated the LCBH.

A Bosnian Islamic revival also developed in the 1960s. A 1954 law on religious freedom eased pressure on Islam. Tito's alliance with Nasser's Egypt and Sukarno's Indonesia (both Islamic states) in the Non-Aligned Movement made the treatment of the Muslim community a diplomatic factor and enabled increased contact with Muslims outside of Bosnia. In contrast to the secular movement, the Bosnian Islamic revival focused on the divisiveness of nationalism and the inadequacies of communism. The most famous statement to come out of the pan-Islamic movement was the 1970 "Islamic Declarations," by Alija Izetbegović, which never mentioned Bosnia-Hercegovina. It tried to reconcile the traditions of Islamic society with the modern world. Using his observations of Islamic societies around the world, Izetbegović argued that society could not progress by abandoning its own traditions in favor of foreign modernity. Citing Turkey as an example of a state that rejected its indigenous Islamic heritage in favor of foreign Western values, he linked its backwardness to the huge gulf between a small group of Westernized elites and the vast majority of traditional Turks. Izetbegović contended that societies must incorporate their own traditions in order to modernize effectively. In Islamic societies, this meant protecting Islam.

In states with both Islamic and non-Islamic populations, it meant protecting minority rights, women's rights, freedom of religion, and freedom of conscience.

The LCY's nationality policy and postwar demographic changes fueled a radical Serbian and Orthodox nationalist revival. By the mid-1960s, Serb emigration out of Kosovo and Bosnia-Hercegovina into Serbia proper had given Bosnian Muslims a plurality in Bosnia and reduced Serb presence in Kosovo. Many Serbs left these rural, underdeveloped regions in search of more opportunity in the more urban and more economically promising areas of Serbia. Anti-Serb riots in Kosovo in 1968 led to a backlash against the Serb minority in Kosovo. As the third largest national group in Yugoslavia, Albanians, who comprised 82 percent of the population of Kosovo in 1991, sought to revise their position as a national minority and gain recognition as a nation and republican status for Kosovo. This proposal was unacceptable to Serbs, who saw Kosovo as part of medieval Serbia that had been rightfully reintegrated into Serbia in 1912. In 1968 the Serb nationalist writer Dobrica Ćosić was expelled from the LCY for proposing that Kosovo Serbs should unite with Serbs into a single state. Since Albanians were mostly Muslim, Serb nationalism also fed anti-Islamic sentiment.

As political reform stagnated, these cultural organizations became politicized, leading to a communist crackdown on Serbian, Croatian, and Bosnian Muslim national (and religious) revivals. As a compromise, Tito offered the 1974 constitution, which increased the authority of the republican and provincial parties at the expense of federal institutions. Autonomous provinces were given political parity with republics. It also provided for an eight-member presidency (one representative from each republic and province) to rule by consensus after Tito's death. The 1974 constitution did not satisfy Albanians' desire for national status. It also enraged Serbs, who saw political parity for the autonomous provinces (both part of the Serb republic) as a direct attack on Serbia.

Many Serbs felt politically underrepresented in Yugoslavia. The Yugoslav capital was in Belgrade, and the Serbs dominated the military. Nonetheless, many Serbs believed that Macedonia (acquired in 1913) should be part of the Serb republic and that the autonomous provinces weakened Serb political authority. Before the Balkan Wars, these areas had not had any Serb rulers for five centuries. In the 1970s Serb nationalists revived nineteenth-century Serb claims to Bosnia and the idea that all Serbs should live in one political unit. Such a scenario (incorporating Serb minorities in Serbia, Croatia, Bosnia-Hercegovina, Kosovo, Vojvodina, and Macedonia with Serbia) could be achieved only within a Serb-dominated unitary state. As long as Yugoslavia was a centralized dictatorship, this question of national representation remained moot. The political devolution in the 1974 constitution reignited these claims and the debate over whether Yugoslavia should be a unitary or federalist state. As in the interwar period, Serbs tended to favor a unitary state and non-Serbs a federal one. As hope for political reform turned to general disillusion, people withdrew from politics, and national resentments flourished.

Tito's death in 1980 left Yugoslavia with a fragmented political leadership and a weak central government, due in large part to the fact that the 1974 constitution strengthened the Yugoslav republics and their regional interests. Political devolution and an unwieldy rotating presidency encouraged politicians to turn to their own nationally defined republics. In the early 1980s the Bosnian government, eager to secure its secular Bosnian Muslim identity, clamped down on "Bosnian nationalism." After Bosnian Muslims showed support for the Ayatollah Khomeni's 1979 Revolution in Iran, the government began to suppress Islam in Bosnia. In 1983 the government tried thirteen people for "hostile and counterrevolutionary acts derived from Muslim nationalism." The most important defendant was Alija Izetbegović, a retired lawyer and building company director, for his "Islamic Declarations" published thirteen years earlier. The government used this position paper as evidence that Izetbegović sought to create an ethnically pure Islamic state in Bosnia-Hercegovina. It also accused him of advocating Western-style democracy and sentenced him to fourteen years in prison (he served six). This trial and the conviction it resulted in gave greater weight to Serb nationalists who denied the secular character of Bosnian Muslims' identity by associating all Bosniaks with the Bosnian Islamic revival, which it claimed was a fundamentalist movement to repress Serbs. This association of fundamentalist Islam with Bosniaks allowed nationalists to claim that Bosnian Muslims were "really" Turks, not Bosnians at all. The LCBH's attempt to curb Bosnian nationalism only further divided the republic.

The Party also became concerned about the Serb nationalist revival, which revised the history of the Četniks and condemned official LCY histories. In the 1980s Serb nationalists called for a new constitution that would create a unitary Yugoslav state and reintegrate the autonomous provinces into Serbia. In 1985 the nationalist writer Dobrica Ćosić published a novel sympathetic to the extreme Serb nationalist Četnik leader, Dragiša Vasić, who advocated the expulsion of Bosnian Muslims from the region and the Serb annexation of Bosnia, Montenegro, northern Albania, and large parts of Croatia in World War II. The prestigious Serbian Academy of Sciences (SANU) gave Serb nationalists respectability in its 1986 Memorandum, claiming that the Party had encouraged anti-Serb Croatian, Slovene, Macedonian, Montenegrin, and Bosnian Muslim nationalism in order to weaken Serbia. The Memorandum contended that ethnic Serb writers were identified as Bosnian authors in Bosnia and Montenegrin writers in Montenegro. Using the nineteenth-century nationalist argument that all members of a nation should reside in one state, the Memorandum called for the political unification of all Serbs. The pursuit of this goal destroyed Yugoslavia and Bosnia-Hercegovina with it.

In 1987 Slobodan Milošević became leader of the Serbian League of Communists (LCS). Using nationalism to mobilize mass political support, Milošević was able to reintegrate Kosovo and Vojvodina into Serbia, giving him enormous political power and control over three votes in the presidency. In Vojvodina, the entire politburo resigned in 1988. In 1989 Kosovo's political autonomy was abolished. Mass protests and a strike in Kosovo were labeled anti-Serb and crushed by Serb security forces. Milošević called a meeting of the LCY for January 1990 to revise the 1974 constitution in favor of a more unitary system. After the Serb delegation blocked discussion of all Slovene reforms (aimed at increased decentralization), the Slovene delegation walked out of the meeting. When the other delegations refused to vote without the Slovenes, the meeting broke up with the LCY in tatters. As a result, each republic held multiparty elections in 1990, in which nationalists dominated.

These elections were the first in a series of events leading to the collapse of Yugoslavia. As in other republics, Bosnian votes divided along national lines, with Bosnian Muslims receiving a plurality. The new president, Alija Izetbegović, formed a coalition government including Bosnian Serbs and Croats. After more than a year of attempting to negotiate increased regional control, Slovenia and Croatia seceded from Yugoslavia in June 1991. This secession precipitated the ten-day war in Slovenia, waged by the Yugoslav National Army (JNA), as well as the JNA's four-month campaign against Croatia. The international community, which had ignored the issues leading up to the war, became involved only as armed hostilities broke out. The Slovenian and Croatian secession left Bosnia-Hercegovina and Macedonia facing Serbian territorial claims without its strongest allies. In January 1992 Macedonia and Bosnia applied for international recognition along with Croatia and Slovenia. A rump state consisting of Serbia (including Kosovo and Vojvodina) and Montenegro was all that remained of Yugoslavia.

The United Nations' recognition of Bosnia-Hercegovina did not lead to independence. The Izetbegović government held a UN-mandated referendum on independence, despite Bosnian fears that it would precipitate bloodshed. The referendum inflamed Serb nationalism. Serbs boycotted the vote, which was over 90 percent for independence. Before recognition, Serb forces in the JNA attacked Bosnia. From April 1992 to November 1995, a war of ethnic cleansing perpetrated overwhelmingly by Serbs engulfed Bosnia-Hercegovina. The war ended in December 1995 with the signing of the Dayton Accords in Paris. Since then, Bosnia-Hercegovina has been occupied by NATO peacekeepers. Despite this military presence, Bosnian Serb and Bosnian Croat leaders responsible for mass murder have not been arrested. The right of return, only recognized for refugees from certain areas, has not been respected. Today, Bosnia remains divided and lacks essential sovereignty. Governed by a UN High Commissioner, Bosnia is also burdened with an excessively complex, unworkable, UN-imposed constitution. The Dayton "peace" seems designed to perpetuate twentieth-century ethnic animosity well into the twenty-first century.

POLITICAL DEVELOPMENTS
ESTABLISHING A COMMUNIST STATE, 1945–1955
The historical narrative has already provided a summary of political events from 1945 to 1995. This section, however,

pays closer attention to the Yugoslav state and covers the events in this period more thoroughly. The three conflicts of the National Liberation Struggle (military occupation, social revolution, ethnic cleansing), together with the victors' vision for the future, defined the basis for the postwar Yugoslav state. Although Tito faced the same dilemmas that had bedeviled the interwar monarchy, he held out the promise of a bright future: "brotherhood and unity" would replace fratricide, social and political equality would replace chauvinism and monarchy, and industrialization and urbanization would replace rural poverty. The Partisans' military success ensured the prominent position of the postwar Yugoslav National Army (JNA). The communist victory over the Četniks enabled the regime to abolish the monarchy in favor of a one-party state and establish a socialist economy. Attempts to accommodate nationalist conflict led to political representation by nationally defined republics. These four features (strong military, one-party rule, national political representation, and an industrial socialist economy) all lent stability to Tito's state and enabled it to survive more than twice as long as the first Yugoslavia.

First, the CPY began establishing a socialist economy as soon as it took power. Since the social revolution had been fought on the basis of delivering both increased wealth and more equitable economic prosperity for all Yugoslav citizens, economic development became and remained one of the regime's top political priorities. Initially, the state pursued economic development using Stalinist strategies. It took control of all major markets and resources to promote industrialization, urbanization, and growth. By 1947, the state controlled 70 percent of industry and 90 percent of retail trade. It did not collectivize completely, but it did control rural markets. In April 1947 the Party formalized this Stalinist economic strategy in its First Five-Year Plan (1947–1951). By 1948, however, a weak economy was contributing to the erosion of the CPY's popular base. Since Tito and the CPY had tied their political legitimacy to economic development, this poor performance compromised the Party's political credibility.

Second, since the Partisans' role in the communists' military victory in World War II had made communist rule possible, the postwar Yugoslav National Army became an integral part of the new regime. In five years the CPY had grown from a tiny political party to the leader of a mass resistance movement and the strongest political power in Yugoslavia. To turn its military success into political support, the CPY promoted unity by extolling the virtues and sacrifices of citizens throughout Yugoslavia, whose efforts expelled fascist, foreign occupiers and defeated the unpatriotic, ultranationalist minority. The Party discredited the Četnik resistance by contrasting the Partisans' heroic battles, dramatic escapes, and multinational fighting force (which included many Serbs) with Četnik passivity, collaboration, and Serb chauvinism. On the other hand, Mihailović's forces were unable to use widespread anticommunism and their own defense of the Yugoslav monarchy to bolster their own domestic political position.

Good Soviet-Yugoslav relations also bolstered the JNA's importance in establishing the Party's domestic and international political authority. The absence of a postwar Soviet occupation to compromise Yugoslavia's national communists allowed the CPY to claim full responsibility for the German defeat. As Stalin's strongest East European ally before 1948, Tito's international standing benefited from his prominent role in the 1947 founding of the Cominform (Communist Information Bureau—a body intended to establish information contacts and demonstrate the unity of the European communist states). By 1948, Tito was poised to become the dominant political and military leader in the Balkans.

Third, the new state opted for a unitary rather than federal government and one-party rule. The CPY, elected by plebiscite in November 1945, abolished the monarchy (1945) and enacted a constitution (1946) that banned political opposition and equated dissent from the Party with treason. Between 1946 and 1949, two hundred Young Muslims trying to organize a political successor to the interwar YMO found themselves on trial. By 1948, the prewar and popular front political parties had ceased any meaningful activity. The CPY had regional affiliates in the republics and autonomous provinces, but Tito and his closest advisors held the real power. Thus, there was no viable political opposition to Tito's government.

Fourth, the Party adopted a new strategy to accommodate nationalism and prevent the violence that had plagued the interwar regime and exploded in World War II. It placed its one-party rule onto a national-federal state structure. The CPY granted each of the five recognized historic nations (Slovenes, Croats, Serbs, Montenegrins, and Macedonians) their own republic based on its historic boundaries. With no dominant nation, multi-ethnic Bosnia-Hercegovina formed a sixth republic based solely on its historic borders. The CPY defined members of nations, whose nation-state existed outside of Yugoslavia (e.g., Albania, Hungary, Romania, Greece, Bulgaria, Italy, Germany) as national minorities. While they had the same individual rights as those belonging to nations, national minorities had no claim to their own republic. This solution was a vast improvement over interwar era policies, but it still ignored the status of many who lived outside their nationally defined republic (such as Serbs in Croatia, Bosnia, and Macedonia, Macedonians and Albanians in Serbia, Croats in Bosnia-Hercegovina). Organizing politics on the issue of national representation served to divide rather than unify the country, as the Party missed opportunities to work on pan-Yugoslav or regional, inter-republic concerns that could have promoted multi-ethnic nation-building.

The case of Bosnia-Hercegovina was especially problematic because no single nation dominated the republic. Restoring the region's historic borders and designating it a republic ended ongoing Serbian and Croatian claims to annex the region. Despite success in recruiting Bosniaks in the regions surrounding their Bihać and Jajce headquarters during World War II, the Communist Party of Bosnia-Hercegovina (CPBH) was small and dominated by Bosnian Serbs. The CPY recognized Bosnian Muslims as a prenational, religiously defined ethnic group, whose members still needed to choose whether they belonged to the Serb or Croat nation (as Muslims in Serbia, Croatia, Macedonia, and Kosovo had). On the other hand, Bosnian Serbs and Bosnian Croats represented only fragments of their respective nations because they lived outside of the respective Serb and Croat republics. With no representative nation, Bosnia-Hercegovina had less political clout and more tenuous claims on resources than other republics.

The state also recognized two historic regions, which Serbia had acquired in the early twentieth century, as autonomous provinces. One of them, multi-ethnic Vojvodina, had a large German and Hungarian population and had been historically Habsburg. The other, Albanian-dominated Kosovo, had been an Ottoman outpost for over 500 years (1389–1912). Serb nationalists viewed the autonomous provinces attached to Serbia (without a corresponding status for Serbian regions in Macedonia, Croatia, and western Bosnia) as an attempt to dismember their nation. Albanian nationalists saw Kosovo's autonomous province status as a way to deny their right to a republic. Until 1974, however, Yugoslavia's unitary state dominated by a centralized dictatorship rendered these issues of national representation moot.

In 1948 conflict with the Soviet Union nearly toppled Tito's government. Growing postwar tensions between the USSR and the Western Allies encouraged Stalin to consolidate his power in Eastern Europe. In 1948 he demanded greater political control over the East European communist parties' foreign and domestic policies. In asserting Soviet power in the region, Stalin targeted the CPY and its ambitious leader as a lesson to the rest of the Cominform and to consolidate his power in Eastern Europe. The ensuing Soviet-Yugoslav conflict brought long-lasting changes to communist Yugoslavia. It strengthened the importance of the JNA, reinforced the one-party political system, and led to economic restructuring.

Stalin attacked the mainstays of Tito's communist regime: the Party, the new economy, and the military. The Kremlin condemned the Party for deviating from the Soviet socialist model (in fact followed more closely in Yugoslavia than anywhere else). When Tito responded with consternation instead of subservience, the USSR recalled its military and civilian advisors and expelled the CPY from the Cominform. To undermine the Party, Stalin also attacked Yugoslavia's weak economy. The Cominform countries reneged on existing trade agreements and boycotted Yugoslavia. Stalin condemned the CPY's unpopular agrarian policies (which he had praised six months earlier) to increase dissension among peasants (70 percent of the population). With the economy in a shambles and the Party isolated and under attack, Tito's leadership was in crisis. However, when Stalin dismissed the Partisans' liberation of Yugoslavia from German occupation as wild exaggeration and claimed credit instead for the Red Army, Tito used this slight to the Partisans and citizens' wartime sacrifices to rally mass support for himself and the Party.

As the Cold War mushroomed, the CPY expanded Yugoslavia's military and reoriented its diplomatic efforts westward. The conflict with the USSR placed Yugoslavia on military alert from 1948 to 1954 for fear of invasion or a coup d'état against Tito's leadership of the CPY. Those suspected of sympathy with Cominform positions were jailed (including entire families). By 1952, the JNA had 500,000 troops and had received hundreds of millions of dollars in direct military grants from the West.

The Yugoslav-Soviet conflict led to contradictory changes in the Party and altered its economic system. It reinforced a centralized, one-party political system and the primacy of security and harsh treatment of dissenters. The crisis also introduced decentralizing legal rhetoric intended to distinguish Yugoslav communism from "Stalinist deviations." In 1950 the Party gave local governments (people's committees, later commune, city, and county governments) greater local control. Formally, it created a less state-directed economy under its worker self-management system. Worker self-management enabled company managers (who were always Party members) to make decisions concerning their individual firms. Like the Partisan liberation, worker self-management became fundamental to Yugoslavia's political identity as a non-Stalinist communist state. Instead of providing tangible changes in 1950, self-management and local political control set out a framework for future challenges to centralized communist power from within the confines of one-party rule.

Soviet-Yugoslav conflict affected Bosnia-Hercegovina's military and economic position within Yugoslavia. With its interior position and difficult terrain, the republic was chosen by the CPY leadership as Yugoslavia's last military stronghold in the event of invasion. The CPY stockpiled weapons and built military bases, oil refineries, and arms factories in Bosnia. The republic remained a strategic military center until 1992. Investment flowed into the republic as its economy was reoriented toward heavy industry and mining. This influx of funds was short-lived, however. Bosnia's mountains, non-navigable rivers, and small skilled workforce made building basic economic infrastructure difficult and expensive. After 1953, investment, production, and jobs found their way to more economically developed republics.

By 1955, a reconstituted Party (calling itself the League of Communists of Yugoslavia, LCY) was firmly in control, a new socialist economic doctrine of worker self-management had become policy, and the JNA's role as the protector of Yugoslavia was more unassailable than ever. In Bosnia-Hercegovina, League of Communists of Bosnia-Hercegovina (LCBH) members pursued their future along multinational, nonreligious, promilitary, worker self-management lines.

THE POLITICS OF DECENTRALIZATION, 1955–1989

From the mid-1950s to the late 1960s, Yugoslav citizens witnessed significant economic and political decentralization. From the mid-1960s, pressure for economic and political reform led Tito to divert liberal opposition from the federal to the republic level. Rather than allowing opposition that might have challenged the political monopoly of the LCY, Tito funneled political dissent through the republics and autonomous provinces. This strategy accentuated nationalist concerns and divisions at the expense of comprehensive Yugoslav solutions for the complex issues facing the country (development, unemployment, growing regional disparity, inequitable resource allocation, and uneven political representation). In the 1960s and 1970s the LCY tolerated cultural associations, which facilitated nationalist political and religious revivals. In the 1970s and 1980s, political power devolved to the republics, and the growing republican power weakened the LCY's central authority. Economic reforms had given republics and autonomous provinces more control over how to spend resources within their jurisdiction. Issues of resource allocation and growing economic disparity between the poorest and the richest regions became increasingly divisive. The great exception to this trend was the military. In 1968 the LCY instituted universal military service and commissioned regionally controlled territorial defense units for each of the republics and autonomous provinces. After briefly lessening the JNA's centralized military authority, by 1980 these territorial defense units had become completely subordinate to JNA command.

The first challenge to the LCY's unitarist party structure came from the national and cultural movements that emerged in the 1960s. Cultural revivals in both Serbia and Croatia encompassed a wide political spectrum of those who were more concerned with national and religious issues as well as those focused on political liberalism. These movements influenced Bosnian Serbs and Bosnian Croats, but held little appeal for Bosniaks because they were infused with Serb and Croat nationalism. In contrast, the Bosniak renaissance split into separate secular and religious movements. By the mid-1960s, secular Bosniaks played an increasingly active role in the LCBH, where they worked to redress the republic's political underrepresentation, which they blamed for relative economic stagnation and slow progress in raising living standards. Thus, they sought national recognition for Bosnian Muslims (achieved in 1971) and increased investment in the region. The Islamic revival, however, was explicitly non-national and at odds with the secular movement that Muslims in the LCBH represented. It looked beyond Bosnia's borders to criticize the divisiveness of nationalism and the inadequacies of communism and to seek a positive role for Islam in modern society. In contrast to the Croat and Serb revivals, which provided national unity, the two Bosniak movements split the Muslim community.

As the 1960s political reform movements expanded, they threatened Tito's political authority and politicized cultural organizations. The LCY responded by crushing the Serb and the Croat movements. It expelled the reformers' political leaders from the Party. After breaking their organization, Tito sought to accommodate the reformers by brokering a new constitution. The 1974 constitution strengthened republic and autonomous province parties' political and economic control over their own budgets and resources and granted the autonomous provinces (Kosovo and Vojvodina) political parity with the republics, strengthening regional political interests. The constitution also provided for an eight-member presidency (one representative from each republic and province) to rule by consensus after Tito's death. It called for the office of the Yugoslav president to rotate among the members of the presidency, each serving a one-year term. One-party rule remained, but the party fragmented into its republic-level organizations.

Instead of mollifying national tensions, the 1974 constitution enflamed them. As the third largest national group in Yugoslavia, Albanians sought recognition as a nation and republican status for the historically and demographically Albanian region of Kosovo. Albanian Kosovars linked the region's continued underdevelopment to its provincial political status and the Serb minority's political domination. However, Serb nationalists saw political parity for Kosovo as an example of the LCY's anti-Serb policies that directly undermined their national rights. Serbs viewed Kosovo as part of their medieval heritage that had been rightfully reintegrated into Serbia in 1912. Kosovo's endemic poverty, overwhelming Albanian majority, and Ottoman culture did not diminish its symbolic importance to Serb national identity.

By the 1980s, the 1974 constitution had become a rallying point for Serb nationalist calls to recentralize the Yugoslav state in order to protect Serb nationhood. In making these calls, Serbs referred to past Ottoman oppressions and the threat of Islamic fundamentalism. The Kosovo question highlighted Serb nationalists' anti-Islamic sentiments. Since Albanians were mostly Muslim, Serb nationalists also associated Bosnian Muslims with Albanians. They denied the secular character of the LCBH and associated all Bosniaks with the Bosnian Islamic revival, which they claimed was fundamentalist. Historically, Bosnia-Hercegovina's religious Sunni and Sufi tradions have incorporated local customs and have no record of fundamentalism. Far from placating nationalist political aspirations, the 1974 constitution allowed Serbs to use anti-Islamic, anti-Ottoman sentiments to challenge Bosnian Muslim identity yet again.

The Bosnian government, eager to defend itself against allegations of fundamentalism and promote Bosnian Muslims' secular national identity, suppressed the anticommunist Islamic revival. In 1983 the government tried Alija Izetbegović and twelve other representatives of the Islamic revival for counterrevolutionary acts. It used his 1970 "Islamic Declarations" to prove the contradictory charges that Izetbegović sought to create an ethnically pure Islamic state in Bosnia-Hercegovina (a region never mentioned in the paper) and that he advocated a Western-style democracy. The court sentenced Izetbegović to fourteen years in jail. This crackdown not only stifled religious freedom, it also had a chilling effect on secular Bosniak political activity. Moreover, it did not refute nationalist charges that the secular LCBH sought to create a fundamentalist state.

In the 1980s the Bosnian government also became concerned about the influence of the Serb nationalist revival among Bosnian Serbs. Serb nationalists glorified their World War I and World War II tragedies, demonized non-Serbs, revised the history of the Četniks, and condemned the official LCY histories. Unlike the Islamic revival in Bosnia, Serb nationalism had the support of some prominent intellectuals and some communist politicians. The infamous 1986 Memorandum produced by SANU (the Serbian

Alija Izetbegović (1925–2003)

Alija Izetbegović is best known as Bosnia-Hercegovina's wartime president and one of the principal signatories of the 1995 Dayton Accords, which ended the country's three-and-a-half-year war for independence. Unlike the other leaders of former Yugoslav republics, Izetbegović had never been a communist. Thus, his political career began only in 1990, when he cofounded the Party for Democratic Action (SDA) in anticipation of the first free general elections in Bosnian history. The SDA appealed to Bosnian Muslims by emphasizing their cultural and historical heritage. Reflecting the republic's national-religious composition, the election returned a plurality for the SDA. As leader of the SDA, Izetbegović formed a coalition government with the nationalist Croatian Democratic Union (HDZ) and the nationalist Serbian Democratic Party (SDS). As president, Izetbegović declared Bosnia-Hercegovina an independent country on 3 March 1992. He spent much of his presidency (1992–1995) in wartime Sarajevo, surrounded by Serb forces in their three-year siege of the capital. The most moderate of Yugoslavia's wartime leaders, Izetbegović negotiated and signed the 1995 Dayton Agreement, which set up the postwar government in Bosnia-Hercegovina. He served as one of the presidencies' three members until 2000, when he resigned, claiming that the postwar settlement had rewarded ethnic cleansing.

Izetbegović was born in Bosanski Samac in 1925, but his family moved to Sarajevo in the 1930s. After Croatia annexed Bosnia-Hercegovina in 1941, he did not affiliate with the nationalist Croat Ustaša, the Serb Četniks, or the communist Partisans.

Izetbegović's long career as a political dissident began when he joined the Young Muslims shortly after World War II. The Young Muslims opposed the postwar communist crackdown on Muslims by attempting to found a non-communist political party to succeed the interwar Yugoslav Muslim Organization. The Communist Party of Yugoslavia, however, tolerated no political opposition in the postwar period. Between 1946 and 1949, the CPY banned the Young Muslims and tried two hundred of its members, including twenty-one-year-old Alija Izetbegović, who served three years in prison. After leaving jail, Izetbegović studied law at the University of Sarajevo and pursued a successful career in law. In the 1970s Izetbegović became an intellectual leader in the anti-communist and anti-nationalist Islamic revival. His 1970 paper, "Islamic Declarations," claimed a place for Islam in the modern world. It rejected Western characterizations of Islam as an inherently primitive religion and argued that replacing indigenous Islamic customs with foreign Western traditions would not help develop or modernize Muslim nations. Citing Turkey as an example, Izetbegović argued that this Westernizing strategy risked creating an unbridgeable void between the poor, traditional masses and a tiny group of Westernized ruling elites, and so causing political instability and economic stagnation. On the other hand, he also called for safeguarding minority rights, women's rights, religious freedom, and freedom of conscience in societies with populations made up of both Muslim and non-Muslim communities. Far from a call for a fundamentalist state in Bosnia as his detractors later claimed, "Islamic Declarations" focused on finding a positive Muslim role in both Islamic and non-Islamic cultures throughout the world. It

(continues)

Academy of Arts and Sciences) asserted that the Party had encouraged anti-Serb, Croatian, Slovene, Macedonian, Montenegrin, and Bosnian Muslim nationalism in order to weaken Serbia. It claimed that Serbian culture was under attack and in danger of extinction. Arguing that Serbs' rights transcended political and geographic divisions, the memo called for the political unification of all Serbs to prevent the extinction of the Serb nation. Although these arguments were not new, the SANU document gave what had been considered nationalist fringe opinions intellectual and political respectability.

Flourishing nationalist resentments in the 1970s and 1980s left politicians unable to confront the effects of economic stagnation and created a more intractable political crisis. In the 1970s the republics gained increased control over resources, but the socialist self-management economy provided little growth. Under Tito, the government had borrowed heavily to maintain rising living standards, jobs, and affordable credit. By the time Tito died in 1980, Yugoslavia was awash in foreign debt and subject to IMF (International Monetary Fund) and World Bank spending restrictions. Political and national resentments rather than economic analysis dominated debate over productivity, resource allocation, and uneven development patterns. In general, Croat and Slovene leaders, demanding increased political autonomy, complained that their republics subsidized the rest of Yugoslavia by generating more than their share of the national income. Croats pointed to the dominance of Belgrade banks, which benefited the most from Croatia's lucrative tourist trade. However, they particularly

(continued)

never mentioned Bosnia-Hercegovina. "Islamic Declarations" became significant to non-Muslims only after the rise of nationalist politics in Yugoslavia. After the rise in fundamentalist states in the Middle East, Izetbegović's detractors charged him with Islamic fundamentalism. His ideas, however, reflected those of the Islamic community in Bosnia, which had never been fundamentalist and had developed in relative autonomy from Istanbul.

In 1983 the government tried Izetbegović for "hostile and counterrevolutionary acts derived from Muslim nationalism." The government's case rested on the thirteen-year-old "Islamic Declarations," which it cited as evidence of two contradictory charges, that of seeking to create an ethnically pure Islamic state in Bosnia-Hercegovina *and* advocating Western-style democracy in the region. The Party sentenced him to fourteen years in prison.

While in prison, Izetbegović wrote *Islam between East and West* (1988), which developed the themes of "Islamic Declarations" more fully. He noted how Islamic study and preservation of ancient Greek and Latin texts served as the foundation of the European renaissance. He also praised Christian ideals, West and Central European philosophy, and Western traditions of democracy and social justice that he believed could positively influence Islam. While maintaining his criticism of Westernizers' rejection of Islamic traditions and culture, *Islam between East and West* praised Islam's historic ability to study other traditions and incorporate some elements into its own. Izetbegović's attempts to discuss how diverse cultures can accommodate each other was the antithesis of fundamentalism and is especially striking in the years leading up to the breakup of Yugoslavia, when Croat and Serb politicians were demonizing both Muslims and each other.

Izetbegović's life as a dissident did not prepare him to become the president of the first independent Bosnia-Hercegovina since 1463. In 1991 he allowed the Yugoslav National Army (JNA) to arm the Serb autonomous regions and disarm Bosnian territorial defense units. When war broke out in 1992, Bosnia was virtually defenseless, losing 60 percent of its territory in six weeks. Nevertheless, Bosnia survived under Izetbegović's leadership, when it could easily have been divided between Serbia and Croatia. He could not have anticipated the ethnic cleansing that made Bosniaks the principal victims of the war and associated them more closely with Islam than at any other time in the past fifty years.

After the war, Izetbegović was elected twice to the Bosnian presidency. In 2000, however, he resigned and retired from politics, because he objected to the postwar political system, which he came to believe had rewarded ethnic cleansing and failed to protect the rights of Bosnian Muslims. Nonetheless, Alija Izetbegović spent his entire adult life fighting for the rights of Bosnian Muslims, first as a political dissident and later within an independent Bosnia-Hercegovina. Unlike the nationalists of his day, Izetbegović strove to work with Bosnia's national communities to preserve Bosnia-Hercegovina. More than anyone else, he is responsible for the survival of the Bosnian state, however imperfect it may be.

---

resented the development fund, which provided investment funds to corrupt public officials in underdeveloped regions with insufficient oversight.

Serb politicians, calling for political recentralization, countered that Slovene and Croat productivity in manufacturing was the result of exploiting below-market raw materials from Serbia and the less developed republics to produce finished goods, which they sold abroad at higher world market prices. They argued that the LCY's investment in heavy industry and mining instead of manufacturing in Serbia demonstrated its anti-Serb bias. The less developed regions (Bosnia, Kosovo, Montenegro, Macedonia) complained that the growing disparity between their areas and the developed regions demonstrated national bias. Because these economic issues were framed in terms of national-republic grievances, and because the Yugoslav presidency was so weak, the LCY made no attempt at a comprehensive solution before Ante Marković's 1989 economic reforms. By this time, the political crisis had spun out of control.

POLITICAL DISINTEGRATION AND WAR, 1989–1995

As the republics grew stronger, the economy continued to plummet, the presidency remained ineffectual, and nationalist politicians gained mass support. The most successful communist in mobilizing nationalist support was Serbia's Slobodan Milošević. In 1987 Milošević had become leader of the Serbian League of Communists (LCS), championing the reintegration of the autonomous provinces into Serbia and a more centralized constitution. In 1989 he reintegrated Kosovo into Serbia proper by abolishing its political autonomy. After labeling participants anti-Serb, the JNA and Serb security forces violently suppressed mass demonstrations and a strike protesting Kosovo's loss of autonomy and imposed martial law. For the first time, one of the republics had deployed the JNA against its own people. (This action was possible because JNA stood out as the primary Yugoslav institution in favor of a strong central government. In the 1980s its political interests had become closely tied to Serbia's.) Milošević was at the peak of his power. The LCS directly controlled three (Serbia, Kosovo, Vojvodina) of the presidency's eight votes, and his influence over the Montenegrin party leadership secured him a fourth vote. In the fall of 1989 Milošević called an LCY meeting to revise the 1974 constitution in favor of the more centralized system that Serbia and the JNA favored.

In the fall of 1989 each of the Soviet bloc communist regimes collapsed. In this climate of political change, the LCY met in January 1990 to amend the 1974 constitution. After the Serb delegation blocked discussion of all of its decentralizing reforms, the Slovene delegation walked out. When the other republics' delegations refused to vote on Milošević's proposals without the Slovene representatives, the meeting broke up, leaving the LCY critically weakened. In 1990 each of Yugoslavia's republics held elections, bringing nationalist leaders to power. All of these politicians were current or former Communist Party members, except for Bosnia-Hercegovina's Alija Izetbegović, who had been released from prison in 1989.

Multinational Bosnia-Hercegovina held its election on 9 November 1990. The three new national parties—Party of Democratic Action (SDA), the Serbian Democratic Party (SDS), and the Bosnian branch of the Croatian Democratic Union (HDZ)—together polled 84 percent of the votes. The results excluded Marković's reform party and Bosnia's communist party from government. The SDA, led by Alija Izetbegović, stressed Bosnian Muslim cultural and historical traditions. The other two parties had their roots in Croatia. Radovan Karadžić's SDS represented Bosnian Serbs and was a branch of the Serbian Democratic Party centered in Knin (in western Croatia's Krajina region) and had close ties to Serbia and the JNA. A Bosnian branch of Croatia's ruling HDZ party (led by Franjo Tudjman) organized a Bosnian branch to represent Bosnian Croats. As in other republics, Bosnians voted along ethnic lines. Bosnian Muslims received a plurality, followed by Bosnian Serbs and Bosnian Croats. As the leader of the largest party, Izetbegović formed an anticommunist government with coalition partners in the SDS and the HDZ.

This coalition survived only four months after Slovenia and Croatia seceded from Yugoslavia in June 1991. This action precipitated a ten-day war in Slovenia and a four-month campaign in Croatia. It also plunged Bosnia-Hercegovina into political crisis. In May 1991 the SDS began establishing "autonomous regions" in Bosnia (as it had in Croatia earlier). After the two republics seceded, Karadžić accused the Izetbegović government of supporting their separation (which it had opposed) and renounced the Bosnian parliament. In September the SDA declared the creation by the SDS of heavily armed autonomous regions (some in Serb minority areas) a violation of the coalition

agreement. Karadžić called on the JNA for military protection of the self-declared "autonomous regions." The military immediately deployed thousands of troops to Hercegovina and Banja Luka. In mid-October Izetbegović enacted legislative sovereignty within Bosnia in an effort to override the JNA's use of its territory in its war in Croatia and to disarm the SDS's "autonomous regions." In October 1991 Karadžić walked out of the assembly, after threatening that Izetbegović's actions would bring a Croat-style war to Bosnia and with it the extermination of the Muslim population, who did not have either a government that could protect them or the weapons to defend themselves. Indeed, the methods of ethnic cleansing later used in Bosnia were being established in Croatia, and Bosnians had already come under sporadic attack. Ten days after the government voted for legislative sovereignty, the SDS formed its own Serb National Assembly in the JNA stronghold of Banja Luka.

Following Karadžić's threats, Izetbegović called on the JNA to conduct joint police and army patrols to defend the republic. Given the strong ties between the JNA, Serbia, and the SDS, Izetbegović's request was astonishing. In Bosnia-Hercegovina, the JNA had supported the creation of extralegal, heavily armed "autonomous Serbian regions" in Serb and non-Serb areas. It helped these autonomous regions construct heavy artillery positions around major towns, and it occupied important communication centers in the fall of 1991. In early 1992 federal army units withdrew from Croatia and were redeployed in Bosnia, where they confiscated Bosnian territorial defense weapons supplies. Neither the Bosnian government nor its citizens had the means to defend themselves.

The European Union (EU) became involved in the crisis in Yugoslavia only when it was on the brink of war. Unprepared for Croatian and Slovenian secession and the subsequent wars, it did not anticipate the course of events in Bosnia or appreciate the distinct interests of Bosnia's three nations. In response to Izetbegović's request for EU recognition of each of the six republics and for peacekeepers in the self-declared autonomous areas patrolled by Serb gunmen, the EU offered recognition to each republic that met its criteria for new states. Bosnian Serbs repeatedly asserted that if the republic were given independence, they would secede. In January 1992 the UN recognized Bosnia and granted it full UN membership, pending a referendum on independence. Yugoslavia had become a rump state consisting of Serbia (including Kosovo and Vojvodina) and Montenegro.

The UN's actions did not lead to Bosnian independence. In January Karadžić promised that independence in Bosnia-Hercegovina would not last a day and that the "autonomous regions" of Bosnia would remain part of Yugoslavia. This area (later called Republika Srpska) consisted of the western side of the Drina River valley in eastern Bosnia (which included heavily Muslim regions) and the Bosnian *krajina* (military frontier) region in western Bosnia, connected in the north by a small strip of land around the Sava River port of Brčko. It included not only areas where Bosnian Serbs predominated but also minority Serb areas. In February 1992 Milošević and Croatia's Franjo Tudjman revisited their discussion of the previous March on dividing Bosnia-Hercegovina between their respective republics.

The Izetbegović government held the UN-mandated referendum on 29 February and 1 March, despite fears that it would precipitate bloodshed. Unable to prevail in or block the referendum, the SDS not only boycotted the vote, it prevented ballot boxes from entering the areas it controlled. With 64 percent of the electorate voting, 99.7 percent voted for independence. The government declared independence on 3 March 1992.

Serbian paramilitary forces in Croatia entered Bosnia. Among the most feared were Željko "Arkan" Raznjatović and his paramilitaries (the Tigers), who dressed in black and khaki, sported neo-Nazi haircuts, and wore tiger insignia. Trained in the Serbian Interior Ministry's Serbian Volunteer Guards, Arkan boasted that every member of his unit was responsible to the Serbian people, the Serbian parliament, and the Serbian president. On 1 April, Arkan's Tigers entered the Bosnian city of Bijeljina. With the JNA nearby, Arkan's Tigers "liberated" the city. They patrolled the streets with machine guns, placed snipers on buildings, summarily executed the city's Muslim leaders, and crushed a small, spontaneous resistance force. By 4 April, Bijeljina's electricity and water supplies had been severed, bodies were lying in the street, and the Muslim population had fled. Although the majority of Bosnians had voted overwhelmingly for independence, Serbs began a war of ethnic cleansing to prevent that independence from coming into effect, even before the EU recognized the state.

The EU's recognition of Bosnia-Hercegovina's independence on 6 April did not confer the political legitimacy that Western diplomats had expected. Instead, Serbian politicians and their Bosnian Serb clients used it as a pretext to launch a war of ethnic cleansing against a disarmed country that the international community was not prepared to defend. Karadžić declared Republika Srpska (with its capital in Sarajevo) on 7 April, and the siege of Sarajevo began a few days later.

On 8 April, the first full-scale ethnic cleansing in Bosnia began. The JNA shelled the city of Zvornik from inside Serbia, and Arkan's Tigers expelled the city's Muslim population (60 percent of the residents). The self-styled "Četnik" paramilitary led by Vojislav Šešelj, a member of the Serbian parliament and leader of the ultranationalist Serbian Radical Party, also participated. Šešelj openly advocated the absorption of Bosnia, Montenegro, Macedonia, and most of Croatia into Serbia. Thousands fled amid gunfire, shelling, and terror. By 10 April, Zvornik lay in ruins, its Muslim population gone. According to Šešelj, Serbian Interior Ministry units had sent special paramilitary forces to carry out this attack (which had been planned in Belgrade). By the end of April, 95 percent of the Muslim population in the eastern Bosnian cities of Foča, Višegrad, and Zvornik had been cleansed. Within six weeks, Serbs controlled 60 percent of Bosnia. By the end of 1992, 2 million Bosnians, mostly Muslims, had fled their homes.

From April 1992 to November 1995, Serbia's war of territorial conquest engulfed Bosnia. Violence and fear gripped all Bosnians, but Serbs (Bosnian and non-Bosnian) committed by far the most atrocities, as they "ethnically cleansed" their mostly Bosnian Muslim targets. Civilians were the primary targets, as Serbs forcibly removed Bosniaks from towns, cities, and villages in order to create an ethnically pure Serb region to claim for a Serb nation-state. To ensure that no Bosniaks ever returned, cleansers systematically terrorized Muslim communities with beatings, thefts, rapes, expulsions, and massacres. They also tried to remove any evidence that non-Serbs had ever existed in the regions they claimed by destroying graveyards, birth records, work documents, churches and mosques, libraries, and museums.

Most scholars agree that the war in Bosnia-Hercegovina was never about "ancient ethnic hatreds." Neither was it a civil war. Bosnian Serbs did not spontaneously rebel against the Izetbegović government, as Milošević asserted. The first attacks had been in peaceful towns with substantial Bosniak populations. However, they formed part of the geographically strategic link between Republika Srpska's claims in eastern Bosnia and the Bosnian krajina in the west. The war in Bosnia-Hercegovina was a well planned campaign of terror and ethnic cleansing initiated and sustained by the JNA, the SDS, and Serbia. In the wake of Yugoslavia's dissolution, these politicians used the principles of national self-determination to claim that much of Bosnia-Hercegovina should belong to Serbia. Since most Bosnian cities were multi-ethnic and rural areas were a mosaic of ethnic communities living side by side, non-Serbs had to be expelled to give validity to these claims of national self-determination. In 1993 the Bosnian Croats adopted the same strategy for pursuing their nationalist claims, as the extreme nationalist Bosnian HDZ leader Mate Boban declared the statelet of Herzeg-Bosna. In contrast, the Bosnian government recruited both Serbs and Croats in its efforts to preserve a multi-ethnic polity. Its forces directed their efforts against secessionists of any ethnicity.

Critical to the success of ethnic cleansing was radicalizing and instilling fear in the local Serb population. For years, Bosnian Serbs had listened to media reports about impending fascist massacres in an independent Croatia and Islamic holy wars. These fears combined with unresolved grievances between neighbors to raise Bosnian Serbs' mistrust and fear of Croats and Bosniaks. Citing the two Bosniak revivals and the 1983 political trials, Serb nationalists argued that Bosniaks were attempting to create a fundamentalist Islamic state. In the process, they transformed the image of the highly secular, urban late-twentieth-century Bosniaks into one of Islamic fundamentalists and brutal eighteenth-century begs.

In addition to radicalizing local Bosnian Serbs, Karadžić and Milošević transformed the JNA in Bosnia-Hercegovina into a Bosnian Serb army. When the war in Croatia ended in early 1992, the JNA, more committed than ever to preserving what was left of Yugoslavia, withdrew its forces to Bosnia-Hercegovina. It took possession of most of Yugoslavia's military industry and weapons installations, which had been located in the republic since the Yugoslav-Soviet conflict. Izetbegović allowed the JNA to disarm the local territorial defense units in an effort to neutralize the Serbian autonomous regions. Although JNA policies required that troops be stationed outside of their native republic,

Muslim men wait behind a police line at the site of a mass grave near Šipovo in western Bosnia, 2002. They hope to find remains of missing loved ones. (Reuters/Corbis)

Milošević ordered Bosnian troops transferred to Bosnia. By 6 April, Bosnian Serbs dominated the officer corps and comprised 85 percent of JNA troops in the country. Disarmed, Bosniaks faced a Bosnian Serb army using the JNA's overwhelming firepower, coordinated with paramilitary ethnic cleansing.

The assault on Bosnia followed a pattern. The JNA shelled cities and villages while paramilitary units terrorized and ethnically cleansed the population. After arriving in an area, paramilitary and JNA forces exploited existing divisions to radicalize the local population. They used suspicion and unfounded fears of Muslim fundamentalist violence against Serbs to recruit local Serbs, who often identified local Muslims and participated in brutalizing their neighbors. Serbs who failed to cooperate or who tried to help their Muslim neighbors often shared their fate. Cut off from the outside and isolated within the community, the non-Serb population became vulnerable to attack, humiliation, and expulsion. After isolating the Muslim community, the paramilitaries entered Bosniak houses de-

manding identification and weapons. After a search of the house, they typically stole money and valuables, beat the residents, and left. Often they returned to take more money before they expelled the residents or burned down the house. Paramilitaries beat and shot young men more than the elderly or women. This violence was part of a scripted campaign of terror repeated throughout the war, all over Bosnia-Hercegovina.

Rape was an especially effective tool of ethnic cleansing. Men of all ethnicities raped women during the war. Serb soldiers and paramilitaries routinely used rape to systematically brutalize and humiliate the entire Muslim population. Serbs raped women and girls in their homes, in front of family members, in public, and during interrogations. In some towns they took women and girls to holding centers and gang-raped them, sometimes for days and weeks. Between April 1992 and February 1993, paramilitaries in Foča ran rape houses for Muslim women and girls. They shaved women's heads, tattooed their bodies with rapists' first names, and committed sadistic acts of sexual violence against women and girls as young as twelve. The Republika Srpska government provided support to rape camps throughout the country. Soldiers claimed they were ordered to rape, a contention some Muslim victims have corroborated. The rapes humiliated and demoralized the entire Bosnian population by clearly showing that the victims' families were unable to protect their families. Many families fled and never returned. Republika Srpska officials have always denied any use of rape, but the European Community estimates that 20,000 women were raped during the war, and the Bosnian government claims more than twice as many victims.

In Serb majority areas such as the SDS stronghold of Banja Luka, city officials, police, and soldiers implemented ethnic cleansing in an orderly way. Banja Luka was the second largest city in Bosnia, with a 1991 population of 143,000. The city and surrounding areas were predominantly Serb but also had deep Croat and Muslim roots. Each of the region's ethnic cultures persisted, but by 1991, 55 percent of Banja Luka was ethnically Serb, and the city had become an SDS and JNA stronghold. The city government set about clearing out the city's 64,000 ethnic minorities, whose families had lived in Banja Luka for generations. To encourage emigration, non-Serbs were intimidated, attacked, tortured, and murdered. They had to register their property (which was then confiscated) and prove that they had no outstanding bills. Security forces destroyed all of Banja Luka's sixteen historic mosques. In nearby Prijedor, officials demolished 47,000 non-Serb houses and forced non-Serbs to wear white armbands.

At the same time, however, Bosniaks who wanted to leave faced great obstacles. In order to leave Serb-held territory, non-Serbs had to pass through the many military checkpoints, through which only official buses could pass. Passengers paid exorbitant bus fares and waited for days or weeks in temporary housing where guards threatened and beat them and extorted money from them. From Prijedor to the nearby Croatian border, buses drove through thirteen checkpoints. At each stop guards beat and extracted valuables from passengers, took men of military age off the buses, killed some, transferred others to prisons, and dumped some in fields several miles from the Croatian border, where they were robbed and beaten again before being shot at as they tried to cross the front line.

Internees from the region were held at Omarska, Keraterm, and Trnoplje camps without adequate food, water, or shelter. In the summer of 1992 Omarska camp guards regularly terrorized prisoners with open killings, rapes, torture, and beatings. At the Keraterm camp outside Prijedor, guards massacred 140 internees using machine guns. They beat children, men, and women so severely that many died or suffered permanent injuries. By October 1995, fewer than 15,000 non-Serbs remained in the region. In Banja Luka, only a few thousand remained, as the city became the postwar capital of Republika Srpska.

In contrast to the Bosnian krajina, Bosniaks constituted the majority nation in much of eastern Bosnia. In these areas, the city administration and police usually did not support the SDS, and the military (commanded by Bosnian Serb Ratko Mladić) attacked while paramilitaries terrorized the local population. Despite their overwhelming superiority in arms, military hardware, and firepower, the Serb army commanded insufficient numbers of soldiers to capture cities without first reducing them to rubble. For example, Mladić besieged Republika Srpska's putative capital of Sarajevo for three and a half years from the surrounding mountains without defeating the city. Before 1991, Sarajevo was known for its distinct Muslim, Serb, Croat, and (pre-1945) Jewish cultures, its cosmopolitanism, and its traditions of ethnic and religious tolerance. Although the Ottomans built the city, Karadžić claimed Sarajevo for Republika Srpska and sought to have its non-Serb population expelled. To "liberate" the city, Bosnian Serb artillery showered the city's civilian targets with an average of 1,000 shells per day. They cut off food and water supplies into the city. The army bombed mosques, libraries, hospitals, schools, and residential neighborhoods.

As in Croatia and Slovenia, Western diplomats were caught off guard in Bosnia-Hercegovina. They could not have anticipated the intensity of the assault against Bosnian civilians. Instead of anticipating events, diplomats reacted to crises and created ineffective ad hoc policies. For example, the UN arms embargo had no effect on Bosnian Serb or Bosnian Croat armies, but prevented Bosnian Muslims from defending themselves. Ignoring clear evidence to the contrary, the UN adopted the position that Serbia's assault on the civilian population was an internal Bosnian affair that was creating a humanitarian disaster. Therefore, the UN sent peacekeepers to quiet the unrest and did not set up a military operation to defend one of its members. The lightly armed, unprepared peacekeepers had the impossible task of treating all "parties" neutrally, as if there was no armed conflict. Since they were unprepared for war, the peacekeepers could not intervene to stop ethnic cleansing and focused instead on minimizing their own losses. The peacekeeping operation failed to stop attacks on civilians, failed to secure food and medical supplies for refugees, and failed to keep UN personnel safe.

The creation of UN-protected safe havens is a prime example of how officials constructed policy in Bosnia-Hercegovina. The UN declared its first safe area on 15 April 1993 in Srebrenica, a predominantly Muslim city in eastern Bosnia. Unlike many towns in eastern Bosnia, Srebrenica initially resisted ethnic cleansing. In 1993, however, after troops from Srebrenica attacked Serb positions, killed civilians, and burned villages, a Bosnian Serb counterattack sent thousands of Muslims fleeing into the city. A blockade cut off food aid and people began to starve. In March, under pressure from residents to relieve the desperate situation, UN Commander Philippe Morillon pledged to protect the city, secure food relief, and end the Bosnian Serb assault. Morillon had not consulted his superiors and the UN did not back up his promises. The bombardment continued and only one aid convoy arrived. Within three weeks, the UN agreed to surrender the city to Mladić and designated Canadian peacekeepers to remove all 60,000 Muslims living there. In this stark reversal, the UN agreed to carry out the biggest act of ethnic cleansing of the war, beginning on 16 April. However, on 15 April the UN reversed itself again and declared Srebrenica a safe area, which prevented the scheduled mass deportation. Since the UN had already surrendered the city, it also declared a cease-fire that left Bosnian Serb forces in place. The 140 peacekeepers arrived and disarmed Bosnian government troops, while the city remained surrounded. Shortly thereafter, the UN declared safe areas in the cities of Sarajevo, Goražde, Tuzla, Bihać, and Žepa.

The creation of the UN safe havens, one of the most important UN policies adopted during the war, was not the result of carefully considered diplomacy. It was a hastily concocted exit strategy to save face. The UN provided the peacekeepers with no mandate and no clear mission. By agreeing to protect the Muslim population, the UN tacitly recognized the Serbs as aggressors for the first time. This broke with the UN's negotiating position that all parties acted on an equal footing and allowed Bosnian Serbs to claim that the UN was acting on behalf of the Bosniaks. When the UN disarmed the Bosniaks, its personnel became responsible for their defense, a task for which the peacekeepers were unequipped and untrained. The UN's refusal to commit combat troops to defend disarmed populations meant that the safe areas could not be protected. They became the most dangerous places in the country.

While the UN was struggling to save face in Srebrenica, U.S. envoy to the UN Cyrus Vance and Britain's Lord David Owen (retired Social Democrat MP) were negotiating a peace plan to divide Bosnia's nations, as both Tudjman and Milošević desired. In March 1993 Bosnian Croat forces demanded that Izetbegović's forces withdraw from territories that the Vance-Owen peace proposal had designated as Croat cantons. When Izetbegović refused, the Bosnian Croat army began its own ethnic cleansing campaign, which ended only when the two armies reunited to battle the Bosnian Serb Army in March 1994. Bosnian Croat forces divided villagers against each other and expelled Muslims. Mate Boban declared the Croat-controlled state of Herceg-Bosna. Like the Serb operations, military attacks were accompanied by paramilitary troops who radicalized

A Bosnian Muslim girl and her mother in a refugee shelter in the central Bosnian city of Zenica after learning that the girl's father was among those executed in Srebrenica, 1995. (David Turnley/Corbis)

Croats and terrorized Bosniaks, who were raped, beaten, killed, expelled, and had their houses burned to the ground. The most infamous site of Bosnian Croat ethnic cleansing was in Mostar, Hercegovina's principal city. Between May 1993 and January 1994, Bosnian Croat forces attacked thousands of Muslims, stole their possessions, and interned men at the Dretelj detention camp in an attempt to create an ethnically Croat west Mostar. On 9 November 1993, following months of shelling, the Croatian Army destroyed Mostar's sixteenth-century Old Bridge, which had linked the city's Muslim and Croat quarters for over four hundred years. As in the Bosnian Serb case, peacekeeping was an inappropriate response to Bosnian Croat offenses. Mate Boban, like Radovan Karadžic, used ethnic cleansing in the name of national self-determination. Each sought to secede from Bosnia and join their respective nation-state after the territory they claimed had been "cleansed." The Vance-Owen peace negotiations not only failed to alleviate bloodshed, they accelerated ethnic cleansing led by Boban's Bosnian Croat forces, who were attempting to secure the proposed canton for Herceg-Bosna.

The creation of safe areas in 1993 committed the UN to protecting these cities. To accomplish this, the UN enlisted NATO support to keep airports open, implement the no-fly zone, and enforce UN policies. In 1994 NATO forces responded to calls for protection in Goražde and in Bihać. However, the UN continued to rely on lightly armed peacekeepers, who did not have the resources or the training to militarily defend the safe areas. In 1995 the Bosnian Serb army took UN peacekeepers hostage in Srebrenica and the UN issued new guidelines to protect its vulnerable peacekeepers at the expense of the local population. In July the UN surrendered Srebrenica to the Bosnian Serb army without resistance, leaving Bosnian Serb general Ratko Mladić a free hand to clear out the Muslim population and massacre 6,000–8,000 men and boys.

Following the massacre in Srebrenica, the Croatian government went on the offensive and launched a successful attack against Serb forces in Croatia, expelling up to 200,000 Croatian Serbs from UN-protected areas. Bosnian Serb control in western Bosnia began to crumble, as Muslim and Croat forces started to advance rapidly. As soon as these forces had displaced the Bosnian Serb Army from more than 50 percent of Bosnia, U.S. officials ordered a cease-fire on 12 October. UN officials estimated that Croat and Muslim forces were three days away from taking Banja Luka, and with it hundreds of miles of plains surrounding it, leaving the Serbs only with eastern Bosnia. The United States wanted to keep Banja Luka under Bosnian Serb control to prevent the possibility of creating 200,000 Serb refugees or

Srebrenica Massacre

In the July 1995 Srebrenica massacre Serbs executed 6,000 to 8,000 Bosniak men and boys in the UN-protected safe area. Srebrenica had been under UN protection since April 1993, when the UN sent 140 Canadian peacekeepers to protect the population. In 1994 600 unprepared and lightly armed Dutch peacekeepers replaced the Canadian delegation. By May 1995, however, the position of Srebrenica had deteriorated. Food was not reaching the enclave and Bosnian Serb forces were violating the military exclusion zone. Following NATO air strikes to enforce the exclusion zone, Bosnian Serb troops took UN peacekeepers hostage. Rather than deploying troops, this crisis led the UN to revoke field commanders' authority to call for close air support and to issue guidelines that UN personnel security would take precedent over its mission to protect Bosnian civilians in safe areas. Bosnian Serb Army commander General Ratko Mladić released the UN hostages in June, but clearly learned that hostage-taking tactics could further his as well as Serb) military aims.

By July 1995, UN generals believed that Srebrenica was indefensible. Mladić took 30 Dutch peacekeepers hostage. On 12 July, Mladić attacked the enclave. Peacekeepers denied local Bosniaks' request for the weapons they had given up when Srebrenica was made a safe area and then stood aside. The UN sent no reinforcements and Bosnian government troops were ordered to stay away. The city fell without resistance. Thousands poured into the peacekeeping headquarters in Potočari. Five thousand were later traded for fourteen peacekeepers. Forty eight hours after the city fell, Mladić's troops had depopulated the area. Men and boys were separated from young children and women. Within thirty hours, Mladić had deported 23,000 women and children. Men and boys over the age of 12 were taken in busloads of sixty and massacred. Thousands fled through the mined woods and mountains to Tuzla. The Red Cross estimates that between 12 and 16 July Mladić's troops executed 3,000 men and boys and hunted down and killed an additional 4,000 unarmed men trying to flee. The thousands missing from Srebrenica make up 38 percent of those unaccounted in the entire war.

The Srebrenica massacre, by far the worst of the war, remains a horrifying and tragic symbol of Bosnia's war and the UN's failed policies there. The UN's unwillingness to commit to protecting Bosnian civilians led it to react to crises as they occurred, creating uncoordinated, ad hoc policies. Over three years into the war, the UN still had no clear strategy, it could not protect its own personnel or Bosnians in the safe havens. In the end, Mladić's Bosnian Serb army succeeded in their efforts to ethnically cleanse three quarters of the city's population and make Srebrenica over into a Serbian city. The 1995 Dayton Accords awarded the city, now predominantly Serb, to Republika Srpska, which denies that any massacre ever took place.

---

derailing its peace initiative. Since united Croat-Bosniak forces depended on Croatian weapons and supplies, government forces had to go along with the Croatian compliance with the cease-fire. On 21 November, Richard Holbrooke and Warren Christopher persuaded a deeply divided Bosnian government to accept the Dayton Accords, which ended the violence but rewarded ethnic cleansing by granting Srebrenica and Žepa, as well as 49 percent of Bosnia-Hercegovina to Republika Srpska. The respective armies maintained territorial divisions between the three main Bosnian nations. Bosniaks were the biggest victims in the war, but the civilians of all three nations were the clear losers in the Dayton Accords signed in Paris on 14 December 1995.

The Dayton Accords created a weak, unstable, and only formally independent federal state. The agreement created a three-member (one from each ethnic group) rotating presidency reminiscent of the rickety, ineffective post-Tito presidency. Each member is elected to a four-year term. The member with the most votes becomes the chairman of the presidency for an eight-month interval, followed consecu-

tively by the other two. The presidency appoints the head of government (similar to a prime minister), who is approved by the House of Representatives. However, the UN's non-Bosnian High Representative oversees the presidency and has the power to dismiss it and to overrule the state's legislature. Further, the federal government's powers are restricted to foreign policy, trade, and monetary policy. Thus, the sovereignty of the Republic of Bosnia-Hercegovina is severely limited.

The federal government is divided into two entities, the Bosnian-Croat Federation (Federation) and Republika Srpska (RS). The RS functions as unitary region, while the Federation acts as a micro-federation made up of separate Bosniak and Croat areas. Deep divisions within the Federation led to an unsuccessful attempt to separate the Croat cantons in March–June 2001. In addition, Sarajevo and the port of Brčko are federal districts, not subject to entity control. Each entity may negotiate treaties. Until 2002, each entity had a separate currency. The failure to create an inter-entity customs union has meant that some domestic trade is more costly than international commerce. Although the military nominally came under a single command in November 2003, each area has maintained its own army. Thus, the Bosnian army controls central Bosnia and the Bihać pocket, Croats provide security for western Bosnia-Hercegovina and part of Posavina, and the army of Republika Srpska still controls RS. Each entity may negotiate its own treaties. Bosnia-Hercegovina is also burdened with an excessively complex, unworkable, UN-imposed constitution.

Since the war pitted armies against civilians, the number of deaths and displaced persons and the amount of property damage were staggering. In 1991 Bosnia-Hercegovina's population was 4.4. million. Since 1992, all population statistics have been estimates and are open to debate. Bosnia was clearly depopulated. Scholars estimate that approximately 200,000 people died and nearly 2 million were displaced during the war. According to Murat Prašo, Bosnia's 1995 population was about 2.9 million, of which 600,000 were internal refugees. Another 1.3 million displaced Bosnians lived abroad at that time (mostly in neighboring Croatia and Serbia, but also throughout Europe, Asia, and North America). Croat areas lost 300,000, RS lost 800,000, and Bosniak sections suffered losses of 500,000. Of those killed, about two thirds were Bosniaks, about one quarter were Serbs, and about 5 percent were Croats.

The cease-fire that allowed diplomats to negotiate the Dayton Accords also validated the ethnic divisions created by ethnic cleansing and gave them international legitimacy. As a result, each of these areas has become more ethnically pure. In Croat-controlled regions, the predominance of Croats surged from 49 percent in 1991 to 96 percent in 1995, while Bosniak and Serb populations fell from 47 percent to less than 3 percent. Similarly, the number of Serbs in the RS-dominated areas rose from 48 percent to 89 percent between 1991 and 1995; at the same time the Croat and Bosniak populations fell from 45 percent to 4 percent. The Bosnian government had no policy of ethnic purification; however, Bosniak flight from areas controlled by Croats and Serbs created a higher concentration of Bosniaks in the areas the Bosnian army controlled, though the changes were more modest. The Bosniak population rose from 57 percent to 74 percent while the Serb and Croat population fell from 34 percent to 20 percent. Thus, the nationalist project of creating ethnically homogeneous territories succeeded.

Since 1995, a fragile peace has been maintained in Bosnia-Hercegovina. Politics is riven with nationalism. Indicted war criminals remain free. The right of refugees to return to their homes unmolested applies only to certain areas and has generally not been respected. Consolidation of wartime ethnic cleansing has split Bosnia-Hercegovina into three increasingly homogeneous ethnic regions (Serbs in RS; Croats in the Croatian part of the Federation; Bosniaks in the Bosnian area of the Federation), which continue to polarize politics. Divisive national politics has slowed economic rebuilding and remains an obstacle to future development. The war and its aftermath have left Bosnia-Hercegovina culturally poorer, economically weaker, and more politically fragmented.

CULTURAL DEVELOPMENT

During the Middle Ages, culture and religion were inseparable. In contrast to many parts of Europe, medieval Bosnia and Hercegovina supported three regional Christian churches rather than one national church. Following the Great Schism (1054), which separated Catholicism and Orthodoxy, states came under the religious jurisdiction of their ruling dynasties. Hercegovina became Orthodox because it lay in the Serbian sphere of influence. In contrast, Bosnia (controlled at that time by Catholic Croatia, which fell to Catholic Hungary in 1102) became Catholic under the auspices of the archbishop in Dubrovnik. In the thirteenth century a third Christian church emerged, following Hungary's crusade to conquer Bosnia and replace the region's clergy with Dominicans. The crusade failed, but the pope designated a Hungarian bishop to administer Bosnia. With their Catholic theology intact, the Bosnian clergy defied the pope, drove the bishop into Slavonia (Djakovo), and established their own Church of Bosnia in schism with Rome.

The state permitted no Catholic clergy in Bosnia until 1342, when the Franciscan Order was allowed to establish a vicariate. Until 1878, the Franciscans remained the only Catholic order officially allowed to work in Bosnia. On the other hand, from 1347 to 1463 all but one of Bosnia's rulers were Catholic. Throughout the medieval period, these three churches operated with only a small number of isolated monks and without any secular clergy or organized parishes. Franciscans worked mainly in northern and western Bosnia, particularly in mining towns and urban areas. The Church of Bosnia was most successful in Central Bosnia, while Orthodoxy was found in Hercegovina and eastern and southern Bosnia. Intermarriage and conversion among these three churches was relatively frequent, fostering a religiously tolerant culture and secular state.

Bosnia's weak religious institutions, its isolation, and its long existence as an independent state allowed its artisans to incorporate influences from many other areas and reshape them with their own local traditions to create a distinctly Bosnian medieval culture. Byzantine, Serbian, and European traditions existed side by side with native crafts: tombstone art *(stećci)*, manuscript illumination, fine silver and metal craftsmanship, and intensive castle building.

The oldest surviving remnants of medieval culture in the region are the inscriptions found on gravestones, royal seals, and in churches. In the medieval period, Greek and Latin alphabets coexisted with local Glagolitic (dating from the tenth century) and later Bosančica (a Bosnian variant of Cyrillic) scripts. These early inscriptions show both Glagolitic and Cyrillic in use through the twelfth century. The tenth-century fragments of the Humac tablet dedicating the Church of the Archangel Michael (in Humac) were written in Cyrillic, but also show Glagolitic elements. Fragments of inscriptions in Kijevac appear in Glagolitic; Cyrillic script was used for the twelfth-century Biškupići church inscriptions near the town of Visoko.

Since the churches were small, noblemen commissioned most written texts. Many nobles, merchants, and craftsmen enjoyed good standards of literacy in the Middle Ages.

Kulin's 1189 charter to Dubrovnik was the first official act written in a national language in the South Slav lands. Nobles commissioned illuminated manuscripts that show great creativity and reflect Old Slav, Byzantine, Coptic, Armenian, and romanesque traditions. The oldest Glagolitic manuscript from Bosnia is the tenth-century Codex Marianus. One of the finest examples of Bosnian illuminated manuscripts is Hrvoje's Missal (written for Duke Hrvoje Vukčić), which shows Hrvoje's portrait, displays his coat of arms, and uses an unusual calendar division. Hrvoje commissioned two copies of the Missal, one written in Glagolitic and one using Cyrillic script. Equally important is the Miroslav Gospel, commissioned by the duke of Hum (today's Hercegovina), which features beautifully illuminated human and animal depictions. Annotations and commentaries on these manuscripts record not only theological interpretations, but also provide a rare window into medieval Bosnian life. For example, the four folios of the Balatal Gospel (fourteenth century) and the Srećkovićev Gospel (fourteenth–fifteenth century) contain questions and answers written in the margins to form a contemporary folk encyclopedia.

These manuscripts were generally commissioned by nobles from one of three political strongholds: Jajce (in western Bosnia, along the Vrbas River); Visoko and Bobovac (in central Bosnia, on the Bosna River); and Hum (Hercegovina). These noble strongholds also became centers of local and political life. In late medieval Bosnia, many builders, stonemasons, and master craftsmen mixed Gothic and romanesque styles but also incorporated architectural elements unique to Bosnia. Churches tended to be small family chapels because there was no parish organization and no Catholic diocese.

The oldest political center in medieval Bosnia was the walled city of Visoko, which the Ottomans destroyed. Nearby, Ban Kotromanić built St. Nicholas Church to be the first center of the Franciscan vicariate. Its ruins house the tombs of both Ban Kotromanić (r. 1322–1353) and King Tvrtko (r. 1353–1391). In 1909 archeologists also discovered the church, dedicatory stone, and tomb of Ban Kulin (r. 1180–1204) underneath St. Nicholas. Visoko is Bosnia's oldest political center, but Bobovac, the site of King Tvrtko's castle on the eastern side of the Bosna River, is generally considered medieval Bosnia's capital. Originally built as a fort with eleven towers (some with drops of over 1,000 meters), Tvrtko's castle was highly defensible. Within its walls, Tvrtko built two palaces, a church, a granary, water cisterns, stables, and many workshops.

In western Bosnia, Jajce was the stronghold of the wealthy and powerful Hrvatinic nobles and medieval Bosnia's last capital. In addition to its castle, Jajce is noted for St. Mary's Chapel and its adjacent fifteenth-century bell tower. St. Luke's Bell Tower incorporates both romanesque and Gothic features. St. Mary's also possesses a unique underground mortuary chapel carved out of rock, associated with knighthood initiation rites used at the end of the fourteenth century.

Examples of fine workmanship can be found throughout Bosnia and Hercegovina. Skilled artisans were known for their glass- and metalware (particularly gold and silver), ceramics, carving, and mural painting. Local artisans' most significant contribution to medieval Bosnian culture, however, consisted of the remarkable thirteenth- to sixteenth-century gravestones known as *stećci,* elaborately carved with anthropomorphic images, crosses, heraldic symbols, fight scenes, reliefs, and inscriptions. Weighing as much as 30 tons, 60,000 of these massive gravestones are found at the burial sites of all three Christian churches throughout Bosnia and Hercegovina, but nowhere else.

Centuries of conquest have diminished the physical remnants of Bosnia-Hercegovina's medieval cultural legacy. Few castles, churches, or manuscripts remain from Bosnia's vibrant medieval period. Despite their presence in Bosnia since 1342, no single Franciscan document concerning the Middle Ages remains in the country. Bosnian illuminated manuscripts have been scattered in libraries and museums throughout Europe. The Čajniče Gospel is the only medieval Bosnian codex that remains in the country. At the close of the medieval period, however, Bosnia-Hercegovina left a cultural legacy of linguistic distinctiveness, religious toleration, and the creative capacity to use disparate influences to fashion a unique Bosnian style.

CULTURAL CHANGE IN THE EARLY OTTOMAN PERIOD

After the Ottoman Empire conquered Bosnia and Hercegovina, the Porte brought both a vibrant urban culture and a dynamic Islamic religion to the region. The peak of Ottoman-era Bosnian culture coincided with the state's great military success and wealth in the sixteenth and seventeenth centuries. Building on their own medieval culture and adapting dynamic Ottoman traditions, Bosnians excelled in architecture, literature, decorative arts, and handicrafts.

In stark contrast to the marginal role religion had played in medieval Bosnia-Hercegovina, the Ottomans made Islam the state church and defined communities by religious affiliation after 1463. Nevertheless, the religious toleration that had been such a marked characteristic of medieval Bosnia continued. There were no forced conversions to Islam in Bosnia and Hercegovina. At a time when Central and Western European states were persecuting Jews, as well as either Catholics or Protestants, the Ottoman state allowed non-Muslims to thrive. Christians did not enjoy Muslim legal privileges, but Sultan Mehmed II formally defended the Franciscans and their nine monasteries. Until Austria's Prince Eugen plundered Bosnia and burned Sarajevo to the ground in 1697, Catholics dominated Bosnian trade and were well represented among crafts and mining. The Ottomans welcomed Jews to Sarajevo after Gazi Husrevbeg built the city's cloth market in the 1530s. As a sign of their importance to the city, in 1577 the Ottoman governor established a Jewish quarter *(mahala)* near Sarajevo's main market, where they built their first synagogue in 1580–1581. Sarajevo Jews worked as physicians, pharmacists, craftsmen, and merchants, as well as in small trades. Ottoman rulers strengthened the weak Orthodox Church by establishing it as the head of the Christian millet and establishing an autocephalous patriarchate for Serbs and Bosnians in 1557. This

Stećci

The medieval Bosnian and Hum gravestones known as *stećci* are huge, carved stone monoliths produced between the thirteenth and sixteenth centuries. Weighing as much as 33,000 kilograms, they are typically shaped as a slab, a chest, or a block with a pitched roof and decorated with intricate calligraphy and designs. Some are set on a base; others are not. Approximately 60,000 stećci survive, but they are found only within the medieval boundaries of Bosnia-Hercegovina (which includes parts of present day Dalmatia, Croatia, Montenegro, and Serbia). Since medieval art and culture was international in character, an art form limited to such a small area is very unusual.

The massive size and the weight of the stones stećak artisans used, the artistic and logistical challenges in working with and transporting the giant stones, and the combination of simple forms with a vast variety of representations make the stećci a fascinating and mysterious art form. Typical of the medieval practice in Bosnia-Hercegovina, stećci graveyards are almost always located on major roads outside of settlements. The gravestones' placement, carvings, and design makes use of available light in all seasons of the year and times of the day, reflecting great sensitivity to the environment. When the sun lights them up, they appear as imposing monuments. At other times they blend into the background almost unnoticed despite their size.

European medieval art greatly influenced stećak art. It combined romanesque or Gothic styles, especially in the use of symbols such as the cross, the sun, crescent moon, stylized lilies, and rosettes. Artists' designs also included twisted braiding, vines with trefoil leaves, and grape spirals found in contemporary Europe. Stećak artists carved animals using both the grotesque or fantastic romanesque style and in the more stylized Gothic style. Scenes of armed combat and tournaments, weapons and shields, hunting landscapes, and animal fights depicted on the stećci are also typical of medieval art throughout Europe.

Bosnian stećak art distinguished itself from other medieval art forms by the way it combined separate European elements, the absence of formalized medieval artistic conventions, and local variations. It combined rural and urban sensibilities with pagan, folk, and Christian (romanesque and Gothic) art forms. However, the stećci did not reflect the widespread medieval cult of death found throughout Europe and they did not show class distinctions. Wealthy families commissioned larger and finer tombs, but many of the details on their stećci were identical with folk designs found in textiles, wood carvings, and tattoos. In addition, engravers carved their own styles and enigmatic symbols (whose meaning has been lost) onto the stećci. Regional creativity provided a number of variants with distinguishing features. Stećci in the Donji Kraj region (north of the Sana and Vrbas rivers) contain the fewest decorations. In some areas, the gravestone design centers around the medieval Bosnian Cyrillic inscriptions. Others are elaborately carved with anthropomorphic images, portraits, and geometric designs.

Most stećci were produced from the thirteenth to the sixteenth centuries. The oldest stećak discovered was on Kulin's crypt (1204), that had been buried under the fourteenth century St. Nicholas Church in Visoko. Ban Kulin was a devout Catholic, but all of medieval Bosnia-Hercegovina's three Christian religions (Catholic, Orthodox, Church of Bosnia) marked their graves with stećci. They continued to be produced after the Ottoman conquest, retaining many of their original motifs and inscriptions. They also influenced Jewish and Muslim gravestones in the Ottoman period. For example, stećci elements such as human portraits, not usually found on Muslim graves outside the region, appear on Bosnian Muslim gravestones. In the Ottoman period, the gravestones became taller and thinner and formed more of an obelisk shape. Beginning in the seventeenth century, religion differentiated gravestones, as Muslim, Catholic, Orthodox, and Jewish communities all developed new gravestone styles.

In the twentieth century, study of the stećci has concentrated on eastern Bosnia and in Hercegovina. The best known stećci graveyard is in Radmilja, near the town of Stolac, where the famous fifteenth century stećak engraversculptor Grubac lived. Grubac's stećci can be found throughout the region. Five hundred years later, Mak Dizdar (another Stolac native) renewed popular interest in the stećci with his best-selling *Stone Sleeper* (1966), which used the tombstones as a metaphor to emphasize Bosnia's common identity and collective consciousness rooted in its medieval past.

support allowed the Orthodox Church in Bosnia and Hercegovina to build new churches, schools, and monasteries. The Church of Bosnia, which Stefan Tomašević had driven out of Bosnia in 1459 at the pope's request, did not survive into the Ottoman period.

Ottoman wealth brought urban culture to Bosnia and Hercegovina. Cities were laid out around a market area (čaršija) organized according to craft and surrounded by religiously defined residential areas (mahala). In keeping with Muslim philanthropic ideals, governors constructed public and sacred spaces. They commissioned mosques, roads, bridges, market centers with fountains, clock towers, inns, and baths. A huge covered market was built in Sarajevo (1537–1555). In the major cities, patrons endowed elementary schools (mektebs) seminaries (medressas), Sufi dervish lodges (tekke), and libraries. This philanthropy particularly benefited Bosnians in the larger cities of Travnik, Banja Luka, and Mostar, as well as in Sarajevo, eventually one of the largest cities in the empire.

Islamic traditions of fine workmanship built on local medieval Bosnian craft traditions. As handicraft trades and decorative arts prospered, Bosnian artisans became especially well known for engraving and embossing, brass work, filigree, and carpet making. Cottage handicrafts of embroidery and wood carving also flourished. In addition to goldsmithing, the Bosnian Orthodox community's finest art found expression in post-Byzantine–style frescoes, icons, and carvings found in sixteenth- and seventeenth-century Orthodox churches and monasteries. The Ottomans brought decorative calligraphy to adorn mosques and schools. For example, Sinova Tekke, a Sufi school built by the wealthy merchant Hadji Sinan, has typical Arabic inscriptions from the Koran in its courtyard. More unusual are the seventeenth-century poems inscribed in the portico and two Ottoman chronograms (dates written with letters) added in 1709 and 1774.

Under Ottoman rule, separate religious traditions encouraged greater linguistic diversity. Bosnians continued to speak their own language, and the Bosančica script remained widespread for at least two centuries. Under the millet system, Christians, Jews, and Muslims were responsible for their members' welfare, including education. As in Western Europe, literacy and literature became part of a male-only religious education based in a foreign language (Latin, Greek, Arabic, Persian, Turkish, or Hebrew), an education that emphasized clerical training, theology, and philosophy. As Orthodox churches and monasteries expanded, literacy and elementary education among its members improved. In 1519 Orthodox Bosnians in Goražde began publishing religious manuscripts on Bosnia's first printing press. Franciscan monasteries provided elementary education for novices, who could later travel abroad as priests for higher education.

Bosnian Jews had no rabbinical schools before the late eighteenth century and recruited rabbis from elsewhere to serve their communities. Despite their small numbers, the most famous surviving religious document from Ottoman Bosnia is a fourteenth century Haggadah, an illuminated manuscript of the Passover seder. Sephardic Jews brought this Haggadah from Spain to Sarajevo. Now known as the Sarajevo Haggadah, it is one of the best examples of medieval Jewish illuminated manuscripts in the world. Muslim mektebs and medressas educated boys in Islamic theology, while the tekke instructed students in the teachings of specific Dervish orders. Bosnian Muslim scholars in Sarajevo, Mostar, and Prusac wrote literature, philosophy, and histories that became part of the Islamic canon. In addition, they wrote classical poetry, histories, chronicles, travel accounts, and biographies. Ottoman Bosnia's reliance on diverse religious education created a linguistic mosaic that included vernacular Bosnian, Arabic, Turkish, Persian, Latin, Greek, Slavonic, Hebrew, and Ladino.

Without universal education, a large gap existed between the tiny number of intellectual clerics and the mostly illiterate laity. Popular literature of all faiths consisted of oral epic poetry and folk songs, which described duels, battles, oppressors (and protectors) of the poor, bandits (hajduks), knights, cowards, and heroes. One of the most popular heroes was Prince Marko, who often outwitted the sultan. In the nineteenth century, Europeans, including Herder, Goethe, and Pushkin, began to translate some of these folk songs. The most popular folk songs originating from the Muslim tradition were the sevdalinka, tragic love songs. The sevdalinka shared the lyrics, symbols, and characters of the Bosnian folk songs, but set them to Islamic melodies. Originally sung by urban women, these songs focused on lost or unfulfilled love and mourning, as well as on great events and tragedies.

In the seventeenth century, separate Franciscan and Muslim movements attempted to establish a vernacular Bosnian literary language accessible to those not fluent in Latin, Greek, Arabic, Turkish, or Persian. Influenced by Counter-Reformation reforms, the Bosnian Franciscan Matija Divković founded a vernacular literary tradition in an attempt to popularize religious teachings and introduce Bosnians to European literature. Divković wrote and published his own sermons, poetry, and dramatic dialogues as well as popular European stories in both Latin and in the vernacular Bosnian-Croatian that he spoke. He revived the Bosančica script and developed standardized spelling rules based on local speech patterns. In 1699, however, the audience for this popular literature declined precipitously, as Bosnian Catholics retreated en masse with Prince Eugen to Austria following his rampage through Bosnia, leaving only thirty thousand Catholics, twenty-nine Franciscan friars, and three working monasteries in the region.

At about the same time, Bosnian Muslim writers constructed Alhamijado, a literary tradition (which continued to be written to the twentieth century) using the Arabic script to write the vernacular Bosnian language. Alhamijado writers earned reputations as defenders of the common people against the Ottoman state.

In the early Ottoman period, the Orthodox Church benefited from its position as head of the Christian millet. Its fortunes further improved under Grand Vizier (chief minister) Mehmed Sokolović, who came from Višegrad. In 1557 Sokolović reconstituted the patriarchate at Peć for Orthodox parishes in Serbia and Bosnia. His brother Marko

Women Writers

The writing by women in Bosnia-Hercegovina has taken a long time to come into its own. Before World War II, very few Bosnian women published at all, and what they did write concentrated on education and the role of women in society. By the 1970s, however, 40 percent of the Union of Writers of Bosnia-Hercegovina were women, and the first anthology of poetry written by women, representing forty authors, was published in 1985.

Noted critic Celia Hawkesworth credits the Bosnian Muslim Nafija Saraljić (1893–1970) with being Bosnia-Hercegovina's first woman prose writer. One of eight children, the Sarajevan native was one of the few girls privileged to receive an education before World War I. She wrote twenty "themes" that she intended to expand, but only published a few prose sketches in the Mostar magazines *Biser* and *Zeman* between 1912 and 1918. She gave up writing in 1918 after one of her daughters died, leaving most of her work unfinished or unpublished. What she did write was witty and humorous, with unexpected twists, and showed her concern with Muslim women's isolation in that era.

After World War I, many more women in Bosnia-Hercegovina began publishing both poetry and prose, especially addressing "the new woman" and women's issues such as education, religion, and tradition. Among these were Vera Obrenović-Delipašić and Laura Papo-Bohereto, who worked among the Sarajevan poor and wrote in Ladino. Papo-Bohereto was killed, along with most of the rest of Sarajevo's Jewish population, during World War II. After 1945, Bosnia-Hercegovina's women writers began to flourish. Obrenović-Delipašić wrote the well-received *Dawn over the Mahale* (1955) about women during and after World War II.

One of the most important communist-era poets is Dara Sekulić. Many of Sekulić's poems concern the traditionally "feminine" topics of women and mothers who lose sons in battle, but she also delves into themes such as death, conflict, reconciliation, belief, and doubt. Sekulić's simple, short poems contain unexpected phrases and twists in meaning. What distinguishes her poetry is her use of regional and Sarajevan vocabulary, speech patterns, and rhythms, which gives her work its distinctive Bosnian, borderland quality.

In a very different style, Mubera Pašić's many volumes of poetry and selected works have been compared to Sylvia Plath and Virginia Woolf for her creation of "powerful human drama" and "powerful creative transformation" (Hawkesworth 2000, 261). Her *Monastic Sketches* (1982) have been especially well received and reflect the importance of the postwar surrealist movement in literature. In contrast to their treatment of earlier writers, Bosnian critics have analyzed her poetry on its own terms rather than in terms of how it conforms to an idealized and abstract notion of "femininity."

Current literature from Bosnian women writers has taken up the theme of the war. Innovative novelist Jasmina Musabegović, who began publishing literary criticism in 1965, published her third novel, *The Bridge* (1996), concerning the Mostar's famous sixteenth-century bridge, destroyed by Croat forces in 1993, dedicating the book to her brother who died in Sarajevo in a Bosnian Serb shelling. The short story writer Alma Lazarevski also published a well-received volume entitled *Death in the Museum of Modern Art* (1996).

The past fifty years of Bosnian literature has seen the emergence of a broad range of women writers. These authors mirror Bosnia-Hercegovina's cultural diversity and reflect its distinct literary heritage.

---

and his two nephews served as its first three patriarchs. For more than a century, the Orthodox Church flourished and built many fine churches and monasteries. These included Sarajevo's Old Orthodox Church, dedicated to the archangels Gabriel and Michael. Many churches and monasteries from this era contain remarkable post-Byzantine style frescoes, representing the peak of early modern Orthodox artistic expression. In 1766, however, the Serbian Church was reincorporated into the Greek Orthodox hierarchy and Bosnian Orthodox cultural life stagnated.

Bosnian Muslim architecture transformed public space with the inns, schools, covered markets, baths, clock towers, fountains, and bridges characteristic of Ottoman towns in this period. Ottoman builders constructed clock towers throughout Bosnia in the style of European bell towers that adjoined churches. Typically, the Ottomans either placed them next to a mosque or incorporated them into the marketplace. Since Ottoman clock towers did not become popular until the nineteenth century, these early ones are notable. Sarajevo's seventeenth-century clock tower, with its unusual clock-face characters written in Arabic script, was particularly unusual. Until it was destroyed in 1992, it was one of the best-preserved in Yugoslavia.

Bosnian bridge design varied greatly because it reflected both the bridge's use and its environment. The two most famous bridges are the Mehmed Sokolović Bridge (1571–1577) that crosses the Drina River at Višegrad and Mostar's Old Bridge (Stari Most, 1566). Mehmed Sokolović commissioned the famed Ottoman architect Sinan to build the bridge in his hometown of Višegrad. Its strong horizontal lines and eleven arches still project strength and solidity. Ivo Andrić celebrated this bridge in his novel, *The Bridge on the Drina* (1959), which portrays the bridge as a unifying symbol for Bosnians. Perhaps even more recognizable is the Old Bridge in Mostar, built by the Ottoman architect Hajrudin, which spans the Neretva River. In contrast to the Višegrad bridge, the Old Bridge crossed the Neretva in a single, graceful arch 27 meters long and 20 meters across. The mathematical precision needed to support such a long, heavy bridge with just one arch was so great that Hajrudin fled before the bridge was completed, afraid that it would collapse and the sultan would kill him.

Secular construction and urban design transformed early modern Bosnia, but its mosques remain its greatest architectural achievement. Typically, sixteenth and seventeenth century Ottoman designers constructed Bosnian mosques with a single dome to cover the sanctuary. Inside, carpets, designs, calligraphy, and Koranic inscriptions decorated the mosque. Outside, slim columns and pointed arches supported the dome-covered front portico. Mostar's Karadjozbeg's mosque (1557) is a wonderful example of the many beautiful single-domed mosques of the period. Every mosque had covered, circular, or polygonal fountains (for ablutions), and many were shaded with trees. In accordance with Ottoman innovations, Bosnians built mosques with one thin minaret for calling the faithful to prayers. In contrast to other Ottoman regions, Bosnian mosques often adjoined cemeteries and mausoleums.

Among the most notable mosques in Bosnia are Gazi Husrevbeg's mosque in Sarajevo and the Ferhadija mosque in Banja Luka. Both are unusual for using both a large dome on an octagonal base and several half domes to cover the interior space. The Ferhadija courtyard contains a dome-covered crypt that surrounds the fountain, and a clock tower stands to the right of the mosque. Gazi Husrevbeg's mosque was designed with typical slim marble columns and pointed arches to support the domed roof covering the outdoor entrance area. Trees shade the front courtyard's large covered fountain. Along one side of the courtyard smaller fountains with warm water are used for winter ablutions.

BOSNIAN CULTURE DURING OTTOMAN DECLINE

The culture of Bosnia-Hercegovina transformed itself between 1500 and 1700. It remained religiously tolerant but became a Muslim state where both Catholicism and Orthodoxy prospered. Ottoman wealth allowed handicraft trades and arts to flourish. Unfortunately, over the next 150 years Ottoman culture experienced a decline as Ottoman military expansion, prosperity, and religious identity gave way to defeat, economic decline, and nationalism. As the Ottoman Empire declined in the eighteenth and nineteenth centuries, elites built fewer mosques and schools, roads and bridges deteriorated, churches decayed, and education stagnated. The wealthy patrons of early modern art and architecture in Bosnia faded. Literature began to reflect the declining support for the empire among all Bosnians, as they called for reform, autonomy, and independence. As national movements swept Europe in the nineteenth century, Bosnian intellectuals, whether Franciscan, Orthodox, or Muslim, focused increasingly on the intertwined issues of national identity and political autonomy.

In France, nationalism had united people sharing a common state and history; in Germany, it united people who shared a common language. Croats and Serbs outside of Bosnia-Hercegovina defined their nations by common language, history, and religion. In Bosnia-Hercegovina, nationalism divided people by religion. It converted Bosnian Catholics into Croats and transformed Orthodox Bosnians into Serbs. Since Catholic, Orthodox, and Muslim Bosnians shared a common history and language (which varied by region, not ethnic group), nationalists within Bosnia focused on confessional differences. In this way, they connected themselves more closely to established national movements in Serbia or Croatia. Both Serb and Croat nationalists claimed Bosnian Muslims as part of their respective nations, but rejected Bosnian Muslim culture. Increasingly isolated, Bosnian Muslims could not forge similar national links with the Ottoman state. In the first place, they were ethnic Slavs, not Turks, and the Ottomans ruled a multinational empire, not a nation-state. In the second place, Bosnian Muslim elites opposed Istanbul's centralizing Tanzimat reforms, which threatened their economic and political privileges. Finally, most Bosnian Muslims were peasants who had little in common with a system that benefited Bosnian Muslim elites and impoverished the countryside. Therefore, Bosniaks had no common ethnic, linguistic, or socioeconomic basis for a national movement that included Muslims from outside Bosnia. Instead of bringing people together as it did in Central and Western Europe, nationalism divided Bosnians by religion and politically isolated the vulnerable Muslim peasant plurality.

As rural Bosnia and Hercegovina struggled with increasing taxes, rising rents, and frequent armed unrest, a middle class emerged, which fostered education and cultural revivals among Jews, Orthodox, Catholics, and Muslims alike. Bosnia's Jews consisted of a small but growing Sephardic community centered in Sarajevo, where they numbered about 330 by the 1720s. The population grew to just over a thousand in 1779 and leveled off at around two thousand for most of the nineteenth century. Bosnian Jews sustained their Sephardic culture through their Ladino language, which they spoke daily and used to write their own folk poetry and romances. Like other Bosnians, Jews learned their distinctive religious heritage—in their case the Torah, the Talmud, and Hebrew—in their confessional schools. In contrast to other Bosnians, Jews had a literacy rate that approached 100 percent.

The Serbian national revival resonated with Bosnia's Orthodox community, the most enserfed and the least literate population in the region. Vuk Karadžić, the nineteenth-century Serbian linguist, standardized Serb, Croat, and Bosnian vernaculars into the modern Serbo-Croatian language. He identified those who spoke any variant of the language as Serbs, whether of Catholic, Orthodox, or Islamic religion, ignoring the importance of religious identity for Bosnians. It held little appeal for Bosnian Muslims or Bosnian Croats but greatly influenced Bosnian Serbs. Karakžuć's linguistic definition of the Serbian nation specifically linked the Bosnian Orthodox population with their more prosperous contemporaries in Serbia, who had gained political autonomy in 1815 and had abolished serfdom in 1833. The Serbian national revival inspired those in Sarajevo and Mostar's religious and literary circles to write their own ethnographies, memoirs, and histories. Since nationalism connects people of different social strata, it incorporated village costumes, folklore, and oral traditions into Bosnian Serb identity.

Many of these writers also began to publish literature and commentaries on Serbian folklore and customs. For example, oral epic poetry, found throughout the region, became increasingly identified as a Bosnian Serb tradition. These poems typically featured an Orthodox hero defeating the enemy Turks in combat. (A small number depict a clever heroine, masquerading as a man, who outwits both the Turks and her Serb comrades.) The Serbian national revival provided the Orthodox population with a Serb national consciousness and improved education, as the number of Orthodox elementary schools rose from ten in 1851 to twenty-eight in 1871. At the same time, it divided Bosnians against each other. In condemning Ottoman rule, nationalists identified Bosnian Muslims as exploiters and foreign enemies, ignoring the history, ethnicity, language, and socioeconomic position that most Bosnian Serbs and Bosnian Muslims shared.

As with the Bosnian Serbs, the Bosnian Croat cultural movement combined religion, literature, and politics. In the eighteenth century, monasteries had maintained the Franciscan practice of publishing homilies, records, and chronicles of everyday life, as well as composing religious poetry and music. Under the influence of the liberal political ideas coming out of the French Revolution, however, Franciscans became instrumental in fostering a nationally oriented Bosnian Croat literary renaissance and establishing a secular political movement among Croats. One of the most important figures in Bosnian Franciscan literature was Banja Luka's Ivan Frano Jukić, who championed liberal issues such as secular education, literature, and politics. He established one of Bosnia's first secular schools, as well as founding and editing Bosnia's first literary magazine, in which he published political polemics, histories, and folk remedies. The sultan exiled Jukić for petitioning for secular education, tax reform, legal reform, and a printing press. Anto Knežević, the author of three histories of Bosnia, called for a politically integrated Bosnia in his book, *The Book of Blood,* which envisioned an autonomous Bosnia with national and religious equality.

In contrast to the Serbian and Croat revivals, late Bosnian Muslim culture is characterized more by continuity with earlier traditions than by innovation. By the eighteenth century, the great age of Muslim architecture had passed, but beautiful mosques continued to be built. Artists added decorative art and calligraphy to many older mosques. The earlier literary traditions written in Persian, Turkish, Arabic, and the Bosnian vernacular continued. Bosnian Muslim political elites made no overtures to the Muslim peasants and serfs, who made up the vast majority of the population. Instead, they tried to preserve landlords' privileges by opposing the sultan's economic and political reforms. Often at great personal risk, the Alhamijado writers denounced corruption and remained critical of Bosnian officials. When Vienna occupied Bosnia-Hercegovina in 1878, the region's most culturally formative period ended.

BOSNIAN CULTURE UNDER HABSBURG RULE, 1878–1918

Ottoman rule left Bosnia-Hercegovina a deeply divided society. These divisions widened under Habsburg occupation, as the region exchanged its position on the western fringe of the Ottoman Empire for colonial status in the Dual Monarchy. During the administrations of Benjamin Kállay (1878–1903) and later Istvan Burián (1903–1914), the region experienced great demographic change and significant cultural development, but little economic and political progress. The great powers justified Habsburg rule of the region by pointing to the Ottoman inability to reform a political and economic system that produced widespread suffering. However, the monarchy maintained the Ottoman's medieval-era system of unfree labor and high rural taxes that impoverished most Bosnians (Muslim, Serb, and Croat). The failure to reform the economy left Bosnia-Hercegovina's national divisions wider than ever.

The population of Bosnian Muslims fell precipitously both during the 1875–1878 war that ended Ottoman rule and the subsequent Habsburg control of the region. No reliable records measure the population loss, but scholars estimate that between 1875 and 1910 the region's Muslim population declined by 300,000. In contrast, the number of Roman Catholics grew substantially. Thus, Bosnia-Hercegovina became more Catholic and less Muslim under the Habsburg occupation.

Vienna's greatest cultural success was its modest progress in elementary education. By 1914, Bosnia-Hercegovina had 200 elementary schools, 3 high schools, 1 technical school, and 1 teacher training school (but no institution of higher education). Still, fewer than 17 percent of school-age children attended school, and the state introduced compulsory primary education only in 1909. Adult illiteracy (overwhelmingly rural) stood at 90 percent. The government in Vienna also introduced interfaith public schools, where children learned secular subjects together but received religious instruction from their own clergy. With more schools and compulsory education, literacy improved.

Habsburg education policies antagonized many Bosnian Serbs and inflamed Serb nationalists. Unlike Bosniaks and Bosnian Croats, the state required Bosnian Serbs to obtain a political reliability certificate to teach in Bosnian schools, which were staffed largely by Croatian immigrants. In 1892 Kállay abolished the state tax supporting Orthodox schools, causing many to close. From 1893 to 1905, Bosnian Serbs campaigned for autonomous schools and churches, and the number of Serbian children attending public schools dropped.

The autonomy movement became an important base of the Serbian cultural revival and political activism, as it laid the foundation for the region's first political party, the Serbian National Organization (1907).

Along with extending education, Vienna increased access and exposure to mainstream European culture. European-style literary journals appeared. European realist and romantic artists, who traveled to Bosnia to find exotic subjects to paint, inspired a generation of Bosnian artists. Modern trends such as art nouveau and the secessionist movement in Vienna greatly influenced the period's architectural styles. At the same time, the administration in Vienna built new schools, train stations, and administration buildings but also encouraged Bosnians to explore their common medieval past and building styles. The Provincial Museum in Sarajevo was opened to study and preserve stećci and medieval artifacts. By the end of the Habsburg era, Bosnian high culture had shifted from an Ottoman to a European orientation.

Kállay tried to create a Bosnian identity (based on shared history in the same territory) to counter Serb and Croat nationalism. However, he also used religious institutions to separate Bosnians and to increase Habsburg control in the region. Since there was no separation of church and state in Austria-Hungary, the emperor dominated Bosnia's religious hierarchies. He appointed the Serbian Orthodox bishops and replaced the position of mufti for Bosnia (formerly appointed by the sultan) with his own *reis ul-ulema* (head of the Muslim religious community). By banning political parties (until 1907), Vienna tried to channel national politics into these state-influenced religious institutions. The strategy of emphasizing Bosnians' diverse religious traditions to counter nationalist politics ignored the strong religious components to national identity. The political curia system, which required voters to choose candidates based on religious affiliation, strengthened religious-national identity rather than building on common Bosnian interests. The failure to address the underlying political and economic bases for national divisions also undermined the Austrian attempt to create a Bosnian-Muslim identity. Believing the Bosniaks were pre-political, the joint administration also ignored the strong Bosniak identity, despite its increasing secularism and distinctive cultural influence.

With Habsburg occupation came immigration, which further increased religious tension within Bosnia-Hercegovina. Both Serbs and Muslims resented immigrant Catholic schoolteachers whom they suspected of proselytizing. Convinced that Bosnians were really Croats, Archbishop Stadler aggressively campaigned to convert non-Catholics. Upon his arrival in Sarajevo, Archbishop Stadler replaced Franciscan friars with his own diocesan priests. (These changes undercut the Franciscans and created divisions in the Bosnian Catholic community that still remain.) Ashkenazi Jews were also among the immigrants to Bosnia. By 1885, these immigrants had swollen Sarajevo's Jewish population. Rather than strengthening the Jewish presence, this new population created a separate community, as the city's well-established, urbane Sephardim looked down on the less educated rural immigrants attending the new Ashkenazi synagogue.

The Habsburg period was critical for the region's cultural reorientation toward Europe and the emergence of separate Bosnian Serb, Bosnian Croat, and Bosniak national identities. European-style educational norms and high culture overtook Ottoman cultural influences. Since the nineteenth century, Bosnian Serbs and Bosnian Croats had defined themselves in contrast to Ottoman and Muslim cultural practices. Yet, for all their differences, Bosnians still shared basic regional similarities. For example, foreign observers noted in 1903 that Catholic and Orthodox Bosnians alike wore turbans, embroidered waistcoats, loose open jackets, loose trousers gathered at the knee, and felt shoes that turned up at the toes. By 1930, these styles were worn only by Muslims, as national identity replaced Bosnian regionalism.

INTERWAR AND WARTIME BOSNIA-HERCEGOVINA, 1918–1945

In 1918 the former Habsburg territories of Bosnia-Hercegovina, Croatia, and Slovenia joined with Serbia and Montenegro to form the Kingdom of Serbs, Croats, and Slovenes. Despite promising Bosnia-Hercegovina economic reform, as well as political and religious autonomy, the state soon gerrymandered districts in 1929 to eliminate any majority Muslim area. After filling most government posts with Serbs, it Serbianized the region and encouraged Bosniaks to declare themselves as Croats or Serbs. Ignoring the indigenous roots of Bosnian Muslims and Bosnian Croats, the regime dismissed non-Serb cultural influences as "foreign."

Interwar cultural life was confined to the region's largest cities: Banja Luka, Travnik, Tuzla, Mostar, and Sarajevo. After World War I, Habsburg-era educational and cultural societies became more nationally oriented. Each community published its own magazine for its members (Croatian *Napredak* [Progress], Bosnian Muslim *Gajret* and *Narodna uzdanica* [National Hope], Serbian *Prosveta* [Enlightenment], and the Jewish *La Benevolencia*). These societies provided Bosnia's cities with entertainment, popular reading rooms, and opportunities for general education, including high school scholarships. However, they did not compensate for an inadequate education system. Overall illiteracy rates dropped to 70 percent, but rural areas were untouched. Aside from basic elementary education and a few very good secondary schools, Bosnians had few educational opportunities. Until the late 1930s, when the state founded an agricultural college, the region still had no higher educational institution.

The Yugoslav monarchy also generated cultural dissent. In addition to the nationally oriented efforts, a small number of artists and writers were influenced by major contemporary European movements, including impressionism, modernism, symbolism, expressionism, abstract art, surrealism, magical realism, political art, and art nouveau. Following World War I, these artists organized art schools and artist colonies. In 1940 a group of painters and graphic artists founded Collegium, an association of artists who synthesized art and left-wing politics.

Nobel Prize–winning novelist Ivo Andrić, 1959. (Bettmann/Corbis)

In the interwar period, the most typical form of Bosnian literature was either poetry or the short story using a realistic narrative. Jovan Krstić, the editor of the influential literary magazine *Pregled* (Review, est. 1927), described this genre as "story-telling Bosnia" (Lovrenović 166). However, not all writers conformed to this style. Many younger writers also explored other genres at this time. Bosnia's Nobel laureate, Ivo Andrić, illustrates the complex, cross-cultural influences of Bosnian society. Raised a Catholic and schooled by Jesuits in Travnik, Andrić lived his adult life in Belgrade, where he worked as a Yugoslav diplomat and was active in Serbian literary circles. He wrote about Bosnia, however, not Serbia, and he represented Bosnia-Hercegovina in the Communist Party until 1953. Andrić's stories show Bosnians of different ethno-religious heritages both cooperating and in conflict. In contrast to the writing of the nineteenth century, the new literature articulated a multifaceted national identity, which recognized both Bosnians' shared characteristics and their cultural distinctions.

Bosnian writers from each of the region's nations and religions created a complex, yet distinct, body of Bosnian literature in this period. The Sarajevo Writer's Group (founded 1928) included not only Krstić, but important literary figures such as Hamza Humo (the modernist poet,

writer, and editor) and Isak Samokovlija (the short story writer, who described daily life for poor urban Jews). Left-wing expressionists produced the 1929 anthology, *Knjiga drugova* (Comrades' Book), which included work by Hasan Kikić, Hamid Dizdar, and later the poets Zija Dizdarević and Mak Dizdar. *Knjiga drugova* inspired Kikić and other Bosniak intellectuals, such as Skender Kulenović and Safet Krupić, to start the journal *Putokaz* (Signpost). Published in Zagreb, *Putokaz* provided a forum for debate on acute economic, social, cultural, and national issues facing interwar Bosnia-Hercegovina.

In 1941 the radical right Independent State of Croatia (NDH) annexed Bosnia and Hercegovina. As in the rest of the NDH, state authorities Croatianized the region. They targeted Serbs for conversion, expulsion, and execution. Jewish property was stolen, and synagogues were ransacked; few Bosnian Jews survived. By 1945, over 700 mosques were destroyed or damaged. Communists and Muslims were deported and interned in concentration camps, along with Jews and Serbs.

Bosnia-Hercegovina's religious and nationalist leaders opposed communism. However, the Partisans' multinational appeal attracted those influenced by multiple cultural traditions. For example, the Bosniak poet Skender Kulenović, who helped found *Putokaz,* became politically active in the Communist Party in the 1930s. His poem "Mother Stojanka of Knežopolje" became a symbol for the Partisans during the war. Other Bosnian Partisans used their wartime experiences as the basis for postwar work. The poet Vladimir Nazor published his 1943–1944 diary, "With the Partisans." Jure Kastelan's poems "The Lake at Zelengora" and "The Typhus Sufferers" were based on his Bosnian Partisan experience. Branko Ćopić wrote wartime humor, which became the basis for future short stories and novels. After 1945, the trauma of Bosnia's wartime experience lived on in literature and profoundly affected the development of Bosnian culture under communism. World War II remained an important subject of literature, songs, and film through 1992.

BOSNIAN CULTURE UNDER COMMUNISM, 1945–1992

After 1945, the new communist state of Yugoslavia recognized Croat and Serb nationhood but identified Bosnian Muslims as nationally "undeclared." This designation meant that Bosnian cultural traditions and the distinct Bosnian character of the region's Serbs and Croats (and the few Jewish survivors) were ignored. Instead, the Party promoted a Yugoslav national identity and persecuted religious institutions. It advanced socialist realism and discouraged social criticism. On the other hand, education made great progress, and political decentralization in the mid-1960s helped the republic revive separate national-cultural and religious traditions.

In the early postwar years, the Party banned all prewar national cultural and educational institutions and targeted Orthodox, Catholic, and Muslim institutions. By identifying Bosnian Muslims solely by religion, the Party also justified nationalizing Bosnian Muslim assets, repressing Bosniak political activity, and closing educational institutions. The distinctive Islamic culture of Bosnia suffered greatly from this program shaped by hostility to Islam, details of which have already been given in the account of the history of Bosnia-Hercegovina. To give just one example, the state shut down the last Muslim printing house in Sarajevo and Yugoslav publishers printed no Islamic texts until 1964.

Socialist realism was the dominant cultural genre in postwar Yugoslavia. The Party had little tolerance for literary nonconformity or pointed social criticism. For example, Branko Ćopić's satirical story, "The Heretic" (1950), faulted the communist elite for its exclusivity and venality. This early attempt at social criticism earned the Bosnian Serb humorist and Partisan veteran widespread condemnation from the highest Party levels, interrogation, and reprimand. Ćopić was never arrested, but the Party eventually revoked his membership, and he soon abandoned satire for less biting forms of humor. Only the Croat writer Miroslav Krleža could openly criticize socialist realism and only the work of Ivo Andrić was beyond Party rebuke.

The communists' greatest postwar success was in basic education. In the early 1950s the Party implemented free primary and secondary education (compulsory from ages seven to fifteen). Its campaign to build 1,000 elementary schools and 1,000 libraries in the republic brought grammar schools to most villages and secondary schools to all of the larger towns. Andrić donated the entire sum of his 1961 Nobel Prize to a book fund for Bosnian libraries. The effect of all these efforts on the republic's literacy rate was stunning. It jumped from 55 percent (compared to 79 percent for Yugoslavia) in 1953 to 85 percent in 1988. By 1981 illiteracy was negligible for both men and women under thirty. In contrast, close to half of the older village women (born before 1941 and therefore educated under a different regime) could neither read nor write. By the early 1980s, Bosnia-Hercegovina also boasted four universities (in Sarajevo, Mostar, Banja Luka, and Tuzla), and the number of students attending institutions of higher education had doubled since 1961. This explosion in education and training beginning in the 1950s helps to explain the Bosnian cultural revival that took place in the 1960s and 1970s.

As the Party began to recognize regional interests and implemented political and economic reform, it began to tolerate cultural associations. These associations fostered cultural revivals, which included those who focused chiefly on religious issues (Orthodox, Roman Catholic, Islamic) and those concerned with economic and political reforms. A reform communist movement among Bosnian Muslims (the largest ethnic group in the LCBH, the League of Communists of Bosnia-Hercegovina) viewed observances of customary religious practices as cultural traditions rather than religious obligations. It sought increased investment, better political representation for the republic, and national recognition of Bosnian Muslims. At the same time, a Bosnian Islamic revival (fostered by the 1954 religious freedom statute and Yugoslavia's diplomatic ties to non-aligned states) focused on the inadequacies of communism and the divisiveness of nationalism.

As part of the 1960s cultural revival and the struggle to achieve parity with the other republics, Bosnians fought for their right to their own Bosnian Academy of Arts and Sciences, their own television station, and recognition of the legitimacy of research on Bosnian culture. The National Museum of Sarajevo sponsored new research in archeology and medieval Bosnian history. Bosnia's medieval gravestones provided material for poets, painters, graphic artists, sculptors, musicians, and filmmakers. The cultural revival strengthened a Bosnian identity and threatened Serb nationalists (from both Bosnia and Serbia, who recognized no separate Bosnian culture) and communist unitarists (including Serbs, Muslims, and Croats). Instead of recognizing Bosnians' common Slavic heritage, history, and language, these groups refocused on Islam and argued that Bosnian Muslims were "really" Turks. After Belgrade recognized Bosnian Muslims as a constituent nation in 1970, nationalists conflated the Bosnian Islamic and cultural revivals and increasingly tarred Bosniak politicians with spurious charges of fundamentalism.

The Bosnian cultural revival profoundly affected literature. In 1945 the Party did not recognize the existence of any distinctively Bosnian literature(s). Despite the distinctiveness of the region's Bosnian Franciscan Alhamadijo, and Bosnian Serb literary traditions, the Party insisted that Bosnian Croats and Bosnian Serbs were to be studied as part of the larger Croat and Serb literary traditions, and Bosniak writers were expected to declare whether they were part of the Croat or Serb traditions. In 1970, however, the Party accepted a Bosnian variant of Serbo-Croatian as having the same status as the Croat and Serb variants. After publishing *Intersections* (1967, 1969), two influential volumes of essays on literary theory, Midhat Begić argued for recognizing a unified, though complex, Bosnian literature.

New Bosnian literature began to pour out in the mid-1960s. Leftist authors trained in the interwar period played an especially important part. Mak Dizdar worked after the war as chief editor of TANJUG (Yugoslavia's official wire service) and editor of Sarajevo's daily, *Oslobodjenje* (Liberation). Dizdar looked to the medieval period for inspiration in his collection of poetry, *The Stone Sleeper* (1966). Dizdar used Bosnian stećci (the best-known stećci site is near Dizdar's hometown of Stolac) to explore Bosnia's pluralistic identity and its collective memory, rooted in the medieval past. Mesa Selimović, a former elementary schoolteacher and communist political organizer from Tuzla, became one of Bosnia's most celebrated novelists. In his best-selling *Death and the Dervish* (1966), he explored the moral, political, and religious dilemmas of an eighteenth-century Bosnian Muslim cleric as he investigates why Ottoman authorities have sentenced his brother to death. These and other works broke with Bosnia's "storytelling" narratives and portrayed Bosnia with its own distinct character. By the 1970s, Bosnian culture flourished not only in literature but also in radio, television, press, film, art exhibits, theater, architecture, and popular culture.

By the 1980s, nationalists, however, believed that the dominance of Bosniaks in the LCBH and the cultural and religious revival among Muslims were leading to the Islamicization of Bosnia-Hercegovina. In the wake of the 1979 Iranian revolution, accusations of fundamentalism against

Bosnian Muslims increased, culminating in the 1983 trial of Muslim intellectuals, including Alija Izetbegović, whose "Islamic Declarations" tried to reconcile traditional Islamic practices with economic and political modernization.

Nonetheless, the 1980s was a culturally dynamic period in Bosnia-Hercegovina, especially for popular entertainment. Coverage of the 1984 Winter Olympics, held in Sarajevo, portrayed the city's modernity as seen through its books, exhibits, performances, films, pop music, graphics, alternative publications, and youth magazines. Bosnian filmmakers attained international recognition, with films that focused on Bosnian experiences in World War II and under communism. For example, experimental filmmaker Ivica Matić became internationally known for his award-winning film, *Landscape with a Woman.* Bato Cengic's acclaimed 1990 film, *Silent Gunpowder,* is based on Branko Ćopić's novel. Set in a Bosnian village at the beginning of the 1941 national uprising, it explores the conflict between revolutionary enthusiasm and a suspicious village through a love story between the Partisan captain and the local priest's daughter. Emir Kusturica became Bosnia's most innovative and well-known filmmaker in the 1980s and 1990s. His award-winning film *When Father Was Away on Business* (1984), based on a work by the poet Abdulah Sidran, examined daily life and betrayal in postwar Bosnia. It brought international attention to filmmakers throughout the former Yugoslavia. By the 1990s, Bosnians had created their own vibrant culture. Increased prosperity, mass education, and continued religious toleration allowed a distinctive Bosnian literary style and film industry to emerge. Its innovative popular entertainment blended internationally popular genres with Bosnian history and traditions.

AFTER COMMUNISM

Yugoslav rule in Bosnia-Hercegovina collapsed in armed conflict in April 1992. With the collapse of communist power, Bosnian writers, journalists, actors, musicians, and scholars struggled to preserve their diverse society by producing plays, film, war photographs, music, and books. Nationalist leaders, however, claimed Bosnian territory and also argued that certain areas should be inhabited only by one national group. To bolster these national aims, Serb and Croat combatants sought to occupy territory and to expunge evidence of whole cultures. They expelled, murdered, and physically destroyed cities, cultural monuments, libraries, graveyards, birth records, and work documents. Since religious institutions had played a vital role in shaping Bosnia-Hercegovina's traditions of high culture, nationalists defined their enemies based on religion. Thus, the war encouraged a turning away from secularism in favor of Islamic, Catholic, and Orthodox particularism.

Serbian forces (1992–1995) and the Croat army (1993–1994) tried to dismantle both the region's Ottoman heritage and (respectively) the Catholic or Orthodox monuments in territory each held. For example, Croat forces not only shelled the Old Bridge in Mostar, they also destroyed the nearby Orthodox monastery at Žitomislići. Similarly, Serbs ransacked Catholic monuments in Republika Srpska.

Banja Luka's Ferhadija mosque (1580), recognized by UNESCO as a world cultural monument, was destroyed in 1993. Bosnia's Islamic community plans to rebuild the mosque despite the Bosnian Serb government's failure to approve permits for reconstruction. (Reuters/Corbis)

They destroyed the Franciscan monastery and church of Plehan with its priceless artwork, as well as the Franciscan monasteries in Jajce and Petrićevac (near Banja Luka). They also laid waste to the Catholic shrine at Podmilačje (near Jajce), destroying its unique, partly preserved medieval Gothic chapel.

In a systematic attempt to erase more than five hundred years of Slavic Muslim influence, Serb and Croat armies separately targeted both Bosniaks and Bosnia's rich Ottoman cultural legacy. They destroyed the most visible signs of the Ottoman heritage. The cities the Ottomans had built, which served as Bosnia-Hercegovina's main cultural centers, were ravaged and declared Serb. For example, Serbs deurbanized Banja Luka, denied its Ottoman history, destroyed its Muslim character, and then declared it the capital of Republika Srpska. Croat shelling reduced Mostar's Old Bridge and its large, historic Muslim quarter to rubble. Sarajevo remained under siege for three years. Serb and Croat forces demolished mosques throughout Bosnia-Hercegovina. Among the most notable were Gazi Husrevbeg's mosque in Sarajevo, the Aladža (colored mosque) in

Foča, and Mostar's Karadjozbeg mosque. All of Banja Luka's sixteen mosques were destroyed in 1992, including the Ferhadija mosque and the Arnaudija mosque (1587), both on UNESCO's list of world cultural monuments. As conspicuous signs of the long-established Ottoman presence in Bosnia-Hercegovina, nationalists shelled clock towers throughout the country.

As the country's largest city since the fifteenth century, Sarajevo's libraries and museums were the principal repository for invaluable Ottoman collections, the region's literary heritage, and its long history. Serb forces shelled the National Museum in Sarajevo. Mortars flattened the National Library of Bosnia-Hercegovina and wiped out its 1.2-million-volume collection, which had contained many extremely rare books and manuscripts. When they bombed the Oriental Institute, its irreplaceable collection of Jewish and Islamic manuscripts (the largest collection in Southeastern Europe) was lost.

Since 1995, national leaders of each of Bosnia's historic cultures have emphasized their own separate national language, religion, and cultural associations. This attempt to disentangle the region's national traditions from their connections to the broader Bosnian culture impoverishes each of them. It ignores the shared history, common language,

Karadjozbeg mosque (1557) in Mostar along the Neretva River. (Otto Lang/Corbis)

Slav ethnicity, constant cultural interaction, and tradition of religious diversity that is uniquely Bosnian. The Bosnian heritage includes multiple languages, scripts, religions (and non-religion), and artistic styles. Intermarriage and religious conversion occurred in Bosnia-Hercegovina more frequently than in other parts of Europe. Bosnians and Hercegovinians have produced unique cultural artifacts that incorporated multiple cultural influences, Ottoman architecture, Bosnian Franciscan literary traditions, Alhamijado

literature, and Orthodox frescoes. In the twentieth century, a complex culture emerged (including Serbs, Croats, Bosniaks, and Jews) that produced distinctively modern Bosnian literature, music, and film. The emergence of such a rich culture could not have developed by relying on an individual Bosniak, Serb, or Croat tradition.

Bosnian culture is the product of dynamic interaction and a balancing of Bosnian identity with national and religious traditions. It is not the sum of its nations or its reli-

Sarajevo City Hall (1896) built in the pseudo-Moorish style during the Habsburg occupation. Austrian Archduke Franz Ferdinand gave his final speech here before embarking on his motorcade through the streets of Sarajevo, where he was assassinated. The City Hall building later became Bosnia-Hercegovina's National Library, housing 1.2 million volumes and a rare book and manuscript collection that included the Sarajevo Haggedah. Bosnian Serb mortars destroyed the library during the siege of Sarajevo, 1992–1995. (Otto Lang/Corbis)

gions. Bosnian writers' simultaneous membership in more than one National Academy of Arts and Sciences illustrates the multifaceted nature of Bosnian culture. This balance between Bosnian identity and national traditions has not been static, nor has it been consistently harmonious in any period. Some artists and writers have harshly criticized Bosnian society and particular national groups within it. Even though these cultural forces have deeply alienated other Bosnians, their voices remain an essential part of the country's cultural landscape. The damage to Bosnia-Hercegovina's patrimony cannot be undone; however, Bosnians are rebuilding their country. For example, the destruction of Mostar's Old Bridge became a wartime symbol of ethnic hatred. With repairs to the bridge now complete, perhaps the Old Bridge can become a symbol of Bosnia-Hercegovina's diverse culture and its centuries-old traditions of accommodating multinational and multireligious traditions.

ECONOMIC DEVELOPMENT
THE MEDIEVAL AND OTTOMAN ECONOMIES, 1400–1878

Bosnia-Hercegovina has been known for its rich silver reserves since Roman times, and silver mining, particularly in Srebrenica, helped the region prosper during the Middle Ages. Bosnia's economy expanded in the fourteenth century. By the early fifteenth century, Serbia and Bosnia produced more than 20 percent of all European silver. Bosnians traded silver and other raw materials with Dubrovnik for high-quality finished goods, especially textiles. Dubrovnik merchants dominated trade in Bosnia-Hercegovina, but German immigrants from Hungary, Transylvania, and Saxony helped develop and expand mining. These Catholic mining and market towns attracted Franciscan monasteries and helped to secure Catholics' trade predominance well into the Ottoman period (until 1700).

Under Ottoman rule, Bosnia-Hercegovina was part of a decentralized, rural, feudal economy characterized by landed wealth. Traditionally, noble estates (*timars*) consisted of state-owned, non-hereditary fiefs that spahis controlled as long as they rendered military service to the sultan. Unlike Europe, there was no legal provision for serfdom. Most Bosnians, Muslim and Christian alike, worked and lived as peasants, who paid some labor dues, an in-kind tithe of 10–25 percent of their produce to the spahi and a land tax to the sultan. Unlike the spahis, however, these peasants enjoyed secure hereditary use-rights and could freely sell their leasehold. In addition, peasant-soldiers living in the Bosnian military frontier zone could also own freeholds, as long as the family defended the region from Habsburg incursions.

Following the period of Ottoman military expansion in the fifteenth and sixteenth centuries, Bosnia-Hercegovina sank into long-term economic decline. By the eighteenth century, Ottoman military losses and the empire's need for cash taxes had transformed the region's economy and created ambiguous property relationships that threatened political stability and stymied economic development. A new landed nobility of begs (upper nobles) and agas (lower no-

bles) replaced the spahi cavalry. In exchange for collecting taxes owed to the sultan (land tax, non-Muslim poll tax), Istanbul treated noble estates (agaluks, begliks) as hereditary private property. As the state became increasingly reliant on cash taxes, these tax farms provided Bosnia's nobles with increasing political power. Agaluks and begliks blurred the distinction between private and state property. Since peasants believed they possessed hereditary control and property rights over the land they worked, they deeply resented these encroachments on their traditional property claims. Rural Bosnians cited the traditional Ottoman property arrangement, to claim that lords had illegally and extralegally usurped peasant land and their rights. Nonetheless, traditional protections for peasants eroded as their taxes and landlord obligations (labor dues and in-kind payments) increased, at the same time as their living standards and personal security declined. Throughout the eighteenth century, villagers rebelled against new taxes and ever increasing landlord obligations, making the region increasingly difficult to govern.

In the nineteenth century, the Ottoman Tanzimat reforms ended tax farming, professionalized tax collections, and replaced the non-Muslim poll tax with a universal tax for those opting out of military service. They also protected begliks by defining them as the landlords' private property and identifying tenants on these estates as freely contracted laborers, despite their obligation to pay taxes, tithes, and labor dues to the beg. Thus, beglik serfs' property claims lost both legal standing and the limited feudal-era legal protection from excessive landlord demands. In contrast, Ottoman reformers defined agaluks as feudal estates. They abolished labor dues (often two to three days of work per week), but raised in-kind obligations and maintained the 10 percent land tax. In most cases, obligations totaled about 40 percent of the sharecropper's harvest (plus the tax in lieu of military service) and required that landlords provide and maintain serfs' housing. These mild reforms failed to clarify property relationships and antagonized everyone. Bosnian landlords begrudged the reforms' infringements on their privileges, while peasants resented the failure to recognize their property rights. Unrest continued and culminated in the 1875 tax revolt, which was the beginning of the end of Ottoman rule in Bosnia-Hercegovina.

THE ECONOMY UNDER HABSBURG AND YUGOSLAV RULE, 1878–1941

After 1878, the Habsburg monarchy occupied Bosnia-Hercegovina and brought significant improvements in economic infrastructure. The monarchy built railroads, developed forestry and coal mining, and began the extraction of copper, iron ore, and chrome. By the 1890s, Bosnia-Hercegovina was growing at an annual rate of 15 percent. In 1883 the monarchy finished building a railroad from Sarajevo to the Croatian border. By 1907, the state had built 121 new bridges, laid 111 kilometers of broad-gauge and 911 kilometers of narrow-gauge railroad, and constructed over 1,000 kilometers of roads to improve trade and communication. Most of the rail connections, however, were on inefficient narrow-gauge lines that led to Budapest. Hungarian officials blocked a proposal to link central Bosnia to the Adriatic port of Split (and access to the Mediterranean). Nonetheless, by the end of Habsburg rule, a small industrial working class of 65,000 had emerged, and unions had organized in many trades.

Vienna missed opportunities to establish clear private property rights. Habsburg officials kept Ottoman property definitions in place, but landlords complained that state officials misclassified their private property as state land (reducing landlord income) when it was re-recorded in the monarchy's new registry. By decreeing all forests state property, the Habsburgs prevented landlords from profiting from the forestry and mining industries on land they claimed to own. The state resolved property claims on a piecemeal, case-by-case basis, using an awkward court system that was slow, highly bureaucratic, and expensive. The system, however, failed to resolve ambiguities over private and state lands. Property remained contested, economic investment stayed out of the region, and political resentments festered.

The 1878 Treaty of Berlin, which gave Austria-Hungary the authority to occupy Bosnia-Hercegovina, charged the Habsburg monarchy with enacting land reform to end serfdom and strengthen the agrarian sector. However, Austria-Hungary did not extend its own 1848 abolition of serfdom to Bosnia, either in 1878 when it occupied the territory or after its 1908 annexation. Instead, it maintained the Ottomans' 1859 and 1876 land reform legislation. Reflecting a narrow electoral base of property-holders, the political parties in the Bosnian parliament (1910–1914) abandoned the 75 percent of Bosnians who worked as free peasants or serfs. By 1914, 93,368 enserfed households (mostly Orthodox) farmed one-third of Bosnia-Hercegovina's arable land.

While forcing serfs to buy their own freedom, the state provided economic incentives to 10,000 households from other parts of the monarchy to "colonize" Bosnia. While providing insufficient credit for Bosnian peasants and banning agricultural cooperatives allowed in other parts of the empire, the state offered "colonists" special tax concessions and a low interest mortgage for the next ten years. In contrast to the colonists' 12-hectare farms (rent-free for three years), Bosnian sharecroppers, serfs, and free peasants typically worked on several scattered micro-holdings that might *total* 1 hectare. Property division required by Ottoman inheritance law had left many agas with little more than smallholdings (defined as 5 to 20 hectares) themselves. Thus, Habsburg rural policies did not address the chronic problems of unfree labor, micro-holdings, and insufficient credit, problems that kept Bosnian farming at a subsistence level.

In the interwar period, the Yugoslav state finally abolished serfdom and redistributed land to peasants. The 1919 agrarian reform limited farm holdings to 50 hectares, affecting less than 40 percent of Bosnian landlords. In contrast to the great estates of the medieval and early modern eras, only seventeen Bosnian families held more than 1,000 hectares. The state compensated landlords for their property with government bonds at below market value. With the loss of rents, tithes, and labor, many landlords did not have enough resources to modernize their farms and sold the bonds for income. When the bonds were traded on the Yugoslav stock exchange beginning in 1925, they were worth less than 30 percent of their original value. The 1919 agrarian reform solely affected agaluk estates (since only these were legally feudal lands). However, in 1921 the state extended the reform to beglik estate peasants, who had worked under de facto feudal tenancy arrangements since 1909. Throughout the interwar period, additional legislation extended the land reform to include (non-peasant) World War I veterans and state forests that peasants had cultivated illegally. Although full implementation remained incomplete by 1941, an estimated 168,000 families (some families counted twice) obtained 1,175,000 hectares of land (1,156,000 arable, 162,000 forest, 47,000 pasture) from large holders, vakufs, "enemies of the state," and peasant encroachments.

The 1919 agrarian reform was a crucial starting point for developing a modern agricultural sector in Bosnia-Hercegovina, but it did not invigorate the economy. Similar legislation had been enacted much earlier in neighboring Serbia (1833) and Croatia (1848). Still, rural poverty and micro-holdings increased in interwar Yugoslavia in general. Peasant smallholders still held their property in scattered micro-plots and still paid a disproportionate share of the tax burden, and farm prices stayed low throughout the period. Farming remained at a subsistence level. Inadequate roads and transportation also discouraged trade and economic growth. The agrarian depression of the 1920s gave way to the worldwide depression in the 1930s. In this period, the main source of industrial investment came from German firms interested in manufacturing and mining in order to extract strategic raw materials. The interwar government took important steps to modernize Bosnia-Hercegovina's economy, but progress was slow.

THE COMMUNIST ECONOMY, 1945–1992

At the end of World War II, the Communist Party of Yugoslavia (CPY) took over Yugoslavia's rural, war-devastated economy. Much of the country's roads, rail, farms, and buildings had been destroyed, creating widespread homelessness and unemployment. Mass starvation threatened. Only 56 kilometers of paved road remained in Bosnia-Hercegovina. By 1947, much of the damaged and destroyed rail and road system had been rebuilt. The Party set about restructuring agriculture and industrializing the economy. The 1945 Agrarian Reform and Colonization Act (completed in 1948) redistributed farmland to smallholding peasants and the state. At the same time, the CPY developed heavy industry and was the first East European state to issue a Five-Year Plan (1947–1951). With the onset of the Cold War, diplomatic tensions with the Soviet Union led to Yugoslavia's expulsion from the Soviet alliance in 1948. The ensuing political and economic crises of 1948–1952 ushered in a period of reform (1952–1968) in Yugoslavia characterized by economic growth, worker's self-management, and increased consumerism. Ultimately, the Party failed to construct a viable agricultural economy or to build adequate industrial infrastructure in Bosnia-Hercegovina. Beginning in the late 1960s, the republic benefited from increased control over its own budgets and special development funds. However, by the end of the communist period, the republic's industries had become outdated, and it remained the second poorest and the least urban republic in Yugoslavia.

In Bosnia-Hercegovina's long history as an overwhelmingly rural economy, grinding rural poverty has contrasted starkly with bustling urban trade. In the postwar period the CPY sought to create an efficient agricultural economy and develop rural industry. Its 1945 agrarian reform completed the work of interwar reforms and redistributed land away from the regime's wartime enemies, large holders, religious institutions, and non-peasants toward veterans and those who actually farmed the land. The postwar Agrarian Reform affected 110,512 hectares in Bosnia-Hercegovina (compared to 1,174,503 hectares in the interwar period). It reduced the maximum size of active farms (from 50 to 35 hectares of arable land), restricted non-peasant holdings to no more than 5 hectares, and limited churches to 10 hectares.

By 1945, there were few large holders left in Bosnia-Hercegovina to expropriate. The lower limits on large holdings accounted for 16 percent of Bosnia's land fund (15 percent in Yugoslavia) but less than 2 percent of holdings. Even fewer Bosnian peasants had farms larger than 35 hectares, and only a handful of Bosnian churches and monasteries held tracts larger than 10 hectares. At half the Yugoslav rate, wealthier peasants provided only 4 percent and religious institutions contributed only 5 percent of the property in the land fund.

Without a significant concentration of landed wealth, communists turned to the smaller properties held by regime enemies and non-peasant holdings over 5 hectares (10 percent of the Bosnian land fund, averaging 7 hectares each). Ethnic Germans residing in Yugoslavia's former Habsburg territories were labeled wartime enemies and deported. Their farms (mostly in the Vojvodina) made up 60 percent of holdings and 41 percent of property in the Yugoslav land fund. German expropriations were less significant in Bosnia-Hercegovina, where seizures averaged only 3.61 hectares and accounted for 12 percent of the land fund, far less than in any of the other former Habsburg regions. Still, many Bosnians benefited from these expropriations, as over 19,000 peasant households left their farms to resettle or "colonize" many of the war-devastated farms in the Vojvodina, Yugoslavia's richest agricultural region. As these peasant colonists emigrated to the Vojvodina, they left their farms (5.31 hectares on average) to the land fund, contributing the largest portion of any group in Bosnia (22 percent of arable land) and far more than the Yugoslav average (3 percent). Bosnia also expropriated a significant amount of property belonging to "immigrants of foreign nationality." These seizures, constituting 13 percent of the land fund and averaging 6.3 hectares each, affected almost exclusively Poles. Thus, the postwar reform in Bosnia-Hercegovina did not transfer land from large holders to small farmers, but shifted smallholdings around, fed ethnic resentments, and reinforced micro-holding.

The 1945 agrarian reform benefited many land-poor peasants (whose land was of poor quality and insufficient in size) and veterans. In Yugoslavia, more than half of the land (51 percent) was redistributed to peasants. In Bosnia, however, the 1945 reform restructured agriculture in favor of the state, with less than one-quarter of Bosnian land (23 percent, 25,106 hectares) finding its way to private sector peasants. Of these, 11,662 peasant households received an average 1.7 hectares each (19,605 hectares total); another 1,620 colonists relocating within Bosnia-Hercegovina received an average of 3.3 hectares. The remaining land went to collective farms (3 percent, 3,258 hectares), state farms (14 percent, 15,233 hectares), state forests and reforestation (31 percent, 34,196 hectares), state offices and ministries (2.5 percent, 2,723 hectares), or was left undistributed (27 percent, 29,993 hectares).

Neither interwar nor postwar reforms significantly improved the agricultural sector, on which 76 percent of Bosnia's population depended. Farms continued to be split into the tiny parcels and peasants still lacked basic farm equipment, features that had characterized the region's land tenure since Ottoman times. The state claimed that the agrarian reform had been fully implemented in 1948, but most peasants remained micro-holders. At this time, official Yugoslav statistics record that 69 percent of Bosnia's peasants were micro-holders (owners of farms smaller than 5 hectares, with 29 percent holding 2 hectares or less), 18 percent were smallholders (farms with 5–10 hectares), 7 percent were middle peasants (10–20 hectare farms), and fewer than 1 percent of farms were larger than 20 hectares. In 1951 there were 637 state farms, 1,496 collective farms, and 359,000 private farms in Bosnia-Hercegovina. Private-sector peasants owned one plow for every 6.4 hectares of farmland (comparable to Macedonia, Vojvodina, and Kosovo), but they possessed only one tractor for every 70,954 hectares, one sower for every 596 hectares, one harvester for every 2,896 hectares, and one thresher for every 3,225 hectares. This lack of basic equipment on private farms reflects the republic's limited agricultural productivity. In contrast, the state created a relatively well-funded, modern state farm sector. By 1951, Bosnia's 113 state farms (averaging 346 hectares each) had grown to 637. State farms owned one tractor for every 130 hectares of arable land, one thresher for every 226 hectares, one sower for every 115 hectares, and one harvester for every 97 hectares. However, this state sector was much too small to transform agriculture as a whole.

In an attempt to rationalize the agricultural economy and gain control over private peasant producers, Yugoslavia became the first East European state to start collectivizing agriculture in 1949. At its peak in 1951, collectives occupied one-quarter of Yugoslavia's farmland. However, collectivization was quite uneven, ranging from 6 percent in Slovenia to 60 percent in Macedonia. On the eve of collectivization, only 3 percent of Bosnian farmland had been in collectives. By January 1951, collective farms took up 18 percent of Bosnia's farmland. Collective farms were much larger than private farms, but since they were made up of members' scattered micro-holdings and lacked sufficient tools and machinery, they were no more productive. More-over, members tended to work on their household allot-ments and ignore their collective farm obligations. Bosnian collectives were among the worst equipped of any repub-lic in Yugoslavia. They owned only one tractor for every 790 hectares, one sower for every 167 hectares, one har-vester for every 441 hectares, and one thresher for every 418 hectares. As on private farms, state attempts to improve productivity, consolidate land holdings, and control the peasant workforce failed.

Within a year, the CPY recognized that its collectiviza-tion campaign had been a disaster. It had brought many peasants into collective farms, but collective farm yields plummeted, and peasants turned against the state. The Party ended its collectivization drive in December 1949 and tried to reform existing collective farms, but the system collapsed as peasants withdrew en masse in 1952. The 1953 Land Re-form legalized peasant withdrawals and reconfirmed rural private property rights. By reducing the maximum size of private farms to 10 hectares, however, and prohibiting pri-vate ownership of farm equipment, the reform also ensured that private agriculture would remain largely subsistence and could not compete with the larger, better-equipped state farms. In Bosnia, the state refocused efforts on build-ing rural industries (mining, hydroelectric power, forestry), food processing, arms production, and vehicle assembly.

In 1945 the CPY sought to transform Yugoslavia (and Bosnia) from an agriculturally dependent economy into a modern industrial one. By mid-1947, the state had control of all transportation, 90 percent of retail trade, and 70 per-cent of industry. In April 1947 Yugoslavia became the first East European state to issue a Five-Year Plan, which em-phasized heavy industry, mining, and manufacturing as the basis for an industrial economy. The 1948 Soviet crisis led to a spurt of industrialization in Bosnia. Fearing a Soviet in-vasion, Tito believed that Bosnia's interior position would protect Yugoslavia's vital industries from possible capture. This encouraged building factories in "splendid isolation from markets, roads, or skilled manpower" (Rusinow 100). Thus, Bosnia-Hercegovina enjoyed a spurt of industrializa-tion despite its lack of infrastructure.

Focusing on heavy industry, communist economic plan-ners took advantage of both well-known and newly discov-ered deposits of iron ore, coal, and bauxite to develop steel, iron, fossil fuel, and armaments industries in Bosnia-Herce-govina. The republic's non-navigable rivers became sources of hydroelectric power, which now produces 61 percent of the country's electricity according to CIA statistics. Banja Luka (in western Bosnia) became a major industrial center. Central Bosnia's Bosna River valley (with heavy industry in Zenica, Sarajevo, and Doboj) became the republic's most in-dustrial and most polluted region. Its plentiful iron ore re-serves enabled Zenica's iron and steel mills to become the biggest in the Balkans. The rich Sredna Bosna coal mines were the largest in Yugoslavia. Lignite and bituminous coal were mined near Sarajevo, Zenica, Tuzla, and in the Kozara Mountains (near Prijedor), providing fossil fuel for 39 per-cent of the country's electricity. Bauxite reserves, primarily mined for aluminum manufacturing in Mostar and

Zvornik, were also used for making bricks for blast furnaces and abrasives for polishing and grinding. These develop-ments industrialized the Bosnian economy. By the 1980s, however, they had become antiquated, unproductive, and responsible for much environmental damage.

As the fear of a Soviet invasion subsided following Stalin's death, the Yugoslav economy began to grow rapidly. Between 1953 and 1968 Yugoslav growth rates were among the highest in the world. The Party attributed this growth to its new worker self-management system, which it had promoted in the wake of the Cominform crisis to distin-guish its socialist economy from the Soviet Union's. In 1949 Tito and his top leaders decided that Soviet-style national-ization of property was only the first step in creating a so-cialist economy. They argued that workers should also control the workplace through an independent labor move-ment, which would manage socially owned enterprises. In contrast to private and state property, socially owned prop-erty (social property) consisted of assets that belonged to so-ciety rather than an individual or the state. Workers would not own their workplace but would control all aspects of how it was managed. Since the Party supervised all enter-prises, worker self management and worker control was se-verely limited. Nonetheless, Yugoslavia's self-management economy (along with the Party and the JNA) was associated with the country's economic boom and became one of the institutional pillars of Tito's state.

Most of the country's economic progress, however, can be attributed to better supplies of raw materials as well as improvements in rail, road, power lines, and mining. The biggest production increases were in heavy industries, such as those favored in Bosnia. For example, Yugoslav produc-tion of steel, iron, and metals tripled between 1947 and 1955. After the Soviet crisis passed, however, the Party shifted much of its industrial investment from Bosnia to more economically developed areas in Slovenia and Croa-tia. Bosnia-Hercegovina's lack of adequate roads, rail, schools, and electricity required a massive influx of capital to sustain economic growth. Since this investment was not forthcoming, the Bosnian economy suffered relative eco-nomic decline during these boom years. By 1960, Bosnian per capita domestic product (GDP) had grown by 152 per-cent. This quick expansion was slower than the Yugoslav av-erage of 192 percent during the same period. From 1952 to 1968, Bosnia-Hercegovina grew more slowly than any other republic or autonomous province. Between 1947 and 1967, per capita GDP in Bosnia-Hercegovina fell from 96 percent to 75 percent of the Yugoslav average. Clearly, Bosnia-Hercegovina was not benefiting from communist economic policy as much as other republics.

Bosnia-Hercegovina's relative decline fit into a larger pattern of widening disparity in income, development, pro-ductivity, social services, and opportunity between the more economically developed and more urban former Habsburg regions (plus Belgrade) and the more rural former Ottoman regions. Communist development policies benefited urban areas most. As the second most rural region in Yugoslavia, Bosnia was second only to Kosovo (the most rural region) in having the highest infant mortality, the most illiteracy, and the largest percentage of people with only three years of elementary education. With greater opportunity elsewhere, 16,000 Bosnians emigrated to other republics every year throughout the 1950s and 1960s.

In the 1960s economic reforms increased the availability of consumer goods and eased restrictions on small business and foreign travel. Living standards also rose. Beginning in 1965, Yugoslavia's Special Fund for the Development of Underdeveloped Areas was expanded to include parts of Bosnia-Hercegovina (as well as parts of southern Serbia proper, and the Croatian districts of Lika, Kordun, and Dalmatia) in an attempt to address growing economic disparities among republics. Officials used this money to electrify towns, lay telephone connections, build food and textile factories, and revitalize craft industries. The 1968 National Roads Loan program sought to connect every town to an asphalt road. Within a few years, it paved 1,800 miles of roads in Bosnia. In the 1970s the republic invested in large industrial projects and added suburbs to the larger urban centers. The Party built new housing complexes, hotels, and office buildings. In preparation for the 1984 Olympics in Sarajevo, the state repaired the city's streets, installed new plumbing, and laid down new tram lines.

In contrast to the "golden 1970s," the 1980s brought mounting debts, inflation, and sustained economic decline to Yugoslavia. By the late 1980s, hyperinflation (120 percent in 1987, 250 percent in 1988, 2,500 percent in 1989) was eroding the economy. Prime Minister Ante Marković's currency reforms cut inflation to nothing in 1990, but the newly elected governments (particularly in Serbia) were unwilling to commit to his austerity program, and inflation resumed in 1991. Bosnia-Hercegovina's antiquated, pollution-spewing industry accentuated this breakdown. For example, the aluminum factory in Zvornik (Europe's largest, employing 4,000 workers) began to import African bauxite because the local reserves could not be processed at the plant. Bauxite processing also polluted the water, generating more costs as the state tried to clean up environmental damage. Bosnia-Hercegovina is still trying to clean up the red sludge from the Mostar aluminum factory that threatens the Neretva River. By the 1980s, much of the republic's industry, badly in need of upgrades, no longer acted as an engine of growth.

Most notorious, however, was the collapse of Agrokomerc, a large poultry processor located in the northwestern town of Velika Kladuša (Bihać district). Originally, Agrokomerc was a small chicken farm with 30 employees. In 1967, Fikret Abdić became its executive director and helped the company grow into one of the thirty largest firms in Yugoslavia, with 11,000 workers by 1987. Unfortunately, however, its expansion had been funded by granting high interest rate loans without collateral. While Agrokomerc was awash in unsecured debt, Abdić and his investment partner, Hamdija Pozderac, had made a fortune. Before it collapsed, Agrokomerc had issued false promissory notes worth $875 million held by sixty-three banks throughout Yugoslavia. The firm's collapse forced the Bank of Bihać to close, leaving the 50,000 workers whose paychecks were automatically deposited there without compensation. The Bihać economy was devastated: shops closed,

workers struck, the state sent food relief, and the chickens starved to death. The Agrokomerc scandal turned political when it was revealed that the fraud had been facilitated at the highest political levels and was well known to senior Party officials. Abdić was a member of the Party's Central Committee in Bosnia-Hercegovina. Pozderac had used his success in Agrokomerc to pursue a very successful political career. In 1987, he was a member of Yugoslavia's presidency, poised to become the country's next president. Pozderac resigned, and Abdić was expelled from the Party, along with two hundred other Bosnians and Croatians implicated in the scandal. The incident was seen as symptomatic of a corrupted system that allowed politically well-connected businessmen to defraud investors and shield insolvent businesses with tacit government approval.

In spite of the economic decline of the 1980s and persistent economic disparities, Bosnia-Hercegovina grew at a historically unprecedented rate for most of the communist era. As the economy industrialized, the agricultural sector contracted to 10 percent of GDP and many of Bosnia's farmers became immigrant guestworkers. Still, by 1990, Bosnians enjoyed more economic opportunities than ever before. The republic had developed chemical manufacturing, energy distribution, oil refining, mining (iron ore, bauxite, coal, lead, zinc, and manganese), metallurgy, vehicle assembly, and the production of electrical appliances, finished textiles, and leather goods. Under communism, Bosnians enjoyed access to basic health care and education that only a tiny group of elites enjoyed before World War II. Infant mortality rates declined from 105 per 1,000 live births in 1960 to 13 in 1990. In 1941 the region had inadequate numbers of elementary schools, a handful of high schools, one agricultural college, and no universities. Under communism, education became comprehensive, with universal access to primary and secondary education, post-secondary colleges, and four universities, which produced a highly educated and skilled labor force. By the early 1990s, Bosnia's average annual per capita GDP was $2,430, and the republic enjoyed a trade surplus with the European Union. This prosperity ended abruptly in 1992.

WAR AND RECONSTRUCTION, 1992–2002

The economic nosedive of the 1980s paled in comparison to the wartime collapse. Each claiming territory for their own national group, combatants shelled cultural monuments, villages, and symbols of communist economic progress, causing tens of billions of dollars in damages. Roads, railroads, ports, electrical and communications infrastructure, factories, warehouses, schools, and housing became military targets. Many Bosnians had spent years working extra jobs and investing their savings to build and improve their homes, only to see them destroyed. By 1995, the war had ruined 80 percent of the economy and most of the country's physical assets, wiped out any private capital, and led to the creation of an extremely weak federal government. Only 20 percent of the workforce held jobs. Bosnia-Hercegovina's annual per capita GDP shrank from $2,430 to $500, and experts estimated the total GDP to be between 10 and 30 percent of its prewar level. In 2003 an estimated six million mines still remained in graveyards, fields, farms, and ports.

The 1995 Dayton Accords officially divided Bosnia-Hercegovina and its economy into two entities: the Republika Srpska (RS), with its capital in Banja Luka, and the Federation of Bosnia-Hercegovina, with its capital in Sarajevo. In addition, Bosniak and Croat regions within the Federation further divided the economy of Bosnia-Hercegovina. These boundaries have divided the already small economy into two economic zones with weak federal controls. Banking and customs regulations are under federal jurisdiction, but each entity creates its own fiscal policies and generates its own economic statistics. Countrywide information is often unavailable and inconsistent, making economic assessment of the country as a whole difficult. The entities' mutual suspicion, as well as significant legal, regulatory, and institutional differences, have prevented economic integration. Since the entities do not even have a customs union, international trade is often easier than official inter-entity commerce. Instead of creating a comprehensive reconstruction or development strategy for all of Bosnia, plans are restricted to the entities, which work at cross-purposes to existing economic infrastructure. Thus, these economic divisions hinder recovery, reconstruction, and future development.

Since hostilities ended in 1995, Bosnia-Hercegovina has experienced strong aid-driven economic growth. Due to the difficulty in data collection discussed above, current economic statistics provide only rough estimates. According to the IMF, total GDP increased 78 percent between 1996 and 1998 and has leveled off at 4 to 10 percent annually since. From 1995 to 1998, industrial production increased at a rate of more than 25 percent per year before average growth slowed to 9 to 11 percent growth in the Federation and between 2 and 6 percent growth in RS from 1999 to 2001. In 1998 the government introduced a convertible Bosnian Mark (BAM). Pegged to the euro, the new currency has kept inflation under control (3.5 percent in 2001); it became the country's only legal tender on 1 January 2002 (it had previously competed with German, Yugoslav, and Croatian currencies).

This strong performance must be seen in the context of Bosnia-Hercegovina's economic collapse by 1995, the base year for these statistics. In 2002 Bosnian GDP, industrial production, wages, and employment remained far below the levels of a decade earlier. Total GDP stood at two-thirds of its prewar level. Average wages have also increased since 1995, but remain low. Annual per capita income has recovered to $1,400–$1,900 in 2002 from its 1995 level of $500 but remains far below 1992 averages. Unemployment,

Reconstructing Bosnia-Hercegovina one nail at a time. A man puts a new roof on his war-damaged home in the Brbavica district of Sarajevo, 1997. (Getty Images)

which dropped to 40 percent by 1998, has not improved since. In contrast to 1990, most jobs are found in the government, in construction sectors, and in international organizations. In 2001 agriculture accounted for 13 percent of GDP, industry made up 41 percent, and 46 percent of the country's wealth came from the service sector. By 1998, the World Bank had expected higher industrial production, higher export levels, and lower import needs. Instead, trade (especially imports) grew faster than industry. As Bosnia-Hercegovina's industrial recovery stalls, its economic growth has become dependent on international aid.

Since 1998, Bosnia-Hercegovina's economy has reached a fragile stability, but living standards have not recovered. In 1998 most Bosnians (61 percent) lived in poverty (unable to buy two-thirds of basic needs). One quarter of those living in poverty were employed. They survive through support from relatives living abroad, humanitarian aid, and black market activity. Delays in and underpayment of pensions and unemployment compensation add to poverty. Despite declines in unemployment, low wages have prevailed in every sector except financial institutions and public administration. Economic data from the entities show that the Federation, which accounts for three quarters of the Bosnian economy, has grown faster and with lower unemployment than the Bosnian average. Average 1998 wages were about 30 percent lower in RS than in the Federation.

More than ten years after hostilities began, Bosnia-Hercegovina continues to rebuild. Ninety percent of trade and travel depends on road and rail. By the end of 2002, 48 bridges and 2,000 kilometers of Bosnia-Hercegovina's 21,000 kilometers of road had been rebuilt. Much of the country's 1,000 kilometers of standard-gauge rail had also been repaired. Highway construction continues. The country has modernized its telecommunications and postal services, but basic reconstruction work on gas and oil pipelines, river ports, and utilities remains incomplete. Mines, harbor destruction, sedimentation from tributaries, and bomb debris have stopped virtually all Sava River transport. The Sava River, Bosnia's largest, is the country's main trade link to the Danube, which flows through Central Europe and the Balkans. As of July 2003, Brčko (with a prewar shipping capacity of 750,000 tons annually of construction materials, coal, iron ores, steel, agricultural products, wood, and fertilizer) was Bosnia's only functional port. Even there, however, lack of dredging, destruction of the quay, and a need for warehouse repairs have prevented vigorous trade from resuming. The ports of Bosanski Samac (coal, iron, raw materials, food, mining, and energy materials) and Bosanski Brod (oil refining and shipments) remain unusable. Dependent on international aid, much of this costly reconstruction is proceeding slowly.

Inter-entity divisions also impede recovery and potential economic development. Without an integrated economy, Bosnian membership in international economic organizations, which could facilitate badly needed development, will be difficult. Bosnia-Hercegovina trades most with Croatia, Italy, Germany, Slovenia, and Switzerland. Existing road and rail service routes goods to Croatia's Adriatic port of Ploče (Croatia), the Sava River ports, to Croatia, and to Yugoslavia.

Entity boundaries crisscross existing roads and railway lines, impeding integration. For example, one of Bosnia's two main rail lines crosses from the Federation (in Bihać) to RS (in Prijedor, Banja Luka, and Doboj) before splitting into two lines. One line ends in Brčko (federal); the other returns to the Federation (in Tuzla) before again arriving in RS (in Zvornik). Roads and rail that run through the economically important Bosna valley connect industrial centers under federal (Sarajevo), Federation (Zenica), and RS (Doboj) jurisdictions to the port of Bosanski Samac.

Three and a half years of war erased fifty years of economic development and rising living standards in Bosnia-Hercegovina. The country continues to remove mines and reconstruct its economy. Recovery from the 1992–1995 war has been strong, but the economy is fragile, and growth has slowed in the last five years. Future development requires economic integration between the entities. These divisions cut through existing trade routes and require developing two separate economies, slowing recovery and darkening the prospects for future development. Economic integration requires stronger federal presence. International bodies call for privatization, but more private wealth must be created before privatization will be beneficial.

CONTEMPORARY CHALLENGES

In the 1970s Bosnians, along with the rest of Yugoslavia's citizens, enjoyed a growing economy, easy credit, and rising living standards. In the years following Tito's death in 1980, massive debt, industrial stagnation, nationalist politics, and a weak, unwieldy federal political system led to a decade of economic decline and political collapse. In 1991 Slovenia and Croatia seceded. The subsequent wars in Slovenia and Croatia fed fears of growing Serb nationalism, prompting Bosnia-Hercegovina and Macedonia to separate from Yugoslavia in 1992. Macedonians avoided hostilities with the Yugoslav government, but in Bosnia-Hercegovina a catastrophic war (1992–1995) destroyed the economy and tore the government apart. In a prewar population of 4.4 million, the war caused hundreds of thousands of Bosnian deaths and left nearly two million refugees. The war ended with an imposed peace that created a quasi-independent and divided Bosnia-Hercegovina. In 2004, after eight years of significant reconstruction and a massive influx of international aid, Bosnia has not made the transformation from reconstruction to development. Along with the rest of the western Balkans, it threatens to become an island of political and economic instability within a European system stretching from Turkey to Ireland. To avoid this fate, Bosnia-Hercegovina must construct an independent political system that protects civil rights, allows for redress of wartime injustices, and reverses its present course of de-industrialization. If these formidable challenges can be met, Bosnians will have a greater chance to shape their own future than at any other time in their history.

To develop a viable, sovereign political system that protects all its citizens, Bosnia-Hercegovina must simplify its complex state structure and strengthen the central government. The current system is far too weak and unstable. The

1995 Dayton Accords imposed a complex state structure consisting of a weak federal government, two autonomous entities (Republika Srpska and the deeply divided Bosnian-Croat Federation) and two federal districts (Sarajevo, Brčko). These entities have a great deal of autonomy vis-à-vis the federal government, enjoying self-rule and deciding policies usually reserved for central government (for example, they maintain their own military and negotiate international treaties). In contrast, the federal government is led by a three-member presidency, whose president rotates every eight months. The UN High Representative can dismiss any member of the presidency at any time. In addition, the UN has ultimate authority over the government and rules by decree. Since becoming UN High Representative in May 2002, Paddy Ashdown has imposed eleven to fourteen decrees per month. Constrained by the nationally defined entities and supervised by the UN, Bosnia's federal government has too little power to rule effectively or provide political stability.

The Dayton Accord's reliance on UN authority allows Bosnian politicians to avoid responsibility for state-building and economic planning. Foreign diplomats, rather than elected Bosnian officials, have drafted and imposed virtually all of the country's "reform" legislation, with little input from local communities. Thus, Bosnian politicians have no stake in or responsibility for implementing these laws and policies, which reflect external priorities rather than the concerns of most citizens, such as the lack of a social safety net and economic development. Moreover, the expectation that non-Bosnians will decide the ultimate shape of the Bosnian state allows local politicians to avoid difficult decisions regarding state building and economic planning. Instead, these politicians continue to rely on nationalist political rhetoric that focuses on historic wrongs, identity politics, and corruption charges. At the same time, the absence of effective leadership and continued economic stagnation is eroding the government's popular legitimacy. Continued reliance on the UN or foreign organizations will delay developing politically stable government institutions in Bosnia-Hercegovina.

Before a viable political culture can emerge, the government must systematically address wartime atrocities. Bosnian politicians must recognize that war crimes occurred, commit to resolving them justly and impartially, and demonstrate their commitment to securing all citizens' civil and property rights. Both Serbia and Croatia attempted to annex parts of Bosnia during the war. While members of each national group committed war crimes, Serbs committed the majority, and Muslims, the principal victims, committed the fewest (an estimated 8 percent). Some politicians, however, deny that the atrocities occurred. For example, an RS government report on the 1995 Srebrenica massacres recognizes a Serb role in only 100 Bosniak murders and claims that another 1,900 Bosniaks were killed in combat or died of exhaustion. This account is sharply at odds with that of the International Red Cross and other estimates, which place the number of unarmed Bosniak men and boys killed at between six and eight thousand.

Creating a consensus about what happened and to whom, as well as about how to provide restitution, is a for-

midable challenge. Yet formally ignoring wartime abuses (as the Communist Party of Yugoslavia did after World War II) or imposing a solution from the outside will not lead to national reconciliation but will inflame national animosity and cripple the state. The December 2003 Serbian elections, which not only returned Vojislav Šešelj (the Četnik paramilitary leader who led many ethnic cleansing operations and is currently being held in The Hague for war crimes) to parliament but gave him a plurality, demonstrate the continuing strength of nationalism.

Bosnians must not only recognize war crimes, they must fairly investigate, punish, and provide restitution for wartime abuses if they wish to create a stable state. Allowing offenders to act with impunity and preventing victims from reclaiming property may lead to vigilante justice, threatening a new cycle of nationalist violence. In prosecuting wartime offenses, transparency and impartiality are essential in order to demonstrate that the procedures serve justice. Otherwise, nationalists may hijack the process to obtain revenge or target ethnic minorities. In both the Federation and RS, local public prosecutors have directed their efforts primarily at minorities. In the Federation, ethnically biased judges and inadequate witness protection have compromised the legitimacy of domestic war crimes trials. In RS, authorities refuse to cooperate with The Hague Tribunal, and no war crimes trials have been conducted. Without justly redressing wartime crimes, the state will not be able to gain its citizens' confidence.

Just as important as holding its citizens accountable for war crimes, the state must also protect citizens' civil and property rights. Widespread violations make a mockery of constitutional amendments for ethnic equality passed in April 2002. The constitution granted Croats, Muslims, and Serbs equality throughout Bosnia-Hercegovina; it established mechanisms for the protection of language, the promotion of cultural heritage, and open access to public information systems. It called for ethnically balanced representation in entity parliaments and high courts, based on the 1991 census. However, individuals (including public officials) continue to occupy other people's property with impunity. RS authorities have encouraged or tolerated Serb construction of houses on land owned by displaced non-Serbs. In 2001 a dozen cars and reconstructed houses belonging to returnees were blown up. Local Serbs vandalized houses and businesses of Bosniak returnees in Prijedor and Bijelina. Violence against returnees also threatens individuals' personal security. In May 2001, 4,000 Serbs beat and stoned 300 elderly Bosniaks visiting Banja Luka for a ceremony marking the reconstruction of the Ferhadija mosque, killing one man. Violence against returnees was also reported in Prijedor, Bijelina, Brčko, Dubica, Zvornik, Doboj, and Bratunac in 2002. In most cases, the police have no suspects and have made no arrests. As of May 2002, national minorities comprised only 15.5 percent of the Federation police force and only 4.9 percent of RS police force. Without securing basic rights, the country cannot be a fully functioning state. It will remain ethnically divided and dependent on UN administrators and peacekeepers.

Bosnia's future political stability is intertwined with the economic challenge of development. Unless the course of

Slobodan Milošević at the International Criminal Court in the Hague. (Corbis Sygma)

de-development begun with the wartime collapse of its industrial economy is reversed, the country will remain politically unstable. After a decade of economic decline in the 1980s, living standards in virtually every Bosnian household have collapsed since 1992. In 2004 Bosnia's human capital remained scattered across the globe, as refugees find it difficult to return to their homes because the state does not guarantee all citizens' property and civil rights. Established firms teeter on the brink of bankruptcy, and potential new businesses lack essential capital. Increasingly, people move in search of elusive employment. Continued economic hardship and the lack of jobs is creating a new wave of political resentment among those who survived the war but have experienced a catastrophic decline in living standards.

The wartime collapse of Bosnia's industrial infrastructure has reversed the astonishing progress in raising social and economic standards and benefits from 1960 to 1990. Since 1995, large amounts of capital have poured into Bosnia-Hercegovina for reconstruction. Much of its infrastructure has been rebuilt, but recreating and developing the economy still lies in the future. By the 1990s, the large, communist-era industrial plants had become antiquated and inefficient. Nonetheless, they were vital to the Bosnian economy. For example, the large Zenica steel mills served as an economic anchor for the entire area by generating thou-

sands of jobs and the attendant services needed to support the population (public works, schools, housing, recreational and medical facilities). Economic prosperity stimulated growth in other sectors. With the mills functioning with less than one quarter of their prewar workforce (and few employees actually receiving their salaries), the local economy has collapsed. Reconstruction aid will not help the Zenica mills return to full capacity or help develop the economy. On the other hand, allowing Bosnia-Hercegovina to stabilize at a much lower economic level will perpetuate the country's political crisis.

The World Bank initially envisioned Bosnia-Hercegovina's economy returning to its prewar levels during reconstruction and then undergoing the process of privatization. However, the new Bosnian economy has de-industrialized. Its physical capital has not been rebuilt, industries have disappeared, and jobs remain scarce. The emerging economy focuses on small-scale, family-owned textile, mining, agriculture, retail, and construction businesses rather than large industry. Resources have shifted from high-tech to low-tech industry, and from industrial to agricultural and commercial sectors. Production of durable goods has given way to single-use commodities and extractive industries. Within agriculture, subsistence farming is replacing market-oriented agriculture. As reconstruction ends, the World Bank has given up its goal of restoring the economy to prewar levels in favor of privatizing inefficient businesses.

International organizations cannot depend solely on privatization to provide economic stimulus in Bosnia-Hercegovina; the country is not attracting investment, and many firms are near bankruptcy. In Republika Srpska only five of the sixty-six companies that have more than four hundred employees (and thus are slated to be privatized) have been sold. Divisions between economic elites with political ties and everyday Bosnians reinforce national resentments and may renew political instability. Unless there is a reorientation toward overall development that reverses this trend, the legitimacy of the political leadership will continue to erode, and the country's fragile political stability will shatter.

Bosnia-Hercegovina's future is closely linked to the rest of Europe. The western Balkans, especially Bosnia-Hercegovina and Kosovo, have the highest level of European Union (EU) involvement of any European region. Its largest trading partners are in Europe (Croatia, Slovenia, Germany, Italy), and most of the UN peacekeepers and administrators are European; the EU is the country's largest donor. By 2006, the EU will phase out its reconstruction aid, despite Bosnia's failure to restore its economy to prewar levels. This withdrawal will result in economic dislocations, as many of the country's well-paying jobs are unsustainable without funding from international organizations. Bosnian development could, however, be facilitated by a constructive relationship with the European Union. Using the EU's structural fund framework, Bosnia-Hercegovina could increase investment and employment, reduce the economic distortions that have accompanied reconstruction aid, incorporate regional and local economic concerns, and bolster political stability. Such improvements would allow the country to compete better with countries in the Middle East and southern Europe.

The EU developed its structural fund framework to promote social cohesion across Europe. In the past, it has addressed industrial decline and rural underdevelopment in Greece, Ireland, Spain, Portugal, and southern Italy. In these countries, the EU helped develop local resources to overcome regional disparity, with great success. It increased productivity by building up existing local labor skills, the physical infrastructure, and innovation potential. It incorporated local priorities by requiring district governments to help plan development projects and the federal government to co-finance them. EU financing added to (rather than replaced) government investment. Thus, co-financing forced the state to make difficult resource allocation decisions. Bosnia-Hercegovina confronts precisely these challenges, and this system could also help Bosnia-Hercegovina move toward the political accountability and economic development it needs. It would force Bosnian municipalities and politicians to prioritize their own needs, and it would give them a stake in their success. It could reduce spending distortions that exist in Bosnia-Hercegovina today, which funds projects that reflect foreign priorities, are unsustainable without foreign aid, have little or no input from Bosnians, and require no accountability from Bosnian officials. The obstacles faced in Bosnia-Hercegovina are similar to those Europeans have faced in other parts of Europe, and the risks of not meeting these challenges are great.

One key to Bosnia's future lies in a positive relationship with the rest of Europe. No matter how long the UN stays in Bosnia, political stability will not be forthcoming without confronting war crimes and offering its citizens some economic and personal security. While only Bosnians can resolve their wartime misdeeds, the country's integration into the European framework would help facilitate economic development and alleviate political divisions. Otherwise, the country risks persistent poverty in each entity, with festering resentments against its neighbors as socioeconomic conditions continue to slide. The UN will continue to control the government to provide a facade of stability. Nationalist hostilities will flourish, and the state will continue to export skilled workers and import peacekeepers. 2003 seems to have marked a turning point in Bosnia's relationship to the European Union. At the beginning of that year, Bosnian leaders feared exclusion from the broader EU project of strengthening economic and social cohesion across the continent. In 2004 Bosnian leaders were discussing negotiations leading to full membership in the EU. Progress toward full membership in the European Union could help reduce the widening gap between Bosnia-Hercegovina (and the western Balkans in general) and the rest of Europe.

SELECTIVE BIBLIOGRAPHY

Allcock, John. *Explaining Yugoslavia.* New York: Columbia University Press, 2000.

Banac, Ivo. *The National Question in Yugoslavia: Origins, History, Politics.* Ithaca, NY: Cornell University Press, 1984.

Bennett, Christopher. *Yugoslavia's Bloody Collapse: Causes, Course, and Consequences.* New York: New York University Press, 1995.

Blanchard, Paul. *Blue Guide: Yugoslavia.* London: A. and C. Black, 1989.

Bokovoy, Melissa. *Peasants and Communists: Politics and Ideology in the Yugoslav Countryside, 1941–1953.* Pittsburgh: University of Pittsburgh Press, 1998.

Bosnia and Hercegovina, Federal Ministry of Physical Planning and the Environment, "State of the Environment—1998." www.grida.no/enrin/htmls/bosnia/soe/html/index.htm (accessed 11 August 2004).

Central Intelligence Agency. "Bosnia and Herzegovina." In *The World Factbook,* http://www.cia.gov/cia/publications/factbook/geos/bk.html (accessed 9 June 2004).

Chaliand, Gerard, and Jean-Pierrre Rageau. *The Penguin Atlas of Diasporas.* New York: Penguin Books, 1995.

"Chronology of NATO's involvement in Bosnia," www.cco.caltech.edu/~bosnia/natoun/natochro.html (accessed 11 August 2004).

Clissold, Stephen, ed. *A Short History of Yugoslavia.* Cambridge: Cambridge University Press, 1966.

Cohen, Lenard J. *Broken Bonds: The Disintegration of Yugoslavia.* Boulder, CO: Westview, 1993.

Djilas, Aleksa. *Yugoslavia: The Contested Country.* Cambridge: Harvard University Press, 1991.

Donia, Robert J. *Islam under the Double Eagle: The Muslims of Bosnia and Hercegovina, 1878–1914.* Boulder, CO: East European Monographs, 1981.

Donia, Robert, and John V. A. Fine Jr. *Bosnia and Hercegovina: A Tradition Betrayed.* New York: Columbia University Press, 1994.

Dubey, Vinod. *Yugoslavia: Development with Decentralization.* Baltimore: Johns Hopkins Press, 1975.

Encyclopedia Britannica. http://www.britannica.com (accessed 3 June 2004).

Encyclopedia Judaica. door.library.uiuc.edu/mdx/jestud/n_jseresources.html.

European Commission. "Regional Balkans Infrastructure Study—Transport: Appendix 15—Final Report: Sava River." July 2003. http://www.seerecon.org/infrastructure/sectors/transport/documents/REBIS/Rebis_FR_App_15_Final.pdf (accessed 3 June 2004).

European Stability Initiative. "Making Federalism Work—A Radical Proposal for Practical Reform." http://www.esiweb.org/reports/bosnia (accessed 3 June 2004).

———. "Western Balkans 2004: Assistance, Cohesion and the New Boundaries of Europe: A Call for Policy Reform." 3 November 2002. www.esiweb.org/paf/esi_document_id_37.pdf (accessed 11 August 2004).

Fine, John V. A., Jr. *The Late Medieval Balkans: A Critical Survey from the Late Twelfth Century to the Ottoman Conquest.* Ann Arbor: University of Michigan Press, 1987.

FNRJ. "Savezni Statistički Ured." *Stanovništvogod* 1, no. 1, Belgrade, 1950, pp. 12–15.

Friedman, Francine. *The Bosnian Muslims: Denial of a Nation.* Boulder, CO: Westview, 1996.

Frucht, Richard, ed. *Encyclopedia of Eastern Europe: From the Congress of Vienna to the Fall of Communism.* New York: Garland Publishing, 2000.

Gačeša, Nikola. *Agrarna Reforma i Kolonizacija u Jugoslaviji 1945–1948* (Agrarian Reform and Colonization in Yugoslavia, 1945–1948). Novi Sad: Matica Srpska, 1984.

Gutman, Roy. *A Witness to Genocide.* New York: Macmillan, 1993.

Hawkesworth, Celia. *Voices in the Shadows: Women and Verbal Art in Serbia and Bosnia.* New York: Central European University Press, 2000.

Hoffman, George. *Eastern Europe: Essays in Geographical Problems.* New York: Praeger, 1971.

Hoffman, George, and Fred Neal. *Yugoslavia and the New Communism.* New York: Twentieth Century Fund, 1962.

Human Rights Watch World Report 2002. "Bosnia and Herzegovina." January 2002. www.hrw.wr2k2/europe5.html (accessed 5 August 2004).

Human Rights Watch World Report 2003. "Bosnia and Herzegovina." January 2003. www.hrw.wr2k3/europe5.html (accessed 5 August 2004).

Hupchick, Dennis, and Harold E. Cox. *The Palgrave Concise Historical Atlas of the Balkans.* New York: Palgrave, 2001.

Jelavich, Charles, and Barbara Jelavich. *The Establishment of the Balkan National States, 1804–1920.* Seattle: University of Washington Press, 1977.

Johnson, Ross. *The Transformation of Communist Ideology: The Yugoslav Case, 1945–1953.* Cambridge: MIT Press, 1972.

Klemenčić, Mladen, ed. *A Concise Atlas of the Republic of Croatia and of the Republic of Bosnia and Hercegovina.* Zagreb: Miroslav Krleža Lexicographical Institute, 1993.

Lampe, John R. *Yugoslavia as History: Twice There Was a Country.* Cambridge: Cambridge University Press, 1996.

Lovrenović, Ivan. *Bosnia: A Cultural History.* New York: New York University Press, 2001.

Magosci, Paul Robert. *Historical Atlas of East Central Europe.* Seattle: University of Washington Press, 1993.

Malcolm, Noel. *Bosnia: A Short History.* London: Macmillan London, 1994.

McCarthy, Justin. *The Ottoman Turks: An Introductory History to 1923.* London: Longman, 1997.

McCarthy, M. Katherine. "Peasant Revolutionaries and Partisan Power." Ph.D. diss., University of Pittsburgh, 1996.

Meier, Viktor. *Yugoslavia: A History of its Demise.* Translated by Sabrina Ramet. London: Routledge, 1999.

Naimark, Norman M. "The Wars of Yugoslav Succession." In *Fires of Hatred: Ethnic Cleansing in Twentieth Century Europe.* Cambridge: Harvard University Press, 2001, pp. 139–184.

Office of the High Representative and EU Special Representative [for Bosnia and Herzegovina]. http://www.ohr.int (accessed 3 June 2004).

Organisation for Economic Co-operation and Development. http://www.oecd.org (accessed 3 June 2004).

Parties and Elections in Europe. http://www.parties-and-elections.de/bosnia.html (accessed 3 June 2004).

Pinson, Mark, ed. *The Muslims of Bosnia-Herzegovina: Their Historic Development from the Middle Ages to the Dissolution of Yugoslavia.* Cambridge: Harvard University Press, 1994.

Poeschl, Josef. "The Economic Situation in Bosnia-Herzegovina." Vienna Institute for International Economic Studies, Bank Austria Creditanstalt. April 2002.

Prašo, Murat. "Demographic Consequences of the 1992–1995 War." July–Oct. 1996, in Bosnia Report. www.bosnia.org.uk/bosrep/juloct96/demwar.cfn (accessed 4 August 2004).

Reiff, David. *Slaughterhouse: Bosnia and the Failure of the West.* New York: Simon and Schuster, 1995.

Rhode, David. *Endgame: The Betrayal and Fall of Srebrenica: Europe's Worst Massacre since World War II.* Boulder, CO: Westview, 1997.

Rothschild, Joseph. *East Central Europe between the Two World Wars.* Seattle: University of Washington Press, 1974.

Rusinow, Dennison. *The Yugoslav Experiment, 1948–1974.* London: C. Hurst, 1977.

Savezni zavod za statistiku. Statiskički bilten no. 14. "Poljiprivredne Mešine i Oredja 1951. Belgrade, 1952, pp. 5–11.

Savezni zavod za statistiku. Statiskički bilten no. 61. Belgrade, 1956, pp. 6–7.

Serbian Academy of Sciences (SANU). "Memorandum" in Gale Stokes, ed. *From Stalinism to Pluralism: A Documentary*

History of Eastern Europe since 1945, 2nd ed. New York: Oxford University Press, 1996.

Silber, Laura, and Allan Little. *Yugoslavia: Death of a Nation.* New York: Penguin Books, 1997.

Singleton, Fred. *A Short History of Yugoslav Peoples.* Cambridge: Cambridge University Press, 1985.

Stiles, Andrina. *The Ottoman Empire, 1450–1700.* London: Hodder and Staughton, 1991.

Stojanov, Dragoljub. "Bosnia and Herzegovina since 1995: Transition and Reconstruction of the Economy." www.esiweb.org/bridges/bosnia/stojanov_ch/v (accessed 10 October 2004).

Tomasevich, Jozo. *Peasants, Politics, and Economic Change in Yugoslavia.* Stanford, CA: Stanford University Press, 1955.

Ulam, Adam. *Titoism and the Cominform.* Cambridge: Harvard University Press, 1952.

UNICEF. "At a Glance: Bosnia and Herzegovina—Statistics." http://www.unicef.org/infobycountry/bosniaherzegovina_statistics.

Woodward, Susan. *Balkan Tragedy: Chaos and Dissolution after the Cold War.* Washington, DC: Brookings Institution, 1995.

World Conservation Union [until 1990, the International Union for the Conservancy of Nature and National Resources]. www.iucnredlist.org.

CHRONOLOGY

Seventh century	Slavs arrive in Bosnia and the rest of the Balkan Peninsula.
Ninth century	Christian missionaries arrive in Bosnia.
1054	Great Schism places Bosnian Christians under the jurisdiction of the Pope in Rome. Bosnian Christians become Catholic.
Tenth–twelfth centuries	Bosnian lands ruled for short periods by Serbia, Croatia, Bulgaria, Byzantine Empire, Hungary.
	Both Catholic and Orthodox churches establish monasteries in Bosnia, but no parish organization or secular clergy.
	Both Glagolitic and Bosnian Cyrillic alphabets in use (as well as Latin and Greek alphabets).
	Codex Marianus (tenth century), oldest Glagolitic manuscript from Bosnia.
1180–1204	Kulin rules Bosnia under the title of *ban* (governor); issues charter to Dubrovnik, first official act written in a national language in the south Slav lands.
1252	Pope places Bosnian Catholic Church under Hungarian archbishop.
	Bosnian Catholic Church defies the pope, expels the bishop, and creates its own schismatic Catholic church, the Church of Bosnia.
1252–1459	Church of Bosnia, one of three Christian churches in Bosnia-Hercegovina; Islam introduced in early 1400s.
	Roma (Gypsies) arrive in Bosnia-Hercegovina.
1322–1353	Kotromanić rules as ban, expands Bosnian territory.
1342	Kotromanić invites Franciscans to establish a vicariate in Bosnia, the first official Roman Catholic presence since 1252. (Franciscans are the only official Catholic presence in Bosnia to 1878.)
1347	Kotromanić converts to Catholicism.
	Kotromanić annexes Hum (present-day Hercegovina).
1391–1463	Power struggle among three powerful nobles and the king weakens the state. Peak of *stećak* art, manuscript illumination, glass and metalware (particularly gold and silver) craftsmanship, ceramics, and mural paintings.
1432	Ottoman forces make first permanent gains in Bosnia.
1443–1461	Stefan Tomaš rules as king.
	Ottoman forces capture Vrhbosna and begin to build Sarajevo on this site.
1448	Stefan Vukčić secedes from Bosnia to form Hercegovina (formerly Hum), calling himself Herceg Stefan; region begins to be known as Hercegovina.
1451–1453	Civil war in Hercegovina.
1459	Tomaš expels Church of Bosnia members and suppresses the church as condition of papal military aid against Ottoman forces. No military aid forthcoming.
1461–1463	Stefan Tomašević rules as king.
1463	Forces of Ottoman Sultan Mehmed II invade Bosnia.
	King Tomašević surrenders to Ottoman forces in Ključ; pockets of resistance continue to fight Ottoman rule.
1463–1878	Bosnia under the Ottoman state. Emergence of distinct religiously affiliated Bosnian cultural identities: Islamic Ottoman culture, Catholic Croat culture, Orthodox Serb culture, Sephardic Jewish culture. Most Roma (Gypsies) were Muslim. As the head of the Christian millet, the Orthodox church represents all Christians in Bosnia.
1482	Hercegovina falls to the Ottoman Empire.
1519–1523	Bosnia's first printing press, in Goražde.
1530–1531	Gazi Husrevbeg's mosque built in Sarajevo.
1530–1565	Sarajevo's cloth market, built in the 1530s, attracts Jewish merchants, who

	establish a Ladino-speaking Sephardic community in Sarajevo, which flourishes until 1941.
1557	Karadjozbeg's single-domed mosque built in Mostar.
	Ottomans establish autocephalous patriarchate for Serbs and Bosnians based in Peć.
1566	Stari Most (Old Bridge) built in Mostar.
1577	Jewish quarter *(mahala)* established near Sarajevo's main market.
1580	Bosnia attains administrative status of an Ottoman *eyalet* (province), held until 1878.
1600–1800	Period of economic stagnation and military decline.
	Rights of Christian and Muslim subject peoples decline as the state's cash needs increase, especially in rural areas. Peasant tax revolts become endemic in eighteenth century.
1766	Ottomans abolish Peć Patriarchate and autocephalous status of Serb and Bosnian Orthodox Church, which is absorbed into the Greek Orthodox Church. Orthodox decline follows.
1778	Austrian Emperor Joseph II conquers Bosnia.
1789	French Revolution. European powers persuade Joseph II to withdraw from Bosnia, but the Habsburg emperor becomes protector of Christians in the Ottoman Empire.
1800–1878	Period of Economic Reforms and Rebellion.
	Vuk Karadžić, a Serbian linguist, standardizes Serb, Croat, and Bosnian vernaculars into modern Serbo-Croatian, which includes variants using Latin and Cyrillic scripts.
1831–1833	Kapetan Husein's revolt for Bosnian autonomy to block Ottoman reforms and restrictions on kapetans.
1836–1850	Series of kapetan-led revolts against Ottoman reforms and authority.
1839	Series of Ottoman military, tax, land tenure reforms known as *Tanzimat* decreed. Bosnian officials resist implementation.
1861–1868	Topal Osman-pasha builds roads, schools, new library for the Begova mosque, first public hospital.
	First printing press since 1523, publishing in Serbo-Croatian and Turkish languages.
	Consultative assembly established with representatives from all faiths.
1875–1878	Tax rebellion in Hercegovina ultimately ends Ottoman rule in Bosnia-Hercegovina.

1878	Treaty of Berlin justifies Habsburg occupation of Bosnia by citing the inability of Ottoman officials to effectively implement land tenure and tax reform.
1878–1918	Austria-Hungary occupies (1878) Bosnia-Hercegovina. Region is administered by Austria-Hungary's Joint Ministry of Finance.
1906	Muslim National Organization (MNO) becomes Bosnia's first legal political party. Consisting mainly of landlords, MNO advocates elected Vakuf Assembly and preservation of Ottoman property law.
1907	Serbian National Organization (SNO) becomes legal political party.
1908	Austria-Hungary formally annexes Bosnia-Hercegovina.
	Croat National Union (CNU) established as a secular, liberal, middle-class political party.
1910	Bosnian Parliament established with no direct legislative powers.
1912	First Balkan War.
1913	Second Balkan War.
1914	Assassination of Habsburg heir to the throne, Archduke Franz Ferdinand, in Sarajevo, by members of Young Bosnia. Austria-Hungary attacks Serbia; World War I begins.
1914–1918	World War I.
1918	Yugoslavia declares itself independent Kingdom of Serbs, Croats, and Slovenes; Bosnian autonomy promised.
1919	Yugoslavia is recognized at the Paris Peace Conference.
1919	Abolition of serfdom throughout Yugoslavia emancipates over 90,000 serf households farming one-third of arable land in Bosnia-Hercegovina. Not fully implemented until 1936.
	Mehmed Spaho founds Bosnian Muslim political party, Yugoslav Muslim Organization (YMO).
1921	Vidovdan Constitution ratified; Bosnia-Hercegovina keeps historic borders, but no autonomy.
1928	Sarajevo Writer's Group founded; includes Bosnia's most important literary figures.
1929	In a successful coup d'état, King Alexander abolishes Yugoslav constitutional state and legislature and bans labor unions.
1929	Anthology of left-wing expressionist writers publish *Knjiga drugova* (Comrades' book).
1929–1941	Historic Bosnia divided for first time since medieval period.

Bosnia is Serbianized; Bosnian Muslims pressured to declare their national affiliation as Croat or Serb.

State dismisses non-Serb cultural influences as "foreign."

1939	Cvetković-Maček *Sporazum* (Agreement) gives Croatia autonomy and divides Bosnia between the Croatian banovina and the remaining Serb-dominated lands.
1941	Yugoslavia signs German Tripartite Agreement; Yugoslav military stages a coup d'état in protest. Prince Paul abdicates in favor of Prince Peter, who renounces the agreement. German and Italian armies defeat and divide Yugoslavia.
	German puppet state, Independent State of Croatia (NDH), annexes Bosnia and Hercegovina.
1941–1945	World War II.
	NDH Croatianizes the region. Serbs converted to Catholicism, expelled, and executed. Jewish property stolen, synagogues ransacked. Few Bosnian Jews survive. Mosques burned, Muslims converted to Catholicism. Serbs, Jews, communists, and Muslims interned in concentration camps.
	Communists, Četniks, German armies, and Croatian armies fight in Bosnia, creating widespread destruction.
1945–1992	Communist Yugoslavia.
1945–1966	Bosnia-Hercegovina is part of a unitary state under leadership of Josip Broz "Tito."
1946	Constitution establishes unitary state, with six republics and two autonomous republics.
	Bosnia-Hercegovina established as a republic with its historic borders, but no dominant nation. Bosnian Muslims designated a special ethnic group.
1947	Majority of economy nationalized; first Five-Year Plan introduces building and industrialization plans.
1949	Collectivization campaign begins.
1950	Muslim elementary schools closed; teaching children in mosques criminalized, Bosnia's dervish orders banned. All but one *medressa* (school for training Muslim clergy) closed.
	Branko Ćopić's satirical story, "The Heretic," early criticism of communist elite culture, published.
1950s	LCY introduces free primary and secondary education, brings elementary schools and local libraries to most

villages and secondary schools to all of the larger towns in Bosnia-Hercegovina for the first time.

1953	Collectivization abandoned; land reform
1966–1992	Yugoslav government decentralizes in favor of its republics.
	Secular Bosnian revival: Bosnian Muslims become dominant in communist party, craft industries revive, large investments in industry, roads (over 3,000 miles), housing, and building.
	Bosnian Islamic revival criticizes communist rule and nationalism.
1971	Bosnian Muslims recognized as a nation.
1974	Constitution makes autonomous provinces equal to republics, weakens the federal government.
1983	Alija Izetbegović sentenced to fourteen years in prison on spurious charges that his "Islamic Declarations" advocated the creation of an ethnically pure Islamic state, at the same time advocating Western-style democracy.
1984	Winter Olympics held in Sarajevo.
1986	SANU Memorandum circulated.
1989	Prime Minister Ante Marković institutes strict currency reforms that end hyperinflation of late 1980s.
1990	First multiparty elections held in communist period; in Bosnia-Hercegovina the Party of Democratic Action (SDA), Serb Democratic Party (SDS), and the Croat Democratic Union (HDZ) defeat the communist party; Izetbegović becomes president.
1991	Newly elected governments (particularly in Serbia) drop Marković's program; inflation resumes.
	Franjo Tudjman and Slobodan Milošević discuss partition of Bosnia.
	Radovan Karadžić and SDS create Serb autonomous regions in Bosnia.
	Slovenia and Croatia secede; ten-day war in Slovenia; four-month war in Croatia.
1992	Tudjman and Milošević discuss partition of Bosnia again.
	Referendum for Bosnian independence passes; government in Bosnia-Hercegovina declares independence.
1992–present	Republic of Bosnia-Hercegovina.
1992	Ethnic cleansing of Bosnian Muslims begins in Bijelina, 1 April.
	JNA and SDS attack Bosnia, 1 April.
	EU and UN recognize Bosnian independence, 6 April; Karadžić declares independent Republika Srpska, 7 April.

1992–1995	Bosnian war for independence, leading to 200,000 killed, 2 million refugees. Systematic ethnic cleansing (including policy of organized rape), especially in areas Serbs claim create three relatively ethnically homogenous regions within Bosnia-Hercegovina. Destruction of cultural heritage throughout region, symbolized by the destruction of Mostar's Old Bridge.
1993	UN declares Srebrenica a safe haven.
1993	NATO protection begins.
1995	UN surrenders Srebrenica; Srebrenica massacre in July. Croatian Serbs expelled from Croatia. August–October become refugees in Bosnia.

	International diplomats halt gains by Bosnian and Croat armies when they are poised to retake most of Republika Srpska. Dayton Peace Agreement signed in Paris. Bosnia-Hercegovina divided into two entities (Federation and RS) and two federal districts (Brčko and Sarajevo), supervised by UN.
1996–2000	Slow progress on refugee return. Massive international reconstruction effort. Period of economic de-industrialization.
2002	Bosnian mark tied to the euro.
2004	Scheduled negotiations for full Bosnian membership in the EU.

ALBANIA

ROBERT AUSTIN

LAND AND PEOPLE

At 28,748 square kilometers, or roughly the size of the state of Maryland, Albania is the third smallest country in Europe, after Slovenia and Macedonia. It is bordered by Montenegro to the northwest, Kosovo to the northeast, Macedonia and Greece to the east, and the Adriatic Sea to the west. The coastline at its nearest point is only 65 kilometers from Italy and 5 kilometers from the Greek island of Corfu. The country owes both its isolation and its relative invulnerability to the natural barriers protecting it: the Dinaric Alps to the north, the Macedonian highland to the east, and the Pindus range to the south. The climate is characterized by cold winters and abundant precipitation. Temperatures vary widely depending on season, geographic location, and altitude. Albania is occasionally subject to violent winds and to summer drought.

Tiny Albania presents an astonishingly varied set of landscapes, from Mediterranean beaches to fertile valleys with fruit orchards and tobacco fields, from arid mountains to oak forests to marshlands harboring a diverse wildlife. A strip of land along the coast, varying in width from 10 to 40 kilometers, is known by geographers as the western lowlands. Much of this area can be characterized as marshland, a good part of which has been reclaimed in the past century through drainage schemes. The reclaimed lagoons and marshlands south of Elbasan offer some of the most fertile land in Albania. The land east of the western lowlands is referred to as the western highlands. Despite its name, this section encloses fertile valleys, especially in the south and southeast, around Korçë and Lake Ohrid.

Although Albania's waterways can be navigated only with difficulty, the country's water resources represent a significant asset in the production of hydroelectric power, as Albania has no other sources of electrical energy. The coastline and Lake Ohrid hold potential for tourism, although the potential has yet to be realized. Albania is limited in its mineral resources, containing only small quantities of low-grade petroleum, low-grade copper ore, low-grade (lignite) coal, and high-quality asphalt bitumen. It also has a large supply of chromite ore, which is difficult to exploit because it is mixed in with other minerals. Unfortunately, Albania is prevented from enjoying whatever benefit it could derive from exploiting its mineral resources because of deficient infrastructure, an absence of large-scale foreign investment, and low prices on world markets.

The transportation network in Albania is primitive. In 1990 there were only 18,000 kilometers of roads, of which only 38.3 percent were asphalt and only 40 percent were usable by motorized traffic. There are 7,450 kilometers of railway, but trains are frequently reduced to speeds of 30 kilometers an hour due to outdated locomotives and poorly laid track. As a result, only 32 percent of freight is shipped by train, with 66 percent shipped by road, and only 37.7 percent of travelers use trains, with the remainder travelling by road vehicle. In 1986 Albania's rail system was linked to the international system when it launched the Shkodër-Titograd (Podgorica)

Albania

Albanian fields, 1995. (Arne Hodalic/Corbis)

line. The hub of the railway is Durrës, which is also the location of Albania's largest port. In 1990 Durrës handled 2,336 tons of goods, accounting for 82.9 percent of Albania's seaport traffic. The other major seaports are located in Vlorë, Sarande, and Shengjin. Albania's international airport is located at Rinas, 20 kilometers north of Tirana.

Because its industrial development during the communist era was so limited, Albania did not have to face the same scope and extent of environmental damage as was the case in other communist countries. Economic collapse in the early 1990s, however, resulted in the closure and abandonment of many chemical production plants, with disastrous consequences. The derelict factories contaminate the surrounding land. Making matters worse, Albanians fleeing poverty have settled near the factories, building their homes with materials taken from the contaminated sites and grazing their animals on the polluted land, exposing themselves to toxin levels several thousand times the accepted level in most European states. The formation of enormous unsanitary shantytowns around major cities is another major concern, as is the air pollution occasioned by rubbish burned at the Sharra garbage dump, near Tirana. Durrës, Sharra, Patos, Vlorë, and Ballsh have been singled out as pollution hot spots. Economic crisis has also resulted in deforestation, as Albanians have taken to chopping down trees indiscriminately for heating purposes.

Albania has a high rate of population growth, relative to other transition countries: 1.5 percent per year, compared with 0.2 percent for Romania and 0.8 percent for Macedonia. This figure is particularly impressive when the high rate of emigration is taken into consideration. The high population growth rate is sustained by a high fertility rate of 2.6 per woman, in contrast to 1.9 for Macedonia and 1.3 in Romania. Albania's population is young: 30 percent of Albanians were under fifteen years of age in 1999, compared to 18.7 percent in Romania and 23.1 percent in Macedonia. This percentage is expected to decrease over time, according to estimates prepared for the World Bank.

At present, Albania's population stands at 3.4 million. Unlike most European countries, Albania is still predominantly rural: roughly 40 percent of the population lives in cities, according to the Albanian Institute of Statistics (INSTAT). This percentage represents a major increase since 1975, when only 37.5 percent of the population lived in cities. The United Nations Development Program (UNDP) projects that the urban percentage of the population will reach 50 percent in 2015. The capital city, Tirana, is by far the country's largest city; in 1995, it had an estimated population of 300,000, although some estimates place it higher owing to large-scale migration from rural areas. The next most populated cities are Durrës, on the coast, with an estimated population of 125,000, and Elbasan, situated at the geographic center of the country, with an estimated population of 101,300. Next are Vlorë (88,000), and Shkodër (81,000). In all, Albania has thirteen cities with a population greater than 20,000.

Communist leader Enver Hoxha's health-care system brought about a dramatic improvement in public health during the communist era, drastically reducing the infant mortality rate, increasing life expectancy, and more than halving the death rate. The postcommunist economic crisis has resulted in some reversals in the quality of health care due to a combination of factors, including shortages in supplies, outdated equipment, and a shortage of doctors. Albania has 1 physician per 668 inhabitants (according to INSTAT), in contrast to Croatia, which has 1 physician for every 435 inhabitants, or the Czech Republic, with 1 per 330. There has also been an exodus of physicians from the countryside to the city, as well as out of the country completely. Three quarters of the population has access to safe water, and only 58 percent to adequate sanitation.

According to health indicators, Albania has improved markedly over the last thirty years, but it still lags behind other transition countries. The infant mortality rate in 1999 was 29 per 1,000 live births, down from 68 in 1970; the under-five mortality rate shows a similarly dramatic decrease from 82 to 35 deaths per 1,000 live births. By comparison, Croatia's infant and under-five mortality rates in 1999 were 8 and 9 respectively, and Romania's rates were 21 and 24 respectively. With a life expectancy at birth of seventy-three in 1995–2000, however, Albania rivals other transition countries: it is the same as in Slovakia, and slightly higher than in Hungary.

Albania's literacy rate lags behind that of other transition countries, at 92 percent compared to 98 percent in Romania, 98.2 percent in Croatia, and 99.3 percent in Hungary. However, illiteracy seems to be a problem mainly with older generations; youth literacy stands at 97.8 percent. The Albanian educational system, like the health-care system, is suffering as a result of economic crisis. Teachers cannot live on their meager salaries, supplies are lacking, and schools have been closed in rural areas as a cost-cutting measure. Furthermore, young Albanians are choosing to emigrate to find work rather than complete their high school education.

As a result of economic backwardness, Albanians are also far behind other postcommunist countries in terms of access to technology. Albanians by and large do not even have access to their own telephone lines: there are only 3.64 phone lines per 100 inhabitants, compared to 9.58 in Bosnia and Hercegovina, 16.69 in Romania, and 36.38 in Croatia. Mobile telephones are no more accessible: Albania has only 3.5 subscribers per 1,000 inhabitants, compared with 60.5 per 1,000 in Romania. Like other countries where obtaining a landline often requires a lengthy wait, cell phone use, although extremely expensive, is growing rapidly. Computer technology is equally out of reach; there are only 6.4 computers for every 1,000 Albanians, compared to 67.0 in Croatia and 26.8 in Romania. It follows that less than 1 out of every 1,000 Albanians is connected to the Internet.

PEOPLES OF ALBANIA

The population of Albania is ethnically quite homogeneous. According to the census carried out in April of 1989, 98 percent of the population was ethnically Albanian. Of the remaining 2 percent, the majority were registered as Greek (59,000 people). This figure has been hotly contested, with primarily Greek sources quoting much larger numbers. There are small numbers of other minorities in Albania, such as Macedonians (realistic estimates vary between 4,700 and 15,000), Montenegrins and Serbs (approximately 2,000), Vlahs (estimated at 35,000), and Armenians. There are also a substantial number of Roma (Gypsies), with estimates varying wildly between 5,000 and 75,000.

Albania is host to three major religions. Islam is by far the most represented faith; it is often claimed that 70 percent of Albanians are Muslims, but this statistic is primarily a pre–World War II figure. It is more realistic to say that 70 percent of Albanians have a Muslim heritage. Some 20 percent of Albanians belong to the Albanian Orthodox

Ethem Bey Mosque in downtown Tirana. (Courtesy of Robert Austin)

Church. Catholicism, which is adhered to by as many as 10 percent of the population, is the last of the three major Albanian faiths. Albania has been surprisingly free of conflict between religious groups. All three faiths were strongly repressed under the communist leader Hoxha, especially after he undertook his Albanian Cultural Revolution, which began in 1966. Places of worship were confiscated and converted to other purposes, and priests were imprisoned.

Following the fall of communism, religion was once again legalized, and the three faiths began to rebuild their infrastructures. The Catholics were in the most advantageous position, as the Vatican was able to provide them with priests and resources. The restoration of the Orthodox Church has proceeded less smoothly. There were no surviving members of the Church hierarchy, and attempts to fill the vacancies with ethnic Greeks provoked nationwide controversy. In their efforts to rebuild Islamic religious life, Albanian Muslims have been supported by Islamic countries such as Saudi Arabia, Kuwait, and the United Arab Emirates. The fall of communism has also witnessed the penetration into Albania of various American-based religious organizations, including Jehovah's Witnesses, Lutherans, Mormons, Baptists, and Seventh-Day Adventists. The appearance of these faiths is disquieting to many Albanians. They are particularly concerned about Evangelical sects, whose exclusivist views they fear may destroy the atmosphere of tolerance that has characterized Albania until today.

The ethnic Albanian population traces its roots to the pre-Hellenic Illyrian tribes, whose presence has been recorded in the Balkans since at least the second millennium B.C.E. Ethnic Albanians can be divided into two groups; the Gegs, or Ghegs, who live in the mountainous north, and the Tosks, who inhabit the plains and mountain basins south of the Shkumbin River. They can be distinguished by their use of different dialects of the Albanian language. The Ottomans colonized the Tosk-inhabited south, transforming its social structures and opening the region to the influence of other cultures, including Islam. The north, however, remained largely impenetrable to Ottoman domination and was allowed a large measure of self-government. Thus, the Tosks and the Gegs evolved virtually in isolation until Albania obtained its independence. Successive generations of Albanian leaders made efforts to break down the cleavage between north and south; for instance, Hoxha put into place various mechanisms to encourage people to move to other parts of the country and to intermarry. Nonetheless, strong regional identities have persisted. In the communist and postcommunist era, these regional identities have played a role in political life: thus, the north felt discriminated against during the rule of Enver Hoxha, who was a southerner. Similarly, southern Albanians considered that the country's first postcommunist president, Sali Berisha, who is from the north, discriminated against them. However, there is no record of unrest ever having resulted from north-south tensions.

Ethnic Greeks are located primarily in southern Albania, near the Greek border. Relations today between ethnic Albanians and the Greek minority are often strained. Although Hoxha did not persecute ethnic Greeks, he barred

The Albanian Language

The Albanian language is part of the Indo-European family of languages and is spoken by approximately 7 million people in the Balkans, predominantly in Albania and Kosovo, but also in neighboring Macedonia, Montenegro, Greece, and Turkey. Some argue that the language has its origins in ancient Illyrian; others hold that it has its roots in the ancient Thracian tongue. The debate over the origins of the language has not merely been an academic one; it has often been politicized, since language claims give rise to territorial ones. The link with Illyrian is especially important for Kosovars, who have long sought to establish their historic presence in Kosovo against Serb nationalist claims that Albanian Kosovars are relative newcomers to a region that was historically Serb. Over the centuries, especially given foreign occupation throughout much of the region's history, foreign words have crept into the language. After the Turks conquered the region in the fifteenth century, the use of written Albanian was banned. Since most of Albanian society was comprised of illiterate peasants, the language remained essentially a verbal one until the twentieth century, when an alphabet was adopted at the Congress of Monastir (now Bitola) in 1908 and a common literary language at Shkodër in 1916.

Albanian is written using thirty-six letters, an alphabet that includes two accented letters (ç and ë) and nine two-consonant digraphs (dh, gj, ll, nj, rr, sh, th, xh, and zh). There are two principal dialects, which correspond to the regional split that existed in the region for hundreds of years. Geg is spoken in the northern region (including Kosovo); Tosk is the dialect of Albanians in the southern areas (south of the Shkumbin River). The communists attempted to create a standardized language beginning in the 1950s. Two decades later, in 1972, a unified language was established, based primarily on Tosk.

Albanian continues to be spoken within émigré communities in North America and Europe.

them from obtaining high positions in the Party and administration. Greek organizations were limited to folkloric groups, and schoolchildren were taught only Albanian history. The Greek Orthodox Church, which plays a central role in Greek identity, was one of the prime targets of Hoxha's campaign against religion. Thus it would be fair to say the regime pursued policies directed against Greek ethnic identification. The fall of communism initially represented an improvement in the rights of ethnic Greeks. The Orthodox Church and cross-border travel were legalized, and political pluralization allowed ethnic Greeks to form a political party, Omonia, to defend their interests and more generally develop ethnic minority rights in Albania.

Despite the easing of restrictions, relations between Albanians and Greeks quickly soured, as Albanians continued to be suspicious of the loyalty of ethnic Greeks. Omonia was outlawed in 1992 on the grounds that it reflected narrow ethnic interests, but was quickly replaced by a nonsectarian successor party called the Union of Human Rights. The nomination in 1992 of ethnic Greek Archbishop Anastasios Iannoulatos to head the Albanian Orthodox Church provoked a great deal of protest from Albanians. The following year, an ethnic Greek Orthodox priest was accused of promoting separatism and was expelled from Albania, and the Albanian Greek community was placed under surveillance. These measures greatly angered the ethnic Greek community. Ethnic Greeks were once again accused of subversion in 1994, when five individuals were convicted of staging an attack on a frontier military post. They were released a year later by order of the Albanian Supreme Court. In 1996 the appointment by the Ecumenical Patriarchate in Constantinople of three ethnic Greek bishops to important positions in Gjirokastër, Vlorë, and Korçë drew fire from Albanians.

Tensions between ethnic Greeks and Albanians in the postcommunist era have also been aggravated by the dramatic improvement in the standard of living of ethnic Greeks, who have gained access to social services in Greece and easily obtain work and residence rights there. This prosperity is in stark contrast to the impoverishment of most Albanians, and to the poor treatment of Albanian workers in Greece. Tense relations between the Albanian government and the Greek minority have been reflected on an international level by often strained relations between Greece and Albania.

ALBANIANS OUTSIDE ALBANIA

One of the peculiarities of Albania is that there are as many, if not more, Albanians living outside of Albania as there are within the borders of the country. Large-scale Albanian immigration began after the Ottoman conquest, with large communities forming in Romania, Bulgaria, Egypt, Turkey, and especially Italy. By 1886, there were 181,700 Albanians in Italy. Large numbers of Albanians also immigrated to the United States in the nineteenth century; by 1907, there were some 60,000 Albanians in the United States, concentrated in Boston and New York. Diaspora communities continued to maintain close ties with the home country and played an important part in the Albanian national awakening. Thimi Mitko, a collector of Albanian folklore and an important figure in the national awakening, was a member of the Albanian community in Egypt. The Albanian Orthodox Church was founded in 1908, not in Albania, but in Boston; its founder was none other than Fan Noli, destined to be prime minister of Albania for six months in 1924. The

Albanian diaspora continued to participate in Albania's political life after the fall of communism, providing a great deal of funding to the nascent Democratic Party in the early 1990s.

The more substantial Albanian communities in neighboring Balkan countries have been an important consideration in the shaping of Albanian foreign policy. There are significant numbers of Albanians in Montenegro (7 percent of the population) and Macedonia (where the most recent census has put the Albanian population at roughly 25 percent). Today, 90 percent of Kosovo's 1.9 million inhabitants are estimated to be Albanian. These communities have existed for centuries. There is also a large community of Albanians in Greece, possibly as many as 360,000, mainly composed of unemployed men who have migrated illegally in the last decade in search of temporary work. The presence of such a large number of often illegal migrants has also added to the frictions with Greece, which blames them for increased criminality in Greece. Equally important, since the Albanian economy is so overwhelmingly dependent on remittances, it provides Greece with tremendous influence in Albanian affairs.

Despite their large number, the Albanians in the Yugoslav province of Kosovo were not among the groups Yugoslavia recognized as constituent peoples of either of the interwar or communist Yugoslav states. (The groups were Serbs, Croats, Macedonians, Slovenes, and later Muslims.) Following the Tito-Stalin split in 1948 and a concomitant rupture with Albania, the Yugoslav regime began to regard the Albanian minority as a threat and attempted to forge a separate Kosovar-Albanian identity in the hope of thwarting the burgeoning Albanian nationalist movement. Initially, Albanians made their demands within the Yugoslav political system, demonstrating in 1968 for the upgrading of Kosovo to republic status, the creation of a university in Priština, equal status for the Albanian language, and economic assistance. Although the demonstrations were put down, all demands except for the status of a republic were subsequently met, and the constitution of 1974 gave the province greater powers, amounting to something close to republic status. Albanians mobilized again in 1981 against Serbian domination; the protests turned violent and were summarily crushed. Serb intellectuals expressed increasing concern over the high birthrate of Albanians, expressing the fear that Serbs would eventually be crowded out of the "cradle of the Serbian nation."

It was in this tense atmosphere that Slobodan Milošević rose to power in Yugoslavia, on promises of restoring Serbian pride and protecting the interests of Serbs wherever they might be. Part of his program was the restoration of Serbian dominance in Kosovo. In 1989, surrounded by the Yugoslav army, the Kosovo provincial assembly was pressured into approving amendments that surrendered much of the province's autonomy, and what was left of that autonomy was abolished in 1990 by the Serbian assembly. Education in the Albanian language was terminated, and Albanian civil servants were laid off en masse, replaced by Serbs. A largely unsuccessful "resettlement program" was put in place to encourage Serbs to settle in Kosovo. In response to these measures, a secret referendum was held, with Albanians overwhelmingly voting for independence. The results of the referendum were not recognized by any country save Albania. A parallel underground state apparatus was put into place. This period also witnessed the growth of the Kosovo Liberation Army (UCK), which practiced armed resistance against the Serb authorities.

Albanians in Macedonia are mainly concentrated in the northwest tip of the country. Until unrest there in 2001 provoked widespread changes, they were not recognized as a constituent nation in Macedonia, but they were recognized as a minority. Neither in the communist Yugoslavia nor later in the independent state of Macedonia were Albanians subjected to the type of repression that characterized life in Kosovo. Until 2000, they largely chose to formulate their demands within the political system. The Party for Democratic Prosperity was formed in 1991 to represent ethnic Albanian interests. Their demands have included equal nation status with Macedonians, proportional ethnic representation in government and the administration, the recognition of Albanian as an official language, and free use of the Albanian flag. Albanians attempted to open a university in Tetovo in 1995, but the government feared that it would become a center of nationalism and did not grant it recognition until 2004. The belief of the Macedonian government seems to be that if they give the Albanians an inch, they will take a mile. The worsening situation in Kosovo gave rise to fears that the unrest would spread to Macedonia, further stiffening the intransigence of the government. Albanians did eventually begin armed resistance in Macedonia, which led to an international settlement known as the Ohrid Agreement in the fall of 2001: the agreement introduced widespread constitutional and other changes designed to address Albanian grievances.

The status of Albanians living in neighboring countries has been a concern for Albanian governments. The Democratic Party from the start expressed support for the plight of Albanians in Kosovo and a desire to forge closer relations with its diaspora in general. Nonetheless, both the Democratic Party and the Socialist Party have adopted a cautious attitude toward the situations in Kosovo and Macedonia and have refrained from making matters worse by stoking nationalist passions in either Kosovo or Macedonia. Relations with Greece have been adversely affected by its harsh treatment of Albanian migrant workers.

HISTORY

Albanians are considered to be descendants of the Illyrians who were the first inhabitants of the Balkan Peninsula; throughout history Albanian lands have been controlled by a succession of foreign empires, from the Roman to the Ottoman. The Illyrianism of the Albanians is not without political implications, especially in a region where who was where first assumes tremendous importance, and not surprisingly the link has been disputed, especially by Albania's Slav neighbors. Thus the Illyrian connection is an important part of the Albanian mentality, and Albanian scholars put considerable effort into ensuring that this connection

is maintained. As well, the struggle of this small nation to survive as a nationality and finally an independent nation, a struggle against often intriguing and meddlesome neighbors, has left an important imprint on the Albanian national character. Albanians are often suspicious of foreigners and, more importantly, deeply nationalistic and patriotic, with an Albanocentric view of the world that verges on the ridiculous.

In the early Middle Ages Albania was nominally under the control of the Byzantine Empire, which saw the region as a forward wall of defense (thanks to the mountainous nature of the region) and a key trade route. It was during this period that the Albanians divided into two main groups: the Gegs in the northern areas, who maintained a tribal structure, and the Tosks in the southern and coastal areas. Never having an independent state, the Albanians were dominated by their neighbors: the Venetians, the Serbs, the Bulgars, and finally the Ottoman Turks.

When the Turkish army defeated the forces of the Serbs (which also included Albanian troops) at Kosovo in 1389, the door was open to the Albanian lands. During the early 1400s, the Albanians resisted the Turks, led by their great national hero, Gjergi Kastrioti (1405–1468), the legendary Skanderbeg. Originally a soldier in the Ottoman army, he later deserted and organized a loose-knit group of Albanian nobles to fight the Turks for the next twenty-five years (1443–1468). Following his death, the resistance collapsed, and the Ottomans gained control of the region.

Because of the nature of the terrain, Ottoman troops garrisoned the towns but allowed a great deal of local control. Most of the population converted to Islam, in part due to taxation policies that favored Muslims. Albanian Muslims became valuable members of the Ottoman army and ruling structure; some thirty Albanians became grand viziers, the second most powerful office in the empire next to the sultan.

Albania thus was isolated from many of the trends taking place in Europe. Turkish control, the sizable Muslim population, peasant backwardness, and cultural isolation, all these factors made it virtually immune to the nationalist yearnings of its neighbors in the Balkans. When a national awakening did begin in the late 1800s, it was born not so much out of a desire for independence, but rather out of the need to defend Albania against the territorial desires of the newly independent Balkan states. When that defense failed, Albania became the last Balkan state to break from Istanbul.

NATIONAL AWAKENING

Albania gained a fragile and premature independence in 1912, after five centuries of Ottoman rule. Although national feeling had come a long way, much remained to be done as far as creating a truly national consciousness among the entire population.

The Albanian national awakening had begun to bear fruit in 1878, when both the Treaty of San Stefano and the Congress of Berlin raised the threat of partition among neighboring powers, as the terms of San Stefano would have severely undermined Albania's ethnic frontiers. Albanian nationalists formed the League of Prizren (a city in present day Kosovo) to defend their national rights and to promote autonomy within the Ottoman framework. The elite in Albania, which consisted of a Muslim landed aristocracy, had been among the most integrated national groups within the Ottoman Empire, and their national aspirations wavered between territorial autonomy within the framework of the empire and outright independence. Turkey's humiliating defeat brought with it questions regarding the empire's long-term viability. In 1912, with the imminent collapse of Ottoman power all too apparent, Albanian patriots sought an early declaration of independence. Whereas in 1878 nationalists felt that Albania's position could be better ensured by remaining in the faltering empire while national consciousness took root, in 1912 the international situation did not allow for such caution.

Albanian nationalism became a much more vital force in the aftermath of the San Stefano Treaty, even though the Ottoman authorities worked hard to prevent this. Any national movement depended on the ability to romanticize, popularize, and legitimize goals through links with historic events and figures, especially Skanderbeg. For twenty-five years (1433–1468) he had managed to free significant parts of Albanian territory from Ottoman control. Despite the fact that Skanderbeg's struggle was in a sense a case of cross against crescent, Christianity against Islam, he became a last-ing symbol of opposition to foreign control. Skanderbeg's image is ubiquitous throughout Albania (and Kosovo).

The Albanian awakening began later than other Balkan countries for several reasons. Aside from high levels of integration within the Ottoman Empire, which saw many Albanians achieve high office within the Ottoman administration, Albania, like Bosnia, also possessed a native Muslim aristocracy. There were also religious and regional differences within ethnic Albanian lands. Unlike elsewhere in the Balkans, where religion had been a unifying factor, in Albania, owing to the Ottoman occupation, some 70 percent of the population adopted Islam, more out of practical necessity than of conviction. The remaining 30 percent included a compact Catholic minority in the north around Shköder of some 10 percent and an Orthodox community of approximately 20 percent in southern Albania. Religion should not, however, be exaggerated as a divisive factor or hindrance to national unity. Albanians showed, and continue to show, a remarkable tolerance for religious diversity.

By far the most significant obstacle to national unity was the existence of strong regional differences between northern and southern Albanians. With the Shkumbin River as the natural boundary between north and south, Albanians form two subgroups. The Gegs inhabit the mountainous regions of the north, while the Tosks inhabit the low-lying regions of the south. The Tosks had been far more subject to

Mural depicting the Albanian struggle for independence on the National Museum in Tirana. (Courtesy of Robert Austin)

foreign stimulus than their northern brethren, who had managed to maintain a quasi independence, even during the Ottoman occupation. The two groups used different dialects, and the Albanian language lacked a standard literary form, factors that also posed an obstacle to national unity. It was only in 1908, at the Congress of Monastir (now Bitola) that Albanians adopted a single alphabet for the language.

Although the Albanian national movement made remarkable gains after 1878, the most important factor in securing Albanian independence was the presence of geostrategic concerns. Austria-Hungary, which subsidized the Albanian national groups, together with Italy, lobbied for the creation of an independent Albania in an effort to block Serbian access to the Adriatic. Independence, as in the rest of East Central Europe, was as much based on the support of one or more of the great powers as on the strength of the national movement. Without that support, Albanian independence would not have been achieved. The borders agreed upon by the great powers in 1913 left substantial numbers of Albanians in present-day Serbia, Montenegro, Macedonia, and Greece. Some 500,000 Albanians were in southern Serbia (Kosovo), and Albania's population approached 1 million. The presence of such a large Albanian community outside the new state's boundaries has remained an unresolved dilemma and a major source of conflict between Albania and Yugoslavia.

INDEPENDENT ALBANIA

The independence achieved in 1913 was by no means complete: Albania became an autonomous principality under the guarantee of the great powers. Prince Wilhelm of Wied was appointed as the country's first sovereign, and he arrived in March 1914 with the best intentions. However, Wied was an alien in the peculiar world of Albanian politics and became an early victim of deception. His goal of creating a unified Albanian state was thwarted, and he fled the country in September. Although his own inexperience was a major factor in his failure, continual interference by neighboring countries, especially Serbia, posed insurmountable difficulties. World War I extinguished Albanian independence, and the process of state building was thus postponed. In the war's aftermath, Albanian independence was again called into question, primarily by Italy, which had received extensive territorial concessions under the Secret Treaty of London in 1915. As well, Greece sought control of southern Albania or, as they referred to it, northern Epirus, in order to imply a link with the Greek region of southern Epirus. Italy and Greece, in the Tittoni-Venizelos Agreement of 1919, supported each other's claims. Owing to the strength of the national movement, however, and some vital support from U.S. president Woodrow Wilson, Albania was able to again embark on the process of nation and state building.

In the face of tremendous difficulty, Albanians achieved remarkable unity at the Congress of Lushnjë in January 1920. The congress was a watershed in Albania's political evolution. With fifty delegates from all regions in attendance, Lushnjë laid the foundations for a new political order in Albania. A new constitution was framed, which placed power in a four-man regency council. Membership was based on religious affiliation, with one member from the Orthodox community, one from the Catholic, and one from each order of Islam in Albania (Sunni and Bektashi, a mystic offshoot of the Shia). Yet the euphoria and unity of the Lushnjë Congress gradually gave way to a return of chaos.

Albania's interwar experience was similar to that of most of East Central and Southeastern Europe; an early experiment with democracy was followed by a drift toward authoritarian rule. External factors were important, insofar as many of Albania's neighbors were unwilling to accept the new state's existence, but it was internal factors that were paramount in the collapse of democracy. To argue that Albanians were unprepared for democracy is inaccurate. Yet it would be fair to note that Albanians for the most part were unfamiliar with democratic norms, and the leaders who emerged were too often most concerned with preserving their own privileges. The conservative beys or landowners who had naturally risen to the top in an independent Albania were determined to retain the economic and political status quo, which was essentially a feudal system.

As elsewhere in the region, then, the majority of elites were only superficially committed to the democratic process. The years 1920–1924 are considered the heyday of Albanian democracy, but even though there were various trappings of democracy, there was also considerable chaos. External pressures along with internal problems served to undermine attempts to achieve democracy. Wide gaps emerged between committed reformers and the more conservative beys who sought to maintain the old order. Reflecting this polarization, political affiliations of a sort emerged in the guise of the Popular and Progressive Parties. The former was committed to modernization and land reform, while the latter sought the maintenance of the old order. As well, differences between Gegs and Tosks were no small factor in undermining attempts to create a unified Albanian state, especially since northerners remained deeply suspicious of central authority. Governments came and went all too often, and no real progress was made in bringing the backward nation into the twentieth century. The most reform-minded government of the era, that of the Harvard-educated Bishop Fan S. Noli, provides an excellent example of the obstacles to democracy, not only in Albania, but elsewhere in Eastern Europe. Noli sought to radically transform Albanian society through land reform.

Imbued with Western ideas and determined to create a democratic Albania, his clique overthrew a conservative government in June 1924. Free elections in December 1923, the last until 1991, had created a tremendous polarization between reformers, headed by Noli, and the more conservative beys, headed by Ahmed Bey Zogu (Zog). Despite the best of intentions, Noli was unable to usher in a new era in Albanian political life. His multi-point program aimed at revolutionizing Albanian society, but it was better suited to a more advanced Western-style democracy, and much of it served to alienate his supporters, who were not entirely convinced of the need for reform. The anti-Zog,

Zog I, originally Ahmed Bey Zogu (1895–1961), king of the Albanians. (Getty Images)

King Zog

Ahmed Bey Zogu, later King Zog, was born in 1895, the son of a chief of the Mati district in central Albania. He came from a Muslim family who had distinguished themselves in Ottoman service. At the onset of the interwar period, Albania was split into two rival camps: one was led by Zogu, who represented the conservative landowners and tribal chiefs; the other camp, led by Fan S. Noli, who was educated in the West and was an Albanian Orthodox bishop, was in favor of installing a liberal democracy based on the American model. In 1922 Zogu became prime minister of Albania, but he faced a series of uprisings and challenges to his leadership. It was not until 1925, when he restored control, sent Noli into permanent exile, and became the president of the newly proclaimed Albanian republic, that his power was secure. In 1928 he proclaimed himself king of the Albanians, as opposed to king of Albania, a move that angered neighboring Yugoslavia because of its large and often restive Albanian community.

Zogu increasingly found himself isolated in the region and beholden to the Italian dictator, Benito Mussolini, for needed foreign support. By 1939, faced with an Italian ultimatum to become a puppet or risk invasion, the Albanian king had no recourse. Zogu, his two-day-old son, Leka, and his wife, Queen Geraldine, were forced to leave Albania in April 1939, with the invasion of the Italian army. Zog offered no resistance to the Italian invasion but tried to raise support for his return outside Albania. His exile was a difficult one, as he moved from country to country; he finally died of cancer in Paris in 1961. His son, Leka, and Zog's wife returned to Albania after their lengthy exile in 2002. Unlike Bulgaria, where Simeon returned to the government in the wake of the collapse of communism, there has been little support for Leka and no substantial support for the restoration of the monarchy.

anti-conservative coalition was rife with dissension, and Noli, like Wied, was an outsider to Albanian political life.

Committing error after error, his coalition slowly fell apart, while his nemesis, Zog, garnered support in Serbia. What Albania needed most was foreign economic assistance, and Noli was unable to achieve either that or international recognition. Moreover, owing to the "revolutionary" nature of his government, he aroused suspicions outside Albania. All the neighboring powers were wary of him, and he was unable to secure financial support from the League of Nations, Italy, or anywhere else. He was at first persuaded to recognize Soviet Russia, then changed his mind. By that time, however, a Soviet delegation had already arrived, and despite its immediate removal, the damage was already done. Also, his failure to deliver on a promised general election only exacerbated the situation and alienated the United States in particular. Nevertheless, Noli remained an important figure in Albanian history, and his brief time in power was exploited by the communists, who saw in his seizure of power Albania's bourgeois-democratic revolution (such a revolution being considered in Marxist thought a necessary preliminary to a revolution of the proletariat). The communists also maintained that his subsequent ouster was part of a wider imperialist agenda.

Unable to impose a new order in Albania, and angering many of their supporters through Noli's planned land reform, the Noli coalition weakened, while Zog strengthened his forces. The majority of neighboring powers were hostile to the Noli experiment, and Zog gained the support of Serbia and refugees from General Wrangel's army (a "White" army that had fought in the Russian civil war to topple the Bolsheviks). Noli fled, and Zog was left a free hand to set up a new order in Albania. Zog, the son of a chieftain from the

Mat district in central Albania, was far better suited to rule in the milieu of Albanian politics. He became president in 1925 and later self-proclaimed king in 1928, and he was the central figure in interwar Albania. Having served as prime minister and minister of the interior in earlier governments, he appreciated the problems of governing Albania. He had lost sympathy for any kind of radical reform and set instead two precise and obtainable goals: the elimination of obstacles to the creation of a central authority in Albania and the maintenance of his own power. Unfortunately, although Zog's achievements were important, his devotion to the latter cause meant that he left the greatest problems that faced Albania largely untouched.

Like Noli, Zog was confronted with desperate economic conditions that required foreign support. Noli's experience had shown that the League of Nations was not viable, and Zog was reluctant to rely on those who had aided his return. He turned his back on the Serbs and opted for Italian support. Italy, with far better resources and less proximity to Albania, seemed a better option. As important, since the presence of large groups of Albanians outside Albania, above all in Kosovo, and the desire to integrate them into Albania—irredentism, in short—remained an important factor in Albanian politics, close relations with the Yugoslavs would alienate important supporters. Regardless, Zog's first year in power saw him return substantial favors to those who had helped him return to power. Zog's dependence on Mussolini's Italy was the single greatest byproduct of the era; although certain gains were made through Italian support, it laid the groundwork for the Italian invasion of 1939. Zog sought to limit Albanian dependence on Italy and many times attempted to escape Italian influence, but the overwhelming financial difficulties faced by the country, along with Western indifference over the fate of Albania, often tied his hands.

Despite the claims of communist historians, Zog was both a nationalist and a patriot. His fourteen years of power saw some significant gains, as the Italians certainly put more into Albania than they got out. It is true, however, that he refused to address the major problems that faced the country. Zog was far more concerned with the establishment of law and order in Albania than with reform, arguing that reform could only come after political, economic, and social stability had been achieved. In the long run, Zog pursued a dictatorial program that sought the maintenance of his own power and eliminated all forms of political opposition. The major problem in Albania was the need for land reform, since over 80 percent of the Albanian population was rural. Zog, owing to his dependence on conservative beys for support, was reluctant to undermine the existing feudal system. In 1930 he did announce a progressive land reorganization program that, had it been implemented, would have fundamentally altered Albania's land distribution. In the end, only a small portion of land was in fact affected.

Zog did manage to make certain improvements in education, transportation, and national stability. Zog was confronted with the same divisive factors as previous governments, but owing to his long tenure, he went further in eliminating these problems. As a Geg, he was able to use programs, largely subsidized by southerners, to slowly bring the previously ungovernable northerners into the fold. He introduced a penal code as well as a civil code, but by far his greatest single achievement was the creation of the first truly national consciousness—of sorts. In 1939 most Albanians began to identify themselves with a central authority in Tirana. This was no small feat when one considers the overwhelming number of factors that worked against national integration. Yet his failure to address the many social and economic problems, together with his obsession with his "kingdom," became fertile ground for the communists during World War II. In 1938 illiteracy was 80 percent, and life expectancy was a mere thirty-eight years. Improvements in national government were offset by drastically limited changes in the national economy.

The imposition of a monarchy, which took place in 1928, is an event worthy of further study. The conversion from republic to monarchy was no spur-of-the-minute decision on Zog's part. Throughout his presidency, he devoted considerable resources to the creation of his own personality cult in preparation for the change. His initials appeared on mountainsides, and in 1927 he had bestowed the title of Savior of the Nation upon himself. Proclaiming that he was responding to popular pressure and that the Albanian mentality was better suited to a monarchy, Zog orchestrated his own coronation. He argued that he had familial ties with Skanderbeg and adopted the helmet of Skanderbeg as his new symbol. In addition, he assumed the title of "Zog I, King of the Albanians," rather than King of Albania. This move, which angered Serbs considerably, with its implied claim to rule Albanians even in other countries, was designed as an attempt to ensure support in the north where irredentism (with its claims on territory outside state boundaries, based upon ethnic, historic, or linguistic factors) was more pronounced. However, aside from making Albania seem somewhat ridiculous, it is doubtful the monarchy had any other lasting effects. Zog set about to create an enlightened Western-style monarchy, but his devotion to outdated methods inherited from the Ottoman system had the greatest influence on his style of rule.

ALBANIAN RESISTANCE AND THE EMERGENCE OF COMMUNIST ALBANIA (1939–1944)

When the Italians invaded on 7 April 1939, Zog, his queen, Geraldine, and their two-day-old son, Leka, fled Albania. This flight did significant damage to his reputation, as he had originally claimed he would stay on to lead the resistance, and also left a dangerous vacuum in Albania. His departure, along with that of large segments of the interwar ruling elite, laid the foundations for a power struggle, which ultimately resulted in a communist takeover.

Desperate for foreign aid, Albania had increasingly become tied to Rome. This dependence gave the Italian leader Benito Mussolini privileges in Albania, including the right to train the country's military. When Zog tried to distance himself from Mussolini in the early 1930s, after Rome demanded that Tirana form a customs union with

Italy (which would have effectively given Mussolini control over much of Albania's economy), the Italians sent a fleet into Albanian waters as a reminder that Italy was not going to allow any independence of action. On 25 March 1939, Mussolini presented Zog with an ultimatum: he could either accept occupation (and the creation of a protectorate) or face invasion. Two weeks later, Italian troops invaded the country.

The Axis occupation of Albania, first Italian and then, after September 1943, German, witnessed the emergence of two key factions seeking the removal of the occupiers and the creation of a new Albania: the communists and the Balli Kombëtar, or National Front (BK). Communism had not been a major factor in interwar Albania, but it had made important gains prior to the Italian occupation, though the movement lacked organizational unity.

The Yugoslav communists emerged as a central force in the creation and subsidization of the Albanian communist movement. Two members of the Yugoslav Communist Party, Miladin Popović, who arrived in Albania in the summer of 1939, and Dušan Mugoša, who arrived in September 1941, played important roles in the formation of the Albanian movement. Though the Yugoslav role has often been exaggerated, owing to a dependence on Yugoslav sources, and in fact Tito's emissaries did not "create" Albanian communism or the Albanian Communist Party (which became the Albanian Party of Labor [APL] in 1948), it is true that their assistance during the war was vital. The Albanian Communist Party's first leader was Enver Hoxha, a southerner from Gjirokastër born in 1908. Having studied in France in the 1930s and served the Albanian consul in Brussels, Hoxha had a certain cosmopolitism, and his experiences abroad had exposed him to the main currents of Marxism in Western Europe. An ardent nationalist who was deeply affected by Albania's historical experiences, as well as an able orator, he was a logical choice as leader of the new party.

The members of the Communist Party in September 1942 formed the National Liberation Movement (NLM) (which later became the National Liberation Front [NLF] in May 1944). The organization was at first made up of a broad coalition of nationalists and communists alike. Seeking to avoid being characterized as a communist front, the NLM based its program rather on nationalist appeals and a commitment to liberal democracy. It drew considerable support from the country's youth and the mass of poverty-stricken peasants, who had seen only marginal improvements in their quality of life under Zog. The Balli Kombëtar

Enver Hoxha addresses delegates of the 4th Congress of the Albanian Trade Union in 1956. (Library of Congress)

(BK), as the national front was called, was founded in 1942, with a program based on calls for the creation of an ethnic Albania and a modern state along Western democratic lines. During the early years of resistance to the occupiers, the NLM and BK were able to coexist.

The Axis incorporation of Kosovo in 1941 (after the occupation of Yugoslavia) had done much to rekindle interest in the question of Kosovo (a territory important to both the Serbs and Albanians), yet at the same time it served to undermine joint resistance efforts. Regardless, the aim of creating an ethnic Albania, one that would include Kosovo, figured prominently in the programs of both parties, but cooperation between the two groups always remained tenuous at best. The NLM became concerned with the BK's growing strength and sought to undermine its influence, first through cooptation, and then through fratricidal conflict.

The key attempt at coordination took place at a meeting in the Albanian town of Mukja in August 1943. The Mukja accord continues to attract attention, and with greater access to party archives, many questions about this subject will finally be answered. What is known is that representatives of both the BK and the NLM met and hammered out a plan for cooperation in the liberation struggle, forming the Committee for the Salvation of Albania. Most important, however, was the agreement that both groups would strive for the creation of an ethnic Albania. Hoxha rejected the accord completely. In the first place, given the Serb attachment to Kosovo, the agreement on Kosovo aroused deep concerns within the Yugoslav Communist Party, and the Yugoslavs no doubt put considerable pressure on Hoxha to reject the accord.

Aside from Yugoslav pressure, it is doubtful that Hoxha envisioned full cooperation with the BK on an equal footing. Also, since Kosovars were both Gegs and anticommunists, Hoxha did not attach much significance to the area of Kosovo as a wartime issue. Instead he felt it better to leave the question of Kosovo until after the war, and documents suggest that he considered Kosovo a Yugoslav problem, not an Albanian one. The repudiation of the Mukja accord, however, ensured that the liberation struggle would also become a civil war.

After the collapse of Mukja, Abaz Kupi, a leading patriot, formed the Legality Organization, which was the only organization in wartime Albania that called for the return of King Zog. The movement had little following, however, owing in part to Zog's position in his homeland, coupled with the fact that so many of his supporters had been forced to flee. The legality of Zog's position on the throne thus remained forever on the fringe of the struggle for Albania's liberation and never received any substantive support from the Allied Powers. The fact that Zog was unable to achieve recognition in exile, along with the disorganization of the BK, thus became important factors in the communist victory.

By late 1943, the rupture between NLM and BK was complete. After the Germans replaced the Italians as the principal occupier of the country, the Germans allowed Albania a measure of self-government; this concession bought off some members of the BK, who viewed the Germans as a more benign force that might even provide assistance in advancing their claims to Kosovo.

As elsewhere in the Balkans, since the communists emerged as the most effective force against the fascists, they were accorded considerable aid from both Britain and the United States. However, the key factor in ensuring the success of the Albanian communists was the incompetence and disorganization of their opponents. Moreover, since Zog had left the peasantry of the population largely untouched, communist calls for social justice and land reform found a very receptive audience. By late November 1944, a communist-dominated provisional government was installed in Tirana. Without Soviet assistance, the Albanian communists had assured victory in their homeland even before the end of the war. This fact was to be of considerable importance to the new regime, whose historical experiences played a large role in the shaping of policy in the years that followed.

COMMUNIST ALBANIA, 1944–1991

Toward the end of November 1944, the last of the German forces left Albania. The NLF was transformed into the Democratic Front (DF), which presented a slate of candidates for elections in 1945. After receiving over 90 percent of the votes, the DF proclaimed Albania a socialist state, and the government's first two years focused on the elimination of potential enemies to the party's program of communization. Despite some early difficulties in consolidating his control over the Albanian communist movement, this entire period was under the domination of Enver Hoxha and shaped by his vision.

The communist era in Albania was in many ways marked and defined by the country's position within the framework of the international communist movement. Owing to tremendous economic backwardness, Hoxha, like his predecessors, sought foreign economic support to reshape Albania. From 1944 to 1948, Albania, owing to its wartime relationship, fell under complete Yugoslav domination. After the Tito-Stalin split in 1948, Hoxha maneuvered his country into the Soviet orbit, where it remained until 1961, when, taking advantage of the Sino-Soviet split, Hoxha made Albania a Chinese satellite. After breaking with the Chinese in 1978, Albania embarked on a peculiar form of self-reliance that lasted until 1990. Hoxha emerged as a shrewd and capable manipulator of international communism, which allowed him not only to preserve his own brand of Marxism-Leninism-Stalinism, but also to maintain his own power.

During the Yugoslav period, Hoxha experienced a substantial attack on his leadership from the number-two man in the party, Koci Xoxe, a tinsmith from the south who was minister of the interior in Albania's first communist government. Xoxe, a proletarian, as opposed to the bourgeois intellectual Hoxha, was favored by the Yugoslavs primarily because of his pro-Belgrade stance. The Yugoslav communist leader, Tito, dreaming of a Balkan federation and a solution to the Kosovo problem, obviously hoped to integrate Albania into Yugoslavia as the seventh republic; accordingly, he supported Xoxe. A moderate faction, which included several key communists such as Sejfulla Maleshova, sought to chart an independent course in foreign affairs and maintain strong ties with both the communist and Western world. Hoxha, true to form, maintained a cautious middle course, but he was eventually forced, at least for the moment, to accept a greater Yugoslav presence. Nevertheless, Hoxha remained concerned that his own position was by no means secure within the Yugoslav framework. Only Tito's break with Stalin in 1948 saved Hoxha, and Albanian independence. Hoxha now carefully maneuvered himself into the Soviet camp and initiated harsh polemics against the Yugoslavs.

The Yugoslavs were now portrayed in official pronouncements as the main threat to Albanian sovereignty, an excellent propaganda device in the hands of a national communist like Hoxha. The Soviets, possessing far greater economic resources than the Yugoslavs, were better able to serve as providers of aid to Albania; Hoxha now emerged as one of Stalin's greatest admirers. Hoxha set about laying the foundations of Stalinism in Albania and eliminating the factors that posed a threat to national unification. The most important of these were the regional variation between Gegs and Tosks and religious differences; in both cases, it was clear that the regime could not afford the luxury of competing loyalties.

The honeymoon with the Soviets, while extremely beneficial on an economic and military level, was only useful as long as the Soviets maintained their commitment to Stalinism and pursued an anti-Tito policy. With Stalin's death in 1953, the subsequent de-Stalinization campaign, and, most importantly, Khrushchev's rapprochement with Tito, Hoxha began to seriously doubt the viability of the alliance.

Since Hoxha's program aimed at creating a siege mentality that would further his own interests by identifying the national cause with his ideological program, hostile relations with the Yugoslavs were almost a prerequisite and were an important tool in his nationalistic program. Also, since both his and the regime's survival were dependent on Stalinism, Hoxha could not afford notions of reform. In the early 1950s, Hoxha for the moment accepted Khrushchev's call for a collective leadership, and long-time comrade Mehmet Shehu became prime minister in 1954 and allowed some minor reforms. Hoxha was, however, unwilling to follow the Soviet example blindly. Again, rifts in the communist bloc came to his rescue, and Hoxha strengthened his ties with the more doctrinaire Chinese throughout the 1950s and early 1960s. Polemics between the Soviets and Albanians assumed almost comical proportions, as Tirana turned away from Moscow and gradually became a Chinese satellite. That the Soviets were now just one more external enemy to be feared only added credence to Hoxha's program, particularly following the events in Poland and Hungary in 1956, when the Soviets crushed all attempts at independence of action in its client states. The Chinese, although not as wealthy as the Soviets, could serve as a viable ally for the Albanians, especially since they were far enough away not to pose a threat. Moreover, both countries pursued similar domestic policies.

Certain features of the alliance between Tirana and Beijing are important to note. In the first place, it is doubtful that Hoxha thought of it as a long-term relationship. Owing to his commitment to Stalinism and his fears of external influence, Hoxha sought a means to avoid foreign entanglements. Barring the success of world revolution, Hoxha was determined to go it alone. On the other hand, the notion that Albania wanted to completely isolate itself is false. What Hoxha sought was relations with others on his own terms, and the relative international insignificance of Albania allowed him to pursue a maverick policy in foreign affairs. After the break with the Soviets, the main thread of Albanian foreign policy remained the dual adversary doctrine, which held that both the United States and the Soviet Union were evil superpowers; thus Hoxha condemned relations with either of them.

The period of Chinese dependence saw Hoxha attempt to impose a more complete control on the nation, to the extent of imposing his own version of the Chinese Cultural Revolution. The Albanian version aimed at the elimination of obstacles to national unity and modernizaton, which entailed a sharp attack on religious institutions and regional differences embodied in the Gegs and Tosks. Responding to "popular appeals," the regime also proclaimed Albania the world's first "atheist state."

Like the Soviet alliance, the Chinese alliance only lasted as long as China's commitment to Stalinism was maintained. The death of Mao, the fall of the Gang of Four (the ideological successors to Mao), and China's growing rapprochement with the United States were all significant in the deterioration of the alliance. Albania, for the first time in its independent history, found itself alone, without a benefactor or patron, a factor that had seemed to be almost a prerequisite to Albanian independence. Self-reliance, embodied in the 1976 constitution, now marked the fourth and final phase in Albanian communism. As became clear during the postcommunist transition, self-reliance devastated the country. By cutting off access to needed foreign technology, Albania allowed the gap to widen between itself and the rest of the world.

Ever since independence, the Albanian state had required extensive foreign support to survive. This need was a central feature of both the interwar and communist periods. As noted, Zog's dependence on Italy was more a product of the economic backwardness of the country than anything else. Had Zog been able to finance programs without dependence, no doubt he would have pursued that course. Yet with the economic collapse in 1929, and the overall global economic climate, dependence was almost unavoidable. In terms of economic development, the Ottoman Empire had left few traces of any progress, so that when Albania embarked on an independent course in the early twentieth century, much of the country remained in the eighteenth century in terms of development and outlook. That Albania remains one of the poorest countries in Europe is a direct outcome of that legacy, as well as of some poorly thought-out economic policies in the communist period.

Enver Hoxha was determined to uproot economic backwardness and create a modernized agricultural and industrial state. In Marxism-Leninism-Stalinism, Hoxha identified a viable program for modernization, yet the appeal of power and control was just as important in his attitude toward the Soviet model. He recognized early that modernization would not be possible without Stalinism and extensive foreign support. Yet he always sought a controlled dependence, since he always perceived interference in Albania's internal affairs as an attack on his rule. Foreign support was crucial to the transformation that Albania underwent under communist rule. Agriculture was fully collectivized, yet never achieved substantial returns. Massive improvements in the infrastructure served to better integrate the country, and there were great leaps forward in education and culture. However, the cost of these gains was extremely high.

The Albanian Communist Party inherited what could be described as a ready-made siege mentality in 1944, a reservoir of nationalism, of sorts, which the regime was able to draw upon in pursuit of its program. The Albanian communists were able to maintain their hold on power through a manipulation of that legacy, coupled with careful exploitation of events during the communist period. Internal and external crises were always used to further solidify the party's control over the country. In the search for legitimacy, which was crucial for Eastern European communist regimes, nationalism was indispensable. Nowhere was this more true than in Albania. The break with Yugoslavia had been based on a realistic fear of absorption, and the successive breaks with the USSR and China were predicated on the need to maintain the primacy of the Albanian Party of Labor (APL) and, more importantly, Hoxha's own position. Events outside Albania helped to drive home the idea that Albania's very survival was at stake. Shifting alliances within the communist bloc were one instrument in fostering a siege mentality, and British and U.S. support of incursions into Albania between 1949 and 1953, designed to overthrow the Hoxha government, further strengthened Hoxha's cause.

The Soviet invasion of Czechoslovakia in 1968, which resulted in Albania's formal withdrawal from the Warsaw Pact, brought notions of siege to new heights. Hoxha suggested that Soviet intervention was imminent, and aside from beginning a massive program that eventually covered much of Albania with military bunkers, he presided over a process that saw Albanian society becoming increasingly militarized at all levels. Propaganda drove home, with a huge measure of success, the idea that Albania was encircled, helping the Party to explain the massive economic problems that were all too apparent. Not only were the bunkers extremely expensive, they absorbed important agricultural land. Also important to the siege mentality that was pervasive in Albania was the condition of the large number of Albanians living outside the state's borders, especially under the repressive policies of the Yugoslav authorities in Kosovo. Doubtless Albanians knew they were much poorer than the rest of Europe, but the official line, probably embraced by much of the population, was that it was better to be poor and independent.

Internally, Hoxha withstood several challenges to his own leadership, the most serious of which was from Xoxe. In the 1950s, because of changes in the USSR following the death of Stalin, some Party members, encouraged by Moscow, questioned Hoxha's adherence to dogmatic Stalinism and sought a slowdown of the economic program. They were subsequently purged. The 1970s witnessed a considerable crackdown on military and cultural elites. Periodic purges, usually coinciding with alliance shifts, were used to perpetuate the myth of internal enemies, solidifying Hoxha's own position and quieting calls for reform, and they served the wider program of a country under siege. The most ridiculous of the events associated with these was the "suicide" of Hoxha's heir apparent, Prime Minister Mehmet Shehu, in 1981, and the subsequent "revelation" that he had been a foreign agent serving multiple governments.

The main beneficiary of Shehu's demise was Ramiz Alia, who became Hoxha's designated successor. Alia had impeccable credentials and had served Hoxha well in the preceding years. Born in the northern city of Shköder in 1925, he became a party member in 1943 and was made a full member of the politburo in 1961. Alia had served as minister of education from 1955 to 1958, when he assumed responsibility for ideology and culture in the Central Committee. Although APL policy had been cloaked in extreme nationalism and strong communist ideology, both were used merely to perpetuate APL control over the country. Stalin-

Enver Hoxha's handpicked successor, Ramiz Alia. (Setboun/Corbis)

ism, more than anything else, was the key to Hoxha's survival, and this mentality was passed on to Ramiz Alia.

With Hoxha's death in April 1985, the direction of the new regime remained unclear. Although there was little doubt that the APL had made important gains in improving the lot of the average Albanian, the dogmatic adherence to Stalinism had in the long run created an almost impossible situation, and Alia's room for manuever was limited. Alia was no doubt more pragmatic than his predecessor, and many suggested that change was in the air. Nevertheless, despite some minor changes, Alia remained committed to Hoxha's legacy. He owed his position to hardliners, who still exercised considerable influence on affairs, and radical change was out of the question until external events forced them.

TRANSITION ALBANIA, 1991–1997

On 22 March 1992, the Albanian population went to the polls in what was their second free election since 1923. In many ways, the second election was the true test for the Albanian population; although the first election (31 March 1991) had been declared "free" by the international monitoring bodies overseeing the balloting, there was still a dominant element of fear in the country, and the rural population remained reluctant to make a hasty and complete break with the past. The result was a substantial victory for the ruling Albanian Party of Labor. In the 1992 referendum, however, an overwhelming majority cast ballots for the fifteen-month-old Democratic Party of Albania (DP), while the renamed Albanian Party of Labor (APL), the Socialist Party of Albania (SP), suffered correspondingly massive losses.

The chaotic state of affairs in Albania's first transitional year of 1992 contributed to the Democrats' success, as the country slid into crisis and was reduced to complete dependence on foreign aid. It was clear that the majority of Albanian citizens felt that Albania could not restore itself without foreign aid and that the DP would be better able to secure that aid.

Albania had begun its transitional phase well after the rest of the former communist states. The Albanian system not only survived longer, but it also survived with most of its Stalinist trappings still in place. Complicating the process, due to the tightness of control exercised over the population, Albania had virtually no experience with indigenous reform movements. The system's tenacity stemmed from several factors, with nationalism assuming prime importance. In essence, the Party was in many ways successful in instilling the idea that Albania's survival was dependent on the Party alone.

During the tumultuous months of 1989, Albania appeared to stand apart from the fundamental changes occurring in the neighboring countries of the Soviet bloc. Although Alia was considerably more moderate than his predecessor, he refused to approve the needed revisions. Hoxha's personality cult had reached ridiculous proportions and Alia continued to pay homage to it whenever possible. Even during 1990, when the bloc was crumbling all around them, no substantive reevaluation of Hoxha's legacy took

place. The Albanian leadership maintained their commitment to the country's peculiar form of Marxism-Leninism-Stalinism, denouncing both the Soviet leader Mikhail Gorbachev's program of reforms (glasnost [openness] and perestroika [restructuring]) and the changes in Eastern Europe that involved the undermining of communist regimes and the call for democratization. But Alia inherited a veritable time bomb. The radical reforms so needed to regenerate the country were simply not a possibility, had Alia even wished to initiate them.

Yet even isolated Albania could not ignore the changes around it. Several events served to contribute to a gradual change in the Albanian political climate. Certainly the events in Romania and the liquidation of Nicolae and Elena Ceauşescu, the most Stalinist leaders in the Soviet bloc, in December of 1989 was a major factor in prompting this reorientation. Similarities between the two regimes were many, and after the events unfolded in Romania, Alia realized that changes were mandatory if the regime was to survive. Adding to that, Albanians were no longer living in complete isolation, and information from abroad was slowly making its way into the minds of the population.

There were some significant changes in 1990, as Alia began to tinker with the ailing economy. Alia sought to orchestrate a top-down revolution, hoping to maintain the primacy of the Party. Early 1990 witnessed the introduction of a program that by Albanian standards was quite radical, calling for greater decentralization of the economy and for greater democracy in political and social institutions. Also, a decision was made that allowed foreign investment. These changes were important, but they were too small and certainly too late. Alia's actions only served to unleash the forces that eventually destroyed the old order. By far the most important in the toppling of the regime were students angry with conditions at the University of Tirana, and their actions provided the spark to what was already a volatile situation. In an attempt to appease the students, Alia sought to meet some of their demands, but he maintained his commitment to controlled change. Eventually bowing to pressure from student demonstrations in early December 1990, Alia finally allowed for the creation of a multiparty system.

The student demonstrations were a reaction to the many crises facing the country. The defection of leading Albanian novelist Ismail Kadare at the end of October was also a major contributory factor in the establishment of a multiparty system. The fact that Kadare was giving up hope for change in Albania appeared to be the final straw for much of the population. With the foundation laid for a multiparty system and the emergence of the Democratic Party under the leadership of two University of Tirana professors, Sali Berisha, a cardiologist, and the economist Gramoz Pashko, Albania formally entered its political and economic transition. Albania's peculiar past program, together with a political and economic backwardness far exceeding that of any other former communist bloc state, served to ensure that its transition would be the most difficult.

The road toward the first multiparty elections was highly precarious, and Albania appeared poised on the brink of

Sali Berisha

Dr. Sali Berisha was born in Tropoje, in Albania's northeast, in 1944. Berisha, a prominent cardiologist, was Albania's first noncommunist president, and cofounder of the Democratic Party, which gained power in elections in 1992. Berisha was a key figure in the transformation of a number of student protests in 1990 into a nationwide anticommunist protest. As president, many of his reforms were unsuccessful, and he was often accused of overextending his power and allowing Albania to return to authoritarian rule. He lost the presidency in 1997, when the Albanian state almost totally collapsed due to the downfall of dubious pyramid schemes and the international community intervened to force fresh elections. Since 1997, despite multiple defeats in local and national elections, Berisha has remained the controversial and combative head of the opposition Democratic Party.

Albania's first year in transition was almost completely wasted, and little was accomplished. A general strike ensued, supposedly an apolitical demonstration, but obviously engineered by the DP; this strike brought the reformist APL government of Fatos Nano down in June. It was followed by the creation of a Romanian-like National Stability government composed of a coalition of the major parties.

The coalition government was doomed from the start. Ridden by conflict, it spent most of its time engaged in polemics while the country slid deeper and deeper into crisis. Although all were in agreement that the old system had to be destroyed, no one had any real ideas on where to go from there. The young DP had only a grab bag of anti-communist slogans, while the APL scrambled to come to grips with its past, eliminate hardliners, and create new programs.

At the June Congress of the APL, in addition to name and leadership changes, the party attempted to redress the past. Open criticism of both Hoxha and Alia occurred, though the criticism of Hoxha was somewhat muted. Several key members, mostly hardliners, were removed from their posts, and a younger, more reform-minded leadership took over the newly formed Socialist Party of Albania (SP). The DP, despite growing disagreements in leadership over the timing of fresh elections and the party's role in the stability government, left the government in December 1991, and a caretaker government of specialists was created to see

civil war as society became deeply polarized between supporters of the old and new orders. Alia, to his credit, refused to condone violence as a means of upholding the system; he emerged as a somewhat able caretaker of the first phase and refused to be drawn into the conflict. That Albania avoided the violence that plagued Romania is a credit to Alia, and given the greater chances for a political explosion, Albania's first few steps must be seen as relatively successful.

As already noted, Albania's first multiparty elections saw an overwhelming victory for the APL. With a 98 percent voter turnout, the APL took 169 seats of the 250-seat legislature. The DP took 75 seats, all in urban centers, and even managed to defeat Alia in his Tirana district. (He was nonetheless elected president by the APL-dominated parliament on 2 May, with 172 votes. In keeping with the draft constitution, which separated party and state posts, he resigned as APL general secretary and was replaced by Fatos Nano at the June Congress.) The Greek minority party, Omonia, won 5 seats and the Albanian War Veterans Party took 1 seat.

Despite the size of the majority vote, the election led to a widespread polarization in the country, primarily between rural and urban voters. In addition to sweeping rural voters, the APL fared better in the Tosk-inhabited south, while they did correspondingly poorly in the northern areas surrounding the Catholic center of Shkodër. What seemed possible after the first election was renewed polarization between northern Gegs and the southern Tosks, a situation that would have further hampered Albania's peaceful transition. The Democrats rejected outright the March 1991 results and were determined to call fresh elections; they therefore refused to cooperate with the elected APL government, a shortsighted policy that only served to worsen Albania's predicament.

Albanian prime minister Fatos Nano speaks at a parliamentary session during which parliament approved a reshuffle of his government after months of political turmoil, 29 December 2003 in Tirana. (AFP/Getty Images)

the country through until new elections were held. Reduced to total dependence on foreign aid for its very survival, the country sought a new mandate.

The election campaign leading up to the March 1992 vote revealed that a deep polarization of the country still remained possible. Throughout the fall and winter of 1991, both major parties appeared to be running almost neck and neck in Albanian political polls, and although a democratic victory was more than likely, it appeared that their majority would be slight, thus throwing the country into another year of near paralysis. All the major parties were committed to market and democratic reforms, and at first glance the programs of all parties appeared almost identical.

The result was a polemical campaign, as the main opposition parties (the DP, the Social Democrats, and the Republican Party) sought to exploit the link between the Socialists and their communist past. Socialist Party leader Fatos Nano was identified whenever possible with former dictator Enver Hoxha and past Party of Labor policies. This was a somewhat hypocritical tactic, given the depth of the ties between all the opposition leaders and the former regime. In fact, since the country had never really possessed an indigenous reform movement of any kind, very few of Albania's new politicians were untainted. The opposition leadership consisted, for the most part, of former APL members.

As the experiences in the rest of Eastern Europe have shown, Albania was confronted with two options: a Polish style "shock therapy," which would mean that reforms would take place immediately despite the hardships, or a more gradual approach toward the creation of a free-market system. The DP argued for a quick transition, facilitated by an expected mass infusion of foreign aid and investment. Sali Berisha argued that, given the nature of Albania's predicament, only speedy change could bring the shattered economy out of the depths of crisis. The Socialists, on the other hand, pointed to the potential for polarization and unemployment associated with rapid change.

In the end, however, the single most important factor in deciding Albania's fate was the nature of foreign aid and investment. Since every party looked westward and sought integration with Europe, foreign investment, and a market economy, the election was essentially a struggle for outside aid. This struggle assumed almost comical proportions, with each party trying to enlist international figures who supported their victory. The opposition portrayed the Socialists as unable to secure Western credit due to their past and argued that a socialist victory would ensure the continuation of Albania's poverty and isolation. All parties declared that they could ensure the arrival of a European standard of living. The second election witnessed a complete reversal of 1991's results and boded well for Albania's transition.

In the reduced 140-seat assembly (100 decided by first-past-the-post and 40 by proportional representation), the DP secured 92 seats and the Socialists 38. The Social Democrats, the Human Rights Union, and the Republican Party won seven, two, and one seats respectively. With a turnout of some 90 percent, the DP received some 62 percent of the popular vote to the Socialists' 26 percent. What is most impressive is that the apparent polarization, especially the Geg-Tosk division of the last election, had been eliminated. The DP victory cut across almost all ethnic, religious, and tribal divisions and succeeded in areas that were traditionally reserved for communists.

Due to grandiose promises during the election campaign, optimism ran high. Sali Berisha, elected by the assembly as the new president, faced an extremely difficult battle. Problems with the economy assumed primary significance, as the new government set out to eliminate the remnants of almost five decades of communist rule. The country's new prime minister, Alexandër Meksi, reiterated his government's commitment to radical reforms to transform the economy.

Such a break from the past, while encouraging, was dependent upon numerous factors—economic, political, and even geographic—that soon became overwhelming, as evidenced by the events in Kosovo in the late 1990s. The Serbian assault on the ethnic Albanian population in Kosovo suddenly made the world aware of the existence of the new Albania and brought its problems into sharper focus.

POLITICAL DEVELOPMENTS

When Soviet leader Nikita Khrushchev opened the door to the Soviet bloc's repudiation of Stalinism in 1956, the Albanian communist leader Enver Hoxha, virtually alone among his Eastern European counterparts, refused to follow suit, declaring himself against revisionism and proclaiming Albania to be the last remaining bastion of Stalinist orthodoxy. Hoxha's rule can be characterized as Stalinist in nature: all decision making was centralized, with Hoxha having the ultimate say; no political initiative from outside the party was tolerated, and dissent within the party was dealt with through purges. Compliance from the general population was assured through terror, via the Sigurimi (the Albanian secret service), and through a system of political prisons. Throughout his rule, Hoxha's personality cult rivaled in its scope and intensity that of Stalin in the Soviet Union of the 1930s, 1940s, and 1950s.

Hoxha intended to transform Albanian society, and his main initiative in this direction was undertaken shortly after the rift with the USSR. He launched the Albanian Cultural Revolution in February 1966. Inspired by its Chinese counterpart, the Albanian Cultural Revolution was more tightly controlled and did not affect the upper echelons of party and governmental activity. Its primary social objectives were to improve the status of women, narrow salary differentials between workers, complete the collectivization of agriculture, and eliminate the practice of religion. This cultural revolution can be viewed as an attempt to create a unified national Albanian identity, as it worked against factors that divided Albanians, such as religion and regional identities like Geg and Tosk. In 1970, convinced that much progress had been made in entrenching socialist values in Albanian society, and aware that Albanians were feeling the strain of living under the pressure of the recent initiatives, Hoxha allowed a relaxation of the political climate, fostering a renewed vigor in artistic expression and the emergence of relatively open debate on such issues as defense and economic policy. But in 1973, dismayed by the flouting of socialist realism in the arts, the Albanians' new taste for Western fashions and music, and the alarming rise in the number of high-school dropouts, Hoxha decided matters had gone too far and reversed his position on the thaw, cracking down on liberal-minded intellectuals and the cultural elite.

When Hoxha died in April 1985, Albania's political life was firmly under the control of an elite, and the participation of ordinary Albanians was limited to demonstrating their support for the Party. Hoxha's handpicked successor and loyal friend, Ramiz Alia, succeeded him without incident. Still, Albanians were becoming more and more disenchanted with the regime, chiefly because the ailing economy was no longer able to ensure their daily subsistence. Self-reliance had only served to impoverish the majority of Albanians. Alia recognized this, and tried to implement some modest economic reforms starting in 1985, largely without result. By 1989, Alia had more important problems on his hands: the fall of the Berlin Wall had triggered popular movements throughout Eastern Europe. One factor that probably had a huge impact on events in Albania was the growing democratization of political life in Kosovo, which came ahead of political changes in Albania. As well, the demise of the Ceauşescu regime, which

shared certain characteristics with Albania in its strict party control, Stalinist core, and cult of personality, had made a particularly strong impression on Albanian public opinion; the Albanian communist elite feared that Albanians would take their cue and mobilize in similar fashion. To counter that risk, Alia announced more thoroughgoing economic reforms and began to dismantle some aspects of the communist apparatus as a gesture of goodwill. Among his acts were the reinstatement of the Ministry of Justice, which had been abolished in the mid-1960s, an easing of penalties for a certain number of crimes, a lifting of the ban on practicing religion, a relaxation of laws dealing with freedom of movement, the de-politicizing of university admissions, and a revision of instructional material in schools.

These measures notwithstanding, Alia was not willing to make political concessions that would compromise the leading role of the Communist Party, such as allowing political pluralism. He began to lose control of the situation in July 1990, when 6,000 Albanians tried to flee the country by taking refuge in the foreign embassies of Tirana. Initially condemning the refugees as traitors and insisting that the embassies return them to Albanian custody, Alia relented a few days later and allowed the refugees to emigrate. The defection of popular writer and intellectual Ismail Kadare to France the following October was a further blow to the regime, as was the continued worsening of the economy.

Democratic Party rally in Tirana's Skanderbeg Square. (Courtesy of Robert Austin)

The weakness of Alia's position became clear at the following APL Central Committee meeting and People's Assembly gathering, when he finally admitted the possibility of political pluralism. Nonetheless, his decision to let representatives of state-recognized organizations run for office in the People's Assembly while preserving the leading role of the Party fell short of establishing a genuine multiparty system.

1990–1992: BEGINNINGS OF TRANSITION

Student demonstrations at the University of Tirana "Enver Hoxha" on 8 December 1990 proved decisive in shifting the balance of power. The protest was at first modest, focusing on students' miserable living conditions; when the police attempted to end the demonstration, the students responded by calling for political pluralism. Hoping to avoid further unrest, Alia agreed to their demands on 11 December. A new draft constitution, which guaranteed civil rights and recognized private property, was presented for discussion on 30 December. The end of 1990 also witnessed an increasing lawlessness in the country, as people stopped showing up for work, city streets became host to noisy and sometimes violent demonstrations, and state property was looted and vandalized.

Following the legalization of independent political parties, five parties registered to take part in the March 1991 elections: the Democratic Party, the Republican Party, the Ecology Party, the Agrarian Party, and Omonia, which claimed to represent the interest of ethnic Greeks. The Democratic Party (DP) was the most significant of these parties, claiming some 60,000 members. The DP platform had as its central focus an aggressive transformation of the economy into a market economy and the establishment of a pluralist society. Furthermore, the DP expressed a desire to promote the rights of Albanians in Kosovo and to work toward unity with Kosovo. The APL, for its part, advocated a more gradualist approach to economic transition, while also affirming its commitment to a pluralist society. The period leading up to the elections witnessed an increase in unrest, prompting Alia to declare a state of emergency and appoint a nine-person presidential council to help him rule the country. Albanians sought to flee the country in ever growing numbers; some 10,000 sought refuge in Greece alone.

Taking advantage of its privileged position and the resources at its disposal, the APL conducted an effective campaign, and was able to limit the amount of exposure for the DP, particularly in the countryside. The APL won 56.2 percent of the vote and obtained 169 out of 250 seats in parliament, and the DP won 38.7 percent and 75 seats. These results highlighted the dominance of these two parties, and indeed they have dominated Albanian politics ever since.

None of the opposition parties was willing to form a coalition with the APL, but it was clear that the APL government, headed by Fatos Nano, would be unable to govern without their support. Faced with pervasive unrest, Alia acquiesced in the creation of a multiparty Government of National Stability comprising twelve APL members, seven DP representatives, and five members from the other parties, signaling the end of one-party rule in Albania. Elections were also scheduled for June of 1992.

The new government faced important challenges in stabilizing the foundering economy and restoring law and order. It took measures to democratize the country, replacing the hated secret police, the Sigurimi, with the National Information Service and depoliticizing the military. The APL also made attempts to revitalize its image, changing its name to Socialist Party (SP) in June 1991 and purging its leadership of hardliners. Despite the SP's efforts to satisfy the demands of its partners, DP leader Sali Berisha became increasingly unwilling to share the spotlight with the SP. On 4 December 1991, he called for the resignation of the DP members of cabinet. In response, Alia appointed a caretaker cabinet and scheduled early elections for March.

According to the new election law, 100 of the 140 seats in the parliament were to be decided by majority vote, and the remaining by proportional representation. The law also banned parties representing ethnic groups, prompting the demise of Omonia. That party was soon replaced by the Human Rights Party, which does not claim to serve an ethnic group (although in practice it represents the interests of ethnic Greeks). The DP was much better equipped to conduct an election campaign than it had been its first time out, in part because of substantial financial support from the Albanian diaspora and international donors. The party based much of its campaign on the promise of attracting foreign aid and of obtaining an increase in immigration quotas for Albanians in European Community countries, highlighting the dire situation in Albania. The voter turnout was high (90.5 percent), and Albanian voters overwhelmingly chose the DP, which got 62.1 percent of the vote and 90 seats. This time the DP obtained strong support all over the country, from both rural and urban constituents. The SP got 25.7 percent of the vote, and 38 seats.

THE ERA OF DEMOCRATIC PARTY HEGEMONY, 1992–1997

In the face of popular rejection of the SP, Alia chose to resign, and Berisha was elected to replace him on 9 April 1992. Alexandër Meksi was appointed prime minister shortly thereafter. The government focused its efforts on implementing a shock-therapy economic reform program and on reestablishing law and order. Victims of persecution under the communists also obtained a significant voice within the DP. The DP did not fare as well in the local elections that were held in July 1992; it obtained only 43.3 percent of the popular vote, while the SP received 40.9 percent. This was probably due to the low turnout among DP supporters. The SP gained a significant voice in local politics and carried over half of mayoral contests. The strong showing of the SP at the local level contributed to growing tensions between the central and local governments.

The disappointing result of the local elections also accentuated the growing dissatisfaction of a number of DP members concerning the direction taken by their party. The growing influence of victims of communism within the party, a perceived ideological drift to the right, and Berisha's domineering leadership were among their grievances. For voicing their concerns, seven prominent members of the

Fatos Nano, Prime Minister of Albania (2004)

Fatos Nano was born in Tirana in 1952. He graduated from the University of Tirana with a degree in political economy and later, in 1989, received a Ph.D. in economics. In 1990 he was the general secretary of the Council of Ministers. He first became prime minister in 1991 (serving both before and after the first elections, in 1991), when Albania began the process of market liberalization and prepared for the country's first multiparty elections. He was later forced to resign his post amid popular protests and strikes. In July 2001 his party, the Communist Party of Labor, changed its name to the Socialist Party.

After losing elections to the Democratic Party in March 1992, Nano led the opposition. In 1994 Nano was found guilty of the misuse of state funds. The trial was highly politicized by the governing Democratic Party. His prison term ended in 1997 when massive civil unrest emptied the country's prisons in the wake of the collapse of the pyramid schemes that cost the Albanian citizens untold sums. He subsequently received a presidential pardon and reentered political life, being again appointed as prime minister. He resigned again following the death of a popular opposition leader, and civil unrest forced him to flee to neighboring Macedonia. After the 2001 parliamentary elections, Nano served as head of the Foreign Affairs Commission.

In 1999 Nano resigned as leader of the Socialist Party, only to be reinstated seven months later. He won the leadership against the then prime minister Pandeli Majko, whom he later voted out, along with Ilir Meta. On 25 July 2002, President Alfred Moisiu appointed Nano as prime minister for the fourth time. In 2003, he was again elected as chairman of the Socialist Party at its congress in December, winning a substantial majority of delegates.

Fatos Nano's political career has made a remarkable comeback over the past decade, but his democratic credentials and leadership abilities are questionable. Before entering politics he worked for the Institute of Marxist-Leninist Studies, constantly opposing political pluralism and the move toward a market economy until the last moments of communist rule. As chairman of the Socialist Party in 1991 he led with an iron hand, often sidetracking reforms. His leadership has led to turmoil and divisions, as Nano has fought successive challenges from younger party members such as former prime minister Ilir Meta.

DP were either expelled or resigned from the party. They later formed the core of the Democratic Alliance Party, under the leadership of Neritan Ceka and Gramoz Pashko. There were also those for whom the DP was not far right enough; their defection resulted in the creation of the Democratic Party of the Right. Overall, however, the DP continued to enjoy the support of the majority of Albanians.

By the end of the first DP term in the mid-1990s, Albania's infant democracy still faced important challenges, some of them coming from the DP itself. The country still had not adopted a constitution, relying instead on the provisional one approved by the first elected government in 1991. Berisha tried, unsuccessfully, to push through parliament a constitution that vested considerable power in the presidency, resorting finally to calling a national referendum to approve the constitution. The result of the November 1994 ballot was negative; with 84.3 percent of the population voting, only 41.7 percent of voters approved the constitution, while 53.9 percent rejected it. Berisha's authoritarian tendencies became more pronounced as his term advanced. He attempted to use legislation and the courts to muzzle press critical of the DP. He also made efforts to oust Supreme Court Chief Justice Zef Brozi because of his outspoken criticism of corruption in government and of civil rights abuses. The DP also pursued a policy of prosecuting former communist leaders, and in September 1995, parliament passed a "Law on Genocide and Crimes against Humanity" to that end.

The 1996 election campaign, by all accounts, was a dirty one, as the DP chose illegal methods to ensure a victory (which they could have won without cheating). The failure of the referendum was a serious blow to Berisha's prestige and created the impression that the DP hegemony was under threat. Fearful of losing power, the DP attempted to stigmatize the SP with the label of "communist." There were bitter debates over changes to the electoral law, which raised the number of majority-vote seats to 115, with proportional representation choosing only 25 seats. The DP's aggressive campaign culminated in serious irregularities on voting day; SP supporters were systematically intimidated and harassed, and the tally of votes was manipulated. The DP won by a wide majority, obtaining 55.5 percent of the vote and 122 seats, leaving the SP far behind with a meager 10 seats. The triumph of the DP was overshadowed by widespread condemnation of the irregularities. Berisha's agreement to rerun the election in seven constituencies did not put to rest international observers' concerns that democracy was being flouted. The DP performed well in local elections the following October, indicating that Albanians by and large still had faith in the party.

The SP refused to recognize the results of the national elections, choosing instead to boycott parliament. The party also undertook a critical self-evaluation to assess what had

Sali Berisha flashing victory sign to supporters, 20 March 1992. (Reuters/Corbis)

gone wrong. As a result, it purged all references to Marxism in its program and pledged to model itself on Western social democratic parties.

THE POLITICAL CONSEQUENCES OF THE COLLAPSE OF THE PYRAMID SCHEMES

Following the 1996 elections, the DP appeared to have a firm hold on Albania, and nothing seemed to be able to challenge its hegemony. But stability eluded Albanian society, and public authority was at best fragile: the legal system was weak and subject to pressure from above; tax collection was ineffectual; and police forces were understaffed, ill-trained, and ill-equipped. Albania remained an extremely polarized society, as the two major political parties fought battles over the past while the Albanian people became isolated and disenchanted with the political process. Furthermore, the state had made no effort to develop the kind of political culture necessary to creating and sustaining a democratic society. Rule of law remained weak, and corruption was rampant. There was no forum in which to discuss social and economic issues of importance to Albanians. Opposition was systematically bullied into silence rather than accepted as a healthy part of society. Like citizens of other postcommunist states, Albanians were also inclined to look

to the state for all their answers, and blame it for all their problems. Thus, democracy in Albania was fragile, so much so that any economic crisis threatened to destabilize it.

The collapse of the pyramid schemes, the massive scandal that devastated the Albanian economy beginning in January of 1997, set back Albania's transition considerably. By early February, there were ongoing protests in several cities, including Tirana, Lushnjë, and Vlorë. Opposition parties seized on the opportunity to mobilize the population and to act as spokespersons for their grievances. Soon the unrest turned into an outright uprising throughout Albania. Some of the violence was uncontrolled: angry Albanians vandalized banks and governmental buildings and libraries, and there were widespread cases of looting and frequent shootings. In short, the country appeared on the verge of civil war. Arms depots were raided, and armed bands appeared in the countryside. However, there was also a political element to this insurgency, with "salvation committees" appearing in various towns, whose membership reflected all walks of life and political persuasions.

The DP government tried and failed to put down the insurgency with military might. In spite of the declining popularity of the DP, Berisha was reelected to the presidency on 3 March. He agreed to the formation of a Government of National Unity in cooperation with the opposition. A wave of Albanian refugees in Western Europe attracted the attention of the West to the increasingly unstable situation in Albania. Concerned that the unrest would spread to neighboring Macedonia, the European Parliament began to consider intervention. By the end of March, the UN Security Council approved a multinational intervention force of nearly 6,000 soldiers. Under pressure from the West, on May 16, Berisha called early elections in the hope of quieting the unrest.

Fatos Nano and Bashkim Fino led the campaign for the SP, and Berisha did the same for the DP. Despite the tense atmosphere, elections took place on June 29 without major incident. The SP did extremely well, receiving 52.7 percent of votes and 101 seats, while the DP only garnered 25.82 percent of votes and 27 seats, and ceded 3 of the proportional seats to 3 smaller parties. The vote was ultimately a rejection of the DP and Sali Berisha, who was blamed by most for the loss of their funds. Berisha resigned as president and was replaced by Rexhep Meidani. Nano became prime minister, and Bashkim Fino took on the position of deputy prime minister. The Socialists' first priority was the restoration of law and order and regaining the confidence of the international community.

GOVERNMENT AND ADMINISTRATION OF PRESENT-DAY ALBANIA

Albania is governed through a mixed presidential-parliamentary system, as defined by a constitution approved by popular referendum on 28 November 1998. The president is the chief of state and is elected every five years. The president's role is largely ceremonial, in marked contrast to the presidency under Sali Berisha. The 140 seats in the People's Assembly (Kuvendi Popullor), up for election every four years, are chosen mainly by direct popular vote, but a few seats are chosen through proportional representation. The party obtaining the most seats determines the prime minister, who is the head of government. He chooses the members of the cabinet, which is then subject to approval by the president.

Albania's most popular parties are still the Socialist Party and the Democratic Party. The Social Democratic party and the Democratic Alliance Party have not posed a significant challenge to the two dominant parties, garnering often less than 3 percent each of the popular vote in the last elections, although they have traditionally taken part in coalitions with the Socialists. Albania's right wing is represented by the Albanian National Front (Balli Kombëtar), a right-wing nationalist party that claims to be a direct descendant of the World War II nationalist resistance movement, and the Movement of Legality Party, which advocates the restoration of the monarchy under Leka Zog, the son of King Zog; each claimed less than 4 percent of the popular vote in the last elections. Leka Zog has sought, without success, the restoration of the monarchy. In 1997 a referendum on the monarchy was held in conjunction with the internationally sponsored vote, and some 60 percent of Albanians rejected a return of the king. In 2002 Leka and his family returned permanently to Albania in hopes of entering political life in

the same way King Simeon has done in Bulgaria. Other parties currently represented in parliament are the Republican Party, the Christian Democratic Party, the Human Rights Party, the Social Democratic Union of Albania, and the Party of National Unity.

Today's Albania is composed of 36 districts, 315 communes, 65 municipalities, and 12,000 villages. Each village and municipality belongs to a commune, and each commune belongs to a district. Districts, communes, and villages have elected councils, whereas municipalities are nominally under the authority of a commune council. While the election of commune and district councils is regulated by standardized procedures, village councils can be formed in a number of ways. Representatives can be chosen through a vote at a public meeting, or can be chosen by the dominant *fis* (family council) of each *mehalla* (neighborhood).

Albania is also divided into twelve prefectures. Prefects are appointed by the president and are responsible for supervising local government councils, with the purpose of ensuring that they do not pass legislation at variance with that of the central government. Critics have noted that the prefect's substantial powers are not sufficiently defined in the constitution. Relations between central and local governments have been strained by the central government's continuous efforts to assert control over the local level. Indicative of this trend, the central government has cut its funding to local government from 22 percent of the national budget in 1995 to 12 percent in 1998, compensating for this by centralizing education, health, and agriculture. Local authorities are prevented from increasing their independence by legislation stating that they must obtain 95 percent of their funding from the central government.

ASSESSING THE HEALTH OF ALBANIA'S POLITICAL LIFE

Social Marginalization   Albania's transition has not been an easy one—in fact, more often than not, it has been a matter of one step forward, two steps back. Albania is not alone in having suffered as a result of its transition; there has been a pattern of initially poor economic performance and impoverishment in almost all countries that have emerged from communism, if only in the first few years. Albania's experience, however, has been exceptionally difficult. Pervasive unemployment, which ranges between 17 and 40 percent, underdeveloped infrastructure, weak governance, and a general breakdown of order have resulted in a degree of human insecurity unparalleled among Eastern European countries, save perhaps the former Yugoslavia. Although insecurity has an impact on the lives of most Albanians, a number of groups have been identified as being particularly vulnerable to social marginalization.

Hoxha's regime claimed to have eliminated gender discrimination, as in other communist countries, and it did succeed in integrating women into the workforce, but it did not tackle traditional attitudes about women's role in the home. This resulted in a double burden for women of household chores and child rearing, on the one hand, and gainful outside employment on the other. The end of communism brought a general worsening in women's status. As unemployment rose dramatically following the end of communism, Albanian women by and large chose to stay at home; only 16 percent work outside the home. The resurgence of traditional values has also meant that women are now seen primarily as caretakers for their families. Divorced women and women abandoned by their husbands, an increasing concern because of mass migration, are at particular risk: they are left without income, become vulnerable to violence, and are sometimes forced into prostitution. The elderly are in a similar position of helplessness. Young women who are unable to marry or to find employment are also at high risk of becoming prostitutes.

In the face of such enormous challenges in the rebuilding of Albania's economy, infrastructure, and administration, the response of government officials to marginalized groups has been limited. Although the government has instituted the Ndhimë Ekonomike to provide financial assistance to some of Albania's poor, many officials cope with marginalization by denying its existence.

Governance and Accountability

Considering that the state has not been able to ensure a minimal standard of living and that its control over some parts of rural Albania is at best tenuous, it is not surprising that most Albanians are wary of government and of political parties. Government is overwhelmingly perceived as corrupt; Albanians expect to pay bribes in order to obtain regular government services. There is also a perception that those regions that support the political party in power are treated preferentially. According to a survey published in 2002 by the World Bank, only 21 percent of those asked whether the government worked well agreed. Despite this dissatisfaction, 62 percent of Albanians claimed that they always participate in elections and referendums, with a further 12 percent participating "quite often." Still, nearly half (47 percent) feel that politics and political parties have no impact on their lives. Thus, while most Albanians appear to value the chance to participate in political life, many are becoming disillusioned with the ability of politics to address the problems they encounter.

The print and electronic media also have an important role in fostering a sense of accountability toward voters by acting as a government watchdog. Under Berisha, media hostile to the regime were systematically bullied. The Press Law passed by the DP was heavily criticized by journalists because its vague wording gave the state too much power. This law was abolished in 1997. Changes in the Albanian media landscape have been monumental since the communists lost their monopoly on information. In fact, Albania may have gone too far, experiencing what can only be called a media explosion, which intensified after Berisha lost power in 1997. There are dozens of options in print and electronic media, simply too many media outlets for a country its size. What are needed are fewer and better sources of information. By and large, Albanians rely on television for news and information, as the national press is expensive, poorly distributed, and considered largely politicized. With a wide variety of private television and radio stations, Albanians no longer need to rely on state-run media, which remain extremely progovernment in their coverage.

Compensating for a Weak State

Albanians have had recourse to a number of mechanisms to stay afloat in the last decade. In the economic realm, emigration has been an essential ingredient in providing families with enough income to survive. The reemergence of traditional institutions such as the *Kanun* and the *fis,* especially in the rural north, have helped to provide a measure of social order, which the state has been unable to ensure. Kanun law is attributed to Leke Dukagjini, a feudal lord from the fifteenth century. It is administered by the fis, a council composed of all the direct male descendants of a clan elder. When dealing with a community matter, several fis may meet to deliberate. They address disputes over land reform, land use, and irrigation, as well as other conflicts.

The reemergence of traditional practices has been considered a generally negative development; it has been associated with the reappearance of blood feuds and the strengthening of traditional values, including a decrease in the status of women. For all its failings, however, this system of law has allowed the reestablishment of order in communities that use it, by offering a body through which to resolve conflict. Furthermore, far from being competition to state governance, it seems that the fis are mainly active in areas where the state is absent and have sought to cooperate with the state where such a possibility arises.

The nonprofit sector has only to a limited degree been able to compensate for the weak state, to monitor its behavior and participate in state building. International philanthropic organizations and NGOs (non-governmental organizations) such as the Soros Foundation run a variety of programs in Albania. Although there are examples of successful domestic NGOs, by and large the nonprofit sector in Albania is not sufficiently developed to have a substantial impact on vulnerable populations. The small size of the nonprofit sector is also a result of its relative novelty in Albania compared to other Eastern European countries; the transitions of states such as Poland and Hungary were fueled by grassroots movements that later provided the backbone of the non-profit sector. Albanians are not well informed about the activities of NGOs and do not share a common view of the role the nonprofit sector should play in influencing governmental policy.

CULTURAL DEVELOPMENT

In the second millennium B.C.E., the Illyrians occupied the western Balkans. Albanians consider themselves to be descendants of the ancient Illyrians, and they believe their language is derived from Illyrian, an Indo-European language at least as ancient as Greek or Latin. Not all scholars accept this derivation, but it is extremely important to most Albanians. For one thing, because of the long period of Ottoman occupation and the nature of Albanian peasant society, illiterate and often isolated, language remained the one defining element of Albanian culture for centuries. Then, once the national awakening began in the nineteenth century, national pride focused on the twin beliefs that Albanians were descendants of the first inhabitants of the region, who had been there long before the Romans, and that they still spoke the language of those ancient inhabitants, despite all the years of domination by other peoples.

The Albanian language today contains numerous foreign words derived from Greek, Latin, Turkish, Slavic, and Italian. The first known Albanian text dates from only 1462. During the occupation of Albania from 1479 to 1912 by the Ottoman Empire, the use of written Albanian was prohibited. The revival of the Albanian written language that took place in the nineteenth century was instituted by Albanian patriots both within and outside Albania.

It must not be forgotten that Albanian is spoken by nearly seven million people, not only in Albania, but in Kosovo, Montenegro, Macedonia, Greece, and Turkey. There are also substantial Albanian communities in Italy, Canada, the United States, Bulgaria, and Ukraine. Owing to Albania's poor economic condition, the best educated and most highly skilled Albanians have often sought better economic opportunities in Western Europe and North America, but they have not forgotten their language or ceased to take pride in it.

An important step in the development of written Albanian was taken in 1908 at the Congress of Monastir (now Bitola in the former Yugoslav Republic of Macedonia), when it was decided that the Albanian language would use a Latin script. This decision demonstrated the desire among Albanians to be connected to the West rather than with the Ottoman Empire.

Though the Albanian language has been the one thread that has bound all Albanians together, it has not always worked as a unifying factor. Albanian has two main dialects. Geg is spoken north of the Shkumbin River, including Kosovo, and Tosk is spoken mainly in the south of the country. (There are also a number of different dialects spoken by Albanian communities abroad, including Arberesh in southern Italy.) Following the Congress of Monastir, there was an attempt to unify the two dialects into one common literary language. Such a language was actually worked out, and those who met in 1916 in the town of Shkodër advocated its adoption, but World War I made the situation unfavorable for further progress. Under the communist regime an outline for the unification of the Albanian language was approved in 1952. However, it was not until 1972, at the Congress of Orthography, that a universal literary Albanian was actually adopted. Although this congress resulted in a language that contained elements of both Geg and Tosk, about 80 percent of that language reflected the Tosk dialect. Thus, even though a standard literary Albanian has finally been achieved, the language issue is far from closed, as some activists and scholars, especially in Kosovo, have sought to resurrect the Geg dialect.

The creation of an Albanian literature did not wait for the adoption of an official standard literary Albanian. The first known written document in Albanian dates from 1462, a Geg baptismal formula. Later in the fifteenth and sixteenth centuries, a number of religious texts began to appear, such as Gjon Buzuku's Missal in 1555. It was only in the later nineteenth century, however, during the beginning of the period of national awakening, that Albanian literature really began to become important. Its leading figure was Naim Frasheri (1846–1900), Albania's national poet, who wrote about Albania's fifteenth-century hero Skanderbeg, the leader in the struggle against the Ottoman armies between 1443 and 1468. (His brothers, Abdyl and Sami, also played important roles in the literature of the second half of the nineteenth century.) Another key figure in early Albanian literature was Faik Konica (1876–1940), who published the journal *Albania* in Brussels in 1897 and later served as Albania's envoy to the United States under Zog in the interwar period.

Although Albanian literature flourished during the interwar period, it never achieved its desired effect, due to the extreme poverty that marked Albanian society during this time. The spread of literature was also impeded by the fact that 80 percent of the population was illiterate and all used numerous subdialects. During this period Ahmed Bey Zogu ruled as prime minister, president, and finally king, and he attached little significance to the growth and development of Albanian literature. In spite of this unpromising situation, figures like Konica, Fan S. Noli (1882 –1965), and the Franciscan father Gjergi Fishta (1871–1940) gained prominence in Albanian literature. Fishta's epic *The Lute of the Highlands* depicts the struggle of the northern Albanians against the Slavs. Noli's contribution to Albanian culture and literature is significant; he wrote history and poetry, as well as translating the works of Shakespeare and other major writers into Albanian. His other major contribution to Albanian life was in developing the independent Albanian Orthodox Church.

In the aftermath of the communist victory in 1944, literature was designed to serve the ideological purposes of the Party. Enver Hoxha, the first communist leader of Albania, moved quickly to abolish intellectual freedom, resulting in a conformist and restricted literature. Under Hoxha, Albanian literature was designed to convey the ideals of socialism, while at the same time reminding the Albanian people of their centuries-long struggle against foreign domination and oppression. Accordingly, Albanian literature reflected a mix of socialist rhetoric and nationalism. All forms of art served the sole purpose of glorifying the partisan struggle of the Albanian people. Artistic expression simply did not fit the ideological mandate of the region. Despite the general sterility of culture, the communists did wage a successful battle against illiteracy; by 1955, they claimed that illiteracy was eliminated for all Albanians under 40 years of age.

During the communist period, Albania was one of the most isolated countries in the world, which meant that foreign influence was very limited at best. The communist regime was highly successful in discrediting prewar literature, and as a result barely any literature of high value was published before 1960. Only after the end of Soviet influence did literature gain merit. Commencing in the late 1960s and early 1970s, a liberal movement materialized, which strove to develop Albanian literature, art, and culture.

Albanian author Ismail Kadare, who wrote the novels The General of the Dead Army *and* Palace of Dreams, *in the 1970s. (Getty Images)*

With the imprisoning of its leaders in 1973, however, the movement failed to gain momentum.

The best-known author outside Albania and the key figure in Albanian literature is Ismail Kadare (b. 1936), whose works have been translated into many languages around the world. Kadare was born in the museum city of Gjirokastër, in southern Albania. He studied at the University of Tirana and at the Gorky Institute of World Literature in Moscow. Kadare's prominent works have included poetry, historical novels, and short stories. Among them, *The General of the Dead Army, The Castle, The Great Winter* (which dealt with the break in relations with the Soviet Union), and the epic *The Concert at the End of Winter* (which was a direct criticism of the socialist system and Albania's break with China in the 1970s) stand out.

Kadare often offered veiled criticism of the communist regime, attacking totalitarianism and the ideology of socialism. In 1982 he came under attack at a Plenum of the League of Albanian Writers. Despite this, Kadare remained relatively protected until October 1990, when he increasingly felt that communist leaders were plotting an attack on him; he fled Albania, seeking asylum in France. Kadare's influence internationally and his exile abroad made him a symbol for those who sought an end to totalitarianism in Albania. His exile thus influenced the political developments that eventually led to the demise of the communist

regime in Albania. Kadare's reputation is international in scope, and he remains the principal figure in Albanian cultural life, with a profound influence on many Albanians. He is also the best-known Albanian writer outside the country.

Other prominent figures in Albanian literature include Dritero Agolli, Sabri Godo, Teodor Laco, Teodor Keko, and Neshat Tozaj. Tozaj's *Thikat tirana* (The Knives), published in 1989, was a clear attack on the Albanian security forces (the Sigurimi), which contributed to the popular insurrection against the communist regime, and so to its subsequent collapse.

An account of Albanian literature cannot, however, do full justice to the basic struggle to create an Albanian culture, or to the role that the communist period played in that struggle. Certainly the Albanian patriots of the nineteenth century knew that they had to use a grassroots approach and pursue an agenda that focused on the development of a national consciousness. First, they had to make Albanians aware they were Albanians before any real progress could be made on a number of fronts. Even though statehood was achieved, the success of their efforts was extremely limited. In fact, the interwar period can be characterized as a time when Albanians as a whole were unaware of the existence of a national culture. Ahmed Zogu did little to promote the development of Albanian culture, although he did make some progress in attempting to undermine regional and religious cleavages. Outside Albania there were numerous attempts to identify Albanian culture with that of the West, through the work of Konica and Noli, who were important figures in the Albanian-American community located in Boston. This community contributed to the growth of Albanian culture through *Vatra,* the Pan-Albanian Federation of America, and their community newspaper *Dielli* (The Sun). Established in 1909, *Dielli* is the oldest Albanian newspaper. Vatra played a principal role in defending Albanian interests and promoting better awareness of Albanian culture.

The really important steps for promoting Albanian culture, however, were taken under the communist regime. The communists' heavy-handed approach may have had a deadening effect on literature, but at least they saw the need to develop Albanian culture in order to build Albanian nationhood. Developments in Albanian culture under the communists included these essential elements: the encouragement and enhancement of national unity; the defeat of the notion that Albania was a backward and primitive nation; and the promotion of the concept that Albanians had fought a long and difficult battle against foreign threats to both their sovereignty and national identity. Their work meant that after the fall of the communist regime Albanians were well aware of their country's culture and history, and thus it has left a lasting impression on cultural norms and mentalities.

The Party of course promoted itself as a vital element of Albanian society, using, for example, the glorification of the wartime liberation struggle, but at the same time it promoted Albanian history and culture. The regime established a network of local museums, as well as numerous monuments, and held festivals celebrating past victories. The central figure in Albanian history and national hero Gjergi

Kastrioti, also known as Skanderbeg, was an important ingredient in this attempt to give Albanians a strong sense of their identity as Albanians, as he had been in the nineteenth-century efforts. Now, however, much more was done. Films, operas, songs, and poems portrayed Skanderbeg's fight against Ottoman forces in the fifteenth century. His importance in Albanian culture can still be seen today: the black double-headed eagle on a red background, his family emblem, is Albania's national flag and symbol. The period of national renaissance is another important aspect of Albanian culture that was celebrated by the communist regime. Its highest embodiment was felt to be the 1878 League of Prizren, which was established to prevent the Albanian lands from being partitioned after the Russo-Turkish War.

The communist regime tended to discredit much of what had happened in the interwar period. Ahmed Zogu was branded a national traitor and scorned for his alleged subservience to Yugoslavia and Italy and his "antinational" and "reactionary" policies. On the other hand, Fan Noli's coming to power in June 1924 was praised in communist parlance as a "bourgeois-democratic revolution"; its failure was blamed on foreign interference by the imperialist powers. Noli became the most important politically correct figure from the interwar period. From an ideological point of view, Noli's success in June 1924 was alleged to have laid the groundwork for the success of Albanian communism in 1944. Regular festivals marked the anniversaries of Noli's seizure of power, the League of Prizren, and Skanderbeg's death. The regime opened a Palace of Culture in Tirana in 1966 and a massive National Museum, which dominates Tirana's Skanderbeg Square. Its mural depicts the Albanians' struggle through the ages. In addition to these initiatives the regime established the Institute of Folklore in 1960, which published several scholarly works and collected thousands of folk songs. There was also a desire to bring a larger culture to the countryside. Outside the major cities, numerous regional museums, cinemas, and small-scale cultural houses were built.

The most significant development in the cultural sphere during the communist era was far less positive: the Albanian Cultural Revolution (1966–1969). This was essentially Albania's own version of China's Cultural Revolution. It aimed to eliminate any form of potential power that could threaten the ruling Albanian Party of Labor and the communist regime. A number of campaigns were undertaken against religious beliefs, traditional customs, Western culture, and foreign influence, with the goal of creating national unity and modernization. In 1967 all religious institutions were closed, and Albania was declared the world's first officially atheist nation. The Albanian cultural revolution spread into the government itself, with the Party of Labor initiating attacks on the state bureaucracy, clan-based habits, and educational institutions. These policies highlighted the desire of Albania's ruling party and its leader, Enver Hoxha, to decrease the influence of the Soviet Union while at the same time promoting Albanian nationhood.

Ironically, the fall of communism has had a negative effect on the cultural sector in Albania. The fact that Albania was one of the most isolated states during the communist era has contributed to the widespread acceptance of foreign culture in Albania today. Attempts by the communist regime to limit foreign influence failed once the regime fell, and the siege mentality that was nurtured under the communists has all but dissipated. Nevertheless, Albanians still believe strongly in their connection to the ancient Illyrians, in Skanderbeg, and in the glory of their national awakening of the nineteenth century.

Financial difficulties, along with the quick embrace of all things Western, may have put strains on cultural developments, but figures such as the popular and often controversial mayor of Tirana, Edi Rama, have made efforts to develop the cultural life of the capital. A regular film festival has been started, and filmmakers like Kujtim Cashku have made their mark on international cinema. Cashku's *Colonel Bunker* (1996) captured Albanian life in the 1970s, as the siege mentality reached new heights.

ECONOMIC DEVELOPMENT
DEVELOPMENTS UP TO 1985: DEPENDENCE AND ISOLATION

The primary legacy of Albania's twentieth-century economic development is dependency. In the interwar period, Italy emerged as the country's main benefactor; in the communist period, Albania shifted alliances from Yugoslavia to the Soviet Union and finally to China, before embarking on a catastrophic period of self-reliance. Transition Albania has once again been forced to rely on outsiders, especially the United States and the European Union. Ordinary Albanians more often than not rely on remittances from family members working abroad.

When Albania obtained its independence in 1912, it was the least-developed country in Europe; it was a feudal society dominated by a few large landowners whose land was cultivated by an impoverished peasantry. Its economy was almost entirely devoted to subsistence agriculture; industry and regional and international trade were nearly nonexistent. The majority of Albanians were landless peasants. Travel through Albania was a daunting proposition: there were only 300 kilometers of road, of which only 185 kilometers were paved. The interwar period witnessed only minor economic development in Albania. Fan Noli's planned agrarian reforms would have resulted in the distribution of land to peasants, but he was ousted by Ahmet Zogu, later King Zog, before he could carry out his reforms.

Zog also undertook some modest agrarian reforms, but they did not significantly modify ownership patterns of the land or promote modern agricultural practices. Zog essentially held out the threat of agrarian reform as a means of keeping the landowning elite on his side. Zog looked to Italy to provide the capital needed for the development of Albania's economy. Italians undertook the exploitation of Albania's mineral resources, provided loans to the government, and financed the development of Albania's infrastructure. Italy secured domination of Albania's banking system, oil and mineral resources, and overseas shipping in exchange for its financial assistance. Nonetheless, the Albanian economy remained the least developed in Europe, and retained its primitive character. Economic changes only minimally impacted the Albanian population, with infrastructure remaining primitive and urbanization low; only 20 percent of Albanians lived in urban areas in 1930. The economy remained primarily based on agriculture, supplemented by the most basic manufacturing activity of the artisanal type. Foreign trade remained low, with Albania importing more goods than it exported, consistently resulting in a trade deficit.

At the end of World War II, the communists assumed control of a territory that was still only marginally developed and that had suffered heavy damage during the war. The major problem remained land reform, as Zog had more or less left the peasantry as he found them and Italian economic assistance was never intended to build the basis of an economically viable Albania. In order to rebuild the country, the communist leadership accepted aid from the United Nations Relief and Reconstruction Agency, the Soviet Union, and Yugoslavia. By 1946, the country's industrial production had caught up with its 1939 level, and by 1947 it had surpassed it by 60 percent, testifying to the narrowness of Albania's prewar industrial base. Lacking the capital necessary to develop the country, the communist leadership turned to more powerful communist states. Albania forged a close relationship with Yugoslavia in the years following the war, which manifested itself partly through the creation of numerous joint ventures. Yugoslavia invested significant sums in developing Albania's oil and mineral sectors, building the railway, and electrifying the country. Relations with Yugoslavia were ruptured in 1948 following the Tito-Stalin break; fear of Yugoslavia's apparent intentions to integrate Albania politically was clearly a factor. Albania then turned to the Soviet Union, becoming a Council for Mutual Economic Assistance (CMEA, or Comecon) partner. With substantial financial support from the USSR, Hoxha embarked on a Stalinist transformation of the economy, concentrating on developing heavy industry and collectivizing agriculture.

The Albanian leadership broke with the USSR in 1961. Soviet leader Nikita Khrushchev's rejection of Stalinism threatened to discredit Hoxha. At the same time, Hoxha feared that Khrushchev's insistence that Albania should specialize in agriculture to fit in with the "international socialist division of labor" would make Albania dependent on the USSR. Albania partnered with China, with which it had been developing relations throughout the 1960s. This reorientation put a heavy strain on the economy, which had been engineered to fit into the CMEA system. While allied with the Chinese, the Albanian government took steps toward making Albania economically self-sufficient by renewing its focus on agricultural development to ensure a sufficient supply of foodstuffs, and by pursuing further development of heavy industry. Driven by Hoxha's fears of military invasion, industrial production was heavily geared toward defense. Chinese aid assisted in the continued industrialization drive, including the electrification of the country, which was completed in 1970. In the late 1970s China reached a rapprochement with the Soviet Union and the United States, which threatened to leave Albania politically stranded. The last straw was China's decision to reduce aid to Albania. Withdrawing from its alliance with China, the Albanian leadership committed the country to a policy of economic autarchy. This period of self-reliance was devastating for the Albanian economy and people. Cut off from vital foreign assistance, Albanians simply became poorer.

The communist era also left a significant mark on the agrarian economy. In 1945 Albania's largest landowners, who held about one-third of the country's land, saw their holdings expropriated, freeing a significant amount of land, which was then distributed to the landless peasantry, before being collectivized in order to create larger units of production. Due to resistance in the countryside, full collectivization was not achieved until 1967. The regime also implemented a program of crop diversification, regional specialization, and increased irrigation. Agricultural production was increased, mainly by expanding the surface area of arable land through desalination of marshlands and terracing of sloped terrain.

During the communist period, the country's transportation network was significantly improved; the highway system in particular was expanded to 6,900 kilometers of roads capable of carrying motorized vehicles. Port facilities at Durrës were upgraded, although they had limited tonnage in comparison to other European ports. A primitive railway system was also created, but rail traffic was exceedingly slow and did not reach most of the country. Domestic air transportation was virtually nonexistent. Through policies of improving health services, sanitation, and diet, the regime also made a significant contribution to raising average life expectancy to seventy-one years. Great emphasis was placed on education, so much so that illiteracy had been nearly eradicated by 1985.

1985–1992: ATTEMPTS TO PRESERVE THE SYSTEM THROUGH CONTROLLED CHANGE

Following Hoxha's death in 1985, the communist leadership, under Hoxha's successor Ramiz Alia, began to implement limited reforms, with the objective of preserving the system by reducing its inefficiencies, rather than transforming it. Albania's economy had shown signs of stagnation during the brief period of autarchy. Hoxha had been unwilling, unlike other Eastern European leaders, to deviate from Stalinist economic orthodoxy, and so in 1985 Albania possessed a highly dysfunctional centrally planned economy. Alia directed his efforts toward reducing the inefficiency of the system by increasing worker discipline and productivity and shifting production to consumer goods and services. He also worked toward improving relations with the West in the hope of establishing trade relations.

The reform process was accelerated by the momentous changes that swept over Eastern Europe in 1989. Albania lost many of its former trading partners within the Eastern bloc. Perhaps more significantly, the success of democracy movements in neighboring countries raised the risk of unrest, all the more threatening as Albania's economy was disrupted by recurring drought. Under mounting pressure, the Alia regime introduced private enterprise as a means of revitalizing the economy, legalizing private handicrafts and family businesses in July 1991.

1992–1997: TRANSITION—THE PRODIGIOUS RISE AND FALL OF THE ALBANIAN ECONOMIC MIRACLE

The Democratic Party was elected in March of 1992 on the promise of carrying out a Polish-style "shock therapy" transition to a free market economy. It immediately set about stabilizing the economic situation by applying restrictive monetary policy, liberalizing prices and foreign trade, and building the embryonic institutions of a market economy. The objectives of these policies were to monitor inflation, minimize the budget deficit, solve the foreign debt problem, and create a two-tier banking system. These measures were in line with the program advocated by the IMF and World Bank for Eastern European countries in transition. By the end of 1992, Albania's macroeconomic indicators had not only stabilized, but showed signs of growth, leading international financial institutions and observers to qualify Albania as an economic miracle.

Privatization of Land   The government also pursued and accelerated the privatization process begun under the previous leadership. The first sector to be privatized was land, with legislation being put in place in 1991. Peasants had already (of their own volition) taken over much of the land and seized machinery during the unrest of the first years. Cooperative land was distributed among the members of each cooperative. An attempt was made to transform some state farms into joint ventures, but most of these enterprises failed, and a decision was made to sell the land to the farms' workers. The progress of land privatization was swift. Only 3 percent of land was in private hands in 1989; by 1996, this percentage had increased to 95 percent, with private farms providing 95 percent of the total agricultural output.

The approach taken to ownership transformation has resulted in the creation of very small properties: more than 95 percent of the land was divided up among some 490,000 individual private farms in at least 1.9 million parcels, with an average of 3.3 separately located parcels per farm, such that the average property size is only 1 hectare. Farms of such small size cannot make use of economies of scale; 42 percent of farms operate with only human and animal power. The prospects for improvement are slim, since the institutions that could promote growth, such as credit-lending institutions, are by and large absent. Legislation freezing the right to buy and sell land has hampered the consolidation of small plots into potentially more productive units. Thus Albania's agricultural industry remains crippled by the small scale of farms and their low productive capacity, in contrast to other Eastern European countries in which large-scale cooperatives, joint-stock companies, and limited liability companies play an important role.

Unlike other Eastern European countries, individuals who owned land prior to the communist land reforms were unable to obtain restitution of their land. The Property with Justice movement, representing the interests of pre-1945 owners, has only succeeded in obtaining either financial compensation or physical compensation in the form of seaside and tourist-site properties. A complete return of land to prewar owners would have spelled disaster for Albania, since the country was essentially feudal prior to 1939.

Privatization of Industry   The new government also launched the process of privatizing industry. Different strategies were employed, depending on the size of the business. Small businesses (primarily retail trade, services, restaurants, warehouses, and independent smaller units of manufacturing firms) were for the most part privatized by allowing their employees to purchase them. The privatization of small and medium enterprises (SMEs), defined as enterprises with a book value of up to 500,000 U.S. dollars or 300 employees, was overseen by privatization boards and was carried out through various means, such as auctions and informal arrangements. The approach adopted resulted in the appearance of a large employee-owned sector, with all its associated problems.

In May 1995 it was decided to use a simplified voucher scheme in the privatization of the large state-owned enterprises (SOEs). A number of enterprises were selected on the basis of their relatively healthy financial status and operation in the more promising sectors of the economy. All citizens over eighteen years of age were eligible to receive vouchers. Plans were made to distribute the vouchers in three installments, originally with the stipulation that vouchers must be used before the next batch was issued, allowing the state to monitor the flow. The program was at first popular: 76 percent of the eligible population collected their vouchers in the first installment. However, the percentage decreased to 64 percent for the next installment, partly because of the unrest following the collapse of the pyramid schemes in 1997 and the very low market value of the shares. Moreover, the voucher system was fraught with irregularities. Few enterprises slated for participation were ever put up for sale, resulting in a significant voucher overhang. A full list of the companies involved was never published, and so buyers were not informed about potential alternatives. The first group of companies was put up for sale before all participating buyers had received their vouchers. Undoubtedly scuttled by the breakdown of order that accompanied the end of the pyramid schemes, voucher privatization was a complete failure. By the end of 1997, only 5 percent of all SOEs had been privatized in this fashion.

In November 1996 the government altered its strategy, putting up large packages of shares in auctions to single buyers. This approach was expected to attract the interest of foreign investors. In March 1998 a law setting out the procedure for the privatization of important branches (such as utilities, telecommunications, and mining) was passed. Strategic partners have been sought, with payment in vouchers limited to a maximum of the value of each company. According to this scheme, partners hold a majority stake. Employees in the companies have been allocated vouchers, different from those already on the market, allowing them to buy shares. This evolution has rendered the vouchers distributed prior to the law worthless.

Other Reforms and Initiatives   Another sector that the new government chose to privatize was housing. The housing that had been produced under communism was of low quality, with most houses lacking running water and central heating. By 1992, there was a chronic housing shortage, and several generations typically lived together in a crowded apartment. The January 1993 Law on Privatization of Housing in Urban Areas provided for the transfer of ownership of some 230,000 flats to their tenants (34 percent of all houses and flats). One-room flats built before 1970 and two-room flats built before 1965 were given to their occupants free of charge. Larger or more recently built flats were transferred to their occupants for a fee of 2,600 lek to 40,000 lek ($26–400). By November 1993, the ownership of 97 percent of flats had been transferred to residents.

Efforts were directed at encouraging investment, both from Albania and abroad. As part of its bid to encourage growth in the private sector, the government offered some financial support to SMEs. New policies were introduced in an attempt to attract foreign direct investment (FDI); in August 1990 a law on joint ventures was introduced, allowing foreign partners to hold up to 99 percent of the company and giving them foreign trade rights, legal protection against expropriation and nationalization, and substantial tax incentives. The need to simplify bureaucratic procedures was also acknowledged. Confusion over land ownership and general instability in the Balkans hindered foreign investment further.

The Albanian government recognized that measures were needed to set up the institutional framework necessary for a capitalist economy. In 1991–1992 a two-tier banking system was put in place. The Central Bank of Albania was given exclusive control over monetary policy, the issuing of money, and the setting of the exchange rate. Three second-tier banks were created to offer commercial banking services: the National Commercial Bank, the Rural Credit Bank, and the Savings Bank.

Behind the Facade, a Weak Economy   Because of their tendency to rely on macroeconomic indicators to evaluate the economic health of a country, international organizations had only praise for Albania, ignoring more worrisome indicators that painted a much bleaker picture of the Albanian economy. Much of the industrial sector had not survived restructuring and privatization, creating massive unemployment. Many of those enterprises that continued to operate officially kept the same payroll, but put many of their employees on part-time or unpaid leave.

To make matters worse, Albania had difficulty in attracting the capital necessary to revive its economy. Despite the government's extremely favorable policy toward foreign investors, FDI came in much more slowly than it has into other Eastern European countries, and was concentrated in export-oriented activities, which do little for the growth of the Albanian economy. For example, Italian investors took (and are still taking) advantage of the cheapness of Albanian labor, importing Italian textiles to be made into clothing, then exporting them back to Italy. Remittances have played (and are still playing) a much larger role in the Albanian

economy than does FDI; revenues from emigrant workers for the period 1992–1996 alone amounted to roughly $1.6 billion, compared to $270 million in cumulative FDI by May 1996. Investment took place primarily in the service sector, particularly in the establishment of restaurants and bars and small trade, prompting observers to warn that Albania has developed a "kiosk economy." The gap between Albania's weak export economy and its imports increased yearly, and has continued to increase. Albania's main trading partners have been EU (European Union) countries, accounting for 78.8 percent of its imports and 85.5 percent of its exports in 2000, according to the Albanian Institute of Statistics.

Because of the government's policy of tightly controlling wages while liberalizing prices, the wages of employed Albanians were not able to keep up with the cost of living. Poverty was (and is) most prevalent in rural and mountainous areas. Furthermore, Albania suffered from high unemployment. The official figures from INSTAT for 2003 was 15 percent; the real percentage of unemployed was most certainly nearer 30 to 40 percent. Albania lost some of its youngest, most skilled, and most flexible labor, as Albanians flooded out of the country to find jobs. The EU has estimated that from 500,000 to 600,000 people have left since 1990, with the vast majority going to work in Greece. The "brain drain" has hit Albania particularly hard, as some of the country's best and brightest have left the country.

Efforts at institutional development to support a market economy were never wholly successful. The banking sector was not able to keep up with the demand for credit, which encouraged the flourishing of informal credit, such as the pyramid schemes that proliferated until 1997. It appears that the informal credit sector was used for illegal activities such as money laundering. Indeed, in part as a result of the sanctions placed on Yugoslavia from 1992 to 1995 and again from 1998 to 2000, Albania has become a hub for illegal activities, ranging from smuggling to the drug trade to prostitution. The NGO (nongovernmental organization) Useful to Albanian Women estimates that there are 10,000 Albanian prostitutes in Italy and Greece alone. Albania is also an important transit zone through which goods and prostitutes make their way into Western Europe. The international community has attached considerable importance to strengthening the rule of law and ending Albania's pivotal role in the illegal trafficking of arms, people, and drugs.

During the period of apparent success, and afterwards, Albanians have shown themselves unwilling to form associations or interest and lobby groups, seeing them as an extension of the hated collective, thus perpetuating another institutional weakness. The agricultural sector, already weakened by the extreme fragmentation of arable land, is kept back by farmers' unwillingness to form associations that could make irrigation, processing, and marketing feasible and affordable. Similarly, trade union activity, which could play an important role in voicing workers' concerns, is very weak.

Collapse of the Pyramid Schemes   The reforms implemented by the government and the changing nature of Albania's economy provided the conditions for the flourishing of pyramid schemes, which ended in disaster for the country. Encouraged by lax banking rules, pyramid schemes began to multiply throughout the country in the early 1990s, as they did in many other Eastern European countries. Some of the funds marketed themselves as charitable organizations; that is the case of Xhaferri, Populli, and Sude, while others such as Vefa, Gjallica, and Kamberri invested some of their earnings in legitimate business activities. Attracted by phenomenal interest rates, Albanians from all social classes invested their savings, mostly remittances sent by their relatives employed abroad, in these schemes. The government did not condemn these schemes, nor did it prevent them from operating by using existing banking legislation. Both the Democratic Party and the Socialist Party have been linked with pyramid schemes, which may help to explain why there was no political debate around the schemes. It seems the government was also afraid of the impact that an action against the schemes would have on the economy, which had become increasingly dependent upon the schemes. Pyramid schemes were allowed to operate unhindered for several years. At the time of the collapse, it is estimated that between one-sixth and one-half of the total population of Albania was involved in one way or another with the pyramid schemes.

Finally, on 12 January 1997, responding to pressures from the increasingly concerned International Monetary Fund and the World Bank, the government made its first move against the funds, freezing $255 million in state-owned banks belonging to Populli and Xhaferri. A week later, it formed a commission to investigate the schemes. Over the next few months, the various funds stopped their operations, some declaring bankruptcy, and their managers were arrested or fled the country. The assets of the companies were found to be much lower than their liabilities, in some cases constituting less than 10 percent.

The popular reaction to the government's decision was immediate. A week later, 3,000 people marched in Tirana to protest the freezing of the funds. Most of the anger was directed at the government; the popular perception was that if the state hadn't intervened people would not have lost their savings. The opposition capitalized on this anger, articulating it into political demands, but failing to quell the fury. However, unrest quickly spread through the country. Widespread rioting resulted in property damage and the loss of some five hundred lives in the following six months. The state lost effective control of the country, leaving some regions at the mercy of armed bands. Albanians fled the country in large numbers, estimated at 14,000. The extent of the crisis garnered international attention, and an international humanitarian intervention force was sent in. Twice in just a decade, Albanians turned on their state and destroyed much of what had been built, and the country's already dubious international image was made worse. The victory of the Socialist Party in the June 1997 elections signaled a return to normalcy.

The collapse of the pyramid schemes and the ensuing chaos had a profound impact on the already fragile Albanian economy. The amount of money lost has been estimated between $300 million and $1.2 billion. Principally, it eliminated the economic progress that Albania had made since 1992. Less tangible, but equally important, was the damage done to Albania's already poor international reputation by the ensuing lawlessness and wanton destruction of property, hardly the type of stability that foreign investors were seeking. The national currency lost significant value, the budget deficit increased, and the economy contracted by 8 percent.

CONTEMPORARY CHALLENGES

The political and economic transition of Albania, which really only started with any seriousness in 1992, has been fraught with setbacks—it had been, at least until 1998, without any substantial gains and very much a matter of one step forward, two steps back. Albanians found that there were always new lows the country could sink to and that even though they had obtained substantial new freedoms, poverty, emigration, and corruption defined their existence. Although the Democratic Party made some gains between 1992 and 1997, all was lost with the pyramid collapse. What is certain is that the legacy of Sali Berisha's rule is not a positive one. Despite the optimism that accompanied his victory in 1992, his government was characterized by intolerance, as he sought to defeat his opposition, not by persuading the voters but by extralegal methods. Despite initially optimistic reports on the economy, success was built on the shakiest of foundations. It remains to be seen if Albania has finally embarked on what can be called a serious transition. Albania's main problem is that its politicians are not all that committed to Albania's transformation; there is a profound lack of political will. If we look at Albania now, we are still confronted with a state that is failing to meet its citizens most basic needs—water, safety, and electricity.

After the chaotic elections in 1997, the Socialists governed for four relatively successful years, until new elections in June 2001. Their main legacy was improved stability and security, although the political climate was extremely polarized between Socialists and Democrats. The issue of the return of the monarchy was solved through a referendum that accompanied the 1997 vote. More than 65 percent of Albanians rejected the restoration of the monarchy, although monarchists claimed the vote was rigged. Zog's son and heir, Leka, returned to live in Albania in 2002. The government gave him a token role, such as opening events and the like, but he has no chance of becoming a serious political figure in Albania in the way that Bulgaria's Simeon II did in 2001.

Despite the resolution of some key issues, organized crime, criminality, and corruption still dominated. Intraparty relations between the Socialists and Democrats were terrible, as neither the Socialist Party chairman nor Sali Berisha seemed able to give up their enmity. After the murder of DP cofounder and activist Azem Hajdari in September 1998, Berisha's militants briefly attempted a coup of sorts, having blamed the Socialist government for Hajdari's "assassination." During the funeral on 14 September 1998, some 2,000 Democratic Party militants took to the streets, setting fire to cars and briefly seizing the office of the prime minister. Nano, who should have

The Pyramid Schemes

In 1996–1997, the dramatic rise and collapse of several huge financial pyramid schemes convulsed Albania. The pyramid scheme phenomenon in Albania is important because its scale relative to the size of the economy was unprecedented, and because the political and social consequences of the collapse of the pyramid schemes were profound. Many Albanians—about two-thirds of the population—invested in them. When the schemes collapsed, there was uncontrollable rioting, the government fell, and the country descended into anarchy and a near civil war, in which some 2,000 people were killed.

The widespread appeal of pyramid schemes in Albania can be attributed to several factors, including Albanians' unfamiliarity with financial markets and the deficiencies of the country's formal financial system, which encouraged the development of an informal market and, within this market, the growth of the pyramid schemes themselves. There were also governance problems, both in the financial sector and more generally. The regulatory framework was inadequate, and it was not clear who had responsibility for supervising the informal market. Even after the approval of a banking act in February 1996 that appeared to give the Bank of Albania the power to close illegal deposit-taking institutions, the central bank could not obtain the government's support. In short, the government did not possess the political will to avoid the looming crisis. There were allegations that many government officials benefited personally from the companies. During the 1996 elections, several of the companies made campaign contributions to the ruling Democratic Party.

In a typical pyramid scheme, a fund or company attracts investors by offering them very high returns; these returns are paid to the first investors out of the funds received from those who invest later. The scheme is insolvent—liabilities exceed assets—from the day it opens for business. Nevertheless, it flourishes initially, as news about the high returns spreads and more investors are drawn in. Encouraged by the high payouts, and in some cases by showcase investments and ostentatious spending by the operators, still more people are drawn in, and the scheme grows until the interest and principal due to the early investors exceeds the money paid in by new investors.

Some of the Albanian companies met this definition exactly: they were pure pyramid schemes, with no real assets. Other cases were more ambiguous. Some of the largest of the companies—in particular VEFA, Gjallica, and Kamberi—had substantial real investments. They were also widely believed to be engaged in criminal activities—including violating United Nations sanctions by smuggling goods into the former Yugoslavia—that were thought to be the source of the high returns they paid.

By November 1996, the face value of the schemes' liabilities totaled $1.2 billion by World Bank estimates. Albanians sold their houses to invest in the schemes; farmers sold their livestock.

Throughout the year, the government was a passive spectator to the unfolding crisis. And despite repeated warnings from the International Monetary Fund and the World Bank, the finance ministry did not warn the public about the schemes until October. Even then, however, it drew a false and misleading distinction between companies with real investments, which were believed to be solvent, and "pure pyramid schemes."

By March 1997 Albania was in chaos. The government had lost control of the south. Many in the army and police force had deserted, and one million weapons had been looted from the armories. Evacuation of foreign nationals and mass emigration of Albanians began. The government was forced to resign. President Berisha agreed to hold new parliamentary elections before the end of June, and an interim coalition government was appointed.

As important as its impact was on the Albanian economy, the collapse of the pyramid schemes had perhaps an even greater impact upon society. The social toll was incalculable, as it seems that almost everyone in the country had some money invested. In addition to the loss of life, thousands of people were impoverished, either by their unwise investments in the pyramid schemes or by the destruction of their property in the ensuing violence. What also suffered seriously was Albania's international image. Before this, many observers had called Albania an economic miracle; now the pyramid collapse and the spiral into mass violence did little to encourage outside investors. Albania, from the point of view of the outside world, remained a dangerous place.

remained during the strife, abandoned his post and fled to neighboring Macedonia.

Nano subsequently resigned from his post as prime minister and was replaced by the thirty-one-year-old secretary general of the Socialist Party, Pandeli Majko, who represented a younger generation of leaders, less compromised by the past. However, Nano's career was far from over, as he remained the principal figure in the Socialist Party, despite growing rifts between him and the younger generation of Socialist Party members. Albanians had thus to contend with a divided ruling party, which meant that there was no continuity in government, but the principal problem in the period was that Albanians still lacked a real opposition party. In fact, the entire transition was marked by the near total dominance of a single ruling party. Berisha's Democratic Party essentially abstained from participating in almost all aspects of government. The boycott, which Berisha had so denounced when the Socialists used it when he was in power, became the DP's principal weapon. Berisha and his increasingly small group of militants preferred the street protest to the parliament.

What became the principal dilemma between 1998 and 1999 was the growing conflict in neighboring Kosovo. As the conflict intensified between the Kosovo Liberation Army and the Yugoslav Army and paramilitaries, followed by the subsequent intervention of NATO in late March 1999, Albania briefly moved again to the center of the stage, as some 450,000 Kosovo Albanian refugees flooded into the country. Despite Albania's acute poverty, unstable domestic policy, and lack of law and order, many Albanians opened their homes to provide shelter to the incoming refugees, and the government organized humanitarian relief and welcomed international humanitarian organizations to aid in provision of basic services for refugees.

The refugee influx had positive and negative consequences for the Albanian economy and political situation. The International Crisis Group (ICG) reported that according to the Bank of Albania, the Kosovo crisis had a positive effect on the Albanian economy. The arrival of Western aid, along with a NATO force that set about fixing Albania's roads and airports, helped the country considerably. The fact that several hundred journalists came along was also a boost, as for the first time, Albania appeared in the international media in a positive light. On the other hand, as soon as the crisis was over and the refugees had left, Albania was marginalized again, as all eyes (and cash) went to Kosovo and then Macedonia, when conflict erupted there between Macedonians and Albanians.

On the foreign affairs front, the Socialist Party government worked hard to make Albania a good neighbor. During the wars in both Kosovo and Macedonia, Albania played a decidedly neutral role. This neutrality was essentially the result of two factors: Albania was no doubt told by its benefactors to avoid making the problems worse, and Albania lacked the power to influence events in either Kosovo or Macedonia. Still, Albania did receive wide international praise for its commitment to a peaceful resolution to both these conflicts.

In the summer of 2001 Albanians again went to the polls, and these elections marked a turning point of sorts.

First of all, the Socialists, with Nano as the Party's secretary general, won easily, in what were not exactly "free and fair" elections. The DP, which ran together with other rightist parties, was easily defeated. For a brief time, it appeared that the much needed third force had finally gained some ground in Albania, as Berisha's former spokesperson, Genc Pollo, who headed up the New Democratic Party, did surprisingly well in the vote. However, Pollo, whose legacy is far from good after serving President Berisha for so many years, has been unable to move beyond the periphery of Albanian political life. The simple fact that Berisha continued to dominate has served to keep the Democrats out of power, as too many people identify Berisha with the loss of their savings in 1997.

As one analyst noted, it was the most tranquil election campaign in ten years of transition. Observers had expected the worst, as the Democrats had made clear that if they did not win, it meant the elections were rigged and there would be trouble. The fact that violence did not accompany the vote merits praise. It seems clear that the international community cautioned Berisha to avoid inflaming the situation. The Democrats did cry foul, and counting took weeks, but in the end, since both sides cheated so much, the result probably reflected the political scene accurately. Voter turnout was surprisingly low, reflecting the general apathy that characterized much of the population. After all, it was ten years into the transition, and the very same figures who had battled it out in 1991 were still there front and center in Albanian political life.

Three big questions loomed after the elections, the answers to which were to determine whether Albania could remain on a path that was inching the country ahead. What was the future role for Socialist leader Fatos Nano? Would the Nano-Berisha conflict continue to dominate Albanian political life? Would the election of a president in 2002 spell the end of the Socialist government and force new elections?

Amazingly, Albania answered all three without chaos, although not without crucial intervention from the European Union (EU). Failure to agree on a new president might well have forced new elections, and the EU wanted to do everything possible to avoid that outcome. After considerable pressure from the international community, especially the European Union, both major parties agreed on a candidate for president—Alfred Moisiu—a relative nobody from the army, on whom everyone could essentially agree. Nano, who endured challenges to his leadership from within, managed to emerge as the country's prime minister in July 2002. This was his third stint as premier. After years of not speaking, Nano and Berisha basically called a truce. Thus, at least on the political level, Albanians had achieved a level of stability that had eluded them to date.

Albania's principal foreign policy goals have been membership in the North Atlantic Treaty Organization (NATO) and the European Union. Albania was one of the first countries to apply for membership in NATO's partnership for peace plan, but NATO membership eluded them, and they were denied admission at NATO's Prague Summit in November 2002. Talks on a Stabilization and

Refugees arrive at the Morine border post between Albania and Kosovo, 6 May 1999. (Les Stone/Corbis)

Association Agreement with the EU began in 2003, but negotiations are expected to be long and comments by EU officials suggest that Albania has much work ahead of it. Most Albanians seem to understand that membership in the EU may well be a long way off. The EU has been especially critical of Albania, demanding Albania take more action in the fight against corruption and organized crime, as well as the strengthening of the judicial system and public administration.

The primary legacy of Albania's twentieth-century economic development is dependency, as it has never proven to be a viable economic entity. In the interwar period, Italy emerged as the country's main benefactor; in the communist period, Albania shifted alliances from Yugoslavia to the Soviet Union and finally to China before embarking on a catastrophic period of self-reliance. During the transition, Albania has once again been forced to rely on outsiders, especially the United States and the European Union. The economic viability of Albania, like that of Kosovo, is doubtful. For both, it is remittances, international aid, and illegal activity that provide sustainability. Economic development in the transition has been extremely uneven—cities like Tirana and Durrës have appeared to thrive, while the north has been largely left in poverty. This split has led to intensive rural–urban migration, as people have sought opportunities, especially in the grey and black markets, in Tirana and other cities. It is estimated that the population of the Tirana district (Tirana and its environs) had grown from 370,000 to 520,000 by 2003.

To return to the background of the current situation in more detail, the collapse of the pyramid schemes and the ensuing civil disorder captured worldwide attention, changing perceptions of Albania from the poster child for shock therapy to the basket case of Europe. For Albanians, however, the transition from the start was a difficult experience; as some have ironically commented, "All shock, no therapy." The high unemployment and underemployment that resulted from the breakdown of the industrial sector, together with the inability of most farmers to translate their land-ownership into meaningful economic gain, have meant that most Albanians must look to other sources of income to earn enough to support their families. Such sources include government pensions, unemployment benefits, private business (not always legal), and remittances, as well as whatever foodstuffs they can grow on their land.

Not all Albanian families are able to muster sufficient income to remain afloat. According to a 2002 World Bank technical report, 29 percent of Albanians say that they do not make enough to feed and house their families, and a further 29 percent estimate that they can attend to these needs but are not able to secure clothing and shoes for their families. Poverty is direst in mountainous and rural areas, particularly in the north, but it is also becoming a major problem in the slum areas that have formed around major cities as a result of the massive rural exodus since the early 1990s. Not only are poor Albanians more likely to suffer from malnutrition, poorer health, and inferior living conditions, their condition is also psychologically stressful, bringing feelings of hopelessness, despair, and vulnerability, and it isolates them from both the social and economic life of their peers. As elsewhere in the region, even in those areas where the transition has been most successful, its impact has been very uneven, and a huge gap has developed between rich and poor. Many people, especially the youth, have opted for the fast money available in various illegal sectors.

The Albanian government is ill equipped to identify and assist families in poverty. The Ndihme Ekonomike (Economic Assistance), created by the government in 1993 as a cash assistance program to assist poor families, reaches only a fraction of those in need, and gives those it does reach much less than they need. Albanians have developed coping mechanisms to stave off poverty. One such system is the "list": shopkeepers allow customers on the list to purchase items on credit, in the expectation that they will pay their debt when they receive some sort of income.

Another very significant strategy, which enables the list to function, is the migration of massive numbers of Albanians in search of employment. Migrants are overwhelmingly young males between the ages of fourteen and forty. Migration occurs internally, from the countryside to the city, and externally to Italy and even more to Greece. Most migrants consider migration to be temporary, and indeed most return to their village with their earnings after less than six months, only to migrate again when the money runs out. Most emigration abroad is clandestine. This strategy allows families to supplement their income substantially. Much remittance money was sunk in the pyramid schemes that collapsed in 1997, and today remittances go toward consumption (especially construction and the purchase of household appliances) rather than investment. In any case, emigration is not an option available to all; it is an expensive proposition, so that wealthier families are more likely to be able to afford it. Larger families with more able-bodied men are also at an advantage.

Although migration allows Albanian families to make ends meet, it comes at a substantial social cost. The encroachment of poverty, combined with the destabilizing effect of mass migration on Albanian social structures, has created a number of vulnerable groups. The departure of able-bodied men from a family leaves women and the elderly vulnerable during their absence. The marginalization of women has manifested itself in the increasing numbers of women drawn into prostitution. Furthermore, youth convinced that schooling will not give them an advantage in the labor market are apt to choose migration over education.

Transition in Albania is thus on the whole a dismal failure, and the blame for that falls on a class of politicians who opted for quick wealth instead of the national interest. In 1992 Albanians were, like Poles, ready to suffer some terrible economic pains for the sake of a better future. The government offered only polemics and an economic revival based on kiosks, along with the same type of rhetoric that had characterized the communist past. Given that the people who rose to the top in Albania were raised in the worst period of Albanian communism, it seems that that was really the best they could do. It is ironic that Albania, which as the most homogeneous country in the region did not suffer ethnic war, needed the international community to come to its aid just as often as states torn by ethnic conflict—only it was to mediate disputes between Albanians. This fact indicates an astonishingly low level of political maturity.

At one point it seemed that there might be light at the end of the tunnel—the compromise between Nano and Berisha calmed things considerably. Unfortunately, however, the truce has lost momentum, and tedious squabbling has again become the norm. One can only hope that the dominance of these two men in Albanian political life cannot last much longer, as the poisoned political atmosphere has virtually devastated the country's transition. Certainly for ordinary Albanians, especially in the villages, life has not improved that much, especially since the state still cannot meet their basic needs, and few governments have succeeded in delivering any optimism to a people who by and large consider emigration as the most likely way to advance themselves. The way ahead will continue to be difficult.

SELECTIVE BIBLIOGRAPHY

Austin, Robert. "Albanian Language." In *Encyclopedia of Eastern Europe: From the Congress of Vienna to the Fall of Communism,* edited by Richard Frucht. New York: Garland, 2000.

Babuna, Ayudin. "The Albanians of Kosovo and Macedonia: Ethnic Identity Superseding Religion." *Nationalities Papers* 28, no. 1 (2000): 67–92.

Bezemer, Dirk J. "Post-Socialist Financial Fragility: The Case of Albania." *Cambridge Journal of Economics* 25 (2001): 1–23.

Biberaj, Elez. *Albania in Transition: The Rocky Road to Democracy.* Boulder: Westview, 1998.

———. "The Albanian National Question: The Challenges of Autonomy, Independence and Separatism." In *The New European Diasporas: National Minorities and Conflict in Eastern Europe.* Edited by Michael Mandelbaum. New York: Council on Foreign Relations Press, 2000, 214–288.

Central Intelligence Agency. "Albania." In *The World Factbook,* http://www.cia.gov/cia/publications/factbook/geos/al.html (accessed 9 June 2004).

Cungu, Azeta, and Johan F. M. Swinnen. "Albania's Radical Agrarian Reform." *Economic Development and Cultural Change* 47, no. 3 (April 1999): 605–619.

De Soto, Hermine, et al. *Poverty in Albania: A Qualitative Assessment.* World Bank Technical Paper no. 520, Europe and Central Asia Environmentally and Socially Sustainable Development Series. Washington, DC: World Bank, 2002.

Economist Group of Publications. *Albania. Country Profile 2000.* London: Economist Intelligence Unit, 2000.

Ethnologue. "Languages of Albania." http://www. ethnologue.com/show_country.asp?name=Albania (accessed 9 June 2004).

Hall, Derek. *Albania and the Albanians.* London: Pinter Reference, 1994.

———. "Rural Diversification in Albania." *Geojournal* 46 (1999): 283–287.

Hashi, Iraj, and Lindita Xhillari. "Privatization and Transition in Albania." *Post-Communist Economies* 11, no. 1 (1999): 99–125.

Holzner, Brigitte M. "Gender, Markets and Transition in Albania." In *The First Decade and After: Albania's Democratic Transition and Consolidation in the Context of Southeast Europe.* Edited by Fatos Tarifa and Max Spoor. The Hague: CESTRAD (Center for the Study of Transition and Development), 2000.

Human Rights Watch. *World Report 1999.* "Albania." http://www.hrw.org/worldreport99/europe/albania.html (accessed 9 June 2004).

International Crisis Group. "Albania." http://www. crisisweb.org/projects/project.cfm?id=1241&l=1 (accessed 9 June 2004).

Judah, Tim. "Greater Albania?" *Survival* 43, no. 2 (summer 2001): 7–18.

La Cava, Gloria, and Rafaella Y. Nanetti. *Albania: Filling the Vulnerability Gap.* World Bank Technical Paper no. 460, Europe and Central Asia Environmentally and Socially Sustainable Development Series. Washington, DC: World Bank, 2001.

Magocsi, Paul Robert. *Historical Atlas of Central Europe.* Toronto: University of Toronto Press, 2002.

Pano, Nicholas. "Albania." In *The Columbia History of Eastern Europe in the 20th Century.* Edited by Joseph Held. New York: Columbia University Press, 1991.

———. *The People's Socialist Republic of Albania.* Baltimore: Johns Hopkins University Press, 1968.

———. "The Process of Democratization in Albania." In *Politics, Power and the Struggle for Democracy in South-East Europe.* Edited by Karen Dawisha and Bruce Parrot. Cambridge: Cambridge University Press, 1997, 285–352.

Pettifer, James. "The Greek Minority in Albania: Ethnic Politics in a Pre-National State." In *The Politics of Nationality Minority Participation in Post-Communist Europe.* Edited by Johnathan P. Stein. Armonk, NY: M. E. Sharpe, 2000.

Poulton, Hugh. *The Balkans: Minorities and States in Conflict.* London: Minority Rights Group, 1991.

Ramet, Sabrina P. *Balkan Babel: The Disintegration of Yugoslavia from the Death of Tito to the War for Kosovo.* Boulder: Westview, 1999.

———. *Nihil Obstat: Religion, Politics and Social Change in East-Central Europe and Russia.* Durham: Duke University Press, 1998.

Republic of Albania Department of Information. http://www.keshilliministrave.al/english/default.asp (accessed 9 June 2004).

Republic of Albania Institute of Statistics. http://www. instat.gov.al (accessed 13 August 2004).

Saltemarshe, Douglas. *Identity in a Post-Communist Balkan State: An Albanian Village Study.* Aldershot, UK: Ashgate, 2001.

Secretariat of the Economic Commission for Europe (ECE). *Economic Survey of Europe 2001,* no. 1. New York: United Nations, 2001.

Southeast European Times, http://www.Balkantimes.com (accessed 9 June 2004).

UNCTAD Handbook of Statistics 2001. New York: United Nations, 2001.

United Nations Development Program. *Human Development Report 2001: Making New Technologies Work for Human Development.* New York: Oxford University Press, 2001.

United Nations Environment Program. *Post-Conflict Environmental Assessment—Albania.* Geneva: United Nations Environment Programme, 2000.

USAID. "Albania," http://www.usaid.gov/pubs/cp2000/eni/albania.html (accessed 9 June 2004).

Van Hook, Mary P., et al. "Responding to Gender Violence in Albania." *International Social Work* 43, no. 3: 351–363.

Vaughan-Whitehead, Daniel. *Albania in Crisis: The Predictable Fall of the Shining Star.* Cheltenham: Edward Elgar, 1999.

Vickers, Miranda, and James Pettifer. *Albania: From Anarchy to a Balkan Identity.* New York: New York University Press, 1997.

World Bank. World Development Report 2002: Building Institutions for Markets. Oxford: Oxford University Press, 2002.

CHRONOLOGY

1403	Gjergi Kastrioti born; later becomes Albanian national hero known as Skanderbeg.
1443	After losing a battle near Niš, Skanderbeg defects from Ottoman Empire, re-embraces Roman Catholicism, and begins holy war against the Ottomans.
1444	Skanderbeg proclaimed chief of Albanian resistance.
1449	Albanians, under Skanderbeg, rout Ottoman forces under Sultan Murad II.
1468	Skanderbeg dies.
1478	Krujë falls to Ottoman Turks; Shkodër falls a year later. Subsequently, many Albanians flee to southern Italy, Greece, Egypt, and elsewhere; many who remain convert to Islam.
Seventeenth–eighteenth centuries	Some Albanians who convert to Islam find careers in Ottoman Empire's government and military service; about two-thirds of Albanians convert to Islam.
1822	Albanian leader Ali Pasha of Tepelenë assassinated by Ottoman agents for promoting an autonomous state.
1835	Ottoman Sublime Porte divides Albanian-populated lands into vilayets of

	Janina and Rumelia with Ottoman administrators.
1861	First school known to use Albanian language in modern times opens in Shkodër.
1877–1878	Russia's defeat of the Ottoman Empire seriously weakens Ottoman power over Albanian-populated areas.
1878	Treaty of San Stefano, signed after the Russo-Turkish War, assigns Albanian-populated lands to Bulgaria, Montenegro, and Serbia; but Austria-Hungary and Britain block the treaty's implementation. Albanian leaders meet in Prizren, Kosovo, to form the Prizren League, initially advocating a unified Albania under Ottoman suzerainty. During the Congress of Berlin, the great powers overturn the Treaty of San Stefano and divide Albanian lands among several states. The Prizren League begins to organize resistance to the provisions of the Treaty of Berlin that affect Albanians.
1879	Society for Printing of Albanian Writings, composed of Roman Catholic, Muslim, and Orthodox Albanians, founded in Constantinople.
1881	Ottoman forces crush Albanian resistance fighters at Prizren. Prizren League's leaders and families arrested and deported.
1897	Ottoman authorities disband a reactivated Prizren League, execute its leader later, then ban Albanian language books.
1906	Albanians begin joining the Committee of Union and Progress (Young Turks), formed in Constantinople, hoping to gain autonomy for their nation within the Ottoman Empire.
1908	Albanian intellectuals meet in Bitola, at the Congress of Monastir, and choose the Latin alphabet as standard script rather than Arabic or Cyrillic.
May 1912	Albanians rise against the Ottoman authorities and seize Skopje.
October 1912	First Balkan War begins, and Albanian leaders affirm Albania as an independent state.
November 1912	Muslim and Christian delegates at Vlorë declare Albania independent and establish a provisional government.
May 1913	Treaty of London ends First Balkan War. Second Balkan War begins.
August 1913	Treaty of Bucharest ends Second Balkan War. Great powers recognize an independent Albanian state ruled by a constitutional monarchy.
March 1914	Prince Wilhelm of Wied, a German army captain, is installed as head of the new Albanian state by the International Control Commission, arrives in Albania.
September 1914	New Albanian state collapses following outbreak of World War I; Prince Wilhelm is stripped of authority and departs from Albania.
1918	World War I ends, with Italian army occupying most of Albania, and with Serbian, Greek, and French forces occupying the remainder. Italian and Yugoslav powers begin struggle for dominance over Albanians.
December 1918	Albanian leaders meet at Durrës to discuss presentation of Albania's interests at the Paris Peace Conference.
January 1919	Serbs attack Albania's inhabited cities.
January 1920	Albanian leaders meeting at Lushnjë reject the partitioning of Albania by the Treaty of Paris, warn that Albanians will take up arms in defense of their territory, and create a bicameral parliament.
February 1920	Albanian government moves to Tirana (Tiranë), which becomes the capital.
September 1920	Albania forces Italy to withdraw its troops and abandon territorial claims to almost all Albanian territory.
December 1920	Albania admitted to League of Nations as a sovereign and independent state.
November 1921	Yugoslav troops invade Albanian territories they had not previously occupied; League of Nations commission forces Yugoslav withdrawal and reaffirms Albania's 1913 borders.
December 1921	Popular Party, headed by Xhafer Ypi, forms government with Ahmed Zogu, the future King Zog, as internal affairs minister.
August 1922	Ecumenical patriarch in Constantinople recognizes the Orthodox Autocephalous Church of Albania.
September 1922	Zogu assumes position of prime minister of government; opposition to him becomes formidable.
July 1924	An insurgency wins control of Tirana; Fan S. Noli becomes prime minister, promising land reform; Zogu flees to Yugoslavia.
December 1924	Zogu, backed by Yugoslav army, returns to power and begins to smother parliamentary democracy; Noli flees to Italy.
1925	Italy begins penetration of Albanian public and economic life.
November 1926	Italy and Albania sign First Treaty of Tirana, which guarantees Zogu's political position and Albania's boundaries.

August 1928	Zogu pressures the parliament to dissolve itself; a new constituent assembly declares Albania a kingdom and Zogu becomes Zog I, "King of the Albanians."
1931	Zog, standing up to the Italians, refuses to renew the First Treaty of Tirana; Italians continue political and economic pressure.
1934	After Albania signs trade agreements with Greece and Yugoslavia, Italy suspends economic support, then attempts to threaten Albania.
March 1939	Mussolini delivers ultimatum to Albania.
April 1939	Mussolini's troops invade and occupy Albania; Albanian parliament votes to unite country with Italy; Zog and his family flee to Greece; Italy's King Victor Emmanuel III assumes Albanian crown.
1940	Italian army attacks Greece through Albania.
October 1941	Josip Broz Tito, Yugoslav communist leader, directs organizing of Albanian communists.
November 1941	Albanian Communist Party founded; Enver Hoxha becomes first secretary.
September 1942	Communist Party organizes the National Liberation Movement, a popular front resistance organization.
October 1942	Noncommunist nationalist groups form to resist the Italian occupation.
September 1943	German forces invade and occupy Albania.
January 1944	Communist partisans, supplied with British weapons, gain control of southern Albania.
May 1944	Communists meet to organize an Albanian government; Hoxha becomes chairman of executive committee and supreme commander of the Army of National Liberation.
October 1944	Communists establish provisional government with Hoxha as prime minister.
November 1944	Germans withdraw from Tirana; communists move into the capital.
December 1944	Communist provisional government adopts laws allowing state regulation of commercial enterprises, as well as foreign and domestic trade.
January 1945	Communist provisional government agrees to restore Kosovo to Yugoslavia as an autonomous region; tribunals begin to condemn thousands of "war criminals" and "enemies of the people" to death or to prison. Communist regime begins to nationalize industry, transportation, forests, and pastures.
April 1945	Yugoslavia recognizes communist government in Albania.
August 1945	Sweeping agricultural reforms begin; about half of arable land eventually redistributed to peasants from large landowners; most church properties nationalized. United Nations Relief and Rehabilitation Administration begins sending supplies to Albania.
November 1945	Soviet Union recognizes provisional government; Britain and United States make full diplomatic recognition conditional.
December 1945	In elections for the People's Assembly, only candidates from the Democratic Front are on ballot.
1946	People's Assembly proclaims Albania a "people's republic"; purges of noncommunists from positions of power in government begin; People's Assembly adopts new constitution, Hoxha becomes prime minister, foreign minister, defense minister, and commander in chief; Soviet-style central planning begins.
July 1946	Treaty of friendship and cooperation signed with Yugoslavia; Yugoslav advisers and grain begin pouring into Albania.
October 1946	British destroyers hit mines off Albania's coast; United Nations (UN) and the International Court of Justice subsequently condemn Albania.
November 1946	Albania breaks diplomatic relations with the United States after latter withdraws its informal mission.
May 1947	UN commission concludes that Albania, together with Bulgaria and Yugoslavia, supports communist guerrillas in Greece; Yugoslav leaders launch verbal offensive against anti-Yugoslav Albanian communists, including Hoxha; pro-Yugoslav faction begins to wield power.
June 1948	Cominform expels Yugoslavia; Albanian leaders launch anti-Yugoslav propaganda campaign, cut economic ties, and force Yugoslav advisers to leave; Stalin becomes national hero in Albania.
September 1948	Hoxha begins purging high-ranking party members accused of "Titoism"; treaty of friendship with Yugoslavia abrogated by Albania; Soviet Union begins giving economic aid to Albania, and Soviet advisers replace ousted Yugoslavs.
November 1948	First Party Congress changes name of Albanian Communist Party to Albanian Party of Labor.
February 1949	Albania joins Council for Mutual Economic Assistance (Comecon); all foreign trade conducted with member countries.
December 1949	Pro-Tito Albanian communists purged.

1950	Britain and United States begin inserting anticommunist Albanian guerrilla units into Albania; all are unsuccessful.
July 1950	A new constitution is approved by People's Assembly. Hoxha becomes minister of defense and foreign minister.
1951	Albania and Soviet Union sign agreement on mutual economic assistance.
July 1954	Hoxha relinquishes post of prime minister to Mehmet Shehu but retains primary power as party leader.
May 1955	Albania becomes a founding member of the Warsaw Pact.
February 1956	After Nikita Khrushchev's "secret speech" exposes Stalin's crimes, Hoxha defends Stalin; relations with Soviet Union become strained.
June 1960	Albania sides with China in Sino-Soviet ideological dispute; Soviet economic support to Albania is curtailed, and Chinese aid is increased; Hoxha rails against Khrushchev and supports China during an international communist conference in Moscow.
February 1961	Hoxha harangues against the Soviet Union and Yugoslavia at Albania's Fourth Party Congress.
December 1961	Soviet Union breaks diplomatic relations with Albania; other Eastern European countries severely reduce contacts but do not break relations; Albania looks toward China for support.
1962	Albanian regime introduces austerity program in attempt to compensate for withdrawal of Soviet economic support; China incapable of delivering sufficient aid; Albania becomes China's spokesman at UN.
February 1966	Hoxha initiates Cultural and Ideological Revolution.
March 1966	Albanian Party of Labor "open letter" to the people establishes egalitarian wage and job structure for all workers.
1967	Hoxha regime launches Cultural Revolution to extinguish religious life in Albania; by year's end, over two thousand religious buildings have been closed or converted to other uses.
August 1968	Albania condemns Soviet-led invasion of Czechoslovakia; subsequently Albania withdraws from Warsaw Pact.
1976	Hoxha begins criticizing new Chinese regime after Mao's death; a new constitution is promulgated superceding the 1950 version; Albania becomes a people's socialist republic.
1977	Top military officials purged after "Chinese conspiracy" is uncovered.
1978	China terminates all economic and military aid to Albania.
1980	Hoxha selects Ramiz Alia as the next party head, bypassing Shehu.
1981	Shehu, after rebuke by Politburo, dies, possibly murdered on Hoxha's orders.
November 1982	Alia becomes chairman of Presidium of the People's Assembly.
April 1985	Hoxha dies; replaced by Alia.
November 1986	Alia featured as party's and country's undisputed leader at Ninth Party Congress.
September 1989	Alia, addressing the Eighth Plenum of the Central Committee, signals that radical changes to the economic system are necessary. Communist rule in Eastern Europe collapses. Ramiz Alia signals changes to economic system.
January 1990	Ninth Plenum of the Central Committee; demonstrations at Shkodër force authorities to declare state of emergency.
April 1990	Alia declares willingness to establish diplomatic relations with the Soviet Union and the United States.
May 1990	The Secretary General of the UN visits Albania. Regime announces desire to join the Conference on Security and Cooperation in Europe. People's Assembly passes laws liberalizing criminal code, reforming court system, lifting some restrictions on freedom of worship, and guaranteeing the right to travel abroad.
Summer 1990	Unemployment throughout the economy increases as a result of government's reform measures; drought reduces electric power production, forcing plant shutdowns.
July 1990	Young people demonstrate against regime in Tirana, and 5,000 citizens seek refuge in foreign embassies; Central Committee plenum makes significant changes in leadership of party and state. Soviet Union and Albania sign protocol normalizing relations.
October 1990	Ismail Kadare, Albania's most prominent writer, defects to France.
December 1990	University students demonstrate in streets and call for dictatorship to end; Alia meets with students; Thirteenth Plenum of the Central Committee of the APL authorizes a multiparty system; Albanian Democratic Party, first opposition party, established; regime authorizes political pluralism; draft constitution is published; by year's end, 5,000 Albanian refugees have crossed the mountains into Greece. Thousands more seize ships at port and sail illegally to Italy.

1991 In multiparty elections, the Party of Labor and allies win 169 of the 250 seats; the newly formed Democratic Party takes 75. General amnesty announced for political prisoners. First opposition newspaper published. Alia reelected president. Prime Minister Fatos Nano resigns after protests against economic conditions and killing of opposition demonstrators.

1992 Democratic Party wins elections. Party leader Sali Berisha, a former cardiologist, becomes first elected president. Aleksander Meksi is prime minister.

1994 Ex-communist leaders, including Fatos Nano and Ramiz Alia, convicted and jailed for corruption. National referendum rejects new constitution, which opponents say would allow president too much power.

1995 Alia released from prison following ruling by appeals court.

1996 Democratic Party general election victory tainted by accusations of fraud.

1997 Leka, son of late King Zog, returns from exile in bid to take throne. Referendum on restoration of monarchy fails. He is accused of trying to stir up an armed insurrection and flees back into exile. Fraudulent pyramid investment schemes collapse, costing thousands of Albanians their savings and triggering antigovernment protests. Government resigns, and Socialist-led coalition sweeps to power. Fatos Nano, now released from prison, returns as prime minister. Sali Berisha resigns as president in wake of financial crisis, succeeded by Socialist leader Rexhep Mejdani.

1998 Escalating unrest in Kosovo sends refugees across border into Albania.

September 1998 Violent antigovernment street protests after prominent opposition Democratic Party politician, Azem Hajdari, is shot dead by unidentified gunmen. Fatos Nano quits as prime minister. Former student activist, Pandeli Majko, named as new prime minister.

1999 NATO air strikes against Yugoslav military targets. In Kosovo thousands flee attacks by Serb forces. Mass refugee exodus into Albania.

October 2000 Majko resigns as prime minister, after losing Socialist Party leadership vote. Thirty-year-old Ilir Meta becomes Europe's youngest prime minister.

January 2001 Albania and Yugoslavia reestablish diplomatic relations broken off during the Kosovo crisis in 1999.

July 2001 Ruling Socialist Party secures second term in office by winning general elections. Meta names European integration and an end to energy shortages as his priorities.

January 2002 Meta resigns as prime minister after failing to resolve party feud.

February 2002 Majko becomes premier and forms new government, as rival factions in Socialist Party pledge to end infighting.

June 2002 Parliament elects Alfred Moisiu president after rival political leaders Nano and Berisha reach compromise, easing months of tension; royal family returns from exile.

August 2002 Nano becomes prime minister after the ruling Socialist Party decides to merge the roles of premier and party chairman.

January 2003 Albania and EU begin Stabilization and Association Agreement talks, seen as possible first step in long road to EU membership.

ROMANIA

JAMES P. NIESSEN

LAND AND PEOPLE

Romania's 237,500 square kilometers make it the second largest country in the area between Germany and the former Soviet Union. Bodies of water constitute more than half of the Romanian frontier. The River Prut and the Danube Delta form the border with Moldova and Ukraine to the northeast, and there is Black Sea coast to the east for 245 kilometers. The Danube separates the country from Serbia, then Bulgaria to the south before flowing northward across the country to the Ukrainian border. The Danube accounts for more than half of the water frontier, and it is navigable for riverine shipping throughout its Romanian course.

Mountains constitute one-third of Romania's territory. The principal mountain chain consists of the Eastern and Southern Carpathians, which form an arc that is more than 750 kilometers in length, open toward the northwest and with its point close to the country's center, extending south-eastward from near the Ukrainian border, then west to the Iron Gate that frames the Danube's entry into Romania. The Eastern Carpathians extend into Romania from the Ukrainian Carpathians to the north, with a spur westward into Transylvania called the Rodna Mountains. Where the Eastern Carpathians extend southward between Transylvania and Moldavia, their western side features Alpine meadows and lakes of volcanic origin, notably Red (Roşu) and St. Ana Lakes. Two major passes pierce them. The first, the Bârgău Pass, connects Bistriţa in northern Transylvania with the valley of the Moldavian river also named Bistriţa and is immortalized in the opening scenes of Bram Stoker's *Dracula*. The second, the Predeal Pass, provides the rail route for most travelers from central Transylvania to Bucharest with dramatic views of the Bucegi Mountains. Smaller passes between these, through the Bicaz Gorge near Red Lake and the valleys of the Oituz and Buzău, connect the Székely region of eastern Transylvania with central Moldova. The Southern Carpathians (or Transylvanian Alps) are less accessible to travelers because they have fewer passes and arc bypassed by major thoroughfares. West of Bucegi, the Făgăraş massif (including Moldoveanu, the country's highest peak at 2,543 meters) presents an almost impenetrable barrier, of which air travelers between Sibiu and Bucharest may gain an uncomfortably close view. Equally hair-raising is the Trans-Făgăraş Highway, built in the 1960s south of Sibiu, which rises up and through the range near its highest point. Further west, the Olt River Gorge provides the only passage of a major Transylvanian river through the Carpathians at Red Tower Pass. The Făgăraş, Paring, and especially the Retezat massif and its national park, west of the Olt, attract hardy mountaineers to their glaciers, lakes, and wildlife: brown bears, chamois, and lynx.

After the Carpathians, lower, older mountain ranges present less substantial

obstacles within the historic provinces: the Moldavian and Getic Subcarpathians to the east and south, and the Western Mountains (Munţii Apuseni, sometimes called the Western Carpathians) in several ranges from north to south, to the east of the present Hungarian border. Only the highest of the Western Mountains, the Bihor range, reach heights above 2,000 meters. Unlike these other mountains, for most of recorded history the Eastern and Southern Carpathians constituted a political and cultural frontier between Hungarian lands and the principalities of Wallachia and Moldavia, where Romanian statehood first arose.

Wallachia (Ţara Românească) arose from the historical regions of Oltenia and Muntenia, to the west and east of the Olt, formerly seats of viceroys but for many centuries no longer distinct administrative units. The northern part of Wallachia is mountainous country populated seasonally by shepherds and their flocks, by occasional hermitages or larger monastic establishments, and the first capital towns of the medieval and early modern era. The Alpine country gives way to hills and tableland, conducive to fruit (especially plums and apples) and viticulture, punctuated by a series of rivers that broaden as they flow south or east into the low, fertile (Romania's maize and wheat are grown here) plain of the Danube: the Motru, Jiu, Olteţ, Olt, Vedea, Teleorman, Arges, Dîmboviţa, and Ialomiţa Rivers. Ancient and medieval accounts reveal that the Danube plain was previously covered with forests, as are the foothills today. The draining and rerouting of river backwaters has also made the Danube plain less productive for fishing than it once was.

Oltenia's principal city, Craiova, rose to prominence as the seat of a viceroy when he moved down from the hills to the newer town on the middle Jiu that was better situated for east–west communications. Its major industries in recent decades have been automobiles, aircraft, and thermal power. Târgu Jiu, in the northwestern mountains, is the country's main mining center. After heavy development under the communists, it is now environmentally blighted and has been the site of industrial unrest in recent decades. Drobeta-Turnu Severin, whose name refers to its ancient origins (remnants of its Roman bridge across the Danube are still visible), is a transport center east of the Iron Gates and known for the rose gardens in its city center. Muntenia constitutes two-thirds of Wallachia's territory. Bucharest (Bucureşti), the capital, is the cultural and industrial center. Other urban and industrial centers are Ploieşti (long one of the major oil-extracting centers of Europe) and Piteşti (auto manufacturing and textiles) to the north and west. Giurgiu is a smaller industrial center (chemicals) and port on the Danube that was heavily polluted under the communists. Several of Romania's largest lakes are backwaters of the Danube in southern Wallachia.

North of Wallachia and facing the Carpathians from the east, Moldavia bears the same name in Romanian—Moldova—and the same historical origin as the independent state to its northeast on the other side of the Prut. As in Wallachia, Moldavia's Carpathian borders slope irregularly to lower mountains, hills, and the plains. Relatively few rivers (the Bistriţa, Oituz, Trotuş, and Buzău) flow down from these mountains, and the principal rivers, the Siret and

Prut, run parallel to them and form a maize-growing plain before emptying into the Danube. Romania's largest Danubian ports are in Moldavia, Galaţi, and Brăila. Galaţi is also an iron and steelmaking center, and its deep harbor enables it to service oceangoing vessels. The hill country of Moldavia boasts two of Romania's most important wine regions, Vrancea in the south and Cotnari northwest of Iaşi. Iaşi, the historical capital of the province, is the country's second largest city and, like Bucharest, a center of diverse branches of industry. The independent nation of Moldova, largely but not completely synonymous with Bessarabia, is a lowland between the Prut and the Dniester. Modest hills in its center are home to major winegrowing regions, but Moldova's principal crops are maize and sugar beets. The capital city is Chişinău (Slavic: Kishinev). The Transdniester (primarily Slavic) and Gagauzi regions of Moldova, near its southeastern border with Ukraine, are virtually though not de jure independent. The area across the border, which was ceded to Ukraine in 1940, has a Romanian minority.

A third major region is Dobrogea (Slavic: Dobrudja) in the southeast, bounded by the Danube, the Bulgarian border, and the Black Sea. The two major coastal towns were founded by the ancient Greeks and contain extensive archeological remains: Mangalia (Greek: Kallatis) near the Bulgarian border and Constanţa (originally Tomis) further north, Romania's largest Black Sea port and near the mouth of the Danube–Black Sea Canal, completed in 1984. The inland of Dobrogea is dry, with a few ranges of hills and a restored Roman monument at Adamclisi to the conquest of the area from the Dacians by Emperor Trajan. Further north, Histria was a Greek port at the mouth of the Danube before it silted up in the seventh century. For most of the modern era this region was ruled directly by the Ottoman Empire, as evidenced by the presence of mosques and Turkish place-names such as Techirghiol and Medgidia, the latter founded under Sultan Abdul Mejid in 1840. Still further north, the Danube Delta is not a part of Dobrogea either historically or geographically but is commonly included with it. East of the port town of Tulcea on the Ukrainian border, the Danube divides into three arms before it reaches the sea. The Chilia arm forms the border and is the longest, frequently branching arm; the Sulina arm, artificially straightened, is favored by shippers but requires periodic dredging, while the St. George arm is furthest south. This is a sparsely populated region of reedy marshes with more than three hundred species of birds. South of St. George, Lakes Razim and Sinoie are salt-water lagoons. After excessive harvesting of the reeds, overfishing, and an ill-conceived project to gain cropland through draining the area, UNESCO inspired the establishment of the Danube Delta Biosphere Reserve Authority in the 1990s that controls development and tourist access.

Bucovina, historically part of Moldavia, was created in 1775 through the cession of this territory northwest of Iaşi to Austria. While it came to united Romania in 1918, its northern part, with a large Romanian population, was ceded to Soviet Ukraine in 1940. Southern Bucovina is in the northernmost part of current Romania, in the upper reaches of the Siret, Suceava, and Moldova Rivers. Due to isolation near the frontier and the Carpathian barrier to the west, the region is relatively undeveloped. This, along with UNESCO designation as artistic treasures, has helped preserve Bucovina's painted monasteries, founded by Moldavian Prince Stephen the Great in the fifteenth and sixteenth centuries. The influence of 143 years of Austrian rule may be detected in a residual German element of the population and in the appearance of some of the towns.

The mountains extending into Ukraine from Romanian Bucovina separate it from the region of Maramureş, known in Hungarian as Máramaros. Maramureş and three other regions formed part of Hungary from the high Middle Ages until 1918: Crişana, Banat, and Transylvania. All four regions already contained a predominant Romanian element at that time. With the assimilating impact of the Romanian educational system and economic development, their adherence to Romania is secure today, but the influence of their earlier history is evident in the religion, work ethic, political preferences, and customs of all groups of society, as well as in the appearance of the towns. Superior rates of economic development benefited the Romanians and the non-Romanian populations, there were superior educational opportunities, and the legal and administrative framework favored the development of civic awareness.

In Maramureş, as in Bucovina, geographic isolation because of the mountains and the proximity of the frontier has limited the development of industry in recent decades and enabled rural communities to maintain their character. The Guţai, Ţibleş, and Rodna Mountains separate the province from Transylvania to the south, and administratively it formed part of Hungary proper rather than the relatively autonomous Transylvania. The earlier self-governing villages of free peasants and minor nobility have retained their separate consciousness, folk customs, and traditional garb to a surprising extent. These villages populate the valleys of the Iza and Vişeu Rivers, while to their north the upper Tisa (Hungarian: Tisza) River forms part of the Ukrainian border before flowing into the Hungarian plain. The major town, Baia Mare (Hungarian: Nagybánya), is a mining center whose population suffered severely through the construction under the communists of metallurgical plants upwind of the city center. The second city, Sighet (Hungarian: Máramarossziget), on the Ukrainian border, was the site of the country's main detention center for political prisoners in the 1950s.

Crişana (Hungarian: Körösvidék), further south, unlike Maramureş and Transylvania, was not a historical region but a term of convenience for parts of several counties separated from Hungary in 1918 around the Someş (Hungarian: Szamos) and the three branches of the Criş (Hungarian: Körös) Rivers. This region is geographically indistinguishable from the great Hungarian plain. It is a maize-, wheat-, and rye-growing area. Its major towns, Satu Mare (Hungarian: Szatmár) on the Someş and Oradea (Hungarian: Nagyvárad) on the Crişul Repede are seats of Roman Catholic bishoprics, hard on the Hungarian border, that bear the imprint of baroque and fin de siècle architecture.

The Banat (Hungarian: Bánát or Bánság) originated as a regional governorship that emerged in the Hungarian Mid-

Religious freedom, 1991: The local bishop of the legalized Greek Catholic Church celebrates a liturgy on the central square in Cluj to remind onlookers that his former cathedral is still in the hands of the Orthodox Church. In the background are the 1903 statue of a medieval king of Hungary and the Gothic St. Michael's Roman Catholic Church (1432). (Courtesy of James P. Niessen)

dle Ages but gained its modern dimensions after the Austrians reconquered the area from the Turks in 1716. Having been depopulated by centuries of Turkish-Christian warfare, it was now colonized by the Habsburgs with German, French, Romanian, Serbian, and other settlers who received incentives to develop agriculture and crafts. The major towns, Arad on the Mureş (Hungarian: Maros) and Timişoara (Hungarian: Temesvár), were largely rebuilt by the Habsburgs, with French-style fortifications and Central European squares. The Mureş and Timiş Rivers both flow into the Danube on Hungarian territory. The southern plain meets the Danube in the Banat by the old town of Oraviţa, while further east the mining town of Reşiţa is a foretaste of Târgul Jiu.

Transylvania (Romanian: Transilvania or Ardeal; Hungarian: Erdély; German: Siebenbürgen) was associated with the Hungarian Crown from its first documented mention in the twelfth century until its union with Romania in 1918.

Alba Iulia and the Mureş River Valley in Transylvania: The towers of the Orthodox and Catholic cathedrals are visible within the citadel of the former Transylvanian capital, partially obscured by the housing developments of the communist era. (Courtesy of James P. Niessen)

The geographic unity of the province greatly contributed to the separate identity it enjoyed over the centuries, and to some extent still does today. The Eastern and Southern Carpathians formed a natural frontier toward Wallachia and Moldavia, while the Western Mountains performed this function to a much lesser extent toward Hungary proper. North of the Bihor Mountains, the hills do not pose much of a barrier. The Someş flows through a wide valley to Satu Mare, while south of these mountains the Mureş, the longest river of Transylvania, flows through an even wider valley before entering today's Hungary near Arad. Central Transylvania is a well-watered plateau with several major river basins, north to south the Bistriţa, two branches of the Someş, two branches of the Mureş, two branches of the Târnava (Hungarian: Küküllő), and the Olt, that helped, along with the defense needs of Hungarian kings, to define administrative and cultural units in this extremely diverse region. In the north, the headwaters of the Someş and Bistriţa became the seat of a Saxon district, while further east the headwaters of the Mureş and Olt formed the core of the Székely or Szekler district, the middle expanse of the Olt formed the bulk of the Saxon zone, and border regiments of Székely and Romanians guarded the Carpathians to the east and south. Central Transylvania too has its characteristic administrative and ethnographic regions. The major towns, Cluj-Napoca (Hungarian: Kolozsvár), Sibiu (German: Hermannstadt), Tărgu Mureş (Hungarian: Marosvásárhely), and Braşov (German: Kronstadt; Hungarian: Brassó) are largely Romanian today but with significant remnants of the ethnic groups associated with much of their older Gothic, baroque, and art nouveau architecture.

Gold, salt, iron, and copper mining are significant in various parts of Transylvania. Partly in consequence, some of the most polluted towns are in the metallurgical centers Zlatna and Hunedoară and the carbon works at Copşa Mică. Transylvania's relatively high altitude means it has shorter growing seasons than the rest of the country does, but it is well watered and hence well suited for livestock as well as rye, maize, plums, and vineyards. Plum brandy *(ţuica)* is the Romanian national beverage, and it is produced in every region.

PEOPLES

The differing history and date of integration into Romania of its regions has contributed in large part to its ethnographic variety. According to the 1930 census, minorities made up 28 percent of the population. Much of the minor-

Modern and ultramodern in Bucharest: The CEC building (Romanian Savings Bank, 1894–1900) with the incongruous Bancorex building behind it. (Courtesy of James P. Niessen)

ity population was permanently lost in 1940 with the secession of Bessarabia, but powerful assimilationist trends have also been at work. Ethnic self-identification, language, and religion must all be considered in describing the population of Romania. In March 2002 Romania held its twelfth census since the beginning of the nineteenth century. In terms of ethnicity, mother tongue, and religious identification, the census showed the following:

Romanians   Romanians are the predominant ethnic and linguistic group in every region of the country. While there is no consensus among scholars about the length of their residence in the country's territories, their presence is documented since the thirteenth century.

Most Romanians belong to the Romanian Orthodox Church, which is contiguous with the territory of the country, led by a patriarch in Bucharest, and divided into thirteen archbishoprics and bishoprics. Romanian Orthodoxy, with its Byzantine rite liturgy chanted in Romanian, rich tradition of icon painting and architecture, and association with dynastic and military history, is closely associated with national identity. The church, having collaborated with communist authorities after 1945, was the

beneficiary of the suppression of the Romanian Greek Catholic (Uniate) Church in 1948. It enjoyed an expansion of Orthodox seminaries and publishing, but it also meekly accepted the destruction of many historic churches in the 1980s. This attitude damaged the prestige of the church among many Romanians, and consequently it has not been in a position to aid in the restoration of Romanian morale in the face of social and economic stagnation since the fall of communism.

Greek Catholics, whose church was organized in 1700 in Transylvania, live overwhelmingly in that province and are mostly Romanian. Their liturgy and artistic traditions resemble those of the Orthodox, but they recognize the authority of the pope. They numbered roughly 1.4 million, about half the Romanian population in the lands formerly part of Hungary, at the time of the suppression of the church in 1948. Although the church was restored to legality in 1990 and its previously clandestine bishops returned to public life, it has failed to regain possession of most church buildings expropriated in 1948. Doubts raised by the Orthodox about the loyalty of the church to the nation (ecclesiastical ties to the Roman Catholics made it relatively open to Hungarian cultural influence, although Uniate schools and writers were generally bulwarks of Romanian culture under Hungarian rule) and stubborn defense of Orthodox Church property have kept the Uniates on the defensive. To some degree neo-Protestant churches have filled the void, attracting members from the traditional but embattled Romanian churches: the more than half million strong Pentecostal, Baptist, Seventh-Day Adventist, and Evangelical Churches have grown rapidly since 1990 and are primarily Romanian. Roman Catholic Church members are mostly Hungarian but include growing Romanian minorities in Moldavia and to a lesser extent in Wallachia, where Latin rite parishes and bishoprics function in the Romanian language.

There are many Romanian ethnographic regions with distinctive folk arts that have inspired writers, painters, and composers. To mention only a few, Vrancea in southwestern Moldavia is known for its folk music, Gorj in Oltenia for its architecture, Țara moților in the Western Carpathians for its carved wooden objects and annual mating fair, and Maramureș for its carved wooden gates. The monasteries and villages of the Carpathians and especially their shepherds *(ciobani, păcurari, mocani)* are powerful images in Romanian culture.

Hungarians   The large Hungarian minority is a legacy of the lands ceded from Hungary after World War I, where Hungarians had settled in medieval times. Though Romanians have predominated in these lands throughout the modern period and into the present, there is a Hungarian majority in two counties of the Székely region of Transylvania and substantial minorities in most other counties that formerly belonged to Hungary. Miercurea Ciuc (Hungarian: Csíkszereda) and Sfîntu Gheorghe (Sepsiszentgyörgy) are the largest towns with Hungarian majorities, but Târgu Mureș (Marosvásárhely) and Cluj-Napoca (Kolozsvár) have large Hungarian minority populations. The decline of

Table 3.1

Ethnic Identity			Mother Tongue			Religion		
Total	21,698,181	100						
Romanian	19,409,400	89.5	Romanian	19,741,356	91	Orthodox	18,806,428	86.7
Hungarian	1,434,377	6.6	Hungarian	1,447,544	6.7	Roman Catholic	1,028,401	4.7
Roma	535,250	2.5	Romanes	241,617	1.1	Greek Catholic	195,481	0.9
German	60,088	0.3	German	45,129	0.2	Reformed	698,550	3.2
Ukrainian	61,091	0.3	Ukrainian	57,593	0.3	Lutheran CA	11,203	0.1
Serbian	22,518	0.1	Serbian	20,377	0.1	Lutheran SB	26,194	0.1
Turks	32,596	0.2	Turkish	28,714	0.1	Unitarian	66,846	0.3
Tatars	24,137	0.1	Tatar	21,482	0.1	Baptist	129,937	0.6
Slovaks	17,199	0.1	Slovak	16,108	0.1	Pentecostal	330,486	1.5
Jews	5,870		Yiddish	1,100		Seventh-Day Adventist	97,041	0.4
Russians/ Lipovans	36,397	0.2	Russian	29,890	0.1	Muslims	67,566	0.3
Bulgarians	8,092		Bulgarian	6,747		Evangelical Christians	46,029	0.2
Croats	6,786		Croatian	6,355		Old Believers	39,485	0.2
Greeks	6,513		Greek	4,146		Evangelicals	18,758	0.2
Czechs	3,938		Czech	3,339		Jews	6,179	

The Stavropoleos Church (1724), Bucharest: Monument of the Brâncoveanu style and the Phanariot era in Wallachia. (Courtesy of James P. Niessen)

the Hungarian population below 1.5 million in the 2002 census is attributed by both Hungarians and Romanians to emigration, especially to Hungary, but economic stagnation and emigration have caused an absolute decline in the Romanian majority as well. The Hungarian political party, the Democratic Union of Hungarians of Romania, provides Hungarians with a large degree of political unity, and their cultural institutions enjoy the support of the Hungarian government, in which the Romanian government increasingly acquiesces. Hungarian churches and bishops have served as protectors of minority culture. Most members of the Roman Catholic, Reformed (Calvinist), Unitarian, and Synodal Lutheran Churches are Hungarians. There are small Hungarian minorities in Moldavia and Wallachia.

Two special ethnographic groups of the Hungarians are the Székely (or Szekler) people and the Csángós. The Székely owe their origins to a Turkic people that was once distinct from the bulk of the Hungarians, but in modern times it has spoken a form of standard Hungarian and expressed Hungarian political consciousness. Székely towns and rural communities are prized by Hungarians for the traditions of their schools and churches as well as (like the Maramureş Romanians) their carved wooden gates. The Csángós (Romanian: Ciangăi) are a Roman Catholic people living in the valley of the Trotuş River and around the towns of Bacău (Hungarian: Bákó) and Târgu Ocna (Aknavásár) in south central Moldavia. The Csángós are probably of Hungarian origin, though today most speak a local variant of Romanian and are distinguished primarily by their strong Roman Catholic faith. A subgroup of Csángós lives in southeastern Transylvania near the town of Braşov.

Romanian Language

Romanian is a Romance language spoken in Romania, as well as by 65 percent of the population of the Republic of Moldova and much smaller portions of the population of Hungary, Serbia, and other parts of the Balkans. Romanian or Daco-Romanian is the largest variety of the Balkan Romance languages. The others, spoken by small minorities to the south, are Aromanian or Macedo-Romanian, spoken in parts of Albania, Macedonia, and northern Greece; Megleno-Romanian, spoken near Thessaloniki in northern Greece; and Istro-Romanian, spoken in some villages in the Istrian peninsula. Traditionally there have been regional variations of pronunciation (rarely a barrier to comprehension) in the Romanian spoken within Romania, which may be placed into three groups, associated with Moldavia and northern Transylvania, southern Transylvania and Wallachia, and Banat. Among these variants, the Oltenian one became painfully well known through the stuttering, interminable speeches of Nicolae Ceaușescu. The Romanian spoken in the Republic of Moldova, and especially in the separatist region of Transdniestria, is strongly influenced by Russian and Ukrainian, with the soft vowels characteristic of those languages. The constitution of the Republic of Moldova designates the state language as "Moldovan" rather than Romanian.

Romania has a greater grammatical similarity to Latin than do Latin-based Western languages such as French and Spanish, thereby buttressing the theory that the ancestors of the modern Romanians resided continuously on their present territory from Roman times. The earliest surviving Romanian text dates from 1521. Statistical analysis of Romanian dictionaries and usage indicates a majority of the words are of Latin origin (this includes modern French imports), but a large minority is not. Many older words that are associated with agriculture and nature have Slavic, Turkish, Albanian, or Hungarian origins and may be paired with Neolatin forms that were preferred by linguistic reformers. The postpositional direct article (as in *Luceafărul,* The Evening Star, a poem by Eminescu) does not exist in other Romance languages.

The spelling of contemporary Romanian is nearly phonetic. The partial exception is due to the application of linguistic reforms in 1994 and prior to 1945 that sought to emphasize the Latin etymology of Romanian words. While the Romance origin of Romanian is not in doubt, until the nineteenth century it was usually written in Cyrillic. The Danubian Principalities introduced the Latin alphabet in 1860. The use of Cyrillic continued longer in Bessarabia, and it was restored there during the period of Soviet rule between 1940 and 1990. Today Romanian uses a Latin alphabet containing thirty characters. Politically motivated changes in orthography during the twentieth century principally affected the vowels *â* and *î,* as in the word *Român,* later *Romîn* (Romanian). The first form has been standard for most of the twentieth century, but the second, emphasizing the possible Slavic origin of the sound, was introduced in 1954. Since 1965 Romania has replaced Rumania as the preferred English form of the country's name. New Romanian spelling rules were instituted in 1994 concerning additional uses of the vowels *â* and *u: sânt* (are) once again became *sunt,* as in Latin.

Roma (Gypsies)   The enumeration of Romania's Roma, or Gypsies, is difficult. The Budapest-based European Human Rights Foundation estimates the Roma population at 1.9 million, the largest in any country. Official census figures are much lower, but it is likely that anti-Roma sentiment in the general population discourages many Roma from declaring this identity to census takers. Market conditions after 1990 have enabled some Roma to do quite well in business or music and to build gaudy "palaces" in the Roma quarters of some towns, but even larger numbers of Roma have failed to establish a firm footing in the Romanian economy. They suffer from poverty, homelessness, and inadequate education. Tens of thousands of Roma from Romania died in the camps in Auschwitz and Transnistria in World War II. Discrimination against Roma today, including mistreatment by the Romanian police, has been documented by Amnesty International.

The variety of ethnic groupings among the Roma also weakens Roma identity. The 2002 census reveals that only half the self-identified half million Roma indicated Romanes as their mother tongue. Most of the others are speakers of Romanian and, in Transylvania, Romanian or Hungarian. The Roma are politically disunited, with at least four Roma political parties in the country and a rival "king" and "emperor" in the Transylvanian town of Sibiu. Roma are distributed among the churches dominated by the Romanians and Hungarians in their respective regions. "King" Florin Cioaba is a Pentecostal minister. The majority of Roma live in settled urban or rural communities, and only a minority still follow a migratory lifestyle.

Ukrainians and Russians   The 100,000 eastern Slavs in the country are concentrated in two regions, the Ukrainians in Maramureș and adjoining parts of Bucovina, and the

Traditional Gypsy (Roma) metalworkers in a Saxon town of southern Transylvania. (Corel Corporation)

(Sachsen) remain in southern Transylvania. Many Germans fled westward at the end of World War II, and a large portion of those who remained were deported to the Soviet Union. Most deportees returned to Romania in the 1950s but began to emigrate in the 1970s with the collusion of the Romanian and West German governments, which paid a ransom (nominally in remuneration for their education in Romania) for each person. Although the ransom system ended with the fall of communism, German emigration became a flood in 1990. Many abandoned Saxon villages have been occupied by Roma, while their historic churches are preserved by foundations based in Germany or have been purchased by Romanian congregations.

Turks and Tatars   Turks and Tatars are remnants of larger settlements in Dobrogea and the Lower Danube that arose during the period of Ottoman domination in Wallachia and Moldavia. Their Muslim religion has proven more tenacious than their language and ethnic identity. Two mosques in Constanţa were built in 1868 and 1910; there are older mosques in Mangalia and Babadag. Romania's growing economic relations with Turkey have helped ensure the preservation of these monuments and modest support for Turkish and Tatar cultural organizations.

Jews   Romania's Jewish population, like that of the Germans, was once much larger. Jews were a majority of the population of Iaşi in the late nineteenth century, and they accounted for much of the commercial activity in Moldavia. Romanian anti-Semitism was correspondingly strongest there. It gained powerful influence in Romanian political life during the interwar period, although Jewish–Christian relations had been relatively peaceful in Bucharest. Jews east and south of the Carpathians were Sephardim, while those in the formerly Habsburg lands were Ashkenazim. The Holocaust took a heavy toll on both these groups, the former being deported by Romanian troops to Transnistria and the latter by the Hungarians to Auschwitz. Still, more Jews survived the Holocaust in Romania than in any other country in the region. As with the Germans, a ransom system (financed by Israel) facilitated the emigration of most survivors by the 1980s. Fewer than 10,000 Jews remain in Romania, but the country's ultranationalists still find anti-Semitism (often paired with anti-Hungarianism) a useful tool.

Russians (Lipovani) in the Danube Delta. The political importance of these minorities is heightened, and their status either worsened or improved, according to the nature of Romania's relations with Ukraine and the Republic of Moldova, where Ukrainians and Russians exercise strong influence over the fortunes of the Romanians living in those countries. The Ukrainians in Romania's northwest adhere primarily to the Ukrainian Orthodox Church, but a minority are Greek Catholics. The Lipovani are Russian Orthodox Old Believers, who came to the delta at the time of Peter the Great to escape religious persecution.

Germans   At its height, during the interwar period, Romania's German minority was ten times larger than its current size. The ancestors of some Germans were brought to Transylvania by Hungarian kings in the thirteenth century to settle and defend the southern borderland of the province, while others came in the eighteenth century to help revive the economy of southeastern Hungary after its liberation from the Turks. Today perhaps two-thirds of the Germans are Roman Catholic Swabians (Schwaben) residing in the Banat, while less than 20,000 Lutheran Saxons

HISTORY

The territories that now compose Romania came together between 1859 and 1918. Although there were intermittent attempts and one brief early success at uniting these lands because of their geopolitical position, the idea that they constituted a Romanian nation arose only in recent centuries. The first published reference to this "Romania" occurred in the early nineteenth century. If we nonetheless project the history of the country further back in time, it is with the understanding that these territories' association with each other was most of the time no stronger than their association with lands that are now outside the borders of Romania. A two-thousand-year history of Romania in this sense is still not totally anachronistic because the cultures in today's country owe much to earlier history. Historians simply disagree about how.

ANCIENT AND MEDIEVAL TIMES

The Thracians, an Indo-European people, lived in much of the area as far south as Homeric Greece in the Iron Age. Greeks established trading colonies along the Black Sea coast of Dobrogea at the end of this period, and reported the presence in the hinterland of Getae and Dacians. They spoke the same language; hence writers today use the term "Geto-Dacians" for this Thracic people that lived in an area resembling modern Romania. Herodotus and other Greek writers have left descriptions of their monotheistic religion and social organization. Small Geto-Dacian kingdoms coalesced into a Dacian "empire" under Burebista in the first century B.C.E., which extended far into modern Hungary and Slovakia. Burebista's capital for a while was Argedava in Wallachia south of today's Bucharest, then later at Sarmizegetusa in southern Transylvania. This empire fell apart after Burebista sided with Pompey in the Roman civil war and was assassinated. The Roman poet Ovid was exiled to the Greek town of Tomis on the Black Sea, at the beginning of the first century. We know he was not happy to be there. A collection of his poems from the years in Tomis is entitled *Tristia* (Poems of Sadness).

Hostilities between Rome and the Dacians increased, in part over control of the rich deposits of gold in Transylvania. Rome annexed Dobrogea to its province of Moesia in 46 C.E. Later in the century, the Dacian kingdoms reunited and fought a series of wars against the Romans before suffering final defeat by the Roman Emperor Trajan in 106, when the Dacian ruler Decebalus (Decebal in Romanian) committed suicide while in flight. In the course of these campaigns, the Romans erected two structures whose ruins have survived to the present: a bridge across the Danube at Drobeta-Turnu Severin in the west, and a monument to the Roman victory in Dobrogea at Tropaeum Traiani, today's Adamclisi. Tropaeum Traiani and the narrative history of the campaign on Trajan's Column in the Roman Forum give us an idea of how the Dacians may have looked. Sources disagree as to whether the Dacian population of the province survived the conquest.

The period of Roman rule over Dacia varied by region: six centuries for Dobrogea, four and a half centuries for southern Oltenia and Banat, 160 years for most of Oltenia, Banat, and Transylvania. Roman rule in Muntenia and southern Moldavia lasted barely a decade. Northern Moldavia and two-thirds of Bessarabia were never occupied, the Romans settling only for military outposts near the mouth of the Danube and nearby Greek colonies, and today's Maramureş was not occupied either. "Free Dacians" in the unoccupied area, Costoboci and Carps, and Germans attacked the Romans repeatedly. Roman Dacia had one of the longest borders of any province facing the *barbaricum*—the Free Dacians and Sarmatians to the north and east and the Sarmatians west of the gold mines in central Transylvania that were the source of the province's wealth.

Given the importance of its mineral treasure and exposed position, Roman Dacia required a substantial military presence. The contested eastern frontier followed the Carpathians, then the line of the Olt River south to the Danube. After the loss of Muntenia, a defensive line was built to the east of the Olt, the *limes transalutanus,* fortified by fourteen military camps from Cumidava, inside the Bran Pass in Transylvania, to Flămânda on the Danube. The frontier of Moesia was similarly defended along the line of the lower Danube, and there were large camps on the Danube south of the Banat and the Mureş, Criş, and Someş in Transylvania. In the interior of Transylvania, Apulum (now Alba Iulia) and Napoca (now Cluj-Napoca) were regional capitals, Apulum housing one legion, while further south Sarmizegetusa, then Berzobis in the Banat housed another. There were up to 55,000 Roman soldiers in Dacia in the late second century, and 10,000–15,000 in Dobrogea.

Most of the estimated 600,000 to 1 million inhabitants of Roman Dacia were civilians, many of them officials brought in from other parts of the empire. After a century of Roman rule, five cities had an estimated population over 10,000, plus three more in Dobrogea. There was extensive construction: aqueducts to supply the major cities, baths, and mineral baths in places like Băile Herculane and Germisara that possessed this resource. The Romans connected their major camps with roads paved in stone, one of which an Austrian map of 1722 suggests was still in use at that time. Inscriptions that have survived on funerary monuments and elsewhere suggest the principal language of the cities in Dacia was Latin and a mixture of Greek and Latin in the towns of Dobrogea, whereas in the rural communities people must have continued to speak Dacian. The objects of religious worship were generally Greco Roman deities.

During an invasion of western Transylvania in 167, workers in a gold mine at Alburnus Maior (now Roşia Montana) hid a number of wax tablets documenting the accounts of the mine. The special conditions in the mine shaft enabled these tablets to survive intact until their celebrated discovery in 1786 and later. The inscriptions, dating between 131 and 167 (mostly in Latin with some in Greek), are often signed by persons who identify themselves as scribes, but other inscriptions are unsigned, suggesting that Latin literacy characterized more than just a narrow segment of the population. The exploitation of gold, begun under the Dacians, was expanded under the control of the imperial treasury with skilled Illyrian miners. Stone, salt, grain, vegetables, and fruit were also produced in Dacia, some on major farms, and exported to other provinces.

Much of the construction and economic growth of Roman Dacia took place in spurts during isolated decades of peace between periods of invasion and war. Disorder at the heart of the empire compounded the impact of the invasions, with new emperors, often imposed by the army, succeeding one another in quick succession. At times, they withdrew troops from Dacia to meet incursions elsewhere. After winning a military victory on another front, Aurelian used the ensuing respite to organize an orderly retreat of his troops and administration from Roman Dacia by the end of his reign in 275. It appears likely that the bulk of the wealthy city dwellers and colonists withdrew with the troops, while there is disagreement as to whether many of the peasantry and common people stayed behind. The central portion of Moesia south of the Danube accommodated many of the refugees.

Roman Dacia survived longest in the south. The bridgeheads on the northern shore of the Danube were maintained and even expanded in the fourth through sixth centuries, and Emperor Justinian built major Christian basilicas in Sucidava (Celei) in the west and Tomis in Dobrogea. Latin remained the language of the Eastern Roman Empire until the late sixth century, or shortly before the Byzantines finally abandoned Dobrogea after a rule of six centuries.

Compared to the extensive written and archaeological remains of Roman Dacia, far less is known about the rulers, and even less about the population, of the non-Roman area and Romania in the following centuries. Funerary practices have given rise to varied conclusions based on the idea that the Romans or Romanized peoples buried their dead, while the Dacians and others cremated them. The ethnic origin of ceramic finds is difficult to establish. Major hoards of fine jewels and weapons from the post-Roman era are more easily identified with the temporary Germanic and Turkic rulers of the day.

Six dominant peoples succeeded each other in much of the region, on either or both sides of the Carpathians, before the arrival of the Hungarians in the ninth century: Goths, Huns, Gepids, Avars, Slavs, and Bulgars. The first successors were the Visigoths, a Germanic people under whom a shadow of Roman urban civilization continued in the area. Many of the Goths adopted Christianity, and their martyr, St. Sava, is venerated throughout the region. Next came the Huns, a Turkic people from Asia who destroyed much of the remaining urban life and exacted tribute as they moved their power center with time from Wallachia to Pannonia in the west. After the defeat of the Huns in 454, the Gepids, another Germanic people who had been their vassals, succeeded them in Wallachia and Transylvania. A century later, they were overturned by the Avars, another Turkic people. The Avars dominated the areas formerly known as Pannonia and Dacia for two centuries, until their defeat in the West by the Franks in 827.

These peoples left virtually no written records, though Ulfila the Goth, an Arian bishop, created the first vernacular translation of the Christian Bible. They kept no archives, had no stable administrative seat on Romanian territory, and erected no buildings that have survived.

The Daco-Roman population left little evidence of its continued existence here. Coin hoards show that Roman coins circulated after the Romans left, as they did in regions the Romans had never occupied. Archaeologists have found graves from the fourth and fifth centuries that followed Roman burial ritual. There is little evidence of the practice of Christianity in Roman Dacia, though subsequently a degree of Christianization of the common people took place after Christianity became the state religion of Rome, thirty years after the legions departed. Altars of Roman origin

were recarved with Christian symbols, and a candelabrum with a Latin votive inscription suggests some of these Christians spoke Latin. Such evidence is lacking for the following centuries. In a Roman envoy's account of his journey through the Banat in 448, he writes that he was given a beverage called "in the local language" *medos,* which might indicate the Latin *medus,* mead. A chronicle reports that a native soldier south of the Danube in 587 was heard to utter a Latin phrase "in the local language," *torna, torna, frater* (turn around, turn around, brother).

The Slavs settled in the Balkans, for the most part peacefully, as farmers. Place-names in Moldavia and Wallachia suggest Romanians and Slavs may have coexisted, as the name of the region Vlaşca (referring to Vlachs) and of the River Dâmboviţa, on which Bucharest is situated, appeared to be of Slavic origin. The large number of words of Slavic origin among Romanian agricultural terms also supports this possibility. In 679 a horde of Turkic Bulgars occupied the Byzantine province of Moesia (with Dobrogea) and subjugated the Slavs who lived there but became assimilated in turn by the Slavic majority. In the ninth century the Bulgars occupied most of the Avar lands, refortifying and renaming Belegrad (Bǎlgrad in old Romanian), the former Apulum. By the 870s, the Bulgarian rulers accepted Christianity and a Cyrillic alphabet from the Byzantine Greeks.

The adherence of the Romanians to the Eastern Church, and use of the Slavonic language in their liturgy, may date from this period of Bulgarian influence. We are not yet on firm documentary ground, however, because the Romanians lacked a state of their own while the lands between the Danube and the Carpathians were under the domination of the Pechenegs, another preliterate Turkic people. This was the state of affairs when the more stable Hungarian rule began to assert itself in Hungary, then by stages and from the west, in Transylvania. Hungarians gave Transylvania this name because it was beyond the wooded hills that formed a modest barrier to their penetration.

Were the Romanians in these lands when the Pechenegs and Hungarians imposed their rule? Modern Romanian historians assert that a Latin-speaking population developed in Dacia under Roman rule and their descendants have occupied the same territory more or less continuously. In support of this thesis are the unquestionably Latin character of the Romanian language, the archaeological evidence of continued Latinate population for a few centuries, and references in Armenian, Byzantine, Hungarian, Norman, and Russian chronicles, beginning in the ninth century, to Vlachs (probably meaning Romance speakers) in the northern Balkans and Romania. Others, however, above all Hungarians, maintain that the thesis of Daco-Romanian continuity on Romanian territory is not proven by available evidence. In support of a countervailing thesis that Romanian-speaking Vlachs came to Romania from the south, they cite linguistic evidence, the substantial absence of German and Turkic elements in modern Romanian that would have resulted from living under the domination of Visigoths, Huns, Gepids, and Avars, and certain similarities to Albanian that would suggest they lived an extended period in the south. In addition, they cite references in Hungarian documents to Romanian immigration from the south after the establishment of Hungarian rule in Central Europe.

THE LATE MEDIEVAL STATES AND OTTOMAN CONQUEST

There can be no doubt of the presence of substantial numbers of Hungarians and Romanians on the current territory of Romania no later than the twelfth century. Fleeing attacks from the Turkic Pechenegs, the Hungarians entered the central Carpathian basin from the north at the end of the ninth century. The chronicle of the anonymous notary of King Béla III, *Gesta Hungarorum,* presents a version of the Hungarian conquest of Transylvania, written in the last decade of the twelfth century and widely accepted by Romanian historians today, in which the Hungarians had to overcome Romanian military resistance to establish control. Hungarian historians question this account, noting that Anonymus wrote more than two centuries after the events he describes and the purported presence of Romanians at the time of the conquest is not corroborated elsewhere. It appears more likely that occupation by the Hungarian king took place over a period of two centuries, overcoming Bulgarian military outposts and local Hungarian leaders of mixed ethnicity. Writing in the late 1190s, Anonymus likely had some contemporary knowledge of the substantial presence of Romanians in Transylvania. The Hungarian documents mention Romanian military servitors on the royal estates in Transylvania, and they were also reported in Hungarian retinues that fought the Bulgarians in the Balkans. These Romanians may have settled in the recent past or their ancestors may have inhabited the region already. From this time on, for most of eight centuries, the Carpathians would constitute a political frontier between the main concentrations of Romanians.

In establishing their control over Transylvania, the Hungarian kings ratified several characteristics of the province that would evolve and survive into the nineteenth century and distinguish it from the lands across the mountains. First, Transylvania was a voivodate (Crown land) with its own voivode (viceroy). Second, it was ethnically diverse, with Hungarians, Székelys (a Turkic people that soon adopted the Hungarian language), Saxons (Germans who came originally not from Saxony but from the Low Countries), and Romanians. Third, conditioned by geography and the local needs of military defense and economic development, these peoples developed distinctive social structures and administrative autonomies within their regions: Hungarian landed nobility dominated the peasantry in the counties, the gentry and free peasantry had self-government in the Székely region, and the Saxons enjoyed autonomy and substantial mercantile privileges in theirs. Romanian regions in the north (Maramureş) and south (Haţeg and Făgăraş) had a more contested constitutional status.

Contention over the Romanians arose from the Catholic policy of the Hungarian kings. The Hungarian kingdom prized the prestige accorded it by papal recognition in the year 1000. The Catholic clergy and faith allied with royal power, demanding religious as well as political fealty from the king's subjects. Participation in the social status and political privileges of the nobility required adherence to Catholicism, prompting the resistance of pre-Christian Hungarians and Cumans in Hungary, then increasingly of the Orthodox Romanians after the East–West church schism of 1054. Romanians participated as one of the four estates in the Transylvanian diet between 1291 and 1355, then they were excluded thereafter. A peasant revolt in 1437–1438, while not exclusively ethnic in character, drew sufficient Romanian support that the three privileged nations responded after its defeat by concluding a *unio trium nationum* that explicitly excluded a Romanian nation from the Transylvanian constitution. But *nation* should not be understood in the modern ethnic sense. Romanian notables could join the Hungarian nobility (primarily through conversion to Catholicism) without assimilating linguistically.

Contemporary sources support the substantial presence of Romanians between the Carpathians and the Danube after the tenth century. The Byzantine Empire experienced a final resurgence in the eleventh and twelfth centuries, defeating the First Bulgarian Empire, regaining the Danube frontier, and recapturing Dobrogea. Their adversaries to the north were the Turkic Cumans and Pechenegs, who occupied most of the land between the Dniester, the Carpathians, and the Danube. The evidence of place-names and archaeological remains indicates there was a mixed population of Slavs, Romanians, and Turkish rulers. In 1185–1186 an anti-Byzantine rebellion established the Second Bulgarian Empire under a Romanian–Slavic dynasty. These circumstances may explain the increased documentary evidence of a Romanian presence north of the Danube.

At the beginning of the twelfth century, the Hungarian king established the Banat (or military province of Severin) and the voivodates of Litovoi and Seneslau as outposts of his power south of the Carpathians. Mongol invasions prevented the Hungarians from consolidating their position and led to decades of disorder in Hungary. Meanwhile, the voivodes in Wallachia sought to increase their autonomy. In 1277 Litovoi refused to pay tribute to the king of Hungary and was killed in battle.

The suppression of the autonomy of Făgăraş and assertion of royal power in southern Transylvania led indirectly to the foundation of the Wallachian state. According to Romanian tradition, a leader in Făgăraş, rather than submit, traveled across the Carpathians with his retinue and established a new authority in the town of Câmpulung. Wallachia was called in Hungarian Havaselve (Across the Mountains) and in Romanian Ungrovlahia or Ţara Românească (the Romanian Land). Wallachia under Prince Basarab (ca. 1310–1352), the founder of the dynasty, recognized Hungarian suzerainty for the first half century of its existence. The Hungarian king sought to suppress the principality's growing autonomy, launching an attack in 1330 on Basarab's second capital, Curtea de Argeş. The Hungarian king failed to capture Basarab and barely escaped with his life after a devastating Wallachian ambush of the retreating Hungarian troops at the battle of Posada, which is recorded in the *Illustrated Chronicle of Vienna*. Basarab united the Wallachian voivodate and the

Banat of Severin, and then asserted independence from Hungary in 1359. Basarab briefly extended Wallachian territory as far as the port cities of the Danube mouth. Hence the territory that would be annexed by Russia in 1812 from Moldavia drew its name from a Wallachian prince.

The foundation of the Moldavian state proceeded like that of Wallachia, but later. Having defeated the Tatars east of the Carpathians in the early fourteenth century, the Hungarians made use of Romanian leaders from Maramureş. According to legend, the founder of the state, Dragoş, came here in pursuit of an aurochs (a European bison), later depicted in the seal of Moldavia. For several decades the region was under Hungarian suzerainty. In 1359 Bogdan, the leader of the Romanians who opposed Hungarian authority, deposed the descendants of Dragoş and established Moldavian independence. Moldavia drew its name from a minor river in the region but was also called Moldovlahia and, by the Turks, the Land of Bogdan. Like Wallachia, the new state created an effective military force with remarkable speed. The first capitals of Moldavia, Siret, Baia, and Suceava, like those of Wallachia, were not far from the mountain frontier. By the end of the fourteenth century, Moldavia controlled the mouth of the Danube.

It is anachronistic to label the three Carpathian provinces "Romanian lands," in anticipation of the later unification of Romania. The ethnic composition of the Transylvanian population in the Middle Ages is hotly contested, whereas the rulers of the province were clearly Hungarians, Szeklers, and Saxons. The term is problematic in the case of Wallachia and Moldavia. Under Basarab and Bogdan, these states established a status close to independence, and Romanians were almost certainly the dominant element in their societies and government. Yet contemporaries did not refer to them as Romanian states. The language of the princely chanceries, reflected in surviving documents from the fourteenth through sixteenth centuries, was Slavonic (the language of medieval Bulgaria and of the Orthodox liturgy) written with Cyrillic characters. Amlaş and Făgăraş, Romanian regions in Transylvania, were held by the princes of Wallachia until 1476, and two years later Stephen the Great of Moldavia referred to Wallachia as "the other Romanian country." But a preferable collective term for Wallachia and Moldavia, which reflects their similar geopolitical situation, is Danubian Principalities.

The political model of the Danubian Principalities was Byzantine autocracy. In styling themselves sovereign ruler and by the grace of God (somoderzhavnoi, bozhiiu milostiu), the prince (voivod or hospodar) asserted independence from erstwhile suzerain powers, but also the native nobility that claimed the right to elect him and his successors. The ruler asserted eminent domain over all the land in the principality and ultimate judicial power as well. The main officials, who all served at his personal pleasure, derived their names and functions from Byzantium and Bulgaria: the chief secretary or chancellor (logofăt), treasurer (vistier), head of the judiciary (vornic), chief diplomat or master of ceremonies (postelnic, portar, uşar), and various household functions (paharnic, stolnic, comis, clucer, sluger, pitar). The chief military adjunct of the prince was named spătar in Wallachia, while in Moldavia his title probably came from the Polish realm, hatman. The prince called occasionally on a princely council, made up of major landowners and, increasingly, officials. Unlike in Transylvania, there were occasional noble assemblies but no periodic diets in the Danubian Principalities or constitutionally established regional autonomies. The only important regional subdivision was Oltenia, whose ban, residing in Craiova on the Jiu River, was the successor of the bans of Severin and a leading member of the princely council who for many decades challenged the Basarab family for the Wallachian throne.

The Principalities also emulated Byzantium in the role assigned to the Orthodox Church. In 1359 the emperor recognized the creation at Curtea de Argeş of an Orthodox metropolitanate for Wallachia, which until the twentieth century was called Mitropolia Ungrovlahiei. Similarly a metropolitanate was established by the Moldavian prince in Suceava in the late fourteenth century with Byzantine sanction. The princes built many churches and monasteries where Greek and Slavonic religious texts were transcribed, and they encouraged their nobility to emulate them. The many Moldavian church foundations of Prince Stephen the Great in the second half of the fifteenth century included the now UNESCO-protected "painted monasteries" of Bucovina, with colorful external murals depicting biblical scenes and the fall of Constantinople in 1453. The church in Wallachia, and to a lesser extent in Moldavia, ordained or consecrated many Orthodox clergy and bishops for the Romanians in Transylvania. The Wallachian princes also became patrons of one of the monasteries on Mount Athos in Greece.

The international position of the fledgling Danubian Principalities was determined in large part by their role in riverine trade. Transit of ships through the Iron Gates of the Danube in the west was not yet feasible, so that an overland connection to the Principalities' entrepôts was crucial for Central Europe. For Wallachia the key port was Brăila, at the point in the river closest to the bend in the Carpathians and the Transylvanian Saxon town of Braşov (German: Kronstadt), while for Moldavia Cetatea Albă (Akkerman), near the mouth of the Dniester and Chilia in the Danube Delta, were the outlets for trade toward Lwów and Poland. The princes' concessions to the merchants of Braşov and Lwów conditioned in large degree the relationship of Wallachia and Moldavia with Hungary and Poland respectively. At times the Principalities recognized the suzerainty of the larger state explicitly; at other times they acted as allies or outright adversaries. These client relationships with the great powers of East Central Europe helped solidify and perpetuate the existence of the principalities as distinct states with their own interests despite their similar Romanian population and Byzantine system of church and state.

The rising Ottoman power confronted Catholic Hungary and Poland and, more directly, their Orthodox client states. A series of princes filled the role of crusader against the Turks on behalf of Christian Europe. Mircea the Old, prince of Wallachia (1386–1395; 1397–1418), fought the Turks at the battle of Rovine in 1395; during the interregnum he joined the Christian forces at the battle of Nicopolis in

1396, and then later he intervened in the Ottoman succession struggles after 1402 to support the less expansionist candidate against the later Mehmed I. After Mehmed's succession to the throne, however, Mircea was forced in 1415 to recognize Ottoman suzerainty and pay an annual tribute. Wallachian princes would contest this suzerainty repeatedly in the coming centuries, often paying for their resistance with their thrones or their lives. The act of 1415, emulated later in Moldavia, guaranteed the Principalities' internal autonomy and statehood, in contrast to the former Christian states to the south, now reduced to pashaliks.

The union of Christian forces was the byword at the meeting at Florence in 1437 that declared a union of the Eastern and Western Churches under the pope, with the retention for the Eastern Churches of the Byzantine liturgy. The bishops from Wallachia and Moldavia, like those from Byzantium, subscribed to the church union. The ensuing Christian military assault, however, led to disaster at the battle of Varna, on the Bulgarian Black Sea coast, in 1444. The Hungarian military leader, a South Transylvanian of Romanian origin known in English as John Hunyadi, won a series of stirring Christian victories over the Turks at mid-century despite the fall of Constantinople, most notably at the battle of Belgrade in 1456, at which he was killed. The brutal Vlad the Impaler (Vlad Ţepeş), Vlad III Dracula, prince of Wallachia (1448, 1456–1462, 1476), continued the principality's crusading tradition with intermittent Hungarian support but against increasing odds, twice forced from the throne by domestic partisans of the Turks but dying in battle. Moldavian Prince Stephen the Great (1457–1504) won a brilliant victory over the Turks at Vaslui in 1475 and was proclaimed Athlete of Christ by the pope. Even so he had to fight the Hungarians and Poles to maintain his position, and in 1485 he recognized Ottoman control over Cetatea de Albă and Chilia.

The successors of Hunyadi, Vlad, and Stephen were forced to recognize Ottoman superiority. Hungarian society was weakened by social conflict. A projected new crusade in 1514 ended in bloody repression when the peasant host turned against the landlords. The suppression of the revolt led to a strengthening of serfdom. A minor Székely nobleman, György Dózsa, led the rebels and the heaviest fighting was in Transylvania. An Ottoman assault on Vienna in 1521 was turned back, but the king of Hungary died fleeing the battlefield after defeat at the hands of the Turks in Mohács, Hungary, in 1526. These events enabled the Turks to formally establish suzerainty over Moldavia in 1535 and establish a pashalik in Hungary and a client relationship with Transylvania in 1541. The role of the Principalities as commercial connectors between the Balkans and Central Europe was at an end. To ensure better control from Constantinople, the Wallachian and Moldavian capitals moved to the lowland towns of Bucharest and Iaşi.

OTTOMAN DOMINATION AT ITS HEIGHT (SIXTEENTH AND SEVENTEENTH CENTURIES)

For over 250 years in the case of Hungary and Transylvania, and more than four centuries in the Danubian Principali-ties, the Ottoman sultans exercised ultimate authority over these lands, directing their trade toward the southeast and draining their resources through financial levies. Unlike Hungary proper and the lands south of the Danube, however, Transylvania, Wallachia, and Moldavia were governed by their own Christian princes rather than Ottoman pashas and local elites. Though the Turks often exercised decisive influence on the selection of the princes, these princes maintained their own armed forces and more or less independent foreign policies. Only relatively small contingents of Ottoman troops were stationed in the principalities, and they were not subject to Islamic law or the child levy (devshirme) for the supply of the Ottoman armed forces. Foreign exploitation was more extreme in the case of the Danubian Principalities than in Transylvania, but even there Romanian culture made important advances. The relatively light Ottoman yoke in Transylvania permitted the Hungarian and Saxon rulers to avoid both Habsburg and direct Ottoman rule, which caused Hungary proper to be divided between the two rival empires.

The outstanding Romanian historian Nicolae Iorga, in one of his most influential writings, characterized the system of rule in the Danubian Principalities during these centuries as Byzantium after Byzantium (Byzance après Byzance). The phrase signifies the remarkable survival of Byzantine tradition in the Principalities after the demise of the Byzantine state as well as the other Balkan Orthodox states that, like the principalities, had been modeled on it, Serbia and Bulgaria. The Orthodox Church continued as before under the authority of Danubian princes, rather than the Greek patriarch in Constantinople, but the ties between the Romanian church and the monasteries on Athos survived and prospered. Greek scholars, noblemen, and merchants as well as churchmen found refuge in the Principalities, and the princes saw themselves as the protectors of Byzantine imperial tradition.

Nomination of the prince originated formally in the noble assembly but was normally contingent on Turkish approval, which required the payment of a fee to the Porte, at times hundreds of thousands of gold ducats, as well as the assumption of the previous ruler's debts. New rulers went into debt to acquire their throne, then sought to recover their investment through the taxation of their subjects. An increasing variety of other payments (pescheşuri) accentuated the tendency toward corruption. The annual tribute to the Porte or haraci, principal symbol of Ottoman suzerainty, rose from 10,000 ducats in the fifteenth century to 65,000 ducats in Moldavia and 155,000 ducats in Wallachia by the end of the next. The principalities were required to supply a percentage of their produce in wheat and livestock to the Porte, a payment that led in time to farmers instead planting American corn or maize, not subject to the levy. The principalities no longer enjoyed the right to their own coinage as earlier. Polenta (mamaligă) became the staple of the Romanian commoner's diet during these years.

The princes' tenure in office tended to be short, both because the Porte sought to collect additional payments and because the princes' repeated involvement in anti-Ottoman alliances led to their execution or death in battle. Despite

Vlad III Dracula, or Vlad the Impaler (ca. 1429–1476)

This medieval ruler of Wallachia is remembered primarily for his role in the bloody struggle against Turkish domination in the fifteenth century, and for a fictitious character with whom he had no connection in fact.

His era was a period of extreme political instability due to the lack of a clear law of succession and the interference of outside forces. Between 1418 and 1476, eleven princes had twenty-nine separate reigns, for an average of only two years. Vlad III Dracula was the son of Wallachian Prince Vlad II Dracul (ruled 1436–1442, 1443–1447), whom Emperor Sigismund inducted into the Order of the Dragon; Dracula meant the "son of the dragon" (or "devil"). The son lived four years as a hostage in Ottoman captivity and became the Turkish favorite for the throne after his father was assassinated at the instigation of the Hungarian commander, János (John) Hunyadi. He had three periods as Prince of Wallachia: (1448, 1456–1462, 1476). The first period was brief: while Prince Vladislav II was away on campaign, he seized power with the support of the Turks. Paradoxically, Vlad chose to take refuge in the Kingdom of Hungary, the great adversary of the Turks, when Vladislav ousted him from the throne. Hunyadi then helped him regain the throne eight years later. During this second reign Vlad achieved a bad reputation for his brutal treatment of internal boiar opponents, Transylvanian Saxon commercial rivals, and Turkish invaders. Impalement was not unique to him; it was practiced elsewhere in the contemporary Balkans. In 1461–1462 Vlad refused to pay tribute to the Porte and attacked Ottoman positions along the Danube and in Bulgaria, winning stunning victories that made him famous in Christian Europe. A massive Ottoman counterattack ousted Vlad a second time and forced him to retreat to the Carpathians, where the Hungarians captured and imprisoned him on suspicion of collusion with the Turks. The Hungarian king helped him regain the throne a third time. Once again his reign was short, and he died in battle during the Turkish counterattack.

For many, Vlad's afterlife is more interesting, and it is certainly better documented, than his confusing political career. German, Russian, and Romanian legends emphasized his cruelty or his sense of justice, while modern Romanian historians seeking national heroes highlighted his military brilliance and political leadership. Vampire beliefs existed in the region too, but it was the British writer Bram Stoker who united them in his novel *Dracula* in 1897. Among the many celebrated dramatic portrayals of Dracula were F. W. Murnau's silent film *Nosferatu* (1922), Tod Browning's talking film *Dracula* starring Bela Lugosi (1931), Carl Dreyer's *Vampyr* (1932), Terence Fisher's *The Horror of Dracula* starring Christopher Lee (1958), John Badham's *Dracula* starring Frank Langella (1979), and Francis Ford Coppola's *Dracula* starring Gary Oldman (1992). Scores of fiction writers have reworked the story as well. Dracula tourism has untapped economic potential for Romania. A businessman formerly employed by the Ministry of Tourism has been marketing "Dracula tours" since 1993. Plans to build a theme park near the picturesque Transylvanian Saxon town of Sighişoara, Vlad's birthplace, were set aside in 2003 after protests by Britain's Prince Charles and other preservationists. However, the government has approved a backup plan to build it in Snagov, where an Orthodox monastery outside Bucharest contains Vlad's grave. An Austrian brewery and a Greek subsidiary of Coca-Cola have signed on in exchange for ten-year concessions.

overwhelming Turkish military superiority and Turkish control of important military installations on the Danube at Giurgiu and Brăila to the south and the former Black Sea outlets of Moldavia to the north, the two states participated in military actions on the side of the less vulnerable, wealthier Transylvania and Poland. In small recompense for these alliances, the central Transylvanian estate and fortress of Cetatea de Baltă (Hungarian: Küküllővár) was deeded to the principalities for extended periods. From 1508 to 1593, twenty-three princes of Wallachia had thirty-four separate periods of rule, while from 1504 to 1606 twenty-one princes of Moldavia had twenty-eight periods of rule. Children of leading politicians were frequently held hostage as a guarantee of political reliability: thus Gabriel Bethlen, prince of Transylvania from 1613 to 1629, and Dimitrie

Cantemir, prince of Moldavia (1693; 1710–1711), both acceded to the throne after many years lived in Constantinople. Still, the principalities' military success and international agreements enabled them to ward off Ottoman plans to annex them, causing the sultan instead to withdraw most occupying troops and recognize the ruling princes.

To the north, Transylvania evolved from an autonomous territory of the Hungarian kingdom to a virtually independent principality. An interregnum in Hungary followed the destruction of the royal army and death of the king at Mohács in 1526. Two claimants to the throne arose: Ferdinand of Habsburg on the basis of an inheritance treaty concluded in 1515, and János Szapolyai, a major Hungarian landowner and military leader, as the choice of home-rule advocates in the Hungarian diet. To prevent a Habsburg occupation of

Gabriel Bethlen, Prince of Transylvania (1580–1629). This Hungarian Protestant was the most successful ruler of independent Transylvania during its 150-year history. (Hulton-Deutsch Collection / Corbis)

Hungary, the Turks occupied central Hungary and in 1541 established direct rule over the region with a pasha in control in Buda. To the north and west, in current day Slovakia and Transdanubia, the Habsburgs established control in so-called royal Hungary. Szapolyai's forces were left with the remainder, out of the reach of the Habsburgs and a strategic backwater for the Turks, who had a negligible military presence in the principalities and could scarcely penetrate the well-defended Carpathian passes, while their main forces faced the Habsburgs to the west. Szapolyai's successors, selected by the Transylvanian diet and confirmed in office by the Porte, thereby achieved considerable freedom of movement, indeed added to their territory parts of Maramureş and Crişana (the Partium) that were part of Hungary proper. A semblance of dynastic succession was achieved among several Transylvanian Hungarian families, a strong princely authority was established, as well as a regularly convoked Transylvanian diet with substantial legislative power. The annual tribute paid to the Porte was a relatively modest 10,000–15,000 ducats.

The Protestant Reformation had a decisive impact on Transylvanian society and the emerging political system. First among the Saxons, then among the Hungarians, Lutherans gained control of many Catholic parishes and their properties. Later, the Reformed or Calvinist faith, then Unitarianism established themselves among the Hungarians. In 1568 the Transylvanian diet at Turda (Hungarian: Torda) proclaimed religious freedom for the four Christian churches of the Saxons and Hungarians: Roman Catholic, Lutheran, Reformed, and Unitarian. Protestant liturgies in the vernacular inspired early Bible translations, as well as religious and secular literature in the Hungarian, German, and Romanian languages, which were printed by new Transylvanian printing presses. The Lutheran Church became something like a national church for the Saxons, since church membership and the Saxon population were essentially the same. The situation of the Reformed and Unitarian Churches was similar in that nearly all their adherents were Hungarians. The churches and regional administrative autonomy became fundamental elements of Transylvanian political life. The tolerance edict of the Turda diet established an important international precedent but arose less from an abstract ideal of religious toleration than from a practical need for political equilibrium. The Romanian Orthodox population of Transylvania stood outside the religious as well as the political system. Transylvania was arguably the center of Hungarian culture in the sixteenth century, but it was not the center of Romanian culture.

International cooperation against the Turks increased after the Spanish naval victory at Lepanto in 1571. Following an appeal by Pope Clement VIII, various Christian states with Spain and the Holy Roman Empire led by the Habsburgs concluded a Holy League, and in 1594–1595 they secured the adherence of Transylvania, Wallachia, and Moldavia. Michael the Brave (Mihai Viteazul), the prince of Wallachia (1593–1601), as the most exposed ally, became the key protagonist in the first phase of the struggle. In the anti-Ottoman revolt led by Michael beginning in November 1595, he captured Ottoman fortresses on the lower Danube and defeated the Turks and their Tatar vassals in Bulgaria. Facing an Ottoman counterattack against Bucharest, Michael won his greatest victory at Calugăreni south of the city, a battle in which, alongside Moldavian and Wallachian forces, many of the troops were Székelys under the command of Sigismund Báthory, prince of Transylvania. Strengthened by these victories and a renewed campaign south of the Danube that was welcomed by the Christians there, Michael concluded a peace treaty with the Porte in 1598 and another with the Habsburgs, in which he recognized Habsburg suzerainty but no new obligations.

The victories were endangered, however, by changes on the Transylvanian and Moldavian thrones. In both lands, the new prince supported Poland and a more conciliatory policy. With the support of his Habsburg and Szekler allies, Michael marched into Transylvania and, after defeating the Transylvanian prince in October 1599, secured the homage of the Transylvanian diet. In May 1600 he ousted the Polonophile prince of Moldavia and secured the throne there as well. Although the Habsburgs reserved the Transylvanian throne for themselves and their descendants, for now Michael was its occupant, and so in the summer of 1600 he styled himself "sovereign of Wallachia, Transylvania, and the whole of Moldavia." Thus for the first time the three lands had a single ruler, and he was a Romanian.

The union was short-lived. Michael increased the authority of the Romanian Orthodox Church in Transylvania;

but, as he had in Wallachia, he protected the interests of the large landowners by strengthening the serfs' bondage to the soil and their masters. In occupying his Transylvanian throne Michael appointed members of his Wallachian boiar retinue to his council and made them grants from the princely estates. This action and Michael's reliance on the Székely element, rather than any support for the Romanian masses and in the absence of any rhetoric about Romanian national unity, prompted the mass of Hungarian nobility to turn against him and, this time supported by the Habsburgs as well as the Poles, to turn him out of power in Transylvania and Moldavia. After a brief change of heart by the Habsburgs in which they again supported Michael, he defeated his opponents in Transylvania and again claimed the throne in Alba Iulia. However, the Habsburg commander had him assassinated in August 1601.

Michael's military exploits prompted considerable contemporary interest in Europe. Some Romanian historians have celebrated him anachronistically as a champion of national unity. Despite the brevity of his Balkan victories and his rule, however, the following decades did bring an amelioration in the status of the principalities. In 1606 the Porte for the first time recognized the Holy Roman Empire in concluding the Peace of Zsitvatorok. The next forty years were ones of relative stability for Transylvania, Wallachia, and Moldavia with longer reigns in each state. The annual tribute paid by Transylvania declined to 10,000 ducats, and the levies on the Danubian Principalities became less onerous than they had been prior to Michael the Brave. Several rulers entertained the thought of uniting the three states under their rule, although none could achieve it. The motivation, as in Michael's case, was the concentration of forces to resist foreign intervention, and this is why the powers opposed it. Transylvania, as the least vulnerable and wealthiest of the three states, was recognized as the most powerful by the Porte, which granted its emissary in Constantinople the right to treat on behalf of all three. Gabriel Bethlen aspired to lead a union of the states called the Kingdom of Dacia. Vasile Lupu, the prince of Moldavia from 1634 to 1653, hoped to gain the Wallachian and Transylvanian thrones, fighting an unsuccessful campaign against Wallachia. He wrote in 1642 that a conquest of Transylvania by Wallachian and Moldavian troops would be possible because "in Transylvania more than a third [of the population] are Romanian, and once they are freed we will incite them against the Hungarians."

Transylvania attained the height of its wealth and independence under Gabriel Bethlen and the two Rákóczi princes, George I (1630–1648) and George II (1648–1657). They strengthened princely power by increasing the amount of land under their own control but also favored urban crafts, economic development, and education. The Transylvanian coinage of the seventeenth century, silver talers and gold ducats minted for the payment of Ottoman tribute and foreign mercenaries, featured striking portraits of the ruling princes. The Protestant character of the principality became more pronounced, the Roman Catholic Hungarian bishop being banished from Transylvania and efforts made through the translation of religious literature into Romanian to convert the Romanians to the Reformed religion. The Orthodox metropolitans resisted these efforts with the help of churchmen on the other side of the mountains. Transylvania participated intermittently on the Protestant side in the Thirty Years' War, gaining territory in northern Hungary from the Habsburgs and recognition, at the Peace of Westphalia in 1648, of Transylvanian independence.

Moldavia under Vasile Lupu and Wallachia under Matei Basarab (1632–1654) experienced their most peaceful and prosperous period of the century. The entry of Greek merchants into the principalities and their acquisition of land and ecclesiastical and political office were facilitated by the Porte, prompting the resistance of native boiars. Basarab came to power as the result of an anti-Greek movement of the boiars. Like Michael the Brave before him, Matei increased the dependence and fiscal obligations of the peasantry. Lupu, an ambitious politician of Albanian origin and Greek education, also came to power as the result of an anti-Greek action of the boiars. He fought several short wars against his Wallachian counterpart but in other respects followed similar internal policies.

The Romanian language, still written in the Cyrillic alphabet, became the standard in the princely chanceries first, then later in the Orthodox liturgy and religious publications. The princes and several boiars were patrons of ecclesiastic and civic architecture, publishing, and schools. The seventeenth century saw the evolution of Romanian historiography from simple chronicle literature to more sophisticated historical accounts. The outstanding innovators were Moldavians who profited from that land's traditional ties to Poland to study in Polish schools and familiarize themselves with the Polish constitution and humanistic scholarship.

The wars of the 1650s brought an end to this period of stability and progress. Vasile Lupu joined a Polish alliance against the Turks but was punished by Tatar and Cossack raids, forced to abdicate by Transylvanian and Wallachian forces and take refuge in Constantinople. The second Rákóczi invaded Poland in a rash attempt to mount the Polish throne; not only was he repulsed but he was then punished by an invasion of Transylvania by the Porte's Tatar vassals and the replacement of Rákóczi by a more subservient leader. Transylvania was also hemmed in by the Turkish annexation of Oradea (Hungarian: Nagyvárad) and the creation of a new pashalic in 1660. Only the more prudent Matei Basarab died while still on the throne, being succeeded in Wallachia by his illegitimate son.

The succeeding decades were a period of aggressive Ottoman military activity on the Polish frontier north of Moldavia and in Hungary to the west. Troops of Transylvania, Wallachia, and Moldavia joined as Ottoman vassals in the siege of Vienna in 1683. The repulse of the siege led to the formation of a new Holy League and an assault on several fronts that achieved notable successes. The liberation of Buda in 1686 led to the establishment of Habsburg rule in central Hungary and an allied advance into Transylvania, where the diet recognized Habsburg rule already in 1687. After changing military fortunes in southern Hungary for several years, by the Peace of Karlowitz in 1699 the Turks were forced to recognize Habsburg control of Hungary and Transylvania.

The Habsburg dynasty secured the adherence of the Transylvanian diet by agreeing to observe its constitution, legislation, and regional autonomies. Habsburg rule in Hungary meant full state support for Catholic restoration, however. The reestablishment of the Roman Catholic bishopric in Transylvania was one aspect of this policy, and the sponsorship in 1697 of a union of the Romanian Orthodox and Roman Catholic Church recognizing the primacy of the pope, on the model of the Union of Florence, was another. While many Saxons welcomed Habsburg rule because it was German and most Romanian churchmen adhered to the union because of the promise of schools and social advancement, these measures were resisted by Hungarian Protestants, the Hungarian and Romanian nobility, and Orthodox believers who rejected the union. The Rákóczi Rebellion, led by the grandson of George II and fought in the Partium and many parts of Transylvania as a civil war, lasted until the conclusion of a compromise peace in 1711.

Russia under Peter the Great joined the alliance against the Turks but had less success. The alliance of Peter's Russia and Dimitrie Cantemir's Moldavia suffered an overwhelming defeat in 1711 at Stănileşti on the Prut and Cantemir's removal from the throne. The long-ruling Constantin Brâncoveanu in Wallachia was more cautious, promising his support for the allies but then withholding it. This enabled him to hold onto his throne for a few more years, but in 1714 he was called to Constantinople to witness the beheading of his four sons before experiencing the same fate himself. The Turks had had enough of patriotic Romanian tendencies, choosing to install loyal subjects (mostly Greeks) from the Phanar district of Constantinople on the princely throne of Moldavia and Wallachia for the next hundred years. Renewed Habsburg attacks were meanwhile crowned with further success: by the Peace of Passarowitz the Habsburgs annexed the Banat of Timişoară and the Wallachian province of Oltenia. A demarcation line between the Habsburg and Ottoman Empires now divided the lands of today's Romania along the Carpathians and the Olt. This line shifted twenty-one years later, in 1739 when Oltenia was restored to Wallachia and Ottoman rule.

IN RIVAL EMPIRES: HABSBURG AND GREEK PHANARIOT ABSOLUTISM

The eighteenth century interrupted the indigenous political and cultural patterns observable in Transylvania and the Danubian Principalities during previous centuries. Despite formal recognition of its constitution, Transylvania was now controlled by Habsburg officials. The Habsburg ruler ended the line of independent Transylvanian princes, absorbed the Transylvanian armed forces into the Austrian army, packed the provincial diet with imperial appointees, and appointed a closely coordinated provincial governing council and court chancellery. Political subjection was resented by the Hungarians and the newly favored position of the Catholic Church by Hungarian and German Protestants, but growing taxation and labor services were especially onerous for

Romanian commoners. An estimated 60,000 of them fled across the mountains, enough to found a series of villages whose names reflect their origin but not enough to alter the ethnic balance in either province.

The new Uniate (or Greek Catholic) Church of the Romanians gained a firm economic base in the landed estates around Blaj in central Transylvania granted it under its energetic bishop, Ion Inochentie Klein. Klein's campaign to secure the social benefits that had been promised to his clergy were rejected by the authorities, however. Exploiting this disappointment, Orthodox clerics insisting on adherence to Oriental tradition led two popular revolts against the union at midcentury. The revolts made little headway against the church union in northern Transylvania, but effectively overturned it in the south. In recognition of this fact, the authorities reestablished the Romanian Orthodox bishopric in 1760. For the next 190 years, Transylvanian Romanians would be equally divided between the two churches.

Partial Westernization to the north of the mountains contrasted with an opposite trend to the south. In the Principalities, the pressure to conform with Constantinople was so powerful that the elites for several generations abandoned Western styles of dress, donning instead oriental caftans and robes. Although the Romanian language was supplanting Slavonic in the Orthodox liturgy, educational institutions founded by the Phanariots helped establish for more than a century the primacy of the Greek language in the Principalities' secular culture. Exorbitant payments, as much as aptitude and loyalty, and not election by the boiars were now required to attain the Wallachian and Moldavian thrones. In 110 years, the throne changed hands forty times in Wallachia and thirty-six times in Moldavia. Once in office, the princes distributed dignities among their family members and plundered the country to recover their investment. While the annual tributary payments to the Porte stabilized, annual and triennial payments by the successful bidders for the throne skyrocketed. Additional contributions (peşcheşurile) and shipments of grain, cattle, and lumber increased dramatically. The export of cattle and animal products was prohibited except to the Ottoman Empire. The widespread cultivation of maize (corn) among the Romanians arose at this time due to the Turks' lack of interest in this food. Peasant flight to escape exploitation occurred here too, less than from Transylvania and primarily across the Danube to the south.

The Phanariot princes abolished the separate military organizations that had permitted the principalities to follow independent foreign policies and even ally with the sultan's enemies. Ottoman forces themselves undertook the defense of the Principalities against Austrian and Russian invasions, fighting no less than seven wars on their territory between 1711 and 1829 and expropriating military supplies from the population each time.

As elsewhere in eighteenth-century Europe, the enhancement of state revenue to support military expenditures was the initial motive for absolutist reform measures. The onset of social unrest and peasant flight prompted further reforms of an ameliorative nature, regularizing monetary exactions and labor services for the common people.

These measures are associated in the Principalities primarily with the name of Constantin Mavrocordat, who alternated on the Wallachian and Moldavian throne between 1730 and 1769. In 1746–1749 serfdom was abolished, though the effect was to stabilize rather than liberate the peasant population. Modest reforms in Transylvania under Maria Theresa and Joseph II could not prevent the violent peasant revolt in 1784 led by a Romanian named Horia. The brutal suppression of the revolt was followed by the abolition of personal servitude, once again not a decisive liberation but a measure that succeeded in stabilizing the rural population. Economic and educational reforms led to an increase in production and well-being in Transylvania, which was spared the frequent military incursions suffered by the Principalities.

The turbulent eighteenth century, while full of hardship for the bulk of Romanian commoners, gave birth to the ideological roots of Romanian unification two centuries later. It is not easy to determine which side of the mountains contributed more to this development. Many historians give the nod to Transylvania, whose vibrant churches and schools provided access to Western education and produced a group of highly influential historians and linguists now known as the Transylvanian School. Phanariot rule and military depredations offered a less promising arena. Yet the Greek schools and culture were conduits for Enlightenment thought, and the declining Ottoman power presented an opportunity for genuine political assertion that was lacking within a Habsburg realm at the height of its power and in provinces dominated by socially advantaged Hungarians and Germans.

One of the intellectual giants of the era was Dimitrie Cantemir (1673–1723), the erstwhile ally of Peter the Great on the Moldavian throne. In Russian exile, he gained international renown and induction into the Prussian Academy for a series of important historical works. Best known of these was his history of the Ottoman Empire (1716, also translated into English), which argued correctly that the Ottoman state was in decline. Cantemir's works on Moldavia and on Romanian origins provided an erudite analysis of current society and the strongest statement yet of the Romanians' descent from the Romans. Works by scholars in the principalities later in the century were less original.

The members of the Transylvanian School, in contrast to earlier historians in the principalities, were not statesmen or associated with the princely court but churchmen. The ecclesiastical connection gave them the opportunity to study in Vienna and Rome, where they gained a strong impression of Roman civilization and the importance of Romanians' connection to it and, even more important, the intellectual arsenal with which to argue the political implications. They would argue that in light of their historical priority Romanians deserved the status of a constituent nation within Transylvania, a status that was denied them. The first modern census of the Hungarian lands that would later join Romania, conducted by the Austrians in 1784–1787, found that more than three-fifths were Romanians. Thus a demand for political emancipation, albeit merely proposing admission to status as an additional feudal nation and equal status for the

Orthodox and Uniate Churches rather than democracy, had radical implications for the established order. The demand was raised in two lengthy Romanian petitions of 1791–1792 entitled *Supplex Libellus Valachorum,* rejected promptly by the authorities. The Hungarian nobility's resistance had already prompted Joseph II to withdraw most of his reforms, and it also sealed the fate of the *Supplex.* The French Revolution and Napoleonic Wars produced a political reaction in the Habsburg monarchy that made it even less hospitable to political change.

Indigenous Romanian and long-settled Greek boiars resented the alien regime of the Phanariot princes, organizing several abortive revolts and petitioning repeatedly for the restoration of the Principalities' independence. During extended periods of military strife when the Phanariot rulers took refuge in Ottoman fortresses, political authority was exercised by a deputized divan of boiar leaders who repeatedly took the opportunity to issue declarations couched in terms of sovereignty derived from the writers of the French Enlightenment. The demand for the restoration of the Principalities' independence was increasingly supported by the Turks' chief enemy, the Russian Empire. The Treaty of Kuchuk Kainardji in 1774 granted Russia the right to intervene on behalf of the Christians in the Principalities. In ensuing years as Russia, Austria, and France established consulates in the Danubian capitals, boiar activists were emboldened to issue a growing stream of manifestoes demanding independence and, from 1772 on, the unification of the two Principalities.

Austria and Russia took advantage of the weakening Ottoman control over the principalities, respectively annexing Bucovina in 1775 and Bessarabia in 1812 and depriving Moldavia of more than half its territory. The real prospect of a complete partition, such as had taken place in Poland, increased the daring of Romanian militants. A conspiracy with the Greek revolutionary movement Hetairia Philiki placed Tudor Vladimirescu, a nobleman possessing military experience fighting the Turks with the Russian forces, at the head of an uprising in Oltenia in 1821. The plan relied on Russian support, but Tsar Alexander I shied away from supporting an antidynastic movement, even one against the Ottoman Empire. After this debacle, Vladimirescu's Greek allies turned on him and killed him. It was the end of the revolt but also the end of the Phanariot regime as the Porte returned to native princes for rulers. Meanwhile the Greek revolt, having foundered in the Principalities, raged on to the south. When it finally ended, the Russian protectors were in a position to fashion a new system in the Principalities.

CREATING THE NATIONAL STATE

The Treaty of Adrianople in 1829, signed after the successful conclusion of Russia's latest Balkan campaign, contained territorial, political, and commercial stipulations. Russia gained a part of the Danube Delta, and the Principalities gained control over Turkish fortresses on their territory as well as administrative autonomy. During an extended occupation, Russian authorities formulated what would become the first Romanian constitution, the Organic Statutes. Finally the commercial clauses reversed the closure of central Europe trade with the principalities by the Turks three centuries earlier. Ottoman suzerainty would remain for another half century. But a new era had begun that made possible the eventual establishment of the rule of law, autonomous political life, and full participation in European developments. The commercial opening led in time to a dramatic social transformation. Landowners and peasantry streamed into the newly secure Danubian plains, and grain production supplanted livestock and corn as the country's chief economic products. By the end of the century, Romania would become the fourth leading wheat exporter in the world.

The Organic Statutes were an imperfect constitution in the eyes of liberals. A narrow base of landowners elected a legislative assembly and an even more restricted body was to elect the two princes—but the Russians simply ignored this clause and appointed two Romanians of leading boiar families in whom they had full confidence. Boiar activists, many of them Greek-educated but now increasingly gravitating toward the French cultural sphere and studies in Paris, demanded the end of political interference by the Russian consuls and the unification of the two principalities. Admirers of everything French were ridiculed with the nickname *bonjuriști*.

North and west of the mountains there was also a liberal challenge to the authorities. The leading liberals here were members of the Hungarian nobility, which clamored in the Hungarian and Transylvanian diets for the observation of existing Hungarian laws, the primacy of Hungarian culture, and the emancipation of the serfs. The Hungarian movement prompted Transylvania's Romanians and Germans to organize their own movements, which under the influence of the Hungarian example increasingly emancipated themselves from conservative ecclesiastical leadership. Hungarians accused them of subservience to Habsburg reactionaries, but in fact many Romanian and German activists supported and stood to gain from proposed Hungarian social reforms.

One of the new features of politics on either side of the mountains was that it was carried out in public, through daily and weekly newspapers in the national languages. Patriots became more aware of events in neighboring countries and their implications for their own. The idea of unifying all Romanians in a single state was now heard occasionally.

The French Revolution of 1848 triggered similar outbreaks across the continent. The liberal opposition in the Hungarian diet, skillfully playing on fears of social upheaval, secured royal sanction for a series of constitutional reforms. Most of these attracted broad support also in Transylvania. In Moldavia, boiar leaders presented a series of liberal demands to the Russian-appointed prince, but they were rejected and the leaders imprisoned or exiled. In Wallachia, the liberal program gained the sanction of the ruler as in Hungary, but he then fled to Transylvania. Increasingly threatened by the Porte and Russia, the Wallachian revolutionary government barely survived the summer of 1848. Events were more dramatic in the Hungarian lands. The proposed union of Hungary and Transyl-

Charles (Carol) I, prince (1866–1881) and king (1881–1914) of Romania. The Catholic Hohenzollern established the modern royal house. (Bettmann/Corbis)

vania caused the brief-lived solidarity among the nationalities in Transylvania to break down. Romanian leaders called, in three popular assemblies in Blaj, for resistance to the union. In October 1848 armed conflict broke out between the Hungarian government on one side and the Austrian authorities and various nationalities on the other. A civil war ensued in Transylvania, with serious atrocities and destruction of property on both sides. The Austrians had to request Russian military intervention to defeat the Hungarians. No upheavals took place in Russian-ruled Bessarabia.

The Russian and Austrian victories were costly and temporary. Defeated in the Crimean War (1853–1856), Russia had to return three counties of southern Bessarabia to Moldavia; then, in 1858, St. Petersburg saw its protectorate over the Principalities replaced by an international one. The powers provided for the coordination of the Principalities but not for their full unification under a single ruler. Romanian leaders took advantage of the opportunity presented by international disunity and French support to gain their optimal demands against Russian and Austrian opposition. Alexandru Ioan Cuza, the Moldavian military commander, was elected in turn prince of Moldavia, then

Carol I (1839–1914, r. 1866–1914)

Romania's second prince and first king was born Karl Eitel Friedrich von Hohenzollern-Sigmaringen, a member of the Catholic branch of the Prussian ruling family. The Prussian army officer came to the throne under adventurous circumstances. The deposition of Prince Cuza in 1866 made it urgent to find a replacement before the Austrians or the Turks could reverse the unification of the principalities. Ion C. Brătianu secured on behalf of the interim authorities the tacit assent of the prospective prince, whose candidacy was then approved overwhelmingly in a plebiscite. Karl traveled incognito through Austrian territory on the eve of the Austro-Prussian war. According to his memoirs, when he hurriedly debarked from a Danube ship at the first Romanian port with Brătianu, someone angrily called out after him: "By God, that must be the prince of Hohenzollern."

Carol I took charge of a totally unfamiliar country, whose domestic and diplomatic situation was very uncertain, and did a remarkable job. He was a strong ruler, but through his tact and circumspection he fostered the development of a stable parliamentary system in which the Liberal and Conservative Parties alternated in power without violence. Through his successful military leadership, Romania secured its independence from the Ottoman Empire after the war against the Turks, and he was proclaimed king in 1881. Carol's good relationship with the Central Powers served the country well both economically and diplomatically, although nationalists increasingly opposed it in his later years. In September 1914 a Crown Council rejected his proposal that Romania enter World War I on the side of the Central Powers. It was a hard defeat for him, but he accepted the decision of the council for neutrality.

Despite his achievements, the king did not establish a warm relationship with his subjects due to his disciplined, formal character. In an intensely Orthodox country, he remained devoted to his Catholic religion, and among his best friends in the country was a Swiss Benedictine, Raymund Netzhammer, who served as Catholic archbishop of Bucharest from 1905 until 1924. Carol's wife, the former Elisabeth von Wied, gained popularity through her fondness for Romanian folk costume and the poetry and collections of Romanian folktales she published under the pseudonym Carmen Sylva. The couple's relationship was strained, however. Because they had no surviving children, Carol adopted his nephew Ferdinand, who became king upon his death. Carol built the beautiful Peleş Castle in Gothic revival style at Sinaia in the Carpathians, which is now a museum.

also of Wallachia, in 1859. During the seven years of his rule, he completed the long-demanded administrative unification of the Principalities with the sole capital now in Bucharest, the secularization of monastic lands, and a land reform that was opposed by the boiars and introduced by decree after the dissolution of parliament. After he was overthrown in a coup, Romanians achieved another major objective, a foreign prince who would stand above the parties and enhance Romania's international standing, by the enthronement of Charles of Hohenzollern-Sigmaringen as Prince Carol of Romania in 1866. In the same year a liberal constitution was proclaimed, modeled on that of Belgium.

In the Habsburg Empire, the Hungarians rather than the Romanians were to profit from Austrian weakness. Austria abandoned a ten-year attempt at centralized rule in 1859, then reluctantly restored Hungarian autonomy. After years of political silence under the centralist regime, Transylvanian Hungarians resumed their political activity and demanded the restoration of the laws of 1848, including the union with Hungary. Austria embarked on a risky game, enfranchising for the first time the Romanian majority of Transylvania to secure its support in the Transylvanian diet against the Hungarian opposition. The experiment was briefly successful, as the diet sent deputies, mostly Romani-ans and Germans, to the central parliament in Vienna. But it was impossible to rule the Habsburg monarchy without the support of the Hungarians, especially after the Prussian military victory over Austria in 1866. Therefore the dynasty concluded the Austro-Hungarian Compromise (*Ausgleich*) in 1867. Transylvania became an integral part of Hungary, and after having tasted political empowerment, Romanians now found themselves a minority in the larger state rather than a majority in Transylvania.

Renewed hostilities between Russia and the Porte in 1877–1878 provided another opportunity for Romania to enhance its international standing. Prince Carol provided Romanian support for the passage of Russian troops to the Balkan front. When the Russian siege of the fortress of Plevna was stalled, Carol answered a call for military assistance on the condition of assuming overall command of the front. After the ensuing allied victory, Romania annexed northern Dobrogea, and was recognized as an independent kingdom. Despite its indebtedness to Romania for its military contribution, Russia insisted on the return of the three south Bessarabian counties it had ceded to Moldavia in 1856. Within Bessarabia, Russification (the promotion of Russian culture) was harsher than anything Romanians had experienced under the Habsburgs. Romania turned now to

Austria-Hungary for an alliance, later increased by the adherence of Germany and Italy, that would be renewed repeatedly until World War I. This alliance was diplomatically and economically advantageous to Romania. Though its precise terms were kept a secret from the public, its existence was not.

Carol I proved effective in a long rule lasting until his death in 1914. The government was the most stable in the Balkans, with Liberal and Conservative ministries succeeding each other at five- to ten-year intervals. Governments ran elections *after* their appointment and the electoral law was restrictive, but the press was uncensored and the system did provide for some responsiveness to public opinion. Romanian education and culture made steady progress. The Brătianu family provided continuity to the Liberal Party and the country through a series of able leaders. A public system of education, decreed by Prince Cuza, began to become a reality late in the century after an energetic school-building program. A Mining Law in 1895 opened Romanian oilfields to foreign investment, as the result of which American, British, and especially German capital became influential in their production and exports. There was a vigorous debate about the proper balance between Westernization and traditional culture. Taking a more conservative position, but not rejecting modernization per se, was the highly influential Junimea literary movement, which warned against superficial Westernization or "forms without content." The greatest Romanian writer, Mihai Eminescu, was associated with this movement.

Romanians also made cultural progress in Hungary. The government took energetic steps after the Austro-Hungarian Compromise to support Hungarian culture in minority areas, founding a Hungarian university in Cluj in 1872 and subsidizing Hungarian education generally. But although national minorities had little political power, they were on average economically better off and enjoyed a higher rate of literacy than in Romania. Their own churches, schools, press, and banks enabled the Romanian minority to maintain and even enhance national identity. The Romanian National Party enjoyed the support of a growing Romanian middle class and produced a number of impressive leaders. While the few Romanians elected to the Hungarian parliament were generally in opposition, they were publicly loyal to Austria-Hungary and not vocal advocates of secession. Romanians were only one-third of the population in Austrian Bucovina, but they participated in the provincial diet and imperial parliament and enjoyed higher education in their own language at the trilingual university in the capital city, Cernăuţi. Romanian culture and political expression was weakest in Russian Bessarabia. Steady Russification reduced the Romanians by 1897 to less than half of the population. They were almost totally absent from political life until after the Revolution of 1905.

The Kingdom of Romania had its darker side, namely the treatment of its peasantry and Jewish minority. The land reform of 1864 gave peasants outright possession of their land, but its amount proved insufficient and had to be supplemented through sharecropping and arrangements that left peasants increasingly dependent and in debt. A peasant revolt in 1888 was a foretaste of a much more serious one in 1907, the worst on the European continent before the Russian Revolution. Thousands of peasants were executed in its brutal suppression. Jewish immigration to the principalities was welcomed during the first half of the century under the Russian protectorate, and this population made a substantial contribution to economic development. For many social conservatives like Eminescu, however, Jewish capitalists seemed to threaten national culture and exploit the poorest Romanians. Jewish farm tenants were a particular target of peasant violence during the outbreak of the revolt in 1907. In Bessarabia, Chişinău was the site of major pogroms in 1903 and 1905; as a result, thousands of Jews emigrated from Chişinău to the United States afterward.

Romania's alliance with the Central Powers (Germany, Austria-Hungary, and Italy) was supported by most politicians of the Conservative Party, but criticized by the Liberals and especially by nationalists who deplored Hungary's minorities policy and even demanded the liberation of Romanians across the Carpathians. On the eve of World War I, rising political tensions in both countries brought the national question to a head. Romania proved itself the strongest of the post-Ottoman states in the Second Balkan War, hosting the Peace of Bucharest in 1913 that awarded it southern Dobrogea (the Quadrilateral), a territory with few Romanians. The Liberal government declined to support the Central Powers when the European war broke out. This decision was a difficult blow for the native German King Carol, who died in the war's first months. His nephew Ferdinand, who succeeded him as king, was more amenable to change.

Romania negotiated an agreement with the Entente in 1916, by which in return for an invasion of Transylvania it was promised protection of its flanks by simultaneous Russian and French attacks and cession of the province after the war. The attacks by the allies did not take place; instead Romania was flanked by the Germans and Bulgarians. Romanian forces had to evacuate Bucharest in November. The court and government retreated to Iaşi, and although it won notable military victories over the Germans in 1917, Romania was forced to conclude a separate peace with the Central Powers in May 1918. The collapse of the Russian tsardom and then of Austria-Hungary created an optimal situation for Romania. The Central Powers recognized Bessarabia's decision to join Romania in March 1918; then in November Romanian troops marched into Transylvania after the collapse of the Austro-Hungarian front. The union of the formerly Hungarian lands with Romania was proclaimed at a mass assembly in Alba Iulia on 1 December, whose anniversary would become Romania's National Day. The longed-for Greater Romania arose suddenly, through a remarkable coincidence of events.

GREATER ROMANIA

Through the demise of Austria-Hungary and the Russian Empire, Romania doubled its territory and its population. While in the prewar census of Romania the population was more than 90 percent Romanian and Orthodox Christian,

Greater Romania was a multinational state with nearly 30 percent minorities, including large numbers of Catholics and Protestants. The urban centers of the new provinces were dominated by the national minorities, who generally enjoyed a higher level of education and wealth than the Romanians and resented the sudden reversal in their political status.

The peasant revolt of 1907 had ushered in an era of social and political reform in the old Romania that was interrupted by the outbreak of war. With the upheaval of the Russian Revolution in his rear in 1917, King Ferdinand promised radical land and electoral reform after the war. Such was to be the case: after the introduction of virtually universal manhood suffrage, the most far-reaching land reform in Eastern Europe was enacted and the Conservative Party disappeared as a political force. More than 2 million peasants received land. Large landholding almost disappeared in all parts of the country, especially in the new territories where Russian and Hungarian aristocrats were targeted. Thus the land reform had its roots before the war but was also applied to the detriment of national minorities and of their cultural institutions.

Alien legal and administrative systems as well as ethnic minorities and their economic power increased the difficulty of integrating the newly acquired territories. Russian, Austrian, and Hungarian laws, civil servants, and currencies were adapted, or accommodated, or eliminated. The government expropriated the schools of the Romanian Greek Catholic and Orthodox Churches of the former Hungarian lands, which had served to preserve minority culture but now had no place in a state where schools were administered by the government. The constitution of 1923, built in large measure on the constitution of 1866, stated explicitly that Romania was a unitary national state. This was a decisive rejection of any notion that Romania's historical regions could best be accommodated by a federal system, which in any case would have been a departure from previous Romanian practice.

The political beneficiary of these reforms was the Liberal Party. It no longer had to alternate power with its Conservative rivals and enjoyed enormous prestige as the original proponent of the electoral and land reforms and the wartime alliance with the Entente that achieved such brilliant success in 1918, and as experienced political partner of the royal house. The Liberal Party and its government officials rapidly and effectively expanded their political organization and membership into the newly acquired territories where they had never existed before. In terms of economic policy, the Liberals were advocates of the urban, industrial, and financial interests of the Old Kingdom and their expansion into the new territories. In support of these interests, they enforced protectionist commercial policies that developed Romanian industries and served to rupture the politically suspect ties of the new territories with their former homelands. Industrial imports declined steadily throughout the interwar period, while the rate of growth in industrial production, at over 5 percent, was one of the highest in Europe.

The hegemony of the Liberal Party began to crumble after the death of its leader, Ion I.C. Brătianu, and King Ferdinand in 1927. As important as their deaths was the emergence of a strong political alternative, the National Peasant Party. It arose in 1926 through the union of two parties, the Romanian National Party, founded in 1881 in Hungary, and the Peasant Party, founded by Ion Mihalache in 1918 on a platform of radical land reform. Throughout the decade, the National Party had attacked the Liberal regime for corruption and excessive centralization that violated the terms under which Transylvania and the new provinces had joined Romania. Transylvanian Romanians never for a moment regretted the unification of 1918 or favored Transylvanian independence, but some proposed that the capital of the country be moved to their province. The Peasant Party, the heir of earlier populist and pro-peasant movements in the Old Kingdom, contested the Liberals' claim as sole architect of the land reform and insisted that commercial and administrative policies take the rural majority of Romania into account. The regency that took office after Ferdinand's death saw no alternative to asking Iuliu Maniu, the Transylvanian president of the new party, to form a government. He accepted on condition that he be permitted to hold truly free elections, which were held in 1928 and returned parliamentary majorities for the National Peasants.

The National Peasant government held office for most of the period between 1928 and 1933. It was genuinely popular at its inception, especially due to the undeniable rectitude of its leadership, the measures it took to facilitate agricultural exports and credit, and a law providing for a modest degree of decentralization. It was difficult for the new party to master a state apparatus that had been created by its ousted rivals or to deal with the world economic crisis that lowered prices for Romanian agricultural exports and made industrial credit scarce. Many historians have faulted Maniu for excessive rectitude in his dealing with the controversy that arose over the eldest of Ferdinand's sons, known in office as Carol II. In contrast to his uncle and father, Carol was an undisciplined individual who liked racing cars and racy women. Twice, in 1918 and 1925, he renounced his succession to the throne after choosing to live with women considered unsuitable for him. Maniu, however, felt Carol had been abused by the Liberals and hence did not oppose his return to Romania after 1928. Once home, Carol ignored a promise to Maniu that he would stay out of politics, and reclaimed his throne amidst considerable popular sympathy for his cause. In protest against Carol's corrupting influence, Maniu resigned three times as prime minister, in 1930 and 1933. Party comrades who succeeded him enjoyed less authority and were no more effective in power. It is impossible to detect any consistent rationale for Carol's political actions, but in effect he undermined the institution of parliamentary democracy and progressively eliminated alternatives to his own personal rule.

As the experience of other Eastern European countries during the 1930s suggests, the weaknesses of Romanian democracy went far beyond the failings of Maniu and King Carol. The land reform of 1918–1921, like that of 1864, failed to permanently satisfy the peasants' hunger for land. The practice of dividing land among sons of the family meant that originally adequate landholdings quickly became less satisfactory. Interwar Romanian governments of all parties sought to assuage rural overpopulation by policies favoring industrialization to create urban workplaces. Industry grew. In the towns, Romanian schools and higher education expanded dramatically, especially in the new provinces where existing institutions were Romanianized and Romanians gained preferential employment in management and the civil service. As the economic motor sputtered, traditionalist voices, questioning the desirability of Western and urban civilization, became more audible. As before 1914, they often associated alien Western civilization with the Jews. Urban, middle class Romania was also strongly committed to defending the country's newly won borders against threats posed by aggrieved Hungarians and Bulgarians abroad and within, and anti-Semitism was also widespread in the urban population. Some followed the corporatist model popular in Central Europe, according to which state and economic production should be reorganized according to occupational groups. What contrasted nationalism in Romania from most surrounding countries was the degree to which the rural, traditionalist ideal prevailed.

Interwar Romanian literary movements, like those before 1914, included liberal, progressive, as well as traditionalist tendencies. As in the case of Junimea earlier, traditionalists produced more striking and influential writers, notably Nae Ionescu, Lucian Blaga, and Mircea Eliade. Unlike the personalities of Junimea, however, many traditionalists questioned the parliamentary system itself and were sympathetic to an outright break with Western models. Many also sympathized with the most distinctive Romanian extremist movement, whose political potential dominated the scene after Iuliu Maniu's second premiership ended in 1933: the Legion of the Archangel Michael, founded in 1927, and its offshoot founded in 1930, the Iron Guard. The leader of the Legionaries was the charismatic "Captain" Corneliu Zelea Codreanu (1899–1938), the former student of an anti-Semitic law professor at the University of Iaşi. Codreanu's student and peasant adherents fascinated contemporaries with their mystical rhetoric drawing on Orthodox Christianity and their rural volunteer work, but horrified them with daring acts of violence against Jews and political opponents.

The Iron Guard's political wing reached its high point in electoral politics (16 percent of the vote) in 1937. The Liberals and National Peasants could provide no strong political alternative to the Guard, in large degree because Carol II excelled in encouraging factions by offering power to secondary figures. The electoral gains of the Guard seemed to indicate that its real popular support was even greater since they were achieved despite the preference of the king (scorned by the Legionaries, among other reasons, because of his Jewish mistress) and his appointed government that ran the election. After this result, Carol proclaimed a new constitution and a royal dictatorship in 1938, with a weak legislature, the judiciary and executive under his own authority, and a National Renaissance Front that superficially resembled the Nazi and fascist parties but lacked any power or social base. Codreanu and 265 followers were arrested and murdered while in prison. Whatever pleasure Roma-

nian democrats may have taken from this act, their own parties had been declared illegal.

Romania's international position had become precarious. As a beneficiary of the peace settlement, it favored strong relations with France, Great Britain, Czechoslovakia, and Yugoslavia. Out of ideological sympathy and in violation of the pro-French dogma of Romanian foreign policy, Corneliu Codreanu declared his support for an orientation toward Germany. This was not the position of King Carol, who declared Romanian neutrality after Germany attacked Poland in 1939. This took considerable courage because Romania had failed to mitigate Soviet hostility over Bessarabia, although it could not know that the secret protocol of the German-Soviet pact placed Bessarabia in the Soviet sphere. The partition that Romanian diplomats had feared ensued even as France was going down to defeat in 1940. In response to a Soviet ultimatum, Romania relinquished Bessarabia and southern Bucovina in June, and after threats from Bulgaria surrendered southern Dobrogea (Dobrudja for Bulgarians) to that country in September. More devastating than either of these events was the Second Vienna Award (known by Romanian historians as the Diktat of Vienna) returning northern Transylvania to Hungary. Facing a likely Hungarian attack and a disinclination by Germany to intervene, the divided Romanian Crown Council agreed to surrender the territory without knowing its exact extent. "Northern Transylvania" was a largely ahistorical creation that included a land bridge for Hungary to its strongest irredenta within Romania, the heavily Hungarian Székely region. Of the 2.5 million people in northern Transylvania, roughly half were Hungarians, half Romanians. Many Romanians and Hungarians fled across the hastily drawn borders. In all, Romania lost close to half of the territory gained since 1913.

Faced with widespread dissatisfaction over the Romanian concessions and an Iron Guard uprising, Carol turned to a war hero and former minister of defense to form a government: General Ion Antonescu. The new prime minister was no admirer of Germany or of the Iron Guard, but he was a realist and he despised Carol. Antonescu quickly demanded Carol's abdication and exile, and announced a National Legionary State with various ministries assigned to Legionaries, but himself in charge. Carol's son Mihai, who had ascended the throne temporarily during the regency of 1927–1930, again became king. He announced the new government, but Antonescu excluded him from real power.

Hitler and Antonescu knew that, in Romania's weakened and vulnerable state, it was dependent on German good favor for any possible border rectification in Transylvania. When they met, Hitler made no promise about rectification but suggested it might be possible after the war. The German interest in keeping Romania in thrall was twofold: access to Romanian grain and oil, and Romanian hostility toward the Soviet Union. Given these priorities, Hitler listened sympathetically when Antonescu reported at the beginning of 1941 on the harmful effects on the Romanian economy of the Iron Guard's mismanagement and use of power to settle scores with Jews and political opponents. Antonescu disarmed his erstwhile allies in short order, with

King Mihai (Michael), leader of Romania (1927–1930, 1940–1947). He lived in exile after his abdication under communist pressure before the 1948 royal wedding in Greece recorded here. (Library of Congress)

the tacit support of the Germans. After a brief Legionary uprising in Bucharest and some other areas, official reports cited 416 casualties, including 120 Jews.

It is doubtful the Germans were disturbed by a series of decrees by the Romanian government to deprive Jews in Romania of their rural (in the fall of 1940) and urban (after the expulsion of the Legionaries from the government in March 1941) property. Official statistics, perhaps intended primarily for German consumption, appear to have exaggerated the scale of the decline in the number of Jewish employees. Romania joined the attack on the Soviet Union with genuine popular enthusiasm. By August 1941, it had reoccupied Bessarabia (with an estimated 130,000 Jews fleeing before the Romanian and German troops into the Soviet Union) but did not stop there, participating in the Axis conquest of Odessa and the advance toward Stalingrad and the Caucasus. In addition to Bessarabia, with Hitler's acquiescence, Antonescu established a Romanian civil administration over a large territory between the Dniester and Dnieper rivers dubbed "Transnistria." Over 100,000 Ro-

manian Jews were deported to Transnistria in 1941–1943, many thousands of whom died from the terrible conditions there. The majority, it appears, survived to be repatriated at the end of the war.

Some historians have engaged in a debate over whether Hungary or Romania treated its Jews more poorly. Contemporaries reported the Germans were horrified by the anti-Semitic violence of local officials in both Transnistria and Hungary during the deportations there in 1941–1943 and 1944, respectively. The mass deportation to Auschwitz of Hungary's rural Jews after the German occupation in March 1944 included those of northern Transylvania. Antonescu's government, on the other hand, was not subjected to military occupation and declined to participate in the deportations to the death camps. It appears likely that he prevented these deportations because, as early as the battle of Stalingrad at the end of 1942, he no longer believed in the prospect of Axis military victory. While Romanian troops continued to fight in great numbers on the retreating eastern front and Antonescu remained a respected collaborator of Hitler, he unofficially sanctioned peace feelers to the Western allies by his foreign minister and Iuliu Maniu. Negotiations intensified as Soviet troops approached prewar Romanian territory. At a point of crisis in the military campaign, on 23 August 1944, King Mihai had Antonescu and his closest associates arrested and declared a unilateral end of hostilities against the Soviet Union. The conspiracy, supported by the parties Antonescu had excluded from power (National Peasants, Liberals, Social Democrats, and Communists), was remarkably successful. Within weeks German forces were forced to vacate Romanian territory.

Romanian troops suffered over 300,000 casualties in three years of fighting on the side of the Axis, then 170,000 more up to May 1945 after changing sides to assist the Soviets in the capture of Transylvania, Hungary, and Czechoslovakia. Just as Antonescu hoped the Romanian contribution would strengthen postwar claims to northern Transylvania, Romania now sought to gain Soviet sympathy for the restoration of the prewar frontier with Hungary, which fought with Germany to the last. There was no question of Romania retaining Bessarabia, which quickly became a Soviet republic (Moldova) once again. The Soviet Union would also exact heavy Romanian war reparations in materiel, demand the extradition of Bessarabian refugees in Romania, and require the forced labor service, for several years, of 80,000 Germans who were Romanian citizens. It turned out that all these contributions were insufficient payment for the return of northern Transylvania; it was also necessary that the government be communized.

After August 1944, Mihai entrusted the government to a succession of coalitions led by nonparty generals and composed, in rough numerical equality, by communist and noncommunist ministers. The popular support of the Communist Party was probably the weakest of any such party in Eastern Europe. In August party membership was no more than a thousand; the leaders had long been tightly controlled by the Comintern and drawn primarily from Romania's ethnic minorities. The party platform, rejecting Romanian control of Bessarabia and characterizing the peace treaties after World War I as imperialist in nature, had severely limited the party's appeal among ethnic Romanians. Now, the presence of the Red Army gave a tremendous boost to the Communist Party. Agitators supported by the communists and radical socialists created stoppages in factories, Communist Minister of Justice Lucreţiu Pătrăşcanu engineered the exclusion of "reactionaries" who were political opponents, and the Allied Control Commission, dominated by the Soviet Union, demanded a leftward reconfiguration of the government. This happened in March 1945 with the appointment of the leftist Transylvanian Petru Groza as prime minister. A radical land reform and the beginning of the transformation of the economy began shortly thereafter. Minor members of the historical parties gave the government a small semblance of legitimacy, leading to its recognition by the Western allies in 1946. Archival records have now confirmed contemporary suspicion that the results of the elections of November 1946, awarding leftist parties 80 percent of the vote, were falsified. In February 1947 the Paris Peace Treaty recognized the return of

territories to the Soviet Union but also Romanian sovereignty over northern Transylvania.

King Mihai opposed the communist takeover but was powerless to resist it. On 30 December 1947, he accepted an ultimatum to abdicate the Romanian throne, and left the newly declared Romanian People's Republic a few days later.

COMMUNIST ROMANIA

High on the agenda of the new regime were the elimination of opposition politicians and centers of power. Antonescu, his foreign minister, and the wartime governor of Transnistria were declared "war criminals" and subjected to a show trial and death by firing squad. Maniu, Mihalache, and many other former government ministers were arrested and concentrated in a special prison in Sighet, in the northwestern corner of the country. Just as the Soviet Union forcibly united the Greek Catholics with the Orthodox Church in its newly annexed western territories, the Romanian government did the same with the Uniates in 1948. The 1.4-million-strong Romanian Greek Catholic Church, which had contributed substantially to the definition and defense of national identity before 1918, found itself forcibly integrated into the Orthodox Church by the decision of a manipulated church synod. By this act and modest state support for its seminaries and publications, the Orthodox Church became an accomplice of the regime. Any social institution recognizing a supreme authority outside the country was unacceptable to the Communists. The Roman Catholic Church, however, enjoyed too much prestige and diplomatic support in the West, and its celibate clergy was relatively immune to blackmail through the intimidation of family members, to suffer the fate of the Uniates. Furthermore, in Romania this church was primarily Hungarian and German in its membership; therefore its outright suppression would have constituted a blatant violation of communist nationality policy. Thus, this church was neither suppressed nor coordinated like the others but survived in a semilegal state. Most Catholic bishops, of both the Latin and Greek rites, joined the former government ministers at the prison in Sighet.

Imprisonment and hard labor was also the fate of social categories such as Serbs and Germans deported from the western Banat to the camps in the Bărăgan Steppe during the crisis in relations with Tito's Yugoslavia, peasants resisting collectivization who were put to work on the massive project to create a canal eastward from the lower Danube to the Black Sea, and ordinary citizens now arrested on trumped up charges to pull reeds in the Danube Delta for cellulose production. Many died or returned home with shattered health.

Terror affected the communists themselves. From a mere thousand in 1944, recruitment among former Legionaries, workers, and other social groups and a fusion with leftist Social Democrats swelled the ranks of the ruling party, renamed Romanian Workers Party in 1948, to over a million in that year. Lucreţiu Pătrăşcanu, the party's first liaison between King Mihai and the Soviets in 1944, was among the first to be purged. Then, following the Soviet-enforced model observable throughout the emerging bloc, broader purges within party ranks were ordained in order to cull undesirable "opportunistic" elements. If many recent recruits were undesirables, it followed logically that the party officials responsible for the recruitment were culpable. This meant for Romania first of all Ana Pauker, the leader of the "Muscovite" (former exile) wing of the party, a visible leader since her return to the country, the most powerful Jewish woman in the bloc, and foreign minister in 1947–1952 before being purged. Was Pauker a victim of an anti-Semitic campaign like the crackdown on the "Doctors Plot" in the Soviet Union? It is likely that being a rival for power of party leader Gheorghe Gheorghiu-Dej, and not a veteran of the same in-country prison clique as the leader, was more important than her ethnic origin. The same is true for purged "Muscovite" communist minister of agriculture Vasile Luca, a Hungarian, and former minister of the interior Teohari Georgescu, a Romanian. The arrest of these leaders occasioned also the arrest and imprisonment of many party members and officials associated with them.

The Stalinist Party leader Gheorghiu-Dej managed to maintain and further concentrate his power after the death of Stalin in 1953 and the onset of de-Stalinization. The execution of Pătrăşcanu in 1954 eliminated the most plausible rival for party leadership; then two potential supporters of Khrushchev were ousted in 1958. Defying the Soviet leader's call for the separation of party and state leadership functions, Gheorghiu-Dej concentrated power in his own hands. Like Romanian leaders during the era of national unification, he adeptly exploited opportunities in the international arena to increase Romanian diplomatic independence. Unlike earlier leaders, he also used national independence to enhance his personal power. The successor chosen after his death in 1965, Nicolae Ceauşescu, learned from and further developed this technique.

In the first years of the communist regime it depended on its Soviet patrons and was totally subservient in its foreign policy. Ana Pauker was foreign minister; Gheorghiu-Dej was chosen above all East European leaders to deliver a speech formally condemning Marshall Tito, and Bucharest was chosen as the headquarters of Cominform, the successor to the Comintern, when Yugoslavia was expelled from this organization. Emil Bodnăraş, a Ukrainian and former Soviet agent, presided as minister of defense over the political coordination of the army. This closeness to the Soviets explains why it was Bodnăraş who first suggested on behalf of the Romanian leadership that Soviet troops were no longer needed in Romania after the conclusion of the Austrian State Treaty in 1955. Romania strongly condemned the Hungarian "counterrevolution" in 1956, and hosted the interrogation of former Hungarian leader Imre Nagy before his execution in 1958. The withdrawal of Soviet troops the same year was to a large degree a recognition of Romanian loyalty and reliability.

Gheorghiu-Dej insisted that the Romanian leadership reject Khrushchev's de-Stalinization initiatives. The crucial opportunity for the expansion of Romanian independence was the Sino-Soviet dispute. Gheorghiu-Dej took a mediating

Nicolae Ceauşescu (1918–1989). He became secretary general of the Romanian Communist Party in 1965 and president of Romania in 1974. The photograph shows his address to the last party congress a month before his ouster and execution in December 1989. (AFP/ Getty Images)

position when the Chinese leadership presented its theses on independent paths to socialism. Romania chose an ideologically impeccable sally, the publication of a collection of research notes by Karl Marx denouncing nineteenth-century Russian imperialism in Bessarabia. The country dissented from a Soviet proposal for a differentiation of economic roles within the East European bloc, whereby Romania would remain a primarily agricultural country, and went public with its opposition to the secret Valev Plan for cross-border economic cooperation that seemed to threaten Romanian sovereignty over Transylvania. Cultural and economic agreements with Western countries further compromised Romania's position within the bloc.

The new party leader, Nicolae Ceauşescu, continued and intensified these policies. During the Prague Spring, the period of liberalization and reform in Czechoslovakia, he declared in public speeches that the party leadership in that country was entitled to pursue its own path without Soviet

Neo-Stalinism: Ceauşescu and the Personality Cult

According to a thesis of the historian Nicolae Iorga, the culture of the Byzantine Empire survived in the Danubian Principalities after the fall of Constantinople, constituting a *Bysance après la Bysance* (Byzantium after Byzantium). The cult of the leader in the era of Nicolae Ceauşescu (1965–1989) constituted what Iorga might have called *Stalinisme après le stalinisme* (Stalinism after Stalinism). Another historian and political observer, Karl Marx, might have commented on this regime by recalling his witticism about the coup that brought Louis Napoleon to power: All great historical phenomena occur twice, the first time as tragedy, the second as farce.

This was a time when market reforms, collective leadership, and party pluralism emerged in other East European countries. In Romania, a policy of rotation of cadres was introduced to prevent the emergence of rivals. An English collection entitled *Romania on the Way of Completing Socialist Construction: Reports, Speeches, Articles* records the dictator's speeches in twenty-nine volumes. Beginning in 1973, several books compiled poetry and prose in praise of the leader and his wife. Two were published in 1981: *The Country with One Voice: Homage to Comrade Nicolae Ceauşescu* and *From the Depth of the Heart: Homage to Comrade Elena Ceauşescu*. Among the most fervent poets was Corneliu Vadim Tudor, the future leader of the Greater Romania Party. The sound track of the *Epoca de aur* (Golden Age) was the hymn, customarily performed with a large chorus, from which the following is an excerpt:

Partidul, Ceauşescu, România

We have in our lead a son of the country
The most loved and most obeyed
Who in the world, to the horizon
Is prized and honored by the people.
And these three wonderful words,

Words worthy like a tricolor,
We carry them engraved in our hearts
Towards Communism, in the coming years.
The people, Ceauşescu, Romania,
The party, Ceauşescu, Romania.

(Unpublished translation by James P. Niessen)

Ceauşescu's visit to the Chinese and North Korean capitals in 1971, followed by the disastrous Bucharest earthquake of 1977, helped inspire the idea of building a new city center. Its centerpiece would be a public palace, the House of the People, at the end of a new Avenue of the Victory of Socialism. The twenty-five-year-old architect Anca Petrescu won a contest to plan it, proposing a building that would be the second largest in the world after the Pentagon. Bulldozers began to clear away buildings from an increasingly lunar landscape beginning in 1984. Forty thousand people were evicted, some on six hours' notice; many committed suicide. Four hundred architects and twenty thousand workers built the outside of the palace in five years; one of their dead bodies was discovered by accident. Considering the victims, some found the spectacular project reminiscent of the construction myth *Meşterul Manole*. There was a call to destroy the palace after the revolution, but since it incorporated high-quality materials and workmanship, it became the Palace of Parliament in 1994. The interior, thirteen stories above ground and four below containing 1,100 rooms and 4,500 chandeliers, was finally completed in 1996. The total estimated cost was $1–3 billion.

interference. The threat that the Soviet Union would intervene militarily in Romania as well as Czechoslovakia in 1968 was apparently genuine. Ceauşescu's defiance of this threat at a mass rally in Bucharest won him enormous prestige among Romanian intellectuals and in the West. Romania established friendly diplomatic relations with West Germany, France, and the United States. Romania never became a true threat to the integrity of the Warsaw Pact, but as with France within NATO, its rhetorical neutralism annoyed the dominant power.

Defiance of the Soviets in 1968 opened for Ceauşescu the prospect of not only asserting domestic autonomy (in order to reduce Soviet interference with his control over the party) but also attaining a degree of popular support outside the party. This option was in marked contrast to the party's disregard for territorial integrity before 1944, as well as to its arrests of prewar political and cultural leaders in subsequent years. After 1948, the party stipulated an official version of history that exaggerated every instance of Romanian indebtedness to the Russian people, enforced socialist realism in literature, established museums, stores, and publishing houses to propagate Russian culture, and made the study of Russian mandatory in Romanian schools. An orthographic reform in 1954 changed the spelling of the Romanian â to î, thereby emphasizing its possible Slavic origin. The new Romanian foreign policy after 1960 found its domestic counterpart in the elimination of the Russian language requirement, the closing of many Romanian-Russian cultural institutions, and the reform of 1965 that restored the letter â and the name of the country from Romînia to România. More significantly, many noncommunist cultural figures were released from prison, and scholars regained the possibility of teaching and publishing. Strict ideological controls and censorship of the media remained in effect but were eased. More nuanced works of history began to appear, and literature dared to touch lightly on taboo subjects such as the worst abuses of Stalinism. After 1965, the party posthumously rehabilitated Pătrăşcanu and restored to the leadership some politicians previously purged. The second half of the 1960s was a hopeful period of relaxed control on public and cultural expression.

After 1971, ideological and political controls were restored and the brief period of liberalization came to an end. Ceauşescu had never been a true proponent of liberalization or pluralism but only accommodated it during a short-lived period of collective leadership. Returning from a visit to China and North Korea, he engineered a series of party resolutions, Romania's "little cultural revolution," modeled on what he had seen there. A less violent version of Stalinism was introduced, with fewer arrests and forced labor than the earlier period. Work on the Danube–Black Sea Canal, however, having been halted, was recommenced and completed in 1984. The party program approved in 1974 made mandatory the theses of the continuity of Romanian territory since ancient times and the unity of the Romanian people.

The revival of national traditions during the period of liberalization survived as an outlet for cultural activity and as a political tool. Some right-wing Romanian writers of the interwar period were republished, and national traditions were celebrated in history works, public speeches, and folklore festivals. The instrumentalization of nationalism was nowhere more evident than in the policy toward Romania's national minorities. The imposition of an anational communist regime had been a precondition for the Soviet authorities agreeing to restore Romanian sovereignty over northern Transylvania in 1945. There was no true national autonomy under these political circumstances, but Hungarian language education and publishing attained a quantitative level not seen in the interwar period. Hungarian was the primary language of administration in a newly established Hungarian Autonomous Region encompassing the bulk of the Szekler Region. Authorities merged the Hungarian university in Cluj with the Romanian one in 1959. The administrative reform of 1967, by which the precommunist era counties replaced the regions, was the pretext for eliminating the autonomous region. A new push to industrialize areas inhabited by national minorities, presented as an initiative to share the benefits of socialism, also worked against the Hungarians: newly established industries attracted large numbers of Romanian workers. Emigration policy also served to further the domination of the Romanian ethnic element. The majority of Romania's remaining Jews and Germans, nearly a million, were allowed to emigrate to Israel and the Federal Republic of Germany in exchange for the payment of a fee in compensation for the cost of their education, usually by both the émigré and the receiving country. Thereby the government rid itself of two minorities and also generated substantial revenue in hard currency.

Emigration to communist Hungary was not an option for the Hungarian minority. This minority still continued to enjoy the use of its language in media and education, but the sphere of this linguistic autonomy was progressively reduced. Hungarian citizens visiting relatives and friends in Transylvania learned firsthand about these changes, and contributed to a growing concern within Hungary about Romanian nationality policy. Beginning in 1978, writers of the two countries and occasionally the party leaders themselves engaged in polemics. A subtext of these exchanges was that the Soviet Union, in its anxiety over Romania's independent foreign policy, was using loyal Hungary as its surrogate. The comparative economic well-being of Hungary, and the historical legacy of the superior educational level of the Hungarian minority in Transylvania, served to exacerbate sensitivities in the Hungarian-Romanian relationship.

The heightening of national tensions in the 1980s occurred at a low point in Romania's economic standing. The nationalized economy and collectivized agriculture served, with only occasional periods of relaxation in the 1950s and 1960s, to progressively impoverish the countryside and attract population to the increasingly industrialized, often environmentally polluted urban centers. Economic policy aimed to decrease reliance on neighboring socialist countries by establishing a strong Romanian industrial base and exports for hard currency. During the early years of Ceauşescu's rule, thanks to substantial Western credits, Romania attained some of the highest rates of economic growth in the industrial world. The development plan relied excessively on the petrochemical industry, however. After Romania's domestic oil production peaked and then declined, it was necessary to import oil at a time when the international price of oil was rising. The result was a rising indebtedness. In 1981 Romania nearly defaulted on its loans from the International Monetary Fund. In an act of national pride and spitefulness, Ceauşescu determined that, rather than accept any controls associated with a rescheduling of the debt, he would establish a harsh austerity regime of rationing and export for hard currency to pay off the debt in the shortest possible time. His last decade in power was one of shortages for the population of food, heat, light, and most necessities. It was also a period of increased scapegoating of national minorities and strained relations with Hungary and the Soviet Union.

Peace demonstration organized by the government, Cluj 1983: The "No rockets in Europe" campaign was ostensibly directed at both the United States and the Soviet Union. (Courtesy of James P. Niessen)

The harshest expression of this dark period was the dictator's systematization plan. In blatant contradiction to the public celebration of Romanian village culture and folk music, the plan sought a drastic reduction in the number of rural communities and the concentration of the population in agro-industrial complexes. A frontal attack on the historic core of the capital city took place, demolishing fully one-third of the territory of the city center, destroying old monasteries and reminders of the nineteenth-century city in order to make way for the huge Palace of the People and the grand Boulevard of the Victory of Socialism. Bulldozers and a startling empty expanse dominated the affected area by 1988. Hungarians suspected the plan was directed against their villages, but the proposed impact on Romanian villages was devastating, and the destruction in Bucharest really happened. Abroad, the Romanian Villages movement raised awareness of rural systematization by pairing threatened villages with sister villages in Western countries.

DEMOCRATIZING ROMANIA

The fall of the regime in Romania on 22 December 1989, when Nicolae Ceauşescu escaped the Central Committee building by helicopter as crowds were entering it, was the only violent overthrow in the former Soviet bloc. The rela-

tive weakness of dissident activity and popular resistence gave rise to the witticism "*mamaliga* [a cornmeal porridge] does not explode," meant to contrast the Romanians with the Hungarians, Poles, and Czechs. The courageous resistance of demonstrators to armed repression, in Timişoara beginning on 17 December and then later in other cities and the capital, gave the lie to this thesis. According to official figures, 689 people died in these events around the country. It is therefore ironic that the political transition has been the most ambiguous and prolonged one in the region.

Romanians saw the new leadership emerge on national television with startling rapidity after the station fell into the control of the insurgents and successfully resisted armed assaults by adherents of Ceauşescu. Alongside a number of military figures and former dissidents, two individuals were more important than the rest: Ion Iliescu, a former communist official who had fallen out with Ceauşescu in the 1970s, and his prime minister, Petre Roman, a professor at the technical university in the capital and son of a prominent communist. They called their umbrella organization, successor to the Communist Party but initially including many noncommunists, the National Salvation Front to capitalize on the resurgence of religious feeling accompanying the fall of the regime. The capture of the Ceauşescus and their execution on Christmas day seemed superficially to also feed into this religious feeling. In fact the trial and execution were hasty and seemed to have been motivated in large part by a desire to obscure the connections between the old and new leadership. There were other trials of leading figures, but the common interest of the leaders and officialdom in self-preservation became increasingly evident. The Timişoara Declaration of March 1990, demanding full application of democratic liberties in the country, came in large degree into effect, but its demand that communists be excluded from the presidency was rejected by the National Salvation Front and, in the first open elections since 1947 in June, by the majority of voters who elected Ion Iliescu as president.

Political history since 1990 may be divided into three periods: the presidency of Ion Iliescu until 1996, that of the anticommunist Emil Constantinescu (1996–2000), and a second administration of Iliescu since then. During the first period, a large degree of freedom in elections and the press was established, but progress in economic reform was slow. Labor unrest was endemic throughout the decade. Iliescu and his allies frustrated reforms through two appeals to the miners of the Jiu Valley (whose two violent incursions into Bucharest in 1990–1991 have been ironically labeled as *mineriadas*), reliance on the self-interest of civil servants, and

Ion Iiiescu (1930–), socialist President of Romania, 1990–1996 and 2000–2004. He was a high party official under Ceauşescu before serving in more modest posts until 1989. (Hulton Archive/Getty Images)

an appeal to Romanian nationalism that branded calls for ethnic tolerance as support for Hungarian separatism. In the elections of 1992 there was a partial return to the interwar electoral pattern, whereby support for the Christian and Democratic National Peasant Party (the descendant of the National Peasant Party) was strongest in the formerly Hungarian regions. Many democrats, ironically, were monarchists who believed that the reestablishment of a constitutional monarchy under King Mihai would enable Romanian's to follow the example of post-Franco Spain. After 1992, Iliescu's government relied on the parliamentary support of nationalist parties.

The 1996 elections brought victory for the Romanian Democratic Convention, a coalition of several anticommunist parties. The new government declared as its main goals economic reform and accession to the European Union (EU) but made more progress on the former than the latter. Disunity in the coalition and continued labor unrest (including three threatened marches of the miners on Bucharest) stymied reforms. The participation of the Hungarian Party in the government signified a breakthrough in interethnic relations, making possible improved diplomatic relations with Hungary and satisfying human rights concerns of the European Union. King Mihai's Romanian citizenship was restored, and after a peaceful visit to the country in 1997 he lobbied NATO member countries for Romanian membership. In 1999 Pope John Paul II visited Romania, the first visit of any pope to a primarily Orthodox country. The Yugoslav conflict inversely affected the economy by interrupting trade with Yugoslavia and along the middle Danube, and there was negative economic growth in 1997–1999. Romania's improved international standing and foreign loans could not prevent rising unemployment, repeated reshuffling of the government, and the collapse of its popularity by the time of the elections in 2000.

The second Iliescu presidency has been a period of greater political and social stability than the first. The threat of ultranationalist Corneliu Vadim Tudor's election in the presidential runoff prompted a pragmatic coalescence around Iliescu by most democratic parties. The new government, while a minority one, dominated the strengthened nationalist opposition with the support of the Hungarian Party. The pro-Western commitments of the Constantinescu presidency have continued. Romania has joined NATO, contributed forces to international peacekeeping efforts, appears likely to host American military bases, and is working steadily toward accession to the European Union.

POLITICAL DEVELOPMENTS

The communist legacy left Romania comparatively ill-prepared for multiparty democracy and economic reform. Extreme centralism in economic policy and political administration, and even in the affairs of the ruling party, prevented the evolution of autonomous interest groups, decision making, and civic awareness. The Communist Party of Romania constituted the relatively largest of any country in the region. In 1988 official membership was 3.7 million or 15.8 percent of the population. The Communist Youth of Romania, pioneers for younger children, women's groups, trade unions, and workers councils of national minorities integrated large numbers of the population into the process of conveying the leadership's directives. The Securitate (secret police) may have included as much as a quarter of the population in the rolls of its employees and informants. The personality cult during the last fifteen years of Nicolae Ceauşescu meant not only that the leader's face and interminable speeches dominated the mass media, but that large numbers of cultural as well as political figures were forced into humiliating expressions of admiration for the "genius of the Carpathians" and the members of his family.

This experience left a deep impact on the Romanian psyche. Scapegoating, the shaping of opinion through rumor and informants, and direction from above were more familiar political techniques than tolerance and open debate. Thus it is not surprising that for the first half of the 1990s Freedom House ranked Romania substantially below other East European countries in terms of democracy and the rule of law. The Freedom House ranking improved dramatically in 1996 with the electoral victory of Emil Constantinescu and his allies. In 2004 Romania was ranked "free," which was good in a worldwide comparison.

Among its "Nations in Transit" ranking of twenty-seven former communist states, Freedom House ranked Romania as intermediate.

Ceauşescu's legacy lends plausibility to the theory that what took place in 1989 was a skillfully engineered coup d'état rather than a revolution. How, given Romania's recent history, could the people have overthrown the regime on their own? The term "revolution" remains fitting because crowds of ordinary people spontaneously braved the danger of armed repression, and genuine dissidents greeted the overthrow of the dictator on national television. It is also true that the only genuinely oppositional voice within the Communist Party during 1989 was that of Silviu Brucan, a former ambassador to the United States and coordinator of official mass media who was demoted after 1965. Brucan was the author of the "Letter of the Six," an open letter released signed by six former communist leaders in the spring of 1989 that called for the replacement of Ceauşescu as party leader. The letter's authors were effectively isolated and not in a position to engineer the events of December, but the document would undermine efforts of anticommunists to tar all participants in the former regime with the same brush. Ion Iliescu was not one of the six, and after his demotion from the top leadership in 1984 he was director of the Technical Publishing House in

The Palace of Parliament in Bucharest. Its construction began under Ceauşescu, but its current name and function were adopted in 1994. (Corel Corporation)

Bucharest. His many connections within the establishment and his reputation as a moderate who had studied with Soviet leader Gorbachev enabled Iliescu to gain the support in December of party and military leaders who distanced themselves from Ceauşescu after his fall.

The transitional leadership, called the National Salvation Front (NSF), included Brucan, literary dissidents Ana Blandiana and Mircea Dinescu, and less-known individuals who gained sudden prominence during the revolution. Iliescu's inner circle made key decisions, excluding these others who in turn were dismissed or resigned. Forgetting earlier promises of nonpartisanship, the NSF transformed itself into a political party that coopted much of the former communist apparatus, and Iliescu emerged as its presidential candidate. Denied equal access to the broadcast media, the revived historical parties and the party of the Hungarian minority could garner only limited support against them in the elections of May 1990, which brought the NSF 65 percent of the votes cast. The new assembly drafted a constitution that was approved in a national referendum in December 1991.

The constitution resembles in many ways the precommunist constitutions of 1866 and 1923. Like these it provides for an elected Chamber of Deputies, a Senate, and a centralized administration with heads of the 41 counties appointed by the minister of interior. The constitution protects private property and the freedom of political parties and established churches. The head of state is an elected president who must not be a member of a political party, and there is no place for the former royal dynasty. A significant change was in the role of elections. Romanian kings had since 1866 appointed new governments that then managed elections so that they would provide the needed parliamentary support, and communist elections were a complete sham. The new constitution provides that the president appoints the prime minister and government only *after* elections have been held. Governments must secure the support of parliament for their confirmation and continued service. The president is elected for a renewable four-year term, chairs a security council, after an amendment in 2003 can call referenda, and can call for new elections if the government loses parliamentary support, but he cannot initiate legislative proposals or veto bills passed by both houses.

The three central bodies of the judiciary branch are the Constitutional Court, the Superior Council of Magistrates, and the Supreme Court of Justice. The Constitutional Court, which may review the constitutionality of all laws of parliament, consists of nine judges who serve nine-year nonrenewable terms; the president, Chamber of Deputies, and Senate each appoint three of its members. The two houses in joint session elect the members of the Superior Council of Magistrates to four-year terms, and the Council in turn proposes members of the Supreme Court of Justice for appointment by the president to renewable six-year terms. The Supreme Court is not only the final court of appeal but must also study and coordinate the activity of all other courts throughout the country.

The Romanian Parliament is today housed in the massive edifice begun before 1989 in a newly cleared area in southern Bucharest, formerly called the Palace of the People and now the Palace of Parliament. Deputies are elected to parliament for four-year terms by universal adult (age eighteen) suffrage based on proportional representation rather than personal mandates. The Chamber of Deputies has 343 members, of whom fifteen are guaranteed seats for recognized ethnic minorities, and the Senate has 143 members. The government or one or another chamber may initiate legislation, and the chambers sitting in joint session may initiate votes of no confidence against individual members of the government, the government as a whole, or the president. The number, names, and popular support of political parties represented in parliament have repeatedly shifted.

The principal socialist party, which formed the government during the first and second Iliescu administrations in 1990–1996 and since 2000, emerged in 1990 under the name of National Salvation Front. After dissociating itself from the former Stalinist regime and supporting the new constitution, the party now favors gradual economic reform. This is the party of Ion Iliescu, although the constitution stipulates that the president not be a member of a political party. Petre Roman, the son of a leading figure in the Communist Party, headed the government in 1990–1991. In September 1991 miners who had descended on Bucharest forced his resignation. His successors were two economists who had not been politically active, Teodor Stolojan and, after the elections of 1992, Nicolae Văcăroiu. The NSF divided in 1992, with Văcăroiu's faction becoming the Democratic National Salvation Front (DNSF) and a faction chaired by Petre Roman retaining the original name. The opposition NSF renamed itself Democratic Party–National Salvation Front (DP-NSF) a year later, and the DNSF became the Party of Social Democracy of Romania (PSDR). There is a small Stalinist party associated more explicitly with the legacy of the Communist Party, called the Socialist Labor Party (SLP) and led by Ceauşescu's one-time foreign minister, Ilie Verdeţ. After the 1992 elections, the government relied on parliamentary support from the SLP and the Romanian nationalists, described below. Later the DP-NSF simply became the DP.

The free market democratic parties originally centered on the historical parties that dominated Romanian politics before 1938, the National Liberal Party (NLP) and the National Peasant Party (NPP). The NLP leadership proved ineffective and it split into many groups, however, so the NPP, which later added Christian Democratic to its name (NPPCD) quickly became the standard-bearer of the opposition. The two principal leaders were Corneliu Coposu, a former secretary of Iuliu Maniu who spent seventeen years in communist prisons, and Ion Raţiu, member of a distinguished Transylvanian political family who had been a leader of the emigration and boasted ties to Western financial and political circles. The government sometimes played on popular xenophobia in emphasizing the NPPCD's foreign connections, support for the restoration of the monarchy, and advocacy for the restoration of its former churches to the Greek Catholic Church. Urban intellectuals not sharing either of these vulnerabilities formed a separate group of the free-market democrats, including the Party of the Civic Alliance (PCA). The NPPCD, NLP, and PCA, along with several smaller parties, formed the coalition Democratic Convention of Romania (DCR) on a platform of anticommunism and support for the principles of the Timişoara Declaration. The DCR's presidential candidate Emil Constantinescu, former rector of the University of Bucharest, lost the presidential elections in 1992 but won in 1996. Two members of the NPPCD served as prime ministers under President Constantinescu, Victor Ciorbea (1996–1998) and Radu Vasile (1998–1999), then were succeeded by the nonparty National Bank Governor, Mugur Isărescu. The DP and the Hungarian Party also participated in these governments.

A week before the overthrow of Nicolae Ceauşescu on 22 December 1989, the spark for this result was given by demonstrations in Timişoara by citizens of various nationalities on behalf of a Hungarian Reformed cleric, László Tőkés. The clergyman's courageous but not chauvinistic defense of human rights in Romania, in particular those of the Hungarian minority, attracted the support of Hungarian congregants, then of Romanian and German residents of this multiethnic city when he was threatened with demo-

Emil Constantinescu (1939–), president of Romania, 1996–2000. The former rector of the University of Bucharest was elected as a candidate of the Democratic Convention of Romania. (Tami Chappell/Reuters/Corbis)

tion and transfer to another town. This act of solidarity, and the Timişoara Declaration of March 1990, signified the hope that the revolution would usher in a new era of tolerance and fraternity in ethnic relations.

László Tőkés became a member of the National Salvation Front during its phase as transitional governing council, but, like other leading noncommunists, he soon left this body. On 25 December 1989, the Hungarian minority established its own political organization, the Democratic Alliance of Hungarians in Romania (DAHR). The DAHR participates in local and national elections and takes positions on countrywide issues, but defines itself as a federation rather than a political party, with autonomy for its territorial organizations and various associated organizations. The first leader of the alliance was Géza Domokos, the former director of Kriterion, the state publishing house for Romania's ethnic minorities, while Tőkés took the position of honorary president. As chief representative of the Hungarian minority, the DAHR has enjoyed the overwhelming support of Hungarian voters in the elections since 1990. As a supporter of free-market democracy and the opening toward the European Union (EU), the alliance joined forces with the DCR in the 1992 and 1996 elections and took a seat in the government during the Constantinescu administration. The policy of collaboration with Romanian democrats has had the support of Domokos, his successor since 1998, Béla Markó, and, according to opinion polls, most Hungarians, but a minority led by Tőkés favors a more militant stance.

There have been three main tendencies of Romanian ultranationalism since 1990: the Legionaries, chauvinists in Transylvania, and Bucharest-based xenophobes. The revived Legionary movement emerged in 1990 under the initial leadership of Marian Munteanu, a charismatic student leader. This movement claims to continue the traditions and platform of the interwar Legionaries and has eschewed collaboration with the other nationalist groups, but it has fragmented into various groups and failed to gain sufficient votes to take a seat in parliament. The Transylvanian group had its origins in the so-called cultural organization Romanian Hearth and civil servants eager to rally Romanians against a supposed Hungarian threat. After Romanian Hearth took a role in the bloody Hungarian-Romanian clashes in Târgu Mureş (Hungarian: Marosvásárhely) in March 1990, the group organized into the Party of Romanian National Unity (PRNU) with the chief goal of opposing Hungarian interests. The PRNU entered parliament in 1992 but gained its greatest notoriety through the flag-waving and Hungarian-bating of former engineer Gheorghe Funar as mayor of Cluj, Transylvania's largest city, since 1992. The party subsequently elected him party leader but replaced him after disappointing results in the 1996 national elections.

The larger Bucharest-based organization is the Greater Romania Party (GRP). Its founder and still dominant personality is Corneliu Vadim Tudor, a poet and journalist who used the newspaper he founded, *România Mare* (Greater Romania), to build his base before establishing the party in 1991. The GRP mirrors the rhetoric of the PRNU equating Hungarian demands for cultural autonomy with territorial separatism but

Graffiti in University Square, Bucharest, 1994: The Monarch saves [i.e., will save] Romania; Neocommunist-free zone; Tien An Men Square II; Long live Romania, Long live the King; Glory to the martyrs. (Courtesy of James P. Niessen)

is anti-Semitic and glorifies wartime leader Marshal Ion Antonescu and Nicolae Ceauşescu. The party included several military officers among its leaders, and for much of the 1990s enjoyed special access to official documents on its political enemies that Tudor used to smear them in the party newspaper. More than the SLP of Ilie Verdeţ, the GRP perpetuates the goals of the last years of Nicolae Ceauşescu to concentrate state authority against all purported enemies in the name of national security and territorial integrity. The PRNU and GRP provided support for the minority government of Nicolae Văcăroiu after the elections of 1992.

After the failure of the NPPCD in its leadership of the coalition government in 1996–2000, in the elections of 2000 the party individually and the DCR as a coalition did not even meet the threshold for representation in parliament. The NLP successfully regrouped and emerged stronger in these elections, but the chief victors were the resurgent PDSR and GRP. Tudor won a surprising second place in the presidential election with his advocacy of radical measures against corruption and separatism, prompting alternative forces to throw their support to Iliescu in the second round. Under the second Iliescu administration the GRP is the strongest opposition party by far but is isolated from the others, with whom it rarely collaborates. The

PRNU also failed to enter the new parliament. With the initial tacit support of the fragmented free market democrats and the DAHR, the PSDR under Prime Minister Adrian Năstase has moved further to the center. In 2001 the PSDR merged with the successor of the prewar socialist party and took its name, becoming the Social Democratic Party (SDP).

Two features distinguished Romanian politics from other postcommunist states after 1990: street violence and the Hungarian question. The politics of the street signified the perception of many Romanians, Hungarians, and Roma that, having played a key role in the toppling of the dictator, they were unable to bring their concerns to bear through the press and formal political structure. In March 1990 Hungarians in Târgu Mureş, the largest city of the Szekler region, were assaulted by Romanians who had been brought into the city in chartered buses to suppress demands for Hungarian cultural autonomy. Several persons were killed in the riots, and the leading Hungarian playwright lost an eye, but official investigations blamed the Hungarians. Demonstrators in University Square in Bucharest established a "Communist-free zone," disrupted traffic in the city center for several weeks during the period of the elections, and attacked a government building on 13

June. In a tactic reminiscent of the communists' assumption of power, after his resounding victory at the polls Iliescu called on the miners to restore order against the "hooligans." Seven thousand miners and others (some were identified as policemen) descended on the capital, capturing the streets, trashing the headquarters of the NPP, killing several, and wounding thousands. More than a thousand were detained by authorities, most of them the aforementioned hooligans. Iliescu thanked the miners for giving the country a "lesson in democracy."

The efforts of Prime Minister Roman to enact economic reform prompted a second assault by the miners on Bucharest in September 1991, this time against the government. The miners demanded that Iliescu and Roman resign, and they ransacked the parliament building. After four deaths and hundreds of injuries in clashes with security forces, however, the miners settled for the resignation of Roman's government and withdrew. After this second lesson in democracy, Iliescu did not call on the miners again. Strikes, marches, and demonstrations were a regular feature of the subsequent years of declining popularity for the Iliescu administration before its electoral defeat in 1996.

Three times during the Constantinescu administration the miners threatened again to march on Bucharest. Privatization and the closure of unprofitable mines were a prominent feature of the coalition's announced program of reforms. An estimated 20,000 workers participated in nationwide strikes in 1997, and miners struck to demand pay raises. In response, the government increased the miners' pay and reversed the decision to close several enterprises. In 1998 and again in 1999, thousands of miners sought to march on Bucharest to protest proposed mine closures and judicial measures against their leader, Miron Cosma. The authorities succeeded in halting both marches, however, and successfully prosecuted Cosma. Labor unrest contributed significantly to the failure of the Constantinescu administration. The reviving economy and the concern of the Iliescu administration for Romania's image have served to reduce street actions and their abuse by the authorities in recent years.

The Hungarian problem is the other enduring, distinguishing feature of politics in Romania. There are also large Hungarian minorities in neighboring Slovakia, Ukraine, and Serbia, but the minority in Romania is by far the largest. As in the neighboring countries, the Hungarians' history of dominance and their sense of cultural superiority have inspired claims for cultural and regional autonomy. The distinctiveness of the Hungarians in Romania is that they live mostly concentrated in a region, Transylvania, with a long tradition of political autonomy that contrasts with the centralism of the Romanian state. During the interwar period, Transylvanianism had been a literary movement of the Hungarian minority that claimed opportunistically (in view of the impossibility of reunion with Hungary) that Transylvania's distinctive history and multiethnic population merited an independent or at least autonomous status. After the wartime division of Transylvania between Hungary and Romania, which prompted the flight of many Hungarians and Romanians across the new border, northern Transylvania returned

to Romanian rule but on the understanding that nationality policy be revised in the Hungarians' favor. A Hungarian university was established in Cluj, and a so-called autonomous Hungarian region was established in the Székely district to the east. These measures were later reversed and there was no true ethnic autonomy in the communist era, but Hungarian language education and media enjoyed considerable latitude within the limits of party ideology.

Since 1990 there have been recurrent demands for enhanced Hungarian cultural autonomy and the devolution of state power to respect local particularities. The DAHR argues that Western European countries offer numerous examples of federalism, territorial autonomy, and the constitutional and institutional protection of ethnic minorities that would be more fitting for Romania than the current centralized and unitary model. The PRNU and GRP are quick to brand these demands territorial separatism, implying that they are a prelude to annexation of part of the country by Hungary. Ion Iliescu's party has repeated these false claims for its own political benefit. Federalism is a sensitive point in Romanian politics, but there has been some movement toward local self-government since 1990.

Ethnic relations improved after 1996 when a bilateral treaty with Hungary was concluded. Since 1996, the DAHR has actively or passively supported the government. Even so, cultural and administrative autonomy remains a sensitive issue. In response to outcries by Romanian nationalists and even moderates, the government backed away from commitments to create a Hungarian university in Cluj. On the other hand, the second Iliescu administration has reluctantly acquiesced in forms of sponsorship for the Hungarian minority by the government of Hungary. Subsidies are distributed to various educational and cultural organizations, and the Hungarian Status Law of 2002 provides for access by Hungarians from Romania and other successor states to education and other services in Hungary. As it did in the interwar period, the idea of Transylvanian regional autonomy even attracts a small amount of Romanian support in the associations and foundations established for this cause. Potentially more explosive are two Hungarian autonomist initiatives that are associated with the nationalist wing of the DAHR led by László Tőkés. They led to the first formal rupture in the organization after they were rejected by the leadership of the alliance.

Romania's foreign policy has been reoriented toward the West. In his early years as national leader, Nicolae Ceauşescu asserted a prominent diplomatic role for the country as intermediary between the blocs with the Israelis and Palestinians and the beneficiary of a special trade relationship with some Western countries. But the collapse of the economy in the 1980s brought an end to this role. The Soviet Union again became Romania's leading trade partner. In fact, Romania had never left Comecon, the Soviet trading network, or the Warsaw Pact and attended meetings of these organizations, though participation was limited in some areas. In 1975 the United States granted Romania Most Favored Nation status in recognition of the country's special opposition. After rising criticism of Romania's human rights record at the time of the annual renewal of MFN in Congress, Ceaușescu renounced it in 1988 in order to preempt its revocation.

Well-publicized human rights problems and delays in economic reform impeded Romania's desire to improve relations with the European Union after 1990. When President Iliescu traveled to Western countries, he was sometimes denied reception by other heads of state. The United States finally restored MFN in 1993 and made it permanent in 1996. Romania pursued an ambiguous policy toward Yugoslavia during its internal conflicts, mostly respecting but sometimes circumventing trade sanctions against that country. Treaties with Ukraine and Russia as well as Hungary have improved trade relations and clarified territorial issues with these countries. The relationship with Russia remains strained by Russia's retention of Romanian state reserves of gold, jewels, and art valued at $5 billion, which were sent to allied Russia during World War I for safekeeping.

Romania has acceded to the Organization of Black Sea Economic Cooperation and the Central European Free Trade Association with the Visegrad countries. The country was formally invited to join NATO in 2002, and is engaged in the protracted process of accession to the European Union with a target date of 2007. The United States is currently considering a move of its military bases from Germany to Romania and Bulgaria that would establish a special strategic relationship with these countries. Romania's two major ongoing issues in foreign relations however remain contentious: EU accession and the Moldovan question.

CULTURAL DEVELOPMENT

The twin foundations of popular and high culture in Romania are the traditions associated on the one hand with the peasantry and rural life, and on the other with Romania's religious communities. The artistic expressions that grew from these foundations are evident in the work of the leading artists and writers of modern Romania. A third foundation, national ideology, arose in the eighteenth century and has accentuated the distinctiveness of national cultures while undermining their commonalities. In addition to these three, external cultural influences have proven increasingly important with the onset of modern communications. Paradoxically, proponents of national integrity have enlisted French, German, and Russian political thought for their purposes.

The secular origins of Romanian folk culture should be sought in migratory shepherds (ciobani) in the Danubian Principalities before the rise of large-scale field agriculture beginning in the eighteenth century. The portrayals of ancient Dacians in Trajan's Column and the Roman monument at Adamclisi suggest they wore the same woolen breeches and fur caps as shepherds do today. It is much more difficult to establish other continuities with the Dacians. It is known that the unsettled military and political conditions south and east of the Carpathians, and the domination of Hungarians and Germans on the other side, left the development of an autonomous Romanian folk culture in the

hands of migratory shepherds astride the mountains. Centuries of transhumance probably account for the lack of dialectal variation in the Romanian language. The archetypical Romanian ballad, *Miorița* (The Little Sheep), has been documented in different versions in many regions. *Meșterul Manole,* on the other hand, is the Romanian variant of a construction myth (walling-in sacrifice) that is well-documented in Southeastern Europe, also among the Hungarians. Landlords are absent from *Miorița,* as they were in the lives of free peasants in the foothill villages who helped preserve the *cioban* culture.

Settled village communities proliferated after the eighteenth century and multiplied the local styles of peasant dress, fabrics, woodcarving, and ceramics. The Hungarian, German, and Slavic communities were more sedentary and concentrated, but also developed variations in their designs as well as some interethnic influence in the use of colors or floral, vegetal, and geometric motifs. Peasant homes and their interiors became more ornate if an agricultural surplus permitted it. Well-off homes would feature little-used rooms heaped with embroidered pillows and bedspreads. Unless sumptuary laws forbade it, wealthier peasants might imitate the clothing and home decoration of the nobility or burghers. In ethnically mixed areas, social climbing prefigured and often motivated linguistic assimilation.

Religious communities were an important marker of ethnic identity in villages of mixed population. First, their ecclesiastical calendars determine the times of major fasts and feasts that set one community apart from the others. Aside from saints and observances particular to one church, the difference of more than a week between the Gregorian and Julian calendars meant that even the major feasts that the Christian churches shared were usually celebrated at different times. Therefore the religious difference between the Orthodox Christians (Romanians, but also Serbs, Ukrainians, and Russians) and the other Christians was particularly strong. Religious differences were at least as important as linguistic ones as an obstacle to intermarriage among ethnic groups in traditional communities. Differences of calendar and diet separated the Christians even more strongly from the Jews.

Liturgy and theology were also important elements in religious differentiation. The Orthodox liturgy is an intensely aesthetic creation several hours in duration, mostly chanted by the priest and congregation without musical instruments, in an environment of icons, murals, and incense. In all churches the clergy preached in the vernacular, but the Western Christian (Hungarian and German) liturgies were progressively less ritualistic and more textual in nature: those of the Catholics, Lutherans, Reformed, and Unitarians. Romanian Greek Catholics lived in two worlds, mostly in that of the Romanians with whom they shared the liturgy and most customs as well as language. They also lived in the Catholic world because of the shared recognition of papal primacy and, in some regions, study in shared seminaries, and the veneration of religious statuary that was atypical of Eastern Christianity. Each church participated through its clergy and bishops in an international communion, cen-

Folk dancers perform on a stage at a folk festival in the Maramureş region in the northwestern corner of the country. (Owen Franken/Corbis)

tered in the case of the Orthodox in the Balkans and Russia, in Rome in the case of the Catholics, in Germany in the case of the Lutherans, in Germany and the Netherlands in the case of the Reformed, and in the Anglo-Saxon countries in the case of the Unitarians. Gregorian chants among the Catholics, organs among the Lutherans, and varied canons of hymnody developed distinctive musical cultures. More than their doctrinal significance, these associations were important for the development of cultural influence in a broader sense. Until modern times the patriarchs of Constantinople consecrated the Orthodox bishops, and the monasteries of Mount Athos were influential in their spirituality and artistic traditions. Western Christian bishops were often educated abroad, and the Saxon Lutheran church of Transylvania even required a university degree from Germany for election to an ordinary pastorate.

Romanian popular religion included pre-Christian as well as Christian elements. The belief in vampires (*muroi* or *strigoi*) was native to Romania as well as many other countries, though widely deplored by Romanian clergymen and others well before Bram Stoker's *Dracula* appeared in 1897. There was a variety of other non-Christian customs. Shepherds celebrated a milking festival before leading the sheep into the mountains in the spring, played tunes called *şireaguri* during cheese making, and called to each other on

the *bucium* (alphorn) or shepherd's horn. Whereas Western Christian villages knew the sound of church bells, in the Romanian ones worshipers were summoned by the drumming of a wooden sounding board called the *toacă*. Christmas, New Year, funeral, and wedding customs contain a mixture of Christian and non-Christian elements. Traditional Romanian funerals may include the procession with open coffin, a colorful ritual called the Wedding of the Dead, and public memorial feasts called *pomana*. Romanian Christmas carols *(colinde)* feature tonalities common to the Orthodox liturgy but, unlike the liturgy, address different occupational groups with distinctive verses. The rituals for the invocation of rain and at the time of the harvest are pre-Christian. Among Transylvanian Hungarians, the counterpart to caroling is the performance of vignettes from the Nativity by groups of young people called *bethlehemesek*. In many Hungarian villages even today, the wearing of elaborate traditional costume on Easter Sunday makes the religious feast an opportunity to celebrate ethnic identity.

There is also a wealth of folk music whose character is not religious. The *doina* is a slow and sad Romanian melody. Its style is different from the Hungarian military recruit's lament or *verbunk;* the word's origin from *Werbung* hints at the Habsburg German authorities who did the recruiting. Many Romanian regions have their characteristic styles of slow and fast melodies and song, which also owe much to styles elsewhere in the Balkans, showing the influence of the Serbs, Jewish *klezmer,* or Islamic music. The ring dance (or *hora)* is commonly practiced in many regions, as are lively dances such as the *sîrba* (its name reflects a Serbian origin) and the *învârtită* or spinning dance for couples. Dancers may shout out humorous, rhythmic verses called *strigături.* In southern Romania and parts of Bulgaria, a ritual involving dance and dramatic plays was called *căluş,* though it is dying out. Gypsy (Roma) music observes many of the same styles practiced by non-Roma but is often more energetic and the singing more high-pitched. The most renowned folk singers in twentieth-century Romania were the female Romanian Maria Tănase and the male Gypsy Fănică Luca. The village of Clejani near the Danube south of Bucharest is the home of some five hundred Gypsy musicians. The best-known ensemble from here, the twelve-piece Taraf de Haiduci or Taraf de Haidouks (Band of Outlaws), has made several acclaimed recordings.

The similarities of Romanian folk music to that of the Middle East owe much to the period of several centuries of the Danubian Principalities association with the Ottoman Empire. There are various forms of flute, bagpipe, and cembalom. The *tekerő lant* (hurdy-gurdy) is peculiar to the Hungarians, while the best-known Romanian folk instrument is the panflute, or panpipe. Ancient depictions, including a passage in Ovid's *Tristia,* indicate the panflute was played by shepherds on the territory of the country already in Dacian and Roman times, though the Romanian term commonly used today for panflute, *nai,* may have come from Persia via the Turks. The earliest professional panflute association was registered in Bucharest in 1843. Fănică Luca was the first internationally known panflutist from Romania. He performed at the world fairs in Paris and New York in 1937–1939 and taught the instrument at the Music Lyceum in Bucharest for fifteen years before his death in 1968. His most famous student was Gheorghe Zamfir, whose recordings and performances are well known in North America. Damian Drăghici-Luca, a grand-grand nephew of Fănică Luca, has performed and recorded since the age of ten.

The documentation of folk customs and songs began in the nineteenth century. Authorities founded the Romanian Folklore Institute in 1949, and ethnography gained a respected place in scholarship. The institute sponsored the excellent folk music orchestra Barbu Lăutaru. The careful collection and study of folk music helped preserve it despite the rapid urbanization and industrialization of the communist era, but the genre also became an instrument of political manipulation. *Doine* of questionable origin lamented the plight of communists in Romanian prisons before 1945. Trade unions and houses of culture had organized a reported 44,000 music, dance, and dramatic ensembles by 1959. In 1975 the government established the cycle of organized music festivals called Cîntarea României (Song of Romania) that performed an amalgam of genuine folk music and paeans to the dictator. The more traditional performances were carefully shorn of any religious or otherwise politically objectionable content and recorded in the most spectacular costumes and scenery with dubbed audio.

Because of the fakery associated with Cîntarea României and an excess of *Tezaurul folkloric* (The Folkloric Treasure) broadcasts on television during that era, many educated Romanians feel distaste for folk music despite the undeniable beauty and originality of the genre.

Formal or higher music owes a debt to ecclesiastical, folk, and Western formal influences. Valentin Bakfark (1507–1576) was a German/Hungarian lutenist from southern Transylvania whose compositions and performances were renowned during his time. Renaissance and baroque music was known in the courts of the Danubian Principalities as well as independent Transylvania. Baron Samuel Brukenthal invited the leading members of eighteenth-century Transylvania and Wallachia to performances of the works of contemporary German composers in his palaces in and near Sibiu. Transylvania's towns became provincial centers of the musical culture of the Habsburg monarchy in the nineteenth century, and philharmonic societies were founded in the principalities as well. In the mid-nineteenth century, Ciprian Porumbescu was the first distinguished modern Romanian composer. His few compositions were influenced by folk music. The foreign visitors Johannes Brahms and Franz Liszt toured the region and became aware of Romanian folk music, but its influence on the Hungarian composer Béla Bartók was even greater. He was born west of Arad and helped establish the folk music archives in the mixed Hungarian-Romanian region of Kecskemét in modern-day Hungary.

The master composer of the Romanians was George Enescu. A composer impressed by his precocity convinced his parents to enroll him in the Vienna conservatory at the age of seven; then upon his graduation he studied in the conservatory in Paris under the tutelage of Jules Massenet and Gabriel Fauré. Enescu composed his best-known works, *Romanian Poem* and the first two Romanian rhapsodies, with their strong folkloric elements, between 1898 and 1901. In addition to composing, Enescu was a distinguished conductor (including at the New York Philharmonic in 1937–1938), violinist, and tutor to Yehudi Menuhin. Other well-known musical performers of twentieth-century Romania have been the pianists Dinu Lipatt and Radu Lupu and the opera singers Ileana Cotrubas and Angela Gheorghiu. Several Romanian cities feature philharmonic orchestras and opera houses.

The key architectural monuments of the country are its churches and monasteries. The monasteries set the tone for Orthodox spirituality, with a clergy that (unlike that of the parishes) is unmarried, renowned for its otherworldliness, and attracts the faithful for festive liturgies in venerable, even grand surroundings. The oldest, fourteenth-century churches in Wallachia at Tismana, Cozia, and Curtea de Argeş are of Serbian and Byzantine inspiration, formed around a square Greek cross. The bishop's church in Curtea de Argeş dates from the early sixteenth century. The ballad *Meşterul Manole* concerns the construction of this church, whose fascinating decoration has Caucasian, Arabic, and Persian elements. The churches of Moldavia also follow the Byzantine model but are longer and higher with pitched shingle roofs and towers with cones at their top, showing a

The Trei Ierarhi Church (1639), Iasi: Architectural masterpiece of the old Moldavian capital, with its ornately decorated façade and conical towers.

Gothic influence in their shape that is unusual in the Orthodox world. This Gothic influence is much more pronounced across the Carpathians. The wooden churches of formerly Greek Catholic Romanian villages in Maramureş share not only the internal plan of other Orthodox churches but also high steeples found elsewhere only in Western Christian churches. Among the oldest surviving such churches is the one in Şurdeşti built in 1724 with a disproportionately high tower of forty-five meters that long made it the highest wooden structure in Europe. Lacking government patronage and even suffering destruction during the religious strife of the eighteenth century, Romanian monasteries were fewer and less influential in Transylvania than in the Principalities.

The elements of an Orthodox church floor plan have Greek names. The *pronaos,* or *exonarthex,* is the first chamber encountered on entry, which was in earlier times the part of the church to which female worshipers were restricted. The *naos* corresponds to the nave in Western churches, and is where the priest, choir, and most worshipers stand to chant the liturgy. At the end of the naos is the icon screen that separates the people from the altar sanctuary. Within each chamber there are standard iconographic elements, from the dedication of the church to scriptural personages and events. The humble wooden churches raised by poorer Romanian communities in Transylvania often contain charmingly naïve and apocryphal scriptural elements in their frescoes and icons. Monasteries produced for worshipers' domestic shrines in workshops for the painting of icons on wood and especially glass. Painting on glass was less expensive and also permitted brighter colors. Glass icons are the most distinctive element of religious folk art among the Transylvanian Romanians. The monastery at Nicula in northern Transylvania, which became a pilgrimage site in the seventeenth century because of a weeping Madonna, later housed one of the most important glass icon workshops.

Western Christian architecture in Transylvania followed the romanesque, Gothic, Renaissance, and baroque models of Catholic Europe. The Catholic cathedral of Alba Iulia has a romanesque tower dating to 1247–1256, a Gothic choir, and two Renaissance chapels. The second Gothic church in Transylvania is St. Michael's in Cluj, completed in 1432 with an impressive buttressed nave that dominates the main square of the city. These and the major Gothic churches of the south Transylvanian towns were actually built by the Saxons. Many Saxon churches, though abandoned by most of their congregants who have emigrated to Germany, still boast impressive winged altar paintings and Turkish carpets on the walls that recall the centuries when Saxon towns were outposts against Ottoman assaults. Saxons, and to a lesser extent Szeklers, fortified their rural churches with thick walls whose apartments could accommodate most villagers and their livestock in case of attack. The most impressive Saxon citadel churches are in Prejmer and Biertan. The focal point of small Hungarian towns in western Romania is often a Reformed church decorated with an ornate wooden cassette ceiling and a carved stone pulpit created by the Renaissance artist Dániel Sípos.

The reign of Stephen the Great in Moldavia (1457–1504) was one of the high points for Romanian ecclesiastical architecture. He built more than thirty churches and monasteries, many of which were in southern Bucovina and subsequently painted on their exterior as well as interior walls. The "painted monasteries" of Moldoviţa, Suceviţa, and Voroneţ are renowned for the brilliant colors and striking images of their exterior frescoes portraying Genesis, the Tree of Jesse, the Last Judgment, and the siege of Constantinople. Moldavian church architecture experienced another great period in the seventeenth century with the construction of the monasteries of Dragomirna (1609) and Trei Ierarhi (1639), notable for their ornate lacework facades. During the seventeenth and eighteenth centuries, the closer relations between the two Danubian Principalities were reflected in greater similarity of their church architecture.

Due to the unsettled conditions in the Danubian Principalities, more important secular buildings survived from earlier times in Transylvania. In the Gothic style, these include the town hall in Sibiu and the castles in Hunedoara (of which a partial replica exists in the Budapest city park since

The Painted Monasteries

All Romanian monasteries have paintings on the inside. The term "painted monasteries" refers to the monastery churches of northern Moldavia that were painted on the outside during the sixteenth century. Moldavia benefited from greater stability than Wallachia, partly because it was not on the direct line between the belligerent Ottoman and Hungarian forces but also because it possessed two remarkable princes during whose long reigns the painted monasteries were created: Stephen the Great (1457–1504) and his son Petru Rareş (1527–1538, 1541–1546). Stephen was a more cautious and savvy politician than his contemporary Vlad III Dracula, navigating successfully between the more powerful Hungary, the Ottoman Empire, and Poland but winning battles against all three of them. He founded one church for each of his thirty-eight victories over the Turks. The largest of these was the monastery of Putna where he is buried, but those in Pătrăuţi, Voroneţ, St. Elijah near Suceava, and Bălineşti anticipated the style and themes of the later external murals through their style and themes. The influence of fifteenth-century Byzantine painting is evident, but there is also a greater realism and liveliness in the figures and harmony of colors and crusading spirit that distinguishes the external murals even more. A distinctive architectural style also developed, with pitched roofs and octagonal towers.

Stephen's first two successors were less able rulers and far less energetic patrons of the arts. Petru Rareş was a more worthy successor, an astute diplomat and military leader, and a well-traveled scholar and art lover. There is some evidence of exterior murals from the reign of Stephen, but they became widespread and characteristic of Moldavia under Petru Rareş. The external murals are brighter, as those inside benefited from few windows and have been darkened by centuries of soot from candles. The murals are better preserved on the south side of the churches than the north, which is more exposed to wind and precipitation. The most remarkable of the painted monasteries are at Humor, Moldoviţa, Arbore, Voroneţ, and Suceviţa. Several of the frescoes depict the siege of Constantinople by the Persians in 626. Although this successful Byzantine defense rather than the disaster of 1453 was the theme, the artists depict the besieging troops as Turks and Tatars. At Humor the artist signed his name below a Moldavian horseman attacking the Turks. Another striking motif is the Last Judgment, which features Turks and Tatars in their distinctive garb among the sinners. The Tree of Jesse appears several times, with a fascinating variety of figures and costumes. The church at Voroneţ is known for the striking blue of its murals and their large size, made possible by wide unobstructed surfaces on this church. It is likely that the political dominance of the Turks after 1550 accounts for the absence of the Siege of Constantinople in the murals at Voroneţ and Suceviţa; the latter was the last of the painted monasteries, completed in 1601. Austrian graffiti have marred the impressive Siege at Moldoviţa since the eighteenth century. In the 1950s UNESCO declared seven of the painted monasteries to be protected cultural sites.

the late nineteenth century) and Bran in the Carpathians south of Braşov. With its angular shape and prominence along the highway to Bucharest, Castle Bran is sometimes referred to as "Dracula's Castle" despite its tenuous connection with Vlad the Impaler. Renaissance monuments in Transylvania include private houses in Cluj and Sibiu and the royal fortress in the middle of the southern Transylvanian town of Făgăraş. Sibiu, whose Saxon inhabitants have largely emigrated, is architecturally the largest German town in Southeastern Europe, with a partially intact city wall and characteristic window vents known as roof eyes (Dachaugen) on the pitched roofs of older buildings. In the Principalities the major sixteenth-century fortress of Piatra Neamţ in Moldavia has survived, but there are only ruins from the Wallachian princely courts in Târgovişte and Bucharest.

Vernacular architecture became the dominant form in the eighteenth century. Wallachian prince Constantin Brâncoveanu (1688–1714) was a great builder and introduced a new style that is named after him, marked by decoration using statuary, columns, arcades, and floral ornamentation.

Notable examples are the Mogoşoaia Palace (1702) north of the capital and the Stavropoleos Church (1724) in central Bucharest. The arrival of the Habsburgs brought the baroque style to Hungary and Transylvania in numerous churches and the large city palaces of the Barons Bánffy in Cluj and Brukenthal in Sibiu, and on a larger scale the Vaubain-style fortresses in Alba Iulia and Arad. Neoclassicism made its appearance in the Principalities under Russian and French influence. The major buildings of the emerging national capital were built in the neoclassical style: the National Theater (1846–1852), the University (1869), and the Romanian Atheneum concert hall (1888).

There were regional styles in the domestic architecture of the common people. The porches in Brâncovenesc buildings may have arisen in imitation of Romanian homes. At the end of the nineteenth century, professional architects began to take more notice of popular styles and attempted a synthesis of folk and modern architecture in their work. The leading representative of this tendency in Romania was Ion Mincu, who built various restaurants and private homes

The "painted" monasteries of Moldavia were built in the fifteenth and sixteenth centuries and present brightly colored biblical and historical scenes. (Gianni Baldizzone/Corbis)

in Bucharest and restored the Stavropoleos Church in 1906. The Transylvania Hungarian Károly Kós studied in Budapest, where he became an advocate of a style that resembled Mincu's in its objectives but sought to revive Hungarian regional styles. His most notable building is the Székely National Museum in Sfântu Gheorghe. The Palace of Culture in Târgu Mureş is another example of Hungarian folk revival architecture, whereas the National Theater in Cluj is an example of Habsburg art nouveau. Many Bucharest houses and even apartment buildings of the interwar period are examples of these styles. After 1920, Kós and the Bucharest sociologist Dimitrie Gusti worked independently for the preservation of folk architecture. Kós published a highly regarded collection of meticulous drawings of Transylvanian village architecture in 1929, while in 1936 Gusti founded the remarkable Village Museum in Bucharest that is a collection of village houses and wooden churches from all over the country. It was the third open air museum of its type in Europe. The Museum of the Romanian Peasant arose from earlier institutions founded in

1875 and 1906–1912. It was associated with the Village Museum after 1978 but became an independent institution once more in 1990.

The dominant trend in Romanian architecture since 1918 has been an international style that is largely functional. The communist era brought the great expansion of most cities, with prefabricated apartment houses accommodating a great influx of population from the countryside. The provision of modern housing and conveniences was a significant benefit to large numbers of people. There was a wide range of quality in these new buildings, both aesthetically and in their building materials and durability. The Scînteia House, the center of Romanian publishing built in the wedding-cake style of the Lomonosov University in Moscow, became the most characteristic monument to communist architecture until the construction of the Palace of the People during the 1980s. The Palace of the People, having been built with the best materials and for the ages, now houses the Romanian Parliament.

Sculpture is a less prominent art form than in many countries because Orthodox Christianity provided no place for religious statuary alongside icons and frescoes. Consequently for most centuries we find sculpted human figures in stone and wood only in association with the Western Christians of the former Habsburg and Hungarian lands. On the other hand, there was a strong tradition of stone carving for external decoration on church and secular architecture across the Carpathians. As previously noted, there was great regional variation in folk ceramics among the Romanians and other peoples. Objects for use were also carved from wood in the mountainous regions. The ornately carved wooden gates of traditional homes are a famous feature of Szekler communities in eastern Transylvania and Romanian ones in Maramureş. Equestrian statues and busts of historical personages arose on the streets of Romanian as well as Hungarian cities in the nineteenth century.

One name stands out among modern Romanian sculptors, Constantin Brâncuşi. Born in a three-room house with a wooden gate in a village in the Jiu Valley in 1876, he gained his first experience of carving in wood while tending the family's flocks. He attended crafts and arts schools in Craiova and Bucharest, winning awards for some of his busts of historical and contemporary personages. After a year in Munich, in 1904 he made a famous walking trip to Paris to study. Sculptures from this period show the strong influence of Auguste Rodin. After 1908, Brâncuşi moved from figurative art to abstract depictions of lovers kissing, birds in flight, and other themes. His most famous works are installed in a public garden in Târgu Jiu: the Endless Column, the Table of Silence, and the Gate of the Kiss. Continuing to live in France after World War II, the sculptor was declared persona non grata by the communist authorities. They tried unsuccessfully to pull down the 27.5-meter-high column, embedded in concrete, with an armored tank. After sixty years in the open air, the installations enjoyed a $3.7 million restoration project in 1999–2000. The studio of the artist, and many of his smaller works, are preserved today in Paris.

Modern secular painting in Romania has closely followed Western models. Romantic and realistic painters of the first half of the nineteenth century favored historical themes but increasingly devoted their attention to the life of the peasantry. Theodor Aman was the founder of modern Romanian painting and director of the art academy in Bucharest. His most famous successor, still known as the greatest Romanian painter of the nineteenth century, was Nicolae Grigorescu. After earning a living briefly as a self-taught painter of icons and then studying in Aman's academy, he spent several months in France where he learned to paint in the style of the Impressionists. Many of his works are pastoral landscapes, but he also painted realistic portraits of the Romanian peasantry and scenes from the War for Independence of 1877–1878, in which he participated as a war artist. Under the influence of the later Impressionists were Ştefan Luchian, Theodor Pallady, and the more abstract Iosif Iser.

Constantin Brâncuşi was the most famous Romanian contributor to the international avant-garde, but others included the painter and architect Marcel Iancu and the poets Tristan Tzara and Ion Vinea. Iancu, Tzara, and Vinea helped found the Dada movement in Zürich in 1916. Iancu returned to Bucharest in 1922 and created a sensation with an exhibition of his post-Cubist paintings. He founded the modernist journal *Contimporanul* (The Contemporary) and organized a notable modernist exhibition in 1924 featuring Brâncuşi, the surrealist Victor Brauner (who lived in Paris after 1930), and the Transylvanian Saxon Hans Mattis-Teutsch, a graphic artist influenced by the German expressionists. Iancu moved to Palestine in 1941 and lived out his days in Israel.

The tank assault on the works of Brâncuşi was inspired by the communist rejection of modernist art in general, many of whose exponents had already left for more congenial environments. The proletarian themes of socialist realism became the standard material of Romanian painters until complemented, beginning in the 1970s, with scenes of national greatness and tasteless images of the dictator with scepter in hand. Since 1990, there has been a modest revival of the interwar Romanian avant-garde.

As elsewhere in Eastern Europe, literary life has played a stronger role than the fine arts in the definition of Romania's ethnic and national cultures. The standardization of literary languages and the presentation of national ideals for popular consumption were necessary components of the process of definition. As with other art forms in Romania, however, the national literatures had their pre-Christian folk elements and Christian forms before they became national. They included sermons, saints' lives, and other religious texts.

The Protestant Reformation in the Hungarian lands inspired an expansion of vernacular publishing among the Hungarians and Germans that also affected the Romanians. Scripture and the liturgy were translated into Hungarian and German, and writings addressing controversial religious issues appeared in these languages. The Saxon scholar and Lutheran preacher Johannes Honterus (1498–1549) became the leading figure in Transylvanian German publishing, while with the patronage of the Transylvanian princes the Reformed preacher Gáspár Karoli translated and published the first complete Hungarian Bible in 1590. Under the influence of these initiatives, Transylvanians also published the first books in Romanian. In the seventeenth century the princes of Transylvania inspired the creation of a Romanian Reformed church, which failed to make lasting converts but further stimulated the use of the vernacular. Vasile Lupu, the prince of Moldavia, founded a printing press to counteract the influence of Protestant propaganda through the dissemination of Orthodox texts. Lupu was not yet printing in Romanian, however; the first publication in this language was a textbook printed in Transylvania in 1699.

The seventeenth century also brought the rise of the first important secular genre, historical chronicles and memoirs. The most important Romanian authors of these chronicles, not yet histories in the modern sense, were Moldavians: Miron Costin and Ion Neculce, while Dimitrie Cantemir, who also briefly ruled as prince of Moldavia, deserves the title of historian because of his much more sophisticated use of sources. His *Description of Moldavia* broke new ground not only in describing the country but in examining its early history. His *History of the Rise and Fall of the Ottoman Empire* was translated into many languages. Notable historians of the Transylvanian Saxons and Hungarians included Johann Troester, Lorenz Töppelt, István Szamosközy, and János Bethlen, often still writing in Latin rather than the vernacular and recording imaginative genealogies and contemporary reports rather than formal history.

French literary models of memoir literature were dominant in the early eighteenth century, mediated in the Principalities by the Greek ruling elite. Later in Transylvania, the influence of the Austrian Catholic Enlightenment was more important, giving rise to a more critical awareness of religious and ethnic identity. Historians give the name Transylvanian School to the group of Romanian linguists and historians active at this time. Its leading figures, Samuel Micu, Gheorghe Şincai, and Petru Maior, presented important findings concerning the Latin origins of the Romanian language and the history of the Romanians in Transylvania. The Transylvanian School had a lasting impact on Romanian national consciousness. The debate between Romanian and Hungarian writers about the theory of Daco-Romanian continuity has raged since this time. The implicit threat in the Romanian arguments to Hungarian cultural predominance in Transylvania contributed in large degree to the vigor of the response.

The center of Hungarian and Romanian literature moved from Transylvania, however, to Hungary proper and the Danubian Principalities. Romanian writers, many themselves graduates of Greek schools, rejected Greek and Russian influence and turned instead to France. Contemporary engravings of notables in the 1830s show an interesting mixture in costume that was emblematic of the culture's reorientation: some men wore Ottoman-style caftans and trousers, while others wore frock coats in the French style. Gheorghe Asachi in Moldavia and Ion Eliade Rădulescu in Wallachia were leading proponents of a national Romanian literature in the era of the Revolution of 1848. Later, but of more lasting influence, was Vasile Alecsandri, the author of popular patriotic verses at key points in the struggle for unification and a major playwright.

A debate about Romania's cultural roots and relationship with the West has enlivened Romanian cultural life since this era. The rejection of Ottoman costumes occurred within a generation, but the new debate lasted longer and was more ambiguous. Some polemics oversimplified the contest as one between Westernizers, who believed Romania must follow liberal, industrial Europe in order to prosper, and traditionalists who wanted to protect indigenous Romanian culture. The opposing camps had their cultural journals, Alecsandri's *România literară* (Literary Romania) on the liberal side and *Convorbiri literare* (Literary Conversations) on the side of the traditionalist Junimea (Youth) literary society, which was based originally in the Moldavian capital but then moved to Bucharest. The debate about language reform added an ambiguous note, with patriots in Transylvania favoring an unnatural spelling of the language to emphasize Latin origins, and the no less patriotic Junimea opposing it. The liberal Alecsandri was a notable collector of folklore, though Junimea placed more emphasis on village traditions. The greatest Romanian writers of the late nineteenth century were associated with Junimea: Mihai Eminescu, Ion Creangă, Ion Luca Caragiale, and Ioan Slavici.

These four classics of Romania's greatest literary era made distinctive contributions. Eminescu is known as the national poet. Influenced equally by his collecting of folk poetry in Moldavia and his study of German philosophy in Vienna, he is best characterized as a late romantic. Creangă recorded his childhood memories of his native village in northern Moldavia. Caragiale was a Bucharest writer of Greek origin who wrote popular plays satirizing the Romanian middle class, living his last years in Berlin when a wealthy inheritance permitted it. Slavici was born in the Banat and studied in Budapest and Vienna, then became a journalist, a leader of the Romanian National Party in Hungary, and author of stories of village life. All four lived tempestuous lives, and only Caragiale died in comfort. Slavici was persecuted by the Hungarian authorities for his political activity but sided with the Central Powers in World War I and documented his year of captivity in Greater Romania in the biting work *My Prisons*. As diverse as the traditionalist camp was among Romanian writers, within Hungary it found itself in ethnopolitical as well as philosophical opposition to the modernist and urban Hungarian writers. The Transylvanian poets of rural opposition to the Hungarian city were George Coşbuc and Octavian Goga. In contrast to Slavici, Goga took his opposition to the Hungarian government into exile in Bucharest in 1913 and lived twenty years in Greater Romania.

The two-sided struggle over Romania's cultural model took new forms after 1918. At one extreme were the modernists, sparked by the Dada movement in Zürich and the journal *Contimporanul* (The Contemporary). Tristan Tzara's irreverent Dada manifesto (1918) set the modernist agenda in Romania in its defiance of conventional ideas, but the author himself stayed in Paris after the war. The journal *Viaţa românească* (Romanian Life) and its leading literary critic, Eugen Lovinescu, represented the Europeanist mainstream of Romanian writers. This mainstream treated urban themes but was also comfortable with rural ones, as evidenced by the novelists who did their greatest work in this period, Liviu Rebreanu and Mihail Sadoveanu. Rebreanu's depiction of the peasant revolt in 1907, *The Uprising* (1932), is arguably the greatest Romanian novel.

The literary journal *Gîndirea* (Thought) had modernist tendencies at first but increasingly served as the focal point for the traditionalists. Among its youngest adherents was Lucian Blaga, the graduate of a Transylvanian Saxon high school who wrote a notable treatise on Romanian culture that idealized Romanian shepherd culture. Other *Gîndirists,* including Octavian Goga and the writer and historian of religion Mircea Eliade, were sympathetic to the fascist Iron Guard. Writers of the Hungarian and German minority in Greater Romania moved uneasily between these extremes. Rather than engage in one or another broad tendency, they aimed to preserve their ethnic communities as socially cohesive blocs. Many Hungarian and German writers, but few Romanians, favored the Transylvanianist movement's vision of ethnic coexistence as an alternative to the national state. The leading writer of the movement was Áron Tamási, whose portrayals of Székely village life are charming and good-natured.

The communist regime put an end to the creative explosion of the interwar years. Many writers of liberal and traditionalist persuasion were imprisoned, while others moved abroad. A handful of prominent interwar writers, including Sadoveanu and the modernist poet Tudor Arghezi, decided to accept the framework of party orthodoxy and flourished. In contrast to the monotony of socialist realism in Romania, the most important Romanian writing took place abroad. Leading writers of the Romanian exile were Mircea Eliade, the absurdist playwright Eugène Ionesco, and the German Jewish symbolist poet Paul Celan (pseudonymn for Paul Antschel). Despite harsh ideological and political controls, the Ceauşescu regime allowed some worthwhile Romanian and Hungarian writers to flourish. The novelists Marin Preda and Augustin Buzura managed to convey implicit criticism of their society in the novels *Most Beloved of Humans* and *Refuges;* the poet Ana Blandiana shocked the censors and the reading public in 1984 with the publication in a literary magazine of her poem "Everything," revealing the banality of everyday totalitarianism. Transylvanian Hungarians for their part used the Hungarian progressive tradition and Marxist principles as a shield for the minority-language publishing house, Kriterion. Chauvinistic writing also survived, in the emigration and increasingly with regime sponsorship, to complicate the revival of cultural life since 1990.

The development of Romanian theater is closely linked to that of literature. Theater provides the opportunity for spontaneous expression in oppressive societies. Traveling troupes of the Romanian minority in Hungary before 1918, and of the Hungarians and Germans after this, served this purpose. Vasile Alecsandri was the first director of the National Theater in Bucharest, and others were founded in Iaşi and Craiova. Theater was especially popular among the urban upper classes, although the comedies of Caragiale pilloried them. Every ethnic minority had its theater; communist Romania even boasted the only Yiddish theater in Eastern Europe.

Mihai (or Mihail) Eminescu (1850–1889)

Romania's national poet was born Mihail Eminovici in Botoşani, in northern Moldavia. His father was a tax collector who sent him for five years to schools in Czernowitz (Romanian: Cernăuţi) in Austrian Bucovina, where he acquired his excellent facility in German. He adopted the name Eminescu at this time in order to sound more Romanian, as he said. His first published poem, in 1866, was an ode to his teacher in Czernowitz, Aron Pumnul. Then a Romanian language newspaper in Hungary, *Familia* (The Family), published several more of his poems. In 1868–1869 Eminescu traveled with an itinerant theatrical troupe under the direction of the dramatist Caragiale, making the acquaintance of many regions of Wallachia, Moldavia, and Transylvania. Then in 1869–1874 he studied at the Universities of Vienna and Berlin, meanwhile publishing poems to growing acclaim in *Convorbiri literare* (Literary Conversations), the journal of the Junimea literary society. After his return from Berlin, for three years he briefly held positions as a librarian, a school inspector, and a newspaper editor. During his longest period of employment, 1877–1883, he worked as an editor for the conservative newspaper *Timpul* (Time) in Bucharest.

Eminescu was a successful conservative journalist, some of whose pieces showed an anti-Semitism and xenophobia that were often part of Romanian nationalism when it was conceived of in terms of race. He also wrote short prose, notably a work of fantasy based on Greek mythology and a romantic love story. His greatest fame and most lasting contribution to world literature came from his poetry. It can be classified into philosophical verse, romantic nature poetry, and poetry that was political and social in character. "Doina" (1883) is his most nationalistic poem, including the central stanza:

> He who loves the foes about
> May his heart the dogs rip out,
> May desert his home efface,
> May his sons live in disgrace!
> (Translated by Kurt W. Treptow and Irina Andone, Treptow 237)

Luceafărul (Hyperion, or Evening Star, 1883) is acclaimed as his masterpiece. Hyperion, the evening star, falls in love with a beautiful princess, but his nature does not permit him to descend to her. Elements of romantic literature, folklore, and Greek mythology are present in ninety-eight perfectly formed four-line stanzas.

Eminescu's travels, work experience, and especially his fluency in German and familiarity with German philosophy, all contributed to his unique literary voice. Also important, and celebrated in Romanian literary lore, was his ill-fated love affair with the poet Veronica Micle (1850–1889). The two became lovers while Micle was married, but after her husband died in 1879 they did not marry for reasons that have never been adequately explained. Eminescu's health deteriorated in 1883 from a combination of work and relationships with women, causing him to resign his position with *Timpul*. Not long after the publication of *Luceafărul,* the poet suffered a nervous breakdown. During his last six years, he experienced alternating periods of insanity and relative health, but he never returned to productivity. Thus ended romantically, and tragically, the hero of Romanian literature.

Cinema developed slowly in Romania. The first notable feature film appeared already in 1912, Grigore Brezeanu's *War for Independence.* Domestic production remained at a modest level however, and filmgoers preferred foreign productions. The communist regime set about creating a substantial film industry, building the Buftea Studios for this purpose outside Bucharest in 1950–1957. Liviu Ciulei won a prize at the 1966 Cannes Festival for his most famous film, *The Forest of the Hanged,* based on the World War I novel by Rebreanu. Sergiu Nicolaescu helped promote Romanian national themes with the epic *The Dacians* and the Oscar-nominated *Michael the Brave.* The darker, visually interesting films of Dan Piţa were notable achievements of the next two decades. One of the most promising producers of the 1960s generation, Lucian Pintilie, was denied the opportunity to direct major films and went into exile. He returned to prominence in 1992 with the French-Romanian production *The Oak,* depicting the moral and physical decay of the country in the last years of Ceauşescu.

The development of Romanian culture and Romanian identity was also tied to education. The earliest schools and colleges in Romania were ecclesiastical institutions, alongside the medieval cathedrals and monasteries. The Hungarian princes of independent Transylvania founded colleges under Reformed and Catholic auspices. The Romanian Orthodox Church established a Romanian school in Braşov in 1559, but it failed to reach the level of the better-endowed Lutheran schools. The Greek Catholic high school founded at the bishopric's new seat in Blaj, Transylvania, after 1754 made a lasting impact on the national sentiment of generations of Transylvanian Romanians, but Romanians also studied in significant numbers in the ecclesiastical schools of the Hungarians and Saxons. The Hungarian state founded the first modern university in Transylvania in 1872, the Hungarian-language University of Cluj. Because it was the policy of the Hungarian state to use its resources for the promotion of Hungarian culture, the government progressively took the place of the Hungarian churches in the administration of elementary schools. The Romanian churches maintained control of Romanian village schools. In defending ecclesiastical autonomy they also helped minority culture to survive.

The first high schools in the Danubian Principalities operated in the Greek language. A Transylvanian Romanian, Gheorghe Lazăr, founded the first Romanian language academy in Bucharest after settling there in the second decade of the nineteenth century. Prince Cuza founded the first Romanian universities, in Iaşi in 1860 and Bucharest in 1864. He introduced compulsory primary education in 1864, but illiteracy remained higher than in Transylvania. The role of the government in education increased further after 1918. The university at Cluj became a Romanian institution, and the government took control of Romanian primary education in the former Habsburg lands that had been run by the Orthodox and Greek Catholic Churches. The position of Romanian and Hungarian education in these lands now reversed, as the Hungarian churches provided institutional support for schools in the vernacular.

The expansion of Romanian education at all levels greatly accelerated in the communist era. There was a great need for training in new branches of the economy, but authorities enforced rigid controls and instituted ideological indoctrination as well. The state schools also took over almost all education in the minority languages, with the exception of a number of seminaries still managed by the churches. There has been continuous reform of the Romanian educational system since 1990. There are more than one hundred institutions of higher education in Romania today. Half of them are private ones founded since 1990, including some for the Hungarian minority, but the majority of students are still enrolled in the state-run universities.

ECONOMIC DEVELOPMENT

The Romanian economy experienced rapid growth and transformation during the communist period. Industrial output grew at an annual rate of 12.9 percent from 1950 to 1977, thanks largely to heavy reinvestment of capital gained by the central control of prices and consumption. The agricultural sector declined from 74.1 percent of the working population in 1950 to 28.6 percent in 1982, while that of industry grew from 12 percent to 36.5 percent in the same period. There was a corresponding shift of population to the cities, the largest of which multiplied in size. The arduous process of collectivizing agricultural land was 90 percent completed by 1962. Collectivization favored the mechanization of agriculture, but it still lagged behind the West because of low productivity and the disproportionate investment in the industrial sector. There was a downturn in the economy after 1976. A massive foreign debt led to rationing in 1981 and a dramatic decline in the standard of living in the following years that made it possible to retire the debt by 1989.

Economic development has been fitful since the revolution of 1989. Overall growth was negative in all sectors until recently, with high inflation and with unemployment hovering around 10 percent. The average retirement age, fifty for women and fifty-four for men, is one of the lowest in the world and serves to distort unemployment figures. Labor unrest, especially in the mining and heavy industry sector that stymied efforts to close unprofitable mines, produced on foreign television screens the horrifying sight of rioting miners on the streets of Bucharest, and helped, along with an unfavorable legal and political environment, to discourage foreign investment. Only during a few years in the middle of the 1990s, then again beginning in 2000, did the economy show positive economic growth. The privatization of land ownership was 75 percent completed by 1995—97 percent by 1999. There has been some privatization in the services sector, but privatization of industrial firms has proceeded much more slowly.

Government sources attributed the recession after 1996 to the democratic coalition's efforts at economic restructuring. Corruption and the mismanagement of state enterprises was a continuing problem in the Democratic Convention as well as socialist administrations. The International Monetary Fund (IMF), World Bank, and European Union (EU) signaled their dissatisfaction with reform efforts by repeatedly suspending financial support packages. By the turn of the century, the level of marketization, foreign investment, and standard of living compared unfavorably with almost all other East European countries. Incomplete reforms due to the successful resistance of many vested interests produced economic imbalances and negative growth in 1997–1999. Reforms became more serious in response to demands arising from the accession to the European Union and caused unemployment to reach 10–11 percent (by various indices) in 2002. The new socialist administration has been more successful in prosecuting balanced structural reform, leading to positive growth after it took office.

The privatization of agriculture, pursued by the socialist governments of the first Iliescu administration, was a popular demand of the opposition National Peasant Party, which completed it once in power, but it failed to achieve the desired improvement in productivity. Agricultural employment rose by varying indices to 34 percent of the labor force (masking industrial unemployment) thanks to privatization but contributed only 13 percent of the gross domestic product in 2000. Many new landowners were unprepared for independent farming, and landholdings were often too small.

The inadequacy of agricultural investment and agricultural markets, including agricultural protectionism in the EU, contributed to the problem. Crops fluctuated wildly due to serious droughts in 2000, 2002, and 2003. Corn (maize) accounts for 40 percent of crop output in metric tons, and potatoes and wheat are each about 20 percent. The leader in meat production is pork, but its percentage of tonnage declined to below half of meat production in 2002 while poultry rose to 30 percent. Despite its large endowment of fertile black earth soil, Romania is a net importer of agricultural goods, and this trade imbalance has increased in recent years.

Mining of coal, salt, iron, and other metals in Transylvania, and the exploitation of petroleum in Wallachia, have historically been sources of wealth. Oil was exploited heavily in support of Nazi Germany during World War II, then subjected to a joint Soviet-Romanian company for a few years afterward. Petrochemical industries were a centerpiece of Ceauşescu's development strategy, but production peaked in 1976 and has declined since then as Romania became a net importer. Production rose slightly after 1990, buttressed by increased exploitation offshore in the Black Sea. Romania remains the largest producer in Eastern Europe and has substantial proven reserves. The largest producer is the state-run SNP Petrom SA. The company has an annual turnover of $2 billion and is the largest taxpayer in Romania. Many domestic and foreign interests are involved in reports of corruption at the company. Discussions about the company's privatization had reached a critical point as this article was completed in 2003. An Austro-Romanian company was privatized in 1998 under the name Rompetrol-OMV group and has a growing number of distribution points and two refineries. The Russian company LukOil is increasingly active in Romania, having acquired a refinery in Ploieşti and many distribution points of its own. In response to price increases and reforms there has been some increase in investment in this sector, the reopening of shut wells, and exploration of new sectors in the Black Sea. Most refineries built under the communists are now considered obsolete, however. Natural gas reserves are also substantial, but production peaked in the 1980s and has declined by two-thirds since then.

Coal mining, concentrated in the Jiu Valley on the border between Transylvania and Wallachia, has provided another major energy source but is plagued by hazardous work conditions that prompt labor unrest that is compensated by wage increases that then endanger the financial viability of enterprises. In 1977 and then again in the miners' marches on Bucharest in 1990–1999, these structural problems produced major social unrest that endangered the political establishment, although miners were less than 2 percent of the civilian labor force in 1999. The government did succeed in closing 209 mines and quarries in 1997–1999, assisted in part by loans from the World Bank. Romanian coal is mostly not of export quality.

More than half of Romania's electrical production (down from over 80 percent in the 1980s) is served by petroleum, gas, and coal, both domestic and imported. There are thermal power plants in many parts of the country, but many are not operational due to damage caused by the de-

clining quality of lignite fuel. The development of hydroelectric power began in the 1960s, with major stations at the Iron Gates on the Danube, Argeş, and elsewhere in the Carpathians supplying 35 percent of electrical production in 1998. The construction of Romania's first and to date only nuclear power plant began at Cernavodă on the Danube with Canadian partnership in 1979. Due to repeated delays the plant was not finally inaugurated until 1996, but by 1998 it accounted for an estimated 10 percent of Romania's energy production. A nuclear plant begun in Piatra Neamţ in 1986 has never been completed. Overall energy production and consumption in Romania has stagnated along with the economy. The country is a net importer of primary energy but has become a net exporter of electrical energy in recent years.

Industry (manufacturing, mining, construction, and power) accounted for 36 percent of gross domestic product in 1998. Bucharest was the leader of the ten most industrialized counties, but half of them were in the lands formerly belonging to Hungary. The largest portion of industry, accounting for 20 percent of the civilian labor force in 1999, was manufacturing in the metallurgical, mechanical engineering, chemical, and timber-processing industries. Industrial production declined by an annual rate of 2 percent in the 1990s, hampered by energy shortages as well as mismanagement and labor unrest. Importation of machinery for engineering industries is a particular source of the current trade imbalance. Most of the progress toward privatization in the industrial section has come after 2000.

Among the better-known industrial firms are Dacia, which has produced cars in Piteşti (Argeş County) with a license from Renault; Oltcit, which has produced cars in Craiova in a joint venture with Citroen since 1977 (the company was renamed Oltena in 1989); and the truck company in Braşov known since 1990 as Roman S.A. It had its origin as a manufacturer of railway rolling stock beginning in 1921, branched out to armaments, machine tools, and mining equipment, and produced its first trucks in 1954. Beginning in 1971, it produced trucks with a diesel engine licensed by the Man Company of Germany; then it became a joint stock company under its new name in 1990. Railroad cars and diesel locomotives have been a major industrial product and export item for decades, with plants in Arad, Bucharest, Caracal, and Craiova. They were heavily exported to the Soviet Union before the revolution but have found fewer buyers since then. Romanian chemical, especially petrochemical, industries were heavily favored but heavy polluters during the communist era but have scaled back due to unprofitability and environmental concerns.

There has been more privatization in the services sector, which accounted for slightly over half of gross domestic product in 2000 and 31 percent of the civilian workforce in 1999. Romanian tourism has failed to flourish despite the splendor of the natural environment and controversial attempts to exploit the interest of visitors in places associated with Dracula, Vlad the Impaler. One-fifth of foreign visitors during the 1990s were from neighboring Moldova. Economic activity in the service sector declined during the 1990s.

Industrial pollution: The iron and steel works in Hunedoara, Transylvania, in 1984. (James P. Niessen)

Transportation and communications are important factors in economic reform. The Romanian constitution stipulates that the transport infrastructure is the property of the state. This is not an unusual situation in Europe, but it does place limits on the flexibility of reforms and the infusion of market forces. A more unique constraint is the Carpathians, whose passes impose substantial detours on long-distance rail and road travelers. The Romanian Railways (Căile Ferate Române, CFR) control the fourth-largest railway network in Europe. The company was reorganized in 1998, with the freight services now open to private companies and denied subsidies but passenger services still subsidized. Ten private operators had gained a 20 percent market share of rail traffic by 2003. Several major routes with international connections are electrified, but most of the network is not. Even the major interurban highways are below international standards. The determination of the railbed through Transylvania to Romania in the nineteenth century had major implications for the development of cities, and the same may be the case with decisions made in 2003–2004 concerning highway construction. Despite the plans of the European Union for a southern route between Arad and Timişoara that would circumvent Transylvania, the Romanian government reached agreement with the party of the Hungarian minority for a highway to be built by the Bechtel Corporation through northern Transylvania. The intention to thereby better connect Transylvania with Bucharest and also with Hungary signified a new level of cooperation between the Romanian and Hungarian governments.

The completion of the Danube–Black Sea Canal in 1984, followed by the fall of the Iron Curtain, buttressed hopes for increased revenue for Romanian ports. Trade sanctions against Yugoslavia, then the closure of transport by American bombing, frustrated these hopes. The subsequent reopening of the Danube has yet to secure dramatic benefits for Romania. Most oil tankers are too large for the main channel of the Danube, let alone for the Danube–Black Sea Canal. The idea of a pipeline through Romania for crude oil shipped from the former Soviet Union to European markets had the double attraction of providing transit fees and even an opportunity for refining within Romania itself. The Romanian plan envisioned a pipeline from the port of Constanţa, which has a refinery and can receive four tankers at the same time, to Trieste on the Adriatic, where it would link to existing pipelines connecting Austria, Germany, and the Czech Republic. Romanian officials expressed optimism about the plan after talks with counterparts in Kazakhstan, Croatia, and other countries, but many diplomatic and financial details still required resolution.

Press and communications have changed dramatically since 1989. The telecommunication infrastructure, as in other countries of the region, is in need of substantial modernization. Not atypically, the total number and per capita telephone lines have risen rather slowly, whereas the number of personal mobile phone subscribers has skyrocketed, but the market is still far from saturated. Personal and institutional Internet use lags far behind Central European countries.

The freedom of the Romanian press has progressed unevenly. In dramatic contrast to the monotonous political press and more interesting but heavily censored cultural press of the communist period, private newspapers soon proliferated, some affiliated with political parties and others not. Censorship was a thing of the past, but the government attempted to limit access to supplies of newsprint for the opposition press. Soon this problem abated, and newspaper journalism critical of the government was important in the turning of public opinion against the socialists before the elections of 1996. Today the daily newspapers with the largest circulation, an estimated 200,000, are *Adevărul* (Truth) and *Evenimentul zilei* (Event of the Day). *Adevărul*, formerly the organ of the NSF and its successors, is a sober independent paper while *Evenimentul* is a tabloid known for investigative journalism of official abuses. Despite the apparent freedom of print journalism, there are serious allegations of violence against journalists who reported corrupt activities of socialist officials. In August 2003 a Romanian reporter won second place in Columbia University's Kurt Schork Awards for investigative journalism for his reports on government corruption.

Broadcast journalism has freed itself with greater difficulty, as licenses and technical facilities were more subject to government control. A National Audiovisual Council, established in 1992, is the sole issuer of licenses and reportedly uses its authority in conjunction with government revenue offices to create difficulty for opposition broadcasters. Private radio stations appeared first, then later in the decade private television stations as well. The emancipation of book publishing has had mixed benefits. Publishing suffered from censorship under the communists but benefited from subsidies that supported literary authors and accepted scholarship. The end of subsidies and the establishment of many new private publishing houses, most notably *Humanitas,* has opened Romania to precommunist and Western intellectual currents but also made the publication of many specialized scholarly works more difficult.

Romania's principal trading partners throughout the communist period were members of the Eastern Bloc, or Comecon. Their percentage share declined with the onset of a more independent foreign policy, from two-thirds in 1960, to under half in 1970, and 34 percent in 1980. Trade with advanced capitalist countries grew in the same period from 22 percent to 36 percent, then declined by 1980 with the onset of harder economic times to 33 percent. Trade with developing countries grew from 8 percent in 1970 to 25 percent in 1980. The Romanian plan to leverage differentiation from the Eastern Bloc for special access to Western technology and markets failed to make progress after 1976. Diplomatic efforts then shifted to the Third World and nonaligned movement, with corresponding commercial agreements. A trade surplus in machinery and industrial consumer goods during the 1980s made it possible to retire the foreign debt in 1989, at the cost of severe domestic austerity.

Trade shifted toward the European Union after 1990. Romania formally associated with the EU and the European Free Trade Association (EFTA) in 1993, then the Central European Free Trade Association in 1997. Germany and Italy vied for the status of leading commercial partner for most of the 1990s, with the latter taking the lead in later years. France supplanted Russia as the third leading source of imports and was consistently the third leading export country. Among the more interesting trends in foreign trade were Hungary's rise to fifth leading country for imports and Turkey to fourth for exports. Romania is pursuing improved diplomatic and commercial relations with these aspirants to EU membership as a complement to its own accession efforts. In contrast to the last years of communism, however, Romania had a serious foreign trade deficit. The country imported machinery and mineral fuels and exported clothing, transport equipment, and chemical products. Substantial remittances from Romanian nationals working abroad redressed the deficit somewhat.

Credits from the IMF and World Bank, along with the creation of joint trading companies with Western companies in the 1970s, fueled Ceaușescu's industrial ambitions but generated foreign debt and austerity later on. After the retirement of the foreign debt in 1989, Romania passed a law prohibiting the incurrence of foreign debt. This law was overturned after the revolution. Romania now also saw foreign direct investment, but its success paled by comparison with former bloc members to the west. Western fast food outlets made their appearance, but the slowness of privatization for larger firms and labor unrest discouraged major investments. Support packages of the IMF, intended to support the ambitious privatization program of the democratic coalition after 1996, were suspended due to failure to reach the agreed targets. In consultation with the World Bank, in 2001 the socialist prime minister announced a plan to privatize sixty-three state-owned enterprises. The second Iliescu administration has proven much more aggressive than the first one in pursuing privatization.

The Romanian economy operated before 1990 without a convertible currency or true market. Domestically, prices were set by administrative fiat and served to subsidize favored goods or accumulate capital for other ends. Foreign trade relied for the most part on bilateral agreements between states. A number of private banks arose after 1990, some of them engaging in pyramid schemes. The most infamous of these was the Caritas Bank. During the time of heavy inflation and unemployment in 1992–1994, an estimated 7 million Romanians and foreigners invested as much as $5 billion in Caritas and were guaranteed an 8-to-1 return as long as they brought new investors into the scheme. As in postcommunist Albania and Russia, the scheme fed on people's ignorance of capitalist finance and eagerness to improve their difficult situation. The survival of Caritas for two years raises questions about the connivance of the socialist government of the time; Caritas arose in Cluj and was allegedly connected to the nationalist Party of Romanian National Unity that was collaborating with the government.

The Romanian currency (singular *leu,* plural *lei*) has been freely traded since 1990, but due to poor budget balances it has fallen steadily against the U.S. dollar until recently. The National Bank of Romania controls the currency. Its governor is a member of the cabinet and served simultaneously as prime minister in 1999–2000. An agreement with the World Bank in 1997 slated six other state-owned banks for privatization. In 2003 the European Bank for Reconstruction and Development (EBRD) and the International Finance Corp (IFC) acquired a 25 percent interest in the largest remaining one, the Romanian Commercial Bank, which controls one-third of the country's banking sector.

Has the economic well-being of Romanians improved since the revolution? The severe rationing that preceded it is a thing of the past. Wages in many sectors remain low, and powerful trade unions in de facto collusion with state firms' officials looking out for their interests long delayed privatization.

Women's health has improved. Ceauşescu's Romania had enacted draconian sanctions against abortion and contraception, including regular, mandatory gynecological examinations, to encourage population growth. The impact on the birthrate was only moderate and temporary; apparently Romanian doctors violated the law. International and Romanian women's groups were relieved to see the legalization of birth control after the revolution. One consequence of pronatalist policies was that many unwanted children were deposited in orphanages. Their number (650 orphanages, with 98,872 children in 1998) and the poor conditions in these institutions attracted foreign investigative journalists, whose television documentaries gained unwelcome notoriety for Romania. Some unscrupulous adoption agencies took advantage of compassionate foreigners eager to adopt unwanted Romanian children despite the cost and in ignorance of illnesses such as AIDS and hepatitis. In response, a strict prohibition on foreign adoptions was enacted, and measures were taken to improve conditions. Romania's high infant mortality rate was reduced by 16 percent from 1996 to 2000.

There has been improvement in the state of the environment. Legislation or government initiative shut down or rehabilitated some of the most serious industrial polluters, notably the chemical and metallurgical plants in Copşa Mica, Zlatna, and Hunedoara in Transylvania. Concerns remain about the state of the fragile Danube Delta, where overharvesting of reeds for cellulose endangered wildlife habitats, and about the quality of water along the Black Sea coast. Concern for tourism, as well as standards imposed by the European Union, have served to encourage remedial measures. As elsewhere in Eastern Europe, emissions into the air per unit of energy produced remain above levels in the European Union. The EBRD is supporting efforts to increase energy efficiency and improve municipal water supplies. Emissions of greenhouse gases have declined significantly, and at the end of 2003 Romania joined other countries of the region in making commitments under the Kyoto Accords to further reduce them.

Romania and especially neighboring Hungary, Yugoslavia, and Ukraine experienced an environmental disaster in January–February 2000. On 30 January, Aurul, a Romanian-Australian joint venture extracting nonferrous metals from mining scrap, permitted cyanide- and metal-laced water to leach from a holding dam to a tributary of the Someş and Tisa (Hungarian: Tisza) Rivers near Baia Mare. From there the plume of water, estimated at close to 100,000 cubic meters, crossed the border into Hungary on 1 February. More than 100,000 kilograms of fish and many birds and other animals were killed in the more heavily populated Hungarian portion of the affected area, and the water supply of the Hungarian city of Szolnok was endangered. Melted snow and heavy rains led to three more spills in the same region later during the same winter and spring. Romanian and Hungarian environmental groups publicized events on their websites and organized demonstrations. This raised the awareness of the international and Romanian press to later cases.

Difficulties with the water supply have caused outbreaks of hepatitis and malaria. There is comprehensive health insurance provided by the state, but serious corruption mars health care delivery. The 2002 census revealed a decline in the country's population of 4.2 percent or one million to 21,680,974 since the census of 1992, due to an excess of deaths over births and to emigration. The emigration of the Hungarian and especially German minority peaked in the years before and after the revolution. Hungarian emigration is ongoing, and according to the census the decline in the Hungarian population exceeded the growth in the Roma population.

The per capita gross national income of Romania in 2003 was half that of Hungary but triple that of Moldova. The World Bank ranks Romania a lower-middle-income country based on this figure, above low-income Moldova but below upper-middle Hungary. The UN Technology Achievement Index ranks Hungary 22nd, Romania 35th, and does not rank Moldova. The same UN agency's Human Development Index, based on a correlation of life expectancy, literacy, and educational enrollment, ranked Romania 72nd out of 175 countries as a Medium Human Development country in 2001, below Hungary at 38th (high human development) but above Moldova (108th) in the same category. Romania's international ranking remained below that of 1985 but had improved slightly over 1990.

CONTEMPORARY CHALLENGES

One of the most prominent contemporary issues for Romania is its accession to the European Union (EU). The country had concluded textile and steel agreements with the European Economic Community in 1978 and a broader trade agreement in 1980. However, the country's steadily worsening economic and human rights situation led to its international isolation. Consequently the idea of a return to Europe attained powerful symbolic importance for Romanian democrats. Romania, the reasoning went, had been a normal, capitalistic European country before, and it should

Hay makers in traditional dress, Şugatag, Maramureş. (Corel Corporation)

become one again. Presumably economic well-being would follow. A trade and cooperation agreement with the EU was signed in 1990 and an association agreement in 1993. Romania also applied to the Council of Europe (a separate organization) and was initially rejected but then accepted after Hungary abstained in the vote. The socialist government submitted a formal application for accession to the EU in 1995.

The EU response to the Romanian application identified areas in which it expected improvement: harmonization of legislation with the EU in the areas of the economy and improvements in the treatment of ethnic minorities and relations with neighboring countries. The poor performance of the first Iliescu administration in these areas was not promising for Romanian accession hopes. In the elections of 1996, the Democratic Convention of Romania announced its intention to work hard for accession to the EU by addressing its concerns. The conclusion of a basic treaty with Hungary before the elections and of a treaty with Ukraine a year later, and improvements in minority policy enacted with the participation of the Hungarian Party in the government, were helpful but insufficient in the eyes of the EU. The organization finally issued a formal response to the application in 1997, which cited various Romanian failings in justification for deferring the start of negotiations. It found that the development of internal market relations and

policy with regard to the environment, justice, and agriculture met a minimum threshold (the Copenhagen criteria) but were still inadequate. Romania lobbied hard to be included in some fashion in the accession process and achieved the establishment of an accession partnership in 1998. This agreement enumerated short-term objectives for the necessary reforms. The government then announced a National Program for Accession to the European Union that committed it to these reforms. Again, however, the annual EU assessment of Romania was critical. It cited government corruption, justice, individual liberties, and the rights of the Roma minority as special problem areas. In the next year's report, the EU asserted that Romania (along with Slovakia, Lithuania, and Bulgaria) was not yet a functioning market economy.

It was a success of the Constantinescu administration that, despite these repeated negative reports, Romania somehow remained on track for accession. His governments failed to deliver on the promised reforms due to internal discord and ineffectiveness. But, fortified by opinion polls indicating strong support for European integration, they created a new Ministry for European Integration and secured a commitment from the EU at the end of 1999 to begin formal accession talks in February 2000. It was a measure of the widespread consensus about accession that it was not a divisive issue in the 2000 elections. The new Iliescu administration, in contrast to the 1992–1996 governments, has taken its commitment to the European Union seriously. This commitment is signified by annual payments by the EU to Romania, for reforms in targeted areas, of no less than 600 million euros. The energetic measures of the second Iliescu administration with regard to privatization can only be explained by EU pressure.

Romania was invited to join NATO in 2002. Despite the temporary annoyance of some West European leaders at Romania's staunch support for American policy in Iraq, membership in NATO appears to add to the inevitability of EU accession. In its annual report for 2003 the EU once again chided Romania for its failure to eliminate corruption and enact administrative reforms and stated that Romania was approaching but had still not achieved a functioning market economy. The European Parliament's special *rapporteur* for Romania, Baroness Nicholson, repeated earlier criticisms in early 2004. She added new, graver details about corruption and adoptions that went counter to the official legal ban on adoptions demanded by the EU and promised by the current government. The response of EU officials seemed to ensure that the country's path to accession could not be derailed. The only uncertainty was whether the parties would adhere to the announced calendar, which called for the finalization of negotiations in 2004 and accession in 2007.

Moldova, and Romania's relations with the newly independent republic, is also a major contemporary issue. This country is constituted of two parts. The largest area, sometimes known as Bessarabia, is between the Prut and the Dniestr (Romanian: Nistru) Rivers. It formed part of the Principality of Moldavia (Romanian: Moldova) until its cession to Russia in 1812; it then was united with Romania in 1918–1940 and 1941–1944. The independent state also includes a strip on the side of the Dniester facing Ukraine that formed part of the Moldovan Autonomous Soviet Socialist Republic (MASSR) between 1924 and 1940 and was then attached to Bessarabia when the Soviet Union annexed Bessarabia. The united area was known until 1991 as the Moldovan Soviet Socialist Republic (MSSR). The state began to call itself simply the Republic of Moldova in English language documents. The name has a half century tradition in its favor but is identical with the name Romanians give to the historical province, half of which is in today's Romania.

The time of domination by imperial Russia, the Romanian kingdom based in Bucharest, and then the Soviet Union contributed to the creation of Moldova's identity. While Romania experienced the union of the Danubian Principalities and the creation of national institutions in the nineteenth century, Bessarabia was a neglected province on the periphery of an alien autocratic state. Local Romanian elites gained little experience in self-governance or access to publications from across the Prut, whose importation was prohibited. Russian was the language of official business and public instruction. Figures from the Russian censuses in 1858 and 1897 indicated Romanians declined from two-thirds to less than half of the population, while East Slavs doubled to one-third. The other major ethnic group, at around 10 percent but much higher in Chişinău (Russian: Kishinev), were the Jews. The Russian anti-Semitic Black Hundreds precipitated pogroms in Chişinău in 1903 and 1905. After the Russian Revolution of 1905, Bessarabian Romanians entered the State Duma in St. Petersburg. In the turmoil of the 1917 revolutions, Bessarabian Romanians formed a provincial council and a year later voted for unification with Romania.

Bessarabian Romanians benefited from Greater Romania's land reform at the expense of local landholders as well as from energetic promotion of local infrastructure and Romanian schools. The region remained relatively undeveloped, however, and subject to administrative abuses by officials from Bucharest and the infiltration of Soviet agitators. The corruption and highhandedness of the Romanian administration in Bessarabia lent some plausibility to the Soviet demand for the liberation of the province, especially within its substantial Slavic minority. In 1924 the Soviet Union created the MASSR in an area of the Ukraine extending from the Dniester to the Bug River that included a large Romanian minority. MASSR would become a showpiece of Soviet-style industrialization and also a laboratory for the promotion of a new Moldovan-Romanian language and national identity that was different from the Romanian one. Soviet scholars conceded that the Moldovan Romanian language was virtually identical with Romanian, although within the MASSR it continued the use of the Cyrillic alphabet that had been abandoned south of the Prut during the nineteenth century.

After the humiliating Soviet annexation of Bessarabia and the execution or deportation of many Romanians in 1940–1941, Romania began its invasion of the Soviet Union alongside the Germans with the appeal by Ion Antonescu: "Soldiers, cross the Prut!" But the soldiers did not stop when they had liberated the province; they crossed the Dniester and even participated in the siege of Stalingrad. Romanian authorities headquartered in Odessa administered a zone between the Bug and the Dniestr that was called Transdniestria (Romanian: Transnistria) and liquidated at least 100,000 Jews there. Many Jews were deported to Transdniestria from south of the Prut, and only a portion of them survived to be repatriated after 1945. After Stalingrad, the Soviets reoccupied Transdniestria and Bessarabia, first exacting reprisals on the population once again, then forcing through Soviet-style collectivization. Economic development in the MSSR proceeded differently on either side of the Dniester. Most of the heavy industrial development took place to the east, attracting Ukrainian and Russian in-migration, while the Bessarabian economy was based on agriculture and light industry and the population was ethnically Romanian. The spoken and written Moldovan Romanian language largely converged with Romanian south of the Prut, despite Soviet ideological controls and the continued use of the Cyrillic alphabet. The MSSR constitution of 1978 made Russian the official language of the republic.

In the years of Soviet glasnost and perestroika (openness and restructuring), Moldovan Romanian activists agitated for a national revival in parallel to the more advanced movements in the Baltic republics. They protested against alleged

Russification and demanded the restoration of the Roman alphabet for Romanian, and the increased use of Romanian in the schools. The Slavic minority opposed this movement, voting in a referendum in 1990 for autonomy in the area beyond the river, or Transdniestria. The Gagauz (Turkish Christian) minority in the southeastern corner of the republic also demanded autonomy. At the time of the coup in Moscow in August 1991, the leadership of Moldova sided with Russian President Yeltsin. On 27 August, the Moldovan parliament declared the republic's independence from the Soviet Union, and four months later the republic joined the Commonwealth of Independent States (CIS). But in the interim, Transdniestria and Gagauzia declared their secession from the republic, proclaiming themselves separate republics within the Soviet Union.

The domestic and international travails of the Republic of Moldova have been a political topic in Romania since 1991. Many in Romania (roughly half in polls taken in 1991 and 1992), and not only supporters of the Greater Romania Party, expected the Moldovan Romanian majority of the new state to demand unification with Romania as it had in 1918. When this did not happen, it was easy to attribute it to the resistance of the minorities within Moldova in collusion with Russia and the post-Soviet military forces in Transdniestria—although opinion was divided among the Moldovan Romanians themselves. Thus Romanian nationalists, always on the lookout for foreign enemies of the nation, had new evidence of machinations by these elements. The situation was also opportune for Hungarian advocates of ethnic autonomy, who praised the autonomist tendencies in Moldova as an alternative to the centralist model in Romania. Various polls taken in Moldova indicate most Moldovan Romanians consider themselves Moldovans rather than Romanians.

The question of unification with Romania was settled fairly early in the decade. The Romanian-dominated Popular Front, later Christian Democratic Popular Front (CDPF), formed the first government of independent Moldova. The CDPF strongly advocated unification and formed a parliamentarian Moldovan-Romanian National Council for Reintegration. Transdniestria opposed reunification and launched militia attacks on Moldovan government outposts in order to back its claim to independence. Following counterattack by the weak Moldovan army, it was repulsed with the support of the heavily armed Soviet Fourteenth Army that was stationed in Transdniestria. Moldova, Russia, Ukraine, for a while Romania, and eventually Transdniestria all participated in the ensuing peace negotiations. The Moldovan government resigned in June 1992, in part because of the unpopularity of its unification stance. The Agrarian Democratic Party (ADP), a group of former collective farm managers, formed a government. The ADP declared its rejection of unification with Romania and support for ties with the CIS. In July 1992 Moldova concluded a peace agreement with Russia that accorded Transdniestria "special status."

The ADP won Moldova's first free elections in 1994. In March 1994 75 percent of eligible voters participated in a national referendum on Moldovan statehood, and 95 percent voted for continued independence. The one-sidedness of the result caused some suspicion that it had been falsified but was sufficient to discourage further referenda. Parliament adopted a new constitution in the summer of the same year. It granted "special autonomous status" for Transdniestria and Gagauzia, without precisely defining this status. The constitution also designated "Moldovan" as the state language. The CDPF protested, and students and faculty organized rallies in 1995 demanding the state language be called Romanian, but the parliament rejected this demand in 1996. Despite the ostensible resolution of these issues, the political situation in Moldova has remained unstable. Progress on economic reform was unequal in the two halves of the bifurcated economy, and the latent civil war between industrial Transdniestria and the rest of the country caused a permanent economic crisis. Moldova had been relatively prosperous while part of the Soviet sphere, but it now declined to the lamentable status of poorest country in Europe. Among the most disturbing manifestations of the country's poverty is the high incidence of trafficking in young women, who are lured abroad and forced into prostitution, and the sale of kidneys by people willing to take this desperate measure.

There have been halting steps toward the stabilization of Moldova's international position. Moldova and Russia concluded an agreement on the withdrawal of Russian troops from Transdniestria in 1994. Their number declined to an estimated 6,000 by 1997, but the final withdrawal of the remaining troops and their substantial weaponry has been repeatedly delayed despite the participation of Russia, Ukraine, and the OSCE in successive agreements and in peacekeeping forces. The arrest by Transdniestrian authorities of the Moldovan Romanian Popular Front activist Ilie Ilaşcu in 1992 and his continued detention, along with four other Moldovans, became a cause celèbre in Romania. Ilaşcu took Romanian citizenship while in prison and was elected to the Romanian Senate in 2000 as a member of the Greater Romania Party. Despite the plight of the prisoners, a basic treaty between Moldova and Romania was concluded in 1999. Ilaşcu was finally released in 2001 and promptly went to Bucharest to take his parliamentary seat. An agreement for the federalization of Moldova was concluded in 2003 that would provide, according to a statement of Moldovan President Voronin, for "an asymmetric federation with one center and two federal units." Half of Moldovans opposed federalization, however, and the communist Voronin backed away from the agreement. The government hoped the EU would participate in a lasting solution.

Finally there is the contemporary issue of history and public memory. In a region where history writing tends to be highly politicized, this is especially true in Romania. The Moldavian aristocrat Mihail Kogălniceanu (1817–1891) founded the first historical journal in Romania and was a leading liberal politician advocating the union of the Danubian Principalities. He served twice as prime minister during the decade of the unification and as foreign minister during the War for Independence in 1877–1878. Nicolae Bălcescu (1819–1852) had a much briefer career but was an even more militant advocate of unification. He was a member of the provisional government during the brief Wallachian Revolution in 1848 and worked unsuccessfully to bring peace between Hungarians and Romanians in Transylvania. In exile, he prepared an important work on the Wallachian prince Michael the Brave, who temporarily unified the Danubian Principalities and Transylvania in 1600. This work is the strongest statement in Romanian historiography of the view, contested by more moderate historians, that Michael prepared the way for the unification of all Romanians through his actions in 1600.

Nicolae Iorga (1871–1940) and Constantin C. Giurescu (1901–1977) were much more prolific historians but also exemplified the continuing strong connection between historical scholarship and political engagement in the twentieth century. Iorga became a professor of history at the University of Bucharest at the age of twenty-three, attaining national and international acclaim for his original research and publication of sources. Incredibly, he authored 1,000 books and over 12,000 articles. Much of this output was serious scholarship, but his boundless energy did not permit him to stand aside from contemporary cultural and political debates. Iorga founded a literary school that glorified traditional peasant culture and a political-cultural journal entitled *Neamul românesc* (Romanian Nation), for which he wrote much of the content himself, directed the irredentist Cultural League beginning in 1908, and in 1910 cofounded the anti-Semitic National Democratic Party. Because of these activities, Iorga is considered one of the founders of Greater Romania. In 1931–1932 Iorga served a brief term as prime minister. To his lasting credit, he put aside his anti-Semitism after 1919 to condemn the Iron Guard and even play a role in the arrest and trial of its leaders in 1938. In retaliation, he was brutally murdered by Legionaries after they came to power in 1940.

Constantin C. Giurescu contested Iorga's leadership of the Romanian historical profession in the 1930s during a celebrated public controversy about errors in Iorga's works. The so-called "New School" associated with Giurescu's revolt against the master of Romanian history was distinguished primarily by its membership from a younger generation rather than substantial differences in philosophy, but its leaders were also active in politics. One member, Gheorghe Brătianu, founded a dissident wing of the Liberal Party, while another, P. P. Panaitescu, was briefly associated with the Iron Guard. Giurescu himself joined Brătianu's party, was an adviser of Carol II along with Iorga during the period of the royal dictatorship, and briefly occupied a cabinet post in 1940. Both Giurescu and Brătianu were imprisoned in Sighet after the communists came to power, and Brătianu died there.

The release of Giurescu from prison in 1955 and his gradual rehabilitation was a barometer of the restoration of national traditions in historiography. While he continued his earlier meticulous studies on medieval Romanian social history, two new works published in 1965–1967 were a marked departure: *The Life and Work of Prince Cuza* and *Transylvania in the History of the Romanian People*. The first was an original work of scholarship on an important but neglected ruler, while the second was a more modest synthesis on a politically charged topic. In each case, Giurescu lent his scholarly authority (and the regime lent its imprimatur) to the restoration of national unity as a legitimate topic of scholarly research.

Giurescu was not responsible for the exaggerations of national communist historiography in the following decades. Other professional historians did contribute to the increasing excursions of Nicolae Ceaușescu into Romanian history in his speeches. A highly selective treatment of Dacian history was prepared for the celebration in 1980 of the "2050th anniversary of the establishment of the first centralized unitary state on Romanian territory." The dictator's brother, Lieutenant General Ilie Ceaușescu, was the putative author of *Transylvania: An Ancient Romanian Land,* a unique compilation of anachronistic statements and maps. The publication in Budapest of a three-volume *History of Transylvania* (1986) provoked (some would say intentionally) an intemperate Romanian response. This response characterized the Hungarian work, which competently synthesized the new research of the best contemporary Hungarian historians, as an instrument of territorial revisionism and "the dangerous game of the falsification of history."

Romanians have struggled since 1990 to achieve an adequate understanding of their recent and more distant past. Former political prisoners stimulated the public debate by the publication of their memoirs and especially by their political engagement. Three of the senior leaders of the revived National Peasant Party had spent long years in prison. Their experience added to the moral authority of the leading opposition party in the early 1990s but also provoked a defensive reaction among former communist officials and ordinary Romanians who had not acted courageously in the face of the many pressures to conform. It is emblematic of the difficulty of assessing recent history that historical museums have little to say about the communist period.

The most notable exception is the Sighet Memorial in Sighetul Marmației, in the northwestern corner of the country near the former Soviet border. It opened in 1997 in the former "prison of the ministers" where various politicians, generals, scholars, and bishops spent years in detention, and where many died. The Civic Academy Foundation, led by former dissident poet Ana Blandiana, founded and maintains the museum. In addition to documenting life in this prison, the museum contains exhibits about agricultural collectivization, hard labor on the Danube–Black Sea Canal, and deportation to the Soviet Union and the Bărăgan Plain within Romania. Giurescu's son, Dinu C. Giurescu, emigrated to the United States in 1988 but returned to Bucharest after 1990 and switched his teaching focus to the history of the communist years in Romania. His new specialty is weakly represented in Romanian university curricula.

Lustration, the identification and elimination from power of former informers of the Securitate and even members of the Communist Party, is perhaps more difficult in Romania than in any other East European country. How can it stop at President Iliescu himself, a former high party official who has three times been popularly elected? The insistence of the Democratic Convention of Romania on lustration in some form certainly made its relationship with the civil service more difficult after it came to power in 1996. Legislation in 1999 created the National Council for the Study of Securitate Records (NCSSR). The NCSSR does not have direct access to the archives of the Securitate, but it has been supplied with voluminous documentation and has identified as informers or agents many prominent public figures. Public dissension among the members of the NCSSR has undermined its work and its authority.

Serious historical research on the communist era is becoming possible, especially for the period prior to the thirty-year limit on access to government archives. The National Archives Law of 1996 improved public access to government records, although the National Archives remain under the supervision of the minister of the interior. This subordination has its advantages for historical preservation because the ministry and its prefects work closely with the county archival inspectors to ensure the proper disposition of the records of enterprises and organizations undergoing privatization or reassignment.

There is continuing, and more focused, controversy about the history of World War II, Marshal Antonescu, and the Holocaust. A partial rehabilitation of Antonescu, who was shot after a show trial in 1946, took place even before 1989. Marin Preda's novel *Delirium* (1975) presented a sympathetic view of the dictator, and in later years documents placing him in a more positive light became available to privileged researchers. Calls for the rehabilitation of Antonescu arose beginning in 1990. The newspaper of the National Salvation Front denied Romanian responsibility for the extermination of the Jews and designated Antonescu a tragic hero in 1991; the parliament dedicated a moment of silence to his memory. In 1993–1994 two cities, Slobozia and Piatra Neamţ, erected monuments to Antonescu, and many other cities named streets after him. Audiences acclaimed a laudatory film about Antonescu by veteran director Sergiu Nicolaescu, *The Mirror*, after it was released in 1994. A public opinion poll in 1995 indicated 62 percent of respondents viewed the dictator positively, and in 1997–2000 the Romanian government rehabilitated several ministers of the wartime era.

The tide turned against Antonescu after 1999. In 1995 members of the U.S. Congress protested against the Antonescu cult in an open letter to President Iliescu, and in 2000 Social Democratic politicians in Germany warned Romania that its glorification of the wartime dictator might make admission to the EU more difficult. Schools introduced the Holocaust into the curriculum in 1999. The Greater Romania Party, as leader of the opposition, increased its campaign on behalf of Antonescu, proposing that military academies be named after him and he be declared a saint. At the end of 2001, Prime Minister Adrian Năstase declared during a visit to the United States his government's intention to have all monuments to Antonescu taken down and to punish "fascist, racist, and xenophobic" symbols. This was done in special government decrees of March and April 2002. Members of parliament, the government, and President Iliescu continued to make controversial statements about the Holocaust, however. A government declaration in June 2003 denied Romanian responsibility for the Holocaust on Romanian territory but then qualified its statement in response to international protests.

In July 2003 the president prompted protests by stating to an Israeli reporter: "There was no Romanian Holocaust, no German or Polish one. It was a general process, and this European phenomenon also had a Romanian complement." In October of the same year he became honorary chairman of an international commission led by Elie Wiesel that was to present a report by June 2005 on the Romanian Holocaust that would provide guidelines for Romanian textbooks. Even the chairman of the Greater Romania Party, Corneliu Vadim Tudor, retreated from his earlier statements. In a public letter in February 2004, he stated that his denial of the Romanian Holocaust had been "a mistake," and that the Romanian government was responsible for an estimated 400,000 Jewish deaths during World War II.

Controversies over the content of history textbooks underline the sensitive nature of public memory. Schools are required by law to teach from textbooks licensed by the Ministry of Education, but it took years to revise those of the previous regime and then distribute them in adequate numbers. New versions distributed in 1994 assessed Marshal Antonescu more positively, however. There were textbook controversies in the Republic of Moldova as well. The Ministry of Education ordained a course on the history of Romania in 1990, but when it wanted to replace it with a course on the history of Moldova in 1995 student demonstrators burned copies of the new textbook and forced the ministry to reverse its decision. In Romania, a competition to approve more democratic textbooks sparked angry debates in the press and parliament in 1999. One of the approved texts, edited by a Jewish Romanian historian in Cluj named Sorin Mitu, attracted most of the ire of the nationalists because it gave minimal attention to the famed princes Vlad the Impaler, Stephen the Great, and Michael the Brave, and highlighted persistent questions about the events of 1989. The attractively illustrated book was printed in 10,000 copies. Opponents, led by Nicolaescu, a senator for the opposition PSDR, demanded that Mitu's textbook be withdrawn. Waving a copy of the book, Nicolaescu declared: "This book deserves to be publicly burned." The minister of education, himself from the University of Cluj, refused to withdraw the book.

Reformers took heavy blows in the textbook controversy of 1999, but historians presenting a more critical view of national history have been gaining a growing audience. The Humanitas Publishing House published many foreign historical works in Romanian translation as well as fresh research by the younger generation of Romanian historians. Lucian Boia wrote a series of well-received revisionist works, including *History and Myth in Romanian Consciousness, The Game with the Past: History between Truth and Fiction, The Scientific Myth of Romanian Communism,* and *Two Centuries of Historical Mythology,* all published by Humanitas. Centers for Jewish Studies exist at three different Romanian universities, and since 1999 the government has required increased attention to the Romanian Holocaust in the schools.

SELECTIVE BIBLIOGRAPHY

Bachman, Ronald D., ed. *Romania: A Country Study.* Federal Research Division, Library of Congress. 2d ed. Washington, DC: GPO, 1991.

Boia, Lucian. *History and Myth in Romanian Consciousness.* Budapest: Central European University Press, 2001.

———. *Romania: Borderland of Europe.* Translated by James Christian Brown. London: Reaktion, 2001.

Brezianu, Andrei. *Historical Dictionary of the Republic of Moldova.* Lanham, MD: Scarecrow, 2000.

Calinescu, George. *History of Romanian Literature.* Paris: UNESCO/Nagard, 1987.

Chirot, Daniel. *Social Change in a Peripheral Society: The Creation of a Balkan Colony.* New York: Academic Press, 1976.

Country Watch. http://www.countrywatch.com (accessed 21 July 2004).

Creanga, Ion, and Mihal Eminescu. *Selected Works of Ion Creanga and Mihai Eminescu.* Boulder: East European Monographs; Bucharest: Editura Minerva, 1991.

Deletant, Dennis. *Ceausescu and the Securitate: Coercion and Dissent in Romania, 1965–1989.* Armonk, NY: M. E. Sharpe, 1995.

———. *Romania under Communist Rule.* 2d ed. Iasi: Center for Romanian Studies/Civic Academy Foundation, 1999.

Eidelberg, Philip Gabriel. *The Great Rumanian Peasant Revolt of 1907: Origins of a Modern Jacquerie.* Leiden: Brill, 1974.

Farnoaga, Georgiana, and Sharon King, ed. and trans. *The Phantom Church and Other Stories from Romania.* Selection, introduction, chronology, and biographical notes by Florin Manolescu. Pittsburgh: University of Pittsburgh Press, 1996.

Fischer, Mary Ellen. *Nicolae Ceausescu: A Study in Political Leadership.* Boulder: Lynne Rienner, 1989.

Georgescu, Vlad. *The Romanians: A History.* Edited by Matei Calinescu. Translated by Alexandra Bley-Vroman. Columbus: Ohio State University Press, 1991.

Giurescu, Dinu C. *Illustrated History of the Romanian People.* Translated by Sonia Schlanger. Edited by Ioana Nestorescu. Bucuresti: Editura Sport-Turism, 1981.

———. *The Razing of Romania's Past: International Preservation Report.* Washington, DC: U.S. Committee on International Council on Monuments and Sites/Preservation Press, 1989.

Hitchins, Keith. *The Romanians, 1774–1866.* Oxford: Clarendon, 1996.

———. *Rumania: 1866–1947.* Oxford: Clarendon, 1994.

Iancu, Carol. *Jews in Romania, 1866–1919: From Exclusion to Emancipation.* Translated by Carvel de Bussy. Boulder: East European Monographs, 1996.

Illyés, Elemér. *Ethnic Continuity in the Carpatho-Danubian Area.* Boulder: East European Monographs, 1988.

———. *National Minorities in Romania: Change in Transylvania.* Boulder: East European Monographs, 1982.

Ionescu, Serban N. *Who Was Who in Twentieth-Century Romania.* Boulder: East European Monographs, 1994.

Jowitt, Kenneth, ed. *Social Change in Romania, 1860–1940: A Debate on Development in a European Nation.* Berkeley: Institute of International Studies, University of California, 1978.

Juler, Caroline. *Romania: Blue Guide.* London: A. and C. Black, 2000.

King, Charles. *The Moldovans: Romania, Russia, and the Politics of Culture.* Stanford: Hoover Institution Press, 2000.

Kligman, Gail. *Calus: Symbolic Transformation in Romanian Ritual.* Foreword by Mircea Eliade. Chicago: University of Chicago Press, 1981.

———. *The Politics of Duplicity: Controlling Reproduction in Ceausescu's Romania.* Berkeley: University of California Press, 1998.

———. *The Wedding of the Dead: Ritual, Poetics, and Popular Culture in Transylvania.* Berkeley: University of California Press, 1988.

Köpeczi, Béla, ed. *History of Transylvania.* Translated by Adrienne Chambers-Makkai. Budapest: Akadémiai Kiadó, 1994.

LexisNexis Academic Universe. http://web.lexis-nexis.com/universe (accessed 21 July 2004).

Livezeanu, Irina. *Cultural Politics in Greater Romania: Regionalism, Nation Building, and Ethnic Struggle, 1918–1930.* Ithaca: Cornell University Press, 1995.

Machedon, Luminita, and Ernie Scoffham. *Romanian Modernism: The Architecture of Bucharest, 1920–1940.* Cambridge: MIT Press, 1999.

Manea, Norman. *The Hooligan's Return: A Memoir.* Translated by Angela Jianu. New York: Farrar, Straus and Giroux, 2003.

Mitu, Sorin. *National Identity of Romanians in Transylvania.* Budapest: Central European University Press, 2001.

Nagy-Talavera, Nicholas M. *The Green Shirts and the Others: A History of Fascism in Hungary and Romania.* 2d. ed. Iaşi: Center for Romanian Studies, 2001.

———. *Nicolae Iorga: A Biography.* Iaşi: Center for Romanian Studies, 1998.

Niessen, James P. "Romanian Nationalism: An Ideology of Integration and Mobilization." In *Eastern European Nationalism in the Twentieth Century,* 273–304. Washington, DC: American University Press, 1995.

Oldson, William O. *The Historical and Nationalistic Thought of Nicolae Iorga.* Boulder: East European Quarterly, 1973.

Popa, Opritsa D., and Marguerite E. Horn, comp. *Ceausescu's Romania: An Annotated Bibliography.* Westport, CT: Greenwood, 1994.

Quinlan, Paul D. *The Playboy King: Carol II of Romania.* Westport, CT: Greenwood, 1995.

Rebreanu, Liviu. *The Uprising.* Translated by P. Crandjean and S. Hartauer. London: P. Owen, 1964.

Ricketts, Mac Linscott. *Mircea Eliade: The Romanian Roots, 1907–1945.* 2 vols. Boulder: East European Monographs, 1988.

Roberts, Henry L. *Rumania: Political Problems of an Agrarian State.* New Haven: Yale University Press, 1951.

"Romania" and "Moldova." *Europa World Year Book.* London: Europa, 2003.

Seton-Watson, R. W. *A History of the Roumanians: From Roman Times to the Completion of Unity.* Cambridge: University Press, 1934.

Siani-Davies, Peter, and Mary Siani-Davies, comps. *Romania.* World Bibliographical Series, 59. Rev. ed. Santa Barbara, CA: Clio, 1998.

Steinberg, Jacob, ed. *Introduction to Rumanian Literature.* New York: Twayne, 1966.

Tismaneanu, Vladimir. *Stalinism for All Seasons: A Political History of Romanian Communism.* Berkeley: University of California Press, 2003.

Treptow, Kurt W. *Vlad III Dracula: The Life and Times of the Historical Dracula.* With original illustrations by Octavian Ion Penda. Portland, OR: Center of Romanian Studies, 2000.

Treptow, Kurt W., ed. *Selected Works of Ion Creanga and Mihai Eminescu.* Boulder and New York: East European Monographs and Columbia University Press, 1991.

Treptow, Kurt W., and Marcel Popa. *Historical Dictionary of Romania.* Lanham, MD: Scarecrow, 1996.

Verdery, Katherine. *National Ideology under Socialism: Identity and Cultural Politics in Ceauşescu's Romania.* Berkeley: University of California Press, 1991.

———. *Transylvanian Villagers: Three Centuries of Political, Economic, and Ethnic Change, 1700–1980.* Berkeley: University of California Press, 1983.

World News Connection. http://wnc.dialog.com (accessed 21 July 2004).

CHRONOLOGY

106 B.C.E.	Dacia becomes a Roman province.
271–273	Emperor Aurelian withdraws troops, administration; rule of the Visigoths.
376	Rule of the Huns begins.
454	Rule of the Gepids begins.
567	Rule of the Avars begins.
ca. 602	Byzantines abandon Dobrudja.
9th century	Rule of the Bulgarians begins.
10th–13th centuries	Hungarian conquest of Transylvania.
1054	East–West Church schism.
12th–13th centuries	Rule of the Cumans and Pechenegs south of the Carpathians begins.
1227–1247	Establishment of Banat of Severin and Voivodates of Litovoi and Seneslau.
1241–1242	Mongol invasions.
ca. 1310	Founding of Wallachia.
1330	Battle of Posada: Wallachian victory over Hungary.
1359	Founding of Moldavia.
1415	Wallachia recognizes Ottoman suzerainty.
1437–1438	Peasant revolt in Transylvania.
1526	Ottoman victory over Hungary at Battle of Mohács.
1538	Moldavia recognizes Ottoman suzerainty.
1541	Transylvania recognizes Ottoman suzerainty.
1600	Michael the Brave rules Wallachia, Transylvania, and Moldavia.
1697	Romanian church union in Transylvania.
1699	Ottoman Empire recognizes Habsburg rule in Transylvania.
1711–1715	Establishment of Phanariot rule in Moldavia and Wallachia.
1718	Establishment of Habsburg rule in Banat and Oltenia.
1738	End of Habsburg rule in Oltenia.
1784	Peasant revolt in Transylvania.
1812	Annexation of Bessarabia by Russia.
1821	Anti-Ottoman revolt in Wallachia led by Tudor Vladimirescu.
1848–1849	Revolutions in Hungary and the Danubian Principalities.
1859–1862	Union of the Principalities under Prince Cuza.
1866	Abdication of Prince Cuza, accession of Prince Carol I.
1880–1881	Recognition of independent Romanian kingdom.
1907	Peasant revolt in the Kingdom of Romania.
1913	Annexation of Dobrudja after Second Balkan War.
1916	Romania enters World War I.
1918–1920	Annexation of lands from Hungary, Austria, Russia, and Bulgaria.
1920	Land reform.
1940	Lands ceded to Soviet Union, Hungary, and Bulgaria under pressure.
1941–1945	Romania in World War II; lands regained from Hungary.
1947	Abdication of King Michael; Romanian People's Republic.
1965	Gheorghiu-Dej succeeded by Ceauşescu; Socialist Republic of Romania.
1989	End of communist rule after disorders in various cities.
1990–1996	First free elections; President Ion Iliescu and socialist government.
1996–2000	President Emil Constantinescu and conservative government.
2000	Second presidency of Ion Iliescu and socialist government.
2004	Romania joins the North Atlantic Treaty Organization (NATO).

BULGARIA

RICHARD FRUCHT

LAND AND PEOPLE

The land of present-day Bulgaria comprises 110,994 square kilometers, an area slightly larger than the state of Tennessee, and contains a population of approximately 8 million. Although Bulgaria became an independent state in the nineteenth century, its current boundaries were not fully established until the end of World War II. Bordered by Macedonia and Yugoslavia on the west, Romania to the north, the Black Sea to the east, and Greece and Turkey on the south, it is a country of varied geographic features, dominated by the range known as the Balkan Mountains (Stara Planina), which divides the country in two.

Much of the country in fact lies at an elevation above 600 meters, even though lowlands comprise nearly one-third of the land surface. The Balkan Mountains (Stara Planina) run approximately 530 kilometers along the 43rd parallel. The width of Stara Planina averages 15 to 20 kilometers. The highest peak in the range is Mount Botev,

nearly 2,400 meters in elevation; other mountains are nearly as high, measuring 2,000 meters in height. Most of the Balkan Mountains, however, are between 700 and 800 meters high, and there are two main gorges that permit travel to flow through the mountains; the passes were instrumental in the migration of peoples and the passage of armies, both factors critical for the development of Bulgaria's history.

The Balkan Mountains are densely populated, with nearly twenty inhabitants per square kilometer, but the towns and cities are comparatively small in size. Lengthy snow cover, which can last a half a year or longer on the highest peaks, is the source of water for a dozen rivers that flow down the mountainsides. Waterpower from these rivers is vital for electrical production in the country. The Balkan Mountains are also a source of coal (anthracite and black coal), as well as other ores. Agriculture, tourism, and forestry are also significant industries found in the region.

Stara Planina divides the country into nearly two equal halves. Hills, lowlands, and the fertile Maritsa Valley are found south of the range, while the often dry Danubian Plain lies to the north.

The Balkans are not the only mountain range found in Bulgaria; the Sredna Gora Mountains lie south of Stara Planina and run essentially parallel to the Balkans for nearly 285 kilometers. The Sredna Gora Mountains do not form a tall range. Its peaks are significantly lower than those of Stara Planina, averaging only about 600 meters in height. The highest peak in Sredna Gora is Golyan Bogdan, at 1,604 meters.

Lying south of Sofia is the Rila-Rhodope Massif, which consists of the Rila and the Rhodope Mountains. Nestled in the Rila Mountains, at an elevation of 1,150 meters, is the historic Rila Monastery, the largest and most famous monastery in Bulgaria. The Rila Monastery was one of a number of

Rila Monastery

Although many of the monasteries of Bulgaria played a role in the cultural and social life of the country, none was more famous than the Rila Monastery, which was designated as a world monument of culture by UNESCO in 1983.

Rila Monastery was founded in the tenth century by John of Rila, a monk born around the year 880. John of Rila became a hermit and moved to a forest cave near the town of Rila. There his message of asceticism attracted many followers, and his tomb became a shrine following his death and subsequent canonization. Around that tomb, the monastery was built.

Rila Monastery sits nestled in the mountains approximately 120 kilometers from Sofia. Construction began in 946, and the first buildings were probably constructed close to the hermit's cave. Aided by generous donations from boiars, construction of a new cathedral began. Seized by the Turks in 1385, the monastery was abandoned in the mid-fifteenth century in the wake of lawlessness in the region. It soon sprang back to life, however, especially after the return of relics of St. John of Rila from Turnovo.

Over the centuries, fires and a lack of funds contributed to a deterioration in conditions. In 1816 renovation began on some of the structures, but in January 1833 a devastating fire destroyed much of the monastery.

In the early days of the national reawakening, funds and master builders were used to rebuild the monastery and restore it as a national treasure. Over the next three decades, master craftsmen created a structure rich in detail (such as the veranda projection on the northwest wing), a fourth floor ornately decorated for visitors, a new kitchen, and new domed chapels. The new cathedral, patterned in part after a similar structure on Mount Athos, the most important monastery in Eastern Orthodoxy, took over twenty years to build. The monastery's Church of the Virgin Mary has elaborate, colorful walls that beautifully capture the spirit of the Bulgarian Orthodox world. Wood-carvers, painters (who made special use of reds and blues), and artisans created a synthesis of design that appealed to the emotions and senses of Bulgarians and visitors alike, an evocation that remains as current in the twenty-first century as it was in the nineteenth. Perhaps the most striking features of the Rila Monastery are the colonnades, arches, and vaults, which capture the essence of nature, beauty, and space in a way that is characteristic of Orthodox architecture.

Apart from the visible architectural design of Rila Monastery, the buildings house some of the finest artwork in all of Eastern Christendom. The library and museum contain numerous manuscripts, many of them illustrated, as well as icons and ethnographic exhibits of embroidery, carpets, and jewelry. The library houses over 16,000 volumes. Manuscripts include a fifteenth-century Psalter, two thirteenth-century Gospels, and numerous histories of the saints. Unique examples of wood carving, such as the doors of the old Hrelyu Church, are found throughout the monastery. But what is most striking is the artwork. The frescoes in the St. John of Rila Chapel, which date from the early fourteenth century, are extraordinary examples of medieval Bulgarian art. The carved wooden iconostasis in the chapel and other frescoes were done with new techniques from the West, thus representing a fusion of past and present.

Among the myriad icons, two of the most famous are the medieval portraits of St. John of Rila and St. Arsenius. Other outstanding icons include St. George Enthroned (sixteenth century) and Our Lady of Tenderness (fifteenth century).

Despite the fires of the early 1800s, and the loss of some of the treasures, the monastery has in a sense lost little; the donations and work of the artistic masters (such as the paintings by the noted Bulgarian artist Zahari Zograf) not only reclaimed the past beauty but enhanced it. Their work spoke volumes about the special relationship between Bulgaria's people and Rila Monastery. Its significance in the lives of Bulgarians is as real today as it was in the days of Paisii of Hilendar, one of the founders of the Bulgarian national reawakening. In his 1762 *Slavonic-Bulgarian History (Istoriia Slavianobolgarskaia),* he wrote that it was the sacred duty of all Bulgarians to safeguard Rila Monastery.

monasteries founded in the mountains and valleys of Bulgaria, and it served as a center of learning and culture throughout the long period of Turkish occupation.

The Rhodope Mountains are the highest range in Europe between the Alps in the west and the Caucasus. Located west and south of the Maritsa Valley, they are often composed of square, leveled ridges, cut by numerous valleys and gorges. The Rhodopes are some of the oldest geographical features in Bulgaria, predating both the Stara Planina and Sredna Gora ranges geologically. They contain the highest peak in the country, Musala, which rises to an elevation of over 2,900 meters. The deep gorges, high peaks (with snow cover that can last as long as six to eight months), and rivers (which provide hydroelectric power) of the Rila-Rhodope Massif meant that parts of the region were often inaccessible to Turkish forces, who preferred to occupy the towns and villages of the lowlands. In fact, this rugged terrain of Bulgaria may have played a role in saving the great city of Vienna from capture in 1529. Swollen rivers, after a prolonged winter, slowed the Turks as they moved through the natural cuts in the mountains toward Vienna, thereby allowing the Austrians needed time to prepare the city's defenses.

The most important river in Bulgaria is the Danube, which forms most of its northern boundary with Romania. Small settlements formed along the banks of the Danube during the time of the Greeks and the Romans. Serving as trading centers, these towns were often razed over the centuries by conquerors, such as the Goths and the Huns. Nevertheless, the Danube, which flows nearly 2,950 kilometers from its source in the Black Forest in Germany to the Black Sea, has served as a vital economic artery from the earliest recorded history to the present. Unfortunately for Bulgaria, the mouth of the river lies outside its territorial boundaries, in Romania, and in the often volatile world of Balkan politics and diplomacy, disputes over water rights and navigation along the Danube have sometimes hampered relations between the riverine states (primarily in the first half of the twentieth century).

There are over five hundred rivers in Bulgaria, most of which flow from the high peaks (where snow is not uncommon for as much as half the year), but generally native rivers are not large (although some of the larger ones, such as the Iskar, which runs for 368 kilometers to the Danube, have been utilized for the production of hydroelectricity). Rather unevenly distributed, due to the nature of the mountain networks, most flow either to the Black or Aegean seas or to large catchment basins (such as the Maritsa Valley). Some of these catchment basins near the Danube River have, like the swamps also situated nearby, been drained for towns and farmland.

There are also few lakes in the country, and of these few, many lie close to the Black Sea coast. There are also glacial mountain lakes high in the various ranges, but many of them are above 2,000 meters in elevation.

Apart from the Danube River, Bulgaria's dominant water feature is the Black Sea, which forms the eastern boundary of Bulgaria. The coastal area is 378 kilometers in length, with a general width of 10 to 30 kilometers. Approximately one-third of the coastline is made up of wide beaches covered by fine yellow and white sand. This naturally beautiful coastal region, combined with affordable tourist facilities, has made Bulgaria's Black Sea coast an attractive vacation destination.

Another contributing factor in the popularity of the Bulgarian coast for European tourists is the climate. Bulgaria has a climate that is classified as "temperate continental," much like other parts of Southern Europe. It is influenced by the Black and Mediterranean seas, which keep the temperatures moderate, and the mountain ranges. This wide diversity of geographical features contributes to warm summers and cold, snowy winters conducive to winter sports.

The average temperature is 10.5 degrees Celsius, and winds, due to the nature and position of the mountains, are constant. Because the winds originate in the northeast in the winter, temperatures can be quite cold (the average winter temperature hovers around freezing) throughout the country. However, the northwest and western breezes of the spring and summer bring warming trends, averaging 24 degrees Celsius, and significant annual rainfall. This precipitation has contributed to the existence of a number of fertile regions in the country, including the Maritsa Valley, the Upper Danubian Plain, and the Dobrudja.

The Maritsa Valley lies between the Balkan and Rhodope Mountains. The Maritsa River, the longest river in the country, flows through the valley before emptying into the Aegean Sea. Rich in forest and agricultural land, the Maritsa Valley is at times plagued by floods, due to the numerous river tributaries that flow through the region. North of Stara Planina is the Upper Danubian Plain. While also fertile, it is drier than the lands south of the mountains and is also relatively treeless. The Dobrudja, in the northeast part of Bulgaria, borders the Danube to the north and the Black Sea to the east. Dobrudja is a hilly region and is one of the richest agricultural regions in Southeastern Europe, thanks in part to a network of irrigation systems from the Danube and local bodies of water. With a mild climate and adequate rainfall, it is ideal for the cultivation of foodstuffs (wheat, fruits, and vegetables). The rich arable land of the Dobrudja was a source of contention between Bulgaria and Romania for decades. The region was taken by the Romanians at the conclusion of the Second Balkan War in 1913, and, after it was briefly retaken by Bulgaria during World War I, was returned to Romania and remained in the hands of Bucharest until 1940, when the southern Dobrudja was returned to Bulgaria.

Many of the cities in Bulgaria have their origins in the distant past. Nevertheless, since the country was primarily a peasant society until modern times, the landscape of many of Bulgaria's cities has taken shape more recently than that of other cities in the region.

The capital of Bulgaria is Sofia, a major metropolitan center with a population of approximately 1.2 million (representing nearly 15 percent of the entire country's 7.9 million inhabitants). Located less than 60 kilometers from the Serbian border in the Iskar River Basin between the Balkan and Rhodope mountain ranges (Mt. Vitosha, rising to a

Beachgoers on a beach in Varna along the Black Sea. (Morton Beebe/Corbis)

height of over 2,000 meters, is a highly visible geographic feature dominating the skyline along the outskirts of the city), Sofia, because of its location, has been a vital center since the time of the Roman Empire. It sat along a key trade route that ran from Constantinople through the mountainous terrain in Southeastern Europe. During the period of the earliest Bulgarian state it was called Sredec. Its present name did not emerge until much later (the fourteenth century) and was derived from St. Sophia Church. Under the Ottoman Turks, who captured the city in 1382, Sofia, because of its location, became a key government center. Numerous mosques were built, symbolizing the town's significance. Although it only had a population of some 21,000 at the time of Bulgarian independence in the nineteenth century, it became Bulgaria's new capital. Over the course of the next century, Sofia expanded dramatically and became the educational center of the country, serving as the home to the Bulgarian Academy of Sciences and numerous museums. With its rapid expansion in the twentieth century, especially during the communist period following World War II, workers' housing, gray and drab, became as much the visible landmarks of the city as the historic older buildings.

Like Sofia, Turnovo was an important medieval city. Inhabited as early as the Neolithic period, it became a Roman fortress town. During the period of the Second Bulgarian Empire (1185–1396), it served as the capital of the Bulgarian state. Turnovo became a center of learning and presently is the home of two universities. Its picturesque location, in the foothills of the mountains along the Yantra River, led to its primacy in the medieval period. It also held a special place in the history of the country; in April 1879 a constitution was promulgated in the city, proclaiming Bulgaria to be a constitutional principality (later monarchy). This constitution remained in effect until December 1947, when a new "people's democracy" was declared. During the communist period, Turnovo became an industrial center.

Approximately 170 kilometers east of Sofia, in the Maritsa Valley, lies Plovdiv. Plovdiv grew from being an ancient fortification into the economic center of central Bulgaria. The city was formerly known as Philippopolis, named for Philip II of Macedon, who captured the town from the Thracians in 342 B.C.E. and made it his capital. In 1878 Plovdiv became the capital of Eastern Rumelia, an autonomous province under Ottoman control. Seven years later, in 1885, Eastern Rumelia and Plovdiv were incorporated into the Bulgarian nation. Currently containing a population of approximately 400,000, Plovdiv serves as a textile and food center.

During the twentieth century, the small fishing village of Burgas became an important port city on the Black Sea. By

People's Square (Plostad Narodno) and the National Assembly (Subranie) in Sofia. In the rear is the Aleksandar Nevski Church. (Sandro Vannini/Corbis)

the 1990s, Burgas had grown to over 200,000 inhabitants and served as a center for fish processing and the refining of petroleum products. Further north along the Black Sea lies the city of Varna, a key maritime port known for its shipbuilding. Located near the site of an ancient Greek trading colony and a later Roman town, Varna grew in importance as railroads linked it to the Danube. During the communist period, the port (briefly called "Stalin," from 1949 to 1956) grew in significance, especially with the completion of ferry train service connecting it to the Ukrainian port of Odessa.

The overwhelming majority of the nation's population of 7.9 million are native Bulgarians, with Turks making up the largest single minority. Other minorities include Romanians, Tartars, Greeks, and Gypsies (Roma); their numbers are very low. Approximately 70 percent of the population live in urban areas, a dramatic shift from the past century, when most Bulgarians lived in the countryside. There are 72 people per square kilometer, and their life expectancies range from 67.1 years for males to 74.8 years for females, according to statistics compiled by *The Economist*. This discrepancy in longevity between men and women has led to a condition in which there are 94 males for every 100 females. The population has stayed relatively stable for over a decade due to a declining birthrate (minus 1 percent from 1995 to 2000), particularly within the Slavic major-

ity. In fact, approximately the same percentage of the population is over the age of 65 as is under the age of 15. The Turkish population, however, has been increasing, always a potential source of tension in Bulgaria after centuries of Turkish rule. Adult literacy is very high (98.4 percent), reflecting an emphasis on education during the period of communism.

Over 85 percent of Bulgarians belong to the Bulgarian Orthodox Church or identify themselves as Orthodox. Although the communists had controlled the church through the Law on Religious Organizations, and the number of priests declined by almost 50 percent from the late 1940s until 1989 (there were not enough priests for the number of churches), during the 1990s the church experienced a revival, a reflection of its historic place within the country. After forty years of suppression (Bibles, for example, were printed, but in such short supply that there were never adequate numbers available), church property, including historic treasures such as the Rila Monastery, was returned to the church.

Muslims make up the second largest religious sect in Bulgaria, accounting for approximately 10 percent of the population. Islam entered the country with the Ottoman conquest; as a result, most Muslim Bulgarians are Sunni, although there are also approximately 80,000 Muslims who

Bulgarian Language

Bulgarian belongs to the Slavic family of languages. Spoken by approximately nine million people, it was exclusively a spoken language for centuries.

The earliest inhabitants of today's Bulgaria used Greek inscriptions for official matters. In 893 an assembly called by Khan Boris officially adopted the Cyrillic alphabet and the Slavic language. Because the great Orthodox churchmen often credited with bringing Christianity to the Slavs, Cyril and Methodius, were from nearby Thessaloniki (Salonika), the dialect chosen for the language of the church was that of the Slavic tribes nearby. This "Old Bulgarian," also known as "Old Church Slavonic" or "Old Slavonic," became the language of the region, as well as the official ecclesiastical language of Eastern Orthodoxy in Southeastern Europe until the 1700s. "Old Bulgarian" thus had an impact on culture and faith far outside the boundaries of the Bulgarian lands.

Over the centuries, Old Bulgarian, or Old Church Slavonic, like its counterpart in the West, Latin, became an anachronism. By the time of the French Revolution in 1789, and the rising of the nationalist tide that was soon to engulf all of Europe, it was little understood or comprehended by the vast majority of Bulgarians.

For the Bulgarian people, like others who chafed under Ottoman Turkish rule, language was critical for national development and identity. Nationalists saw that modernization required linguistic changes. Thus, during the period of national revival in the nineteenth century, the modern Bulgarian language began to emerge, based heavily on a regional dialect from the eastern part of the country. The first Bulgarian grammar was written in 1835 by Neofit Rilski. Changes continued to take shape well into the twentieth century (such as spelling reforms initiated in 1945).

Bulgarian, which is similar in many respects to Macedonian, uses a modern Cyrillic alphabet and has two principal dialects (eastern and western). Although it is rooted in the Slavic linguistic tradition, it differs from the other Slavic languages in a number of ways. Bulgarian does not use a noun case system, and prepositions are critical in defining the relationship between different parts of sentences. In addition, Bulgarian uses a definite article (like the word "the" in English) that falls at the end of the noun. Although there are numerous verb tenses in the language, the infinitive form of verbs is no longer used.

The modern Bulgarian alphabet is comprised of thirty letters. Most of these represent one specific sound. Three letters (ш [sht], я [yǎ], and ю [yu]) have combinations of sounds. In addition, ь is not pronounced, but is a softening sound for some preceding consonants.

Most Bulgarian words are spelled phonetically; however, some are spelled etymologically, often due to the fact that they are still spelled as they were more commonly pronounced in the past, a clear case in which Bulgaria's traditions still have the power to shape its present, even in the area of language.

---

identify themselves as Shia. Many Muslims are descended from Turkish colonists who entered the region when it came under Turkish occupation; at the same time, some native Bulgarians converted to Islam. This minority, known as Pomaks ("helpers"), are considered by many Bulgarians to be Turks as well, even though they have continued to wear native dress and speak the native tongue. Although nearly twelve hundred mosques were located in Bulgaria in the 1980s, persecution of Muslims, beginning in the 1940s and continuing through the last days of the communist regime of Todor Zhivkov in 1989, led to the imprisonment and emigration of many Muslims. Following the fall of communism, religious persecution of the Muslim population eased. New mosques were built, and new Muslim publications appeared.

Small communities of Protestants, Roman Catholics, and Jews also reside in the country. Under the communists, Roman Catholic priests were charged with being agents of the Vatican. Four priests in fact were executed, after being tried and convicted in 1951–1952 on the specious charges

that they were spies for the West. Church property was also confiscated. In the 1990s approximately 44,000 Roman Catholics and 18,000 Uniate Catholics (those who accept the pope's authority but practice the rite of the Eastern Orthodox Church) remained.

Although Catholics were a target of the communists, no group was more persecuted than the Protestants, due to their perceived links to the West, especially the United States. During the period of national revival in the late 1800s, Methodists and Congregationalists came to the Balkans. Their activities led to the first translation of the Bible into Bulgarian in 1871. Many Bulgarian leaders, especially ministers, were in turn educated at Robert College, a nondenominational institution in Istanbul, or in the West. In 1949 thirty-one clergy were charged as spies and sent to prison. Although the "mainstream" Protestant churches were allowed to hold services, Protestants were nevertheless considered to be both alien and Western. This continuous persecution left the Protestant community fractured into small denominations.

In 1990 the Jewish population of Bulgaria was small. During the preceding four decades, nearly 90 percent of the Jewish population had emigrated, primarily to Israel or to the United States. Jews had been an important part of Bulgarian life since the early days of the Ottomans, when the early toleration of the Turks saw numerous Jews flee persecution in the West (especially during the Spanish Inquisition) for the relative safety of the Ottoman Empire. Jews often assimilated into Bulgarian life. During World War II, King Boris blocked their deportation, instead passing anti-Jewish legislation that assuaged the Nazis in Berlin, but which either allowed Jews to emigrate with visas to Palestine or which sent them to camps inside Bulgaria, which were internment rather than death camps. Under the communists, however, Jews were classified as being members of a nationality rather than of a religion and were encouraged to leave.

Although cities and towns have long been important to the Bulgarian lands, from the time of the ancient trading villages established by the Thracians and Greeks, to the fortress towns of the Romans, to the cities of the medieval Bulgarian empires, to the industrial complexes created during the communist period, in fact for most of Bulgarian history, the essence of the state was the peasantry.

The term "Bulgar" was derived from an old Turkic word meaning "to mix." This name connoted the migratory nature of the peoples who arrived in the lands south of the Danube River during the sixth and seventh centuries. When they settled into the mountains and valleys that define the Bulgarian lands, the terrain offered protection and a means of preserving their way of life. This was especially true after the Ottoman conquest, when Bulgaria was ruled from Constantinople, but Bulgarian culture was preserved in the day-to-day lives of the peasants.

Peasant life defined Bulgaria for a millennium. Traditional Bulgarian society was composed of three groups: peasants, the *chorbadzhii* (larger landowners), and the *esnafi* (tradesmen). Only the twentieth century, with the twin forces of urbanization and industrialization, especially following the communist takeover and the social disruption and environmental disaster that accompanied that painful chapter in Bulgarian history, changed the peasant nature of the country.

For centuries, peasant life revolved around the family, the village, and subsistence agriculture. The center of that world was the *zadruga,* the communal extended family (generally comprising ten to twenty families), which was a central part of the life of Bulgaria (as it was of Serbia). Family members lived under one roof or in close proximity to one another. The eldest male, sometimes called the "lord of the house" or "the old man," headed the family and made all the decisions for it. The family revolved around him. No one ate before him, and everyone rose when he entered the room. His wife, by virtue of their marriage, likewise took on a position of primacy among the women.

Modernization however brought about the breakup of the *zadruge* (plural). Newer inheritance laws in the mid-1800s and the movement of the peasant class to the cities led to disintegration within the larger group. The breakup of the zadruge however did not end the patriarchal nature of Bulgarian society. Husbands continued to maintain most property rights. Arranged marriages also continued until well after World War II.

Bulgaria was (and remains) a male-dominated, patriarchal society. Leadership positions historically were exclusively male. In the waning years of Ottoman control, some women did become involved in the national renaissance, but their numbers were few and their impact upon national life generally minimal. In the villages, women were considered to be as much possessions as they were people. They were to be seen and not heard. Men, for example, often rode while women walked and did the carrying.

This pattern continued until the 1940s when, ironically, the imposition of communism, which was to shackle the country for four decades through the loss of personal liberties, partially "liberated" women. Women became an integral part of the labor force, comprising half of workers by the end of the 1980s. The areas open to female employment and opportunity greatly expanded, and education led to significant increases in women joining fields outside those considered to be traditionally female. Although many women continued to work in "traditional" occupations such as education, office work, and childcare, they also became engineers and construction workers.

Despite the fact that women became contributors to the economy, the patriarchal nature of Bulgarian society did not disappear. Women were still expected to obey their husbands; to question a male's decision was frowned upon. Women took care of the homes, even after workdays that were as lengthy as that of males. Few women obtained positions of real authority, either in the government or in the economy. Perhaps the most visible woman was Liudmila Zhivkova (the daughter of the president, Todor Zhivkov), who served as minister of culture from 1975 until her death in 1981 from a car accident.

Although the constitution declared full equality for women, that equality created strains within the system. The marriage rate, for example, remained steady until the 1970s but then began to decline. Divorce, which was rare before World War II, increased dramatically, especially for those who lived in the cities. This led to a low or declining birthrate. Large families became rare. In response, the regime, which saw women as mothers more than workers (again reflecting the deeply rooted paternalism in Bulgaria), tightened rules for divorce and increased incentives (though with little effect) for having children.

After the fall of communism and the resulting economic problems of the 1990s, some of the support given to women by a communist regime desirous of promoting childbirth (through maternity leave and day care) declined. Women also lost jobs, as work was no longer guaranteed. Under communism, there had been only one organ for women, the Movement of Bulgarian Women, but women's organizations now sprang up to promote women's rights. Although progress has been made, equality in real terms remains elusive.

Just as the twentieth century saw changes for women, it also witnessed progress in education. During the eighteenth and nineteenth centuries, cell schools and reading rooms *(chitalishta)* extended primary education to some segments of the Bulgarian population. Many of the leaders of the Bulgarian revolution against the Turks in the 1870s were teachers. Following national independence, education spread. In 1878 a law established free education that was to stress reading, writing, and arithmetic. By the beginning of the 1900s, one-third of the villages in the country contained an elementary school, but schooling was sporadic, in part due to the lack of teachers. Under communism, literacy and education expanded dramatically. The communist regime saw education as critical for industrialization (thus, technical education was emphasized) and to promote the ideology of the state. By the 1990s, Bulgaria could boast 98 percent literacy.

Education during the communist era, however, was often rote and political. Following 1989, the school system had to be depoliticized, a difficult process owing to decades of ideologically driven textbooks and the fact that most teachers were members of the Party (the renamed Bulgarian Socialist Party). The system for a half-century had stressed doctrinaire learning with little creativity. In 1991 a Law on Public Education, which made education compulsory for all children between the ages of six and sixteen, sought to remove politics from the curriculum. Still, the transition was slow, as many textbooks continued to reflect the past. Many students in higher education had failed to develop critical computer and business management skills. This failure to create a revolution in education to match the one that occurred in 1989 with the fall of the Soviet bloc meant that the shift from communism to capitalism faced as much an educational barrier as a capital one. Nevertheless, significant progress, especially in the area of computers, has taken place in the past decade, leading to an increasing number of high-tech jobs flowing to the country.

Like education, the quality of health care also improved dramatically in the twentieth century. Life expectancy increased as the number of available health practitioners grew. However, the mortality rate was still high (nearly twice that found in Western Europe), especially in the villages, a reflection of the spotty nature of health care delivery. Many in the villages, in fact, continued to rely on herbalists and healing mineral springs as they had done for centuries. Bulgarians also had a high rate of stroke, attributable to smoking (Bulgaria has one of the highest rates of tobacco usage in the world) and alcohol (the average Bulgarian consumes over seven liters of alcohol per month, and that rate continued to grow throughout the 1980s and 1990s), as well as a high consumption of animal fats and sugars. Another contributing factor to the higher mortality rate was the polluted environment. Pollution will be a legacy of communism for decades to come, and it has contributed to severe respiratory problems for many. The communist economic system was unconcerned about the environmental toll of rapid industrialization. Cities were dirty. Toxic wastes were dumped into the air, water, and soil. Many of the country's forests are either dying or have been irreparably harmed. Factories had few, if any, antipollution devices. In fact, the toll from the disregard for environmental safety may never fully be known (although it was estimated that over one-third of the population in the 1990s had health problems related to environmental pollution).

It is estimated that by 2020 Bulgaria will have one of the highest median age populations in the world. In 2000 it already had the seventh highest percentage of elderly population, while having the second lowest birthrate and lowest fertility rate, according to *The Economist*. This will create significant additional pressures upon an economy that will have to provide for this aging demographic.

HISTORY

Like many, if not most, of the peoples of Central and Southeastern Europe, the Bulgarians are often overlooked in histories published in the West. This is often due to a twofold problem: limited written source material from much of Bulgaria's past, certainly prior to the eighteenth century, and the fact that much of what has been written has not been in Western languages. Nevertheless, despite certain limitations, such as the need to rely on chronicles that are often notoriously myopic for much of Bulgaria's earliest history, much is known about Bulgaria's rich past, and it is clear that it is integrally entwined with its present.

The Balkan region witnessed habitation as early as the Stone Age (ca. 700,000 B.C.E.). Valleys were used for cultivation, and by the time of the Bronze Age (3500–1000 B.C.E.), during the so-called Thracian period, the region moved beyond isolated communities to a greater sense of integration. For nearly a millennium, despite periods of disruption from invaders, the Thracians were a creative and unifying force in the lands within the present geographical boundaries of Bulgaria. Although Thracian civilization, which experienced its peak in the sixth century B.C.E., never rose to the level of that of neighboring Greece and Macedonia, the Thracian language, part of the Indo-European family of languages, continued to be spoken long after the power of Thracian civilization was eclipsed by the Greeks and the Romans.

During the reigns of Philip II of Macedon and his son Alexander (the Great), in the fourth century B.C.E., the region fell under Greek rule in the form of the Macedonian Empire. Greek colonies also could be found along the Black Sea coast. However, direct Greek control over the territory was relatively short-lived; after Alexander's death, the Macedonian Empire declined, and a new Thracian kingdom was established in the third century B.C.E.

During the first century C.E., the Romans began to push toward the Danube River, building roads for troops and trade. One important crossroads was in an area near present-day Sofia. About that time, the Goths began to weaken the fringes of the Roman Empire, and Christianity made its first inroads into the region.

Beginning in the third century, barbarian raids began to take their toll on Roman holdings in the Balkans, causing disruption in trade and dislocation in some of the more populated regions. The division of the Roman Empire into two parts in 395 for the moment stabilized the situation, with the establishment of the Eastern Roman Empire, which later came to be called the Byzantine Empire. On the other hand, wars conducted by Constantinople depleted the empire's resources, forcing higher taxes on the peasants, which only caused the latter to flee to the mountains to escape. Ironically therefore, defense of the empire (as when Justinian, for example, constructed a series of fortresses along the Danube to keep out the barbarians) in the end only served to weaken the empire in the Balkans, thereby opening the door to further incursions.

Of the various invaders of the Bulgarian lands in the sixth and seventh centuries, it was the Slavs and the Bulgarians who in the end had the greatest impact; most of the other invaders, from the Huns to the various groups of Goths, raided the countryside but had little permanent influence beyond the temporary devastation they caused.

The term "Bulgar" is derived from an old Turkic word signifying a people of a mixed nationality. The Bulgars were a nomadic people of Turkic origin originally from the area near the Sea of Azov. According to some legends, they were descended from Attila the Hun. By the 630s, a loose federation of Bulgar tribes had been established. In the late 600s, led by their khan (prince), Asparuh, the Bulgars crossed the Danube, possibly due to pressure from another steppe people, the Khazars, and occupied what is today's modern Bulgaria. In 681, the date generally held to be the beginning of Bulgarian history, the Byzantine emperor, Constantine V, was forced to sign a treaty establishing a Bulgarian state (the First Bulgarian Empire) under Asparuh with its capital at Pliska, near the present city of Shumen.

The area that now fell under the control of the Bulgars was already occupied by a number of peoples, including the Slavs. The origins of the Slavs have long been a matter of historical debate. They probably originated in the region of the Ukraine, and by the mid-500s they had migrated into northern Bulgaria. Within another half-century, large-scale settlements, whose population spoke an old form of today's Bulgarian language, had begun to form. Along with the Avars, another group that had moved south of the Danube, they presented a military challenge to Constantinople. Although the Byzantine Empire failed to collapse in the face of the attacks from the north, the warfare weakened the state, thus making it easier and more inviting for the Bulgars to expand their holdings; these wars also led to the weakening of the Avars in the 630s, which eventually led to Slavic dominance in the region.

With the entrance of the Bulgars into the lands south of the Danube, the interplay between the Bulgar leadership and the Slavic population began, which was to have an important effect upon the course of Bulgarian history. Although the Bulgars were the political leaders, they were not a numerous people, and thus in the end it was the culture of the Slavs, the majority population, that came to dominate the leadership and define the state. The other inhabitants of the land, the pre-Slavic peoples, had little impact on either the Slavs or the Bulgars.

THE FIRST AND SECOND BULGARIAN EMPIRES

From 681 until 1018, the First Bulgarian Empire was a powerful state in Southeastern Europe, one that saw the state move from an identity that was not Slavic to one that

was. Pliska was built on a plain, and at first the ruling Bulgars sought to keep their distance from the Slavs. They often built new towns rather than inhabit or build on the old. The Slavs, on the other hand, were a loosely structured, pastoral people. As long as they paid their tribute to the Bulgars, they were allowed to keep their customs. In fact, until the ninth century, writers (often from Constantinople) regularly distinguished between the two groups. Wars between the Bulgars and the Byzantines throughout the mid-700s, however, may have begun the process of bringing the Slavs and Bulgars closer together.

In 803 Krum, a warrior khan, came to the throne, and the Bulgars again found themselves at war with the Byzantine Empire, under the emperor Nicephorus, who captured and plundered the capital at Pliska. After his victory at Pliska, however, Nicephorus left his army in a vulnerable position in the mountains, allowing Krum's forces to attack the exposed Byzantine army; a massacre ensued in which Nicephorus was killed (his head became the khan's drinking cup), and his son was mortally wounded, dying after a few agonizing months. Although Krum himself was to perish three years later (814) on a new campaign aimed at seizing Constantinople, the power of the Bulgarian state was established.

In 852 Boris became khan. By the time of his coming to power, the Bulgarian khanate had departed from its past nomadic roots. With their military successes had come political stabilization (although civil wars to see who would become khan were a constant threat). Moreover, the Turkic elite had long since adopted the language of the Slavs. This Slavization of the Bulgars solidified the state internally. What was not solidified was the religious nature of the people.

Bulgaria was a land of religious plurality. Apart from native paganism, there were contacts with Roman Catholic areas in the West, as well as with the Eastern Orthodox Byzantine Empire. Khan Boris, realizing the need to bring religious unity to the kingdom, now turned to the Eastern rite in 864 (after briefly contemplating turning to Rome), and forcibly converted the population to Christianity. This momentous act not only shaped the religious and cultural future of the state, it created a Bulgarian people by symbolically uniting the inhabitants. Moreover, the Slavic-based language, Old Bulgarian, or Old Church Slavonic, used for the liturgy, gave a linguistic unity to the people that provided the basis for modern Bulgaria.

Boris became a devout Orthodox Christian. Although he built numerous churches, his basilica in Pliska was the grandest, said to be the size of a football field. He brought in translators and scholars, built monasteries, supported the work of architects and artisans, and, perhaps most importantly, replaced the Greek clergy and rite with a Slavonic clergy and a Slavonic rite. Boris even briefly abdicated his throne and retired to a monastery. When his son, Vladimir, reverted to paganism, however, even destroying the great basilica, Boris left the monastery, deposed and blinded his son, and convened a council at Preslav (near his monastery) to recognize his younger son, Simeon, in 893 as khan and Christianity as the religion of the state.

The Bulgarian Orthodox Church

Central to the lives of most people in Southeastern Europe, the Eastern Orthodox Church is a conservative faith that sees itself as the preserver of true Christianity. The very word "Orthodox" itself means true or right worship. Believers hold that the Orthodox Church preserves the true revelation of God to humankind. That revelation is based upon the books of the Old and the New Testaments and is expressed in the early doctrines of the church, most notably the words of the Nicene Creed.

The Nicene Creed and the Trinity (Father, Son, and Holy Spirit) are the cornerstones for the faithful. Jesus of Nazareth, as the son of God, is the redeemer and the hope for salvation. A true believer must read the Bible and, most importantly, accept the mysteries of faith (including the sacraments of baptism, communion, repentance, confession, and marriage). Of greatest significance is the Eucharist, which creates a fellowship in Christ for believers, just as Christ united with his disciples. For the Orthodox, Father, Son, and Holy Spirit are of the same essence. The writings of the early church leaders and the work of the seven Ecumenical Councils (385–787) form the essence of Orthodox doctrine, by establishing the traditions that a Christian must follow.

Churches in the Orthodox world reflect the traditional nature of the faith and its adherents. Whether simple or ornate, large or small, churches are houses of God, and all are equal in that house. In the front of the church's interior is the iconostasis, a wall adorned with icons (holy images that depict important scenes in the life of Christ and of the saints) that are viewed as windows between heaven and earth. Along the wall is the royal door, through which the religious leader passes at key points in the service (as if moving from the earthly to the heavenly, again reflecting the mysteries so central to Orthodoxy).

As Orthodoxy spread into the Balkans from Constantinople, rulers began to adopt it and convert the population. This process took place in Bulgaria in 864 under Khan Boris. An independent Bulgarian Patriarchate was established in 917 and recognized by Constantinople in 927. From its earliest days, the Bulgarian church became central to the lives of the people. After the destruction of the First Bulgarian Empire, the seat of the church moved to Ohrid (creating the Autocephalous Archbishopric of Ohrid). However, with the destruction of the Second Bulgarian Empire by the Turks in the late fourteenth century, the Bulgarian church's independence disappeared as the Ottomans placed Orthodox Christians under the jurisdiction of the patriarch in Constantinople. This resulted in the "Hellenization" of the Bulgarian Church in the eighteenth century and a struggle within the Church to break free of Greek influence.

Even during the long period of foreign domination, the Orthodox Church served as the preserver of much of Bulgarian culture. Orthodox monasteries, including those at Hilendar and Rila, became vital in the national reawakening of the nineteenth century; they had guarded and preserved the Bulgarian past. Monks played a critical role in the creation of "cell schools" that served as the genesis of the intellectual renaissance. In 1870 the Ottoman Empire restored the authority of the former Bulgarian Patriarchate under the title "Bulgarian Exarchate." However, the Greek Orthodox patriarch refused to accept the creation of an independent Bulgarian church. Following World War II, the Bulgarian Patriarchate was again officially recognized by the patriarch in Istanbul (Constantinople). In 1953 Cyril of Plovdiv was officially ordained as Bulgarian patriarch in the Aleksandar Nevski Church in Sofia.

Like other religious institutions in the communist world, the Bulgarian Orthodox Church suffered under the socialist regime, especially through the confiscation of church property. Following the fall of communism, the 1991 Bulgarian constitution recognized the Bulgarian Orthodox Church as the "traditional religion in Bulgaria."

The Bulgarian Orthodox Church is governed by a Holy Synod made up of the patriarch (who also heads the diocese of Sofia) and the bishops of the other dioceses within the church. Over 85 percent of the Bulgarian population identify themselves as Orthodox

The symbol of Simeon's reign, the height of the First Bulgarian Empire, was the construction of a new capital at Preslav in eastern Bulgaria. The greatness of Preslav was fitting for the new ruler, who took the title of Tsar of the Bulgarians and Autocrat of the Romans (that is, Greeks associated with the Eastern Roman Empire) and sat on his throne in his purple robes. The city became a center of learning and culture, and out of Preslav Greek culture and Orthodoxy spread to other parts of Southeastern Europe. Simeon himself respected Greek culture and had numerous works of literature translated into Old Bulgarian. During his thirty-four year reign (893–927), Simeon the Great, as he came to be known, was a far different man from the kind his background (he had been

The Last Judgment [detail], located in the Church of the Assumption, Monastery of Rila. (Paul Almasy/Corbis)

in a monastery prior to his being chosen) would have foreshadowed.

Although Simeon had been schooled in Constantinople, much of his reign was dominated by conflict with the Byzantine Empire. His armies reached the Adriatic and Aegean seas, taking Albania, Macedonia, and Belgrade, and even attacking the great walls of Constantinople itself in 913. Although his forces could not take the great walled city of Byzantium, to give it its ancient name, his power led the

emperor to recognize him as tsar, which connoted equality with the emperor himself. Moreover the emperor granted the head of the Bulgarian church the title of patriarch, again symbolizing power and distinction. Simeon's state also developed a structure and a ruling hierarchy, headed by the great landowners *(boiars),* who also served as his military commanders.

However, despite the achievements of the First Bulgarian Empire, its dominance proved to be fleeting. Like most states in Southeastern Europe, the Bulgarian Empire faced predators (Croatians, Serbs, Russians, Pechenegs, and others) on its borders, and Simeon's conquests had taxed the resources of the state. In 969, for example, the Kievan prince, Sviatoslav, took Preslav and made the tsar, Boris II, his prisoner. Moreover, internal economic, political, and religious weakness had set in. Boiars in the southwest even broke away, challenging the authority in the capital. The patriarch moved the seat of the church to Ohrid. And finally, the state was split by the Bogomil heresy.

Bogomilism was a religious and social movement that grew out of the question of good and evil. Bogomilism held that there was a dualism in the world. To Bogomils, the material and bodily world was evil, the spiritual world divine. To avoid evil, a believer had to avoid the material world as much as possible and instead work for social justice. The nobility and the clergy, however, were impediments to justice, since their interests required their protection of their material possessions. Thus the church and the state were seen by the Bogomils as both evil and tools of the devil. Accordingly, Bogomils rejected rituals, symbols, relics, and the sacraments. This heresy split the population, as the state now fought against its own people.

Whether the internal weakness brought on by the Bogomil movement alone would have destroyed the state is a matter of conjecture, but certainly it provided an inviting target for the Byzantine emperor, Basil II, who defeated the Bulgarian army near Thessaloniki in 1014. Basil's destruction of the Bulgarians was so complete (he blinded almost all of the 14,000 survivors, leaving only a few [one in one hundred] with one eye so that they could guide their comrades home) that he earned the title "the Bulgar Slayer." (Tsar Samuil was said to have died upon seeing the destruction of his army.) Within four years, the Byzantine Empire had reclaimed the Bulgarian territories, thereby bringing an end to the First Bulgarian Empire in 1018.

Although Constantinople had regained control of Bulgaria, the cost of administering a larger empire led to increased taxation of the peasantry and resulting unrest. Additionally, the Crusades mortally weakened Byzantium. In 1185 an uprising against the Byzantines, led by two aristocratic brothers, Asen and Petûr, led to the creation of a second Bulgarian state with its capital at Turnovo. From Turnovo, the Bulgarians resisted and defeated the Byzantines (which in turn weakened the Byzantine state to the point that it was seized by the forces of the West in the Fourth Crusade in 1204). Under John Asen II, "Tsar and Autocrat of all Bulgarians and Greeks," many of the lands Simeon had taken during the time of the First Bulgarian Empire were reconquered.

During the period of the resulting Second Bulgarian Empire (1185–1396), which at times stretched from the Adriatic and Aegean seas to the Black Sea and the Dnieper River, Bulgaria was an important trade route to the east, and Turnovo became an important commercial center and a seat of the arts. Now, however, whereas the First Bulgarian Empire had been the dominant state in the Balkans in the tenth century, other states in the region, most notably the Serbian Empire, held a position of primacy. Moreover, numerous other states, from Hungary to the Latin coastal states, competed for trade. As a consequence, the power of the Second Bulgarian Empire was short-lived.

Internal squabbling and Tartar incursions from the east soon weakened the state. In the early 1300s a brief revival occurred under Mihail Shishman. Then seemingly constant warfare, especially with Serbia, cost Shishman his life and economically crippled the state. It was left vulnerable not only to Serbia, which, led by its great ruler Stefan Dušan, defeated Bulgaria in 1330 and made it a virtual vassal for the remainder of its existence, but more importantly to the growing power of the Ottoman Empire in the southeast.

Beginning in the 1360s, Ottoman armies advanced steadily in Southeastern Europe against the forces of the Byzantine Empire and the Balkan states. When the Bulgarian tsar Ivan Alexander split Bulgaria between his two sons, Ivan Shishman (in Turnovo) and Ivan Stratsimir (in Vidin), it further weakened the state's ability to resist the Turkish invasion. In 1389 the Turks destroyed the army of the Serbs at Kosovo, leaving the final conquest of the Balkans in little doubt. Sofia had already fallen to the Ottomans in 1385. Eight years later Turnovo fell, despite a defense led in part by the patriarch himself. Finally, in 1396, Bayezid's army conquered Vidin in a campaign that saw the destruction of the last crusading army in European history (at Nicopolis). Bulgaria had ceased to exist as an independent state.

BULGARIA UNDER THE OTTOMAN EMPIRE

For almost the next five centuries, Bulgaria was under the control of the Ottoman Empire. The Ottomans were the dominant military power in the fifteenth century. The empire's military prowess was exemplified by the conquest of Constantinople on 29 May 1453, an event that stunned Europe and is sometimes considered to mark the end of the Middle Ages. Although by the end of the 1500s the seeds of the eventual weakening and collapse of the Ottomans had already begun to sprout, its control and domination of Bulgaria, as with much of the Balkans, had a profound effect upon the Bulgarian lands and the people who inhabited them.

The old Bulgarian state structure was destroyed by the victorious Turks, and much of the nobility died. Even the separate Bulgarian church ceased to exist, as the Turks placed all the Orthodox peoples within their empire under the authority of the patriarch in Constantinople. The Ottoman Empire was in the beginning perhaps the most tolerant state in Europe, and the Christian inhabitants of the empire were seen as "people of the book" (as Jews and Christians were called, who, because they shared Abraham with Islam as the common father of their religions, were tolerated by their Muslim overlords). Nevertheless, Orthodox Christianity was now controlled by the Turks, through the office of the patriarchate in Constantinople. This loss of religious autonomy in many respects paralleled the destruction of Bulgaria's political independence.

The Ottoman conquest of Southeastern Europe was based upon a combination of factors: military innovation, talented sultans, and the weaknesses of their opponents.

After 1204, and the taking of Constantinople by the forces of the Fourth Crusade, the Byzantine Empire failed to recover, even after the Crusaders were driven out. In 1360 Murad I took the city of Adrianople, which essentially cut the Byzantine capital off from the Balkans. The conquest of Adrianople also gave the Turks a base for operations in Southeastern Europe. In 1371 the Turks defeated Bulgarian forces at the Maritsa River. At first, defeated princes were permitted to remain as long as they paid tribute to the Turks, though they had become, in effect, vassals of the Turkish sultan. By 1396, however, all pretensions of independence were gone.

From 1396 until the end of the nineteenth century, Bulgaria's fate was linked to the fate of the Ottomans, who, in 1453, moved their capital to the great city of Constantinople. Thus, to understand Bulgaria under the Turks, one has to also understand the nature of the Ottoman state itself.

The Ottoman Empire was a warrior state, whose aim was expansion both for itself and Islam. Muslims saw the world as being divided into two houses, that of the faithful (Sunni Islam) and that of war (nonbelievers). When they conquered a territory, however, the Turks did not force conversion of the population to Islam. Turkish forces entering the Balkans were generally tolerant of the indigenous population. A populace that did not convert in fact had benefits for the Ottomans, since non-Muslims paid additional taxes.

Beneath the ruling elite, all peasants, Muslim and non-Muslim, were the *reaya*. However, only the non-Muslim reaya were subject to the *devshirme,* the "child-tax," children taken from the village according to a quota. These children, whose ages ranged from eight to twenty, were then converted to Islam, divided by talent, and taken into the service of the sultan. Some became administrators; others became soldiers in the elite janissary corps, the infantry units that (along with the cavalry, the *sipahi,* who were rewarded for their service with grants of nonhereditary land [*timars*]) were responsible for Ottoman success on the battlefield.

When the Turks first conquered a territory, a careful assessment of the land was made for the purposes of taxation and the granting of timars. Thus, toleration of the population was beneficial to the state; as long as taxes were paid and wealth flowed to the state's coffers, the ideal of harmony, one of the tenets of Turkish rule, could be maintained.

At first, although the Bulgarian lands were more closely administered than other parts of the empire (due to their close proximity to Constantinople [now Istanbul]), conditions were not harsh. Commerce continued with little disruption. The Turks were on the whole tolerant of their subject peoples, save for some restrictions on things such as church buildings. There was no attempt to convert the population to Islam or to impose Turkish culture upon the people. Taxes were not onerous. In other words, Turkish rule, at least for the moment, seemed at the worst to be benign.

Unfortunately, however, the Ottoman system was a hierarchical one, dependent upon the talents and whims of the sultan. Through the reign of Süleyman the Lawgiver (who was also known as Süleyman the Magnificent), who died in 1566, the sultans had proven to be excellent administrators and military commanders. But the system turned out to have flaws. Less able sultans were captivated by the vast wealth of the empire. In addition, in order to prevent the kind of palace intrigue that proved to be so devastating to other states, upon the death of a sultan, the oldest heir would assume the throne and execute his brothers (with a bow-string). This practice of fratricide was later changed to imprisonment (in what came to be known as the Cage), but what was seemingly more humane often turned out to have worse effects, when sultans took the throne after decades of imprisonment that had resulted in dementia. The early Ottoman rulers had been warrior kings; after Süleyman they ceased being warriors, and expansion, the key to Ottoman rule, turned into retreat.

Increased military costs for the janissaries, coupled with the need to maintain the lavish lifestyle of the palace, meant that once expansion ceased, taxes, which had, when the Turks first entered the Balkans, actually been reduced for many, now had to be raised. As the sultan became more and more immersed in the material pleasures of the palace, local officials, especially the janissaries, were in charge of collecting taxes. The opportunity for corruption was great. By the seventeenth century, the once vaunted and feared military units were rife with corruption.

This debilitation in the military paralleled an economic decline as well. As trade routes shifted following the "discovery" of the New World, the economy of the empire suffered. Trade that had previously run through the Balkans declined, putting further pressures on the state to raise taxes to cover the shortfall. And as the empire weakened, the Ottoman system of dividing the state administratively into *millets* (religious communities), with each religious community administered by its own hierarchy, meant that despite centuries of rule, the population had never developed an identification with Istanbul.

The millet was an institution unique to the Ottomans. With the collapse of the old ruling authorities after Ottoman conquest of a territory, the Turks organized local affairs through the millet, in which they identified a people not by geography but by religion. There was a Muslim millet, a Roman Catholic millet, an Armenian millet, and an Orthodox millet in the European lands occupied by the Turks. The head of the Orthodox millet was the patriarch in Constantinople. At first, two autocephalous churches were permitted to exist, one in Peć for the Serbs, and the other in Ohrid for the Bulgarians, but the patriarch over time abolished them. Over the years, the patriarch became the de facto leader of the Orthodox peoples, even responsible for the actions of his "flock." The patriarch was a part of the Ottoman governing structure, and his powers were wide, even including judicial matters in the Orthodox millet. However, the church (including the patriarch himself), like the Ottoman government it had come to serve, came to experience the same corruption that defined the Ottoman state itself. The office of the patriarch was bought through bribery, a corruption that led to higher taxes upon the peasantry to offset the costs of procuring the office.

Aside from the authority of the church in Istanbul, Bulgaria was at first considered to be part of a single administrative unit. Later it was subdivided into smaller units that varied in name over the centuries. For the average Bulgarian, however, day-to-day society continued along traditional lines, especially through the institution of the *zadruga* (the communal extended family that defined peasant life). Villages had their own organizational structure, and their leaders were often the intermediaries who dealt with the Ottomans. Although these village leaders had opportunities for corruption and did tend to live better lives than the average Bulgarian, it was they who provided leadership during the national revival of the 1800s.

The peasants formed the lowest stratum of society, and in the remotest areas of Bulgaria they could live their lives with little contact with Ottoman authorities. Over the centuries, however, the lot of the Bulgarian peasant declined dramatically. At first, they could maintain their possessions, and taxes were actually reduced. But as the nonhereditary timars were converted to *chiftliks* (private estates), taxes increased substantially. As Ottoman power receded and local authorities became the dominant everyday force in the region, conditions for the reaya declined even further. Many peasants took flight to the mountains. *Haiduk*s (bandits) became heroes in peasant folklore for resisting the authorities, but the realities of the lawlessness in the countryside caused by their activities was that villagers were just as likely to be the victims of haiduk activities as administrators or landowners.

Making matters even worse for Bulgarians was the fact that as the empire ceased expanding, the inability (and refusal) of the Ottomans to change and innovate to meet the reversals on the battlefield meant that while the outer reaches of the empire (Hungary, for example, during the seventeenth century) were under attack from Ottoman neighbors, the peasants in Bulgaria were under a different kind of assault: taxation and corruption.

During the eighteenth century, the Porte (the name often used for the Ottoman government) fought a series of wars with its great power neighbors, Russia and the Habsburg Empire. These conflicts weakened the Ottoman state and, in retrospect, doomed it, not only through the loss of territory, but by awakening the Balkan peoples. In 1774, after six years of warfare against the Russians, the Turks signed the Treaty of Kuchuk Kainardji, a devastating agreement that territorially opened the Black Sea to the Russians, but more importantly granted St. Petersburg the power to act as the protector and guarantor of the Christian peoples in the Balkans, as well as the right to open consulates in the region. Kuchuk Kainardji represented a vague, open-ended grant of power to Russia that, in part, led to a century of repeated wars between the Turks and the Russians. For many in Russia, the lure of becoming the emancipators of the Orthodox Christian population in Southeastern Europe was intoxicating. For others in the Balkans, the presence of Orthodox Russia as a great power presented the opportunity to gain that independence.

NATIONAL REAWAKENING

Bulgaria was one of the last states in the Balkans to obtain national independence. During the centuries of Ottoman occupation, because of the close proximity of Bulgaria to Istanbul, the Bulgarians felt a more pronounced Turkish presence. Partly this was due to the sizable number of Turks who had come to Bulgaria following the Ottoman destruction of the Second Bulgarian Empire in 1396. In addition, many Bulgarians converted to Islam over the years (coming to be known as Pomaks [helpers]). But for most Bulgarians, culturally there was no identification with the Turks. Although outwardly life went on as it had for centuries, the failure of the Turks to create any sense of identification among the majority of the population with the rulers in Istanbul meant that the Turkish capital was as foreign to the people in the eighteenth and nineteenth centuries as it was in the fourteenth. Moreover, what was at first a mild occupation by the Turks had degenerated. The army, increasingly corrupt and beset by low morale and poor discipline, used the Bulgarian lands through which it passed as an opportunity to steal. The weak Ottoman administration left the countryside unprotected, both from the corruption inherent in the landowning chiftlik system, which caused many peasants to flee to the mountains, and from the armed bands *(kirdjalis)*, which became a threat to the inhabitants north of the Balkan Mountains (as well as to the officials, who could not, or would not, eliminate them). The combination of the chiftlik system and the banditry caused severe economic

Bulgarians defend a mountain pass against the Turks in 1876. (North Wind Picture Archives)

and social dislocation throughout the country, but especially within the grain-producing lowlands.

Although the economic and social problems that plagued the Bulgarian lands in the eighteenth century might have by themselves led to rebellion, what in many respects precipitated the reemergence of a Bulgarian national identity was the belief that the very core of the nation's cultural link to the past was under assault. In 1767 the archbishopric was abolished in the wake of scandals, and all ecclesiastical matters passed under the complete jurisdiction of the patriarch in Constantinople. In the process, Greek replaced Old Church Slavonic, or Old Bulgarian, as the language of the church, and the Greek language and Greek culture became dominant, while the Bulgarian church, which had preserved much of Bulgaria's culture, from the liturgy to folklore, lost its identity. It was this challenge to Bulgaria's cultural heritage that led to the national revival.

The process of rebirth in Bulgaria began at the Hilendar Monastery atop Mount Athos (the most important monastery in the Orthodox world). At Hilendar, a monk named Paisii wrote a history of the Bulgarian people entitled *Istoriia Slavianobulgarskaia* (A Slavonic-Bulgarian History) in 1762. Paisii's work reflected a hostility toward what he perceived to be Greek interference in the lives of the Bulgarians. He argued that Bulgaria had a rich and glorious past and that the Greeks were alien to the culture of the people. While his "history" was in many respects little more than a polemic against the Greeks, his defense of Bulgarian culture was a call to arms.

Paisii's protégé, Sofronii Vrachanski, the bishop of Vratsa, continued the attack upon Greek culture by promoting the use of the Bulgarian vernacular, printing his sermons in Bulgarian in Wallachia, the first of a number of such works that were to be published outside of Bulgaria. Histories, translations, and other works printed in the Bulgarian language now found their way into the land, and the linguistic and educational revivals were the first steps in gaining independence.

Another early figure in the movement to reawaken Bulgarian nationalism was Neofit Bozveli, who, after training at the Hilendar Monastery, returned to the town of Svishtov, where he organized a school. Instrumental in the publication of textbooks, by the 1840s he was banished to Mount Athos by Greek officials who viewed him as an agitator for an independent Bulgarian church.

At the dawn of the nineteenth century, the few schools that existed in Bulgaria were clustered around churches and monasteries and often narrowly focused on the needs of the church. Outside the church, school curriculum was usually taught in Greek or in Old Church Slavonic. Until the nineteenth century, little emphasis was placed on the real world, especially commerce. The Greek schools, however, did introduce students to the emerging ideas of nationalism in Europe.

By the early 1800s, a native educated elite began to emerge. Other students, educated abroad, returned with ideas of liberalism. However, perhaps the greatest influence on the early movement came from Russia, where Pan-Slavs (those who believed in the cultural unity of the Slavic peoples under Russian leadership) formed a Slavic Benevolent Society, which brought Bulgarians to Russia to study. There, Bulgarian students were exposed to the ideals of revolution as well as nationalism.

Ironically, as the beginnings of a quest for national independence began to take shape within the minds of some Bulgarians, conditions within Bulgaria were improving. Confronted by bandits (such as Pasvanoglu Osman Pasha, who, until his death in 1807, carved out a virtually independent domain in Vidin, as well as the kirdjalis, who terrorized the population in the countryside, and rebellious military units who defied their authority, the Ottomans embarked on needed reforms in the 1820s. Moreover, with the revolt in Greece in the 1820s, Greek influence in Ottoman affairs, especially in the economy, declined, leaving the door open for Bulgarian merchants to make greater inroads in the Ottoman economy. As Bulgaria became one of the principal suppliers of grain and manufactured goods for the Ottoman Empire, economic benefits were felt in many parts of the country. During the 1830s, Bulgarian cities served as centers for the manufacture of textiles, notably wool and linen products. A number of Bulgarians in turn became wealthy, and their newfound wealth spilled over into publishing, schools, and a reemphasis on culture. Their patronage of the arts, for example, led to the refurbishing of the Rila Monastery and new architectural designs.

Bulgarians also began to study or live abroad (notably in Bucharest and Odessa). This renewed emphasis on education abroad led to the creation of a strictly Bulgarian school in Gabrovo. Opened in 1835, thanks to the aid of wealthy merchants led by Vasili Aprilov, the school was a Bulgarian one in every respect, from the language of instruction to the textbooks. The Gabrovo school became the model for other such institutions, which began to open throughout the country.

But despite improvements in the economy and a growth in education, as well as Bulgaria's increasingly important position within the Ottoman Empire, Bulgarian nationalists continued to focus on the issue of the church, steadfastly opposing perceived Greek usurpation of culture. With the aid of the patriarch in Constantinople, Greek had become the language of both the church and the majority of schools in Bulgaria. Many who saw oppression at the hands of the Greeks probably made exaggerated claims, but in an atmosphere of charged nationalism, scapegoats and myths are inevitable byproducts of emotion. Certainly, the demand for a national church was a critical aspect of the national revival.

In 1860 Bulgarians living in Constantinople disavowed the authority of Greek prelates over the Bulgarian church, setting in motion a decade-long struggle to bring back a Bulgarian church after almost a century. The patriarch, Ioachim, at first offered linguistic concessions to the critics, but was immediately rebuffed. His successor, Gregory VI, offered to create an autonomous Bulgarian church, but only with a jurisdiction limited to the Bulgarian lands, thereby keeping it out of Macedonia. This too was rejected. Finally the Ottomans issued a *firman* (decree) on 11 March 1870 (against the wishes of the patriarch) establishing a Bulgarian Exarchate, which, although limited territorially at first, provided for the possibility of later expansion (with clear implications for Macedonia). The exarchate, finally established in 1872 even though the patriarch declared it to be a heresy, proved to be the living symbol of a growing national consciousness.

Bulgarians were generally divided politically between those who wanted reforms within the Ottoman governing system and others (many of whom lived in the Danubian Principalities [Romania]) who sought full independence. Beginning in the 1830s, a number of revolutions occurred. Although they failed badly, a few of the leaders, notably Georgi Rakovski, Khristo Botev, Vasil Levski, and Liuben Karavelov, in defeat became the legendary leaders of Bulgarian independence.

Levski, a monk, joined a paramilitary group of Bulgarian émigrés in Serbia (along with Rakovski) and helped establish the Bulgarian Revolutionary Central Committee (BRCC), an organization devoted to fostering an armed insurrection in Bulgaria. Botev was educated in Odessa; while living in Romania, he published a number of newspapers, including one in collaboration with Karavelov, before joining the BRCC. Although Rakovski died in 1867 and Levski was hanged in 1873, the work of émigré radicals inspired a number of Bulgarians to believe the time was right for a rebellion. To spark that revolution they formed *cheti,* small groups whose aim was to attack the Ottomans and gain independence for Bulgaria. Unfortunately their first efforts failed, just as others had failed before.

In May 1876 a revolt broke out in central Bulgaria. Like other such uprisings, including one the year before, the Turks quickly put down the insurrection. However, in stopping the uprising, the Turks utilized irregular forces *(bashi-bazouks)* who exacted a harsh revenge on the local population for previous attacks upon Muslims. Their assaults came to be known as the Bulgarian Massacres, actions that inflamed the West and set the stage for Bulgaria to win its independence.

INDEPENDENCE

In 1875 a revolt in Bosnia-Hercegovina led to a call by Russian Pan-Slavists to aid their Christian Slavic brethren against the Turks. St. Petersburg was caught in the unenviable position of being drawn into war by a small but vocal minority while trying to avoid further chaos in the Balkans that might lead to a wider conflict.

Unable to withstand the calls by the Pan-Slavists to intervene in the Balkans, in April 1877 Russia went to war against the Turks yet again (the Russo-Turkish War of 1877–1878) and at first gained military success. By July, they had seized the Shipka Pass in central Bulgaria, and the door to the south temporarily appeared open. Turkish defenses, however, stiffened at Plevna, leading to months of intense fighting. By the time the Russian forces broke through, the war had become an issue for the great powers, not just the region; it was clear that Britain had no intention of allowing Russia to reach the sea (thus potentially threatening British interests in the eastern Mediterranean), and Britain made its feelings known. The Russian forces halted, and on 3 March 1878, St. Petersburg signed the Treaty of San Stefano with the Turks.

Among the numerous territorial provisions of the San Stefano treaty, an autonomous Bulgaria was to be created, with its borders stretching from the Danube River to the Aegean Sea. This "Big Bulgaria," as it came to be known, violated earlier pledges by Russia not to create a large client state. It also angered Serbia and Greece, which had claims to parts of the territory. And British fears of unfettered Russian access to the Mediterranean remained. Under pressure from numerous quarters, Russia now had to agree to meet in Berlin to revise the territorial provisions of San Stefano.

In June 1878 the Congress of Berlin convened. San Stefano Bulgaria was now divided into three parts: an autonomous Bulgarian state north of the Balkan Mountains; Eastern Rumelia, between the Rhodope and Balkan ranges, as a semiautonomous territory under Ottoman jurisdiction; and Macedonia and Thrace, which were returned to Ottoman control. While this division satisfied the desires of the Western powers to control both the disintegration of the Ottoman Empire and the perceived designs of Russia in Southeastern Europe, the treaty was a bitter disappointment for Bulgarian nationalists who refused to accept the new territorial boundaries.

Meanwhile, Bulgaria had attained autonomy, but not by the actions of any one internal political group, which meant that no national leadership had emerged to lead a successful revolt. Rather, those who had long run local affairs found themselves the national leaders by default. Moreover, Russia, which was, according to the Berlin treaty, granted the right to occupy Bulgaria for up to nine months, was made responsible for the formation of a new national government. Prince A. M. Dondukov-Korsakov, the Russian commissioner, now drew up a constitution; after it had been examined in St. Petersburg, it became the framework for the delegates who met in Turnovo in February 1879 to finalize a new government.

The Turnovo constitution called for the creation of a strong unicameral legislature (the Subranie), which was to be elected by universal manhood suffrage. Although the initial ruler was to be chosen by the great powers, special assemblies would have the power to confirm the ruler and amend the constitution. The document centralized power, but also granted significant powers to local areas, a recognition of the long tradition of local authority in the country.

Alexander of Battenberg, a twenty-two-year-old prince from Hesse in Germany (who was also related to both the royal houses of Russia and Great Britain), was selected as the new prince. Although a capable man, Alexander found himself suddenly enmeshed in both Bulgarian and great power politics, neither of which he was prepared to address. The latter proved to be the most troublesome, since the Russians, having failed to create a client state at San Stefano, now looked to maintain their influence in Bulgaria through a loyal Bulgarian army. All officers above the rank of captain, in fact, were of Russian origin. In 1881, with the assassination of the Russian tsar Alexander II, Alexander III came to the throne determined to exert influence in Bulgaria, which he believed owed loyalty to him and his government. This belief naturally irked many in Bulgaria, including Alexander of

Battenberg, who, despite being a relative of Alexander III, was neither close to St. Petersburg nor prepared to surrender authority to it.

This quarrel between the two Alexanders rather quickly spilled over into the matter of Eastern Rumelia. Although the latter was returned to nominal Ottoman oversight in 1878, it was generally understood that union with Bulgaria was a certainty. Societies inside Eastern Rumelia immediately formed demanding unification. Russia at first countenanced such a move, since it was the first step in restoring what it had lost at Berlin when San Stefano Bulgaria was partitioned. Then Alexander III grew reluctant to support any movement that would bring acclaim to what he perceived as a less-than-grateful Bulgarian prince.

In September 1885 a revolt in Eastern Rumelia and calls for unification with Bulgaria placed Alexander of Battenberg in an awkward position. According to the Treaty of Berlin, unification would require great power approval, and Russia was certain to oppose the union. But Bulgarian nationalists demanded Alexander of Battenberg's support, which he gave. Alexander III now withdrew his officers from the country, thus making Bulgaria an inviting target for Serbia, which sought to use the situation, especially a weakened Bulgarian army, to gain land. In November 1885 Serbian prince Milan ordered an invasion of Bulgaria, believing victory would be swift. It was, but not as Milan envisioned. To the surprise of most, the invaders were defeated, and as a result, the powers recognized the personal union of Bulgaria and Eastern Rumelia, that is, the joining of the two areas through the personage of the prince.

Despite the fact that this was supposed to be a personal union, Prince Alexander unified the assemblies of Bulgaria and Eastern Rumelia and began to rule one country. By now, Russia, which had hoped to be the promoter of unification, only to find itself at odds with a prince who received the credit, looked to end their problem with the prince by organizing a conspiracy to overthrow him.

In August 1886, a coup led by a conspiratorial group of officers forced Alexander of Battenberg to resign and leave the country. Despite Russian convictions that most Bulgarians were pro-Russian, however, the new government failed to gain support and was quickly removed by a countercoup led by Stephen Stambolov, a leading Liberal politician. Alexander of Battenberg was invited to return, but before doing so he erred. He wrote a letter to Alexander III, which, in effect, offered subservience to St. Petersburg. Resentful Bulgarian nationalists now forced him to abdicate for the second time, leaving Stambolov in charge of a regency to find a new prince.

Because of the precarious position in which Bulgaria found itself vis-à-vis Russia, finding a candidate willing to accept the throne was hardly a simple task. Finally, the special assembly called to name a prince offered the position to Ferdinand of Saxe-Coburg. He accepted, but becoming prince was one thing; ruling was quite another. Ferdinand had a throne but no great power support. He also had to contend with the powerful Stambolov, who until his resignation as prime minister in 1894 (and his subsequent assassination in 1895) was the most powerful figure in the

country. Finally, Ferdinand had to deal with the matter of Macedonia, the territory that inflamed the passions of Bulgarian nationalists.

Ferdinand had some success. He was able by 1896 to reach a rapprochement with St. Petersburg and thus finally gain international recognition. But the resolution of that international problem was easy in relation to the Macedonian Question.

At the Congress of Berlin in 1878, the great powers returned Macedonia to Ottoman authority, an action that angered both Macedonian nationalists, who hoped to create an independent state, and Bulgarians, who looked to regain the "Big Bulgaria" of the San Stefano treaty. Parts of Macedonia were claimed by Bulgaria, Greece, and Serbia. Organizations within Macedonia (as well as outside) formed to support the various claims, organizations such as the Cyril and Methodius Society, formed by Bulgarians in 1884. It was the Internal Macedonian Revolutionary Organization (IMRO), however, founded in Thessaloniki (Salonika) in 1893, which was to have the greatest impact on the region as well as on Bulgarian politics.

IMRO's membership was often split on the organization's objectives. Initially some supported incorporation within a larger South Slav federation. Others sought complete independence, launching a rebellion (the Ilinden Uprising) in August 1903, which, after some initial success, was put down by the Turks. Yet another group, called the Supremists (or the Macedonian External Organization), advocated annexation by Bulgaria. The Supremists had the support of the government in Sofia, and Bulgarian territory served as a base of operations for attacks against officials inside Macedonia. Violence was not, however, confined to Macedonia. Those who failed to back the goals of the Bulgarian and Macedonian nationalists became targets of IMRO and its supporters. Thus, no matter what progress Bulgaria seemed to make in the international arena, the danger of conflict, political or military, that surrounded the question of Macedonia and its relationship to Bulgaria was a millstone around the neck of the country, a situation that eventually led to disaster on multiple occasions.

Meanwhile, during the 1890s, thanks to its rapprochement with Russia, Bulgaria pursued a policy of modernization. Unfortunately, however, the expense of economic development fell heavily upon a peasantry little able to bear additional tax burdens. In the late 1890s poor harvests brought on by bad weather led to increased discontent in the countryside. Although the government met the demonstrators with violence, Ferdinand was forced to appoint a new ministry under Petko Karavelov to deal with the situation. Karavelov lowered the new taxes, but still the problems in the countryside had led to a new peasant movement, the formation of the Bulgarian Agrarian National Union (BANU, or BZNS). Although the Bulgarian Agrarian National Union was organized by intellectuals rather than peasants, it was a popular movement that sought to raise the quality of life in rural areas. At its first national meeting in 1899, BANU's delegates called for increased education and reform of the tax system. By 1901, when it actually adopted the name Bulgarian Agrarian

Ferdinand I (1861–1948) in his chauffeur-driven Mercedes convertible, ca. 1910. (Hulton-Deutsch Collection/Corbis)

National Union, it had become more political, and by 1908, led by Aleksandûr Stamboliiski, it had become the largest opposition party in the country. Although it was still a small voice in Bulgarian affairs, international events soon changed that.

In 1908 the annexation of Bosnia-Hercegovina by Vienna, which a weak government in Istanbul was unable to prevent, led to the formal independence of Bulgaria. Ferdinand declared himself tsar of Bulgaria. He saw himself as the ruler of a state that had been deprived of its rightful lands (primarily Macedonia), a view that led to a disastrous policy of war.

Although the Young Turk revolt in the Ottoman Empire in 1908 hoped to revitalize the once proud state, the dismemberment of the Turkish state quickened. In 1912 Bulgaria, Serbia, Greece, Montenegro, and Serbia formed a Balkan League, an alliance fostered by St. Petersburg as a counterforce to Austria-Hungary in the wake of Vienna's annexation of Bosnia-Hercegovina. St. Petersburg, however, did not foresee the Balkan League as an aggressive alliance;

that was a miscalculation. In October 1912 League armies attacked the Turks and quickly drove them back. Bulgarian troops even reached the outskirts of Istanbul before the parties reached a cessation of hostilities. At the London Conference in May 1913, Istanbul relinquished most of its remaining Ottoman possessions in Europe, including Macedonia, which was divided between the Greeks, Serbs, and Bulgarians.

Still, Bulgaria felt slighted by the territorial provisions of the Treaty of London. On the night of 29–30 June 1913, only a month after the signing of the treaty, Bulgaria attacked into Macedonia in a disastrous attempt to gain what it claimed as rightfully Bulgarian land. Not only did Sofia's former Balkan League allies counterattack, but Bulgaria also faced Romanian and Turkish troops. On 13 August 1913, Bulgaria was forced to sign the Treaty of Bucharest, losing most of its Macedonian lands to its former partners, as well as the rich agricultural land of the southern Dobrudja to Romania. Bulgaria was now isolated in the region as well as humiliated.

WORLD WAR I AND INTERWAR BULGARIA

As World War I broke out in Europe in the late summer of 1914, Bulgaria found itself increasingly drawn toward the Central Powers, led by Germany. In part this was due to its failure in the Second Balkan War. Equally important, the Entente, specifically its members Britain and France, had courted Serbia and Greece, the former because of its struggle against the Habsburg monarchy, the latter due to British concerns for the Mediterranean. Bulgaria, defeated by both Serbia and Greece in 1913, did not offer the Western allies the same advantages and might even threaten the Entente's position in Belgrade and Athens. By 1915, however, Britain, sensing the danger that prolonged war against the Ottoman Empire might create in the eastern Mediterranean, reversed its policy and began to court Sofia with offers of land in Macedonia (even telling Serbia to abandon some of its Macedonian territory so as to preclude the entrance of Bulgaria on the side of the Central Powers).

Britain's change in policy was futile. On 6 September 1915, Bulgaria signed a series of agreements with Berlin, which called for a Bulgarian attack on Serbia within thirty days. The Central Powers had decided to eliminate the Serbian front immediately, and Bulgarian military intervention in the rear would ensure victory. Seeing this move, the Entente countered by opening a front (the Salonika Front) in Greece that was intended to protect Serbia's southern flank; their efforts failed. Although Bulgarian actions in Macedonia were not crucial in the defeat of Serbia, they successfully kept the British and French from aiding their Balkan ally. Bulgaria had its land in Macedonia, and for the next three years the war in the south became a stalemate along the Salonika Front.

In 1916 Bulgaria turned its attention to the northeast. In August Romania entered the war on the side of the Entente with promises of territory (at Hungary's expense). While the initial Romanian attacks into Transylvania went well, German troops soon bolstered the forces of their Austro-Hungarian allies and drove the Romanians back. Bucharest had miscalculated by sending most of its troops against the Habsburg armies, leaving Romania's southern border exposed. On 2 September 1916, Bulgarian troops moved into the Dobrudja, pinching the Romanian army and forcing the abandonment of Bucharest.

Bulgaria had by 1916 forgotten the defeat of 1913. Territories lost had become territories regained. But the euphoria of victory proved to be fleeting, as the war ground on, weakening all parties. In the summer of 1918, Bulgarian defenses broke along the Salonika Front. As the Bulgarian armies retreated, troops mutinied at the headquarters in Kiustendil in the village of Radomir (near Sofia). The rebels demanded an end to the war, the release of political prisoners (including the Agrarian leaders Aleksandûr Stamboliiski and Raiko Daskalov), and punishment for those who had been responsible for the war.

On 27 September, Daskalov declared himself the commander of a new republic and marched toward Sofia. Although the government succeeded in defeating the insurgents, it was clear that Bulgaria had to withdraw from the war. On 29 September 1918, Bulgaria signed an armistice in Thessaloniki (Salonika); four days later, on 3 October, Ferdinand abdicated and left the country.

Bulgaria's defeat in World War I was the second military debacle to befall the country within five years. The Balkan Wars and World War I had resulted in the deaths of over 150,000 in only six years of fighting. This represented nearly 20 percent of the nation's male population between the ages of twenty and fifty. A comparable number of civilians also perished, due in large part to the outbreak of epidemics, notably the pandemic of flu that swept the globe after 1918. Thus, Bulgaria entered the postwar negotiations in a position of defeat and despair.

The Treaty of Neuilly, one of a series of treaties concluded between the victorious allies and the defeated Central Powers, was signed on 27 November 1919. In it, Bulgaria lost another 10 percent of its territory. But it was the geographic and economic significance of the loss that left the country bitter and politically divided throughout the interwar period. Not only was Sofia forced to cede strategic areas along the nation's borders, it lost important food-producing land in the southern Dobrudja, an area that had heretofore provided a significant portion of the country's agricultural harvest. This loss was compounded by the fact that during the war the nation had lost a significant portion of its livestock; it took decades to recover the breeding stock that had died. On top of the loss of territory, Bulgaria was, like its Central Power allies, forced to reduce its military and pay reparations to the victorious Allies.

All of the former Central Powers bridled at the conditions imposed by the peacemakers in Paris. For a nation that had fought two Balkan wars over territorial claims, the loss of additional land was a blow that was unacceptable, not only to nationalists but to the average Bulgarian as well. Nationalists now claimed that the number of "Bulgarians" living outside the boundary of the "homeland" numbered in the millions. These "foreign" Bulgarians (mostly Macedonians), they asserted, represented nearly one-third of all their countrymen and -women. To accept the provisions of Neuilly was anathema to any patriotic Bulgarian. Thus, revisionism, the desire to free themselves from the burdens imposed by Neuilly, and irredentism, the fixation on reclaiming territory that they believed wrongfully sat outside the true territorial boundaries of the country, drove Bulgarian nationalists even more passionately than before.

The most important issue for Bulgarian nationalists was what they perceived to be the continuing sore of Macedonia. Despite Sofia's claims to large portions of Macedonia, it held little more than 10 percent of the region, as compared with the 90 percent that was divided between Greece and the Kingdom of Serbs, Croats, and Slovenes (renamed Yugoslavia in 1929). Exacerbating Bulgarian resentment over the already volatile Macedonian Question was the fact that Yugoslavia administered its Macedonian lands poorly, while the Greeks used the territory as a place to resettle Greeks displaced from Turkey in 1922, following Greece's disastrous war against the Turkish nationalist leader Mustafa Kemal (Ataturk).

The emotional draw of Macedonia, combined with the continued influence of IMRO upon Bulgarian politics (still, in many ways, in a manner disproportionate to their numbers within the general population), left Bulgaria, its politicians, and its citizens captive to an issue that could only serve to divert the nation from its real, immediate problems. Worse, intimidation aimed at keeping the Macedonian Question at the forefront of the nation's agenda poisoned Bulgarian politics and destroyed any chances for regional rapprochement. Few Bulgarians were willing to be seen as "soft" on Macedonia. IMRO's tactics ensured that Macedonia was on the lips of all. Even when IMRO engaged in terrorist activities that worked against the interest of the nation and destabilized the country and the region, Bulgaria's politicians failed for decades to crack down on the organization, thereby guaranteeing that instability would be the norm.

The history of interwar Bulgaria was thus marked by numerous changes in government but few solutions to its problems. The political parties, over forty of which obtained representation in the national assembly, were often little more than personal mouthpieces for leading political figures. Even the peasant party, the Bulgarian Agrarian National Union, failed to become a magnet for reform, as it too fell prey to IMRO and the nationalists.

In 1919 association with the military failure in World War I led to the discrediting of the prewar and wartime "bourgeois" parties. After the first postwar elections, a coalition government was formed by the peasant leader and agrarian idealist Aleksandûr Stamboliiski. Stamboliiski's plan, unlike the course pursued by some of his peasant party counterparts in Central and Southeastern Europe, was to reduce the power of the cities and what he believed to be their ahistorical trends, and return Bulgaria to its village roots. In some respects, this program paralleled that of the failed Populist movement in the United States, with its attempt to turn the clock back to a perceived idyllic past. To that end, Stamboliiski mobilized the party's paramilitary organization, the Orange Guard, to suppress a communist-led general strike. Named for the colors of the BANU, the Guard organized in the rural areas, and when the strike broke out, thousands converged on Sofia to combat the strikers. Having broken the workers' movement, Stamboliiski called for new elections, which saw his party gain additional seats in the Subranie. Although his party at first fell short of gaining an absolute majority in the parliament, he invalidated the elections of three rival delegates, thus giving him the numbers he needed.

Stamboliiski envisioned the creation of a "Green International" to reconfigure relations in the region. This federation of like-minded peasant parties would serve as a bulwark against Western capitalism and Soviet Bolshevism. Guided by this dream, Stamboliiski overlooked the reality of Bulgaria's domestic and international position. First, the king, Boris, saw his own powers being eroded by the charismatic peasant leader. Second, Sofia's neighbors, especially the Kingdom of Serbs, Croats, and Slovenes, had little desire (or even incentive) to follow Stamboliiski's lead. Finally, in seeking a restructuring of the situation in postwar Southeastern Europe, Stamboliiski knew he had to avoid pursuing the matter of Macedonia; that realization however,

Tsar Boris III (1894–1949) presiding at a national festival. (Library of Congress)

although correct, ignored the emotional attachment to Macedonia that was felt by many in the country, especially those in positions of leadership, and the single-minded determination of IMRO to assassinate anyone who dared to stand in the way of their sole purpose in life, the restoration of Macedonia. Thus, whatever progress Stamboliiski made in the international arena paled next to the personal danger he incurred.

Stamboliiski's government was able to create a series of land, tax, and legal reforms that offered greater hope to the peasantry. In addition, he expanded educational opportunities to a nation that, despite the progress that had been made since the late 1800s, still failed to provide universal compulsory education. In the end, his reforms failed, not because they were not well intentioned, but because they fell victim to Stamboliiski's inability to deal with the Achilles' heel of irredentism.

Nationalist opposition to Stamboliiski and BANU grew in the early 1920s. In 1921 the minister of war was assassinated. Stamboliiski's opponents began to unite in a parliamentary bloc to oppose the government. The Orange Guard, which had become the paramilitary arm of the government, was unable to stem demonstrations by the Internal Macedonian Revolutionary Organization against BANU rule.

On 9 June 1923, a coup was initiated against the government. The coup was led by a shadowy clandestine organization of military officers known as the Military League *(Voenen Suiuz)*. Founded after World War I, the Military League had been ordered dissolved by Stamboliiski a year later; it quickly reorganized underground. The Treaty of Neuilly had required Bulgaria to cut the size of its military to 1,650 officers and 20,000 soldiers. The League thus initially was founded to preserve the camaraderie of the officer corps so as to be ready to defend the country against Bolshevik Russia. By 1922, it had joined the opposition coalition, the Constitutional Bloc. Although the exact details of the coup may never be entirely known (such as whether or not the conspirators had the tacit approval of Boris), the League quietly prepared to act, and when it struck, it did so with brutal force. Five days after the coup began, Stamboliiski died at the hands of the conspirators. He had been tortured before being beheaded and dismembered.

Although idealistic and demagogic, Stamboliiski had been a national leader. His conclusion that the fixation on Macedonia and the politics of the past could never serve a Bulgaria that had severe economic problems, a peasant agricultural base, and hostile neighbors wary of Bulgarian irredentism was at least pragmatic. With his death, perhaps Bulgaria's one chance to gain a measure of stability during the interwar period was lost.

As the coup of 9 June 1923 unfolded, a new government formed under the leadership of Aleksandûr Tsankov. Both the Peasant and Communist Parties were excluded from the new government and were repressed in a form of "white terror" (conservative attack) that targeted them for political reprisal. The Military League formed a special group to carry out assassinations of its political opponents.

A communist uprising in September 1923 was unable to rally the surviving remnants of the Stamboliiski regime or those who had been isolated by the Tsankov coalition. The uprising failed badly, giving Tsankov an anti-Bolshevik aura within many Western circles. The white terror that followed the aborted uprising witnessed a bloody suppression of the "Left" by the conservative forces that was reminiscent of the reprisals that followed the overthrow of the communist government of Béla Kun in Hungary in 1919. (Although suppressed and eventually outlawed in 1924, the Bulgarian Communist Party remained the strongest of the interwar communist parties in Southeastern Europe, often operating clandestinely through various "fronts.")

The wave of assassinations and political retribution following the events of June–Sepember 1923 resulted in a period of political chaos in Bulgaria. And even though the fall of the Tsankov government in 1926 led to an easing of the internal repression, IMRO's actions abroad continued to leave the country isolated within the region. As the 1920s drew to a close, the disastrous combination of political atrophy, regional isolation, and the economic effects of lost territory and markets left Bulgaria in an even more weakened position as the Great Depression spread throughout Europe.

Following World War I, the economies of all Europe's states felt severe strains. The creation of new countries, territorial revisions and the resulting revisionism that sought to reclaim the land, massive debts, and the desire to isolate the Bolshevik revolution in Russia, all served to destabilize the already fragile Balkans. Trading patterns shifted, as past markets disappeared. Countries tried to protect their own economies by creating high tariff barriers against foreign competition. The onset of the Great Depression only worsened the already tenuous position of the Bulgarian economy.

For a country like Bulgaria, heavily dependent upon agricultural exports, the loss of foreign markets was particularly devastating. As exports of tobacco and other commodities plummeted, so too did faith in the government. On 9 May 1934, a group of army officers (led by colonels, many of whom had been members of the Military League) and an ultranationalist secret society known as *Zveno* (Link), which had formed in 1927, initiated a coup against the government. Led by Colonel Damian Velchev, the coup succeeded in making Kimon Georgiev premier; despite their success in gaining power, however, the conspirators lacked both political experience and acumen. Espousing national regeneration was one thing; running the country was quite another. Their failure played right into the hands of the king.

In 1935 Boris suspended the constitution, which had been in place since 1879, thereby giving him virtually full power in the country. He outlawed political parties and created a legislature made up of approved deputies. Boris marginalized the influence of the Military League (many of whose members were antimonarchists) in the affairs of his government, and the organization quickly faded from influence. High-ranking appointments were mere tools of the king. He also placed the press and labor unions under government supervision. Perhaps the only positive step in his authoritarian regime was the suppression of IMRO, but that was hardly a sufficient answer to the nation's various maladies.

Although Boris ruled through a series of ministers until his death in 1943 at the age of forty-nine, his most significant decision was perhaps his pursuit of a pro-German foreign policy. Outwardly this seemed logical. Boris was pursuing a rightist agenda, like many countries in the region, and fascist Italy and Nazi Germany seemed to be models to emulate. More importantly, during the mid-1930s, Germany had stepped up its purchases of Bulgarian goods, thus tying Sofia more and more to the dictates of Berlin. Finally, Germany seemed to be the most powerful state in Europe, able to advance its agenda and destroy its opponents. Sensing this, Bulgaria's neighbors, Romania, Greece, Turkey, and Yugoslavia, formed a regional Balkan Pact to guarantee the boundaries of 1919. Bulgaria's isolation within Southeastern Europe made it obvious that being the ally of Germany offered benefits to Bulgaria, notably the return of land.

Boris's courtship of Berlin in 1940 proved fruitful, as Bulgaria was rewarded with the return of the southern Dobrudja (from Romania) in the Vienna Award. On the other hand, although German-Bulgarian diplomacy had reaped a territorial dividend, German operations against Greece in 1941 meant that Bulgaria would be drawn further into the war.

In March 1941 the head of Boris's puppet government, Bogdan Filov, signed the Tripartite Pact, thereby formally allying Bulgaria with Germany and Italy. As the German Wehrmacht entered Greece through the territory of its Bulgarian ally, Bulgarian troops deployed along the Turkish border so as to protect German operations on their left flank. Hitler, in turn, presented Boris with the portion of Macedonia that had been under Yugoslav control as well as Greek lands in western Thrace. For the moment, Bulgaria, as it had in 1915–1916, had obtained almost everything it had sought in the past. Boris was hailed by his propaganda organs as the unifier of the state. But success was fleeting.

Boris lobbied with Hitler to keep Bulgarian troops out of military operations in the Soviet Union. Past ties with Russia, he argued, were too strong. Despite his pleas, however, although Bulgarian troops did not enter Soviet territory, he had no choice but to join the Anti-Comintern Pact, the alliance aimed against the USSR. On 18 December 1941, Boris further blundered by declaring war against both Great Britain and the United States. Thus, while German troops were being halted in the snow outside Moscow, Bulgaria had declared war against two great powers and allied itself with Germany against a third, the Soviet Union.

To his credit, despite his alliance with Nazi Germany, Boris was able to find a way to send Bulgaria's Jewish population (which numbered almost 50,000) to rural areas in the country rather than deport them to the death camps. Although they lost their homes and possessions, Bulgaria's Jews were able to avoid the fate that befell so many others before war's end.

After meeting with Hitler on 14–15 August 1943 to discuss strategy, Boris returned home. Within days of his return, he fell ill, and he died shortly thereafter. A regency was quickly created for his son Simeon, who was six at the time of his father's death. For the moment, the cabinet remained steadfast in its support for Germany, but that was soon to change.

In early 1944 Allied bombing raids began to strike Sofia from air bases in Italy, causing a sizable portion of the population to flee and causing significant damage to the city. Although the cabinet continued to voice support for the Germans, Bulgarian leaders, like their counterparts in Romania (another German ally), now began to look for a way to avoid the inevitable. Bulgarian diplomats opened talks with the Allies, even offering to withdraw from the lands it had retaken. But the efforts were futile. On 5 September 1944, the Soviet Union declared war on Bulgaria. Four days later, a coup organized by the Fatherland Front, a coalition made up of the Bulgarian Communist Party, splinter groups of the Agrarian Union and the Social Democrats, Independents, and Zveno (a group of intellectuals and army officers), succeeded in toppling the government. Bulgaria's flirtation with Nazism had come to an end; its encounter with Marxist-Leninist Stalinism had just begun.

COMMUNISM AND POSTCOMMUNISM

Although the communists were never as large a party as the postwar propaganda claimed, the Bulgarian Communist Party (BCP) had advantages over their partners in the Fatherland Front. Of greatest help was the presence of the Soviet Red Army, which gave them cover and support. The communists also successfully marginalized their partners early; immediately following the takeover on 9 September, they began to use the police apparatus of the Interior Ministry to arrest, try, and execute political opponents under the guise of accusations that they were war criminals. These attacks upon the political opposition fractured the tenuous unity of the Fatherland Front, and an anticommunist movement now coalesced around Nikola Petkov, a leader of the Bulgarian Agrarian National Union. As a counterforce to the communist program, Petkov's popularity forced BCP temporarily to ease their crackdown. But behind the scenes, the communists continued to consolidate their power.

In 1946 a plebiscite was held that called for the creation of a republic. In elections in October, the Fatherland Front, dominated by BCP, won over 70 percent of the vote. Despite legitimate questions whether the vote count was accurate, and whether Petkov would have succeeded in truly free elections, Petkov had become the lightning rod for the anticommunists and the enemy of BCP. His fate, though, was sealed as much by events in the West as by the situation in Bulgaria. The day after the United States ratified the peace treaty formally ending the war against Bulgaria (1947), Petkov was arrested; communist officials no longer had to be cautious with political foes once the ink was dry on the treaty. In September 1947 he was hanged. Other opposition politicians were either arrested or fled abroad.

Clearly the West had written off Bulgaria (as well as much of Eastern Europe). In 1944 Winston Churchill had negotiated the so-called Percentages Agreement with Stalin, whereby the USSR was to play the preponderant role in postwar Bulgaria. By 1947, the communists were prepared to take 100 percent. In December 1947 a draft constitution, patterned after the Soviet model, formally codified the reality.

Georgi Dimitrov, the prime minister (and secretary general of BCP), who had returned to Bulgaria from the USSR, had been the principal mover behind the fall of the monarchy and the institution of the communist regime. Dimitrov now acted quickly to put in place a socialist agenda, nationalizing private property, cracking down on the independence of the Bulgarian Orthodox Church, closing Western schools, and setting up tribunals to punish political criminals. He also briefly explored the possibility of allying Bulgaria in a federation with Tito's Yugoslavia. Stalin, however, refused to countenance such a move, and Dimitrov, while conferring in Moscow with the Soviet leader before his death in July 1949, abandoned the plan.

With the death of Dimitrov and the break between Stalin and Tito, Bulgaria now was subjected to a new hunt for political enemies, that is, "Titoists." Anyone who had contacts with the Yugoslav leader or who had even remotely suggested pursuing a course not countenanced by Stalin was branded a traitor, a nationalist, or a deviationist. The most visible victim of the resulting reign of terror was Traicho Kostov, who had been in charge of economic affairs under Dimitrov. Because Kostov had advocated pursuing the national economic interests of Bulgaria rather than merely

Portrait of Georgi Dimitrov (1882–1949), Bulgarian communist leader instrumental in establishing communist rule in Bulgaria following World War II. (Hulton Archive/Getty Images)

supporting a Soviet-style program, he was denounced by Dimitrov prior to his death, tried in December 1949, and executed.

Leadership of Bulgaria now fell to Vulko Chervenkov, a relative of Dimitrov and a disciple of Stalin. Chervenkov immediately embarked on a political purge of the Party designed to cleanse it of those who had been "infected" by Kostov. Economically, he also pushed a rapid program of collectivization, much as Stalin had done. He also forced over 150,000 ethnic Turks out of Bulgaria, and the numbers would have been much greater had Turkey not closed the border. Although Chervenkov saw himself in the mold of the Soviet dictator, the would-be Stalin did not long survive the death (in 1953) of his mentor.

In 1954 Chervenkov, having allied himself with the wrong side in the power struggle that took place in Moscow after Stalin's death, was replaced as general secretary of the Party by Todor Zhivkov; two years later he yielded his post of prime minister as well to his longtime rival Anton Yugov. For the next five years, Zhivkov, a seemingly drab figure, consolidated his hold on the Party apparatus through the power of appointment. In 1961 he ousted

Chervenkov from all positions of authority for his past errors and his "cult of personality." A year later, Zhivkov did the same to Yugov, charging him with a list of offenses ranging from incompetence to rudeness. For the next twenty-seven years, Todor Zhivkov was the face of the Bulgarian leadership.

In May 1971 Zhivkov promulgated a new constitution to replace the "Dimitrov Constitution" of 1947. In it, he made official the role of the Bulgarian Communist Party as the guiding spirit of the state and the Soviet Union as Bulgaria's inseparable friend. Moreover, despite encouraging economic growth, due in large measure to détente in the international arena and foreign investment, increasingly Bulgaria under Zhivkov tied its economic fortunes to the Soviet model and the Soviet trading system, Comecon. As a consequence, the nation fell further and further behind the West, and even some developing nations, economically and technologically. A stagnant economy produced heavy borrowing from the West but no real reform. Rather than dealing with the realities of a failed system, Zhivkov instead resorted to ethnic jingoism by renewing the attack upon the Turkish and Muslim minority; officials even charged that unless measures were taken the Turks would take over the country, due to their higher birthrate.

By the 1980s, the economy had not only stalled but was in severe decline. Even the Soviet Union could no longer be counted upon, as the reforms of Mikhail Gorbachev (glasnost [openness] and perestroika [restructuring]) were generally ignored in Bulgaria. Frustration with conditions grew. Demonstrations began, demanding changes. Human rights and environmental groups chronicled the regime's abuses. And as the fissures in the Soviet bloc widened in 1989, leading to the collapse of communism in one country after another, Bulgaria's Party leaders, led by Zhivkov's foreign minister, Petûr Mladenov, came to believe that only the removal of the leader could save the Party. On 10 November 1989, Zhivkov resigned. In the final analysis, despite this shift in power, Zhivkov had been ousted by his former colleagues in the Party not so much because of what he was doing, but rather in an attempt to save their own political positions, even if their power could only survive in another form and by another name. The era of Soviet-imposed communism had come to an end. The often painful transition to a democracy, the reintegration of Bulgaria into the wider world community, and the creation of a civil society had begun.

The political stranglehold over the country by the communists had ended, but at first the change was little more than cosmetic. The Bulgarian Communist Party changed its name to the Bulgarian Socialist Party (BSP) and succeeded in winning a majority (albeit bare) in the June 1990 elections behind slogans calling for reforms and greater economic freedoms. Even though this was a multiparty election, the first in a half-century, it was the communists who, for the moment at least, had the political apparatus to deliver the vote.

Despite the victory of the BSP at the polls, demonstrations continued in the streets. The Union of Democratic Forces (UDF), a coalition of opposition parties, formed and pressed demands for the "former" communists to resign. The Socialists responded by naming a UDF leader, Zheliu Zhelev, a former Communist who had become a popular symbol of the need for change due to his earlier opposition to the policies of Zhivkov, as president. This new coalition now set about to write a new constitution.

While Bulgarian political leaders looked to create a workable political structure, ethnic and economic problems continued. The past attacks by the Zhivkov regime on the country's ethnic Turkish and Gypsy populations remained sores. Moreover, when the government announced a program of economic austerity to deal with the nation's foreign debt, demonstrations took place demanding higher wages and guarantees of employment. A vicious cycle now had emerged. To correct the legacy of economic neglect and poor decisions, the government had to make hard choices that caused pain. When that pain was felt, demonstrations forced the government to increase wages and pledge to keep open unproductive enterprises, the latter one of the root causes of the economic malaise. This in turn resulted in higher inflation and the need for economic measures that required austerity and pain. Keeping open failed industrial complexes meant that resources were sapped and the overhauling of a system that in many ways had already died in the 1980s was delayed.

In 1991 parliamentary elections resulted in the defeat of the BSP, officially removing Bulgaria from communist control, but what replaced it failed to bring the stability and change that many in the country myopically thought would follow. Parliamentary democracy meant coalition governments with different constituencies and different demands. It also meant that governments could rise and fall quickly, thus lessening the chances for continuity and increasing the chances for inertia. This was quickly obvious in the rapid collapse of the first government, under Philip Dimitrov, by 1992. A second coalition under Liuben Berov likewise failed, and in elections in 1994 the Socialists returned to power.

The Socialists won in 1994 because UDF had failed to deliver improvements in living standards. The new prime minister, Zhan Videnov, was a disciple of Mikhail Gorbachev's belief in the need for restructuring. However, that required loans from the World Bank and the International Monetary Fund, monies Videnov was unable to procure because the international agencies demanded actions that would have required economic austerity to reduce the 100 plus percent inflation rate. To take such actions would have incurred the wrath of the population; the failure to do so, however, meant that conditions continued to deteriorate, thereby further incurring the wrath of the population.

By the mid-1990s, Bulgaria was in many respects a Third World nation economically. Real wages had declined, inflation had eroded the lifestyles of many, banks had collapsed and foreign loans and credits had failed to materialize (thus making capital difficult to obtain), and health care had declined. New elections now returned the UDF to power, as the political carousel continued to spin.

The new leader, Ivan Kostov, called for economic reforms designed to gain foreign aid and, more importantly,

pave the way for admission into the European Union. To gain that admission required a better record on human rights. Overtures toward the Turkish minority proved to be a positive sign. While substantive steps were being taken on one human rights front, however, on another, namely freedom of the press, there was a regression. A new law limited freedom of speech in the name of protecting domestic tranquillity.

Almost a decade after the fall of Zhivkov, Bulgaria began to move ahead with the difficult matter of privatization and inefficient industries. Long overdue, the program succeeded in stemming the economic downhill spiral.

In 2001 new parliamentary elections were held. As elections neared, it appeared as if it would again be a struggle between the BSP and UDF. However, the former king, Simeon II, announced that he was heading a new political party, the Simeon National Movement (SNM), which provided an alternative for those disillusioned by the failures of the two principal parties. In June SNM won 50 percent of the seats in parliament, and Simeon was asked to become prime minister and form a government.

Made up of reformers, many of whom were educated in the Western capitalist environment, the new government cleverly allayed the fears of foreign investors by its pragmatic program of reform. And even though in November the country elected as president the BSP leader, Georgi Parvanov, who made it clear that he was going to ensure that the new parliament did not abandon Bulgaria's social commitments in favor of a rush to capitalism, Bulgaria had a new public face.

Symbolic of that new direction was Bulgaria's improved international standing. Despite tensions that are always a danger in the Balkans (Bulgaria, for example, was the first state to recognize Macedonian independence in 1992, but refused to admit the existence of a Macedonian language, insisting it was really Bulgarian), Bulgaria has avoided the inter-Balkan squabbles that so strained relations and resources in the past. Moreover, progress was made in gaining admission to the EU (European Union) and NATO (the North Atlantic Treaty Organization). Bulgaria made a calculated move to improve relations with the United States by supporting American intervention in Iraq in 2002–2003. This support furthered the possibility of Washington moving bases from Western Europe to the Balkans so as to be closer to vital interests in the Middle East; such an action would provide an economic boost to the country as well as accelerate the chances for entrance into the EU and NATO.

Thus, at the beginning of the twenty-first century, Bulgaria, at least to outward appearances, seemed to have begun a process that in one way or another had eluded the country for centuries, namely full integration into the European and global communities.

POLITICAL DEVELOPMENTS

Ironically, the most stable period in Bulgarian political history was the four decades of communist rule (1947–1989). This is not surprising, given the late emergence of an independent Bulgarian state in the late nineteenth century, a

Ivan Kostov, prime minister of Bulgaria (1997–2001). (Reuters/Corbis)

state formed after years of struggle against the Turks but with few developed political institutions that could serve as the foundation of a successful political state. Much of Bulgarian political history has been a search for political stability, a goal that remained elusive even at the dawn of the twenty-first century.

For centuries after the destruction of the Second Bulgarian Empire in 1396, the Ottoman Turks ruled the Bulgarian lands. Because of Bulgaria's close proximity to Constantinople, the Turks controlled the territory more closely than they did some of their more distant lands (although the Turks were content to leave many of the local regions relatively alone if the taxes were paid). The destruction of the past ruling elite left the country with few native leaders outside of the village. A native nobility did not exist, as it did in some of Bulgaria's neighbors. Village leaders certainly continued to run local affairs, much as they had before. But, for most Bulgarians, the political elite was often little more than the head of the *zadruga,* the extended family unit around which the lives of most Bulgarians revolved. The Turkish overlords were just that. Day-to-day life and politics remained local, and they were to remain that way for centuries.

The modern Bulgarian state did not emerge until the nineteenth century. A small elite group of wealthy Bulgarians and intellectuals, many of whom lived abroad, became the leaders of a movement that, in large part owing to the Russo–Turkish War of 1877–1878, brought a Bulgarian state into being.

In 1879 an assembly gathered in Turnovo and drew up a constitution that created a unicameral parliament (Subranie) with a German prince, Alexander of Battenberg, to serve as monarch. Although at first Alexander had the backing of St. Petersburg, he quickly lost favor with the Russian tsar, Alexander III, and in 1886 the prince was deposed by a faction of pro-Russian officers.

A new prince, Ferdinand of Saxe-Coburg, accepted the throne in 1887, but the real power in Bulgaria was in the hands of Stefan Stambolov, who had headed a regency to find a successor to Alexander of Battenberg. Stambolov pushed a program of modernization, including an expansion in education internally, and an external program of making inroads in Macedonia with the eventual aim of incorporating it. His strong-armed policies however fell out of favor with many, especially the prince, and a year after he resigned (in 1894), he was assassinated by Macedonian revolutionaries.

With the death of Stambolov, Ferdinand was able to govern more directly. He successfully expanded the Bulgarian economy and education, and Bulgaria earned the praise of many, including the former U.S. president Theodore Roosevelt. However, his reign also saw an increase in foreign debt, political assassinations, and a devastating defeat in the Second Balkan War, which cost the country the valuable agricultural land of the southern Dobrudja (as well as the lives of over 60,000 Bulgarian soldiers combined in the two Balkan wars).

In 1915 Ferdinand and his prime minister, Vasil Radoslavov, entered into an agreement with Germany allying Bulgaria with the Central Powers in World War I. While initially Bulgaria regained lands lost in the Second Balkan War and occupied most of Macedonia, by 1918, the war had turned against the Bulgarians. Troops revolted, and Ferdinand and his new foreign minister, Aleksandûr Malinov, sought an armistice with the Entente, which was signed on 29 September. It was, however, too late to save the crown for Ferdinand, who abdicated in favor of his son Boris days later.

Politicians who had supported the wars that had so debilitated the country were discredited by 1918. This enabled the agrarian leader Aleksandûr Stamboliiski, the head of the Bulgarian Agrarian National Union (BANU), to form a coalition government. Stamboliiski now pursued a program designed to support Bulgaria's peasants, pursue economic recovery, create a Green International to act as a counterforce to Western capitalism and Soviet Bolshevism, and promote regional stability. The latter however proved to be his undoing, since it required him to direct Bulgaria away from its obsession with Macedonia.

For Bulgarian politicians before and after World War I, Macedonia was their Achilles' heel, and IMRO (the Internal Macedonian Revolutionary Organization) the joker in the deck. Members of IMRO supported either full autonomy for Macedonia or its incorporation into the Bulgarian state. With Serbia, Greece, and Bulgaria all holding claims to the region, the "Macedonian Question" was one of the most divisive issues in the southern Balkans. Its emotional appeal drowned out rational discussions. For IMRO and Bulgarian nationalists there could be no surrender on the issue. Stamboliiski's move to promote better regional relations with Bulgaria's neighbors meant that the Macedonian issue would not be pursued, and therefore Stamboliiski would be pursued, by IMRO and conservative factions within Bulgaria. For anyone who opposed IMRO, assassination was an omnipresent danger.

In June 1923 a coup, led by elements of IMRO and the army, the so-called Military League, bloodily overthrew Stamboliiski, who was tortured and dismembered. A new rightist government, headed by Aleksandûr Tsankov, initiated a wave of terror against its opponents. In 1926 Andrei Liapchev formed a new cabinet and pursued a more moderate policy, even granting new rights to opposition parties.

For a brief moment, Bulgarian politics seemed to stabilize. Although political assassinations on the part of IMRO continued, Liapchev was able to maintain his government

Through the Bulgarian Agrarian National Union, Aleksandûr Stamboliiski (1879–1923) became the champion of peasant rights and the founder of the Green International, an organization of European peasant parties. A prime minister following World War I, he was assassinated following a coup in 1923. (Hulton Archive / Getty Images)

for five years. However, by the early 1930s, with the economic downturn brought on by the onset of the Great Depression, Bulgaria was isolated in the region.

In 1931 Liapchev's coalition lost decisively in free elections. A new "People's Bloc," a broad-based coalition, took control of the government, but not the worsening situation in the country. On 19 May 1934, a political group known as Zveno (Link), formed by Dimo Kazasov, and the Military League (*Voenen Suiuz*), a clandestine group of disaffected army officers led by Damian Velchev, overthrew the government and formed a new one under the leadership of Kimon Georgiev. The new cabinet, called the Nineteenth of May Government, dissolved the Subranie and banned political parties. They even succeeded in disarming IMRO. Factional infighting, however, forced the resignation of Georgiev, thereby permitting the king, Boris, to rule with virtually no opposition.

Aleksandûr Stamboliiski

Born in the town of Slavovitsa in 1879, Aleksandûr Stamboliiski never forgot his peasant roots. Although Southeastern Europe's economy at the beginning of the twentieth century was based heavily on peasant agriculture, and peasant parties were important political movements in every country, no one came to represent the interests of peasants more visibly than Stamboliiski.

After studying agriculture in Germany, Stamboliiski returned to Bulgaria with a firm commitment to peasant rights. That belief in the peasant movement led to his creation of a Green International in 1920. Only an international organization of peasant parties, he believed, could ensure social justice and economic prosperity for the peasant class. Such an organization would be a bulwark against Bolshevism in the East and capitalism in the West. These forces were in his view antithetical to peasant welfare and traditions.

In 1903 Stamboliiski became the editor of *Agrarian Banner* (*Zemledelsko zname*), the party organ of the Bulgarian Agrarian National Union (BANU [Bulgarian: BZNS]), and eventually rose to head the party. The Bulgarian Agrarian National Union, like other peasant parties, formed in the late nineteenth century (1899), calling for easy credit for peasants and an end to oppressive taxation. Stamboliiski saw the peasants not as a class but rather as a distinct occupational group. As time went on, peasant agrarian parties, including BANU, grew more political in their approach as commercialized agriculture disrupted traditional agrarian society. But, like other such political movements, the party had little power before World War I.

Stamboliiski was elected to the Bulgarian parliament (Subranie) in 1908. A vocal critic of his country's military actions in the Balkan Wars and again in World War I, he was imprisoned by King Ferdinand during the latter. Bulgaria's defeat in 1918 left the conservative parties discredited, and Stamboliiski rode the wave of disillusionment brought on by the country's defeat to become prime minister in 1919. He represented Bulgaria at the peace conference in Paris that formally ended World War I.

Concerned about the state of Bulgaria's economy, Stamboliiski worked for agricultural reform and the agrarian movement abroad. Land reform, education, and revision of the tax code that fell heavily on the peasants became the cornerstones of his activities. In addition, he promoted the idea of compulsory national labor service. What he failed to do, however, was to understand the power of the Bulgarian irredentist dream of regaining Macedonia. Despite three failed wars begun, in large measure, to reclaim Macedonian lands, the nationalistic appeal of a Macedonia incorporated into a greater Bulgaria was still alluring to many. Stamboliiski correctly realized that peace with his neighbors, especially with the Kingdom of Serbs, Croats, and Slovenes (the future Yugoslavia), was essential for the country's future. This required international peace and thus a cessation in the activities of IMRO (Internal Macedonian Revolutionary Organization), which supported armed bands in the region and was a powerful political force in Bulgaria.

In 1923 a conspiratorial group composed of conservatives, the military, and members of IMRO organized a coup that overthrew Stamboliiski. After being tortured for days, the peasant leader was killed. With his death, the country reverted to a state of instability that was to define Bulgarian politics throughout the interwar period.

Boris named officials who would follow his dictates and do his bidding. He allowed elections in 1938, but they were almost scripted, as candidates were not even permitted to represent parties. The election gave him the appearance of allowing political discussion, but the reality was that Bulgaria was being run by the king's personal rule.

In the late 1930s Boris and Bulgaria drew closer to Nazi Germany. In February 1940 a new cabinet formed under the leadership of the pro-German professor Bogdan Filov. The move toward alliance with Germany offered the temptations of land, notably the southern Dobrudja, Thrace, and Macedonia. The former was restored to Bulgaria by the German-imposed Vienna Award. After German actions against Greece and Yugoslavia, Bulgarian troops occupied significant por-

tions of the other two areas. By siding with Germany again, however, again above all because of the lure of resolving its territorial demands, Bulgaria had joined a conflict in which defeat would have a profound effect upon the nation's future.

By 1943, when Boris died unexpectedly at the age of forty-nine, German troops were in retreat in Russia, and the Allied landings in Italy opened the door to air attacks upon Sofia itself. Defeat was inevitable. So too was the political future of the nation, as the Soviet Union declared war on Bulgaria on 5 September 1944. The resulting Red Army invasion and occupation inaugurated over four decades of communist control of the nation.

Following the publication of the *Communist Manifesto* in 1848 and, more importantly, *Das Kapital,* the first volume of which appeared in 1867, the ideas of Karl Marx spread from the industrial countries of Western Europe into the Balkans. In 1891 the Bulgarian Social Democratic Party was founded, under the leadership of Dimitûr Blagoev. Blagoev was drawn to Marxism while studying in Russia. After his expulsion from Russia in 1885, he returned to Bulgaria and began his political activities. In 1903 he broke away from his own creation to form the Bulgarian Workers' Social Democratic Party (BWSDP, the "Narrow Socialists") rather than compromise his "pure" Marxism by reaching out to the rural areas; such an action would, he believed, violate his dedication to the proletariat. This single-mindedness, strengthened in 1917 by the success of the Bolsheviks in Russia, even caused him to refuse to come to the aid of the agrarian government of Stamboliiski when it was overthrown by a rightist coup in 1923.

Given the peasant nature of Bulgaria before World War I, it is not surprising that the fledgling socialist party, based on the industrial working class, grew slowly, but by 1919, when it officially became the Bulgarian Communist Party (BCP), it had become a significant force in the Subranie. Its power, however, was short-lived. Following the violent overthrow of the Stamboliiski government, and the subsequent September uprising (organized by the communists), the Party was officially outlawed in April 1924. A number of the Party's leaders were killed, and many others either went underground or fled abroad. Although it attempted to reformulate itself under different names, it continued to operate clandestinely (especially after the banning of all political parties in 1934) and continued to take its directions from Moscow.

After World War I, the Bulgarian Communist Party joined the Comintern, the Third Communist International. The BCP, like other such movements, henceforth took its marching orders from Moscow. In the 1930s that meant fealty to the directives of Josef Stalin.

During the interwar period, the most prominent figure in the BCP was Georgi Dimitrov, who had been elected to the central committee of the Bulgarian Workers' Social Democratic Party and became a member of parliament in 1913. Following the failure of the poorly organized workers' uprising of September 1923, which he had helped organize, he fled Bulgaria and eventually moved to Moscow in the mid-1930s, where he was elected the head of the Comintern. Although many foreign leaders suffered at the hand of Stalin during the purges of the late 1930s, Dimitrov succeeded in not only surviving but directing the Comintern's antifascist policies.

In August 1943 the Bulgarian Communist Party, led by Dimitrov (who had returned to Bulgaria), organized an underground coalition of antifascist parties, the Fatherland Front. On the night of 8–9 September 1944, the Fatherland Front conducted a coup that overthrew the government and installed a coalition cabinet composed of Communist, Agrarian, Social Democratic, and Zveno members.

With Bulgaria out of the war, the Fatherland Front gave the BCP the cover it needed for its political activities. BCP was highly organized and had the support of the occupying Soviet Red Army. BCP supervised political and economic activities in local areas under the direction of the new prime minister, Georgi Dimitrov. Despite the existence of an Allied Control Commission, made up of Soviet, American, and British representatives, Moscow, which had secretly negotiated the so-called Percentages Agreement with British prime minister Winston Churchill earlier that year (which granted the Soviet Union a preponderance of power and control in Bulgaria), watched as Dimitrov repressed political opposition with impunity. In early 1945 BCP forced the Fatherland Front to endorse the creation of a single list of candidates for the Subranie, thereby ensuring their electoral success. Meanwhile, working within the system for the moment, BCP placed its members in key positions in the government, while at the same time eliminating independent organizations and banning opposition parties. In elections in 1946, the communists won the majority of seats in the parliament.

In December 1947 the parliament issued a new constitution for Bulgaria, which simply codified the new political reality; the communist takeover was complete. By the following year, its coalition partners in the Fatherland Front had either been ousted, sworn loyalty to BCP, or merged with it. Now firmly in control, the Party embarked on the classic Stalinist program of industrialization, collectivization, central planning, and the creation of a new society. Along with that overturning of Bulgarian society and politics came terror and political purges.

The new constitution continued the unicameral national assembly, but it was little more than a body designed to endorse the actions of the Party. Modeled along the lines of the Soviet constitution, it guaranteed freedoms on paper (from speech and press to religion) but those liberties were mere words. Churches were placed under state control. Independent organizations were brought under Party control.

In 1949, following the death of Dimitrov, Vulko Chervenkov, who had joined the Party in 1919, became prime minister. Like other Stalinists in Eastern Europe, he ruled with an iron fist and a cult of personality. After the death of Stalin in 1953, Chervenkov eased the terror campaign in an attempt to maintain power, but he was forced to step down as Party general secretary in 1954. Two years later, he was forced to resign as prime minister. For the next five years, Chervenkov shared power with Anton Yugov, the new prime minister, and Todor Zhivkov.

In 1962 Zhivkov, an advocate of industrialization and collectivization, was able to oust his two rivals from the Party. He cleverly began to place his own followers in key positions, while purging those who might prove to be a counterforce to his program and position. By the middle of the decade, new restrictions had been placed upon the arts. In 1968 Bulgaria supported the Soviet actions in Czechoslovakia that ended that country's brief flirtation with a more liberal socialism. Firm internal control and support for Soviet policies abroad were the mainstays of BCP policy through the 1970s.

A new constitution was written in 1971, which defined the Party as the leading force in society. The liberties of the previous constitution were continued, but only as they applied to the interests of the nation. Almost all private property was abolished. A new State Council was created, now headed by Zhivkov after he resigned as prime minister, and the new council had broad powers over legislation.

Although the early 1970s saw an easing of international tensions (détente) and a rise in foreign investment, the Helsinki Accords of 1975 raised hopes that greater freedom would follow at home. Like the rest of the world, Bulgaria felt the pinch of rising energy costs after the oil embargo of 1973. Discontent in Bulgaria resulted in antigovernment demonstrations. Zhivkov responded with cosmetic reforms and demagoguery.

During the 1981 celebration of the 1,300th anniversary of the first Bulgarian state, Zhivkov announced the rehabilitation of political foes and eased restrictions on the church. However, the Party also launched a renewed campaign against the ethnic Turkish minority. Early actions in the 1950s and 1970s had limited Turkish language instruction and closed schools. This new wave, which lasted until Zhivkov's last days in office, forced Turks to adopt Bulgarian names and even outlawed circumcision, as part of a full-fledged assault on Turkish Muslim culture. By 1989, hundreds of thousands of Turks had been forced from the country.

As cracks appeared in the Soviet empire in the 1980s, dissent grew, even within the Party. Some leaders looked to follow the program of glasnost and perestroika (openness and restructuring) advocated by the Soviet leader Mikhail Gorbachev. Zhivkov promised reforms, including decentralized planning, but there were few tangible moves to change the system. In a speech to the Party in October 1989, Zhivkov admitted that his plan to renew society and the economy had largely failed.

In 1989, throughout Eastern Europe, regimes fell, emboldening those in other countries to take to the streets. Pressure began to build on Zhivkov. A group, which included the prime minister, Georgi Atanasov, defense minister Dobri Dzhurov, and foreign minister Petûr Mladenov, received the support of the Party and of Moscow to move against Zhivkov. On 3 November 1989, a mass demonstration took place in Sofia. One week later, a plenary meeting of the Party's Central Committee announced that Zhivkov had resigned. The Party had tried to save itself, but it was too late; communist control over Bulgaria was over, and a search for a new political stability had begun.

Following Zhivkov's ouster, the Bulgarian Communist Party changed its name to the Bulgarian Socialist Party (BSP) in April 1990 in an attempt to preserve power. Mladenov, the foreign minister for the better part of two decades and the successor to Zhivkov as president from November 1989 until he was replaced in July 1990, was a disciple of perestroika. Such a program, BCP hoped, would reform the state within a socialist structure. (Hard-liners, however, gathered the remnants of the "true believers" in a new Party of the Working People; in June 1990 they retook the name BCP.)

By appearing to support democratization (the Party had renounced Marxism-Leninism at its Fourteenth Congress in January-February 1990), BSP had ended the communist monopoly on Bulgarian political life.

In April 1990 the Subranie ratified a new electoral law. Of the 400 seats in the National Assembly, half were to be elected directly, and the other half would be proportionally elected from the parties that obtained at least 4 percent of the vote. In June the first free elections in a half-century took place, with over a 90 percent turnout.

Despite abandoning the past communist program in favor of democratic pluralism, BSP was the first former communist party to succeed in winning in multiparty elections (with 211 seats). The Union of Democratic Forces (UDF) finished second (144 seats), and the Movement for Rights and Freedoms (MRF, the "Turkish Party") received 23 seats. The once-powerful Bulgarian Agrarian National Union received only 16 seats.

BSP now moved to create reforms needed for foreign credits through the International Monetary Fund, but a coalition of opposition groups, the Union of Democratic Forces (UDF), refused to endorse the Socialist program. By the autumn of 1990, street demonstrations and strikes had led to the resignation of the prime minister, Andrei Lukanov, and the installation of the first noncommunist prime minister in over four decades. New elections were scheduled for the following year. In addition, the UDF leader Zheliu Zhelev succeeded Mladenov as president.

In October 1991, out of the 240 seats elected by proportional voting (following a new electoral law promulgated in September 1991), UDF won a narrow victory (110 seats) over the Socialists (106 seats), who were identified with a program of austerity. Led by the new prime minister, Filip Dimitrov, UDF had secured its victory only by forming a coalition with the MRF, representing the Turkish Muslim minority, which had won 24 seats. Genuine reform and change now appeared to be a distinct possibility. Zhivkov and other high-ranking members of the communist regime were put on trial. Zhivkov himself was sentenced to seven years in prison (although he only served four under house arrest before his sentence was commuted). But the new government, like its predecessor, failed to answer the myriad economic problems facing the nation, and by late 1992 Dimitrov fell from power as a new parliamentary coalition formed.

In December 1994 the Socialists returned to power, winning over half the seats (125) in the Subranie. Despite the lack of real economic progress, Bulgaria was a nation of firsts. Just as it had been the first to elect a communist government in multiparty elections and later to sentence former officials, now it was the first to return the former Communist Party, albeit with a different name, to power. For the next year there was relative political quiet. The new prime minister, Zhan Videnov, a critic of his Socialist colleagues' failures to reform the system, now pursued aid from the IMF and the World Bank. But in order to obtain such assistance, Bulgaria had to make choices that would alter social spending in order to bring down inflation, something a Socialist government could not do.

In 1996 the economy suffered a steep decline. Unrest grew, symbolized by the assassination of former prime minister Lukanov. Grain shortages, runaway inflation (over 300 percent), a steep decline in real wages and the gross domestic

Demonstration by opposition in Sofia, 4 January 1997. (Jacques Langevin/Corbis Sygma)

product, and street demonstrations undermined the government, and in April 1997, six months after the Socialists lost the presidency, the revolving door that was Bulgarian politics turned again. The Union of Democratic Forces formed a coalition and, led by Ivan Kostov, returned to power.

Only in 1996 did Bulgarian politicians begin a concerted effort to address the lack of reform that so crippled the country. Of greatest importance was the failure to develop a true program of privatization that would return land to farmers and revitalize the industrial sector by closing outdated plants and creating an entrepreneurial environment conducive to attracting investment. Equally significant was the stifling rate of inflation, which undermined chances for critical foreign investments and caused internal discontent.

By 1996, governments had risen and fallen at a bewildering pace, but little of substance had occurred. Victories were narrow, thus giving successive governments no real mandate for governing. Frustration grew while wages declined. Kostov was thus placed in a delicate position, but one that required action.

Kostov pushed through parliament laws cracking down on crime, encouraging foreign investment, and pushing the pace of privatization. He granted NATO (the North Atlantic Treaty Organization) the right to use Bulgarian airspace to fly missions against Serb positions during the 1999 crisis in Kosovo. He was criticized for his crackdown on the press, but inflation was brought under control, and productivity rose.

As elections scheduled for June 2001 neared, the country was still divided between UDF and BSP. Then a surprise

occurred, with the announcement by the former king, Simeon II, that he had formed a political organization, the Simeon National Movement (SNM), which received the endorsement of the Turkish party. Other voters too were excited by a party that not only offered something new, but that, due to the presence of Simeon, created a sense of nostalgia. Kostov's shock therapy had admittedly improved the economy, but the pain felt by many naturally brought resentment. The BSP, while offering a safety net, had failed to make the necessary changes when it had been in power. Simeon promised improvements in living standards within three years.

On the first ballot, Simeon's party won half the seats in the Subranie; with the MRF, they held a clear majority. Simeon, the ex-king, became the new prime minister. By virtue of his past experience outside the country, Simeon was able to bolster foreign confidence in Bulgaria's ability to tackle its problems. Simeon also displayed a deft touch in foreign affairs, continuing Kostov's policies aimed at strengthening regional and European ties with the ultimate goal of gaining admission to both NATO and the European Union.

Despite this enhancement of its international position and achievement of a measure of internal stability, politics in Bulgaria remained volatile. Months after what seemed like a decisive victory by SNM, the BSP candidate for president, Georgi Parvanov, was elected, defeating the incumbent, who was a supporter of Simeon's program. This led to continued inertia, as the new president was in a position to veto bills that he and the Socialists believed moved the economy too fast. Although his votes could be overridden, Parvanov's position as president remained an indication that gridlock, which had hampered progress for a decade, was still not far from the surface in postcommunist Bulgaria.

CULTURAL DEVELOPMENT

Much of the history of Bulgaria is the story of the average Bulgarian. For hundreds of years, Ottoman domination of the Bulgarian lands dictated that national life should revolve around the village and the peasant. It was that world that preserved the culture of the people and led to a cultural life that was rich, deep, and diverse.

Culture is often viewed through a narrow definition of art (typically painting), music, and literature. In a society that was heavily peasant in nature and often isolated, that definition is too restrictive. It ignores characteristics unique to a people or to a region by relying on a single, often externally defined paradigm that overlooks internal dynamics. Moreover, it often paints that which does not conform to the model definition as "backward."

Cultural life in Bulgaria dates to the ancient Thracians. The Thracians were skilled at metallurgy, and their tombs, some of which continue to be unearthed, contained frescoes that exhibited characteristics reminiscent of their Greek contemporaries. Thracian contacts with the Greeks, Macedonians, and later the Romans led to a greater sophistication in the region, notably in terms of architectural styles that grew more elaborate and ornate (including mosaics, pillars, and murals). Tombs dating from the time of the Thracians and Romans contain remarkably preserved frescoes.

As the Slavic tribes penetrated Southeastern Europe, one might argue that artistic styles reverted to a more "primitive" state. Such a view, however, would ignore the quality of the woodwork (especially in architecture) and ceramics that were part of Slavic society. When the Bulgars migrated to the region from their ancestral lands, they brought the handicrafts so typical of a nomadic people. Then, as the Bulgarian kingdom took root, the culture of the Slavs and Bulgars merged, and the palaces of the rulers, especially at the new capital at Preslav, came to embody the power of the state.

Preslav was a city adorned with churches and palaces. Craftsmen—from wood-carvers to goldsmiths—worked within the walls of the city. They erected buildings that included unique stylized animals carved into the walls. Ceramic tiles were also distinctive features of the art in Preslav. The city's churches were equally distinctive, as beauty and the celebration of nature were always dominant themes in the Orthodox Christian world. The church was a place that brought comfort to the churchgoer, not merely through the words of the liturgy but also through the beauty of the art.

In many respects, Bulgarian culture was born with the country's conversion to Christianity by Khan Boris in 864. By unifying the people under a common faith, Boris quelled the possibility of further divisions among the two principal groups in the region (the Slavs and the Bulgars), and even more importantly, the common language chosen for the liturgy, Old Bulgarian, or Old Church Slavonic, united the people linguistically.

The Slavonic alphabet had been introduced into Southeastern Europe by the monks Cyril and Methodius during the second half of the ninth century. With its introduction, the Slavic-based language of the region remained distinct from the Greek despite the ties of the Bulgarian Church to Constantinople. In turn, the Bulgarian Church was autocephalous, that is, it maintained a quasi independence.

With the conferring of the title of patriarch upon the head of the Bulgarian church by the Byzantine emperor (owing, in large measure, to the emperor's recognition of the power of the Bulgarian tsar Simeon the Great, who ruled from 893 to 927), the center of Bulgarian culture was established. Bulgarian church and cultural centers came to thrive at Rila, Ohrid, and Preslav. This cultural self-realization sustained Bulgars, even after the destruction of the First Bulgarian Empire at the hands of the Byzantine emperor Basil II ("the Bulgar Slayer") in 1018. Without a sense of cultural distinctiveness, the preservation of a Bulgarian cultural and political identity would have been less successful.

When the Second Bulgarian Empire was created in the late twelfth century, Turnovo became not only the state's new political center, but its cultural one as well. Illustrated manuscripts, including perhaps the most famous, the Gospels of Tsar Alexander, and church art, including the frescoes at the church at Boyana, considered by many to be Bulgaria's most renowned and artistic treasure, left a legacy that continued to stand long after Turnovo ceased to be the center of Bulgarian rule.

From the beginning of Bulgaria's Christian heritage, the art and architecture of the churches were the cornerstones of the nation's culture. This was especially true with regard to icons, which became a central focus and feature of Bulgarian art for centuries. The mystical nature of Orthodoxy and the traditional stylized features of Byzantine art became central motifs in the Bulgarian lands. Even the monumental art that was so characteristic of the cities like Turnovo and Preslav (as well as its predecessor, Pliska) gave way to the newer, more decorative religious art form of iconography (religious paintings on wood or glass, sometimes encased in silver, that are part of the mysteries that are so central to Orthodoxy).

Monasteries become the centers of artistic life in Bulgaria even before the coming of the Ottoman Turks in the late fourteenth century. Adorned with scenes of the life of Christ and the lives of the saints, the monasteries and churches were magnets drawing the people not only to the faith but also to the beauty associated with it. Depictions of the fall from Grace and the descent into Hell were reminders to parishioners of the lives that the righteous should lead and the penalties that awaited those who strayed. Art played a role in the lives of all believers, since it celebrated the beauty that God provided and offered a message of salvation. Accordingly, when the Bulgarian lands fell to the Turks, the church's role as preserver and promoter of culture took on a heightened role.

When the Turks destroyed the Second Bulgarian Empire in 1396, they razed many churches over the course of the next five centuries. However, the church as an institution kept alive Bulgaria's heritage. Churches were rebuilt or constructed and painted in secret, and faith became a passive form of resistance to Turkish rule. Icons now took on an even more important function, since they continued to affirm the true faith. The suffering of the Passion story, the themes of Redemption and Salvation, and the Virgin Mary as a mother figure became refuges in a world in which the rulers were Muslim and the Bulgarian identity seemed lost.

The monastery at Mount Athos in Greece (as well as other monasteries) became centers of church art. Manuscripts and works of art were hidden and preserved. It is not surprising then that when life under the Ottomans deteriorated and national feeling began to reawaken, the first manifestations of national self-consciousness were seen in the church. Secluded in the mountains, monasteries, such as that at Rila, had kept traditional Bulgarian culture alive.

It was in the monastery at Hilendar that the Bulgarian national revival may be said to have begun. In the 1740s a young man named Paisii entered Mount Athos. There he was exposed to culture and history unavailable to him in his native land. In Greece and Serbia, a revival in culture was in its infancy, but Bulgaria, it was said by many, had no past. Paisii, who was ordained at the age of twenty-three, rejected this notion. He worked in the library at Hilendar, collecting material on Bulgaria. In 1762 he wrote his *Slavonic-Bulgarian History* (*Istoriia Slavianobolgarskaia*), the first modern Bulgarian history.

Typical of many works in the revivals of the various nationalities in Southeastern Europe, the tome is as much polemical as it is factual. Filled with errors that are often

Rila Monastery. (David Ball/Corbis)

self-serving, the short book, written in Old Bulgarian (or Old Church Slavonic) glorified everything Bulgarian, while blaming others, notably the Byzantines, for the travails faced by the people. It was Constantinople, for example, that failed to defend the West from the Turkish onslaught. Paisii's emotionally charged anti-Greek bias (he was especially critical of the Hellenization of the church) was a critical step, both in creating the beginnings of a national identity and in inspiring the reemergence of the Bulgarian Orthodox Church in the nineteenth century. He elevated the medieval Bulgarian tsars and the people to positions of glory, while calling for the oppression from Ottoman overlordship and Greek ecclesiastical domination to be lifted. Only then would the people be able to see their past greatness and work toward a better future (which could only come through love of the homeland and the language).

The work of Paisii of Hilendar was carried forward by his student Stoiko Vladislavov, who became better known by his ordained title, Bishop Sofronii Vrachanski. Like his mentor, Bishop Sofronii attacked Greek influence in Bulgaria and within the church. It was Sofronii who promoted literacy in the Bulgarian lands, stressing the Bulgarian vernacular rather than the Old Bulgarian, or Old Church Slavonic, that was the language of the church. Although he was forced to flee to Wallachia in the early 1800s (due to attacks upon him by both Greek and Turkish officials) and he lived his remaining years in Bucharest, Sofronii's calls for the use of the Bulgarian language, almost always a first step in national rebirth, were critical in Bulgaria's national development.

Prior to the eighteenth century, the Old Church Slavonic, or Old Bulgarian, was the written language in Bulgaria. Codified by the missionaries Cyril and Methodius in the ninth century, it was very familiar to the people, due to the fact that it was based on the dialect around Thessaloniki. In the medieval period, schools grew up in Pliska, Preslav, and Ohrid, among other cities, and the early literature of Bulgaria was devoted to the church, especially the lives of the saints. During the thirteenth century, the school in Turnovo was the center of a vibrant culture, but it had come to an abrupt end with the Ottoman conquest. Bulgarian writing and creativity had lain dormant for centuries.

In the early nineteenth century, literature and art began to emerge from years of slumber, and their influence not only inspired a revival in native culture but also the movement toward liberation from Istanbul. The new writers and artists also freed the country from the domination of the church over Bulgarian cultural life. Although the church had served as a valuable bulwark, keeping Bulgarian culture alive after the Turkish invasion, it was at the same time resistant to change and innovation. Now, however, what began as a linguistic reawakening that was in many respects an attack upon Greek influence soon spread into a full-blown artistic revival.

By the early 1800s, wealthy merchants and craftsmen began to support art and architecture. Building projects were the first outward manifestations of this movement, as the homes of the wealthy soon contained prominent displays of colorfully painted rooms, carved ceilings, and ornamental facades.

It may seem surprising that architecture played such a prominent role in the artistic revival. After all, unlike many of the other nations of Central and Southeastern Europe, Bulgaria is rarely thought of in terms of architecture. Lacking the imperial splendor of Budapest, the classic lines of Prague, or even the broad avenues of Bucharest, Bulgarian architectural masterpieces were rooted in traditional forms and styles, but they still had great value.

Bulgarians relied heavily upon wood and stone for their homes. Decorations included carved wooden ornaments, often depicting shapes or stars. Ceilings were often carved as well. The homes, multileveled, were also colorfully painted. This style continued even after the Turkish conquest, and it formed the basic architectural model during the nineteenth century. Woodcarvings remained distinctive features of Bulgarian design, as well as the use of color to represent beauty and nature. And even when Bulgarians traveling and studying abroad returned with new styles, such as the use of columns, these new techniques were blended with the older traditional ones.

Only in the twentieth century, with the growth and expansion of cities heavily dependent upon manufacturing, did a new form of architecture, epitomized by the Stalinist-style apartment blocks and large concrete buildings so typical of Soviet architecture, come to predominate. Monumental in style and austere in appearance, such buildings were found throughout the communist bloc, often blurring the distinctiveness of cities or even regions. Housing, for example, although utilitarian, was often constructed rapidly with poor workmanship. Only the villages maintained a traditional appearance.

The other great source of inspiration for the artistic revival in Bulgaria was the church. The architectural design of the Bulgarian churches, like most such structures in the Orthodox world, emphasized beauty. During the early medieval period, churches in Bulgaria were a synthesis of color and space. Interiors were open, with depictions of church events adorning the walls. This vitality, some have argued, represented a blend of Orthodox Christianity with the pagan background in Bulgaria prior to Boris's conversion. Even after the Turkish conquest, styles stayed the same. Perhaps the highest achievement of Bulgarian church architecture was the Rila Monastery, founded in the tenth century and nearly entirely rebuilt in the 1800s, with new techniques brought in by craftsmen. Not surprisingly, the monasteries at Rila, Dragalevski, and other locations were more than mere architectural masterpieces. They were also magnets for those who would lead the national revival, even if their activities became more secular in scope.

Along with the new synthesis in architectural design found during the nineteenth century, a greater emphasis on secular art emerged in the country. With the growth in national consciousness and increasing ties with Europe, it was only natural that more secular, Western-style art accompanied Bulgaria's transition to modern statehood. That is not to say that the past was forgotten. The schools of art at Debur, Trynava, and Samokov, among others, continued to produce outstanding altarpieces and works in Renaissance and Baroque styles (with a distinctive Bulgarian emphasis on nature, especially birds, leaves, and fruit). But a greater realism had begun to dominate Bulgarian art. Even icons, always a bastion of tradition, began to feature images of real life and ordinary people, rather than merely reproducing past iconic images.

Among the early artists who led this transition away from the traditional were Zahari Zograph (whose work marked a move toward Western styles), Nikolai Pavlovich (who studied in Vienna and Munich), and Stanislav Dospevskii (a student in Moscow and St. Petersburg). Each drew inspiration from different schools in Europe, and together they infused a new vibrancy into Bulgarian art. Although most artists continued to paint portraits, increasingly new themes, such as Pavlovich's historical subjects, changed Bulgarian art. In a way, this art was as revolutionary for Bulgaria as the political winds that led to national independence. And just as Bulgaria formed new political institutions, so too did a new artistic synthesis emerge.

Anton Mitov, who had studied in Florence, became one of the founders of a School of Painting in Sofia in 1896 (later renamed the Art Academy in 1908). Although international in its scope, the institution also emphasized Bulgarian themes, especially folk subjects.

Reflecting the growing internationalization of Bulgarian art was the emergence of impressionist painters such as Nikola Petrov and symbolist-expressionist artists such as Ivan Milev and Vasil Zakhariev in the late nineteenth and early twentieth centuries. Bulgarian artists studied abroad in increasing numbers and brought back new techniques from their studies; others came from Europe to work in Bulgaria. Although at first few Bulgarians attended art exhibitions, a magazine entitled *Art,* edited by Ivan Mrkvichka and Mitov, began publication in the 1890s. Mrkvichka, a Czech, had come to Bulgaria in his twenties and painted vibrant village and market scenes.

Perhaps the three most renowned Bulgarian artists—Vladimir Dimitrov-Maistora, Nikola Petrov, and Tsanko Lavrenov—worked in the period during and following World War I. After attending the Sofia School of Art, where he became known as "the master" *(maistora),* Vladimir Dimitrov-Maistora became a painter for the military during the Balkan Wars as well as World War I. After 1918, Dimitrov-Maistora returned to his native region (the Kiustendil valley), where his focus became the people. His subjects, such as young lovers and nature, reflected the simple lives of Bulgarians. His landscapes blended with his human subjects to form a synthesis of nature and humanity, all in broad strokes and bright hues. A contemporary of Dimitrov-Maistora, Nikola Petrov cofounded the Contemporary Art Society in 1903. Also a landscape artist, Petrov painted a wide variety of subjects, from street scenes in Sofia to the primitive mountains of the interior. Unlike Dimitrov-Maistora, however, Petrov's brushstrokes were more delicate and soft, displaying a deft subtlety of subject and treatment. The third noted artist of the period was Tsanko Lavrenov. Lavrenov at first drew inspiration from iconography and later moved to expressionism. His street scenes were particularly emotional and evocative.

World War II and the subsequent communist takeover of the country had as a consequence a loss of artistic independence and creativity. Art, like most forms of culture, became an instrument of the state. Independent organizations and artist guilds were abolished and their members placed under the umbrella of a national artists' union. "Socialist realism," which was devoted to the celebration of the worker and the new socialist world, emphasized "revolutionary struggle." It was designed to "educate" the average Bulgarian artistically and politically. Art was not pursued for its own sake, but rather for the state's. Statues of leaders such as the Bulgarian communist leader Georgi Dimitrov, antifascist paintings, and Stalinist architecture fit the model of art for the proletariat masses. It was not until the fall of communism that art was again freed from the dictates of the state and the Party that demanded conformity and political purity.

The same trends that defined the development of art in Bulgaria during the nineteenth and twentieth centuries were also found in literature. What was vibrant during the period of national revival and the interwar era suffered from the stifling of expression during the years of communism.

At the height of the first medieval Bulgarian empire, schools of learning could be found at Preslav and Ohrid. In fact, these schools had an impact upon the development of literature in both Serbia and Kiev Rus. Later, during the second empire, a new school at Turnovo (which also had an impact within the lands of Russia) dominated Bulgarian literature until the Turkish occupation.

The Ottoman conquest of Bulgaria was catastrophic to the development of a national literature. Although an educated middle class did emerge, its loyalties were primarily to the ruling elite. Its ties to the average Bulgarian were little more than linguistic. Since Bulgaria was more closely supervised than most of the other regions in the Balkans, due to its close proximity to Istanbul, learning was more confined to the monasteries. There church works and documents were reproduced, and "cell schools" were established to provide rudimentary education to some segments in Bulgarian society. Beyond the very basics, the most important contribution of the monasteries was the preservation of the language that formed the basis of the national revival. Until then, most of the key literary events actually took place outside the Bulgarian lands, including the first printed Bulgarian work, which appeared in Romania in the early 1500s.

In the early nineteenth century, following the call to arms from Paisii of Hilendar and Bishop Sofronii, Bulgarian writers (such as Liuben Karavelov and Nayden Gerov), partly inspired by the rich native folklore, emerged. Simultaneously, *chitalishta* ("reading rooms" or "community centers") were organized to provide weekend classes for those outside the institutions of traditional educational instruction. Through the libraries and reading rooms, works in Bulgarian, particularly those that emphasized cultural and nationalist themes, became important in the struggle for national independence. Thus the chitalishta served as clandestine organizations to promote national interests (though they also continued to operate long after independence was won).

Two writers, Khristo Botev and Ivan Vazov, serve as examples of the synthesis of literature and nationalism. Botev collaborated with Karavelov on two newspapers (*Svoboda* [Freedom] and *Nezavisimost* [Independence]) in the early 1870s. Although he was killed in a battle in 1876 against the Turks, Botev's poetry, rich and romantic, made him the voice of a people. Vazov, Bulgaria's national poet (in 1920 he received the title "People's Poet"), published his first works in Bucharest, after fleeing Bulgaria in the early days of the 1876 uprising against the Turks. Following his return to his native land, he began to publish novels and poetry; his most famous work, *Pod igoto* (Under the Yoke), written in 1889–1890, gave an account of Bulgaria as it moved toward revolution. Vazov believed that contemporary European trends clashed with the nature of the Bulgarian soul.

After World War II, literature in Bulgaria suffered the same fate as art. Socialist realism led to a stifling of creativity. One indication of the sterility that characterized Bulgarian literature over the four decades of communist rule was the fact that bookstores tended to be full of works that fit the needs and rules of the state, but did not sell, while any older literature that might be printed was quickly purchased. Only the fall of communism removed the bonds on writers.

Ironically, folk culture, which had declined as the central component of the nation's culture during the modernization and urbanization of the twentieth century, was perhaps the aspect of Bulgarian culture that was best able to survive communism. Rich and deeply rooted in the Bulgarian past, folk culture—from folk songs to the folk arts—has served as a timeless expression of the people. In fact, the rich cultural traditions are as varied as the topography, ranging from intricate wood carvings, to folk embroidery, to music.

Wood carving falls into three main categories: general architectural, church, and shepherd. There were a number of Bulgarian wood-carving schools, most notably at Samokov, Debur, and Trynava. In the medieval period an-

Christo

Of all the cultural figures born in Bulgaria, perhaps the best known internationally is Christo. Born Javashev Christo in 1935 in the town of Gabrovo to an industrial family, Christo studied at the Fine Arts Academy in Sofia from 1953 to 1956. After briefly residing in Prague, he studied in Vienna before finally settling in Paris. There he met his future wife, Jeanne-Claude, with whom he has collaborated ever since. In 1964 they moved to New York, and they have made that city their home.

Since husband and wife have always worked together, their art belongs to both of them. Nevertheless, the focus here is naturally on the Bulgarian half of the team. From the beginning, Christo's art revolved around objects. In 1958 his first major rendering involved the wrapping of bottles in fabric. Such conceptual art asks the viewer to visualize the object as it was; the observer is challenged to distinguish that which is real from that which is not.

Although his work includes prints, Christo became internationally famous for his monumental wrappings. These are temporary works, at best lasting several weeks, in which highly visible objects or landscapes are transformed by fabric into what he calls gentle disturbances, thereby giving the viewer a fresh perception of something seen so often that people no longer really see it. Christo has said often that he doesn't like labels, but prefers "environmental" to "conceptual," because his work is actually created out there in the environment, not just conceived.

From 1961, when he prepared his first major outdoor exhibit, *Stacked Oil Barrels, Dockside Packages at Cologne Harbor,* through his latest projects, including the placement of over 7,000 "gates" (woven fabric similar to flags placed 4.9 meters high on poles) throughout New York's Central Park, the works have perhaps become more elaborate and been undertaken on a grander scale, but they have always demanded the attention of those who came in contact with them.

A year after the *Stacked Oil Barrels* presentation (which lasted three weeks), Christo rendered *Iron Curtain-Wall,* 240 barrels stacked 4.3 meters high and 4 meters wide in Paris. However it was not until the late 1960s that his monumental style took flight. In 1968 his *Wrapped Kunsthalle Berne* saw approximately 2,500 square meters of fabric and over 3,000 meters of rope used to cover a façade in Berne. A year later, over 900 square meters of fabric covered the Museum of Contemporary Art in Chicago. Later that year, another 93,000 square meters of cloth was used to cover fifty-eight kilometers of Turtle Bay near Sydney, Australia, a display that melded his art and the environment.

Since the 1960s, from Italy (numerous projects, including the wrapping of a portion of the Roman Wall in 1974), to California (a "running fence" 40 kilometers long in Sonoma and Marin counties in 1976), to the wrapping of the Pont Neuf Bridge in Paris (1985) and the Reichstag in Berlin (1995), and the exhibition entitled "The Umbrellas Japan—USA (with 1,340 blue umbrellas in Japan and 1,760 yellow ones in California), his works have captured the attention and imagination of millions. His conceptual artistic projects transform a world that people think they know into one that causes them to rethink reality, a world in which the observer is transported to a place in which art takes on almost musical flowing qualities.

thropomorphic designs predominated. However, by the nineteenth century, newer styles, particularly floral designs, were emphasized. Wood-carvers, in turn, were held in the highest esteem.

The exteriors of Bulgarian village homes, distinctive by their colors, often have carved designs around doors and windows. These are usually geometric in design (such as stars) and reflect patterns dating from the time of the arrival of the Bulgars in Southeastern Europe in the seventh century.

Churches always reflect the faith of a people, but Bulgarian churches are especially distinctive in that regard. Throughout the churches, the wood-carving prowess of the craftsmen, who were often men of the villages, immediately catches one's eye. Most striking are the ornate, deep-cut iconostases (the front walls of the interiors).

Most wood-carvers, unlike the artisans who beautified the churches, were anonymous and amateur. But, while their skills varied, their work epitomized the life of their villages. They produced carvings that ranged from plates, bowls, and other such "ordinary" everyday objects to the ornate "crooks" (staffs with rams' heads for handles and lower ends shaped like curved snakes) that the shepherds carried into the fields. What they produced was art that was as rich as anything produced on canvas. The peasant's knife was his brush, and wood was merely the medium.

Another highly visible aspect of peasant life was the colorful embroidery often associated with folk costumes. While the costumes varied by region, all contained similar characteristics, including the red, black, and white color patterns. A woman wore a shirt (a *riza*), a tunic-like dress (a *soukman*), and an apron (a *prestilka*). Head coverings might include a kerchief (a *karpa za glava*), and a vest was often worn. A man wore trousers *(benevretzi),* shirt, belt, and (usually) a jacket or vest; the predominant colors were black and white. Men also usually wore a fur cap (a *kalpak*) as well. The clothes were homemade, and were usually constructed of wool, hemp, cotton, flax, and silk. Embroidery, primarily geometric but often containing small lines of birds, flowers, or even humans, elaborately adorned the sleeves, fronts, and backs of the shirts. The *soukman,* often sleeveless, was also embroidered in numerous colors and was worn with a belt (a *pafti*). The apron was, in most cases, the most decorative part of a woman's costume and made each costume distinctive.

Aside from the regional costumes, Bulgarian peasants were also skilled in decorative textiles (such as tablecloths) in floral and geometric designs. Rugs, made of goat hair, were decorated in geometric patterns and stripes. The dyes, made from plants, blended with the materials to create rich colors that did not quickly fade.

Another aspect of Bulgarian peasant culture that was preserved was music. Bulgarian music admittedly is much less well known than the music of other countries in the region. It lacks the internationally known composer that one associates with Hungary (Béla Bartók) or with the Czech and Slovak lands (Antonín Dvořák or Bedřich Smetana, to name but two). Bulgarian music may not be known within the world of classical music, but it has a rich tradition that derives from its peasant roots. Whereas many folk traditions have either died out or are merely remembered on days of celebration, this folk music tradition is an exception.

Bulgarian folk songs have always reflected the experiences in Bulgaria and within the village. They are filled with joy and sorrow, moods that reflect the difficulty of life and yet the pleasures that life brings. What is most unique about Bulgarian music is the sound of its women, and Bulgarian women folk choruses have become internationally famous during the last two decades of the twentieth century, thanks, in part, to the State Ensemble for Folk Music and Dance, founded by Philip Koutev. Although these choruses do reflect an amalgamation of the folk past with new professional training, the sound produced is still unlike that found anywhere else. Melodies have limited range, but there is a power and expressiveness in their distinctive harmonies. Songs feature sounds that seem to float in the air; they deal with aspects of village life, such as the harvest, with heroes defending the people from oppressors (the songs of the *haiduk* tradition, which glorified the bandits who resisted authority), religious celebrations, feasts and festivals, and love. The choruses are often accompanied by instruments derived from the village, such as the *kaval,* a flute-like instrument used by the shepherds, the *gadulka,* an upright fiddle that is perhaps the oldest instrument used in Bulgaria, and the *gayda,* a bagpipe that is a centerpiece of wedding music.

Thus, while perhaps not internationally known, culture in Bulgaria is deeply rooted in its past, rich in its variety, and, in a way that illustrates the vitality of the people, a synthesis of the old and new.

Traditionally dressed men and women celebrate the Rose Festival. (Michael Freeman/Corbis)

ECONOMIC DEVELOPMENT

At the beginning of the twenty-first century, Bulgaria's decade-long transition from the command economy of the past half century to capitalism had achieved at best mixed results. The average annual growth from 1995 to 2000 fell slightly over 1 percent. Adding to other economic woes was the continued high inflation rate. Although these rates had declined from the early 1990s, inflation from 1995 until the end of the decade continued to average 5.7 percent annually; in 2001 it rose again to 7.4 percent. Similarly, the rate of unemployment, already high (averaging above 14 percent from 1995 to 2000), rose to 16.3 percent in 2001 (the twelfth highest rate in the world according to *The Economist*).

Certainly the transition from communism has proved to be painful for many Bulgarians, a fact that has affected Bulgarian politics. An economy already underdeveloped during the early twentieth century, then suddenly placed under the constraints of the communist command system (1945/7–1989) in which the failure to innovate was partly responsible for the collapse of the regime in 1989, faced the daunting challenge of suddenly integrating into a world economic system. Even its former trading patterns within the Soviet bloc had been disrupted. As a result, Bulgaria found itself confronted by a competitive system for which it was little prepared. In almost all measures, from gross domestic product (GDP) to purchasing power to deficits and foreign debt (Bulgaria had the thirty-fifth highest deficit in the world in 2003 and the fortieth largest foreign debt), Bulgaria lagged behind most of the other nations in Europe and even some countries normally associated with the undeveloped Third World.

Communist leaders stressed the need for rapid industrialization. The very philosophy of Marxism itself, and certainly its form as Marxism-Leninism, diverted resources into the transformation of an agrarian state into an industrial, one with little regard for the social or environmental ramifications of the planning. Since Bulgarian indices were low in the 1950s, at first the growth rates, especially in the early 1970s, appeared to be dramatic. But the progress was illusory, and by the late 1970s the economy not only stagnated but rapidly declined. Following the collapse of the Iron Curtain in 1989, the already poor performance of the economy continued. The clearest indication of the painful legacy of communism was a negative 12.6 percent growth in annual real percentage growth in industrial output during the 1990s.

It would be myopic merely to lay the blame for Bulgaria's economic woes on the communist dictatorship, even if there were few economic positives during the period. Rather, the stagnant economy was a by-product of numerous factors that had stifled growth over the centuries.

Before the fall of communism, people in Bulgaria (as well as other countries in Southeastern Europe) often attributed their nation's economic problems to a backwardness brought on by centuries of control by the Ottoman Turks. It is human nature to seek scapegoats for problems, and the Turks provided an ideal excuse. Certainly Ottoman rule had retarded economic progress, but to blame the Turks for failures in Bulgaria a century after the fall of the Ottomans would be equally myopic. Still, some account of the economic situation under the Ottomans and after provides a necessary background for understanding the economic situation in Bulgaria today.

For centuries, Bulgaria's economy was tied to Istanbul. Turkish landlords controlled large estates *(timars)* in return for military service. These estates produced grains, such as barley, wheat, and rye, as well as vegetables and livestock. Well into the early nineteenth century the essentially feudal nature of the Bulgarian economy changed little, save for the increasing oppression of the peasant class as the Ottoman Empire became more stagnant and corrupt.

Modern economic development in Bulgaria had its infancy in the early 1800s. As the Turks confronted numerous problems, both internally and externally, reforms were enacted that greatly benefited Bulgaria economically. The loss of direct control over Greece and indirect control over the Romanian Principalities created new opportunities for Bulgarian merchants and manufacturers. In 1839 Bulgarians received the right to trade freely throughout the Ottoman Empire. As a result, Bulgaria now became one of the principal suppliers of goods and materials for the Turks. Bulgar-

ians supplied the reformed Turkish army with both food and military uniforms. Cloth production spread, primarily in the form of small woolen handicraft industries. This in turn led to a rise in the population of towns and cities, such as Plovdiv, Gabrovo, and Sliven, which served as manufacturing and commercial centers. Bulgarian merchants traded primary products such as grain, salt, and livestock through offices in Istanbul and other regional centers. Grain exports to Western Europe began in the 1840s. Other products traded included honey and pig iron. Land reforms, especially after the beginning of the largely unsuccessful *Tanzimat* (reform) period in the Ottoman Empire in 1839, saw the establishment of some small, private farms. Tobacco became a key agricultural product for export as well as for consumption within the empire.

While this small economic boom was relatively short-lived, partly owing to foreign competition (primarily from England) following the Crimean War, and partly because of Istanbul's failure to achieve real reforms either politically or economically, a small stratum of middle-class wealthy Bulgarians did come into being. This development, however, had perhaps a greater impact on the movement toward revolution and independence than it did on the economic situation. Artisans and merchants now pushed for education in the form of primary schools (the first such school began in Gabrovo in 1835). For the bulk of the country, however, life, which revolved around a subsistence peasant agricultural system, went on relatively unchanged, and conditions within the entire economy made only sporadic improvement.

Peasants, who constituted over 80 percent of the population, for the most part used archaic equipment, such as wooden plows pulled by oxen. Modern methods of planting, as well as the use of fertilizers, were rare. Illiterate and rooted in tradition, governed by the rules and ideals of the village and the *zadruga* (the communal, extended family that formed the center of peasant society), peasants were reluctant to innovate. Moreover, their lack of income and possessions meant that they were not consumers, thus retarding economic development elsewhere in society.

National independence created both new opportunities and new problems in the economic sphere. Liberation created a euphoria that led to a doubling of land devoted to grain. But an overdependence on wheat, a rise in the peasant population that in many ways offset the increase in arable land, poor soil management, and poor weather at the turn of the century combined to produce an agricultural depression. Reliance on one crop, such as wheat, meant that if things did not go well, the resulting problems would have effects throughout the economy.

Much of Bulgaria's export trade after independence continued to flow toward the Ottoman Empire, a reflection of past trade patterns (although access to these markets became more difficult after 1878, when the country gained autonomy from the Turks), while imports came primarily from Great Britain and the Ottoman Empire. With independence came tariffs that led to a decline in the total trade with the Ottoman Empire, thus further retarding development.

Mechanization, which had revolutionized agriculture in countries with which Bulgaria now found itself in economic

A Bulgarian ethnic Turk hangs up strings of tobacco leaves to dry in the village of Fotinovo in the Rhodope Mountains in 2002. Bulgaria is a major producer of tobacco and tobacco products. Tobacco is grown heavily in southern Bulgaria. (Reuters/Corbis)

competition, proceeded slowly. Yield per acre in fact did not increase, but rather stabilized or declined. Moreover, peasants were forced to pay for the land, thus reducing the size of their holdings (most peasants owned less than twenty hectares, often in unconnected smaller strips of land) and contributing to high levels of debt. A vicious cycle thus developed, one in which peasant income was too small to buy more land and equipment, which only increased the need for land and machinery in order to combat the low income levels. This situation in turn led to peasant dissatisfaction, especially with the lack of government support for projects aimed at lifting the agricultural sector, and so to the rise of the Bulgarian Agrarian National Union (BANU, or *Bulgarski Zemedelska Naroden Soiuz* [BZNS]) led by Aleksandûr Stamboliiski. Although shut out of the political power structure before World War I, BANU nevertheless was able to create cooperatives and insurance funds, as well as gain credits through the Bulgarian Agricultural Bank (Bulgarska Zemedelska Banka).

Any hope for a rapid improvement in economic conditions in Bulgaria in the period before World War I was hindered by the difficulty in raising investment capital, as well as

the unrealistic approach of governments lured by the dream of economic development and restricted by fiscal realities (conditions faced by all countries in Southeastern Europe). The government borrowed heavily to finance projects (such as railroads) that crippled state budgets by consuming a significant portion of the state's revenues (the debt service reached 20 percent of state revenues). Promoting manufacturing, although perhaps commendable, ignored the reality of the difficulty of finding markets. Bulgarian goods could not compete with the higher quality products from Western Europe. Although labor was available, much of it was unskilled, and wages remained low. As a result, industrialization remained but a small part of the overall economy for decades.

This is not to say that the economic picture was entirely bleak. The construction of a transportation network, despite its costs, was critical for future development. Tobacco remained a profitable commodity, and the foodstuff industry remained a bright spot. The expansion of education both within the country and abroad also led to new economic innovations and opportunities.

Bulgaria's defeat in the Second Balkan War (1913) and World War I cost the country valuable resources as well as the loss of land, most notably the southern Dobrudja (to Romania). Fortunately, the country had not suffered physically (only minor fighting took place on Bulgaria's soil during World War I) during the conflicts, thus reducing dislocation. This situation enabled the manufacturing sector to grow throughout the decade following World War I; even so, despite a significant rate of growth, the low levels of manufacturing in the first place make the changes seem far more important than they actually were.

Bulgaria was (and remained throughout the interwar period) an agriculturally based country, and with the loss of the rich lands of the Dobrudja and the changes in markets, the agricultural sector suffered long before anyone spoke about the Great Depression. (One of the few bright spots was the fact that Bulgaria was already a nation of small landholders and was thus able to avoid the painful land redistributions that afflicted some of its neighbors.) Critical to the underlying weakness in the economy, especially in terms of agriculture, was the fact that as the recovering nations of Europe placed high tariff barriers on imported grains in order to bolster their own agricultural sectors, Bulgaria lost potential markets for its agricultural produce. Only tobacco and rose oil (exported to France for the production of perfume) continued to be in demand.

As a defeated state in World War I, Bulgaria, like other members of its alliance, was forced to pay reparations. While not crippling, the payments placed an additional burden on already shaky budgets (until the reparations were renegotiated in 1930). State debts, a prewar problem, thus remained a burden, as it hindered the state's ability to raise capital and promote projects.

With the coming of the Great Depression, Sofia confronted a collapse in the agricultural sector. Markets, already limited, dried up. Although Bulgaria weathered the Depression better than some of its neighbors, it still faced the need for markets. That need was filled by Germany, which better than doubled its share of Bulgarian grain exports between 1929 and the outbreak of World War II a decade later. By 1939, three-fourths of Bulgarian food exports were bought by the Third Reich. Payment for these products was often made by credits or products, thereby increasingly tying Sofia to Berlin economically, a contributing (although not crucial) factor in the alliance that developed in World War II between Bulgaria and Nazi Germany.

As the forces of the Soviet Union defeated the German Wehrmacht, the advancing Red Army entered and occupied Bulgaria in 1944, providing the basis for the imposition of communist rule that was to follow the end of the hostilities. The coming to power of the Fatherland Front, a coalition of center and left parties, in September 1944, began the three-year transition to complete communist rule, which included the full direction of the economy. Symbolic of the subordination of the nation's economy to the Soviet model was the dissolution of the Bulgarian Agrarian National Union as an independent organization. For the next four decades, Bulgaria was a prisoner of a command economy, as the new system reversed past policies of decentralization in favor of central planning and state ownership.

In order to build a Soviet-style economic system based upon large-scale industrialization and collectivized agriculture, a 180-degree shift in the economy away from one driven by market forces was required. From 1944 to 1947, as the communists solidified control politically, they moved to nationalize industries. In December 1947, months after Cominform, the Communist Information Bureau that served as the propaganda organ for Moscow, announced that the pace of nationalization would quicken, all private firms in Bulgaria were seized. In addition, all independent banks, of which there were few even before the war, were incorporated into the national system. And the first steps aimed at state planning were announced with a shift in funds from agriculture to industry.

Before World War II, Bulgaria was a nation of small landholders. Nearly 80 percent of the population was engaged in agriculture. Like Stalin in the Soviet Union, the new Bulgarian leaders saw agriculture as potentially providing revenue needed for industrialization, and collectivization as the means to gain that objective. At first, collectivization was encouraged as a voluntary movement, but the policy of suasion produced limited results at best by 1947. With the consolidation of the regime in December of that year, Sofia increased pressure on peasants to join. Over the course of the next decade, either through intimidation or economic pressure, over 90 percent of Bulgaria's agricultural land was brought under the collective system.

Originally modeled after the Soviet system, over the next decade the collective farms decreased in number, while consolidation increased their size. What had been a nation of smallholders had become one of large agricultural complexes. Although these complexes were largely inefficient, as evidenced by the fact that the small plots of land granted to farmers for personal use accounted for nearly 25 percent of the overall production, Bulgaria remained an exporter of agricultural products, one of the leaders in such exports in the entire Soviet bloc. Tobacco remained the most lucrative export; Bulgarian cigarettes, high in tar and nicotine, could be found throughout Europe. In addition, Bulgarian fruits and vegetables (such as tomatoes and grapes) found markets across the continent. France continued to import rose oil for its perfume industry. Although the agricultural sector stagnated in the 1980s, in part due to a series of poor harvests that resulted in the need to import grains, agriculture, although not the primary focus of government planners, remained Bulgaria's economic bright spot.

Communist planners, however, had unflagging faith in heavy industries and central planning. With control of capital and resources, they could build sectors virtually by decree, no matter the cost in valuable resources or in damage to the environment. This freedom for the planners created inefficiency and ultimately economic stagnation.

Symbolic of the disastrous decision making that accompanied central planning was the massive Kremikovtsi Metalurgical Complex, which was built near Sofia. Constructed in the belief that huge deposits of iron ore existed in the area that would provide the needed materials for steel making, the plant in fact had to import iron ore, with much of it coming from the Soviet Union, when the supplies failed to meet initial expectations. The Kremikovtsi works failed to meet production targets, and rather than becoming a contributor to the economic health of the country, it drained it.

Inefficiency was visible throughout the industrial sector. Although industrial production rose impressively from the 1950s through the 1970s, when the industrial sector surpassed agriculture as the leading sector of the economy, fealty to the Soviet model and the five-year plans stripped away at innovation. Gains were made in the chemical and machinery sectors, and major improvements were made in electrical generation. Bulgaria exported heavy machinery, especially forklifts. Large plants were constructed throughout the country, from petrochemical plants at Pleven and Burgas, to shipbuilding at Varna, to machine tools at Gabrovo. Western investment offset the nonconvertibility of the Bulgarian monetary unit (the leva). Nevertheless, the fact that the economic sector was dependent upon the health of the Soviet bloc, since most of its industrial exports were sold to fellow members of Comecon (the Council of Mutual Economic Assistance, the Soviet Union's answer to the Common Market in the West), meant that Bulgaria was, in effect, a prisoner of a system that began to unravel in the 1980s.

Although on the surface Bulgaria had seemingly achieved "modernization" in just a short span of time, the economy stagnated, in part due to problems in the agricultural sector, as well as to an inability to generate new foreign investments. Prior to the 1980s, Western capital had masked some of the internal weaknesses, such as a poor infrastructure and the uncertainty of Zhivkov's reforms aimed at reviving the economy. Although Bulgaria had avoided the severe foreign debt burden that plagued some of the other countries in the region (notably Romania), capital generation became critical. In addition, productivity began to decline, causing a greater reliance on state subsidies. Energy production was inadequate. The economy was over-reliant on its trading partners within the Soviet bloc, which absorbed the vast majority of Bulgaria's exports. Most of that went to a Soviet Union that was experiencing its own economic malaise, the malaise that resulted in the Soviet leader Mikhail Gorbachev's calls for restructuring (perestroika). The combination of these factors fueled discontent within Bulgaria, which in turn led to the collapse of the regime in the fall of 1989.

With the fall of Zhivkov and the shift away from the command economy, the legacy of the communist economic system to Bulgaria was clear (both in visible and not so immediately apparent terms). Outwardly, the existence of large unproductive enterprises that required excessive energy resources and continued to produce substandard goods that had no market was an obvious problem. In addition, the environmental legacy of four decades of centralized planning that emphasized growth at the expense of health could be seen almost everywhere. In 1990 numerous Bulgarian cities, including Ruse (due to chlorine gas emissions from the Romanian city of Giurgiu that lies across the Danube) and Plovdiv, were declared to be environmentally damaged regions. The power grid remained dependent on a nuclear fa-

Cooling pond at Kozloduy Nuclear Power Plant. (Ed Kashi/Corbis)

cility at Kozloduy that had been constructed along the model of Chernobyl in the Soviet Union. Even after the Chernobyl disaster in 1985, the Bulgarian reactor, which leaked radiation, still could not be closed, despite several near catastrophes in the 1970s and 1980s, because the economy was too dependent on the energy.

While the communist political system crumbled throughout Eastern Europe, so too did the trading patterns that had governed the economies of the Comecon nations. Over 80 percent of Bulgarian trade prior to 1990 had taken place within the bloc. Removal of the overarching economic system in the region left Bulgaria without markets, while having to pay market prices for imports. A year later, the Gulf War destroyed Bulgaria's trade with Iraq, one of its most valuable prewar non-bloc economic partners.

Less visible, but still clear, was the psychological impact of the communist era upon the average Bulgarian. The explosion in urban growth brought on by rapid industrialization and modernization had changed the character of Bulgaria. Old ways and old ties had been broken with little to replace them. The inefficient use of labor (there were in many sectors of the economy too many workers for jobs) and the lack of pay incentives led to a diminution in the work ethic (the old joke throughout the Soviet system was "You pretend to pay me and I'll pretend to work") that is difficult to overcome. Although workers wanted more material goods (one of the dreams of many Bulgarians after the collapse of the Zhivkov regime in 1989), the psychological shift that was necessary to make that even a long-range possibility was virtually impossible for those who had toiled so long under the old system.

Thus, the post-1989 Bulgarian economy has been beset by continuous difficulties, problems that cannot be divorced from the immediate past. Integrating into the world system with outdated plants, poor quality goods, few natural resources, a weak infrastructure (such as an outdated transportation grid), little investment capital, a lack of entrepreneurial innovation, an outdated educational system that discouraged initiative and creativity in favor of ideology, technology that was years if not decades behind the nations of Western Europe, and the reemergence of independent labor unions, which demanded benefits that the state simply could not deliver, all together have constituted a daunting challenge, despite the expectations of the people that things would quickly improve.

An immediate need was to figure out how to handle property. Since the state had owned virtually everything (despite some limited privatization during the 1980s for small areas of the economy such as restaurants), the redistribution of land and other property became vexing issues. Money was unavailable for investment, especially since former high-ranking officials knew where the money was and often expropriated it for their own use.

Moreover the reversion to a market system brought severe economic dislocation, which continued throughout the 1990s. Inflation was high, and wages fell. The country continued to fail to attract foreign investment due to continued bureaucratic red tape (especially in the economic sector) and limited opportunities for a profitable return on those investments. Midway through the 1990s, Bulgaria attracted only one-fourth of the foreign investment that went to neighboring Romania, for example. Inflation remained a constant problem. And the continued power of the restructured communist party has in some respects stalled progress.

In 1992 Bulgaria's parliament passed a privatization law that legislatively paved the way for change, but the reality was that privatization proceeded slowly. By the mid-1990s only about 10 percent of agricultural land had been privatized (although on a positive note, nearly 90 percent of housing had been turned over). And while the pace of privatization quickened, beginning in the spring of 1996, most private farms remain less than ten hectares in size. State cooperatives and farms continued to predominate. Thus, those who use the land continue not to own the land. This in turn has led to a situation in which farm incomes remain low (in part due to a significant decline in production of numerous crops brought on by land degradation caused by a half-century of poor management and soil acidification), thus reducing the domestic market for all products. Lack of credit leaves all farmers short of capital needed to purchase needed equipment.

On the industrial side, the government continued to move at a slow pace away from the state-run economy to a market one. The absence of capital markets hampered stock generation. Outdated large firms continued to operate in part because there was no economic alternative. While small privately owned businesses and shops opened (a striking sight to anyone who had been in the country during the years of communism was the changes in the shop windows from the formerly drab and indistinguishable display of products to a more attractive consumer-friendliness), the legacy of years of heavy industrialization continued to cast a pall over the country.

The government in the early 1990s attempted to sell shares in the state-run industries, but found few takers. Productivity continued to decline, while unemployment increased. Most Bulgarians supported state-run economic endeavors as a means of maintaining employment and price subsidies. But Western banks and international monetary funds demanded a speed-up in privatization and fewer government subsidies to outdated enterprises.

By 1995, inflation was 122 percent, and a year later over 300 percent according to World Bank statistics. Six governments took power between 1989 and 1997, providing few substantive economic answers to the country's problems. Retirees could barely survive on their pensions. People even turned off their heat the following winter because the bills were too high. And economic output continued to decline until 1997, when a few positive signs of increasing productivity, sales, and lower inflation were seen. Still, the failure (or unwillingness) of the government to make a clean break from the past policies of state sponsorship remained a serious problem, lessening hopes for future economic vitality.

Critical for the future of the country at the turn of the century was the prospect of joining the European Union (EU). Talks with the EU began in the spring of 2000. But four years later, Bulgaria had still not met many of the requirements for membership (including administrative and judicial reforms). The government's slow pace of reforms, including barriers to foreign investment in industrial development and budget deficits, continue to hamper the country in fulfilling the requirements for membership.

The burden of ensuring Bulgaria's economic future thus ironically still lies with the government. For nearly a half-century, false hopes were placed on a command economy that shifted the country's economy from the West to the East. For over four decades, governmental decisions hampered the country. With the collapse of communism and a return to a market economy, the government has continued to make choices that have slowed economic regeneration. Despite recent hopeful signs, that failure to meet the challenges and opportunities presented by the collapse of the communist bloc has led to hardship and political dislocation and an almost Third World economic status.

CONTEMPORARY CHALLENGES

With the collapse of the Soviet empire, the greatest threat to stability and prosperity in Central and Southeastern Europe is no longer the possibility of external conflict, but rather internal. Two forces have long plagued the region, especially in the Balkans: irredentism and nationalism. Ironically, during the Cold War these forces, so potentially destabilizing, were generally held in check by the imposed communist ideology. After the fall of the Iron Curtain, the restraints fell as well.

Irredentism is the belief or perception that neighboring territory lies unjustly outside the boundaries of the nation. Such a belief may be derived from historic, ethnic, or cultural claims. Given the emotionalism engendered by the issue, irredentism often becomes an instrument of state policy, as political leaders see the opportunity to use the claims for their own political purposes, or are obliged to play to the public clamor for "justice." Irredentist sentiments and demands are tied to nationalism, which for centuries has proved to be the Achilles' heel of the Balkans. Nationalism is an emotional attachment to and identification with a group that sees itself as distinct and possibly threatened by others not part of the group. Historians have long debated the exact nature of nationalism and its variant in Eastern Europe, where ethnic homogeneity is rarely found (unlike many of the nations of Western Europe), and where ethnic divisions have led to genocidal bloodshed, most notably in Yugoslavia during World War II and again during and following the dissolution of the Yugoslav state in the 1990s. What is clear is that the appeal of nationalism has turned neighbors into enemies in the twinkling of an eye. Hot spots are not confined to Kosovo and Bosnia, the most visible problem areas of the 1990s. Transylvania, although quiet as the twentieth century came to an end, has long been a thorn in the side of relations between Romania and Hungary. And Macedonia remains a source of bitter conflict between Bulgaria, Serbia, and Greece, over a hundred years after the onset of the "Macedonian Question."

Macedonia dominated Sofia's foreign and domestic agendas for decades. Statesmen who ignored Bulgarians' emotional attachment to the region risked stirring up nationalist passions. The greatest Bulgarian interwar statesman, Aleksandûr Stamboliiski, was killed in a coup in 1923, in large measure because of his belief that the country had greater needs than a nearly obsessive, almost paralytic, preoccupation with Macedonia; instead, he focused on domestic matters, in the belief that they were far more pressing for the future welfare of the state. It made little difference that boundaries in Southeastern Europe, given the shifting movements of people and the various states that existed before the coming of the Ottoman Turks in the 1300s, were often at best ethnic approximations. Claims that were a thousand years old (or more) remain essential to the national soul. Even today, the thought of an independent Macedonia is beyond the imagination of those Bulgarians, Greeks, and Serbs who see the region as part of their historic lands.

Energies in the region thus have often been sapped by inter- and intrastate preoccupation with real and perceived grievances and injustices. Nationalism has often trumped all other needs and made progress much more difficult for a region often termed backward; nationalism has become a millstone around the neck of progress in countries that have far more pressing problems.

If there was one positive effect of the communist takeover in Bulgaria and Eastern Europe in general, it was the apparent cooling of irredentist and nationalist passions by the new ideology of communism and the dream of a socialist future mandated by the new political masters. For four decades, nationalism, at least on the surface, was ideologically anathema, utterly foreign to the rhetoric of internationalism and the socialist fraternity.

In fact, however, the replacement of the old prewar governments with a communist state apparatus could not douse the flames of nationalist aspirations; even during the heyday of communism, nationalist problems continued to arise, a reminder (albeit infrequent) that the past never lurks far beneath the surface in Southeastern Europe. As communism began to unravel in the 1980s, nationalism, as so often in the past, again became a convenient tool for regimes that had lost favor and credibility with the people. Nationalism provided a means of diverting attention away from the realities of economic decline and material shortages.

Marxist claims of a new world in which internationalism would create a new order failed to take into account the fact that nationalism in Eastern Europe was often ethnic in origin, with ethnic minorities living in countries that considered them as "outsiders" and "alien." Romania's Nicolae Ceauşescu used the ethnic divisions within Transylvania (where 30 percent of the population is Hungarian) to prop up his unpopular dictatorship in the 1980s. Likewise, Slobodan Milošević came to power in Belgrade by playing to the memory of the great Serb defeat at Kosovo in 1389.

In the 1980s nationalism also made positive contributions to the lives of the people of Eastern Europe. Poles rallied behind shipyard workers (the Solidarity movement) and a Polish pope (John Paul II) to lay bare the hollow claims that communism had led to a "workers' paradise." Their actions led to the eventual toppling of the house of cards that was the Soviet empire. Moreover, the overthrow of communism was more than merely a political change; it also represented the removal of a kind of foreign overlordship and the restoration of national sovereignty. Yet in the wake of the collapse of communism, a vacuum was created that invited a reversion to past policies. For a "new" Bulgaria, the danger that nationalist sentiments at home and irredentist claims abroad would undermine its efforts at reintegrating the state into Europe was a threat not to be overlooked.

During the 1980s, the economy of Bulgaria was flagging and public discontent was growing; political jokes, always a barometer of public opinion in countries in which the only public voice was the state-run media, became darker and more bitterly directed toward the regime. The Bulgarian government, led by Todor Zhivkov, responded by turning its attention not to the economy (the real focus of the discontent) but to the Turkish minority.

After almost five centuries of Ottoman domination, a small Turkic and Turkified population existed within Bulgaria at the time of national liberation in the nineteenth century. Some were native Bulgarians who had converted during the long period of Turkish overlordship. These Pomaks ("helpers," from a Bulgarian word [*pomagach*] that denoted a traitorous renunciation of the Bulgarian Orthodox heritage for the Muslim faith of the ruling elites) were considered to in fact be Turkish, due to the Ottoman millet system that differentiated the population on the basis of religion. In addition, Turkish settlers had colonized parts of Bulgaria in the 1400s, moving into towns and serving as administrators or irregular military forces. Others populated urban areas as part of the ruling bureaucracy.

When the Ottomans lost control of the Balkans in the nineteenth century, many Turks left, but sizable numbers of Turks and Pomaks remained in the towns and valleys they had inhabited for centuries. The two largest pockets of Muslims could be found in the northeastern part of the country between Ruse and Varna in the Dobrudja and in the valley south of the Maritsa River. Although a minority, they were not an insignificant one. By the 1980s, Turks made up approximately 10 percent of the total population (although the numbers vary depending upon the source; Amnesty International claimed that there were 900,000 ethnic Turks in Bulgaria in 1986).

After World War II, the new constitution of 1947 provided for minority rights and the protection of language and culture. For a Turkish population that numbered some 675,000 out of a total of 7 million and that had seen close to 220,000 leave during the interwar and war years, the guarantee of minority rights was critical. But, like so much written in socialist constitutions, words did not necessarily match reality.

From 1949 until 1951, 155,000 Turks either left the country or were expelled (as Ankara charged) after the new communist government announced that 250,000 Turks would be "allowed" to leave. This exodus placed enormous strains on the Turkish government, which had to absorb this population. Twice, in fact, Ankara had to close the borders with Turkey lest the exodus overwhelm Turkey's capacity to deal with the problem. The majority of the Turks who left Bulgaria came from the southern Dobrudja, the richest agricultural region in the country, which the regime hoped to collectivize. Town names in Turkish in the Dobrudja were replaced by Bulgarian ones.

In 1958 the government closed schools for the Turkish minority and began to crack down on the religious life of Muslims. Turkish schools were replaced with Bulgarian ones. The number of imams (religious leaders) began to decline. By 1965, the census did not even distinguish between ethnic groups, and six years later a new constitution dropped references to ethnic minorities altogether. In 1968 Turkish language publications had been reduced to two (one newspaper and one journal). In 1972 Turkish language classes were banned, and fines were issued for speaking Turkish in public.

In 1971 the Party began the process of assimilating the country's minority population. Pressure was placed on Pomaks (as well as the Roma [Gypsies]) to become Bulgarian. Pomaks with Turkish family names were ordered to change them to Slavic or Bulgarian (that is, Christian) ones or suffer imprisonment. Many Pomaks resisted and were sent to labor camps; they had become enemies of the state by clinging to their names. Effectively, the Pomaks had ceased to exist. By the 1970s, even the use of the word "Pomak" was banned, despite the fact that there were an estimated 170,000 Pomaks in Bulgaria.

For the moment, however, save for the language restrictions, the regime left the ethnic Turkish population alone, perhaps owing to concerns about international reaction. (Bulgaria, like the other states in Eastern Europe, was working toward gaining foreign economic credits and investments.) Instead the regime continued to "encourage" emigration. From 1968 to 1978, an agreement between Sofia and Ankara reopened the border, and another 130,000 Turks left Bulgaria.

In the early 1980s the campaign against the Turks resumed. "Historians" began to assert that the Turks were really ethnic Bulgarians (that is, Pomaks) who had lost their cultural and historic consciousness during centuries of occupation or had been forced to convert to Islam by the Turks.

In 1984–1985, after a few years of quiet, the regime initiated a new campaign designed to end the Turkish presence in Bulgaria. Whatever the motivation for the policy, the effects were catastrophic. All Turks (as well as other Muslims) were ordered to adopt Bulgarian names, as had been done earlier with the Pomaks. This action was intended to signal that they were voluntarily taking the names so as to return to their true ethnic roots. If one refused to comply, a name was assigned, and those who resisted were punished. And the campaign went far beyond names. Towns and villages were occupied. Citizenship cards (with the new names) were issued, and the cards were required for obtaining salaries and pensions. Those who resisted were imprisoned, and some (the numbers range from 500 to 1,500) were killed.

The assault was also cultural. Despite the requirements of Islamic law, circumcision was banned, as was the hajj, the pilgrimage to Mecca, one of the five pillars of the faith. Birth certificates and marriage licenses could only be issued in Bulgarian. Speaking Turkish became a criminal offense. Muslim sites were destroyed and mosques closed. Even the traditional Turkish peasant costume was forbidden. Nationalism had become both xenophobic and demagogic.

Like much of the propaganda that filled the airwaves or appeared in the newspapers (an old joke in the socialist world was that people preferred not to read the papers; the newsprint merely got their hands dirty), the reasoning issued by Sofia was stunningly brazen. Charges were made that unless something was done and done quickly, the Turkish birthrate was so much higher than the Slavic birthrate that Turks would swamp Bulgarians and the nation would cease to exist. Another angle in the propaganda campaign was that the attack on the Turkish population was really for their own good. The return to their true national culture was the end that supposedly justified the means. In fact, however, this campaign was clearly tantamount to a declaration of war upon the culture of the Muslim minority, requiring the largest single military exercise employed by Bulgaria in decades to enforce the dictates.

Zhivkov perhaps believed that if he could use the Turks to rally ethnic Bulgarians in a nationalist crusade, he could divert the public's attention from the regime's economic failures. Whatever his motivation, the plan backfired. Bulgaria, reeling under the weight of international credits it was unable to repay, and unable to secure new loans or to attract new business or investment, now felt the wrath of the international community. The United Nations, the Islamic Conference, and other organizations swiftly condemned Bulgaria's actions. Zhivkov's campaign was a clear violation of the 1975 Helsinki Accords, which prohibited such violations of human rights. International condemnation did not, however, halt the campaign or its negative effects.

Beginning in May 1989, the government began the forcible removal of Turks from their homes; they were permitted to take only what they could carry. By August, over 300,000 refugees were either in Turkey or in camps along the border waiting to be processed. Although most in the West took little notice (in the summer of 1989, much of the world was transfixed with the rapidly unfolding events in the Soviet bloc that led to the collapse of the empire), this exodus took an enormous toll on both the people and the Bulgarian and Turkish nations directly involved.

Since the Turkish inhabitants of Bulgaria were often agricultural workers or employed in low-paying construction jobs, a labor shortage quickly developed, primarily in the countryside. With the fall harvest season approaching, others had to be recruited to fill the void. The effects upon the economy, including the tobacco crop (one of the country's leading exports and thus a source of essential hard currency), were catastrophic. An already failing economy had just worsened.

Although Zhivkov could not help being pleased with his success in driving so many Turks from Bulgaria, he had clearly isolated himself politically, even within the ranks of the Party. This fact was not lost upon the Soviet leader, Mikhail Gorbachev, whose needs for glasnost and perestroika (openness and restructuring) in the Soviet Union required that international attention not be focused on the abuses of communism but rather on his attempts at reformism.

Within a matter of months, Zhivkov was toppled from power by the Party, and a new National Assembly (Subranie) moved to retreat from the policy of cultural assimilation and assault. In 1991 lawmakers decreed that those who wished to restore their names could do so (for a period of three years). Slavic endings to ethnic names could also be removed; this decree was directed not just at the Turks but at other groups, such as the Roma, who had been forced to alter their familial spellings. In addition, limited language instruction in Turkish was reinstated. At the same time, however, the Socialists, who controlled the parliament, added a measure to the new constitution that prohibited the formation of political parties on the basis of religion or ethnicity, a provision clearly directed at the Turkish minority. Thus, although some of the provisions of the campaign against the minorities were repealed, and a new friendship agreement was concluded with the Turkish government, the effects and lessons of the xenophobic exercise in nationalism have lingered.

Despite the restrictions on the formation of political parties, a political organ, the Movement for Rights and Freedom (MRF), formed to represent the voice of the Turkish population, which increased with the return of over one-half the Turks who had emigrated in 1989. Although the MRF has been courted to participate in coalition governments, criticism of the human rights record toward the Turkish minority (as well as the Roma) has continued to be a barrier toward admission to the European Union and NATO. In the late 1990s the leadership of the dominant political party in the country, the Union of Democratic Forces (UDF), made overtures to the Turkish population. It was clear that as Bulgaria moved toward full integration into the European system, the problems of aggressive nationalism would be detrimental to the greater cause of economic progress and international respect. Nevertheless, the dangers of nationalism and irredentism, as evidenced by what has occurred in the former Yugoslavia as well as in the case of the Turkish minority in Bulgaria, are always potentially sources of division and hostility that linger, influenced by the past. Whether the moves by Bulgarian leaders to deal with the problems of the Turkish minority are sincere or based solely on expediency thus remains to be seen. For Bulgaria to make progress in the third millennium, that part of its past has to stay buried.

SELECTIVE BIBLIOGRAPHY

Barford, P. M. *The Early Slavs: Culture and Society in Early Medieval Eastern Europe.* Ithaca, NY: Cornell University Press, 2001.

Bell, John D. *The Bulgarian Communist Party from Blagoev to Zhivkov.* Stanford, CA: Stanford University Press, 1986.

————. *Peasants in Power: Alexander Stamboliski and the Bulgarian Agrarian National Union, 1899–1923.* Princeton: Princeton University Press, 1977.

Bokov, Georgi, ed. *Modern Bulgaria: History, Policy, Economy, Culture.* Sofia: Sofia Press, 1981.

Bozhkov, Atana. *Bulgarian Art.* Sofia: Foreign Language Press, 1964.

Brown, J. F. *Bulgaria under Communist Rule.* New York: Praeger, 1970.

Bulgarian Arts. www.arts.omega.bg (accessed 24 August 2004).

Carter, F. W. "Bulgaria." In *Environmental Problems in Eastern Europe.* Edited by F. W. Carter and D. Turnock. London: Routledge, 1993, 38–62.

Chirot, Daniel, ed. *The Origins of Backwardness in Eastern Europe: Economics and Politics from the Middle Ages until the Early Twentieth Century.* Berkeley, CA: University of California Press, 1989.

Crampton, Richard. *A Concise History of Bulgaria.* New York: Cambridge University Press, 1997.

————. *A Short History of Modern Bulgaria.* New York: Cambridge University Press, 1987.

Crampton, Richard, and Ben Crampton. *Atlas of Eastern Europe in the Twentieth Century.* New York: Routledge, 2001.

Curtis, Glen E. *Bulgaria: A Country Study.* Washington, DC: Library of Congress, Federal Research Division, 1993.

Detrez, Raymond. *Historical Dictionary of Bulgaria.* New York: Rowman and Littlefield, 1997.

Economist Books. *Pocket World in Figures, 2003*. London: Economist Books, 2003.

Fine, John V. A., Jr., *The Early Medieval Balkans: A Critical Survey from the Sixth to the Late Twelfth Century*. Ann Arbor: University of Michigan Press, 1991.

———. *The Late Medieval Balkans: A Critical Survey from the Late Twelfth Century to the Ottoman Conquest*. Ann Arbor: University of Michigan Press, 1994.

Frucht, Richard, ed. *The Encyclopedia of Eastern Europe: From the Congress of Vienna to the Fall of Communism*. New York: Garland, 2000.

Glenny, Misha. *The Balkans: Nationalism, War, and the Great Powers, 1804–1999*. New York: Penguin Books, 1999.

Goldman, Minton F. *Russia, the Eurasian Republics, and Central/Eastern Europe*. 9th edition. Guilford, CT: McGraw-Hill/Dushkin, 2003.

Hristov, Hristo. *Bulgaria: 1300 Years*. Sofia: Sofia Press, 1980.

Human Rights Watch. "Bulgaria." World Report 2002. http://www.hrw.org/wr2k2/europe6.html (accessed 12 June 2004).

Hupchick, Dennis P. *The Balkans: From Constantinople to Communism*. New York: Palgrave, 2001.

Hupchick, Dennis P., and Harold E. Cox. *A Concise Historical Atlas of Eastern Europe*. New York: St. Martin's, 1997.

Jelavich, Barbara. *History of the Balkans: Eighteenth and Nineteenth Centuries*. New York: Cambridge University Press, 1983.

———. *History of the Balkans: Twentieth Century*. New York: Cambridge University Press, 1983.

Jelavich, Charles, and Barbara Jelavich, *The Establishment of the Balkan National States, 1804–1920*. Seattle: University of Washington Press, 1977.

Keegan, John. *The First World War*. New York: Alfred Knopf, 1999.

Kinross, John Patrick. *The Ottoman Centuries: The Rise and Fall of the Turkish Empire*. New York: Quill, 1977.

Lampe, John R. *The Bulgarian Economy in the Twentieth Century*. New York: St. Martins, 1986.

Lampe, John R. and Marvin R. Jackson, *Balkan Economic History, 1550–1950: From Imperial Borderlands to Developing Nations*. Bloomington: Indiana University Press, 1982.

Macdermott, Mercia. *A History of Bulgaria, 1393–1885*. London: George Allen and Unwin, 1962.

Magocsi, Paul Robert. *Historical Atlas of East Central Europe*. Seattle: University of Washington Press, 1993.

Mihailov, Dimiter. *Bulgaria*. New York: Hippocrene Books, 1992.

Mitchell, B. R. *European Historical Statistics, 1750–1970*. Abridged edition. New York: Columbia University Press, 1978.

Moser, Charles. *A History of Bulgarian Literature, 865–1944*. The Hague: Mouton, 1972.

Oren, Nissan. *Bulgarian Communism: The Road to Power, 1934–1944*. Reprint. Westport, CT: Greenwood Press, 1985.

Perry, Duncan M., "New Directions for Bulgarian-Turkish Relations." *RFE/RL* (Radio Free Europe/Radio Liberty) *Research Report* 1 41 (1992): 33–39.

———. *The Politics of Terror: The Macedonian Liberation Movements, 1893–1903*. Durham, NC: Duke University Press, 1988.

———. *Stefan Stambolov and the Emergence of Modern Bulgaria, 1870–1895*. Durham, NC: Duke University Press, 1993.

Pounds, Norman J. G. *Eastern Europe*. London: Longman, 1969.

Pundeff, Marin. "Bulgaria." In *The Columbia History of Eastern Europe in the Twentieth Century*. Edited by Joseph Held. New York: Columbia University Press, 1992.

———. "Bulgarian Nationalism." In *Nationalism in Eastern Europe*. Edited by Peter F. Sugar and Ivo Lederer. Seattle: University of Washington Press, 1969, 93–195.

Rossos, Andrew. *Russia and the Balkans: Inter-Balkan Rivalries and Russian Foreign Policy, 1908–1914*. Toronto: University of Toronto Press, 1981.

Rothschild, Joseph. *East Central Europe between the Two World Wars*. Seattle: University of Washington Press, 1974.

Rothschild, Joseph, and Nancy M. Wingfield. *Return to Diversity: A Political History of East Central Europe since World War II*. 3d edition. New York: Oxford University Press, 2000.

Sedlar, Jean W. *East Central Europe in the Middle Ages, 1000–1500*. Seattle: University of Washington Press, 1994.

Stavrianos, L. S. *The Balkans since 1453*. New York: Holt, Rinehart and Winston, 1958.

Sugar, Peter F. *Southeastern Europe under Ottoman Rule, 1354–1804*. Seattle: University of Washington Press, 1977.

Todorova, Maria. *Imagining the Balkans*. New York: Oxford University Press, 1997.

Tzvetkov, Plamen S. "The Politics of Transition in Bulgaria: Back to the Future." *Problems of Communism* 41, no. 3 (1992): 34–43.

Vassilev, Rossen. "De-Development Problems in Bulgaria." *East European Quarterly* 37, no. 3 (September 2003): 345–364.

Wyzan, Michael L. "The Political Economy of Bulgaria's Peculiar Post-Communist Business Cycle." *Comparative Economic Studies* 40, no. 1 (spring 1998).

CHRONOLOGY

Fifth century B.C.E.	Thracian kingdom established in Bulgarian lands.
352 B.C.E.	Conquest of the Bulgarian lands by Philip of Macedon.
First and second centuries B.C.E.	Conquest by the Romans.
Sixth and seventh centuries C.E.	Migration of the Bulgars and the Slavs into the region south of the Danube and settlement there.
681	Following his victory over a Byzantine army, Bulgarian khan Asparuh is recognized by Constantinople as the head of a Bulgarian state with its capital at Pliska.
681–1018	First Bulgarian Empire.

Eighth and ninth centuries	The slow assimilation of the ruling Bulgars by the larger Slavic population, who in turn adopt the term Bulgarian for themselves.
803	Bulgar forces, led by Krum, defeat a Byzantine army led by the emperor Nicephorus.
852	Boris becomes khan.
864	Conversion by Boris to Orthodox Christianity.
886	First translations of religious texts into Old Bulgarian, or Old Church Slavonic.
893–927	Height of First Bulgarian Empire under Simeon the Great, with his capital at Preslav.
917	Simeon takes title of "Tsar of the Bulgarians and Emperor of the Romans" after failed siege of Constantinople in 913.
927	Recognition of the Bulgarian Patriarchate by Constantinople.
946	Death of John of Rila; construction of Rila Monastery begins.
Tenth and eleventh centuries	Bogomil "heresy" weakens Bulgarian state.
1018	Fall of First Bulgarian Empire to Byzantine forces led by Basil II ("the Bulgar-Slayer").
1185	Creation of Second Bulgarian Empire with capital at Turnovo, after successful revolution led by Petur and Asen.
1185–1396	Second Bulgarian Empire.
1218–1241	Territorial height of empire under Asen II.
1371	Bulgarian tsar becomes a vassal of the Ottoman Turks; Bulgaria is divided into two parts, with capitals at Vidin (west) and Turnovo (east).
1393	Turnovo taken by Ottoman forces; Bulgarian Patriarchate abolished.
1396	Ottomans take Vidin, ending the Second Bulgarian Empire.
1396–1878	Ottoman rule of Bulgarian lands.
1453	Forces of Mehmed the Conqueror take Constantinople.
1762	Paisi of Hilendar publishes *A Slavonic-Bulgarian History (Istoriia Slavianobolgarskaia),* which attacks Greek influence in Bulgaria.
1774	Treaty of Kuchuk Kainardji grants Russia authority to protect Christians in the Ottoman lands.
1792–1807	Warlord Osman Pasvanoglu rules from Vidin over parts of Bulgarian lands.
1806	First work in Bulgarian published in Bucharest.
1809	Bishop Sofronii establishes a Bulgarian center in Bucharest.
1835	First Bulgarian school established at Gabrovo.
1839	Beginning of *Tanzimat* (reform) period in Ottoman Empire, aimed at revitalizing the empire. Reform period lasts until 1876.
1856	First *chitalishta* (reading rooms) are established.
1860s	*Cheti* (armed groups) form in Romania to fight for liberation. Key revolutionaries include Georgi Rakovski, Liuben Karavelov, Khristo Botev, and Vasil Levski.
1870	Ottoman sultan offers the creation of an autonomous Bulgarian church, the Exarchate.
1876	Failed April Uprising.
1877–1878	Russo-Turkish War.
March 1878	Treaty of San Stefano creates an independent "Big Bulgaria."
July 1878	Congress of Berlin revises the provisions of San Stefano. A semi-independent Bulgaria and an autonomous Eastern Rumelia (under Ottoman jurisdiction) are created.
1879	Turnovo Constitution written, which will remain in force until the "Dimitrov Constitution" of 1947.
April 1879	Alexander of Battenberg elected monarch.
1885	Union with Eastern Rumelia.
November 1885	Serbo-Bulgarian War.
8–17 August 1886	Coup led by pro-Russian officers in the Bulgarian army forces Alexander to abdicate; countercoup, led by Stefan Stambolov, invites Alexander to retake throne.
26 August 1886	Alexander formally abdicates.
June 1887	Ferdinand of Saxe-Coburg is elected as new monarch.
1891	Bulgarian Social Democratic Party founded.
1893	Formation of the Internal Macedonian Revolutionary Organization (IMRO).
1894	Resignation of Stambolov government.
1895	Assassination of Stambolov.
1899	Bulgarian Agrarian National Union (BANU) founded.
1903	Failed Ilinden Uprising in Macedonia.
1903	Formation of Bulgarian Workers' Social Democratic Party by Dimitûr Blagoev.
1908	Bulgaria gains complete independence; Ferdinand takes the title of tsar.
1912	Formation of Balkan League with Serbia and Greece.
October 1912–May 1913	First Balkan War.
May 1913	Treaty of London ends First Balkan War; Bulgaria does not feel properly compensated in Macedonia.
June–July 1913	Bulgaria attacks Macedonia, precipitating Second Balkan War.

August 1913	Treaty of Bucharest ends Second Balkan War; Bulgaria loses territory, including southern Dobrudja.
October 1915	Bulgaria enters World War I on the side of the Central Powers by declaring war on Serbia.
September 1916	Bulgaria attacks Romania.
September 1918	Salonika Front breaks, leading to armistice and Radomir Rebellion.
October 1918	Ferdinand abdicates for son Boris.
November 1919	Treaty of Neuilly signed. Bulgaria loses land to Serbia, Romania, and Greece.
1920	Aleksandûr Stamboliiski forms a government led by the Bulgarian Agrarian National Union.
June 1923	Coup overthrows and murders Stamboliiski; government led by Aleksandûr Tsankov forms.
September 1923	Failed September Uprising against rightist government.
1930s	Effects of Great Depression cause severe economic dislocation.
1934	Greece, Turkey, Romania, and Yugoslavia form Balkan Pact aimed at containing Bulgarian territorial revisionism.
May–June 1934	Boris overthrows government and bans all political parties and organizations; Turnovo Constitution is suspended.
1933–1941	Growth in economic dependence on Nazi Germany.
March 1941	Bulgaria joins the Tripartite Pact.
April 1941	Bulgarian troops occupy Yugoslav Macedonia and western Thrace.
1943	Coalition of parties, led by the Communist Party, forms the Fatherland Front.
August 1943	Boris dies.
September 1944	Soviet army crosses into Bulgaria. Bulgaria declares war on Nazi Germany.
8–9 September 1944	Coup d'état by Fatherland Front overthrows the government.
1946	Fatherland Front candidates control the National Assembly.
November 1946	Communist leader Georgi Dimitrov named prime minister.
1947	Peace treaty with Allied powers ratified; opposition leader Nikola Petkov arrested, tried, and executed; new constitution, the "Dimitrov Constitution," promulgated.
1949	Dimitrov dies; replaced by Vulko Chervenkov, a hard-liner who will purge the Party of "deviationists."
1949–1951	First campaign against the Turkish minority leads to the flight of 155,000 Turks.
1953	Death of Soviet leader Josef Stalin; Chervenkov increasingly isolated politically.
1954	Todor Zhivkov named first secretary of the Bulgarian Communist Party (BCP).
1958	Turkish schools in Bulgaria closed.
1962	Zhivkov consolidates power.
1971	Zhivkov issues new constitution.
1981	Celebration of the 1,300th anniversary of the First Bulgarian Empire.
1984–1985	Campaign against the Turkish minority intensifies.
1989	Renewed campaign against the Turkish and Muslim minority.
November 1989	Zhivkov replaced as Party secretary at plenary Party session by Petûr Mladenov; days later he is replaced as president as well.
January 1990	BCP gives up exclusive political power; in April it will rename itself the Bulgarian Socialist Party (BSP).
1990	First free elections in the postcommunist era; despite BSP victory, a coalition of opposition parties, the Union of Democratic Forces (UDF), refuses to endorse BSP program.
22 November 1990	The People's Republic of Bulgaria is renamed the Republic of Bulgaria.
1991	Zhelyu Zhelev elected president.
1992	Privatization laws adopted.
April 1997	Elections lead to UDF government headed by Ivan Kostov.
June 2001	A new party, the Simeon National Movement, headed by the former monarch Simeon II, wins elections. Simeon becomes new prime minister. Later, Georgi Parvanov, from the BSP, elected president.

GREECE

ALEXANDROS K. KYROU

LAND AND PEOPLE

At varying times in their almost 4,000-year-history, the Greeks have populated diverse areas of the larger Mediterranean world. The earliest Greek communities emerged within a geographic pale corresponding roughly to Greece's current territory and extending across the Aegean Sea to the central and southern portions of Asia Minor's western coast. At the height of their distribution of settlement in antiquity, Greeks dominated the southern Balkans and the peninsula's surrounding islands, western and northern Asia Minor, southern Italy and Sicily, and Cyprus. At the same time, Greek populations, especially in urban communities, were widely dispersed along the shores of the Black Sea, the Libyan coast in North Africa, and throughout much of the Near East; meanwhile, Greek colonies in Western Europe dotted the Mediterranean coasts of France and Spain, and networks of Greek settlement stretched as far as Iran and Afghanistan in Southwest Asia. During the Middle Ages,

Greek society, and its population, consolidated through the Byzantine Empire to form a geographic and population core anchored in, first, the peninsular landmass of Asia Minor and, second, the southern Balkans, as well as the Aegean Islands and Cyprus. Greek communities continued to cling to southern Italy and Sicily, as well as other places, but these particular historic Greek centers steadily declined under the pressures of foreign conquest and assimilation.

During the early modern period, and largely as a result of the Greek world's conquest by the Ottoman Turks, a major territorial contraction of the Greek population took place. In Asia Minor, most of the region's Greek population, despite its survival in considerable numbers along the Aegean and Black Sea coastal areas, as well as places in the interior, was displaced or assimilated by the Turks. In the Balkans, although Greeks continued to dominate the south of the peninsula and even expanded northward into urban settlements throughout the region, Ottoman conquest of Southeastern Europe brought with it Turkish settlement and consequent displacement of many Greek populations, especially in large parts of Macedonia and Thrace. The contraction of Greece's geographic space and population distribution was accelerated in the modern era. Although the Greek nation-state emerged in the early nineteenth century as the first successor to the Ottoman Empire, it proved incapable of liberating and incorporating all of the Greeks' geographic patrimony. Today, in fact, the Greek world is geographically smaller than at any other time in its history. In its present form, the country's territory of 131,957 square kilometers is overwhelmingly mountainous, shaped by a complex coastline exceeding 15,000 kilometers in length, and includes as many as 2,000 islands and islets that dot the surrounding Aegean, Ionian, and Mediterranean Seas.

The Acropolis, Athens. (PhotoDisc, Inc.)

Given Greek society's exceptionally long history, it is not surprising that Greece's geographic stage, and corresponding population landscape, experienced such dramatic change. What is remarkable, however, is that the Greeks managed for over three millennia to maintain or reassert their constant, dominant position in the southernmost Balkans, their historic homeland and geographic base. Often identified as the Greek peninsula, this region, comprising the lands of the modern Greek state, are traditionally divided into nine geographic regions that are differentiated by historic frontiers but not by political administration. The six mainland regions are Epirus, Macedonia, and Thrace in the north, and Central Greece, the Peloponnesus, and Thessaly to the south. The three island regions consist of the Aegean Islands, in the Aegean Sea between mainland Greece and Turkey, the Ionian Islands, in the Ionian Sea immediately west of the mainland, and the island of Crete, straddling the Aegean and Mediterranean Seas.

Greece's most underdeveloped area, Epirus, is the Greek part of a larger territory, which extends into Albania. Dominated by a mass of complex mountain lines known as the Pindus Range, Epirus is the most mountainous region in Greece and, by virtue of its rugged topography and limited passageways, the country's historically most isolated area. Because there are no major valleys between its steep ridges, Epirus is also a poor agricultural region, suitable mainly for

pasture. The chief city, Ioannina, which enjoyed considerable cultural and political influence in Ottoman times, functions today as the region's primary commercial center. Although the population of Epirus played an important role in the Greek Revolution against Ottoman rule in the 1820s, most of Epirus was not incorporated into Greece until 1913.

East of Epirus, south of the border with the former Yugoslavia and bounded by the Aegean Sea, is Macedonia, the largest region of Greece. Macedonia is the Greek portion of a geographically larger area that also includes the lands comprising southwestern Bulgaria and the Former Yugoslav Republic of Macedonia (FYROM, or the Republic of Macedonia, which until 1991 was the southernmost republic in Yugoslavia). Macedonia's terrain is defined primarily by rugged mountains interspersed with fertile river valleys and an extensive coastal plain shaped by the Axios (Vardar) River, which empties into the Aegean Sea. Western Macedonia, an area dotted with several large lakes, is the mountainous source of Greece's longest flowing river, the Aliakmonas, which meanders eastward to form a swampy delta shared with the mouth of the Axios River. The fertile Strymonas (Struma) River valley is nestled in eastern Macedonia. Central Macedonia's plain is one of the most agriculturally productive regions in the Balkans and a resource crucial to Greece's economy. Greece's second largest city,

Thessaloniki, is also located in central Macedonia. Thessaloniki possesses one of the most strategic ports in Southeastern Europe and the city serves as an important commercial center, linking Balkan markets with international trade. Founded in the fourth century B.C.E., Thessaloniki was for many centuries, both in the Byzantine and the Ottoman Empires, the most important economic and cultural center in the Balkans after Constantinople. Southeast of Thessaloniki, one of Macedonia's most prominent geographic features, the Chalcidice peninsula, extends three subpeninsulas into the Aegean Sea. The rugged easternmost of these three long arms of land is home to the autonomous religious community of Mount Athos, a legendary Orthodox Christian monastic enclave that has provided seclusion to its male-only members for more than a millennium. Athos, although preserving its status as a self-governing territory, was, like the rest of Greek Macedonia, incorporated into the Greek state in 1913.

Thrace, like Epirus and Macedonia, is the Greek part of a larger geographic and historic region. Greek Thrace is sometimes distinguished as Western Thrace to differentiate it from Turkish Thrace, also known as Eastern Thrace or European Turkey. Thrace's eastern border is defined by the Evros (Maritsa) River, which separates Greece and Turkey, while the Greek border with Bulgaria serves as the region's northern frontier. To the south, Thrace meets the Aegean Sea, and to the west the Nestos River sets the regional border between Greek Macedonia and Thrace. While most of northern Thrace is dominated by the Rhodope Mountains, Thrace's southern lands encompass three alluvial plains, running along the coast of the Aegean Sea and the valley of the Evros River. Thrace became part of Greece in 1919.

The region of central Greece, known historically as Rumeli, extends from the Ionian Sea on the west to the Aegean Sea on the east, and from Epirus and Thessaly in the north to the Gulf of Corinth on the south. The main range of the Pindus Mountains extends southward into the western part of Central Greece, where it connects with another mountain system, the Parnassian Range, which extends southeastward toward the historic area of Attica and the city of Athens. Greece's capital, Athens, is surrounded by its largest metropolitan area and neighbors the country's chief port, Piraeus. Greater Athens is the hub of Greece's lucrative international trade and investing activity and the center of the country's largest industrial complex. Leaving an enormous intellectual, cultural, and political imprint on the development of civilization, the legacy of ancient Athens continues to overshadow much of the modern city, which, like its ancient ancestor, has developed a reputation for rapid growth, overcrowding, an inadequate transportation structure, a frenetic pace of public and private life, and a creative and resourceful population. Center-stage along with the Peloponnesus in the course of the Greek Revolution, fought in the 1820s for liberation from Ottoman rule, Rumeli, or Central Greece, was one of the core territories comprising the independent Greek state established in 1832.

The southernmost part of mainland Greece, as well as the Balkan Peninsula, is a mountainous landmass connected to central Greece by an isthmus only four miles wide at its narrowest point. The isthmus connecting the Peloponnesus to central Greece, is, in fact, cut by the Corinth Canal. Since the canal's completion in 1893, the Peloponnesus has been made a virtual island surrounded by the Gulf of Corinth on the north, the Ionian Sea to the west, the Mediterranean Sea on the south, and the Aegean Sea in the east. The Peloponnesus, like much of Greece, is renowned for its physical beauty, which also reflects an intensely complex concentration of diverse topographical features. The Peloponnesian networks of mountains extend southward to form three peninsulas that make up the southernmost points of the landmass. In the center of the Peloponnesus, surrounded by mountains, rests the Plateau of Arcadia. Lowlands stretch along the northern and western coasts, along inland river valleys, and in several spring-fed mountain basins, while fertile alluvial plains are found in the northeast. All the same, much of the peninsula is arid during summer, requiring irrigation in many agricultural areas. The centrally located city of Tripolis aside, most of the Peloponnesus's population is located on the periphery of the peninsula. Still home to several cities, such as Argos, Corinth, and Sparta, renowned for their importance in the ancient world, today the Peloponnesus's largest and most important city is the thriving industrial, commercial, and port city of Patras on the north coast. A major source of early nationalist revolutionaries and the first region to be liberated from Ottoman rule during the Greek War of Independence, the Peloponnesus was a core territory of the modern Greek state created in 1832.

The region of Thessaly occupies the east side of the Pindus watershed, extending south of Macedonia, north of Central Greece, and on to the Aegean Sea. Thessaly's major river, the Pinios, originating in the Pindus Range and emptying into the Aegean, flows through the region's most important topographical feature, its central plain. The fertile, and relatively large, Thessalian Plain constitutes one of Greece's most vital agricultural areas, particularly for the production of grains and livestock. Another of Thessaly's most prominent geographic features is a spur of mountains extending southeastward from Mount Olympus in Macedonia along the Aegean coast, forming and terminating in the Magnesia peninsula. The peninsula envelops the Gulf of Pagasai along which rests one of Thessaly's two major urban centers, the port city of Volos. The nearly landlocked gulf provides metropolitan Volos with a natural harbor for shipping the agricultural products from the plains just to the west. Thessaly's second large city, Larisa, makes good use of its geographic position in the center of the region's productive plain and at the nexus of major transportation corridors to function as one of Greece's largest food-processing centers. The Ottoman Empire was forced to cede to Greece most of Thessaly in 1881; the remainder of the region's territory was incorporated in 1913.

Greece's islands have long held a special place in the imagination of Greeks and foreigners alike. Like the mainland, however, the islands are geographically and topographically far more diverse than they are popularly represented. Most of the islands are geological extensions of the mountains of the Greek mainland, forming regional clusters in the Aegean Sea. In the northern Aegean the densely forested island of Thasos is part of Macedonia, dry Samothrace belongs to Thrace, and the lush chain of the Northern Sporades make up part of Thessaly.

In the western and central Aegean are a large group of some twenty-four islands comprising the Cyclades. Excluding Naxos and Siros, which benefit from fertile and well-watered valleys, most of the Cyclades Islands are dry, rocky, and infertile. A historic bed of piracy and a source of decisive opposition to the Ottomans for control of the sea during the Greek Revolution, the Cyclades were an integral part of independent Greece established in 1832. East of the Cyclades and close to the Turkish coast is another archipelago known as the Dodecanese Islands, the largest of which is Rhodes. The Dodecanese, wrested from the Ottoman Empire by Italy in 1911 and awarded to Greece in 1947, comprise the last territories added to Greece. North of the Dodecanese are the relatively large islands of Samos, Ikaria, Chios, Lesbos, and Lemnos, the first of which is remarkable for its green forests, the fourth of which is notable as one of Greece's most economically developed islands, known for its enormously profitable olive production. All of these islands were acquired by Greece in 1913.

Shielding the Aegean Islands from the Mediterranean Sea is Crete, Greece's largest island. Crete's location in the eastern Mediterranean and on the cusp of the Aegean has made it historically significant as a natural and vital link in the exchange and diffusion of cultures between Europe and the Near East. Conquered by the Ottomans in 1669, Crete had been a Venetian possession for more than four centuries. After several uprisings against the Ottomans, Crete secured autonomous status in 1897 and was incorporated into Greece in 1913.

Finally, beyond the Aegean and immediately west of the Greek mainland are the Ionian Islands, which share the name of the sea in which they are found. Corfu is the northernmost of the main Ionian Islands, as well as the archipelago's most populous, most prosperous, and most strategic island. In fact, its strategic position, which commands the strait between Italy and the Balkans where the Ionian and Adriatic seas meet, had placed it for several centuries at the mercy and occupation of several foreign powers such as Venice, Russia, France, and Britain. Corfu is the only part of Greece never to have been subject to Ottoman conquest and rule. Corfu, as well as the other Ionian Islands, was ceded by Britain to Greece in 1864. Despite their many differences, the Greek islands share a set of distinctive features that have defined the broader Greek historical experience—the geographical markers of sea and mountains.

NATURE AND ENVIRONMENT

Greece's environment is significantly influenced by its climate, which is largely Mediterranean but with considerable regional variation. There are essentially five main climatic regions in Greece: Attica and the Aegean, the continental northeast, the mainland mountainous interior, the Peloponnesus, and the west (including the Ionian Islands). Considerable local variation within these zones results from differing elevation and distance from the sea. The dominant condition of Greece's climate is the alteration between hot dry summers and cold damp winters typical of the larger Mediterranean climatic belt. Continental climatic and weather influences are, as could be expected, felt more in the north and in the center of the country than in other parts of Greece. In winter, low-pressure systems originating in the North Atlantic reach Greece, bringing rain and drawing cold winds from the eastern Balkans over Macedonia and Thrace. In summer, low-pressure systems decline, allowing for hot and dry conditions throughout most of the country. Precipitation throughout the year is influenced appreciably by elevation, with high mountain regions from Macedonia, in the north, to Crete, in the south, covered with snow for several months during the year.

The rapid modernization that swept Greece in the postwar period also produced severe pressures on Greece's natural environment. Several of the problems associated with ongoing economic development have had a deleterious effect on Greece's ecological system. The considerable expansion of industrial activity, a dramatic increase in the number and use of motor vehicles, poor controls over land use, and massive waves of regular tourism have lowered air and water quality and placed enormous strains on Greece's environment. Athens, for example, has become known for acutely poor air quality and frequent severe incidents of smog. The city's climatic conditions and topography favor formation and trapping of pollutants close to the ground, a condition created in large part because the rapid postwar urbanization of Attica has proceeded without any systematic plan for traffic and industrial expansion. The same conditions contribute to air pollution in Thessaloniki, albeit to a lesser extent. In addition, sulfur dioxide, created chiefly by industrial manufacturing, has severely damaged monuments and stone buildings in Athens and Thessaloniki and generated acid rain that has injured the health of forests in Epirus, Central Greece, and Macedonia.

Water pollution and soil conservation have likewise become serious problems. Greece has shared in the general postwar deterioration of water quality in the Mediterranean basin. Bodies of water adjacent to industrial centers, especially the Saronikos Gulf south of Athens, where virtually half of Greece's industrial complex is located, receive large amounts of untreated industrial waste and municipal sewage. Greece's soil, most of which is naturally poor in organic matter, has been degraded in recent decades by the extensive, and in some instances uncontrolled, use of fertilizers as well as by soil erosion, the latter a problem plaguing Greece since antiquity. Furthermore, together with chronic and apparently increasing droughts, erosion has caused semi-desertification in many agricultural areas. Finally, rural vegetation has been stripped by overgrazing and urban sprawl construction, further contributing to soil erosion. The major agricultural plains of Macedonia and Thessaly have, however, been largely immune to soil erosion problems.

In response to the mounting crises, which became clearly apparent in the 1970s, Greek governments have produced a mass of environmental regulations. Greece's 1975 constitution gives the state authority over the country's environment and natural resources, while the 1986 Law on the Protection of the Environment sets the basic principles of

Greece's environmental policy. However, rather than establishing an efficient, centralized apparatus for implementing and enforcing such principles, the 1986 law provides for no autonomous regulatory environmental agency. In place of such an agency, the law requires nearly one hundred implementation decisions by multiple government agencies before going into full effect. The unwieldy nature of this structure has promoted bureaucratic inaction and even obstruction as much as it has led to any tangible problem solving. Often, for example, government ministries responsible for infrastructure projects and linked construction industries oppose land-use and conservation initiatives.

Despite the state's largely failed attempts to introduce effective environmental protection policies on its own, significant progress has been made on this front in Greece since the early 1990s. This progress is largely the result of the convergence of a number of sources of pressure and activism that have compelled, or forced, government and industry in Greece to undertake measures to tackle the country's environmental problems. The Greek media have been instrumental in this area by increasing attention to escalating problems. Pressure beginning in the early 1990s from the European Community (EC), and later its successor, the European Union (EU), on Greece to uphold national and international environmental obligations were important in motivating the Greek government to act more responsibly. Likewise, major decisions made by the Council of State, the highest administrative court in Greece, overturning antienvironmental policies had a decisive impact on the advancement of environmental concerns. In addition, during the 1990s several grassroots nongovernment environmental organizations emerged, and have continued, to mobilize public opinion in support of specific environmental issues. Moreover, such activist groups have brought environment-driven legal proceedings successfully before the Council of State in Greece and relevant agencies of the EU. Despite steadily increasing successes, Greece's environmental movement remains fragmented and highly localized, beginning only recently to coordinate and coalesce its efforts on a national level comparable to the "Green" groups of Western Europe.

Agriculture, the backbone of the Greek economy since antiquity, has experienced steady proportional decline as a sector of the country's overall economy in the postwar period. This trend, of course, is representative of the transition to an increasingly more developed economy and general modernization. The shrinkage of the agricultural sector, relative to other sectors, has been accelerated especially during the last two decades. For instance, whereas agriculture (together with forestry and fishing, the so-called primary sector) contributed approximately 20 percent of gross domestic product (GDP) around 1980, by the year 2000 that figure had declined by half to about 10 percent. Nevertheless, agriculture remains comparatively more important to Greece than to most other EU countries. In the EU as a whole, the agricultural sector contributes 6–7 percent of GDP. Notwithstanding, employment in agriculture has declined as the primary sector's role in the Greek economy has receded. While in 1980 persons employed in agriculture represented 28 percent of national employment, two decades later that figure had declined by almost one-third to approximately 20 percent.

Despite the modern transformation of Greece's agricultural sector toward export crops, the millennia-old tradition of fragmented, non-contiguous, and small-scale landholdings continues to persist. This pattern of land tenure was reinforced in the nineteenth and early-twentieth centuries by state land distribution programs that divided national lands to be given to landless peasants. The state's commitment to universal land ownership for the peasantry spared Greece much of the social instability, hence the absence of a significant agrarian political movement, that was common throughout much of the rest of prewar Eastern Europe. Nonetheless, the application of these policies often sacrificed efficiency in land use for equity in land distribution.

Greece's total agricultural utilization area is 3.7 million hectares (one hectare equals approximately 2.5 acres) of land, of which roughly 60 percent is in the plains and 40 percent is in the semimountainous or mountainous areas. While two-thirds of the land under cultivation is used for crops, and about one-quarter for orchards, the remaining agricultural land is used for pasturage and vineyards. In the EU as a whole, the average area per holding is approximately fourteen hectares, while in Greece the average is below four hectares. The small size of individual landholdings is the primary cause of lower agricultural productivity in Greece compared with other EU countries. The economies of scale offered by the most recent advances in farming methods have a limited impact on small plots of land characteristic of the Greek agricultural sector.

Greece's diverse topography and climatic conditions have led to differences in agricultural practices and cultivation methods throughout the country. For example, in Macedonia and Thessaly approximately 85 percent of agricultural land was cropland, while in Crete two-thirds of the island's agricultural areas were occupied by vineyards and orchards. Meanwhile, in the Peloponnesus two-thirds of agricultural land was used as cropland and one-third was used for vineyards and orchards. The approximate shares of major crops in total agricultural production are as follows: 16 percent from cotton, tobacco, and sugar beets; 11 percent from wheat and other grains; 11 percent from fruits and vegetables; 11 percent from olive products; and 6 percent from grapes. Livestock and livestock production constitute roughly 30 percent of the total value of Greece's agricultural output. The largest components of the country's livestock population are sheep and goats, whose meat and milk, respectively, account for 6 percent and 7 percent of the agricultural total. Whereas most of the sheep, goats, pigs, and poultry are evenly distributed among the agricultural regions of the country, about half of Greece's cattle are concentrated in the plains of Macedonia. Beef and milk provide 6 percent of the country's agricultural output, while poultry and eggs account for 6 percent, and pork for 4 percent.

POPULATION

At the time of the 2001 census, the population of Greece was 10,964,020, marking an increase of approximately

700,000 since 1991. The de jure population by region was approximately as follows: 490,000 in the Aegean Islands; 4.6 million in Central Greece; 580,000 in Crete; 400,000 in Epirus; 220,000 in the Ionian Islands; 2.32 million in Macedonia; 1.18 million in the Peloponnesus; 800,000 in Thessaly; and 370,000 in Thrace. Greece's largest urban area is metropolitan, or Greater, Athens with a population of 3,761,810 in 2001. Metropolitan Thessaloniki's population exceeds 740,000, followed by Patras with a population of approximately 175,000. Only three other cities, Heraklion on Crete and Larisa and Volos in Thessaly, have populations over 100,000. According to the most recent statistics, Greece has a population density of 78 persons per square kilometer. As for most other EU countries, the Greek birthrate has been declining steadily in the postwar period from its peak of 20.3 births per 1,000 inhabitants in 1951 to an estimated 9.82 in the year 2000. At present, 18 percent of the population is 65 years and over, 67 percent is 15–64 years, and 15 percent is under 15 years of age. Females, making up 51 percent of the country's population, have an average life expectancy of seventy-nine years, three years longer than that for males. Greece has a literacy rate of 95 percent.

According to official statistics, Greece's ethnic composition consists of a 98 percent Greek population and minority populations totaling only 2 percent. The latter figure typically does not include the small Vlach population, of fewer than 80,000, concentrated primarily in the central Pindus Range area and the even smaller Macedonian Slav population, numbering less than 40,000, located in northwestern Macedonia, both of which have been viewed culturally, if not linguistically, as Greek. Greece's largest minority comprises approximately 130,000 Muslims in Thrace, half of whom are ethnic Turks, one-quarter of whom are Pomaks (ethnic Bulgarian, or Bulgarian-speaking, Muslims), and the remainder of whom are Roma (Gypsies). Greece's indigenous population is one of the most ethnically homogeneous in Europe. Notwithstanding, during the 1990s Greek society experienced increased ethnic diversification through the influx of significant numbers of foreign workers. Historically a net exporter of labor, as the Greek economy developed during the preceding decade, Greece was transformed into a net importer of labor. Whereas a million persons emigrated from Greece between 1944 and 1974 to industrialized countries such as Australia, Canada, and the United States, since 1991 the trend has been reversed, with the number of immigrants to Greece far exceeding emigrants, the latter's once substantial numbers now altogether insignificant. By 2001 there were perhaps as many as 500,000 to 600,000 foreign citizens living in Greece. Although a significant proportion of that population consists of ethnic Greeks from Albania and the former Soviet Union, the overwhelming majority was made up of laborers from the former East Bloc and developing countries.

Perhaps the most significant postwar change in Greece's demography has been the rapid urbanization of the country's population. Whereas in 1940 only 32 percent of Greece's population resided in urban areas, by 1971 only 35 percent remained in rural communities, and in 2001 only 28 percent of Greece's population was categorized as rural. This dramatic shift of the majority of Greece's population from rural to urban and semiurban life in one generation has also produced dramatic social changes. Furthermore, Greece's population has also shifted into a new geographical axis defined by Athens in the south and Thessaloniki in the north. Through a pattern of expanding chain migration, village families established lives in the city, with migrants to Athens coming mainly from southern Greece and the islands and their counterparts in Thessaloniki coming from the north of the country. The highest rates of this postwar wave of migration took place between 1950 and 1967. Although the trend slowed during the late 1960s and through the 1970s, in those two decades alone Athens grew by 37 percent and 19 percent, respectively, and Thessaloniki grew by 46 percent and 27 percent, respectively.

RELIGION

Reflecting Greece's ethnic and cultural homogeneity, an estimated 97 percent of Greece's population identifies itself as Orthodox Christian, while 1.3 percent is Muslim. The country's remaining religious communities comprise small groups of, in order of their size, Catholics, Protestants, and Jews. With Greek philosophy, language, and ideas so decisively informing the development of Christianity in Late Antiquity, with Orthodox Christianity functioning as the chief source of inspiration for cultural production and worldview among the medieval Greeks, and with the imprint of the Orthodox Church as the primary Greek institution for the organization and preservation of collective identity under Ottoman rule, it is not surprising that Orthodoxy remains closely intertwined with national identity in Greece today.

Orthodox Christianity is based on the theology of Christianity as codified in the canons passed by the first seven church councils of the Byzantine (Christian Roman) Empire, as well as by the Christian Church's patristic foundations, established by Christ, the Apostles, and the early Church Fathers. In contrast to Western Christianity, which has developed a largely legal and functional approach to theology, Orthodoxy has consistently emphasized the experiential and mystical dimensions of theology. Furthermore, unlike Western Christendom, which was by the Early Middle Ages preoccupied with conflicts over papal religious versus secular supremacy, Eastern Christendom remained committed to the principle of ecclesiastical unity, but with a decentralized administration. This principle had been realized in practice with the creation of the five patriarchal sees of (in order of their establishment) Jerusalem, Antioch, Alexandria, Rome, and Constantinople. Eastern Christendom's tradition of cultural and administrative decentralization as a basis for ecclesiastical organization led to the formation, concurrent with the creation of an independent Greek state, of the Autocephalous Orthodox Church of Greece (Church of Greece) in 1830; the autocephaly of the Church of Greece was recognized by the Ecumenical Patriarchate of Constantinople in 1850.

During much of its history, the relationship between the Church of Greece and the Greek state was characterized by simultaneous partnership and ambivalence. One of the means by which the early Greek state sought to legitimize itself and

The Greek Language

Greek is the official language of the Greek state, and the primary language spoken by virtually all of the almost 11 million inhabitants of Greece, as well as the more than a half million Greeks of Cyprus. Greek continues to be spoken in some villages of Apulia and Calabria in southern Italy, throughout much of southern Albania, and among the dwindling Greek community of Istanbul. Greek is also spoken around the world in a global diaspora of 4–6 million Greeks. In terms of native speakers, Greek ranks well down the list of world languages. However, culturally and intellectually its importance is disproportionate to its number of native speakers. As the language of classical Greek philosophy and literature and later as the language cauldron for the development of early Christianity, Greek has profoundly shaped Western thought and world civilization.

Like any other language, Greek has evolved over time, but modern Greek can trace its pedigree to the first attempts at recording ideas in writing. An Indo-European language, Greek, in its several variations, has been used to shape a continuous literary tradition stretching back almost 3,500 years, a role no other European language has played. The earliest records of written Greek, in the archaic Mycenaean dialect, are dated around 1450 B.C.E. Ancient Greek, however, is most associated with Attic Greek, the language of fifth and fourth century B.C.E. Athens, in which most of the surviving classical Greek literature was written. Later, Greek, as it was most widely spoken in the Hellenistic Near East and throughout much of the Roman Empire, became known as *Koine* (Common). This was the form of Greek in which the New Testament was written, and from this version of Greek emerged the medieval Greek that became the official language of the Byzantine Empire and finally modern Greek.

Although its inter-intelligibility with ancient Greek is a matter of debate, modern Greek retains many of the linguistic qualities of its ancient form and a high degree of unity with it. In spite of this basic continuity, until recently the chief linguistic problem for Greece has been a conflict and dichotomy between use of the vernacular language and the literary language. As Greek intellectuals became increasingly influenced by nationalist ideas in the late eighteenth and early nineteenth centuries, language emerged as an important political issue. As they envisioned an independent Greek state, populist nationalists debated the merits of standardizing the spoken vernacular, demotic Greek, to serve as the language of a future Greek state. In contrast, elitist nationalists sought to return to a form of Greek closer to classical Greek, a literary (or artificial) language, fashioned by intellectuals and known as Katharevousa (pure) Greek. Katharevousa was accepted as the official language of the newly independent Greek state in the 1830s. The adoption of Katharevousa over demotic did not resolve the tensions between the vernacular and higher literary forms. In fact, demotic Greek experienced a creative renaissance beginning in the late nineteenth century and enjoyed increasing support from intellectuals and writers who championed it as a natural expression of the Greek people's nationhood. Although Katharevousa stimulated advances in the sophistication of demotic Greek, the dual-language system tended to reinforce social and economic divisions in Greek society to such an extent that it eventually became associated with a kind of antiquated conservatism. After a long rivalry that contributed as much to its own transformation into a new literary language as to its eventual triumph, in 1976 demotic Greek replaced Katharevousa as the official language of Greece.

its nation-building agenda was by co-opting the Orthodox Church. Meanwhile, the Orthodox Church sought to safeguard its influence in Greek society by virtue of its privileged position vis-à-vis the Greek state. In short, both institutions were interested in the subordination and exploitation of the other; consequently, the Greek state recognized Orthodoxy as the official state religion in 1833. This status for the Orthodox Church ensured that it would have a decisive role in the nation-building process of the nineteenth and early-twentieth centuries, but it did not resolve the complex tensions between church and state, which continue, despite fairly recent changes in the status of the Church.

The constitution of 1975 changed the status of Orthodox Christianity and the Orthodox Church from the official "state religion and state Church" to the "prevailing religion and established Church" of Greece. This seemingly minor change, in fact, marked a major reform in church-state relations. By drafting the Orthodox Church as Greece's established but no longer official Church, the state recognized the country's religious majority while acknowledging its religious pluralism. Like several similar constitutionally "prevailing religions and established Churches" in Western Europe, the Orthodox Church of Greece enjoys certain benefits, such as financial support from the state. However, it no longer, especially following additional church-state reforms initiated in the 1980s, wields the kind of influence through the state that it was associated with in the past.

In terms of its administrative structure, the Church of Greece is divided into seventy-eight dioceses, eight dioceses comprising the semiautonomous Church of Crete, four additional dioceses in the Dodecanese Islands, and the monastic community of Mount Athos, which enjoys constitutionally guaranteed autonomy. The Church is governed by a Holy Synod made up of all the diocesan bishops, who convene annually under the chairmanship of the archbishop of Athens, the Church's primate. Twelve bishops, chosen from the Holy Synod on a yearly basis, and the Archbishop of Athens form an executive body responsible for day-to-day Church administration. The dioceses of Crete, the Dodecanese Islands, and, nominally, the monastic community of Mount Athos are officially administratively dependent on the Ecumenical Patriarchate of Constantinople in Istanbul, Turkey. Mount Athos, given its constitutional protections, is formally organized as the Monastic Republic of Mount Athos and is administered by a committee of twenty monks, each representing one of the community's monasteries.

After Greece's 130,000 Sunni Muslims in Thrace, the country's remaining religious minority groups are made up almost entirely of small Western Christian communities. Chief among these other religious populations are Catholics. Organized into four archdioceses, in 2003 approximately 52,350 Roman Catholics lived in Greece. Most of the members of this community are descendants of Venetian settlers in the islands. Two other Catholic Churches, the Byzantine Rite and the Armenian Rite, have 2,300 and 550 communicants, respectively. The largest Protestant group in the country is the Greek Evangelical Church, which has thirty parishes and approximately 5,000 members. There are also small numbers of Jehovah's Witnesses and Mormons in Greece.

Before World War II, Greece had a Jewish population of approximately 75,000. That population, however, like the Jews of every country in Eastern Europe, was devastated by the genocide of World War II. Home to the first Jewish settlement in Europe, Jews have lived in Greece since the fourth century B.C.E. The oldest Jewish communities in Greece, with roots in antiquity, were Romaniote, Greek-speaking, Jews concentrated primarily in Athens and Ioannina. The largest Jewish population in Greece, however, was made up of Sephardic, Ladino-speaking, Jews who first arrived in the Balkans as religious refugees from Spain in the fifteenth century. Before World War II, Sephardic communities of more than a thousand Jews each could be found on Corfu, Crete, and Rhodes, as well as in the towns of Kastoria and Volos. Nonetheless, the overwhelming majority of Greece's Jews resided in Thessaloniki, where they played a dynamic role in the city's rich cultural and commercial life. In 2003 the Athens-based Central Board of the Jewish Communities of Greece, the main administrative body of Judaism in the country, estimated Greece's Jewish population at about 5,000.

NATIONAL SYMBOLS

The most important official national symbol of Greece is the Greek national flag. Although there is no consensus on the exact origins of the flag, it is clear that it was in use by Greek revolutionaries within the first year of the Greek War of Independence. The newly established Greek state adopted the revolutionary flag as Greece's official flag in 1833. The flag consists of five blue and four white alternating stripes set against a canton, which occupies the upper left corner of the flag. The canton contains a white Orthodox cross over a blue background. The cross symbolizes the Orthodox Christianity of the Greeks and their struggle against the Muslim empire of the Ottoman Turks. The use of nine stripes is deliberate, each stripe representing one of the nine syllables in the revolutionary phrase, *Eleutheria e Thanatos* (Freedom or Death), which served as a motto of determination for liberation from Ottoman rule. According to convention, the flag's two colors represent the blue of Greece's seas and the white of the restless Greek waves. Another view posits that the use of white in the flag was intended by the revolutionaries to symbolize the purity of their cause for freedom.

An unofficial flag, consisting of a simple white cross on a blue background, also dates from the first year of the Greek Revolution. This flag has been used in the past as an alternative national flag but only on land, not at sea. However, from June 1975 until December 1978, this same flag was used as the only official national flag. The law of 1978 reversed this situation, making the striped flag the only official national flag, although the alternative flag can still be seen in unofficial use.

In addition to the country's flag, the Greek national anthem also enjoys official recognition. Inspired by the Greek Revolution against the Ottoman Turks begun in 1821, the Greek national anthem is based on the "Hymn to Freedom," a lengthy poem written in 1824 by the distinguished poet Dionysios Solomos, a native of the Ionian island of Zakynthos. In 1828 the eminent composer, and native of the Ionian island of Corfu, Nikolaos Mantzaros, wrote the music for Solomos' Hymn. Although the words and music were an instant sensation and enjoyed immense popularity throughout both liberated and unredeemed Greece, the work of Solomos and Mantzaros was not adopted as the country's official anthem until 1864, when their Hymn, in words and song, finally replaced an unpopular royal anthem that had been imposed on Greece by the Great Powers in 1832.

Rudyard Kipling completed the most popular English-language translation of the national anthem in 1918, as follows:

We knew thee of old,
Oh, divinely restored,
By the lights of thine eyes,
And the light of thy Sword.

From the graves of our slain
Shall thy valor prevail
As we greet thee again—
Hail, Liberty! Hail!

Long time didst thou dwell
Mid the peoples that mourn,

Awaiting some voice
That should bid thee return.

Ah, slow broke that day
And no man dared call,
For the shadow of tyranny
Lay over all:

And we saw thee sad-eyed,
The tears on thy cheeks
While thy raiment was dyed
In the blood of the Greeks.

Yet, behold now thy sons
With impetuous breath
Go forth to the fight
Seeking Freedom or Death.

From the graves of our slain
Shall thy valor prevail
As we greet thee again
Hail, Liberty! Hail!

HISTORY
ANCIENT GREECE

People appear to have first entered Greece as hunter-gatherers from southwest Asia about 50,000 years ago. With the development of agriculture, Neolithic settlers began to establish village life in Greece by 7000 B.C.E. By the third millennium B.C.E., these Stone Age communities were transformed by advances in metallurgy. The subsequent emergence of Bronze Age culture and technology laid the foundations for the rise of Europe's first civilization, Minoan Crete. The Minoans, named for King Minos, a legendary ruler in Greek mythology, had by 2200 B.C.E. created a sophisticated urban society. The Minoan Greeks built considerable prosperity for themselves through maritime trade in the Aegean and eastern Mediterranean and innovative agricultural methods at home. Much of their wealth, in fact, was displayed in palace structures and a dramatic architectural and artistic style. The Minoans knew how to write and mastered multiple technologies, including shipbuilding and sailing. The Minoans continued to prosper until about 1450 B.C.E., when the combined pressures of a succession of natural disasters, beginning with a huge volcanic eruption that ravaged the Aegean fifty years earlier, and attacks from neighbors north of Crete brought down Minoan society.

The vulnerable Minoans were attacked and destroyed by the Mycenaeans, probably over control of the lucrative trade routes in the Mediterranean. Greek-speaking people like the Minoans, the Mycenaeans, named for the palace at Mycenae in the Peloponnesus, were settled in the southern Greek mainland as well as most of the Aegean and Ionian islands. Mycenaean culture developed later than Minoan, but by 1400 B.C.E. it had become quite prosperous. Like the Minoans, the Mycenaeans lived in independent communities organized around palaces and ruled by kings. The Mycenaeans had a warrior culture that enabled them to conquer the Minoans, but the Mycenaeans' preoccupation with fighting also contributed to their eventual downfall. By 1200 B.C.E. they began to fight each other in a succession of civil wars that lasted until about 1000 B.C.E., a period that coincided with the arrival in the southern Balkan Peninsula of a new wave of Greek tribes known as the Dorians, who, in turn, were quick to overcome the weakened Mycenaeans and seize many of their lands.

The "invasion" by the Dorians, the Mycenaeans' internecine conflicts, and other still undetermined calamities had major repercussions for the Greek world. These events appear to have caused a major migration of the Mycenaeans across the Aegean to the western coast of Asia Minor and Cyprus. More importantly, and whatever the cause, the entire economic system, kingship and centralized bureaucracy, cities and urban life, art and craftsmanship, as well as literacy disappeared, while population plummeted. For 300 years, from roughly 1050 to 750 B.C.E., after the collapse of Mycenaean civilization, a veritable dark age descended on Greece. Recovery came slowly, with the earliest revivals in agriculture and trade occurring in a few locations by 900 B.C.E. Shortly thereafter an innovation in metallurgy helped Greece escape its Dark Age. Greeks acquired from Near Eastern traders the skills necessary for the production of iron and applied this technology to produce, among other things, highly efficient and relatively inexpensive agricultural tools. Plentiful tools helped increase food production and thus stimulated population growth and economic activity.

Technological innovation paved the way for the cultural and political revival of Greece during the eighth century B.C.E. but it was not the only factor behind the rapid redevelopment of Greek society. Other significant stimuli were, first, the restoration of trade with the advanced societies of the Near East, one of the consequences of which was the development of the Greek alphabet from the Phoenician script, and, second, the Greek colonization of much of the Mediterranean and Black Sea coasts. In response to the pressures produced by a sudden and rapid population growth in a country with relatively limited arable land, large numbers of Greeks left their homeland for livelihood elsewhere. As a result, throughout the eighth century B.C.E. and beyond, Greeks established a network of colonies on the Mediterranean coasts of France and Spain, the Libyan coast of North Africa, the southern and northern shores of the Black Sea, and especially in southern Italy and Sicily, where eventually Greek cities were so densely concentrated and the Greek population so large and dominant that the region would come to be called *Magna Graecia,* or Greater Greece, by the Romans.

The reemergence of cities, among other things, marked the transition from the Dark Age to what is commonly labeled the Archaic Period, lasting from about 750 to 500 B.C.E. The poverty and insecurity of the Dark Age had forced people to cooperate in order to defend themselves, and gradually the Greeks established political power-sharing practices. By the beginning of the Archaic Period most Greeks had organized themselves into independent

Mural, palace of Minos, Knossos. (Corel Corporation)

city-states *(poleis)*. Breaking the tradition of kingship, the Greeks created new kinds of political organization for their growing communities. Initially, most of the city-states were dominated by an oligarchy, a limited elite, which was often overthrown by tyrants who temporarily seized sole power on behalf of the people. By the close of the Archaic Period this process of political evolution led to a political innovation that replaced most tyrannies and remaining oligarchies. In short, driven by the goal of avoiding a strong central authority, and utilizing long-established power and decision-making practices, the Greeks created democracy, a system involving shared self-government by all of the state's citizens. The Greek city-state, or polis, was a political and social organization based on the concept of citizenship, which guaranteed shared rights and responsibilities to its free members. Citizenship made, at least in theory if not always in practice, free men, regardless of their social status or wealth, political partners who shared equal privileges and duties under the law. In Greek democracies, all free adult male citizens, including the poor, shared in government by membership and voting in a political assembly, where laws and policies were decided. Although Greek society was decidedly paternalistic, giving only men the right to participate in politics, women were citizens legally, socially, and religiously, meaning women could own property, were

equal before the law, and enjoyed privileged positions in Greek religion.

It was largely within the dynamic of the democratic city-state that Greek culture, especially during the sixth, fifth, and fourth centuries B.C.E., produced a flood of intellectual and artistic creativity that established the foundation of Western civilization. This period saw the emergence of not only the principle of citizenship and the practice of democracy but philosophy and science as well. Some of the world's most influential thinkers, Aristotle, Plato, Pythagoras, to name but a few, essentially created our understanding of logic, ethics, and science during this time. Moving beyond their seminal inheritance of Homer, these critical centuries also produced great literary innovations in poetry and theatrical drama and comedy, as well as the first historical writing. In addition, Greek artistic brilliance expressed itself through unparalleled accomplishments in complex and beautiful architecture, as well as masterful sculptures. The works of this period exercised enormous influence in shaping subsequent notions of beauty and excellence in the creative arts and aesthetic concerns, making its own norms and values synonymous with classical standards and ideals. This remarkable confluence of creativity from so many quarters in such a relatively short period of time altered dramatically the trajectory of civilizational development.

Parthenon, Athens. (Corel Corporation)

At any rate, although democracy, most well-represented by the city-state of Athens, was the most common political system among the many Greek polities, by the beginning of the so-called Classical Period, lasting from 500 to 323 B.C.E., kingdoms survived in some parts of Greece, such as Macedonia in the far north, while elsewhere some states blended monarchy with democratic principles to create elite democratic monarchies, such as the militarist city-state of Sparta in the far south of the mainland. What all the Greek states shared in common, however, was a fierce commitment to their respective independence. The continual demand of each city-state for its complete autonomy, combined with Greek geography, which fragmented the country by its mountain complexes, hampered Greek political unity and impeded interstate cooperation even in the face of external threats.

The most serious challenge to Greek freedom, theretofore, arose in the beginning of the fifth century B.C.E. The huge Persian Empire, the most powerful state thus far in existence in the Near East, had conquered the large and prosperous Greek cities and territories in western Asia Minor around 550 B.C.E. Encouraged and supported by Athens, the Greeks in Asia Minor revolted against Persian rule in 499 B.C.E. The revolt was unsuccessful and served only to elicit the wrath of the Persians who now planned to destroy Athens. In 490 B.C.E. a large amphibious force was sent across the Aegean by the Persian emperor Darius to attack Athens. The Persian force did not reach its destination and was instead crushed by the much smaller Athenian citizen-army at the battle of Marathon. For the Athenians the victory was a remarkable demonstration of the superiority of their city-state, and it reinforced the people's confidence in democracy. The Persians, for their part, suffered a severe blow to their prestige that Darius's successor, Xerxes, would attempt to avenge a decade after Marathon. Toward that end, the Persians launched a massive invasion of the Greek mainland in 480 B.C.E., overrunning northern Greece and penetrating as far south as Athens, which had been evacuated before the Persians burned the city. All the same, allied Greek forces led by Sparta, the country's fierce military city-state, had successfully slowed the Persian advance, giving other Greek forces led by Athens, the country's leading naval power, time to consolidate their strength and defeat the Persian navy at the battle of Salamis. A year later, in 479 B.C.E., the Greeks completed their triumph by decisively defeating the Persian army at the battle of Plataia. This string of unexpected Greek victories against the Persians preserved Greek independence and further reinforced their confidence, especially that of the Athenians.

Before the Persian Wars, Sparta was the most powerful and feared city-state in Greece. Athenian power and influence, however, had grown enormously as a consequence of its major role in the defeat of the Persian invasion. Both Athens and Sparta were soon competing with each other for primacy among the Greek city-states. Athens used its wartime fleet to become an aggressive power rivaling Sparta, while Sparta maintained its alliance with other city-states in the Peloponnesus as a counterbalance to the growing influence of Athens. The Delian League, made up largely of the Aegean maritime city-states, brought Athens unprecedented power and wealth. Athens, having established hegemony over the Delian League gradually through the use of force and political controls, converted the alliance into an empire and the erstwhile allies into subject peoples.

As resentment grew against the Athenian misuse of power, the city-state's perhaps most dynamic political leader rose to prominence. Pericles, an Athenian from a distinguished family, and the originator of Athenian monumental public works and building projects, including the Parthenon, became the era's leading politician in the 450s B.C.E. by promoting Athenian dominance within the Delian League and expansionist goals outside the alliance. He sponsored far-flung expeditions in the Black Sea and eastern Mediterranean and engaged the Athenian navy in a confrontation with Sparta. Despite a brief stabilization of relations with Sparta, the aggressive policies of Pericles so threatened the balance of power between Athens and Sparta that any crisis soon acquired the potential to provoke a major conflict. In fact, in 431 B.C.E. tensions erupted when Athens pressured Corinth, a crucial Spartan ally, which was a rival with Athens for maritime trade. Sparta came to the defense of Corinth and the subsequent fighting led to the Peloponnesian War.

Ultimately involving virtually all of the states comprising the Greek political world, and fought in two phases between 431 and 404 B.C.E., the Peloponnesian War began well for Athens, which used its large fleet to good effect against Sparta and its allies. However, the death of Pericles and the superior Spartan army produced a military deadlock. In an effort to break the armed stalemate, the Athenians undertook increasingly bold, risky strategies. In 415 B.C.E. Athens launched an ill-conceived large-scale campaign against Sparta's allies in Sicily, which ended in a catastrophic defeat of the Athenian army outside the city of Syracuse in 413 B.C.E. Athens did not recover from this defeat, and the Spartan victory on land was followed by the destruction of the Athenian navy in 404 B.C.E. and the surrender of Athens in the same year.

Before the victorious Spartans withdrew to their home territory in the Peloponnesus, they imposed a harsh peace on the Athenians. The Athenian empire was dismantled and the Delian League ended. Moreover, Athenian democracy was abolished and replaced by a brutal puppet government made up of an autocratic group of oligarchs. However, with Spartan troops gone from Athens, the oligarchs were unable to keep their hold on power and were overthrown in 403 B.C.E., less than a year after being installed. Athens restored its democracy, rebuilt some of its strength, and entered into a new phase of competition for leadership in Greece. From 403 to 338 B.C.E., Athens, Corinth, Sparta, and Thebes competed with each other for hegemony in Greece, with Sparta wielding more power during the first half of this period followed by Thebes during the last half. None of these rivals, however, was strong enough to decisively defeat all of the other competitors and fully dominate Greece. As a result of this intense interstate rivalry, these city-states drove each other to exhaustion by constant warfare, creating instability, weakness, and a veritable power vacuum in central and southern Greece.

The Kingdom of Macedonia stepped into this competition for hegemony in Greece during the reign of Philip II, which began in 359 B.C.E. Despite its comparatively large territory and population, Macedonia had historically been underdeveloped and politically weak. As a consequence, Macedonia rarely played a significant role in Greek politics. In addition, Macedonia's geographic position as Greece's northernmost state had long forced the kingdom to devote most of its attention and resources to the defense of its porous northern frontier against the non-Greek peoples of the central Balkans, the Illyrian and Thracian tribes, who continually raided and sometimes invaded Macedonia's territory. Furthermore, although the Macedonians were ethnically, culturally, and linguistically Greek, they were viewed disparagingly by many southern Greeks as barbarous and even foreign because of their unsophisticated customs and lack of urban ways. Undaunted, the ambitious Philip was committed to asserting Macedonia's leadership in the Greek world. Macedonia emerged as a powerful force when Philip II built up a large, highly disciplined army, which he used to secure the kingdom's northern flank by neutralizing the Illyrians and Thracians and then turned south against his Greek rivals. Effectively employing diplomacy, bribery, and, when faced with resistance, his army and war, by 338 B.C.E. Philip forced the weakened city-states to acknowledge Macedonia's leadership and hegemony in Greece.

Philip's ultimate goal, to lead an allied Greek army in a war of revenge and conquest against the Persian Empire, was taken up by his son, Alexander, who succeeded his father after Philip's assassination in 336 B.C.E. Alexander the Great began the invasion of the Persian Empire in 334 B.C.E., defeating a Persian army near historic Troy, liberating the Greek cities of western Asia Minor, and overrunning Anatolia. Alexander continued his astonishing campaign and added to his growing string of victories through Syria and Egypt, before turning his advance against Mesopotamia, where he demolished the Persian emperor Darius III's final field army in 331 B.C.E., and eventually the heart of the Persian Empire in Iran. After destroying the Persian capital, Persepolis, in an act of vengeance for the Persian burning of Athens almost 150 years earlier, Alexander and his forces resumed their eastward march, conquering former Persian lands in Central Asia and beyond into India. The unity of Alexander's far-flung empire, which he colonized with Greek settlers in a string of newly established cities throughout the eastern Mediterranean and Near East, and within which he had planned to create a new global hybrid society of blended

Greek and Persian peoples and cultures, did not survive his premature death in 323 B.C.E.

The death of Alexander the Great resulted in a power struggle and division of his empire into kingdoms established by his senior generals. Antigonos formed a kingdom encompassing the historic Greek territories in the southern Balkans and Asia Minor, while Seleucus established rule over Mesopotamia, Iran, and the Central Asian provinces, and Ptolemy seized Egypt and initially Syria and Palestine. These absolutist Greek monarchies encouraged the continued Greek colonization of their cities and towns and witnessed the integration of Greek and local Near Eastern cultures to produce a new cultural environment in which the Greek language functioned as the lingua franca for culture, commerce, and administration throughout the Near East. Greek art, architecture, and thought, as well, became prevalent in the eastern Mediterranean during the three centuries following the death of Alexander the Great, a period typically known as the Hellenistic Age.

Macedonia's ongoing domination of the city-states of central and southern Greece, as well as the absolutist rule of the Hellenistic kingdoms, disturbed many Greeks, who remembered their history of political freedom and democracy. Consequently, during the second century B.C.E., when the Hellenistic kingdoms had been weakened by internecine wars, some mainland Greeks appealed for help from the western Mediterranean's emerging superpower, Rome. The Romans, who had begun their steady expansion into the Greek world by conquering the Greek states of southern Italy and Sicily and invading the Greek lands in the western Balkans a century earlier, took advantage of the new opportunity to interject themselves in Greek affairs. After defeating the Macedonians in 197 B.C.E. and declaring the rest of Greece liberated, the Romans proceeded to impose their will on Greece. The Greeks consequently rebelled, but a Roman army invaded the country, burned the city of Corinth in 146 B.C.E., and placed mainland Greece under Roman rule. The Romans continued their expansion into the Greek world, and within about a hundred years Rome conquered the last remaining Hellenistic kingdom with the fall and annexation of Queen Cleopatra's Egypt in 31 B.C.E.

The conquest of the Greek world ensured that the fortunes of the Greeks and Romans would be intertwined for the rest of the Roman Empire's existence. During the two centuries that followed Rome's conquest of Hellenistic Egypt, uninterrupted peace and security in the Mediterranean created the conditions for considerable cultural creativity and economic growth in the Greek world, as well as the emergence of Greek scholars as the empire's intellectual elite and the integration of prominent Greeks into Rome's ruling class. In addition, Greek cities became the administrative and economic centers of the eastern half of the empire. Greek cities such as Alexandria, Athens, Corinth, Ephesus, Miletus, Smyrna, and Thessaloniki flourished, producing a new urban, and often wealthy, Greek elite. At the same time, life in Greek cities incorporated certain Roman features, and new generations of Romanized Greeks emerged. Concurrently, Roman elites and even emperors embraced Greek culture, actively promoting the Hellenization of much of Roman culture and drawing from Greece to produce architecture, art, education, and literature. Meanwhile, and moreover, the Greek cultural, demographic, intellectual, and linguistic landscape, which had been grafted onto the Near East by Alexander the Great and the Hellenistic kingdoms, was only further embedded and expanded in the region under Roman rule. Greek language and thought, interacting with local religion, created the foundations for the cultural and intellectual development and spread of Christianity, leaving a lasting Greek philosophical influence on the theology and ecclesiology of the Christian Church.

BYZANTIUM AND MEDIEVAL GREECE

The peace and prosperity that the Greek world enjoyed during the first two centuries C.E. began to break down as the result of a series of Roman civil wars and foreign attacks against the empire in the third century. The responses to the growing pressures on the imperial system highlighted the disparity in strength and resilience between regions rather than the unity of the empire as a whole. Such conditions set the Latin West and the Greek East onto separate historical trajectories. When the Emperor Constantine I chose to relocate the empire's capital from Rome to the Greek city of Byzantium (later known as Constantinople) in 324 C.E., he not only advanced the growing separation of the eastern and western halves of the empire, he explicitly acknowledged the superior cultural, economic, and military resilience of the east. This move did not represent a break with Rome; the Roman Empire would continue but under a revised political structure, with a different geographic anchor, and, in time, an entirely new cultural and religious foundation. In short, Constantine established the foundations for the transition of the Roman Empire to the Eastern Roman, or Byzantine, Empire, an essentially Medieval and Christian Greek state.

Marking this transformation, in 325 Constantine proclaimed Christianity the empire's official religion and presided over the First Ecumenical Council in Nicaea. This gathering of the hierarchical leadership of the early Christian Church, as well as subsequent councils, formalized the faith's doctrines and defined the theology of Orthodox Christianity. During the next two centuries Christianity supplanted the final vestiges of pagan tradition in the Greek world, producing a culture founded on Orthodoxy and Roman identity within a Greek-speaking society. Notwithstanding the fact that the Byzantines were ethnically and linguistically Greek, they thought of themselves as Romans and their empire, quite legitimately, as the direct inheritor of classical Rome. Constantinople in time became the cultural, economic, intellectual, and political center of the Medieval Mediterranean world, and the Byzantines regarded their capital as the center of a theocratic state meant to represent God's heavenly order on earth.

For the Byzantine Greeks, their confidence in the superiority of their state was affirmed by the survival of their empire. The Greek East faced many of the same barbarian waves in the late fourth and through the fifth centuries that would also descend on the West. The Byzantines had even suffered some military losses to the barbarians, but their army succeeded in either destroying or pushing out the invaders. The Latin West, conversely, did not fare as well. By the late fifth century, the western part of the empire had been overrun by Germanic invasions and its lands had been transformed into a patchwork of barbarian successor states. Although Constantinople and the Byzantine Empire eventually triumphed over the Germanic threat and demonstrated a remarkable ability to withstand and survive serious external threats, something that would be repeated continually for many centuries, parts of mainland Greece were devastated by the barbarians. The Visigoths, who had been pushed across the Danube by the Huns, defeated an imperial army at Adrianople in 378 and marched southward wreaking havoc in peninsular Greece, sacking several cities, including Argos, Corinth, and Sparta in 395, before being driven out of the Balkans. Almost a century later, in 465, the Vandals attacked northern and central Greece but were quickly defeated. The Greek mainland recovered some prosperity and the population thrived once more during the following hundred years. However, this peaceful interlude ended with the massive Slav migrations into the Balkans beginning in 582.

Shortly before the Slav invasions took place, the Byzantine Empire launched a major series of military campaigns aimed at the reconquest, or liberation, and reunification of the Roman imperial lands lost earlier to the barbarians in the West. Emperor Justinian I, who ruled from 527 to 565, inaugurated this policy and succeeded at restoring imperial control over Italy, much of Spain, and northwest Africa. However successful Justinian's campaigns may have been in the short term, his policy of reconquest of the West left a vastly reexpanded but perilously overstretched empire, in both financial and military terms. Consequently the empire's core Greek territories in Asia Minor and the Balkans were more vulnerable to external threats after Justinian's reign than they had been before it. This fact was made evident when beginning in the late sixth, through most of the seventh, and into the eighth centuries Slavs broke through Byzantium's northern defenses, entered the Balkans, overran enormous stretches of the peninsula, and penetrated as far south as the Peloponnesus. Meanwhile, the empire's longtime nemesis in the east, Persia, occupied Byzantine Syria and pushed into Asia Minor.

Unlike the previous Germanic invaders, who had been content to raid and loot in the Balkans and Greece, the Slavs established permanent settlements. The Slav migration and occupation of the central Balkans, as well as much of western mainland Greece and parts of the country's interior, had been aided by a plague, which had depopulated and made available much of the region's territory to the Slavs.

Byzantine city of Mistras in the Peloponnesus. (Corel Corporation)

Hagia Sophia

Considered the finest example of Byzantine architecture and perhaps the most impressive building achievement of Late Antiquity and the early medieval world, Hagia Sophia in Constantinople, a cathedral overlooking the Bosporus, was constructed on a scale unprecedented in human history. For more than a thousand years it stood as the world's largest structure, with an interior space unrivalled by any other building in both total mass and height. Although there is no available physical evidence confirming it, early accounts suggest that Hagia Sophia was built on the site of an ancient pagan temple appropriated for the service of the Eastern Roman Empire's new official religion, Christianity.

The church underwent three major phases of construction before attaining its final form. The first church on the site was built by Emperor Constantius I, son of Emperor Constantine, and was consecrated in 360. Although little is known about this structure, it is generally accepted that it was a basilica-type building with a rectangular floor plan, circular apse, and timbered roof. The structure was first named Megali Ekklesia (the Great Church) because it was the largest church in the Christian world at the time. Before Constantius's reign ended, the church became known as Hagia Sophia (Holy Wisdom), a name attributed to Christ by Greek theologians in the fourth century. In 404 the church was destroyed by rioting mobs protesting the emperor's illegitimate exiling of the patriarch of Constantinople. In 415 Emperor Theodosius I rebuilt the church, but it was destroyed by a rebellion of heretics in 532. After putting down the rebellion, Emperor Justinian I, a firm defender of Orthodoxy, ordered the construction of an entirely new church that was to surpass in magnificence all earlier churches.

Driven by his ambition to make his church the greatest structure in the world, Justinian personally supervised the construction of Hagia Sophia and made full use of the empire's resources. The finest and rarest materials from throughout the Mediterranean world were brought to Constantinople to be used in the building of the church. The two most famous architects of the Greek world at the time, Anthemius of Tralles and Isidorus of Miletus, were entrusted with the design of the church and execution of its construction. They oversaw the work of 100 master builders and 10,000 laborers. Launched in February 532, the construction of Hagia Sophia was completed in December 537. The new building was like no other structure that had been built before it. In fact, the grand basilica represented a major revolution in architecture. In grappling with how to build a circular dome atop a square base, Anthemius and Isidorus arrived at an unprecedented solution and thus created a brilliant, creative outcome. They built four massive columns, each measuring approximately 33.45 square meters, at the base, positioned at each corner of the foundation, and on top of each column they built four arches. The architects then filled the spaces between the arches with masonry to create curved triangular shapes called pendetives, which, once structurally integrated with the arches, created an incredibly strong base of support for Hagia Sophia's most remarkable feature, its huge dome with a diameter of 33.5 meters. The church measures 79.25 by 82.3 meters, and the dome rises 64 meters above the floor. Pierced by forty single-arched windows set at the dome's base, light entered the structure in a way that created the visual sensation that the dome actually floated over the church. In addition, twelve large windows in two rows flooded the building with streams of light, producing the impression of infinite space. Having been damaged by three earthquakes in the sixth century, another in the ninth, and again by one in the tenth century, the church was made progressively stronger and more resilient with each set of repairs and additional architectural buttressing.

Hagia Sophia, the mother church of all Orthodox Christians and the greatest architectural triumph of the Byzantine Empire, even survived foreign conquest. In 1204 Roman Catholic Crusaders attacked and sacked Constantinople. Hagia Sophia was not spared as the crusaders looted and defiled the church, while purposely damaging much of its interior. With the restoration of Greek control in Constantinople in 1261, Hagia Sophia was repaired and again functioned as the cathedral of the patriarch of Constantinople. After the Ottoman conquest of Constantinople in 1453, Hagia Sophia was converted into a mosque. In 1935 it was converted into a Turkish state museum. Albeit Turkey's most visited museum and the country's most famous tourism resource, Hagia Sophia has not enjoyed government support comparable to that extended to Muslim historical sites in Istanbul and elsewhere. Furthermore, the structure is aggressively marketed and increasingly subjected to the vulgarities of the tourist trade, whereas the religious sanctity and historical integrity of other sites are safeguarded. UNESCO and other international organizations have expressed serious concerns about Turkey's insufficient attention to the preservation, restoration, and management of Hagia Sophia. This crisis of indifference led World Monument Watch to include Hagia Sophia on its list of one hundred most endangered sites.

Nonetheless, this rugged part of Greece had historically been the most sparsely populated area of the country and, given its limited agricultural potential, could never sustain a large population, either Greek or Slav. All the same, most of the Greek population from these territories was displaced and pushed toward the coasts and the eastern part of the country, where imperial defenses held. Where Greek communities survived in the interior, they had been able to do so because they had withdrawn to defensive geographic positions before arriving at local understandings for coexistence with the Slav tribes. By 750, despite the fact that the Greek population in the region had remained intact and was still larger than that of the Slavs, most of northern and central Greece, and even parts of the country's south, had been overrun and occupied by Slav tribes. At the same time, the empire's territories in the Near East had been seized by a new enemy that proved to be an even more serious threat than the Persians, the Arabs, who also raided Asia Minor in depth and threatened Constantinople.

Again demonstrating its resilience, the Byzantine Empire reversed many of these losses by going on the counteroffensive against the Slavs in Greece and pushing the Arabs out of southeastern Asia Minor. Political stability internally, the beginning of a new period of economic growth and expansion in the late eighth century, and dissension among their enemies, enabled the Byzantines, by the year 800, to reestablish control over all of Asia Minor and to reassert the empire in the Greek mainland territories formerly overrun by the Slavs. Once these territories were again under imperial administration, the Byzantines implemented a resettlement policy, like that used earlier with considerable success in parts of eastern Asia Minor, to ensure that the reconquered, or liberated, lands would contain only loyal populations. Consequently, following the expulsion of considerable numbers of Slavs, the Greek communities that had been displaced by the invasions of the preceding century were returned to their original lands, while Greek refugees from southern Italy and surplus Greek populations from densely populated western Asia Minor were also settled in these areas. Pockets of Slavs remained scattered in the Greek territories, but their isolated condition and reduced numbers led in time to their assimilation and absorption by the much larger surrounding Greek populations.

Although the empire had been successful in reconquering mainland Greece and restoring, more or less, the historic Greek ethnological frontier in the south Balkans, Greek security problems in the region were far from over. The Bulgars, a Turkic people assimilated by the Slavs, settled south of the Danube and began to pose a serious threat to Byzantium by the late ninth century. In the early tenth century, under the aggressive leadership of their khans, they established a rival empire and invaded much of northern Greece and the central Balkans. The Byzantines and Bulgars were soon locked in a long series of brutal wars that culminated in 1014, when the dynamic and formidable Emperor Basil II led his army in a string of brilliant actions, decisively crushing the Bulgars (earning the nickname Bulgar Slayer) and conquering all of their lands. Before destroying the Bulgars, Basil had defeated the Arabs in a series of equally dazzling military campaigns beyond southeastern Anatolia, restoring parts of northern Mesopotamia, northern Syria, and the Syrian coast to the empire.

Basil II's reign from 963 to 1025, the longest of any Byzantine Roman emperor, marked the zenith of both the empire's power and the prestige and influence of the Medieval Greek world. All of the Balkan Peninsula south of the Danube was firmly back in Byzantium's grip; even the Croats and Serbs in the region's northwest had voluntarily submitted to vassal status rather than risk the fate that had befallen the Bulgars, total conquest and subjugation. On the eastern frontier, with the Arabs defeated and the Byzantines having established forward defense positions in Syria, Asia Minor was well protected, at peace, and prospering. In order to create an additional geographic shield for the empire's most valuable territorial base, Anatolia, Basil expanded his control of formerly independent Armenian and Georgian principalities. Although the empire under Basil was smaller than it had been under Justinian, it was more territorially cohesive and fundamentally stronger. Protected by border conquests and an innovative system of layered and territorial defense, Byzantium's core, historic, and Greek-populated lands—Asia Minor, the southern Balkans, and southern Italy—now formed a more compact, homogeneous, manageable, and powerful territorial unit than at any previous time.

Byzantium's large, professional, well-led, yet still primarily citizen-soldier army was the most efficient and feared fighting force in the Mediterranean world, but the empire's power and influence was not limited to military affairs. The empire experienced a dramatic revival of intellectual life beginning in the ninth century that continued through the tenth century. During this period, ancient manuscripts were recopied and disseminated in large quantity, reference works and encyclopedias were compiled, and astronomy, literature, mathematics, and philosophy received new attention. The revival of classical learning was accompanied by a conscious return to classic models in art and literature, which were found to complement rather than conflict with Byzantium's dominant religious aesthetic in the creative arts. The empire also experienced a remarkable, steady economic expansion during this period, fueled in large part by intensified trade in the Mediterranean and Black Seas. Byzantium so effectively dominated international trade, accumulated such incomparable wealth, and enjoyed such fiscal stability, that its coinage was for centuries accepted as the international hard currency standard for trade throughout the Mediterranean world and beyond.

Moreover, Byzantine cultural, religious, and intellectual influence radiated throughout Eastern Europe, the eastern Mediterranean, and much of Italy. It was during Basil's reign that the state of Kiev converted to Christianity and a new era of development began for Russia. Two centuries earlier, the Greek monks Cyril and Methodius had been instrumental in establishing the foundations for the conversion to Orthodoxy of the Bulgars, Serbs, and East Central European Slavs by creating a literary language, Church Slavonic, for liturgical use among all Slavs. The Medieval Greeks, from their cosmopolitan centers of Constantinople and Thessaloniki transmitted modes of art, architecture, and thought that were embraced and reproduced by the peoples newly converted to Orthodoxy. In short, these Eastern European and Russian peoples, like the historic Christian populations of the Near East earlier, were drawn into a kind of Greek cultural commonwealth that extended far beyond the empire's political borders, leaving a lasting Byzantine civilizational imprint on their societies.

By the death in 1025 of Emperor Basil II, the empire was once again the paramount economic, cultural, political, and military power in the Mediterranean world, rivaled only by the Arab caliphate in Egypt and Syria. Byzantium's accomplishments and monumental wealth created unparalleled grandeur and prestige for the empire, often articulated through a tradition of imperial statesmanship and adroit diplomacy. Notwithstanding, sometimes Byzantium's image was greater than its actual strength, and it often disguised the empire's problems, both small and large. After Basil's death, the empire enjoyed continued economic expansion and prosperity but suffered from a series of mediocre emperors who neglected the state's needs and allowed the army to deteriorate. Increasing state demands for revenue clashed with short-sighted aristocratic resistance to tax paying, while political factionalism in the imperial court led to policy failures, the dangerous overestimation of military strength, and neglect of defenses. Paradoxically, these structural problems, which rapidly sapped the empire's real power and ability to respond to serious threats, went largely unnoticed because of the universal perception of Byzantium's presumably unshakable prowess.

Byzantium's image as an invincible superpower was so great that even the magnitude and implications of the strategic disaster that befell the empire in 1071 could not be fully understood or appreciated by both belligerents in this clash, Greeks and Turks. When Seljuk raiding parties were able to defeat a major (but inadequately trained and poorly led) imperial force at the chaotic battle of Manzikert in Armenian Anatolia in 1071 and capture the emperor, Romanus IV, the empire could offer no organized counterattack. As a result, the interior of Asia Minor was open to invasion by the Seljuk Turks, and central Anatolia was lost permanently to the empire. Asia Minor, the empire's agricultural breadbasket, the source of most of its soldiers, and the core of its population base, would now be vulnerable to attack and invasion. For centuries the Byzantines had relied on the rugged, mountainous, excellent natural defense lines created by the geography of eastern Anatolia to defend the rest of Asia Minor. Other invaders had penetrated Asia Minor in the past, but the empire had always been able to respond with successful counteroffensives that forced the Arabs or Persians back across the eastern frontier defenses. Now, however, conditions changed as the Turks could not be dislodged from the central Anatolian plateau. This strategic turn began the steady multicentury transformation of Asia Minor from an entirely Christian and Greek-populated region to a predominantly Muslim and Turkish one.

Ironically, in their relations with their fellow Christians in the West, the imperial majesty, prestige, and wealth that the Byzantines enjoyed proved to be as much a liability as an asset. The Latin, and from the perspective of the Byzantines, semibarbarous, Westerners, increasingly resented the power and influence of Byzantium, while they coveted the Greek world's spectacular wealth. Furthermore, many of the petty princes and kings of Western Christendom had irritated the Byzantines since the ninth century by seizing the empire's lands in Italy and, more menacingly, by challenging the legitimacy of Constantinople's emperors as heirs of the Roman Empire and affecting the pretense themselves as inheritors of the Roman Crown, thus implicitly threatening Byzantium. The bishop of Rome, or pope, contributed to the growing tensions between Western and Eastern Christendom by aligning his see with the political ambitions of Germanic and other imperial pretenders to the Roman Crown in exchange for their political and military support to press his own objective of papal supremacy over the entire Christian Church. Although the early Christian Church reserved, among its ancient ecclesiastical sees, primacy of honor for Rome, this primacy was honorific among equals, not administrative over subordinates. Consequently the early Christian tradition of ecclesiastical autonomy, cooperation, and decision making in ecumenical councils, still vibrant in Eastern Christendom in the ninth century and beyond, necessarily required the sees, or patriarchates, of Alexandria, Antioch, Constantinople, and Jerusalem to reject the growing autocracy and imperial ambitions of the pope. More immediately for Byzantium, after centuries of growing tension, the expanding political and cultural gulf between Eastern and Western Christendom reached a crisis with a formal schism between the papacy and the patriarchate of Constantinople in 1054. This mutual excommunication would have significant political implications for Byzantium and the freedom of the Medieval Greeks.

As relations between the Latin West and the Greek East deteriorated, an atmosphere of hostility emerged that many Western adventurers, with their attention focused on Byzantium's wealth, were quite willing to exploit. Violence was initiated by the Normans, who began raiding Byzantium's western territories in 1080 from their base in Sicily. In 1146, and underscoring the serious nature of the threat posed by the Latin West, the Normans attacked mainland Greece, ravaged much of the countryside, and sacked the city of Thebes, which had been targeted because of the wealth it had acquired from the silk trade. Approximately forty years later, the Normans once more invaded Greece and sacked the great cultural and commercial center of Thessaloniki, Byzantium's second largest city. The Byzantine emperor turned to the growing naval power of Venice for help in interdicting the Normans at sea. The Venetians agreed to assist the Greeks but only in exchange for access to the lucrative trade markets of the empire. Once the Venetians penetrated the empire's economy, they ruthlessly and systematically exploited their privileges. Although the Byzantine emperors attempted to curtail predatory Venetian policies, Byzantium found its former ally a deadly threat embedded within the empire.

The Greeks' fears of the West's intentions materialized during the Fourth Crusade. The Venetians exploited Western prejudice against the Greeks and persuaded the Crusader army, mobilized earlier by the pope and organized in France, to attack Constantinople rather than go to the Holy Land. In 1204 the Fourth Crusade besieged and sacked the empire's capital, Europe's and the Mediterranean world's largest and wealthiest city. Constantinople's population was brutalized and much of the city was burned while most of its treasures and wealth were looted and carried off to Western Europe. The Crusaders then proceeded to partition many of the empire's territories into a ring of Latin kingdoms, principalities, and duchies based in Constantinople, the Greek mainland encircling the Aegean, and the Aegean islands. These occupation states imported Western feudalism and Catholic hierarchs to exploit the Greek subject populations economically and to oppress them religiously. The actions of the Crusaders ended the possibility of any ecclesiastical reconciliation or political cooperation between the Greeks and the West.

Their general incompetence at governance, coupled with the popular hatred against them that their conduct produced, ensured that most of the Latin occupation states would be short-lived. Moreover, as soon as the Crusaders began their occupation of Greece, resistance against them was organized. From their territorial bases in western and northeastern Asia Minor and Epirus in the Balkans, Greek Byzantine successor states waged a war of liberation and reconquest against the Latin occupation forces in and around Constantinople. Led by the new Paleologos dynasty, in 1261 the Greeks recovered Constantinople, much reduced in population and condition by the Latin regime's abuses, and reestablished the city as the capital of the Byzantine Empire.

Although the empire was revived, the events of 1204 had so weakened Byzantium that it was no longer a great power. The empire consolidated most of its territorial base in northern Greece and western Asia Minor during the late thirteenth century but was unable to assert itself beyond this area. Furthermore, the empire's Balkan territories remained caught in a strategic pincer during the fourteenth century, with the Bulgars and Serbs, having reasserted their independence after 1204, pressing on Byzantine Macedonia and Thrace from the north and the surviving Latin states clinging to parts of central Greece to the south. At the same time, the Byzantine position in Asia Minor was threatened by the emerging strength of the Ottoman Turks.

Under these overwhelming conditions, the much truncated and weakened empire could not have expected to survive much longer. The empire's resources after 1261 were acutely limited in terms of finances, territory, and military strength. Remarkably, despite the ongoing depredations of the West, the continual loss of territory to rival Balkan states, followed by the loss of virtually all of Byzantium's remaining lands to the expanding and powerful Ottomans, Late Medieval Greek society experienced an astonishing outburst of artistic, cultural, and intellectual creativity. The empire's waning years saw another major revival of Greek classicism as Greek scholarship and increasing numbers of Greek intellectuals found their way to Italy, where both would have a significant impact on the Renaissance. Nonetheless, by the middle of the fifteenth century, Byzantium had been reduced to little more than Constantinople

and its outlying villages, the historic Spartan portion of the Peloponnesus, and a few Aegean islands, all surrounded by the Ottoman Empire. The end came in 1453 when, after a two-month siege, an Ottoman force of 200,000 overcame Constantinople's 8,000 defenders and captured the city. Although the Ottomans had conquered most of the Greek lands in Asia Minor and the Balkans years earlier, and although it was some years before all Byzantine territories were conquered, the fall of Constantinople marked the end of the Greek medieval empire and the Greeks' freedom.

MODERN GREECE

During the three centuries after the Turks first entered Southeastern Europe, the Greek world came almost entirely under the control of their Islamic and dynastic empire. Between 1354, the year the Ottomans crossed the Straits into Thrace, and 1461, the year the final Byzantine fortifications in the Peloponnesus fell to them, the Ottomans had not only conquered all of mainland Greece but virtually the entire Balkan Peninsula as well. With their own state destroyed, the Greeks now became spectators and victims in a struggle for dominance of the eastern Mediterranean between the Ottoman Empire and Venice. Although much smaller Venice lacked the military resources that the huge Ottoman Empire possessed, the apparently unequal struggle was sustained by a potent combination of the Italian republic's wealth, diplomacy, naval power, and religious fanaticism. The rivalry between the Ottoman Empire and Venice was fought out almost entirely on Greek soil, and the fate of much of the Greek population was determined for the next several centuries by the fortunes of these aggressive rivals. Control of strategic positions on the coasts of the Greek mainland and in the islands of the Aegean and Ionian Seas was fiercely contested and was regarded by both the Ottomans and Venetians as essential to their survival.

The first Turko-Venetian War broke out in 1463 and ended in 1479. The war did not produce a change in the strategic balance between the Ottomans and Venetians, but it did establish a pattern of conflict and fighting between the two protagonists, which resulted in more injury to the local Greek population than to either of the belligerents, that would be often repeated. Renewed wars were fought on the Greek islands, as well as in coastal and southern Greece, from 1499 to 1502 and again from 1537 to 1540. Between 1566 and 1669 the Ottomans and Venetians fought each other without respite. This brutal, protracted phase of the Ottoman-Venetian rivalry over Greece led to a series of Ottoman victories culminating in the Turkish conquest of Venetian-held Crete and Cyprus, as well as the Aegean islands not already under their control. Emboldened by the Ottoman failure to capture Vienna a year earlier, the Venetians launched a counteroffensive war in 1684. The Venetians successfully reoccupied the Peloponnesus and advanced into central Greece, positions they would hold onto until their final defeat in 1715. It was during this campaign that the Parthenon, largely intact since antiquity, atop the famed Acropolis, was seriously damaged by Venetian cannon fire.

The near destruction of the Parthenon, caught between Venetian cannonballs and exploding Ottoman gunpowder magazines, served as a symbolic analog for the fate of much of Greece during the Turko-Venetian Wars. For the Greeks, both the Turks and Venetians were foreign masters who denied them their freedom, exploited them and their lands, and imposed often violent and arbitrary rule. The greatest impact of the two-century-long conflict was on the physical condition of the hapless Greek population. Most of the crews, in both the Ottoman and Venetian navies, that fought each other were made up of Greeks pressed into service by their respective occupiers. Greeks also had to provide military levies to both belligerents. But the enormous loss of life among Greek sailors and soldiers paled in comparison to the level of destruction experienced by the general population. The savage intensity of these wars, the marching of armies back and forth over the same territories, and the depredations of both Turks and Venetians against local villages and towns left much of central and southern Greece depopulated, while many Aegean islands were made entirely uninhabitable.

The Greek populations in Asia Minor and those north of the fighting in the Balkans escaped the devastation that affected other parts of the Greek world during the Turko-Venetian Wars. These communities, which experienced uninterrupted Ottoman rule, may not have been exposed to fighting but they did not escape the dictates of the Ottoman state, which was, in its classic form and function, an Islamic war machine whose purpose was constant expansion. The lives of ordinary Greek people were, accordingly, structured to satisfy the interests and needs of the Ottoman system. The Greeks, as the empire's most populous and important subject peoples, were profoundly affected by this situation. Their taxes paid for the sultan's wars and their agriculture was organized to sustain the economic needs of a feudal Ottoman military caste. They built, captained, and crewed the sultan's fleet. Finally, through the *devshirme,* a human tax on the subject Christians, Greek children were taken from their families, converted to Islam, and trained to form the elite corps of the sultan's army, while others ascended the imperial system to serve as the highest officials and diplomats of the Ottoman state. The non-Muslim inhabitants of the sultan's territories were regarded by the Ottoman state as *reaya* (cattle), a resource to be tapped for manpower and material in pursuit of Islamic and imperial expansion. The customs, social structures, and religious institutions and hierarchies of the Greeks (as well as other Christians) were of no interest to the sultan, so long as they provided the resources to serve the empire's policies and did not challenge the state's total authority and Islam's supremacy.

As an Islamic polity, Ottoman society was organized into millets (nations), in effect, administrative units based on religious identity. Thus, over time, the Patriarchate of Constantinople functioned simultaneously as an ecclesiastical institution and an administrative, civil, and judicial apparatus for Orthodox Christians in the empire. The patriarch, as head of the Orthodox population, answered to the sultan, for whom he administered the Orthodox populations, and was responsible for ensuring the subject Christians' loyalty and obedience to the empire. As a result of this situation, the Orthodox Church was put in the paradoxical position of acting to advance the interests of the Ottoman Islamic theocracy while trying to preserve through limited autonomy the survival of Christian culture and Greek society. This delicate balancing act did not always work, as more than one patriarch paid with his life for his coreligionists' resistance to the sultan's rule and as significant numbers of Orthodox Christians converted to Islam in order to escape the devshirme, discriminatory taxes, abuses, and restrictive and demeaning regulations that accompanied the Ottoman separate but unequal *millet* system.

Many Greeks suffered while others benefited from this system of contemptuous tolerance. So-called Phanariot Greeks, members of a small group of families originating in the Phanar quarter of Constantinople, came to hold important administrative and diplomatic positions in the service of the sultan, forming an influential elite and, for a period, exercising considerable autonomous authority in the Ottoman Romanian provinces of Moldavia and Wallachia. In the Greek countryside local elites, especially in the Peloponnesus, enjoyed some social status and privileges in exchange for controlling their peasant counterparts. Finally, given the Muslim Turks' disdain for the usurious aspects of commerce and investment, Greeks were allowed to dominate trade and eventually banking in the empire. Their involvement in commerce within the empire led to the emergence of a prosperous Greek merchant class that was dispersed throughout the urban centers of Asia Minor and especially the Balkans. Furthermore, Greek networks of trade expanded beyond the empire to link Ottoman markets and Europe's economies, with Greeks operating as the commercial middlemen in the process. The subsequent growth of international trade activity led to the demand for a large Greek merchant marine that, by the end of the eighteenth century, dominated Mediterranean ports. These conditions eventually combined to create a Greek diaspora of wealthy business families settled throughout Europe's commercial, urban centers.

Increasingly influenced by exposure to the ideas of the Enlightenment, the French Revolution, and the radical concept of nationalism, some members of the wealthy Greek diaspora, along with an émigré intellectual community that their patronage had helped create, began to explore the idea of Greek political independence. In 1814 a secret revolutionary organization, Philike Hetairia (Friendly Society), was formed by Greek nationalists in the Russian port city of Odessa with the aim of overthrowing the Ottoman Empire and liberating the Greeks. The group enrolled members and began to collect resources and organized plans for a revolt. Alexandros Ypsilantis, a Greek general in the service of the Russian tsar Alexander I, accepted leadership of the organization, and early in 1821 launched an attack from Russia into Ottoman Moldavia. Ypsilanti's revolutionary forces, however, were defeated when the assistance the revolutionaries expected from the tsar did not materialize. Nonetheless, and almost simultaneously, another uprising broke out in the Peloponnesus and soon spread to other parts of Greece.

The Greek War of Independence, or Greek Revolution, began in March 1821 and initially went well for the Greeks. In the early stages of the revolution, the Greek insurgents achieved some striking successes against the Ottoman army while the Greek revolutionary fleet won a string of impressive naval victories. Continued Greek advances, however, were undermined by factional struggles among the insurgents that led to a veritable civil war within the liberated Greek territories in 1824. Capitalizing on the Greek internecine conflict, and the arrival of a large army from Egypt, the Ottomans launched a major counteroffensive against the Greeks in 1825 and retook most of the gains the Greeks had made. Responding to growing public support for the Greek cause in Europe, the Great Powers overcame their initial hostility to the Greek Revolution, and in July 1827 Britain, France, and Russia signed the Treaty of London, which called for the establishment of an autonomous Greek principality. However, the unplanned, spontaneous battle of Navarino in October 1827, resulting in the destruction of the Ottoman navy at the hands of a combined British-French-Russian fleet, impressed the Great Powers to move beyond mere autonomy to support Greek independence.

The Great Powers proclaimed the independence of Greece under the London Protocol of February 1830, which also placed the new kingdom under their protection. Greece's boundaries were subsequently established by the Treaty of Constantinople (July 1832). The new state contained only the Peloponnesus, Rumeli, or Central Greece, and the Cyclades in the Aegean, meaning most of the Greeks in the Balkans and none of the Greeks in Asia Minor were liberated. Also in 1833, Prince Otto of Bavaria, whom the Great Powers had chosen a year earlier, arrived in Greece to become the independent country's first king.

Otto did not prove to be a popular monarch. The Bavarian administrators he brought with him to Greece alienated most of the population. Furthermore, Otto's refusal to grant a constitution, his failure to convert to Orthodoxy from Catholicism, and his inability to produce an heir to the throne culminated in a military coup in 1843, which led to a reduction of the king's powers. In 1844 Otto was forced by military and political leaders to accept a liberal constitution, which defined the country's political system as a constitutional monarchy. Nevertheless, Otto continued to act as an autocrat, only producing more opposition to his rule. In 1862 growing dissatisfaction with King Otto led to an uprising and finally his abdication. The Great Powers offered the throne to Prince William of Denmark, who in 1863 was crowned George I King of the Hellenes.

The Battle of Navarino on 20 October 1827, during the Greek War of Independence, where the Turkish and Egyptian forces were defeated by Greek allies Great Britain, France, and Russia. (Archivo Iconografico, S.A./Corbis)

George's title, King of the Hellenes, not merely King of Hellas, expressed the popular nationalist sentiment that all Greeks, not only those in the limited territory of the Greek kingdom, should, along with their historic lands, ultimately become part of a larger fully unified Greek nation-state. The fact that only one-fourth of the Greeks who had been under Ottoman rule were included in the territories composing independent Greece in 1832 all but guaranteed that irredentism would become Greece's chief political preoccupation for the first century of its existence. Greek elites and common people alike passionately supported the *Megali Idea* (Great Idea) of uniting the unredeemed Greeks still under Ottoman rule in the Balkans and Asia Minor within a single state. Greeks cherished this goal despite the fact that it was bound to bring the small and comparatively weak Greek kingdom into conflict with the Ottoman Empire.

Independent Greece's first territorial gain came not from the Ottomans but from the British. In order to mark the beginning of King George's reign, Britain ceded the Ionian Islands in 1864, over which they had exercised a protectorate since 1815. Following the defeat of the Ottomans in the Russo-Turkish War of 1877–1878, the sultan was forced by the July 1878 Treaty of Berlin to cede most of Thessaly and a portion of southern Epirus to Greece in 1881. As part of the same settlement, Britain acquired the right to occupy and administer the predominantly Greek-populated island of Cyprus beginning in 1878. During the last two decades of the nineteenth and the first decade of the twentieth centuries, Greece's expansionist ambitions focused on the Ottoman territories of Macedonia and Crete. In Macedonia, Greek insurgents and Bulgarian guerrillas fought each other in a complex, protracted, and savage contest for domination over the region before its liberation from the Ottomans, while in Crete, Greek nationalists expressed their fervent desire for union with Greece through repeated rebellions against Ottoman rule, eventually sparking a brief, failed Greek war against the Ottoman Empire in 1897.

The lesson of the humiliating defeat of 1897 was not lost on the Cretan politician and ardent nationalist, Eleutherios Venizelos, who, as leader of the Liberal Party, became prime minister of Greece in 1910. Venizelos realized that Greece could not unilaterally challenge the still considerable power of the Ottoman Empire, and he therefore sought to develop alliances with the other Ottoman successor states in the Balkans, particularly Serbia. Consequently, in October 1912 the First Balkan War began when an alliance consisting of Bulgaria, Greece, Montenegro, and Serbia launched a coordinated attack against the Ottoman Empire, defeating the Turks and pushing their army to the outskirts of Constantinople. Unsatisfied with its territorial gains in Macedonia, in June 1913 Bulgaria attacked its former allies, Greece and Serbia, only to be defeated by them, Romania, and the Ottoman Empire one month later. This Second Balkan War ended with the August 1913 Treaty of Bucharest, which awarded southern Macedonia, most of Epirus, Crete, and the Aegean Islands to Greece. Under the leadership of Venizelos, Greece increased its territory by 70 percent and almost doubled its population.

When World War I broke out in August and September 1914, Venizelos, emboldened by the victories of the Balkan Wars, was confident that Greece was poised to achieve the *Megali Idea* at the expense of the Ottoman Empire. At the outset of the war, Venizelos advocated Greece's entry on the side of the Entente Powers, or Allies, who were arrayed against the Central Powers, which eventually included the Ottoman Empire and Bulgaria. However, King Constantine I, who had succeeded his father, George I, in 1913, favored neutrality. The differences in foreign policy perspective between the king and the prime minister led to increasingly hostile confrontations between the two leaders. Forced to resign twice in 1915, Venizelos broke with King Constantine in October 1916, and with the support of Allied forces already in Greece, he established a rival government in Thessaloniki. This serious rupture between Venizelos and the king marked the beginning of a national schism that would divide Greek politics and society into two rival camps, Liberals versus Royalists, for at least the next two decades. Intervening in Greek domestic affairs, in June 1917 British and French troops occupied Athens and forced Constantine to resign in favor of his second son, Alexander.

Constantine I, King of Greece. (Corbis)

Eleutherios Venizelos (1864–1936)

Generally regarded as the greatest Greek statesman of modern times, Eleutherios Venizelos was born in Chania, Crete, on 23 August 1864. After studying law in Athens, Venizelos returned to his native Crete, then part of the Ottoman Empire, and became involved in the island's liberation movement. He was politically active during the Cretan revolt of 1897 in favor of union with Greece. When Crete became autonomous as a result of international intervention following the revolt and the Greek-Turkish War of 1897, Venizelos played a major role in drafting the island's constitution. As a member of Crete's assembly, he actively promoted the cause of union with Greece. After making his mark in the politics of Crete, he was projected onto the stage of national politics by the military coup of 1909 in Athens, becoming the choice of the coup leaders, or Military League, for prime minister and assuming office in October 1910. As founder and leader of the Liberal Party, Venizelos dominated Greek political life for the next quarter century, serving as prime minister for twelve of those turbulent years.

During his first two years as prime minister, Venizelos presided over a vigorous reform program that extended to the administration of the state, public education, and the national economy. Simultaneously he led Greece into an alliance network with Bulgaria, Montenegro, and Serbia aimed at wresting from the Ottoman Empire its remaining Balkan territories. Indeed, Venizelos first achieved international prominence as the architect of Greece's spectacular victories against, first, the Ottoman Empire in the First Balkan War in 1912 and, second, against Bulgaria in the Second Balkan War, fought in 1913. As a result of Greek successes in the Balkan Wars the country doubled its territory. Encouraged by these successes, Venizelos was committed to Greece's entry into World War I on the side of the Entente as a means to liberate the Greeks and their territories still under Ottoman rule. Venizelos and King Constantine, who favored neutrality in the war, soon clashed over foreign policy differences. The subsequent feud between the two leaders resulted in Venizelos's forced resignation twice in 1915 and the eruption of a crisis that divided Greek politics and society between supporters of Venizelos and supporters of the king. This division, or National Schism, became irreversible when Venizelos established a rival government in Thessaloniki in 1916. In 1917 King Constantine was forced to leave Greece under British and French pressure, and Venizelos returned to Athens to lead a reunified but bitterly divided country.

Restored to office by British and French military intervention, as prime minister, Venizelos brought Greece into World War I on the side of the Entente in June 1917. Representing Greece at the Peace Conference in Paris, he secured Allied consent to occupy the important Anatolian city of Smyrna in 1919, and a year later he obtained major territorial concessions for Greece against the Ottoman Empire in Eastern Thrace and western Asia Minor. Venizelos's apparent postwar achievements were, however, short-lived. In 1920 he was defeated in national elections and went into self-exile. By 1922, Venizelos's policy of involvement and expansion in Asia Minor ended in disaster when the Greek army was defeated by nationalist Turkish forces and over 1.3 million refugees poured into Greece.

Venizelos represented Greece at the 1923 Lausanne Conference, ending hostilities between Greece and Turkey, before returning to Greece to serve briefly as prime minister from 1923 to 1924. During his last term as prime minister, from 1928 to 1933, his regional diplomacy significantly improved Greece's bilateral relations with Romania and Yugoslavia and built a rapprochement with Turkey. Faced with the repercussions of the international economic crisis, Venizelos fell from power in 1933. An abortive March 1933 coup by pro-Venizelos army officers tarnished his controversial reputation, and his involvement in another attempted coup two years later forced him to go into self-exile once more. Fleeing to France in March 1935, he lived the last year of his life in Paris, removed from politics. Shortly before his death on March 18, 1936, Venizelos urged his followers to cooperate with King George II, who had recently returned to Greece, for the sake of stability and national unity.

That same month Venizelos returned to Athens in triumph as prime minister of a reunited Greece, declared war against the Central Powers, and began a purge of royalists from government and the state bureaucracy.

After the Allied victory in 1918 and Greece's subsequent diplomatic successes at the postwar settlements in Paris, Venizelos's policies appeared to be vindicated. The November 1919 Treaty of Neuilly required Bulgaria to transfer Western Thrace to Greece. Moreover, after long negotiations, many of Venizelos's territorial aspirations against the Ottoman Empire seemed to be obtained with the signing of the Treaty of Sevres in August 1920. According to the provisions of Sevres, Greece acquired all of Eastern Thrace, excluding Constantinople, the rest of the Aegean islands,

Eleutherios Venizelos. (Bettmann/Corbis)

presence of Greek troops in Asia Minor aroused a Turkish backlash and helped to fuel the growing armed Turkish nationalist movement led by Mustafa Kemal in the Anatolian interior. With British encouragement, in October 1920 Venizelos ordered the Greek army to advance from Smyrna in order to put down expanding Turkish nationalist resistance to the Treaty of Sevres. A month later a war weary electorate voted Venizelos out of office, returned the Royalists to power, and restored Constantine to the throne, Alexander having died only weeks before the election. Venizelos's electoral defeat proved to be a blessing for his political career. Having put Greece in an increasingly untenable diplomatic and military position, Venizelos now went abroad and did not have to preside over the disastrous outcome of his Asia Minor policy.

Locked now in an irreversible conflict, with no meaningful opportunity for negotiation, the Royalist government continued to pursue a military solution to Greece's Anatolian dilemma. In early 1921 the Greek army began a sweeping offensive deep into Anatolia with the goal of decisively defeating Kemal's illusive nationalist forces. Securing a series of victories along its advance, the Greek operation reached the outskirts of Ankara where it engaged the Turks in a fierce but indecisive battle in September. Unable to overpower the Turkish forces, the Greek army withdrew to and held defensive positions between Smyrna and Ankara during the winter and spring of 1922. Isolated and weakened by the Allies' abandonment and declaration of a policy of neutrality and now realizing that a military victory was impossible, the Greeks were left paralyzed. In August 1922 Kemal's now large and powerful nationalist army launched an enormous, well-coordinated offensive, quickly routing the Greek army, pushing a mass of Greek refugees ahead of its advance, and burning Smyrna in its wake. Meanwhile, Constantine, who was blamed for the fiasco in Anatolia, abdicated in favor of his son George II, after a military coup took place against the Royalist government.

The Treaty of Lausanne, signed in July 1923, formally ended the Greek-Turkish War and introduced a new, draconian principle to the resolution of international conflicts—forced population exchange. Along with fixing the boundary between Greece and Turkey, which required that Greece relinquish all territories awarded to it earlier by the Sevres Treaty, Lausanne dictated the exchange of minority populations between Greece and Kemal's Turkish republic, which had succeeded the Ottoman Empire. Accordingly, 1.3 million Greeks, many of whom had already been uprooted by the Turks, were expelled from Asia Minor and Eastern Thrace, in exchange for 350,000 Turks who were expelled from Greece. The only exceptions to this compulsory exchange of populations were the 80,000 Muslims, half of whom were ethnic Turks, in Western, or Greek, Thrace, and the 120,000 Greeks left in Istanbul. The Greek disaster in Asia Minor, remembered by the Greeks as the Great Catastrophe, ended the *Megali Idea* in a tumult of chaos and human suffering and shattered forever the goal of a fully restored Greece encompassing all its historic lands. Greece and the Greek people were exhausted, confused, defeated, and demoralized. Although the circumstances probably

excluding Rhodes, and a mandate to administer Smyrna and its hinterland in western Asia Minor, pending a plebiscite in five years to determine the area's permanent status. It now appeared that realization of the *Megali Idea* was within reach. However, Venizelos's diplomatic triumph in Paris was illusory. Overwhelmed by opportunity, Venizelos overestimated the Allied, especially the British, commitment to the postwar treaty, especially once the Turks proved unwilling to ratify Sevres. Furthermore, he underestimated the challenges facing the Greek position in Asia Minor, and he dismissed all counsel, civilian and military, that advised him that Greece did not possess the resources necessary to act unilaterally against Turkey, the fundamental principle that had guided his earlier more restrained foreign policy.

Before any treaties regarding the status of Ottoman territories had been concluded, Venizelos had involved Greece militarily in Asia Minor. At the behest of Britain, France, and the United States, who sought to use Greece as a counterweight against another ally, specifically Italy and its expanding sphere of influence in southwestern Anatolia, Venizelos landed Greek forces in Smyrna in May 1919. The could not have been worse, the population exchanges, iron-ically, resulted in the unification of the Greek people, albeit in a smaller and poorer Greece than most Greeks could have foreseen a decade earlier.

A country of barely 5 million people before the popula-tion exchanges of 1923, Greece's interwar problems neces-sarily focused on the economic and social integration of the nation's refugees. Greek society's ability to tackle the serious issues that confronted it was, however, undermined by po-litical instability. The leaders of the military coup that had removed Constantine from the throne yielded in January 1924 to a democratically elected government led by Venize-los, recently returned to Greece. In March of that same year the parliament declared Greece a republic, and the procla-mation was confirmed by a subsequent plebiscite. Although the constitutional issue of the monarchy appeared to be re-solved, the political polarization created by the wartime Constantine-Venizelos dispute continued into the 1920s and 1930s between the Liberal and Royalist parties and their supporters. Intense factionalism precluded political di-alogue and led to repeated breakdowns of the parliamentary system. The interwar period was wracked by multiple mili-tary interventions in the political process, with pro-Liberal coups followed by pro-Royalist countercoups and vice versa. Practically the only thing the two major political par-ties could agree on was their opposition to, and fear of, the small but exceptionally well-organized and disciplined Greek Communist Party (KKE), which capitalized on the economic distress and social discontent of the interwar years. Finally, the republic's domestic problems were too great and its institutional foundations not strong enough to withstand the international turn toward authoritarianism that affected most of Europe and virtually all of Eastern Eu-rope by the close of the 1930s. The failure of an anti-Roy-alist coup in 1935 led to the end of the republic with the restoration of the monarchy under King George II, whose return to Greece and exaggerated fears of a communist seizure of power paved the way for dictatorship. In August 1936 a retired general, Ioannis Metaxas, seized power, sus-pended parliament, and abolished all political parties.

Despite Metaxas's authoritarian governance and affinity for fascism, he maintained a foreign policy oriented toward Britain, which soon brought Greece into direct conflict with Germany and Italy. Metaxas's efforts to keep Greece out of World War II ended in October 1940, when fascist Italy attacked Greece from its bases in Albania. Against over-whelming odds, the Greek army repulsed the Italian inva-sion and pushed Mussolini's forces, which were saved from a complete rout by weather and poor communications, deep into Albania. Hitler intervened to rescue Mussolini from his widening fiasco and German forces invaded Greece in April 1941. The country was quickly overrun and divided into German, Italian, and Bulgarian occupation zones.

The brutality of the Axis occupiers provoked resistance. In fact, several resistance movements soon emerged in the mountains. By far the largest of these was the communist-led National Liberation Front (EAM) and its military arm, the National Popular Liberation Army (ELAS). Of the

smaller armed movements, the most significant was the National Republican Greek League (EDES), a nationalist organization that supported restoration of the republic. In an effort to monopolize control of the resistance move-ments in anticipation of liberation, the ELAS, in the midst of the occupation, attacked its noncommunist rivals in Oc-tober 1943, provoking a civil war that was halted by an un-easy truce in February 1944. In August representatives of the surviving resistance organizations joined in support of a government of national unity established in Cairo under the leadership of a Liberal Party prime minister, George Papandreou.

Despite the agreement arrived at in Cairo and the Ger-man withdrawal from Greece in October, the prospects for political reconciliation were ended shortly after liberation. A ministerial crisis between the Papandreou government and EAM over the disarmament of ELAS led to violence in December and quickly escalated into a full-fledged battle for the control of Athens fought between the small Greek government forces, police, and allied British units on one side and ELAS forces on the other side. Meanwhile, in the rest of the country the ELAS returned to the offensive against the EDES and other noncommunist resistance

Bird's-eye view of large crowd jamming University Street, off Constitution Square in Athens, Greece, as the EAM stages a protest rally on the eve of the first free Greek elections in ten years, March 1946. (Library of Congress)

forces. The ELAS, however, lost the battle of Athens and signed an armistice in January 1945. Responding to the events in Athens and the brutal ELAS suppression of opponents in the countryside, all of which had the appearance, if not the substance, of an armed communist attempt to seize power, a rightist reaction descended on Greece. A cycle of retributions and counter-retributions created a state of chaos and lawlessness throughout the country. The restoration of King George II to the throne by plebiscite in September 1945 further polarized the Greek Left and Right. The KKE ultimately responded by organizing a guerrilla army and launching a civil war in March 1946. Implementing the Truman Doctrine, the United States intervened in Greece against the communists precisely one year later and provided the national government with economic aid and military supplies sufficient to turn the tide. After more than three years of intense fighting, the death of 160,000 combatants and civilians, and the dislocation of over 800,000 people, the communist insurgency was defeated in August 1949.

Although the decade-long ordeal of war, invasion, occupation, and civil war left Greece devastated, the country recovered quickly during the 1950s. In 1952 Greece became a member of NATO (the North Atlantic Treaty Organization), and with significant aid from the United States the conservative government that dominated the decade of the 1950s inaugurated a rapid economic and social modernization of the country. This period of growth was primarily associated with the policies of Prime Minister Constantine Karamanlis, leader of the National Radical Union, a conservative party despite its appellation.

Many of Karamanlis's domestic achievements, however, were overshadowed by an increasingly bitter conflict over Cyprus, a British Crown colony since 1914 with an 80 percent Greek population. During the 1950s, British colonial forces brutally suppressed the Greek Cypriots' growing struggle for self-determination expressed through demands for union, *enosis,* with Greece. The problem of Cyprus soured relations between Greece and Turkey. The British, pursuing a policy of divide and rule, encouraged Turkey, which had abandoned its interest in Cyprus since 1878, to interject itself in the Cyprus issue as the protector of the Turkish Cypriot minority, which composed 18 percent of the island's population. Moreover, in order to manufacture a rationale for a continued colonial presence, British policy deliberately created intercommunal conflict that led, for the first time, to violence between Greek and Turkish Cypriots. In 1959, as an alternative to the wishes of the majority of Cypriots, who continued to favor enosis, Britain, Greece, and Turkey, all acting as protecting powers, reached an agreement that Cyprus would become an independent republic within the British Commonwealth. In 1960 Cypriot independence was established under the leadership of the new country's president, and its Orthodox primate, Archbishop Makarios. Within a few years, the dysfunctional constitution and arcane power-sharing political system that the British had imposed on independent Cyprus led to a paralysis of government and subsequent intercommunal tensions and ultimately violence.

Portrait of Constantine Karamanlis, prime minister (1955–1963, 1974–1980) and president (1980–1985, 1990–1998) of Greece. (Embassy of Greece)

Meanwhile, events in Greece were pushing the country toward another period of instability and crisis. Karamanlis, who had clashed with King Paul and Queen Frederika, resigned in 1963 and went into self-exile. In the elections of February 1964 the Center Union Party, led by wartime leader George Papandreou, defeated the conservatives, winning a clear majority in parliament. Against a background of renewed crisis in Cyprus, Papandreou found himself embroiled in a conflict with King Constantine II, who had succeeded his father, Paul, in March 1964. In an apparent effort to protect his son, Andreas, whom some conservatives alleged had been involved in a conspiracy with radical military officers, Papandreou moved to assume control of the Ministry of Defense. The king refused to sanction the older Papandreou's attempt to take control of the ministry and thus Papandreou resigned in protest in July 1965. For almost two years, parliamentary democracy steadily broke down as a succession of weak, coalition caretaker governments failed to function effectively, while polarization between Left and Right reached a fevered pitch in countless massive demonstrations. Finally, when Panayiotis Kanellopoulos became prime minister in April 1967, he dissolved parliament and announced that elections to form a new national government would be held the following month.

Before the planned elections that would have finally replaced the string of unstable caretaker governments with an elected government could took place, a group of army officers led by Colonel George Papadopoulos seized power in a bloodless coup on 21 April 1967. The junta, whose members became collectively known as the Colonels, claimed that they had acted to thwart a communist takeover. In reality their primary motivation was to forestall the May elections, which they feared would return George Papandreou to power, who was expected, at the behest of his son, Andreas, to purge ultraconservative officers such as themselves. The junta suspended the constitution, abolished political parties, imposed censorship, and arrested thousands of opponents from across the political spectrum. The dictatorship was extremely unpopular and did not even enjoy support among the military. In December 1967 King Constantine launched a countercoup with units of the army. The attempt to topple the Colonels failed and Constantine fled into exile. In May 1973 elements of the navy tried to bring down the junta but their mutiny failed. When anti-government demonstrators headed by university students tried to end the dictatorship through a massive protest in November 1973, they were brutally suppressed with tanks and troops. When the junta finally fell, it was the result of its own bungling. In July 1974 Turkey invaded and occupied northern Cyprus following a short-lived coup against Archbishop Makarios that had been instigated by the junta. Paralyzed by incompetence and international isolation, and unable to mobilize Greece's armed forces in response to the Turkish invasion of Cyprus, the junta collapsed.

Within days of this critical juncture, Constantine Karamanlis was recalled to Greece from Paris and sworn in as prime minister. Karamanlis quickly reestablished civilian government and brought the seven-year military dictatorship to an end without bloodshed. In November 1974 the first general election in a decade resulted in an overwhelming victory for Karamanlis's conservative New Democracy Party. In December 1974 a plebiscite abolished the monarchy, ending definitively the historically vexing constitutional issue, and in June 1975 the parliament approved a republican constitution. Emphasizing economic modernization, political pluralism, and integration within the evolving framework of European cooperation as the keys to the consolidation of democracy, growth, and security in Greece, Karamanlis achieved one of his primary long-standing objectives when he helped secure agreement for Greece to enter the European Community (EC), the precursor to the European Union (EU), in 1981.

When Andreas Papandreou's Panhellenic Socialist Movement (PASOK) won the elections of 1981, the new government continued along the EC policy lines established by Karamanlis while simultaneously instituting sweeping social reforms that promoted further modernization and broadened political participation at the grassroots level. Growing economic problems, coupled with scandals in the government and in Papandreou's private life, contributed to the defeat of PASOK in the parliamentary elections of 1989,

but after a brief coalition government and then a New Democracy Party interlude, Papandreou and the socialists were returned to power in 1993. Managing (not always satisfactorily) a worsening state of relations with an increasingly revisionist Turkey and struggling to maintain security in the troubled central Balkans after the dissolution of Yugoslavia, Greece's domestic development was often overshadowed by foreign policy crises during the 1990s. By the turn of the century, however, it was clear that the government of Costas Simitis, who succeeded the ailing Papandreou in 1996 and represented the modernizing, technocratic wing of PASOK, was beginning to enjoy the results of successful economic modernization policies, an improved foreign relations and security environment, and steady progress toward full integration within the European Union. Although Greece's path to its current position was difficult and it continued to face many challenges, the country's entry into the Economic and Monetary Union of the EU in January 2001 capped Greece's ultimately successful effort over two centuries, if not longer, to build a modern, stable, and democratic nation-state.

POLITICAL DEVELOPMENTS

Greece, the oldest and most stable democracy in Southeastern Europe, is a parliamentary republic whose president is the official head of state and whose prime minister is the head of government. The government and political system is based on the constitution of 1975 and the 1986 revisions to the constitution, with the former concretizing the establishment of a representative republic and the latter curtailing presidential power. The 1975 constitution marked the resolution of the so-called constitutional question, the conflict over a monarchy versus a republic, which plagued countless governments and had been at the center of political instability in the country since the establishment of an independent Greece in the 1830s.

The country's constitution was drafted by a legislature elected through popular elections held after the fall of the last military dictatorship in Greece in 1974. The document, reflecting the overwhelming vote of the national referendum of December 1974, abolished the monarchy and established the basis for a democratic republic. Based on the fundamental view that the state's legitimacy stems from the self-determination and will of the nation, the constitution notes that sovereignty rests with the people. Employing the principle of checks and balances, the constitution establishes a governmental structure, and accompanying functional responsibilities, dividing the state into three branches—executive, legislative, and judicial. The president of the republic, who is placed above the three branches of government and is intended to be above partisan politics, functions as a titular head of state, especially since the constitutional amendments of 1986.

As in most nations in the European Union (EU), but to a lesser extent than most Eastern European countries, the ethnic model, not the citizenship model, remains the chief informal norm for identity in Greece. Nonetheless, the constitution grants equal rights to all persons residing in

Portrait of Costas Simitis, prime minister of Greece (1996–). (Embassy of Greece)

Greece. The full range of human rights is protected under the constitution, which notes that all citizens of Greece may enjoy "full protection of their life, honor, and freedom, irrespective of nationality, race, or language and of religious or political beliefs." While every adult citizen has the right to participate in the economic, political, and social life of the country, the Greek state and all its agents are to ensure that individual rights and liberties are protected and exercised fully. The constitution specifies that basic rights and liberties include freedom of speech, of the press, of peaceful assembly and association, and of movement; furthermore, basic rights extend to economic freedom and ownership of property, the inviolability of privacy, and equality before the law, as well as legal due process. Also guaranteed by the constitution are the rights to social security and housing, to education, and to health care, as well as the right to petition the state for redress of grievances. In addition, the constitution states that work is a right, and that all workers are entitled to equal compensation for equal labor or services performed. The freedom of workers to organize (including the right to strike) is protected, but judicial functionaries and members of the state security forces are prohibited from striking.

While the basic articles of the constitution, such as those defining Greece as a parliamentary republic, those guaranteeing fundamental rights and liberties, and those establishing and distributing respective powers to the three branches of government, remain unalterable, all other parts of the constitution may be amended. In order to amend the constitution, a proposal for change must be introduced into the parliament by at least fifty of the three hundred members of the legislature. The next step in the amendment process requires that 180 (the equivalent of three-fifths) of the members of parliament vote in support of the amendment on each of two ballots held at least one month apart. Finally, the next session of parliament enacts the amendment by a majority vote of the total legislature's membership, at least 151 out of 300 representatives. At any rate, constitutional revisions cannot be made before a lapse of five years from the completion of a previous revision. These methodical, incremental, and reflective provisions are designed to ensure the stability of constitutional order in Greece and have succeeded.

Inspired by the modern systems of government in Western Europe, especially the French model of state organization, Greece is a unitary state based on a system of parliamentary democracy. In order to prevent the concentration of power in a single authority, the powers and functions of the state are separated into three branches of

Parliament, Athens, Greece. (Corel Corporation)

government. Despite constitutional provisions to strengthen local administration and the 1994 inauguration of direct local elections for provincial governors (formerly appointed by the central government), real power rests overwhelmingly with the central government in Athens.

At the head of the central, or national, government is the president. As the principal link among the executive, legislative, and judicial branches of government, the president is insulated from direct political pressure by virtue of his election by the parliament for a term of five years, and a maximum number of two terms. The presidency, especially after the constitutional amendments passed in 1986, enjoys largely ceremonial functions as a sort of representative national figurehead. The day-to-day governance of Greece is conducted by the three branches of government arranged according to the elected parliamentary system, with an independent judiciary and an executive branch that operates with the approval of the legislature.

The executive branch, or government, consists of the prime minister and his cabinet, which includes twenty-two departmental ministers, thirty-one alternate or deputy ministers, and one cabinet-rank minister to the prime min-

ister. All major cabinet ministers are members of the parliament, while others are chosen by the prime minister and formally appointed by the president. Led by the prime minister, the executive branch is collectively responsible to the parliament for the formulation and implementation of general government policy, while each minister is also individually responsible for the work of his respective office as an agency of the national government. The cabinet must receive and maintain the confidence of the parliament. A confidence vote by the legislature is required whenever a new cabinet is established. This vote, which is determined by an absolute majority, focuses on the broad outline of the government's proposed policies and programs. If a government is forced to resign as a result of a no-confidence vote, a nonpartisan caretaker government must be formed to administer new elections. Although two attempts have been made, in 1988 and 1993, no government has been censured by a no-confidence vote since the adoption of the constitution of 1975.

The National Assembly, or Parliament, is a unicameral body of three hundred deputies elected through direct universal ballot to a term of four years. The parliament elects its own officers and a committee that organizes the body's legislative work agenda. At the beginning of each annual session, which convenes in early October, committees are formed to examine bills, with committee membership proportional to party representation in the parliament. Bills may be introduced by the government or by any member of the parliament. In practice, however, the vast majority of legislative initiatives originate with the government. Bills become laws by a majority vote in the full assembly or by a majority of a proportionally representative section of parliament that continues to meet while the remainder of the assembly is in recess.

The current legal system, with roots in ancient Greek, Roman, and Byzantine civil law, as well as modern French and German models, is administered by an independent judiciary, which is divided into civil, criminal, and administrative courts. Underscoring the independence of the judiciary, judges enjoy personal immunity and are subject only to the constitution and the law in discharging their responsibilities. Judges and other judicial personnel are appointed and promoted by presidential decree, based on the prior decisions of the Judicial Council. The Judicial Council comprises the presidents of the three highest courts in Greece—the Supreme Court for civil and criminal justice, the Council of State for administrative cases, and the Comptrollers Council for fiscal matters. All legal proceedings are public and, depending on their severity, are decided by juries, judges, or magistrates. At the top of the judicial system is the Special Supreme Tribunal, comprising the presidents of the Supreme Court, the Council of State, and the Comptroller's Council, as well as four members of the Supreme Court chosen by lot every two years, and two distinguished professors of law also chosen by lot. The Special Supreme Court Tribunal interprets and rules on the constitutional validity of laws in cases where the Supreme Court, the Council of State, and the Comptroller's Council have rendered conflicting judgments. In these instances, the ruling of the tribunal is irrevocable. Constitutional interpretation in other cases is left to the legislature, not the judiciary.

The foundational linchpin and primary legitimizing instrument of the entire Greek political system is the principle of democratic representation, which is practiced through the electoral system. Except for the period of military dictatorship between 1967 and 1974, the electoral process has provided the country's citizens a tangible (if sometimes imperfect) structure for the exercise of democratic choice in postwar Greece. Elections, which are direct, universal, and achieved through secret ballot, are held every four years for both parliamentary and municipal elections unless the dissolution of the parliament necessitates an interim election.

The three hundred members of the parliament are elected from fifty-six local districts, which are represented by from one to thirty-two seats according to their population. Candidates are elected under a so-called reinforced proportional representation system in which 288 members of the parliament are chosen directly from the fifty-six constituency districts, while the remaining twelve seats of the assembly are occupied by so-called national deputies, elected not in any of the electoral districts but at large from political party lists in proportion to the popular vote the parties receive. Thus these national deputies, who enjoy the same rights and functions as directly elected representatives, represent the entire country. In one form or another, the reinforced proportional system has been in operation since the 1920s, with virtually every successive government modifying the system to maximize its own electoral prospects. As a result, the proportional system has consistently worked to the advantage of Greece's larger, dominant political parties. The justification for such a practice is that the proportional system helps to preserve political stability and, more importantly, functional one-party governments. Reinforced proportional representation, usually expressed through the allocation of most or all national deputy seats to a plurality party, makes it possible for a parliamentary majority to be formed even if a winning party fails to secure a majority of the popular vote. This outcome is made possible by awarding extra parliamentary seats to the larger parties that obtain more than a minimum percentage of the national vote.

Despite its demonstrated capacity for promoting stability, the proportional representation system has been controversial since its implementation. The proportional system has been consistently opposed by Greece's small political parties, especially those representing the ideological left, to whom reinforcement has been an exclusionist instrument that minimized their numbers in parliament between the 1950s and 1970s. As the fear of the Left receded in the 1980s and 1990s, the country's two dominant political parties, the conservatives and socialists, reached a consensus in favor of a system that made representation more in proportion to the direct vote but still significantly favoring the largest parties. Despite its problems, the electoral system has provided remarkable political stability in Greece. Since the restoration of democracy in Greece in 1974, of the nine parliamentary elections held, only two held in 1989 failed to produce a one-party majority government.

LOCAL GOVERNMENT AND CIVIL SERVICE

Although important in traditional and historical terms, Greece's nine geographic regions have no administrative significance. They are, however, the basis for subdividing the country into fifty-two prefectures, or provinces, which are the main local administrative units and the chief links between central and local government. The prefect, or *nomarch,* operating as a provincial governor, oversees local administration and functions as the principal agent of the central government. It is the prefect's responsibility to coordinate the activities of the ministerial field offices within his jurisdiction. The office of the prefect works in concert with a provincial council. For its part, the provincial council consists of the mayor of the prefecture's administrative capital, two representatives drawn from the province's municipalities and communes, and representatives of mass organizations for farmers, workers, professionals, entrepreneurs, and public corporations. Provincial councils may also meet with senior officials of the central government ministries on matters of shared local interest.

At the lowest level of local administration, the provinces are subdivided and organized around the country's approximately 350 municipalities and 5,600 communes. Typically, a municipality is a city or town with a population exceeding 10,000 residents, while a commune is a town or village containing fewer than 10,000 persons. Municipalities and towns elect councils headed by a mayor and president, respectively. The tenure and mandate of these councils is renewed every four years through popular election. Membership in the local councils varies from five to sixty-one deputies, depending on population.

Traditionally, through the entire Ottoman experience and most of the modern Greek state's history, local government had been popularly viewed as the exclusive domain of wealthy elites. The concept, let alone prospect, of popular participation in local administration was seen as remote until fairly recently. In 1982 Greece's first socialist government, which had promised to fully democratize local decision making by enacting the conditions necessary for popular involvement in provincial administration, passed legislation that began the profound transformation of local government. A new legal framework was created that began the transfer of considerable decision-making authority from the central government to the prefectures, municipalities, and communes. Although the decentralization initiatives, which had lost momentum by the mid-1980s, stalled with the return to power of the conservatives in the early 1990s, the socialists, on returning to power in 1993, renewed the agenda for decentralization. The now continuing strides forward in this area were made especially evident in 1994, when provincial governors, formerly appointed by the central government, were for the first time determined by direct popular local elections.

With major reform goals achieved in virtually all areas of government, the state's civil service remains the most intransigent challenge to Greece's state evolution. Like other modern governments, the Greek state is entrusted to a network of public personnel within a vast civil service bureaucracy. Entry into the civil service is generally made possible by competitive state examination. However, government ministries often bypass the regular recruitment system and engage personnel, without benefit of civil service examinations, by individual contract. The logic behind this accepted practice is based on the need for governments to employ specialists to fulfill certain tasks that the existing civil service pool cannot address as effectively. Such contract specialists are hired through a noncompetitive procedure at higher salaries than the mainstream ranks of the civil service bureaucracy. Furthermore, after several years of service, contract personnel are entitled to receive civil service tenure, or guaranteed permanence of position and salary. Precisely because these contract positions depend on the discretion of each minister, the practice is highly conducive to political patronage and favoritism. Furthermore, the effective internal division of the state bureaucracy into two unequal categories of recruitment and compensation has promoted resentment and often undermined professionalism and efficiency within the ranks of the regular civil service.

Despite periodic attempts to rationalize the goals and the methods of the system, the civil service apparatus is the single most visibly inefficient sector of the Greek governmental process. Since 1974 both ruling parties, the conservatives and socialists, have offered various programs to deal with the problems endemic in the civil service, especially in the area of personnel recruitment. However, the impact of these legislative reforms has been minimal, apart from broadening the immediate political influence of the governing party. In the final analysis, continued reliance on subjective criteria and personal connections in state agencies is a (perhaps throughout the Balkan region) practice rooted in the late Ottoman experience, a norm reinforced during most of the history of the independent Greek state. This pattern has cultivated in Greek citizens a general distrust for formal criteria such as exams, inspectors, and objective qualifications. Yet, at the same time, the consequent inefficiency associated with the civil service has bred almost universal contempt for its agencies.

THE PROBLEMS OF POLITICAL EVOLUTION

Although the ancient Greeks invented democracy, their nineteenth- and twentieth-century descendants had to struggle for generations to create a viable and truly representative government, a modern version of a democratic political system. Although the current Greek political system still grapples with serious flaws, the transition to and solidification of democracy since 1974 is often cited for the effectiveness with which it has dealt with political problems lingering from the past. Political development in nineteenth-century Greece was forestalled by the continual interference of the Great Powers in the country's domestic affairs. Political evolution in the first half of the twentieth century was handicapped by war, a pervasive culture of political patronage, polarization and schism between liberals and royalists, and a collapse of constitutional order.

The chief postwar political problems in Greece were the final disposition of the monarchy and the legalization of the Communist Party. By resolving both of these issues within

one year after the fall of the junta in 1974, Prime Minister Constantine Karamanlis removed two of the major issues of the postwar political environment that had made the accession of a military dictatorship possible in 1967. The immediate result of World War II had been a brutal civil war fought between communists and the national government from 1946 to 1949. The trauma of the conflict left Greece with a succession of repressive rightist governments and a stunted parliamentary system characterized by a meddling monarchy, pervasive domestic surveillance, and a Cold War–driven, paternalistic, interventionist U.S. ally throughout the 1950s and most of the 1960s.

After seven years of highly unpopular military rule and political isolation, let alone decades of parliamentary dysfunction, preparing Greece's political system for vigorous democratization and long-term stability was a formidable task. The conservative, decidedly democratic government of Karamanlis's New Democracy Party that came to power in 1974 tried to recover the economic momentum that had propelled a rapid political evolution in the late 1950s and made possible the liberal policies of the mid-1960s. The military dictatorship's pariah status and its general incompetence had separated Greece from the developmental path followed by its Western European counterparts, leaving the economic system that emerged from the early 1970s unprepared to cope with the monumental social changes and political demands of the remainder of the century.

The establishment of a republic and the legalization of the Communist Party and other leftist parties under the Karamanlis government cleared the way for the consolidation of democracy in Greece. The expanded political spectrum stimulated calls for further democratization, a goal vigorously embraced by New Democracy's chief opposition party, the Panhellenic Socialist Movement (PASOK). Founded as an anti-junta organization by the Greek diaspora intellectual and member of a prominent political family, Andreas Papandreou, PASOK was transformed into a political party in 1974. Seven years later, the new party and its charismatic leader came to power to form the first socialist government in Greece's history. PASOK's rapid rise and its electoral success in 1981 confirmed that government power could pass in orderly democratic fashion from one party to another, even between parties of quite different ideology.

The first socialist government launched a wave of jarring and controversial social and political transformations. Central features of the early 1980s were an environment of increasing openness and a concurrent sense of disorientation. PASOK's initial fiery rhetoric created high public expectations that were frustrated by deepening economic problems and by the socialists' unfocused long-term agenda. Nonetheless, PASOK's first term brought new segments of society, which until that time had been marginalized in the political life of the country, into the political mainstream. This process of expanding democracy and political participation stalled under mounting economic pressures during the socialists' second term, which ended in 1989 amid malaise and scandal. A subsequent New Democracy gov-

Portrait of Andreas Papandreou, prime minister of Greece (1981–1989, 1993–1996). (Embassy of Greece)

ernment was unsuccessful in both domestic and foreign affairs, so the electorate again turned to Papandreou's Socialist Party, which returned to power in 1993.

Following Papandreou's death in 1996, Greece's newly elected prime minister and leader of PASOK, Costas Simitis, began a restructuring of policy, which has produced considerable success in achieving his government's primary goals. Simitis's government, reelected in 2000, is committed to economic stability and modernization, monetary integration into the EU, and security through multilateral and cooperative international structures. Under Simitis's technical and sophisticated (if not charismatic) leadership, Greece has achieved most of its goals in these areas. Moreover, Simitis's approach to expanding domestic political life has been crucial in stimulating another vital evolutionary step in Greece's political development. Although the process is not entirely complete, the country's major political parties have been transformed to a considerable extent from exclusively elite organs to instruments for popular participation in the increasingly urgent process for reforming and modernizing national institutions.

CULTURAL DEVELOPMENT
FAMILY AND FOLK TRADITION

Reflecting the enduring influence of traditional culture, Greek society, for the most part, continues to prioritize collective over individual identity in assigning social status to persons. The family remains paramount in society's perception of an individual's public standing and value. Because of its patriarchal structure, Greek culture defines family membership through patrilineal descent, but bilateral kinship remains a factor in determining family relationships. Although mitigated by the growing imprint of Western culture, two basic categories of kinship exist simultaneously within the larger family system. The basic, primary category is based on notions of bloodline, or biological bonds, and is composed of the nuclear and extended family. The second category of relationships is established through sacramental sponsorship in weddings or baptisms and thus unites different families into so-called affinal, or nonbloodline, networks of kinship. The two categories of kinship—primary and affinal—are denoted in the conceptual terms *oikogenia* (family) and *koumbario* (affinal relation), respectively.

Breaking from the centuries-old pattern of multigenerational households, the nuclear family has for the last few decades constituted the basic domestic unit in Greek society. Consistent with general demographic trends among the EU countries, the average nuclear Greek family in the 1980s and 1990s consisted of four people (husband, wife, and two children) who generally occupied a common residence apart, although often close to, extended family households. Marriages arranged by parents or trusted intermediaries were typical in Greek culture as recently as the first half of the twentieth century but have been replaced by largely independent unions. Traditionally marriages functioned, at least in part, as economic mergers and alliance structures between families and thus tended to be arranged. Courtship rules, which once were appropriate only to engaged couples, have been relaxed since the 1970s but remain (at least formally) restrictive, especially as applied to girls and women in rural communities.

Underscoring the general continuity of roles and values, male heads of household are chiefly responsible for engaging the public on behalf of the family's interests, while their female partners are typically responsible for most of the family's domestic management. Mothers tend to be the primary caregivers in most Greek families, although grandparents and elder siblings are often actively involved in child rearing. Although early childhood is associated with considerable freedom, behavioral controls that are intended to protect family reputation and status are applied to children and are expanded and adjusted with age. Consistent with traditional patriarchal norms, male children generally enjoy more autonomy and privileges than do female children and are subject to less family and community scrutiny in terms of social conduct. Primary and secondary education is prized from the perspective of most traditional families as a system for inculcating children, especially boys, with competitive principles. Social elites aside, higher education is valued almost exclusively as an instrument for children's economic advancement, leading to an emphasis on professional and vocational training, often at the expense of creative and intellectual pursuits.

Although material factors such as individual wealth and education operate as the primary factors in the acquisition of status and influence in community life, intangible yet culturally significant factors can build or undermine social status regardless of personal wealth and power. The basis for this dynamic, as well as the source for the attendant mechanisms of social control, lies in the integrated principles of honor and shame. Although less openly pronounced at present than in earlier periods, these principles continue to resonate within Greek society. Honor functions as a moral commodity defining, or at least contributing to, a family's status. Family honor, and hence respectability and status, can be compromised and lost by the deviant actions of any member of the family. The collective, corporate nature of honor consequently requires that individuals conform to the interests of the family in abiding by the norms of the community. Acting otherwise brings shame not only to oneself but to one's entire family. Shame, in the form of public derision and social marginalization, thus works as an inducement for conformity and a deterrent against aberrant behavior.

THE VISUAL AND PERFORMING ARTS

Despite their enormous influence and presence in the lives of most Greeks, folk art and popular aesthetic tradition did not attract the interest of modern Greece's first artists. The post-Byzantine tradition of religious art that prevailed before the Greek Revolution was ultimately challenged by a Western influence that came to Greece with the Bavarian monarchy and administration imposed on the independent Greek state by the Great Powers in the 1830s. The majority of nineteenth-century Greece's most important artists studied or completed their training or education in Bavaria. The most prominent of these artists, Nikolaos Ghizis, became an influential professor of art at the Munich Academy and gained considerable fame abroad. Other leading artists making up the cohort of talent known eventually as the "Munich period" artists included George Iakovides, Nikiforors Lytras, and Constantine Volanakis, who returned to Greece to accept appointments at the School of Fine Arts in Athens. Heavily influenced by Western European sensibilities, the only Greek element in the work of these artists was the subject matter, which was sometimes drawn from folklore. Although less influential, a more indigenous tradition came from the local artists of the Ionian Islands, which became part of Greece in 1864.

The work of Greek artists living in Western Europe during the first half of the twentieth century was affected significantly by postimpressionism. The most accomplished among this group of artists was Constantine Parthenis, who returned to Greece to teach at the Athens School of Fine Arts, where he influenced a generation of artists that studied under him. As a symbolist and exponent of modern trends, Parthenis's work demonstrates a strong interest, emulated by his students, in Greek light and color. An equally influential but opposite artistic influence came from a refugee from Asia Minor, Photios Kontoglou. Committed to reviving the tradition of Byzantine religious art, Kontoglou rejected Western influences and urged his students to seek out creative roots in Greek culture. Eventually the cross-fertilization of Parthenis and Kontoglou produced a postwar generation of artists with a unique hybrid vision of Greece and Greek culture.

When Greece became independent in the 1830s, it enjoyed two dominant musical traditions, colored by countless regional variations. The first of these traditions was so-called demotic music, which had originated in the Ottoman period and was heavily influenced by liturgical music. The second tradition was found in the music of the Ionian Islands, which escaped Ottoman rule and was influenced by Italian forms. In the twentieth century the musical folk tradition divided into the older demotic songs of the countryside and a new type of urban song, known as *rebetika* or *rebetiko,* which appeared mostly among Asia Minor refugees and Greek immigrants in the United States.

Once Greece obtained its independence, many Greeks living in Western Europe returned home to introduce Western musical culture. Moreover, Greece's first monarch, King Otto of Bavaria, established bands, imported Western musical instruments, initiated musical education in schools, and sponsored musicians from Germany, Italy, and the Ionian Islands to perform in Athens. Opera was introduced, and by the middle of the nineteenth century, Greece was home to numerous orchestras, choirs, and musical societies. Among the most respected representatives of the Western musical tradition, expressed through the Ionian school of composers, were Nikolaos Mantzaros, who wrote the music for the Greek national anthem, Pavlos Karrer, and Napoleon Labelette and Dionysios Lavrangas, the founders of the Greek National Opera. Under the creative composition of the Asia Minor Greek, Manolis Kalomiris, Western and Greek folk traditions merged to form a new orchestral style. The most revered of Greece's operatic performers, and perhaps the most renowned twentieth-century master of classical voice, was the diaspora Greek Maria Callas, born Maria Kalogeropoulos, who enjoyed a brilliant career in Greek opera before being discovered in the West.

Regardless of its unique classical composers and unmatched operatic artists, Greece is best known abroad for its popular music. Manos Hatzidakis was the first of a generation of composers who introduced themes from *rebetika* in their work and, in the process, legitimized nonmainstream music. Hatzidakis's compositions and Greek popular music gained global recognition through international film, beginning with *Never on Sunday* (1960). This phenomenon was magnified with the film *Zorba the Greek* (1964), which showcased the music of the influential and politically controversial Mikis Theodorakis, whose compositions became widely known throughout Europe and beyond.

Greek filmmaking first drew international attention through the work of Cypriot-born Michael Cacoyannis, the director of the immensely popular *Zorba the Greek* and the critically acclaimed film *The Trojan Women* (1971), as well as other major features. Another filmmaker who has achieved recognition as one of Europe's most original cinematic artists is the director Theo Angelopoulos, the recipient of countless awards for works that entered the European canon of classic films during the 1980s and 1990s.

THE LITERARY ARTS

Of all the aspects of cultural and artistic creativity associated with modern Greece, literature and everything connected with language was the most lively and perhaps most important realm of expression. Although Greek writing in the early nineteenth century depended largely on the formal and rigid literary tradition of the Ottoman-era Constantinopolitan elites, the incorporation of the Ionian Islands into an independent Greek state in 1864 marked a critical turn in the development of a modern Greek literature. Ionian poet and author of the words of the Greek national anthem, Dionysios Solomos, and his contemporary Andreas Kalvos experimented with a largely unexplored, yet vibrant and potentially rich vernacular. In doing so, Solomos opened the way to poetic emancipation from the formal, stilted idiom. Although the formal idiom, Katharevousa, produced a large group of nineteenth-century prose writers, the only impressive and lasting craftsman of this medium was Alexandros Papadiamantis, a short story writer of considerable genius. The son of a poor priest and a native of the island of Skiathos, Papadiamantis studied briefly at the University of Athens before earning a modest living as a translator and prolific writer. He led an ascetic life, dominated by the Orthodox religious calendar, for whose traditions his writings reflected admiration and nostalgia. Papadiamantis's short stories and novels centered on historical and cultural themes. They appeared in serial form in periodicals during his lifetime and were published as books only after his death.

The late nineteenth and early twentieth centuries saw a wellspring of extraordinary poetic writing flowing from both formal and vernacular camps. The most talented of the vernacular poets during this period and a celebrated exponent of demotic was Kostis Palamas, whose approach to verse was highly original and unrestrained by convention. Palamas was one of the best known and most loved Greek poets of his time. Born in Patras and educated in Mesolonghi, he worked as a journalist and literary critic before publishing his first collection of verses, *The Songs of My Fatherland,* in 1886. After the publication of his second collection of poems in 1897, he was appointed secretary-general of the University of Athens, a position he held until his retirement in 1926. On the opposite end of the stylistic spectrum was the understated poetry of diaspora Greek Constantine Cavafy. A native of Alexandria, Egypt, Cavafy spent much of his childhood in Constantinople and England before settling permanently in Egypt in 1885. He

Adamantios Koraes

The leading figure of the eighteenth-century Greek Enlightenment, a Western-inspired intellectual revival, Adamantios Koraes (1748–1833) was born in Smyrna, the son of a merchant from the island of Chios. Although Koraes obsessively identified with Chios, there is no evidence that he ever visited the island from which his family originated. While a young man in Smyrna, Koraes was introduced to Latin and exposed to Western classical scholarship by Bernard Keun, a Dutch Protestant pastor. Between 1771 and 1778, Koraes attempted to pursue the family trade as a merchant in Amsterdam. His experience of freedom in Holland fueled his hatred for the Turks, whom he considered nothing more than barbaric oppressors. Not finding fulfillment in his life as a merchant, Koraes studied medicine at the University of Montpelier from 1782 to 1786. Nonetheless, his real interests lay in ancient literature, and he soon developed into one of the foremost classical scholars of his day in Europe. From 1788 until his death in 1833, Koraes lived in Paris, experiencing at close quarters the turbulent events of the French Revolution and the Napoleonic wars. Alarmed by the violent excesses of the revolution, mob rule, and Napoleonic despotism, Koraes embraced the virtues of moderation.

Koraes's passions were manifest in his private pursuit of classical scholarship and his public effort to raise the educational level of his fellow countrymen and instill in them an awareness of a glorious past that was universally admired in Europe. Toward achieving the latter, Koraes conceived the idea of publishing the *Hellenic Library,* consisting of editions of ancient Greek authors and aimed at a Greek audience. Koraes believed that the Greeks would never attain freedom from the backwardness of Ottoman bondage unless they became versed in the knowledge of their ancient heritage. As a result, he thought the outbreak of the Greek Revolution in 1821 was premature by a generation, since the Greeks had not yet reached the educational level required to make them truly free. Nonetheless, he published works in support of the revolution, as well as pieces aimed at ensuring that his fellow countrymen did not merely substitute native tyrants for their Ottoman masters. A central participant in the debates of the early Greek intelligentsia over the form of the language appropriate to an independent Greece, Koraes was one of the chief architects behind the formal language, or what became known as Katharevousa.

made a living as a bureaucrat in the British Imperial Irrigation Office of Alexandria, but his poetry was his private life and all-consuming obsession. The 154 poems that compose Cavafy's completed works fall into three categories, which the poet himself identified as philosophical, historical, or hedonistic reflections. The poems of the first category, all published before 1916, often displayed a didactic imprint. The historical poems, the first of which was published in 1906, explored the unity and continuity over time of the Greek experience, paradoxically by setting them in the Hellenistic age. In this context Cavafy drew considerable inspiration from the decline of Hellenism and the conflict between Christianity and paganism. As for the third category, Cavafy's hedonistic poems first saw publication in 1911 and by 1918 had become increasingly explicit but also expressive of a social dimension as they depicted life on the margins of society.

The period between the two world wars witnessed the emergence of Greece's most dynamic and influential crop of poets and novelists. This new wave of intellectuals and writers, who would dominate Greek letters during the rest of the twentieth century, vacillated in their outlook between the complete despair and isolation of the suicidal Kostas Karyotakis and the sophisticated resignation of George Seferis, born George Steferiadis, to the exaltation of the senses in the vision of Odysseus Elytis, born Odysseus Alepoudhelis. The poetic medium in Greek culture, an international literary form, marked a high point of achievement with the award of Nobel Prizes to Seferis and Elytis in 1963 and 1976, respectively. Seferis, a professional and senior diplomat as well as an accomplished poet, developed an international following thanks to skillful translations of his work that retained his poetry's brilliant lyrical quality. Elytis became world celebrated for his poetry's vigorous commitment to the struggle for freedom and creativeness. Closely associated with this group of poets, who all began their long careers during the interwar period, was an important cadre of intellectuals who became known as "the generation of the 1930s." Prolific and thoughtful advocates of liberal democracy and political moderation, the most prominent members of this group were Constantine Dimaras, Kosmas Politis, and George Theotocas.

Kostas Karyotakis, born in Tripoli in the Peloponnesus, was the son of a rural engineer, whose family moved continually from one provincial town to another in pursuit of work. Karyotakis spent most of his lonely childhood in Crete, where he began to publish his writing, his first poems appearing in children's magazines when he was only sixteen years old. After completing his law degree in Athens, he was posted as clerk to the prefecture of Thessaloniki. Openly contemptuous of his superiors and unwilling to accept the conventions of bureaucratic life, Karyotakis was dismissed from his position and assigned to a series of demeaning positions, many in the countryside. These experiences added to his existing sense of misery and alienation, themes that dominated his poetry. In 1919 Karyotakis published his first book-length collection, *The Pain of Man and Things*, which was dismissed by literary critics. Two years later he published his second book of poetry, *Nepenthe*, a term denoting free-

Adam, Church of the Holy Apostles, Thessaloniki, Greece. (Corel Corporation)

dom from sorrow and grief. His last book was published in 1927; a year later, consumed by depression, he killed himself. Marking the influence of the nineteenth-century French symbolist poets on Greek writing, Karyotakis's haunting, complex verse was appreciated as a reaction against the emotionalism of romanticism only after his death.

George Seferis, the son of an accomplished university literature professor, was born in Smyrna and educated in law in Athens and Paris before studying English in London. Although his real interest was in philology, Seferis pursued a diplomatic career while writing and publishing poetry. In 1931 he published a small collection of thirteen poems. Despite the booklet's brevity, it was important in marking Seferis's desire to shed new light on the existing Greek poetic landscape and overcome the shadows of Palamas and Karyotakis. Other poems soon followed this first publication, many of them built on the intermingling of Greek history and mythology, a theme that would inspire much of Seferis's writing for decades. During World War II, when Seferis served with the Greek government in exile in Egypt, his poetry was deeply influenced, as Cavafy's was earlier, by Alexandria's climate of cosmopolitanism and diaspora Hellenism. The decade after the war was a particularly successful one for Seferis as both a poet and diplomat. In 1947 he published his most mature work, *The Thrush*. Meanwhile, Seferis's diplomatic career skyrocketed with a series of prestigious assignments, culminating in 1957 with his appointment as ambassador to London, where he would finish his career in the Greek foreign service corps. In 1963 Seferis became the first Greek author to be awarded the Nobel Prize for Literature. Seferis achieved international recognition not only because of the extraordinary quality of his poetry but also because of the creative ways that his work explored intellectual concerns. In the final analysis, Seferis was concerned with the dynamic interrelationship between the ancient and Modern Greek language, between the power of Greek civilization and its modern expression, and finally between tradition and innovation.

Greece's second Nobel laureate, Odysseus Elytis, was born in Heraklion, Crete, to a family from the island of Lesbos. During the 1930s, Elytis was influenced by French surrealist poetry and adopted surrealism's rejection of traditional modes of poetic expression. These qualities were manifest in the publication of Elytis's first collections of poetry, *Orientations* (1939) and *Sun the First* (1943), joyous celebrations of the Greek landscape as an ideal world of sensual enjoyment and moral purity. Elytis's experience of war, when he served as a junior officer on the Albanian front, where the Greek army thwarted the fascist Italian invasion in 1940, marked a departure from the sunny atmosphere of his early poetry. From this point, Elytis began to identify himself, through more sorrowful writing, with the loss and suffering of the Greek nation. This direction in his writing reached its zenith with the publication in 1957 of his most ambitious and important work, *Axion Esti*. This monumental work is a three-part composition of intricate structure, aiming to present Modern Greek consciousness through the development of a first-person narrator who is simultaneously the poet himself and the voice of his country. In this poem Elytis attempts to identify the vital elements of Greece's long history and complex tradition. In all of his poetry Elytis consistently emphasized humanity's innocence, dismissed guilt and fate, and professed the redeeming quality of light. He criticized the vulgarity and materialism of contemporary society and culture, showed the possibility of a different relation with the things of the world, and reformulated the fundamental and minimal essentials of life.

GREECE'S CHIEF CULTURAL EXPORT: NIKOS KAZANTZAKIS

Any review of modern Greek culture must include Nikos Kazantzakis, a prolific novelist, poet, essayist, and author of plays, who was arguably the most important Greek writer and philosopher of the twentieth century. Kazantzakis, the Greek author with the most translations in several languages, is more known to people outside Greece than any other writer from the world of Greek letters. Thanks to highly successful film adaptations of some of his most popular novels—including *Christ Recrucified* by French director Jules Dassin, *Zorba the Greek* by Greek director Michalis Ca-

Odysseus Elytis. (Bettmann/Corbis)

coyannis, and *The Last Temptation of Christ* by American filmmaker Martin Scorsese—Kazantzakis achieved world recognition.

Born in Heraklion, Crete, to an entrepreneurial couple, Kazantzakis was raised in a provincial town under Ottoman rule and teeming with revolutionary fervor. On completing his secondary education at the Gymnasium of Heraklion in 1902, Kazantzakis studied law for four years, receiving his law degree from the University of Athens in 1906, the year of his first publication, a narrative entitled *Snake and Lily,* and his first stage play. The following year he went to Paris and studied philosophy until 1909 under Henri Bergson. After his studies in France, Kazantzakis authored in 1910 a tragedy, *The Master Builder,* based on a popular Greek folktale. Returning to Greece, he began translating works of philosophy and in 1914 met and formed an influential friendship with the lyric poet and prominent playwright Angelos Sikelianos. Together with Sikelianos, whose enthusiastic nationalism served as a wanderer's guidepost among Greek communities in Europe and the Middle East, Kazantzakis traveled for two years in places where Greek culture, outside Greece, flourished. His personal knowledge of the Greek diaspora was put to practical use in 1919 when, as recently appointed director general of the Ministry of Public Welfare, Kazantzakis undertook the humanitarian relief and relocation of Greek populations from the Caucasus to Greece. By 1927, when Kazantzakis resigned from his post, he had been responsible for rescuing 150,000 ethnic Greeks from famine, revolution, and civil war in the southernmost region of the Soviet Union.

Kazantzakis's experience in the Caucasus became the beginning of a continuous global wandering. Like his hero, Odysseus, Kazantzakis lived most of his artistic life, excluding the years of World War II, outside Greece. Driven by an intense internal urge, Kazantzakis spent short periods of time in Europe, the Middle East, and East Asia until his death from leukemia in 1957 in Freiburg, Germany. His numerous journeys inspired Kazantzakis to publish the series *Travelling,* which included books on China, Egypt, England, Italy, and Japan and became known as masterpieces of Greek travel literature. Kazantzakis himself considered *The Odyssey: A Modern Sequel,* a massive book informed by his humanitarian involvement in the Caucasus, to be his most important work. Written seven times before being finally published in 1938, this immense spiritual exercise followed the structure of Homer's *Odyssey,* divided into twenty-four rhapsodies and comprising 33,333 verses. During the interwar period and through his travels, especially to Germany and later the Soviet Union, Kazantzakis was attracted to communism but never became a communist. Kazantzakis became increasingly disillusioned with revolutionary materialism and rationalism. Yet his exposure to communism tempered his earlier nationalism and replaced it with a more universal ideology. Bringing his views back to public service, as minister of state in the Greek government from 1945 to 1946, he tried in vain to reconcile the factions of left and right in Greece between the end of the Axis occupation and the outbreak of the civil war. During the 1950s, his career, especially as a novelist, reached its most creative and prolific peak, and in 1957, the year of his death, Kazantzakis came close to winning the Nobel Prize, ultimately losing by a single vote to the French writer Albert Camus.

ECONOMIC DEVELOPMENT

Like most of the countries of Eastern Europe, Greece had an economy that was dominated by agriculture until the postwar period. Throughout the first half of the twentieth century, Greece drew most of its income from the export of a few highly profitable agricultural products, such as tobacco and dried fruits, and from its expansive shipping industry. After the 1940s, the Greek economy underwent significant transformation. Driven largely by government policies, and the results of membership in the European Community (EC), later the European Union (EU), manufacturing and services emerged as the chief areas of economic activity, accounting, by the 1990s, for roughly 85 percent of the gross national product (GDP). By 2001, it was estimated that Greece's labor force of approximately 4,590,000 people was divided into a primary, or agricultural, sector employing 18 percent of workers, a secondary, or industrial and manufacturing, sector engaging 23 per-

cent of labor, and a tertiary, or service, sector utilizing 59 percent of the country's workforce. Greece enjoys the highest proportional level of entrepreneurial self-employment and family-based small business ownership in the EU. This employment characteristic has limited, compared to most of the EU, the growth of labor unions outside the public sector. Nonetheless, approximately 600,000 members of the Greek workforce are members of private or public sector labor unions.

Reflecting the modernization and progress of the economy, per capita income in Greece has increased from $500 in 1960 to $19,100 in 2002, the highest in all of Eastern Europe. Despite the fact that the Greek economy is ranked as one of the lowest performers in the highly developed and industrialized EU, in the world it is ranked twenty-third in per capita income and is placed in the top 10 percent of the world's national economies. Furthermore, despite slowing, or, according to some analysts, stagnant trends in the early 1990s, since 1995 the overall economy produced an annual average growth rate of 3.6 percent, exceeding the average rate achieved by the EU. According to 2002 statistics, Greece's GDP had reached $203 billion, an increase of 33 percent in only four years. These comparatively impressive figures do not, however, tell the full story of recent economic development and national wealth creation. Such official statistics understate Greece's actual prosperity because an estimated 40 percent of all economic activity in the country takes place in an unofficial, unrecorded, market outside the tax and social security systems.

Despite its remarkable postwar accomplishments, the Greek economy continues to grapple with serious problems and potential threats to its long-term growth. The significant size of the unofficial, or underground, economy is an obstacle to complete economic modernization, as black market merchants rarely make improvements to their businesses or comply with commercial regulations. Another problem confronting the economy is the large size of the public sector, which, in expenditures, constitutes one-third of Greece's GDP. Although attempts were made in the 1990s to reduce the size of the public sector through privatization, these efforts were only partially successful when confronted by severe opposition from powerful public sector unions opposed to reform.

The Greek government in the late 1990s sought to tackle many of the Greek economy's impediments to long-term growth by prioritizing monetary integration, seen as a necessary building block for attacking structural problems. Consequently in 1996 the government undertook efforts to qualify Greece to share a proposed single European currency, the euro, with other EU member states. These initiatives involved the implementation of austere and unpopular measures aimed at reducing Greece's chronically high rate of inflation, at 18 percent throughout the 1980s and early 1990s, and increasing its tax revenues. By the close of 1999, Greece had effectively reduced its deficit to an acceptable EU standard and had reduced its rate of inflation to 2.6 percent, thus meeting the qualifying criteria to join the EU single currency system. In January 2001, Greece, marking an economic and political threshold in its development and

Olive grove on Euboea. (Yann Arthus-Bertrand/Corbis)

modernization, adopted the new euro currency, thereby fully integrating its economy with the EU.

During the nineteenth century, the most important developments in the Greek economy were in the agricultural sector, which employed more than three-quarters of the labor force. Prior to liberation from Ottoman rule, of the 120,000 peasant families residing in the lands that would compose independent Greece by 1832, approximately 85 percent were landless and worked as sharecroppers for Turkish large landowners. Independence, however, changed the structure of land ownership and therefore the nature of agricultural production in the newly liberated regions of Central Greece, the Peloponnesus, and the Cyclades Islands. Although it was not completed until 1871, the Greek state's distribution of the former Ottoman estates to the peasantry led to the replacement of formerly large estates by relatively small family plots. Furthermore, before the Greek Revolution the large Ottoman estates had produced wheat for export, while after independence the proliferation of small family plots, not conducive to profitable wheat farming, caused the currant (the "raisin of Corinth"), a comparatively viable commodity for small landholders, to become Greece's major export item. Thus the production of currants dominated Greece, especially in the Peloponnesus, at the expense of wheat and other grains. During the 1870s, in fact, currant exports constituted more than half of the value of all exports. Wheat, the chief export before the 1830s, had declined to 41 percent in the 1840s, to 38 percent in 1860, and plummeted, following the completion of the land distribution process, to 23 percent by 1880. The lands of independent Greece, which had been exporters of wheat at the beginning of the nineteenth century, had become dependent on the importation of wheat before the close of the same century.

Demand and price fluctuations of the currant, nineteenth-century Greece's major export item, had a significant effect on the condition of individual peasant cultivators, as well as the national economy. Single-crop cultivation in southern Greece was especially encouraged by the blight that devastated French vineyards in the 1870s and spurred Greek farmers to fill the vacuum in the international market for currants. As a result, currant production increased from 43,000 tons in 1861 to over 100,000 tons in 1878. Once the French vineyards recovered and production returned to normal, surpluses emerged that, combined in 1892 with the French imposition of high tariffs on imports from Greece, triggered a plunge of 70 percent in the price of Greek currants. Despite the efforts of the Greek state to relieve the plight of financially devastated peasants, thousands of villagers were forced to migrate, thus setting into motion the largely economically driven exodus of over 500,000 Greeks to the United States between 1891 and 1922.

Despite the disaster that befell Greece's economic sector at the end of the nineteenth century, the decades that followed independence saw significant progress in the development of other areas of the national economy, especially in a crucial sphere long ignored by the former Ottoman rulers—the country's infrastructure. The profitability of export crops such as currants depended largely on the Greek merchant marine fleet, which had expanded, thanks in large part to favorable international treaties, to dominate much of the carrying trade in the eastern Mediterranean during the last several decades before the Greek Revolution. After independence was achieved in 1832, domestic growth of Greek commerce was a further stimulus to expansion of the merchant fleet.

Expanding trade in agricultural products, chiefly currants, provided the impetus for the development of the first post-Ottoman Greek financial networks, as well as the creation of a variety of domestic economic infrastructures. The establishment of the National Bank of Greece in 1841 marked a significant development in building the country's financial system. Authorized to issue banknotes and able to deal in both domestic and foreign currency, the National Bank of Greece fostered the gradual unification of a national market by making a uniform national currency available throughout the country. This critical development greatly facilitated domestic and foreign trade, saving and investment, availability of credit, and access to capital from abroad. By the 1870s, the National Bank of Greece had emerged as the country's leading economic institutional force, and a major international financial actor.

Thanks in large part to the success of the financial and capital systems, other parts of Greece's economic infrastructure could be improved or, where they did not exist, created. In the 1880s and 1890s paved roads and modern bridges, the first network of railroads, the opening of the Corinth Canal, and the construction and rehabilitation of several port sites all contributed to Greece's growing infrastructure, as well as to the movement of Greek goods in domestic and foreign markets. The country's first manufacturing facilities also appeared during this time, in conjunction with Greece's large infrastructure projects. Nonetheless, major industrial growth was hindered by the instability of the agricultural export sector, government debt, and resulting economic crises.

Greek industry, plagued by sluggish growth in the nineteenth century, was not successful at attracting either domestic investors or foreign capital at the beginning of the twentieth century. World War I brought commerce to a halt and produced the adoption of trade barriers to protect Greek industry from foreign competition, but the end of the war revived the adverse factors that had originally impeded industrial growth. The majority of early twentieth-century industries were involved in food processing or the production of consumer goods that required neither technological nor organizational modernization. Furthermore, manufacturing enterprises typically were small-scale operations, as evidenced by 1920 statistics indicating that workshops with fewer than six workers made up 92 percent of the industrial sector, while those with more than twenty-five workers represented less than 2 percent. Although the Greek state was committed to a policy of economic modernization, its programs were interrupted by a decade-long series of wars beginning in 1912.

As a result of these conflicts, Greece experienced a rapid and dramatic transformation of its economic and social structures. Beginning in 1915 and culminating in 1923, Greece, with a population of around 5 million, was forced to absorb almost 1.5 million refugees, mainly from Asia Minor, whose displacement and resettlement acted as a catalyst for profound change. The financing of the resettling of the refugees expanded the involvement and power of the state in the country's economy, as well as increasing the importance of such institutions as the National Bank of Greece. Wartime activities and public projects generated an enormous increase in government expenditure and a corresponding rise in taxes and state borrowing. Between 1914 and 1926, the external national debt tripled and outstanding debts to foreign creditors became an obstacle to contracting new public and commercial loans. Nonetheless, and after faltering under multiple domestic and foreign pressures, the economy experienced a revival beginning in 1927. The sophisticated entrepreneurial and modern farming skills introduced to Greece by the refugees, as well as increased domestic demand for goods, combined to stimulate a period of growth and industrialization. This growth was reinforced by financial reforms that included the stabilization of Greece's currency, the drachma, and the establishment of the Agricultural Bank of Greece. All the same, these institutional changes aimed primarily at improving the allocation of resources, not the extension of the benefits of economic growth to broader segments of the population. Consequently, despite growth, widespread economic hardship persisted in interwar Greece.

In 1931 the onset of the Great Depression ended Greece's interwar growth cycle. A year later, under the weight of the international market collapse, Greece was obliged to suspend interest payments on its foreign debt. This development consequently forced the country to dedicate the remainder of the decade of the 1930s to the management of the financial crisis caused by the default. A new period of economic stagnation, together with urban poverty, stimulated social tensions, the growth of political militancy, widespread labor unrest, and finally the imposition of an authoritarian dictatorship in 1936. Responding to the international economic depression and anticipating war in Europe, the Greek dictatorship of the late 1930s was committed to the goal of national self-sufficiency. Through price-support measures and various debt moratorium policies, the state restored considerable stability to the economy, especially its agricultural sector. Furthermore, the state succeeded in promoting significant increases in the production of vital, strategic crops. The output of wheat, for example, rose from 30 percent of domestic consumption before the dictatorship to 60 percent by 1939.

Fascist Italy's attack on Greece in 1940 upset the balance of the economy, but the Nazi invasion of the country in 1941 and subsequent Axis occupation destroyed the basis of Greece's productive capacity. Given Greece's low level of industrialization and the prevalence of small-scale manufacturing, the Axis occupation authorities saw no incentive to maintain the country's production plants and enforced an extractive policy in Greece. In short, Greece's economic resources were systematically plundered between 1941 and 1944. In addition to pillaging the Greek economy, the Axis authorities exacted payment from Greece for the enormous cost of the Bulgarian, German, and Italian occupation of the country. This deliberately cruel policy had the effect of unleashing a wave of hyperinflation that destroyed the value of Greece's currency, created a destructive web of black markets, and pushed the economy down to a barter level system for goods and services.

Unlike the rest of Europe, Greece's economic recovery did not begin with the end of World War II. The postwar reconstruction efforts of the Marshall Plan in Western Europe provided no immediate benefit to Greece, which underwent a bitter civil war from 1946 to 1949. A new round of violent conflict produced yet another period of physical destruction, inflation, and economic instability. Although Greece was a major recipient of American aid under the Marshall Plan, beginning in 1947, the overwhelming majority of this support was dedicated to either military assistance or war-related economic needs. At the close of the decade of the 1940s, the country's shattered economy had not yet had a chance to recover from the combined destructive impact of world war and civil war.

Although the Greek Civil War ended in 1949, economic stabilization was not achieved until 1953. A critical threshold in the country's postwar recovery, restoration of public confidence, and economic development was a package of economic measures implemented by the Greek government in 1953, which included the devaluation of the drachma and the lifting of most controls that impeded exports. The package also included new banking regulations to counter inflation and speculation, as well as new laws for the protection of foreign investment. These monetary and trade reforms were followed by an ultimately successful policy to attract foreign investment, and by an equally ambitious program that produced significant achievements in rebuilding, modernizing, and expanding the country's infrastructure, including not only Greece's roads and seaports but its airports and electric power and telecommunications networks. The initiatives launched in 1953 began a twenty-year-long period of sustained and high growth rates, low inflation, effective industrialization, export expansion, urban growth, and significant, albeit uneven, prosperity.

The period from the late 1950s to the late 1960s is often characterized as an era of unprecedented growth, the so-called Greek economic miracle. During these years, Greece's GDP grew at the fastest rate in Western Europe, averaging almost 8 percent annually. Meanwhile, industrial production grew at an average annual rate of 10 percent, exceeded in Western Europe only by Spain. Marking a major turning point, in the 1960s manufacturing exports surpassed agricultural exports for the first time in Greece's history. Yet the dramatic changes produced by economic growth, especially those associated with rapid urbanization and inequities in the distribution of Greece's growing wealth, also caused social tensions in the 1960s. The basic

weaknesses of the Greek economy, including the lack of competitiveness in the country's manufacturing sector, remained untreated. Neither the conservative government of the 1950s and early 1960s that was the architect of the economic recovery, nor the centrist government that led the country in the mid-1960s, nor the military junta that seized power in 1967 resolved these problems.

After two decades of growth, the global energy crisis of 1973 and the ensuing international monetary turmoil had a profoundly adverse effect on the Greek economy. One of the most pernicious and lasting results of the economic disruption was the unleashing of high rates of inflation. Running for more than a decade at only 3 percent, the annual rate of inflation jumped to 16 percent in 1973 and 27 percent in 1974. The negative effects of the economic recession brought on by the crisis of 1973 were magnified by the ineptitude of the military junta in managing Greece's problems. The collapse of the junta in 1974 and the restoration of democracy marked another major turn in Greece's economic development. With a civilian government returned to office, in 1981 Greece became a full member of the European Community, the tenth member in the economic alliance of European states to join the community. As a community member, Greece began to eliminate its protectionist policies, leading eventually to full liberalization of trade and the movement of capital and labor within the EC.

The democratic governments of the 1970s and 1980s inherited the accumulated economic and social problems that had been either ignored or suppressed by the junta. Issues that needed to be tackled before the structural adjustments necessary for long-term economic growth and modernization could be made possible included labor legislation, social insurance, education reform, and the provision of public health care. Furthermore, the state had to address the serious problem of a rising inflation rate that damaged business competitiveness, caused increasing energy costs, and triggered escalating pressures for higher wages. Adding to the state's challenges, the policy requirements for resolving Greece's economic and social problems were often contradictory. Modernization of social protection required increased public spending while economic stabilization and adjustment, an urgent need with the internationalization of the Greek economy through the EC, required spending restraints by government.

The conservative government that restored democracy in Greece in 1974 and secured the country's membership in the EC was unable to hold on to power in the 1980s. Reflecting the frustrations of those in the middle and lower classes who felt that they had missed out on the boom of the late 1960s and 1970s, when the annual growth rate averaged around 7 percent, the socialists were handed a major electoral victory over the conservatives in the national elections of 1981. After decades of sustained growth, it fell to the socialists to preside over the beginning of a decline in the Greek economy. The rate of growth in the 1980s fell to approximately 1.5 percent. The government under the socialists failed to restructure the economy at a time when most developed countries were moving away from labor-intensive industries toward those based on higher technology. Such readjustments caused significant increases in unemployment, which the new government was unwilling to face. Consequently, instead of taking measures to continue the modernization of the economy and make the Greek marketplace more competitive, the state sought to cushion the impact of the decline on the electorate by expanding welfare programs. The entire economic policy orientation of the socialist government in the early and mid-1980s prioritized political expediency and day-to-day survival over the interests and needs of long-term development and growth.

The mounting economic crisis, characterized in the public sector by high budget deficits, public borrowing, and an erosion of tax compliance in combination with economic stagnation, created serious problems that persisted into the early 1990s. Long overdue stabilization policies finally implemented in 1986 and 1987 began the arduous and difficult process of rebuilding the economy. From 1990 to 1993, a conservative government undertook more systematic efforts at stabilization accompanied by a government austerity agenda and a privatization program for state-owned firms, all measures aimed at increasing marketplace efficiency and competitiveness.

The socialists, back in power in late 1993, did not reverse the economic policies set into motion by the preceding conservative government. In reality, the socialist governments of the 1990s had considerably less economic policy latitude than in the 1980s. Greece, as a signatory of the Treaty on European Union, known as the Maastricht Treaty of February 1992, was now bound to a set of standards of state policy and economic performance. Indeed, EU membership imposed strict rules and disciplines on the economic behavior of the Greek state, and introduced long-term structural changes that no government could have achieved outside the larger European framework. Motivated by the new EU architecture, which promised greater integration of member states, a goal that Greece supported, both the conservative and socialist parties began to move to a common economic policy outlook.

The Maastricht Treaty had a profound effect on Greek policies and the Greek economy. In pursuit of the goal established by Maastricht for the increased integration of EU states through a monetary union, a common euro currency, the Greek government successfully implemented policies aimed at producing positive structural changes in the Greek economy. Chief among these policies were a reformed, more efficient tax structure and a pragmatic course of privatization of major segments of the public sector. The impact of this approach was positive, finally breaking Greece's perennial inflation problem and stimulating a vigorous revival of economic growth that has outpaced EU averages since the mid-1990s. Problems such as unemployment and a troubled, albeit reduced, public sector persisted, but the recent dynamism of the Greek economy reflected favorable domestic structural changes that also underscore the importance of, and are to a large extent the product of, EU membership. The changes undertaken to achieve successful integration into the supranational EU, magnified by entry into the Euro single currency system in January 2001, reflected a new and remarkable level of responsible and disciplined state-economy relations and leadership in Greece. By the late 1990s, after almost two decades of decline or stagnation and vacillating, indecisive policy directions, Greece had rebuilt the foundations for sustainable growth and, for the first time in its modern history, enjoyed a political consensus and common vision for the county's economic future.

CONTEMPORARY CHALLENGES
DOMESTIC CHALLENGES: IMMIGRATION AND ITS CONSEQUENCES

Since the 1990s, Greece has undergone a significant transformation from a land that was for centuries associated with the emigration of its own population to a country that is now a major European recipient of foreign immigrant populations. The late-twentieth-century influx into Greece of economic and political refugees from foreign countries marks a striking reversal of the historic pattern of population movement in Greece. For the first time, in at least its modern past, Greece has attracted the immigration of not only uprooted ethnic Greeks from abroad but people from Eastern Europe, Asia, and Africa.

Greece has drawn significant numbers of immigrants because of the opportunities that the country's growing economy and its free and open society offer to the destitute and oppressed. Yet the new immigration is also characterized by several problems and challenges: immigrants are mostly employed in the informal or tertiary economy, their social position is at the end of the social scale with little opportunity for advancement, they are not organized in trade unions or other collective structures, and most of them are illegal, clandestine immigrants with no documentary record. The immigrants' status depends on several factors, including whether they are in Greece as political refugees, in which case they are granted temporary residence in the country. In addition, there are many nonpolitical immigrants that come to Greece with temporary work or tourist visas. Nevertheless, the overwhelming majority of immigrants who reside in Greece are there illegally and remain undocumented.

The number of overall immigrants, legal and illegal combined, has never been determined with any accuracy. Nonetheless, Greek government estimates in 1999 indicated that there were between 500,000 and 600,000 immigrants in Greece, while some unofficial estimates suggested that the number was actually closer to 800,000 persons. In the beginning of the 1980s Greece accepted the settlement of some 200,000 ethnic Greeks who were displaced by turmoil in a host of African and Middle Eastern countries and were thus considered political refugees. During the same period, approximately 50,000 ethnic Greeks from the Soviet Union were permitted to immigrate to Greece, beginning a pattern of migration that continues to the present at an annual rate of around 10,000 ethnic Greek immigrants largely from Georgia, Russia, and Ukraine. Ethnic Greeks from Albania, especially from the country's southern region where a sizable Greek minority is concentrated, represent another large body of political immigrants who settled in Greece in the beginning of the 1990s.

Because of their status as ethnic Greeks, and often as political refugees, most of these immigrants obtained Greek citizenship. Nonetheless, the adjustment to life in Greece has not been without its difficulties for many of these immigrants. Approximately half of the ethnic Greek refugees from the former Soviet Union spoke little or no Greek, making their assimilation into a familiar culture but a forgotten language particularly challenging. Although most ethnic Greek immigrants from Albania were Greek speaking, they had fled from one of the world's most closed societies and one of its most oppressive, isolated regimes. As a result, not all Greek immigrants from Albania were equipped to cope with a modern, open society and marketplace that required initiative and creativity for success. The displaced Greeks from the former Soviet Union have been received in Greece better than the Greek immigrants from Albania. The Greek authorities, concerned by declining domestic birthrates, have generally welcomed this injection of Greeks from the former Soviet Union but have not provided adequately for their settlement. With the exception of modest language instruction programs to promote their facility in Greek, and some assistance to meet initial expenses, most of these immigrants have been left to their own devices. Working chiefly in low-wage manual labor or service positions, and settled largely in Athens and Thessaloniki, these "Russian Greeks" remain socially marginalized and are often economically exploited by unscrupulous employers. Despite these significant hardships, the problems stemming from the integration of ethnic Greeks into Greek society have been considerably less complicated than the problems confronting other immigrant groups.

Ethnic Greeks may constitute the largest group of legal immigrants in the country, but Albanians are the most prominent group of illegal migrants in Greece, probably forming a plurality of the overall immigrant (legal and illegal) population. Reliable estimates indicate that there are between 250,000 and 350,000 ethnic Albanians in Greece, most of them illegal economic immigrants and migrants. The collapse of the communist regime in Albania in the early 1990s triggered a flood of Albanian migrants who crossed the border into Greece in pursuit of economic opportunities. Most of this initial stream of destitute, desperate people found low-skilled service employment in Greece's urban areas, while much of the subsequent wave of Albanian movement into Greece has been characterized by migratory and seasonal patterns of employment related to the labor needs of Greece's agricultural and construction sectors. As a result, Albanians constantly cross the border into Greece illegally and are immediately deported by the Greek authorities, only to return to Greece as soon as they can again reach the border. This problem, although it continues into the present, reached its peak in 1993, when the Greek government reported that over 220,000 Albanian citizens were apprehended entering Greece illegally.

Never having experienced such an influx of foreign migrants, the Greek state was not prepared to cope with this unprecedented phenomenon. During most of the 1990s there was no coherent migration policy, as Greece was still considered to be a net exporter of population. Institutions such as support centers for the legal, social, and economic orientation of immigrants barely existed. Furthermore, illegal Albanian (and other) immigrants were excluded from aid by the public social service system, especially regarding the provision of housing, health care, and personal safety, which historically were provided by the Greek state only to Greek citizens and documented foreigners.

Albanians were prepared to assume the risks associated with illegal migration because of their dire economic plight. The legacy of the inefficient communist economic model, the breakdown of economic structures, the closure of 90 percent of Albania's factories during the early 1990s, and the chaotic revolts of 1990–1991 and 1997 were just a few of the many factors responsible for the exodus of hundreds of thousands of unemployed workers to Greece. The importance of economic migration for Albania is paramount because it functions as a kind of development aid through the export of labor and the import of capital. Remittances from Albanians abroad are an indispensable financial source for the development of Albania's domestic economy, especially as other sources such as export revenues and foreign investment have remained insignificant. Moreover, since 1991, the majority of Albanian families have depended on remittances for their survival. Since 1991, most of these payments have come from Greece, averaging annually 80–85 percent of the Albanian national total. In addition, technical knowledge and work experience obtained by Albanian migrants in Greece has been used to modernize the private sector as many of these workers have returned to Albania.

The employment of foreign workers in general, and Albanian workers in particular, has also had a significant impact on the Greek economy. One of the positive consequences, for the economy but not necessarily for workers, is that Albanians are employed with lower wages and without social security, thus reducing production costs and increasing the competitiveness of Greek exports. In addition, Albanian workers and their families help increase the private consumption of goods and services, thereby stimulating growth of domestic markets. Furthermore, undocumented workers form a readily available, flexible, and unorganized labor force that benefits countless small Greek enterprises, whose survival could be threatened without occasional, seasonal, and above all inexpensive employees. The majority of Albanians are employed as unskilled workers at building sites, as transient agricultural workers, and, in the case of most women, as household domestics.

Although Albanians, like most immigrants in Greece, exert a positive influence on the Greek GNP, some negative consequences have also been produced by the large and rapid influx of migrant labor. The skilled labor sector has been largely unaffected by these new conditions, but increases in unemployment among manual and unskilled Greek workers is directly linked to the growth of immigrant labor. In many cases, the low salaries paid to Albanian immigrants have pushed away Greek workers, especially those in the industrial and construction sectors. As a result, there has been a general decline in wages in these sectors, and the position of the working class has become weaker, as a consequence of the abundance of alternative and cheaper employees. In order to meet the costs associated with massive repatriations of illegal migrants and the editing of visas, Greek public spending is increasing while tax revenues are lost to Albanian workers, whose incomes are usually unreported. Finally, it is impossible to estimate the moral costs to Greek society associated with the exploitation of foreign workers, especially women and children.

Since 1991, both of Greece's conservative and socialist governments have focused on security as their primary concern in relation to the immigration question, especially regarding the country's Albanian migrants. Apart from the obvious security concerns that the routine violation of the Greek border with Albania poses, illegal Albanian immigration is linked, although much exaggerated in its scope by the Greek media, to Albanian crime cells that prey on undocumented immigrants and utilize the illegal flow of migrants to traffic in narcotics and exploited human beings. The failure of Greek authorities to deal effectively with Albanian organized crime networks, a problem confronting much of the western and southern Balkans, has contributed to the common public perception that criminality is rife within the Albanian immigrant community, thus promoting considerable mistrust and misunderstanding of Albanians in Greece. Greek feelings toward the Albanian immigrants are overwhelmingly negative. Although the 200,000 to 250,000 Arabs, Bulgarians, Filipinos, Kurds, Pakistanis, Poles, and Romanians making up the remainder of the immigrant population have not been integrated into the mainstream of Greek society, unlike the Albanians, these groups are not perceived as a threat to public security and hence have not encountered the kind of prejudice and negative stereotyping that characterizes popular views of Albanian migrants.

Greek public opinion is beginning to adjust to the growing realization that Greece has become a more heterogeneous society than it was before the 1990s. Xenophobic and even racist sentiments, although real in some quarters, are tempered by countervailing attitudes, which emphasize the need to extend legal status to immigrants, as well as the historic dynamism and resilience of Greek culture and identity often expressed through the historic assimilation of non-Greeks. Increasing economic interaction between Greeks and immigrants has also contributed to the erosion of group barriers, the growth of mutual familiarity, and declining prejudice. The Greek state, in 1999 and again in 2001, began the complex process of establishing a coherent immigration policy through new parliamentary legislation. Finally, despite many shortcomings in dealing with its immigrant question, Greek society has demonstrated a considerable capacity for tolerance and flexibility in accommodating itself to a new cultural landscape. There have been no efforts to endanger the security of immigrants, there is no anti-immigrant political movement in Greece, and there are no parties in the parliament that hold an anti-immigrant or anti-immigration stance, all phenomena that have been observed in Austria, France, Germany, and Italy, as well as in most of Greece's other EU partner states.

FOREIGN CHALLENGES: GREEK-TURKISH RELATIONS, THE EU, AND NATIONAL SECURITY

It is commonplace to argue that Greece and Turkey have been constant rivals. After Greece achieved independence from the Ottoman Empire in the 1830s, its diplomatic history in the nineteenth and early twentieth century was dominated by irredentist wars and rebellions against the declining empire. These conflicts led to the formation of Greece's borders and embedded the view that Greek and Turkish interests could only be antithetical. Nevertheless, the establishment of the nationalist Turkish republic in the early 1920s led to an interwar reconciliation and period of détente between the two countries.

Cordial relations, however, were disrupted by a massive pogrom against the Greek minority in Istanbul and the emergence of the Cyprus issue in the 1950s. The frustration of self-determination on Cyprus by the British colonial authorities, the establishment in 1960 of a nonviable state system for an independent Republic of Cyprus, and the consequent deterioration of relations among the Greek majority and Turkish minority communities on the island directly affected Greek-Turkish state relations. The process reached a critical threshold in 1974 when a botched nationalist coup instigated by the Greek junta against the Cypriot government was used as a pretext by Turkey to invade and occupy the northern part of the island.

Greece and Turkey came to the brink of war during the Cyprus crisis, and this tension had a spillover effect fueling disputes in the Aegean and beyond. The invasion of Cyprus, a fait accompli achieved with little international protest, was a watershed in Turkish foreign policy. For Ankara's military and diplomatic elites, the invasion, occupation, and partition of Cyprus established the lesson that war can accomplish foreign policy objectives and that the principles of international law should not act as a restraint on Turkish interests and actions. Thus encouraged by its experience in Cyprus, Turkey confronted Greece with a new set of contested issues, or revisionist demands, beginning in the 1970s. Ankara insisted that the international status quo regarding three issues in particular was unacceptable—control of air traffic over the Aegean, the allocation of operational responsibility for the Aegean and its airspace within the NATO framework, and, most important, the delimitation of the Aegean continental shelf, an issue that brought Greece and Turkey close to war in 1976 and 1987. Athens has viewed these demands as incremental steps aimed at the gradual dismantling of Greek sovereignty in the eastern Aegean, and has thus responded with proposals to have the growing disputes between Greece and Turkey resolved by the International Court of Justice. Turkey has consistently refused to accept the jurisprudence of any international mediation and, instead, has increased coercive pressure on Greece by inaugurating an armaments buildup and simultaneous concentration of armed forces along the border with Greece. Greece's response to the increasing military threat from Turkey has been to develop a deterrent through its own military buildup. At the same time, Greece has used diplomacy to safeguard its security.

Problems in Higher Education

Greek culture historically placed a high value on formal education. In the postwar period the public demand for education grew with the increasing modernization of Greek society, which since at least the nineteenth century has viewed education as the key to upward social mobility and status. The national educational system established shortly after Greece gained independence in the 1830s was the result of a combination of the contemporary French elementary school model, the Bavarian system of education, and the late-nineteenth-century German university system. Many elements of that original system have survived with very little change, especially in the sphere of higher education.

Greece's first modern university, known eventually as the National and Capodistrian University of Athens, was established in 1837. The University of Athens opened a new era in Greek education, producing the first modern indigenous Greek intelligentsia and professional class, as well as serving as a model for the development of other educational institutions in the other Balkan countries. At present there are nineteen Greek state universities, the largest being the University of Athens, with over 70,000 undergraduate and graduate students, followed by the Aristotle University of Thessaloniki, the University of Crete, the University of Thrace, the University of Patras, the National Polytechnic University of Athens, the University of the Aegean, and the University of Macedonia.

Several private universities and colleges, all of foreign origin, also operate in Greece but are not recognized by the state, leaving their graduates with no official credentials in the public arena. The rationale for this constitutionally mandated policy is that education should not be commercialized, not even at the level of higher education, nor should the marketplace determine access to education. Nonetheless, the state system has not provided a sufficient supply of higher education in response to increased demand. The high social status and competitive advantage associated with a university education have produced an enormous increase in the demand for the relatively small number of student positions in the university system. During the 1990s, on average, annually there were 150,000 applicants for only 40,000 state university and technical college slots.

The intense demand for higher education has had several problematic results. Secondary students with sufficient means utilize the large network of supplementary private schools throughout the country to prepare themselves for university entrance examinations. This practice undermines the official principle of equal access to higher education by producing inequities of opportunity among university applicants. Many students who are not accepted into the Greek university system go abroad to study. Underscoring the impact of this situation, in the 1980s Greece had the highest ratio of foreign to domestic university enrollment in the world. Moreover, a significant number of these students remain abroad, establishing careers outside Greece, depriving their homeland of their expertise and creating a brain drain. Furthermore, because of their very limited funding, Greek universities offer few graduate programs, and faculty have little incentive to pursue advanced research. Finally, despite efforts initiated in the 1980s to make the administration of the country's universities more professional, university and departmental administration has actually become more politicized by reforms inspired more by the governing socialists' populist agenda than the university system's practical needs.

Membership in the EU, and earlier the EC, has served as Greece's chief asset in its relations with Turkey. Turkey's persistent violation of Greek sovereign rights and disregard for international law and norms had not, until fairly recently, attracted any significant international support for Greece's positions as other states defined their policy in the region on the basis of their own interests. In that environment Greece had to rely on its own resources and options against Turkey—thus its emphasis on the EU as an instrument for the protection of its national security and sovereignty. As Turkey's main strategic objective is integration into the European political, economic, and cultural architecture, its campaign to join the EU has become critically important and this has increased Greece's leverage in

using its EU membership to exert counter pressure on Turkey.

Until the late 1990s, Greece exploited Turkey's ambitions for EU membership by conditioning its consent to the improvement of EU-Turkish relations on the modification of Turkey's revisionist policies in the Aegean and a resolution of the Cyprus problem. As Turkey proved unwilling to alter its policies, EU-Turkish relations suffered a stalemate, as any decisions that could improve EU-Turkish relations were blocked by Greece's EU member veto. Nonetheless, as a gesture of goodwill, and in exchange for a commitment from the other member states to discuss Cyprus's future EU membership application, Greece lifted its objections to Turkey's entry into the EU customs union agreement in

Turkish soldiers stand on a tank outside Kyrenia ten days after they launched their invasion of Cyprus, July 1974. (David Rubinger/Corbis)

March 1995. The Greek move, which satisfied an important demand of the Turkish government, elicited no positive response from Ankara. In fact, Greek-Turkish relations sharply deteriorated after the customs union agreement came into force at the beginning of 1996.

Having already threatened Greece with war in June 1995 if Athens were to exercise its legal right according to international law conventions to extend the country's territorial waters from 9.66 to 19.3 kilometers, Turkey renewed the threat of war by launching a provocative incident in January 1996. Executed during the first twenty-four hours of the administration of a new government in Greece, the Turkish action on the barren Greek islet of Imia ultimately led to Ankara's official claim to the islet as well as to several other islands in the Dodecanese complex and beyond, extending as far into Greece as the island of Gavdhos, south of Crete. The crisis was defused through American mediation, but a Turkish claim to actual land had now been added to the weighty list of Greek-Turkish problems. No longer able to ignore the seriousness of Greek-Turkish troubles, not only the United States but NATO too became involved in efforts to mediate between the alliance's two southeastern states, the organization proposing confidence-building measures to avoid future crises. The EU added its voice to the issue in July 1996 when its Council of Ministers issued a declaration stating that relations between Turkey and the

EU should be guided by respect for international law, international agreements, and the sovereignty and territorial integrity of the EU member states.

Clearly an important factor governing Greek-Turkish relations is the perception that each side has of the other. Where the Aegean is concerned, Turkey believes that Greece is interested in transforming the area into a "Greek lake," while Greece believes that Turkey aspires to make inroads in the region at the expense of Greek sovereignty in the eastern Aegean islands. Furthermore, Turkey's political instability, its ongoing occupation of Cyprus, its poor human rights record, the systematic obliteration of its Greek minority, routine threats of war against multiple neighbor states, its blockade of Armenia, and Ankara's response to the Kurdish autonomy movement have made Greece suspicious of Turkish motives in the region. Finally, the tendency of the Western powers to view what Greece considers to be Turkish provocations as merely a dispute between two allies has been interpreted by Athens as Western tolerance of aggression. More important, given Turkey's enhanced strategic role in the region, most Greek political leaders believe that the United States has adopted a policy of appeasement vis-à-vis Ankara at the expense of the potential victim, Athens. In response, and on the whole, Greece's policy is centered on defending the territorial status quo, while Turkey appears committed to challenging certain legal aspects regulating Greek sovereignty and rights in the region.

Again, given these conditions, Greece has seen its membership in the EU as its chief asset in defending its sovereignty vis-à-vis Turkish revisionism. Adversely affecting Turkey's primary strategic goal of EU membership, in the EU Copenhagen summit of June 1993 the EU leaders agreed on a set of conditions to be met by all states aiming to accede to the European Union. These requirements, known as the Copenhagen criteria, included, among other things, the stability of institutions guaranteeing democracy, the rule of law, human rights, and respect for and protection of minorities, as well as the existence of a functioning market economy and the ability to take on the aims of political, economic, and monetary union. Despite Turkey's failure to meet any of the Copenhagen criteria, Greece had to routinely use its veto power to block Turkey's request for official EU candidacy status during most of the 1990s. Greece's EU partners, although generally unenthusiastic about the prospects of Turkish membership, were also dissatisfied by the way Greece appeared to undermine EU official policies with respect to Turkey. Although Greece was effectively depriving Turkey of any closer relations with the EU through its consistent veto policy, this objective was being achieved at increasing political cost to Greece's image within the EU.

In 1996 Greece's newly elected prime minister, Costas Simitis, began a restructuring of domestic and eventually foreign policy aimed at rebuilding Greece's position within the EU. A pivotal part of the foreign policy restructuring necessarily involved policies toward Turkey. Toward that goal, in May 1999 Athens launched a dialogue initiative with Ankara on low-profile bilateral issues, such as environmental protection, tourism, and trade. The display of mutual goodwill at both the governmental and popular levels during the earthquakes that hit Turkey and Greece in August and September 1999, respectively, contributed to a dramatic reversal of hostile attitudes in the press and public opinion of both countries.

The growing rapprochement between Greece and Turkey had a positive influence on EU-Turkish relations. Ankara had suffered a severe setback at the EU Luxemburg summit of December 1997, when Turkey was omitted from the list of states awarded candidate status. In this instance, and again as Ankara resumed its effort to achieve candidate status, Greece was decreasingly hostile toward Turkey's EU membership process, while other states such as Germany and Sweden, which could no longer conveniently take advantage of Greece's veto and simultaneously express consternation with Athens, were revealed as staunch opponents of Turkey's candidacy. Nonetheless, with active support from Greece, the EU Helsinki summit of December 1999 extended official recognition to Turkey as a candidate state for accession to the EU. The Helsinki summit also established that before the start of EU accession negotiations, Turkey should settle its disputes with Greece or, alternatively, bring the disputed issues before the International Court of Justice, while substantial progress was the least to be expected for the Cyprus problem. In short, under the Simitis government, Greece was now using the EU as a

more nuanced asset, offering Turkey a set of structured incentives in exchange for corresponding changes in Ankara's behavior instead of simply imposing punishment for its unflinching policies.

Greece's position toward the prospective accession of Turkey to the EU marked a critical turn in Greek diplomacy. In 1995 Greece had abandoned its veto policy against any improvement of EU-Turkish relations and conceded to the customs union between the EU and Turkey. This did not mean, however, that Greece would support the prospect of Turkey's membership in the EU. The latter was to happen only after the December 1999 Helsinki EU summit, when active support for Turkey's efforts toward EU membership became a key component of Greek foreign policy strategy. This policy came to its culmination during the EU Copenhagen summit of December 2002, when Turkey's compliance with the 1993 Copenhagen criteria was evaluated by the EU member states. Although Turkey failed to meet the established standards, Greece, along with Italy and Spain, argued that the EU should reconsider Turkey's progress in the implementation of the Copenhagen criteria within 2003, so that Turkey's accession negotiations could start in 2004, provided that compliance with the Copenhagen criteria was achieved. In response, the European Council decided to reconsider Turkey's progress in December 2004 and to not set a date for accession discussions.

Although Greece's proposal on dealing with Turkey's candidacy was not accepted by the Council, the fact that the state that had kept EU-Turkish relations frozen for more than a decade had emerged to lead the minority of EU member states that supported acceleration of Turkey's accession process was characteristic of the change in the Greek view of EU-Turkish relations and the role of the EU in Greek-Turkish relations. By February 2004, the Simitis government could claim that its policy of support for Turkey in the EU succeeded in creating the necessary inducements for Ankara to agree to finally support a UN-sponsored plan for the reunification of Cyprus, regardless of the plan's unresolved implementation questions or actual viability. Nonetheless, although Greece under Prime Minister Simitis played a decisive role in promoting Turkey's EU vocation, a significant gesture of reciprocity regarding the basic issues of Greek sovereignty and concerns for international law in the Aegean has yet to materialize in Ankara.

SELECTIVE BIBLIOGRAPHY

Agnold, Michael. *The Byzantine Empire, 1025–1204: A Political History.* New York: Longman, 1997.

———. *Church and Society in Byzantium under the Comneni, 1081–1261.* Cambridge: Cambridge University Press, 1995.

Allison, Graham, and Kalypso Nicolaidis, eds. *The Greek Paradox: Promise vs. Performance.* Cambridge: MIT Press, 1997.

Augustinos, Gerasimos. *The Greeks of Asia Minor: Confession, Community, and Ethnicity in the Nineteenth Century.* Kent, OH: Kent State University Press, 1992.

Boardman, John, Jasper Griffin, and Oswyn Murray, eds. *The Oxford History of Greece and the Hellenistic World.* Oxford: Oxford University Press, 2002.

Browning, Robert. *The Byzantine Empire.* Washington, DC: Catholic University of America Press, 1992.

———. *The Greeks: Classical, Byzantine, and Modern.* New York: Thames and Hudson, 1985.

Carabott, Philip. *Greek Society in the Making, 1863–1913: Realities, Symbols, and Visions.* Aldershot, UK: Ashgate, 1997.

Cartledge, Paul, ed. *The Cambridge Illustrated History of Ancient Greece.* Cambridge: Cambridge University Press, 1997.

Cheetham, Nicholas. *Medieval Greece.* New Haven: Yale University Press, 1981.

Clogg, Richard. *A Concise History of Greece.* Cambridge: Cambridge University Press, 1992.

Dakin, Douglas. *The Greek Struggle for Independence, 1821–1833.* London: Batsford, 1973.

———. *The Greek Struggle in Macedonia, 1897–1913.* Thessaloniki: Institute for Balkan Studies, 1966.

———. *The Unification of Greece, 1770–1923.* London: Ernest Benn, 1972.

Errington, R. Malcolm. *A History of Macedonia.* Berkeley: University of California Press, 1990.

Fine, John V. A. *The Ancient Greeks: A Critical History.* Cambridge: Harvard University Press, 1983.

Frazee, Charles. *The Orthodox Church and Independent Greece, 1821–1852.* Cambridge: Cambridge University Press, 1969.

Freris, A. F. *The Greek Economy in the Twentieth Century.* London: Croon Helm, 1986.

Gallant, Thomas W. *Modern Greece.* New York: Oxford University Press, 2001.

Hondros, John Louis. *Occupation and Resistance: The Greek Agony, 1941–44.* New York: Pella, 1983.

Hornblower, Simon. *The Greek World, 479–323 BC.* London: Routledge, 2002.

Hussey, Joan. *The Orthodox Church in the Byzantine Empire.* Oxford: Clarendon, 1986.

Iatrides, John O., ed. *Greece in the 1940s: A Nation in Crisis.* Hanover, NH: University Press of New England, 1981.

Iatrides, John O., and Linda Wrinley, eds. *Greece at the Crossroads: The Civil War and Its Legacy.* Philadelphia: Pennsylvania State University Press, 1995.

Issawi, Charles, and Dimitri Gondicas, eds. *Ottoman Greeks in the Age of Nationalism: Politics, Economy, and Society in the Nineteenth Century.* Princeton, NJ: Darwin, 1999.

Kazhdan, A. P., and Ann Wharton Epstein. *Change in Byzantine Culture in the Eleventh and Twelfth Centuries.* Berkeley: University of California Press, 1984.

Kitromilides, Paschalis. *The Enlightenment as Social Criticism: Iosipos Moisiodax and Greek Culture in the Eighteenth Century.* Princeton: Princeton University Press, 1992.

Kofos, Evangelos. *Nationalism and Communism in Macedonia: Civil Conflict, Politics of Mutation, National Identity.* New Rochelle, NY: A. D. Caratzas, 1993.

Koliopoulos, John S., and Thanos Veremis. *Greece: The Modern Sequel from 1831 to the Present.* New York: New York University Press, 2002.

Leontaritis, George. *Greece and the First World War: From Neutrality to Involvement.* Boulder: East European Monographs, 1990.

Llewellyn Smith, Michael. *Ionian Vision: Greece in Asia Minor, 1919–1922.* London: Hurst, 2000.

Mavrogordatos, George. *Stillborn Republic: Social Coalitions and Party Strategies in Greece, 1922–1936.* Berkeley: University of California Press, 1983.

Mazower, Mark. *Greece and the Inter-War Economic Crisis.* Oxford: Clarendon, 1991.

———. *Inside Hitler's Greece: The Experience of Occupation, 1941–1944.* New Haven: Yale University Press, 1993.

Mazower, Mark, ed. *After the War Was Over: Reconstructing the Family, Nation, and State in Greece, 1943–1960.* Princeton: Princeton University Press, 2000.

McGrew, William W. *Land and Revolution in Modern Greece, 1800–1881: The Transition in the Tenure and Exploitation of Land from Ottoman Rule to Independence.* Kent, OH: Kent State University Press, 1985.

McNeill, William H. *The Metamorphosis of Greece since World War II.* Oxford: Blackwell, 1978.

Nicol, Donald. *Church and Society in the Last Centuries of Byzantium.* Cambridge: Cambridge University Press, 1979.

———. *The Despotate of Epirus, 1267–1479: A Contribution to the History of Greece in the Middle Ages.* Cambridge: Cambridge University Press, 1984.

———. *The Immortal Emperor: The Life and Legend of Constantine Palaiologos, Last Emperor of the Romans.* Cambridge: Cambridge University Press, 1992.

———. *The Last Centuries of Byzantium, 1261–1453.* Cambridge: Cambridge University Press, 1993.

Osborne, Robin. *Greece in the Making, 1200–479 BC.* London: Routledge, 1996.

Papacosma, Victor S. *The Military in Greek Politics: The 1909 Coup d' Etat.* Kent, OH: Kent State University Press, 1977.

Petropoulos, John Anthony. *Politics and Statecraft in the Kingdom of Greece, 1833–1843.* Princeton: Princeton University Press, 1968.

Pomeroy, Sarah B., et al., eds. *Ancient Greece: A Political, Social, and Cultural History.* Oxford: Oxford University Press, 1998.

Runciman, Steven. *The Fall of Constantinople, 1453.* Cambridge: Cambridge University Press, 1965.

———. *The Great Church in Captivity: A Study of the Patriarchate of Constantinople from the Eve of the Turkish Conquest to the Greek War of Independence.* Cambridge: Cambridge University Press, 1968.

Sealey, Raphael. *A History of the Greek City States, ca. 700–338 B.C.* Berkeley: University of California Press, 1976.

Treadgold, Warren. *The Byzantine Revival, 780–842.* Stanford: Stanford University Press, 1988.

———. *A History of the Byzantine State and Society.* Stanford: Stanford University Press, 1997.

Tritle, Lawrence A., ed. *The Greek World in the Fourth Century: From the Fall of the Athenian Empire to the Successors of Alexander.* London: Routledge, 1997.

Woodhouse, C. M. *Modern Greece: A Short History.* London: Faber and Faber, 1992.

Vacalopoulos, Apostolos. *The Greek Nation, 1453–1669: The Cultural and Economic Background of Modern Greek Society.* New Brunswick, NJ: Rutgers University Press, 1976.

———. *History of Macedonia, 1354–1833.* Thessaloniki: Institute for Balkan Studies, 1973.

———. *Origins of the Greek Nation: The Byzantine Period, 1204–1461.* New Brunswick, N.J.: Rutgers University Press, 1970.

Vryonis, Speros. *The Decline of Medieval Hellenism in Asia Minor and the Process of Islamization from the Eleventh through the Fifteenth Century.* Berkeley: University of California Press, 1986.

Yiannias, John J., ed. *The Byzantine Tradition after the Fall of Constantinople.* Charlottesville: University of Virginia Press, 1991.

Zakythinos, D. A. *The Making of Modern Greece: From Byzantium to Independence.* Oxford: Basil Blackwell, 1976.

CHRONOLOGY

3000 B.C.E.	Bronze Age culture replaces Neolithic culture on the Greek mainland, the Cyclades, and Crete.
2200 B.C.E.	Minoan Greek culture emerges in Crete.
1450 B.C.E.	Minoan society is destroyed by natural disaster.
1600–1150 B.C.E.	Mycenaean Greek civilization flourishes in the southern mainland. Mycenaean communities are destroyed by a wave of human and natural catastrophes (Homer's Troy destroyed in 1184).
1050 B.C.E.	An "invasion" of most of the mainland by Dorian Greek tribes begins. Dorian and Ionian Greek populations spread across the Aegean and Mediterranean to settle the western coast of Asia Minor and Cyprus.
1050–750 B.C.E.	A highly limited record of cultural activity characterizes this so-called Dark Age (776 traditional date for the first Olympic Games).
800–700 B.C.E.	City-states emerge throughout most of Greece.
700–500 B.C.E.	Greece's many polities are ruled by aristocratic elites during the so-called Archaic Period. In the sixth century many of these elites are overthrown and replaced by tyrannies, which in turn are overthrown and supplanted by oligarchies.
500–400 B.C.E.	The century known as the Classical Period produces Greek democracy and an unparalleled flood of intellectual and artistic creativity to form the foundation of what develops into "Western civilization," as well as a complex of foreign wars and city-state rivalries and conflicts.
490 B.C.E.	After conquering the Greeks of Asia Minor fifty years earlier, the Persians attack mainland Greece and are defeated by an Athenian force at the Battle of Marathon.
480 B.C.E.	The Persian Empire launches a massive invasion of mainland Greece, penetrating as far south as Athens. Greek forces led by Sparta slow the Persian advance, giving other Greek forces led by Athens time to consolidate and defeat the Persian navy at the Battle of Salamis and, a year later, the Persian army at Plataia.
478 B.C.E.	Athens forms the Delian League, an alliance of city-states, to pursue the war against the retreating Persians.
478–431 B.C.E.	Athens, subjugating its erstwhile allies, uses the Delian League to create an empire for itself in the Aegean. Led by Pericles, Athenian power and influence grows.
431 B.C.E.	Resentment against Athenian hegemony over other Greek states leads to the outbreak of the Peloponnesian War.
431–404 B.C.E.	The Peloponnesian War, ultimately involving most of the Greek world's city-states and kingdoms, ends with the defeat of Athens by its chief rival, Sparta.
404–371 B.C.E.	Sparta wields political and military domination over most of the Greek mainland.
371–338 B.C.E.	The city-state of Thebes defeats Sparta and establishes its own period of hegemony over Greece.
338–336 B.C.E.	Thebes and its allies are overpowered by Greece's northernmost state, the kingdom of Macedonia, which, as the Greeks' final hegemonic power, forcibly unites most of the Greek world under its leadership.
336–323 B.C.E.	Succeeding his father, Philip II, as king of Macedonia, Alexander the Great launches a Greek war of revenge against the Persian Empire, invading and conquering all of its vast territories throughout the Near East.
323–146 B.C.E.	Alexander the Great's successors establish several Greek dynastic states in the conquered lands of the former Persian Empire. Greek populations, the Greek language, and Greek culture spread into the Near East, creating the foundations for the emergence of a hybrid Hellenistic civilization, the cultural cauldron in which the emergence and spread of Christianity later takes place.

197–86 B.C.E.	The Romans defeat Macedonia and progressively annex all the remaining Greek states in Europe and Asia.
30–300 C.E.	The convergence of Greek philosophy and Jewish religious thought within the framework of a politically united Roman Mediterranean and a Greek-speaking East create the conditions for the development and expansion of Christianity.
324	The Roman emperor Constantine relocates the empire's capital from Rome and the Latin West to Byzantium, eventually known as Constantinople, and the predominantly Greek East, establishing the foundations for the transition of the Roman to the Eastern Roman, or Byzantine, Empire, a medieval Greek state.
325	Constantine, declaring Christianity the empire's official religion, presides over the First Ecumenical Council in Nicaea, which formalizes Christian doctrine. This and subsequent councils define the theology and ecclesiology of Orthodox Christianity.
325–550	Christianity supplants the final vestiges of pagan tradition in Greece (Olympic Games are suppressed in 395; Athenian pagan philosophical schools are closed in 529).
550–750	The Byzantine Empire's control over most of the northern and western Balkans collapses as Slavic raids and settlement extend into central and southern Greece, displacing much of the Greek population from the interior and pushing it toward the coasts and the eastern part of the country.
800–900	Byzantium reasserts control over the Greek lands previously lost to the Slavs. Greek populations are resettled in these territories, while most of the Slavic tribes not destroyed are either pushed northward or gradually Hellenized. Cultural differences between Eastern and Western Christendom begin to take on an increasingly political dimension.
900–1025	The Byzantine Empire reaches the zenith of its power with the destruction and conquest of the Bulgars in the Balkans and the decisive defeat of the Arabs in the Near East.
1054	After centuries of growing tension and mutual suspicion, the expanding cultural and political gulf between Eastern and Western Christendom reaches a crisis with the formal ecclesiastical rupture between the See of Rome (the emergent Roman Catholic Church), on one hand, and the Sees of Alexandria, Antioch, Constantinople, and Jerusalem (the Orthodox Church), on the other hand.
1071	The Byzantine Empire suffers a major defeat at the Battle of Manzikert in eastern Anatolia, opening the interior of Asia Minor to invasion by the Seljuk Turks. This strategic turn begins the steady multicentury transformation of Asia Minor from an entirely Christian and Greek-populated center to a predominantly Muslim and Turkish region.
1080	The Normans, from their base in Italy, begin raiding the western territories of Byzantium. These raids escalate to a series of wars fought for Byzantine land and wealth that continue until the Fourth Crusade.
1185	Underscoring the serious threat posed to the Byzantine Greeks by the Catholic West, a Norman army sacks the great cultural and commercial center of Thessaloniki, Byzantium's second largest city.
1204	The Fourth Crusade sacks Constantinople, breaks up the Byzantine Empire, divides most of its territories and spoils, and subjects most of its population to the feudal exploitation of a series of petty Western occupation states. These actions end the possibility of ecclesiastical reconciliation or political cooperation between the Greeks and the West.
1204–1261	From their territorial bases in Asia Minor and the Balkans, Byzantine Greek successor states wage a war of liberation and reconquest against the Western occupation forces in and around Constantinople.
1261	The Greeks recover Constantinople and reestablish the Byzantine Empire, which still enjoys enormous prestige and influence but in its weakened state and reduced domain is no longer a major power.
1261–1453	Despite the ongoing depredations of the West, the continual loss of Byzantine territory to rival Balkan states, and the loss of virtually all of Byzantium's remaining lands to the expanding and powerful Ottoman Turks, late medieval Greek society experiences an incredible outburst of artistic, cultural, and intellectual creativity.
1453	After a desperate siege, on 29 May Constantinople falls to the Ottoman

	Turks, who make the city the capital of their expanding Islamic empire.
1453–1821	Under Ottoman rule, the Greeks are organized according to Islamic political principles and placed under the administrative authority of their religious leaders while simultaneously subject to the absolute authority of the sultan and his government.
1463–1479	The first Turko-Venetian war takes place, ravaging the population of southern Greece and the islands.
1499–1502/ 1537–1540	The second and third Turko-Venetian wars continue to devastate Greek populations on the mainland and the islands.
1566–1669	Greek populations are further reduced by Ottoman wars in the Aegean and Mediterranean that lead to the conquest of the Aegean Islands, Crete, and Cyprus.
1684–1715	The Venetians occupy the Peloponnesus and raid Central Greece (the Parthenon, largely intact since antiquity, is seriously damaged by Venetian cannon during a siege of the Athens Acropolis in 1687).
1774	The Treaty of Kuchuk Kainardji ends the Russo-Turkish War of 1768–1774 and gives Russia considerable concessions in the Ottoman Empire, which fuel early Greek nationalist aspirations for freedom.
1774–1821	The Greek commercial diaspora throughout Europe begins to shape the intellectual foundations for a Greek nationalist revival.
1814	The secret nationalist revolutionary organization Philike Hetairia (Friendly Society) is established by Greek nationalists in Odessa with the aim of overthrowing the Ottoman Empire and liberating the Greeks.
1821	The Greek War of Independence against Ottoman rule breaks out.
1822	The first constitution for an independent Greece, a liberal and democratic document, is drafted by the revolution's leaders.
1827	The unplanned, spontaneous battle of Navarino sees the destruction of the Ottoman fleet at the hands of a combined British, French, and Russian fleet, producing Great Power support for Greek independence and a Russian invasion of the Ottoman Balkans.
1830	Britain, France, and Russia recognize the independence of Greece under the London Protocol (3 February), which also establishes the three Great Powers as protecting states over Greece.
1832	The Treaty of Constantinople (21 July) between Britain, France, Russia, and the Ottoman Empire formally establishes Greece's boundaries.
1833	Prince Otto of Bavaria arrives in Greece to become the independent country's monarch.
1834	Relocating it from Nafplion, Athens becomes Greece's capital.
1843	In a bloodless revolt, King Otto is forced by the troops of the Athens garrison and a popular demonstration by the capital's citizens to grant a constitution.
1844	Otto officially accepts the new constitution, which defines the political system as a constitutional monarchy.
1853–1857	Popular Greek support for Russia against the Ottoman Empire during the Crimean War leads to a blockade and eventual occupation of Piraeus by British and French troops, enforcing strict neutrality on Greece.
1862	Growing dissatisfaction with Otto leads to an uprising in Athens and Nafplion against his rule, and produces his abdication.
1863	Prince George of Denmark becomes "King of the Hellenes."
1864	Britain cedes the Ionian Islands to Greece through the Treaty of London (29 March). The new constitution defines the political system as a "crowned democracy."
1866–1869	An uprising in Crete fails to liberate the island from Ottoman rule.
1870	The Ottoman sultan recognizes the autonomy of the Bulgarian Exarchate Church, which inspires a Bulgarian nationalist reaction against Greek cultural and ecclesiastical dominance, as well as ethnic presence, in Macedonia.
1878	According to one of the terms of the Treaty of Berlin (13 July), Britain occupies and assumes administration of Cyprus, which officially remains part of the Ottoman Empire.
1881	As an addendum act to the 1878 Treaty of Berlin, which established Romanian and Serbian independence, along with an autonomous Bulgaria's borders, Britain forces the Ottoman Empire to cede most of the province of Thessaly and the region of Arta to Greece.
1883–1893	The reformer Charilaos Trikoupis and the expansionist Theodoros Deliyannis alternate in power during this decade, marking the heyday of the two-party system and establishing a dynamic of political rivalry that will be repeated by

	other politicians to more divisive results in the twentieth century.
1896	Cretan rebellion against Ottoman rule.
1897	Set into motion by the rebellion in Crete, a Greco-Turkish war breaks out. The Greeks are quickly defeated and Athens is forced to surrender some strategic border territories in Thessaly.
1893–1908	Local Greek armed bands, some supported by Greek officers, organize to counter the Bulgarians' guerrilla forces operating in Ottoman Macedonia. Both sides fight each other for the liberation and future control of Macedonian territory.
1909	Frustrated by the lack of effective political leadership in Athens, a group of officers organizes a Military League and coup that force the government to draft reforms.
1910	The liberal nationalist Cretan Eleutherios Venizelos, the Military League's political adviser, wins an overwhelming popular mandate in general elections and launches extensive reforms.
1911	Italy attacks the Ottoman Empire in Libya and occupies the Dodecanese Islands in the Aegean.
1912	Venizelos and his Liberal Party enjoy a landslide election victory. Greece and its allies, Bulgaria, Montenegro, and Serbia, defeat the Ottoman Empire and push its army to the outskirts of Constantinople in the First Balkan War.
1913	Dissatisfied with its territorial gains in Macedonia, Bulgaria attacks its former allies, Greece and Serbia, only to be defeated by them, Romania, and the Ottoman Empire in the Second Balkan War. Greece doubles its territory with the acquisition of the Aegean Islands, Crete, most of Epirus, and southern Macedonia in the Treaty of London (30 May) and the Peace of Bucharest (10 August).
1914	World War I begins, Britain declares war on the Ottoman Empire, an ally of the Central Powers, and annexes Cyprus.
1915	Prime Minister Venizelos and King Constantine clash over Greek foreign policy in response to the outbreak of World War I. Venizelos advocates a Greek alliance with the Entente Powers (the Allies), while Constantine remains committed to neutrality. Bulgaria joins the Central Powers. Venizelos resigns under pressure from the king.
1916	A national schism develops as Greece is divided between north and south with a revolutionary government under Venizelos backed by the Allies in Thessaloniki and the official government in Athens appointed by Constantine.
1917	Under Allied pressure, Constantine abdicates and is succeeded by his second son, Alexander. Venizelos reestablishes his government in Athens and Greece severs relations with the Central Powers who declare war on Greece.
1918	The Greek army, alongside other Allied forces, scores major successes on the Macedonian front, defeating the Bulgarian army and forcing German forces to retreat. Bulgaria and Turkey sign armistices.
1919	Venizelos takes his place among the victors of World War I and puts forward Greece's territorial claims against Bulgaria and the Ottoman Empire at the Paris peace conference. At the behest of Britain and France, Greek forces land in Smyrna. The Treaty of Neuilly (27 November) requires Bulgaria to transfer Western Thrace to Greece. Mustafa Kemal declares his independence from the Ottoman sultan and establishes a Turkish nationalist movement and army in Anatolia.
1920	Under the Treaty of Sevres (10 August) Greece acquires Eastern Thrace, the rest of the Aegean Islands, and a mandate to administer Smyrna and its hinterland in Asia Minor, pending a local plebiscite to determine the area's future status. With Allied backing, Venizelos orders the Greek army to advance from Smyrna to put down growing Turkish nationalist resistance and forcibly impose the terms of the Sevres Treaty. King Alexander dies prematurely. Venizelos is defeated in the ensuing elections, and the royalists return to power and restore Constantine to the throne.
1921	The Greek army's offensive against Kemal's nationalist forces reaches the outskirts of Ankara but is blocked from further advance. The Allies, abandoning Greece, declare a policy of strict neutrality.
1922	The Turks launch a massive offensive, routing the Greek army in Asia Minor and sacking Smyrna. Constantine abdicates in favor of his eldest son, George, after a military coup against the royalist government.
1923	The Treaty of Lausanne (24 July) fixes the boundaries between Greece and Turkey and imposes an exchange of

populations. Almost 1.5 million destitute ethnic Greek refugees arrive in Greece, a country of barely 5 million people. Venizelos's Liberal Party wins almost all the seats in parliament after the royalists abstain from the national elections.

1924
Venizelos accepts the premiership and Greece is declared a republic.

1924–1926
The republic is destabilized by a series of pro-royalist and pro-Venizelist military coups.

1926–1928
In order to curb instability, an all-party government takes office.

1928–1932
Venizelos returns to power and initiates a Greek-Turkish diplomatic rapprochement.

1932–1936
Renewed rivalry between liberals and royalists erodes the republic's stability.

1935
The failure of an antiroyalist coup leads to the restoration of King George.

1936
Greece's leading senior politicians, including Venizelos, die in quick succession. King George suspends the constitution and enables retired General Ioannis Metaxas to assume dictatorial powers.

1936–1940
Metaxas establishes a nationalist authoritarian regime but enjoys little popular support.

1940
Greek resistance to the thwarted Italian invasion from Albania results in the first Allied victories in Europe during World War II.

1941
German forces invade and overrun Greece. A Greek government in exile is established in Egypt.

1941–1944
Greece is occupied by German, Italian, and Bulgarian forces. Armed resistance obliges the Germans to maintain a large number of forces in Greece. Internal strife and political rivalry between Communist-dominated and nationalist resistance groups erupts into a short-lived civil war.

1944
Greece is liberated but an armed rebellion of the Communist-dominated resistance leads to intense fighting in Athens and deepening political polarization.

1946–1949
A large-scale civil war is fought between the Communists' insurgent army and the national government and its armed forces.

1947
In accordance with the Treaty of Paris (10 February) Italy cedes the Dodecanese Islands to Greece. Under the Truman Doctrine, the United States grants massive aid to Greece.

1952
Greece becomes a member of NATO, and a reconstruction program of the war-ravaged country is launched with significant aid from the United States.

1955
A massive state-sponsored pogrom against the Greek community of Istanbul takes place as Turkish nationalists demand the annexation of Cyprus by Ankara.

1956
Elections are won by the newly formed conservative party, National Radical Union, led by Constantine Karamanlis. British colonial forces suppress the Greek Cypriots' growing struggle for self-determination, expressed through demands for union with Greece.

1959
Finalizing a British compromise involving Greece and Turkey, Greek and Turkish Cypriot leaders, the former under British pressure, sign the London agreement on the independence of Cyprus.

1960
Cyprus, albeit saddled with a nonviable constitution and political system, becomes an independent republic with Archbishop Makarios as president.

1963
Karamanlis and the conservatives lose the national elections to George Papandreou, leader of the Center Union, a party formed by the coalition of all of Greece's center factions. Papandreou, however, refuses to form a coalition government with the political left and resigns. As the state system begins to fail, violence breaks out between the Greek and Turkish communities in Cyprus.

1964
In new elections the Center Union wins an absolute majority. The Turkish air force bombs Cyprus after a series of violent incidents between the Greek and Turkish communities.

1965
King Constantine II, who came to the throne a year earlier following the death of his father, King Paul, clashes with Papandreou over ministerial appointments, leading Papandreou to resign in protest and demand new elections.

1965–1967
Political conditions deteriorate as the monarchy interjects itself in parliamentary affairs and tensions grow across party lines.

1967
A junta of colonels stages a coup against the civilian government and establishes a military dictatorship. King Constantine flees Greece after an abortive effort to oust the colonels.

1973
Units of the Greek navy launch an abortive coup against the military dictatorship.

1974	Turkey invades and occupies northern Cyprus following a short-lived coup against Makarios instigated by the dictatorship in Athens. On the heels of its disaster in Cyprus, the junta collapses. Democracy is restored and Karamanlis returns from self-exile in France to lead his New Democracy Party and to be elected prime minister. The monarchy is abolished and Greece becomes a republic after a national referendum.
1975–1976	Following the entrenchment of the Turkish occupation in Cyprus, Greek-Turkish relations are further strained by a series of Turkish provocations against Greek sovereignty in the Aegean.
1979	Karamanlis signs a Treaty of Accession (28 May) to the European Community (EC) with the nine EC member states.
1981	Greece officially joins the EC. The Panhellenic Socialist Movement (PASOK), led by Andreas Papandreou, the son of George Papandreou, wins the national elections. The new socialist government launches a wave of populist reforms.
1985	Papandreou and PASOK retain power following victorious parliamentary elections.
1987	Greek-Turkish relations face a crisis over renewed disputes in the Aegean.
1988	Papandreou and Turkish Premier Turgut Ozal meet in Davos, Switzerland, to defuse tension between their two countries.
1989	A deadlocked election leads to the formation of a short-term coalition government made up of the conservative New Democracy Party and the Communist Party. Papandreou faces serious financial corruption charges. Subsequent to inconclusive elections, an all-party caretaker government is formed.
1990	New Democracy, under Constantine Mitsotakis, wins the national election. Mitsotakis's government introduces an economic austerity program to overcome economic malaise.
1992	The issue of diplomatic recognition of the newly independent Former Yugoslav Republic of Macedonia (FYROM) dominates Greek foreign policy under the Mitsotakis government. General strikes over privatization and social security reforms paralyze the economy. Mitsotakis dismisses his entire cabinet after disagreements over economic policy and the Macedonian issue. Andreas
	Papandreou is acquitted of corruption charges.
1993	Greece accepts international arbitration to resolve state name and other disputes with FYROM, the name under which the country is admitted into the UN. Mitsotakis government falls with the defection of some New Democracy Party members. PASOK is voted back into office and Papandreou again becomes prime minister.
1994	In reaction to the FYROM policy of diplomatic intransigence, Papandreou imposes a nominal trade embargo. Although this assertive policy backfires, creating significant international antipathy for Greece, it succeeds in forcing Skopje to negotiate with Athens.
1995	Greece and FYROM resolve several disputes and agree to begin normalization of relations. Turkey threatens Greece with war over sovereignty issues in the Aegean.
1996	Failing in health, Papandreou resigns and is replaced by Costas Simitis. Greece and Turkey come close to war over disputed islets in the Aegean. Simitis and PASOK win national elections.
1997	The Simitis government pursues decisively its convergence policy, ensuring that Greece will meet criteria to qualify to participate in the EU Economic and Monetary Union.
1998	Greece's relations with its Balkan neighbors continue to improve while Greek-Turkish relations reach a new low amid tensions over Cyprus, the Aegean, and Greek complicity in the international passage of the anti-Turkish Kurdish independence movement's leader, Abdullah Ocalan.
1999	Although Greece does not take part in military operations against Yugoslavia, the Simitis government, facing strong public opposition, maintains solidarity with its NATO partners. Greece becomes the strategic linchpin for the deployment and supply of American and other forces into Kosovo. Greece and FYROM sign a series of important cooperation agreements.
2000	Simitis and PASOK remain in power after a narrow election victory.
2001	Having satisfied all criteria, Greece officially joins the Economic and Monetary Union of the EU.
2004	PASOK, now led by George Papandreou, the American-born son of

the party's founder, Andreas Papandreou, suffers a major defeat in national elections. PASOK, which dominated the Greek political system more or less since 1981, is succeeded by the conservative New Democracy Party. Costas Karamanlis, the nephew of New Democracy's founder, Constantine Karamanlis, becomes Greece's new prime minister.

2004   Olympic games are once again held in Athens.

Index

Note: Numbers in **bold** indicate chapters.